ALSO BY THE EDITORS AT AMERICA'S TEST KITCHEN

The New Family Cookbook
The Complete Vegetarian Cookbook
The Complete Cooking for Two Cookbook
The America's Test Kitchen Cooking School Cookbook
The Cook's Illustrated Meat Book
The Cook's Illustrated Baking Book
The Cook's Illustrated Cookbook
The Science of Good Cooking
The America's Test Kitchen Menu Cookbook
The America's Test Kitchen Quick Family Cookbook
The America's Test Kitchen Healthy Family Cookbook
The America's Test Kitchen Family Baking Book
The Complete America's Test Kitchen TV Show Cookbook

THE AMERICA'S TEST KITCHEN LIBRARY SERIES

The Best Mexican Recipes
The Make-Ahead Cook
The How Can It Be Gluten-Free Cookbook
Healthy Slow Cooker Revolution
Slow Cooker Revolution Volume 2: The Easy-Prep Edition
Slow Cooker Revolution
The Six-Ingredient Solution
Pressure Cooker Perfection
Comfort Food Makeovers
The America's Test Kitchen D.I.Y. Cookbook
Pasta Revolution
Simple Weeknight Favorites
The Best Simple Recipes

THE TV COMPANION SERIES

The Complete America's Test Kitchen TV Show Cookbook 2001–2015
America's Test Kitchen: The TV Companion Cookbook (2009 and 2011–2015 Editions)

AMERICA'S TEST KITCHEN ANNUALS

The Best of America's Test Kitchen (2007–2015 Editions)
Cooking for Two (2010–2013 Editions)
Light & Healthy (2010–2012 Editions)

THE COOK'S COUNTRY SERIES

Cook's Country Eats Local
From Our Grandmothers' Kitchens
Cook's Country Blue Ribbon Desserts
Cook's Country Best Potluck Recipes
Cook's Country Best Lost Suppers
Cook's Country Best Grilling Recipes
The Cook's Country Cookbook
America's Best Lost Recipes

THE BEST RECIPE SERIES

The New Best Recipe
More Best Recipes
The Best One-Dish Suppers
Soups, Stews & Chilis
The Best Skillet Recipes
The Best Slow & Easy Recipes
The Best Chicken Recipes
The Best International Recipe
The Best Make-Ahead Recipe
The Best 30-Minute Recipe
The Best Light Recipe
The Cook's Illustrated Guide to Grilling and Barbecue
Best American Side Dishes
Cover & Bake
Italian Classics
American Classics

For a full listing of all our books:
CooksCountry.com
CooksIllustrated.com
AmericasTestKitchen.com

PRAISE FOR OTHER AMERICA'S TEST KITCHEN TITLES

"The entire book is stuffed with recipes that will blow your dinner-table audience away like leaves from a sidewalk in November."
San Francisco Book Review on **The Complete Cook's Country TV Show Cookbook**

"This book upgrades slow cooking for discriminating, 21st-century palates—that is indeed revolutionary."
The Dallas Morning News on **Slow Cooker Revolution**

"The 21st-century *Fannie Farmer Cookbook* or *The Joy of Cooking*. If you had to have one cookbook and that's all you could have, this one would do it."
CBS San Francisco on **The New Family Cookbook**

"The sum total of exhaustive experimentation . . . anyone interested in gluten-free cookery simply shouldn't be without it."
Nigella Lawson on **The How Can It Be Gluten-Free Cookbook**

"Even ultra-experienced gluten-free cooks and bakers will learn something from this thoroughly researched, thoughtfully presented volume."
Publisher's Weekly on **The How Can It Be Gluten-Free Cookbook**

"One bag, three meals? Get the biggest bang for your grocery buck."
Fox News on **The Make-Ahead Cook**

"The go-to gift book for newlyweds, small families or empty nesters."
Orlando Sentinel on **The Complete Cooking for Two Cookbook**

"A one-volume kitchen seminar, addressing in one smart chapter after another the sometimes surprising whys behind a cook's best practices. . . . You get the myth, the theory, the science and the proof, all rigorously interrogated as only America's Test Kitchen can do."
NPR on **The Science of Good Cooking**

"Scrupulously tested regional and heirloom recipes."
The New York Times on **The Cook's Country Cookbook**

"Carnivores with an obsession for perfection will likely have found their new bible in this comprehensive collection."
Publisher's Weekly (Starred Review) on **The Cook's Illustrated Meat Book**

"This book is a comprehensive, no-nonsense guide . . . a well-thought-out, clearly explained primer for every aspect of home baking."
The Wall Street Journal on **The Cook's Illustrated Baking Book**

"Buy this gem for the foodie in your family, and spend the extra money to get yourself a copy too."
The Missourian on **The Best of America's Test Kitchen 2015**

"Some 2,500 photos walk readers through 600 painstakingly tested recipes, leaving little room for error."
Associated Press on **The America's Test Kitchen Cooking School Cookbook**

"Cook-friendly and kitchen-oriented, illuminating the process of preparing food instead of mystifying it . . . . the perfect kitchen home companion."
The Wall Street Journal on **The Cook's Illustrated Cookbook**

"If this were the only cookbook you owned, you would cook well, be everyone's favorite host, have a well-run kitchen, and eat happily every day."
Thecitycook.com on **The America's Test Kitchen Menu Cookbook**

"Further proof that practice makes perfect, if not transcendent. . . . If an intermediate cook follows the directions exactly, the results will be better than takeout or Mom's."
The New York Times on **The New Best Recipes**

"There are pasta books . . . and then there's this pasta book. Flip your carbohydrate dreams upside down and strain them through this sieve of revolutionary, creative, and also traditional recipes."
San Francisco Book Review on **Pasta Revolution**

THE COMPLETE
Cook's Country
TV SHOW COOKBOOK

EVERY RECIPE
EVERY INGREDIENT TESTING
EVERY EQUIPMENT RATING
FROM
ALL 8 SEASONS

BY THE EDITORS AT AMERICA'S TEST KITCHEN

PHOTOGRAPHY BY KELLER + KELLER

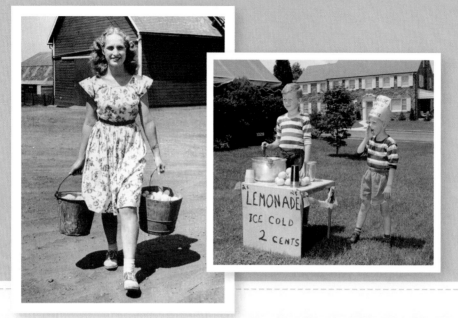

America's Test Kitchen
17 Station Street
Brookline, MA 02445

The Complete Cook's Country TV Show Cookbook
Every Recipe, Every Ingredient Testing, Every Equipment Rating
From All 8 Seasons

ISBN 978-1-940352-17-6
ISSN 2330-5762
Paperback: US $29.95 / $35.00 CAN

Manufactured in the United States of America
10 9 8 7 6 5 4 3 2

Distributed by Penguin Random House Publisher Services
tel: 800-733-3000

facebook.com/americastestkitchen

twitter.com/TestKitchen

youtube.com/AmericasTestKitchen

instagram.com/TestKitchen

pinterest.com/TestKitchen

americastestkitchen.tumblr.com

google.com/+AmericasTestKitchen

Editorial Director: Jack Bishop
Editorial Director, Books: Elizabeth Carduff
Executive Editor: Lori Galvin
Senior Editor: Debra Hudak
Editorial Assistant: Kate Ander
Photography by: Keller + Keller
Staff Photographer: Daniel J. van Ackere
Additional Photography by: Stephen Hussar and Carl Tremblay
Cover Photo: Kate Kelley
Photography Director: Julie Cote
Associate Art Director, Photography: Steve Klise
Food Stylists: Mary Jane Sawyer, Marie Piraino, Catrine Kelty, and Daniel Cellucci
Design Director: Amy Klee
Art Director: Greg Galvan
Associate Art Director: Taylor Argenzio
Designer: Jen Kanavos Hoffman
Production Director: Guy Rochford
Senior Production Manager: Jessica Lindheimer Quirk
Project Manager: Britt Dresser
Production Management Specialist: Christine Walsh
Production and Imaging Specialists: Heather Dube, Sean MacDonald, Dennis Noble, Lauren Robbins, and Jessica Voas
Historical Researcher: Meg Ragland
Copy Editor: Cheryl Redmond
Proofreader: Amanda Poulsen Dix
Indexer: Elizabeth Parson

Credits for archival photography are listed on page 564

AMERICA'S
TEST KITCHEN
RECIPES THAT WORK®

CooksCountry.com
AmericasTestKitchenTV.com
CooksCountryTV.com
AmericasTestKitchenFeed.com

CONTENTS

PREFACE

The farmhouse where *Cook's Country* is filmed was originally part of the Sheldon farm and later became known as the Carver house. The house required major renovation and was also moved back 12 feet from the main road.

Dear Home Cook,

For years I had driven by the Carver house (the current home of *Cook's Country from America's Test Kitchen*) when it was in a state of serious disrepair. Although just 12 feet back from the road, it was hidden in a jungle of bushes and poplar, the clapboards were chipped and stained, and the foundation was sinking down badly on the right side. But having some experience inspecting old houses, I noticed that the roofline was straight and that the lines were good. Little did I realize that some day I would purchase the old farmhouse and strip it back to pretty much the bones. It needed a thorough rehabilitation, except for the straight roofline of course!

Today, we use the Carver house for shooting *Cook's Country from America's Test Kitchen* on public television. It is just down from the post office (which is about the size of a 10-yard dumpster), across the street from one of three churches in our town, and a few doors up from the town library, where, in summer months, you can go see a movie on Saturday night. It is also a stone's throw from the firehouse where we celebrate Old Home Day in August and where numerous barbecues and chicken dinners are given throughout the year to raise money for the all-volunteer squad.

All of this history is by way of saying that this is a real house with a real past, not some set constructed for a television show. The same can be said for the magazine, *Cook's Country,* and the TV show.

This is one of the three churches in town and it sits right across the street from the Carver house.

This is real regional American food, from the past as well as the present, and it comes from a real place where it was cooked by your grandmother or my great uncle. As they say in the art business, this food has "provenance."

Our goal is to assemble and rehabilitate America's culinary past and present by seeking out lost and regional recipes—Colorado Green Chili, Natchitoches Meat Pies, "Impossible" Ham and Cheese Pie, Italian Cream Cake—and bring them up to date and freshen them up for a new audience. This isn't "meals in minutes" or four-ingredient suppers—this is real cooking for real cooks. Sometimes we make up new favorites such as Skillet Lasagna or find better ways to use appliances such as the slow cooker, but the cooking we do at *Cook's Country,* just like the old house, starts with a good foundation.

For almost 50 years, I have seen the sun rise over Minister Hill and gone fishing in the Green River. I have seen Charlie Bentley and his father before him drive by in an old Ford pickup. I have watched the yellow farmhouse where I had dinner as a kid go through changes

The farmhouse also has a horse barn on the property that is built on a marble foundation. A large dairy barn in back is in poor shape but is still standing.

I often sit on the porch during breaks in the filming—one of the many benefits of filming in a real farmhouse!

over the decades from working farm, to homestead, to a rental property with clothes hanging on a line on the side porch.

Good recipes like good places have good bones and they wear well. That's what this collection of recipes is all about: not just a complete collection of all of the recipes that have appeared on our TV show along with an ingredient and equipment shopping guide, but a group of dishes that tell a story about who we are and where we came from. Now that these recipes have been put through our exhaustive test kitchen process, you can also rest assured that the food will turn out just right, even the first time you make it.

As a kid, I remember sitting in the front parlor of the yellow farmhouse listening to Floyd Bentley, rheumy eyes looking downward, a deep cough in his chest from smoking, tell story after story about the brothers who jacked a deer and got caught, or "Little Man," who was bigger than a refrigerator, or the one about the Butler sisters, who had just one pair of false teeth between them so they traded off every Saturday night.

All of the recipes in this volume have stories, too, and yet they have been updated, tested, and spruced up to work in your kitchen tonight. The food will surprise you when you get a good taste of it; it's as modern and fresh as the day it was first put together.

That reminds me of the story of a farmer during the Depression. He went down to Hoosick Falls to get breakfast at the diner and he brought along two bull calves. He left them by the side of the road in a makeshift pen with a FREE sign on it. After breakfast, he went out and found three calves, not two. He couldn't even give them away!

A lot of recipes are like that these days; they are so commonplace that nobody wants them. But as with a good horse or a well-trained dog, once you find a good one, you never let go. That's how we feel about this collection of country recipes—once you try a few, you'll stick by us. It's worth every mouthful.

So that's our story. That's where we come from. And that's why we care so much about the food in this book and on our television show. We invite you to take a taste of our past and our present and to join us in a renewed appreciation of what the American kitchen has to offer.

Cordially,
Christopher Kimball
Founder and Editor,
Cook's Illustrated and *Cook's Country*
Host, *America's Test Kitchen* and
Cook's Country from America's Test Kitchen

WELCOME TO COOK'S COUNTRY

This book has been tested, written, and edited by the folks at America's Test Kitchen, a very real 2,500-square-foot kitchen located just outside of Boston. It is the home of *Cook's Country* and *Cook's Illustrated* magazines and is the Monday-through-Friday destination for more than three dozen test cooks, editors, food scientists, tasters, and cookware specialists. Our mission is to test recipes over and over again until we understand how and why they work and until we arrive at the "best" version.

Filmed in a renovated 1806 farmhouse, *Cook's Country from America's Test Kitchen* features the best regional home cooking in the country and relies on the same practical, no-nonsense approach to cooking that has made *Cook's Country* magazine so successful.

Christopher Kimball, the founder and editor of *Cook's Country* and *Cook's Illustrated* magazines, is the host of the show and asks the questions you might ask. It's the job of our chefs, Julia Collin Davison, Bridget Lancaster, and Erin McMurrer, to demonstrate our recipes. The chefs show Chris what works and what doesn't, and they explain why. In the process, they discuss (and show you) the best examples from our development process as well as the worst. Jack Bishop continues to challenge Chris to live tastings of kitchen staples like egg noodles, blue cheese dressing, and orange juice, while Adam Ried reveals the test kitchen's top choices for equipment, including cookie sheets, slow cookers, aprons, and more.

Although just six cooks and editors appear on the television show, more than 60 other people worked to make the show a reality. Executive producer Melissa Baldino conceived and developed each episode along with co-executive producer Stephanie Stender and lead production assistant Kaitlin Hammond. Lynne Olver and Meg Ragland assisted with all the historical recipe research. Debby Paddock assisted with photography research.

Along with the on-air crew, executive chefs Erin McMurrer, Christie Morrison, and Dan Zuccarello helped plan and organize the 13 television episodes shot in September 2014 and ran the "back kitchen," where all the food that appears on camera originated. Hannah Crowley, Lauren Savoie, Kate Shannon, and Lisa McManus organized the tasting and equipment segments.

During filming, chefs Morgan Bolling, Cecelia Jenkins, Lawman Johnson, Lan Lam, Ashley Moore, Russell Selander, Dan Souza, Diane Unger, and Anne Wolf cooked all the food needed on set. Kitchen assistants Ena Gudiel and Erica Sheridan also worked long hours. Chefs Daniel Cellucci, Sebastian Nava, Leah Rovner, and Stephanie Pixley helped coordinate the kitchen with the television set by readying props, equipment, and food. Assistant test kitchen director Leah Rovner and senior kitchen assistants Michelle Blodget and Alexxa Grattan were charged with making sure all the ingredients and kitchen equipment we needed were on hand.

Special thanks to director Jan Maliszewski, director of photography, Michael McEachern, and editor and assistant director Travis Marshall. We also appreciate the hard work of the video production team, including Rena Maliszewski, Alisa Placas Frutman, Ken Fraser, Stephen Hussar, Tom Robertson, Peter Dingle, Roger Macie, Gilles Morin, Joe Christofori, Brenda

Coffey, Jim Hirsch, Jeff Hamel, Jeremy Bond, Bob Hirsch, Marc Jameson, Ken Bauer, Kelly Emerson, Eric Joslin, and Brian Depaul Carey. Thanks also to Dexter Media and Nick Dakoulas, our second unit director.

We also would like to thank Nancy Bocchino, Bara Levin, and Victoria Yuen at WGBH, and Judy Barlow at American Public Television, which presents the show.

DCS by Fisher & Paykel, Blue Apron, Chef's Catalog, and Valley Fig Growers sponsored the show and we thank them for their support. We also thank Michael Burton, Deborah Fagone, Kate Zebrowski, and Morgan Mannino for serving our sponsors and Deborah Broide for managing publicity.

Aprons were made by Crooked Brook. Props were designed and developed by Ross MacDonald. Thanks to music supervisor Christopher Sabec, Aaron Redner, and the band Hot Buttered Rum. Thanks also to kitchen designer Paul Worthington.

We also thank Doug Armstrong, Axel and Donna Blomberg, Charles and Rachael Armstrong, Fred Pickering, Al Ducci's, Rupert Rising Bread, Sherman's Country Store, Depot 62, Dutton Farms, Someday Farm, the Community Food Cupboard, George's Dry Cleaning Service, T&N Builders, Vermont Kitchen Store, rk Miles, Scott Dicky and Cheryl Smith of Shaw's supermarket in Manchester, Vermont, J.K. Adams, Mettowee Mill Nursery, Rupert United Methodist Church, Barrows House, The Dorset Inn, Roche Bros. E-commerce Department in West Roxbury, Massachusetts, and Whole Foods Market.

AS GOOD AS GRANDMA'S

NOSTALGIA ISN'T THE ONLY REASON MOST OF US THINK OUR grandmother's (or mother's) dishes tasted best. Most likely our forebears in the kitchen really were experts at what they cooked—after all, they cooked the same dishes over and over again. It can seem hard to believe today, but most home cooks cooked out of the same book (or two) during their entire lifetime: books like *The Joy of Cooking*, *The Boston Cooking-School Cookbook* (later known as *The Fannie Farmer Cooking School Cookbook*), *The Settlement Cook Book*, and just a handful of others. Outside of cookbooks, newsstands didn't bulge with dozens of cooking magazines either. Women were more likely to turn to women's service magazines, such as *Ladies Home Journal* and *Good Housekeeping*, which tackled all manner of domestic issues, not just cooking. These publications came on the scene after the Civil War and were a terrific resource when family was not at hand to show a new bride the ropes of running a home. Thus, with access to a fairly small universe of recipes, most home cooks prepared the food they grew up eating—macaroni and cheese, meatloaf, and smothered pork chops—and along the way, clipped the occasional recipe from a newspaper, magazine, or back of the box, often fancy restaurant dishes that became simplified for home cooking, such as Chicken Divan and Chicken Florentine. In this chapter, we give you those recipes, made as good as we remember—and maybe even a little better.

✓ WHY THIS RECIPE WORKS

To pack our mac and cheese with bright tomato flavor, we discovered that undercooking the pasta and adding petite canned diced tomatoes with their juices to the drained macaroni allowed the macaroni to soak up more of the tomato flavor. Returning the pasta to the heat afterward allowed the noodles to absorb some of the tomato juice. Finally, to avoid a curdled sauce, we added fat in the form of half-and-half (cut with some chicken broth) and a mix of sharp and mild cheddar cheeses.

Macaroni and Cheese with Tomatoes

SERVES 8 TO 10

Let the finished dish rest for 10 to 15 minutes before you serve it; otherwise, it will be soupy.

1	**pound elbow macaroni**
	Salt and pepper
1	**(28-ounce) can petite diced tomatoes**
6	**tablespoons unsalted butter**
½	**cup all-purpose flour**
¼	**teaspoon cayenne pepper**
4	**cups half-and-half**
1	**cup chicken broth**
1	**pound mild cheddar cheese, shredded (4 cups)**
8	**ounces sharp cheddar cheese, shredded (2 cups)**

1. Adjust oven rack to middle position and heat oven to 400 degrees. Bring 4 quarts water to boil in large Dutch oven. Add macaroni and 1 tablespoon salt and cook, stirring often, until just al dente, about 6 minutes. Drain pasta and return to pot. Pour diced tomatoes with their juices over pasta and stir to coat. Cook over medium-high heat, stirring occasionally, until most of liquid is absorbed, about 5 minutes. Set aside.

2. Meanwhile, melt butter in medium saucepan over medium heat. Stir in flour and cayenne and cook until golden, about 1 minute. Slowly whisk in half-and-half and broth until smooth. Bring to boil, reduce heat to medium, and simmer, stirring occasionally, until mixture is slightly thickened, about 15 minutes. Off heat, whisk in cheeses, 1 teaspoon salt, and 1 teaspoon pepper until cheeses melt. Pour sauce over macaroni and stir to combine.

3. Scrape mixture into 13 by 9-inch baking dish set in rimmed baking sheet and bake until top begins to brown, 15 to 20 minutes. Let sit for 10 to 15 minutes before serving.

TO MAKE AHEAD: The macaroni and cheese can be made in advance through step 2. Scrape mixture into 13 by 9-inch baking dish, cool, lay plastic wrap directly on surface of pasta, and refrigerate for up to 2 days. When ready to bake, remove plastic, cover with aluminum foil, and bake for 30 minutes. Uncover and bake until top is golden brown, about 15 minutes. Let sit for 10 to 15 minutes before serving.

AN AUTOMAT CLASSIC

Home cooks have long put their stamp on plain-Jane macaroni and cheese, stirring in such items as hot dogs or diced ham and peas. One appealing, old-fashioned variation, however, is practically endangered: baked macaroni and cheese with tomato. The genius in the recipe is that the bright acid of the tomato cuts the richness of the cheese. Today, people of a certain age remember tomato mac and cheese fondly from Horn and Hardart's automats.

Automats started in Germany in 1896 as a way to quickly feed hundreds of thousands of workers during their lunch hour. The idea was very much like a vending machine. Rather than ordering their meals through a server, patrons would drop coins into a slot to open a glass door in front of a compartment holding a menu item. Frank Hardart brought back the automat idea after a visit to Germany. Hardart, along with his partner, Joseph B. Horn, hired an engineer to further simplify the German system so they could transform their traditional lunch counter into an automat in 1902.

As for one of their most popular menu items, macaroni and cheese with tomatoes, most of us have never heard of it, much less tasted it. Automats may be a thing of the past, but a good recipe for macaroni and cheese shouldn't be.

✓ WHY THIS RECIPE WORKS

Unlike many macaroni and cheese recipes, our Best Potluck Macaroni and Cheese is creamy, sturdy, and rich. We prevented the sauce from separating and clumping when baked by using evaporated milk and American cheese—the stabilizers in these ingredients kept the sauce from breaking, so that it emerged from the oven satiny smooth. Homemade bread crumbs, enriched with melted butter and Parmesan cheese, created a flavorful, crisp topping.

Best Potluck Macaroni and Cheese

SERVES 8 TO 10

Block American cheese from the deli counter is best here, as prewrapped singles result in a drier mac and cheese.

4	slices hearty white sandwich bread, torn into quarters
4	tablespoons unsalted butter, melted, plus 4 tablespoons unsalted butter
¼	cup grated Parmesan cheese
1	pound elbow macaroni
	Salt
5	tablespoons all-purpose flour
3	(12-ounce) cans evaporated milk
2	teaspoons hot sauce
1	teaspoon dry mustard
⅛	teaspoon ground nutmeg
8	ounces extra-sharp cheddar cheese, shredded (2 cups)
5	ounces American cheese, shredded (1¼ cups)
3	ounces Monterey Jack cheese, shredded (¾ cup)

1. Adjust oven rack to middle position and heat oven to 350 degrees. Pulse bread, melted butter, and Parmesan in food processor until ground to coarse crumbs, about 8 pulses. Transfer to bowl.

2. Bring 4 quarts water to boil in large pot. Add macaroni and 1 tablespoon salt and cook, stirring often, until just al dente, about 6 minutes. Reserve ½ cup macaroni cooking water, then drain and rinse macaroni in colander under cold running water. Set aside.

3. Melt remaining 4 tablespoons butter in now-empty pot over medium-high heat. Stir in flour and cook, stirring constantly, until mixture turns light brown, about 1 minute. Slowly whisk in evaporated milk, hot sauce, mustard, nutmeg, and 2 teaspoons salt and cook until mixture begins to simmer and is slightly thickened, about 4 minutes. Off heat, whisk in cheeses and reserved cooking water until cheese melts. Stir in macaroni until completely coated.

4. Transfer mixture to 13 by 9-inch baking dish and top evenly with bread-crumb mixture. Bake until cheese is bubbling around edges and top is golden brown, 20 to 25 minutes. Let sit for 5 to 10 minutes before serving.

TO MAKE AHEAD: The macaroni and cheese can be made in advance through step 3. Increase amount of reserved macaroni cooking water to 1 cup. Scrape mixture into 13 by 9-inch baking dish, cool, lay plastic wrap directly on surface of pasta, and refrigerate for up to 1 day. Bread-crumb mixture may be refrigerated for up to 2 days. When ready to bake, remove plastic, cover with aluminum foil, and bake for 30 minutes. Uncover, sprinkle bread crumbs over top, and bake until topping is golden brown, about 20 minutes longer. Let sit before serving.

KEEPING IT TOGETHER

Using already stabilized ingredients like American cheese and evaporated milk ensures that this cheesy sauce doesn't break in the oven.

WHY THIS RECIPE WORKS

Grits are a southern staple, but their appeal can be lost in bland, gluey incarnations. To take this down-home dish from dull to delicious, we needed to work on both texture and flavor. Replacing some of the cooking water with milk gave a creamy sweetness to the unadorned grits. As for the cheese, we found that a combination of Monterey Jack and sharp cheddar lent both smoothness and pronounced cheesy flavor. To give the dish more depth, we sautéed scallion whites and added real pureed corn for an extra boost of corn flavor.

Creamy Cheese Grits

The grits are ready when they are mostly creamy but still retain a little bite. If the grits get too thick, whisk in a little water. If you are using frozen corn, thaw it first.

½	cup fresh or frozen corn kernels
3½	cups water
4	tablespoons unsalted butter
4	scallions, white parts minced, green parts sliced thin
1	cup milk
½	teaspoon hot sauce
	Salt and pepper
1	cup old-fashioned grits
4	ounces Monterey Jack cheese, shredded (1 cup)
4	ounces sharp cheddar cheese, shredded (1 cup)

1. Puree corn and ¼ cup water in blender until smooth, about 1 minute; set aside. Melt 2 tablespoons butter in medium saucepan over medium heat. Add scallion whites and cook until softened, about 2 minutes. Stir in remaining 3¼ cups water, milk, hot sauce, ½ teaspoon salt, and ½ teaspoon pepper and bring to boil.

2. Slowly whisk grits into saucepan until no lumps remain. Reduce heat to low and cook, stirring frequently, until thick and creamy, about 15 minutes.

3. Off heat, stir in Monterey Jack, cheddar, pureed corn, and remaining 2 tablespoons butter until incorporated. Season with salt and pepper to taste. Serve sprinkled with scallion greens.

KNOW YOUR CORN

CORNMEAL: Cornmeal is corn kernels that are dried and ground to a powder.
GRITS: Grits are cornmeal, but the name also refers to the cooked porridge so popular in the South.
HOMINY GRITS: Hominy grits are corn kernels with the hull and bran removed before grinding.
POLENTA: Polenta is cornmeal, but the name also refers to the cooked Italian porridge, which is traditionally enriched with butter and Parmesan.

WEIGHING CHEESE

Our recipes specify cup amounts of cheese to reflect the habits of the typical home cook. But cheese is sold by weight, so it can be hard to determine how much to buy. Also, one person's measure may not precisely equal another's. To complicate matters, we classify cheese into three categories: hard, such as Parmesan and Pecorino Romano; semisoft, such as cheddar and Monterey Jack; and soft, such as feta, blue, and fresh goat cheeses. Each packs into cup measures differently. To develop a standard weight for each cheese category, we gathered 10 test cooks and had each weigh out 1-cup samples of each type. We averaged the weights to account for the heavy and light hands of different individuals. We found that 1 cup of grated hard cheese equals about 2 ounces, while the same measure of soft and semisoft is about 4 ounces. And remember, when measuring cheese, lightly pack measuring cups meant for dry ingredients; don't use liquid measuring cups, which will give you an inaccurate measurement for dry ingredients.

✅ WHY THIS RECIPE WORKS

To restore chicken Florentine to its elegant roots, we started with fresh spinach. To prevent the water from the spinach from washing out the other flavors in the dish, we drained excess liquid from the cooked spinach by pressing the leaves with the back of a spoon in a colander. For flavor, we seared the chicken breasts first and then poached them in the sauce before broiling. We used cream to make the sauce silky and built volume with equal amounts of chicken broth and water. We also added a squeeze of lemon juice and a hit of zest, along with Parmesan cheese for its nutty, savory punch.

Chicken Florentine

SERVES 4 TO 6

We like tender, quick-cooking bagged baby spinach here; if using curly-leaf spinach, chop it before cooking.

2	**tablespoons vegetable oil**
12	**ounces (12 cups) baby spinach**
4	**(6-ounce) boneless, skinless chicken breasts, trimmed**
	Salt and pepper
1	**shallot, minced**
2	**garlic cloves, minced**
1¼	**cups chicken broth**
1¼	**cups water**
1	**cup heavy cream**
6	**tablespoons grated Parmesan cheese**
1	**teaspoon grated lemon zest plus 1 teaspoon juice**

1. Adjust oven rack to upper-middle position and heat broiler. Heat 1 tablespoon oil in 12-inch skillet over medium-high heat until shimmering. Add spinach and cook, stirring occasionally until wilted, 1 to 2 minutes. Transfer spinach to colander set over bowl and press with spoon to release excess liquid. Discard liquid.

2. Pat chicken dry with paper towels and season with salt and pepper. Wipe out pan and heat remaining 1 tablespoon oil over medium-high heat until just smoking. Cook chicken on both sides until golden, 4 to 6 minutes. Add shallot and garlic to skillet and cook until fragrant, about 30 seconds. Stir in broth, water, and cream and bring to boil.

3. Reduce heat to medium-low and simmer until chicken is cooked through, about 10 minutes; transfer chicken to plate and tent with aluminum foil. Continue to simmer sauce until reduced to 1 cup, about 10 minutes. Off heat, stir in 4 tablespoons Parmesan and lemon zest and juice.

4. Cut chicken crosswise into ½-inch-thick slices and arrange on broiler-safe platter. Scatter spinach over chicken and pour sauce over spinach. Sprinkle with remaining Parmesan and broil until golden brown, 3 to 5 minutes. Serve.

DRAINING SPINACH

As it cooks, spinach releases a lot of moisture, which can make dishes like our Chicken Florentine watery. To prevent that, we transferred the spinach to a colander and pressed the leaves with a spoon to force the liquid out. We drained nearly ¼ cup of liquid from the 12 ounces of spinach used in this recipe.

ENCHANTING CHICKEN– WITHOUT A WAND

The idea of chicken Florentine as a dish made from chicken, spinach, and a cheesy cream sauce appeared in print as early as 1931, when *The Lowell (Mass.) Sun* breathlessly described Chicken Mornay Florentine as served at the Manhattan restaurant, Divan Parisien: "They make magic passes over spinach, then cover it with breasts of chicken and a Mornay sauce." In the "Tables for Two" column of *The New Yorker*, April 25, 1931, the Divan Parisien was described as "a quiet and extremely civilized restaurant with an assorted clientele. . . ." What a shame then, that one of their most popular dishes morphed to a 1960s casserole (made with frozen spinach, margarine, packaged bread crumbs, and condensed soups) and then to wedding banquet fare in the 1970s and '80s (breasts stuffed with spinach, rolled, fried, and served with a cheesy sauce). We wanted to deconstruct the casserole, unroll the spirals, and return chicken Florentine to its earliest version: a bright, elegant, streamlined sauté with a pan sauce. No magic passes involved.

THE DIVAN PARISIEN RESTAURANT

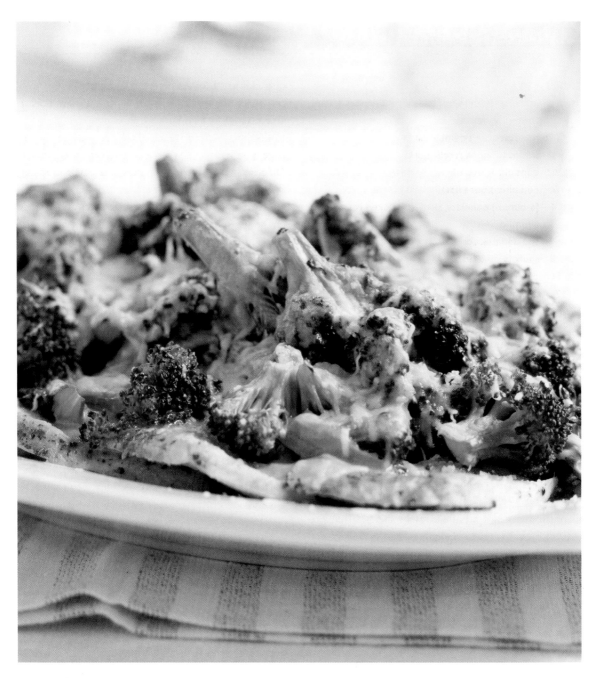

✓ WHY THIS RECIPE WORKS

Once-trendy chicken Divan's original recipe calls for many different components and even more cooking steps. We wanted to stay true to the original flavor of the dish but streamline the cooking process. To do this, we batch-cooked the broccoli first, then the chicken. While the broccoli and chicken rested, we used the same pan to prepare our sauce. And instead of making a separate hollandaise sauce, like the traditional chicken Divan recipes demand, we whisked egg yolks and lemon juice together, then tempered the mixture with the hot pan sauce, and whisked in butter at the end.

Chicken Divan

Use one small onion instead of the shallots, if desired.

- 3   tablespoons vegetable oil
- 1   pound broccoli florets, cut into 1-inch pieces
- 2½   cups chicken broth
- ¼   cup all-purpose flour
- 4   (6-ounce) boneless, skinless chicken breasts, trimmed
-   Salt and pepper
- 2   shallots, minced
- 1   cup heavy cream
- ½   cup dry sherry
- 2   teaspoons Worcestershire sauce
- 3   ounces Parmesan cheese, grated (1½ cups)
- 3   large egg yolks
- 1   tablespoon lemon juice
- 3   tablespoons unsalted butter

1. Adjust oven rack to lower-middle position and heat broiler. Heat 1 tablespoon oil in large skillet over medium-high heat until just smoking. Add broccoli and cook until spotty brown, about 1 minute. Add ½ cup broth, cover, and steam until just tender, about 1½ minutes. Remove lid and cook until liquid has evaporated, about 1 minute. Transfer broccoli to plate lined with paper towels; rinse and wipe out skillet.

2. Heat remaining 2 tablespoons oil in now-empty skillet over medium-high heat until smoking. Meanwhile, place flour in shallow dish. Season chicken with salt and pepper and dredge in flour to coat. Cook chicken until golden brown on both sides, 4 to 6 minutes. Transfer chicken to plate.

3. Off heat, add shallots to skillet and cook until just softened, about 1 minute. Add remaining 2 cups broth and cream and scrape browned bits from bottom of pan. Return chicken to skillet and simmer over medium-high heat until cooked through, about 10 minutes. Transfer chicken to clean plate and continue to simmer sauce until reduced to 1 cup, about 10 minutes. Add sherry and Worcestershire and simmer until reduced again to 1 cup, about 3 minutes.

4. Stir in 1 cup Parmesan. Whisk egg yolks and lemon juice in small bowl, then whisk in about ¼ cup sauce. Off heat, whisk egg yolk mixture into sauce in skillet, then whisk in butter.

5. Cut chicken into ½-inch-thick slices and arrange on broiler-safe platter. Scatter broccoli over chicken and pour sauce over broccoli. Sprinkle with remaining ½ cup Parmesan and broil until golden brown, 3 to 5 minutes. Serve.

BROCCOLI MAKES IT TO THE BIG TIME

BROCCOLI
ITALIAN GREEN SPROUTING
Everett's Seed Store
INDIANAPOLIS, IND.

It can seem hard to believe today, but broccoli, a key ingredient in chicken Divan, an elegant chicken dish from Manhattan's Divan Parisien restaurant (see page 9), was a relative latecomer to the American diet. This headline from *The New York Times* in 1926 attests to its arrival on the scene: "New Vegetables Vary our Menus: Broccoli, Artichoke, and Avocado Naturalized, and Fennel Enters Under Foreign Name—Homely Carrot Is Still in Demand." Broccoli aside, the restaurant's recipe required a whole poached chicken and a sauce made with béchamel, hollandaise, Parmesan cheese, and whipped cream. The ingredients were combined *à la minute* (just before being plated) and broiled to perfection. Sounds good, but if we're counting right, that's at least five pots, four recipes, and more time than we'd care to spend in the kitchen. No wonder most "modern" recipes rely on canned soup. We wanted to bring Divan into the 21st century without compromising the flavors of the original dish.

✅ WHY THIS RECIPE WORKS

For our old-fashioned meatloaf, we cut ground beef with an equal portion of sweet ground pork for better flavor. As for seasoning, we stuck with tradition: salt, pepper, Dijon mustard, Worcestershire sauce, thyme, parsley, sautéed onion, and garlic. To add moisture and structure, we used a panade (paste) of milk and saltines. Combining the panade in a food processor and then pulsing it with the meat gave the loaf the most cohesive, tender structure. To evaporate the surface moisture that was inhibiting the formation of a crust, we broiled the loaf prior to baking and glazing.

Glazed Meatloaf

SERVES 6 TO 8

Both ground sirloin and ground chuck work well here, but avoid ground round—it is gristly and bland.

GLAZE

1	cup ketchup
¼	cup packed brown sugar
2½	tablespoons cider vinegar
½	teaspoon hot sauce

MEATLOAF

2	teaspoons vegetable oil
1	onion, chopped fine
2	garlic cloves, minced
17	saltines
⅓	cup whole milk
1	pound 90 percent lean ground beef
1	pound ground pork
2	large eggs plus 1 large yolk
⅓	cup finely chopped fresh parsley
2	teaspoons Dijon mustard
2	teaspoons Worcestershire sauce
½	teaspoon dried thyme
	Salt and pepper

1. FOR THE GLAZE: Whisk all ingredients in saucepan until sugar dissolves. Reserve ¼ cup glaze mixture, then simmer remaining glaze over medium heat until slightly thickened, about 5 minutes. Cover and keep warm.

2. FOR THE MEATLOAF: Line rimmed baking sheet with aluminum foil and coat lightly with vegetable oil spray. Heat oil in nonstick skillet over medium heat until shimmering. Cook onion until golden, about 8 minutes. Add garlic and cook until fragrant, about 30 seconds. Transfer to large bowl.

3. Process saltines and milk in food processor until smooth, about 30 seconds. Add beef and pork and pulse until well combined, about 10 pulses. Transfer meat mixture to bowl with cooled onion mixture. Add eggs and yolk, parsley, mustard, Worcestershire, thyme, 1 teaspoon salt, and ¾ teaspoon pepper to bowl and mix with hands until combined.

4. Adjust 1 oven rack to middle position and second rack 4 inches from broiler element; heat broiler. Transfer meat mixture to prepared baking sheet and shape into 9 by 5-inch loaf. Broil on upper rack until well browned, about 5 minutes. Brush 2 tablespoons unreduced glaze over top and sides of loaf and then return to oven and broil until glaze begins to brown, about 2 minutes.

5. Transfer meatloaf to lower rack and brush with remaining unreduced glaze. Reduce oven temperature to 350 degrees and bake until meatloaf registers 160 degrees, 40 to 45 minutes. Transfer to cutting board, tent with foil, and let rest for 20 minutes. Slice and serve, passing remaining reduced glaze at table.

KETCHUP–THE TRUFFLE OIL OF THE '20s?

Say "meatloaf" and most Americans think 1950s comfort food and Mom, but this humble recipe has surprisingly elegant roots in a now-forgotten dish called "cannelon." A typical cannelon recipe from the original *Boston Cooking-School Cookbook* calls for chopping and seasoning beef, shaping it into a log, and basting with melted butter as it bakes. The wide availability of meat grinders and the advent of reliable refrigeration made ground beef a household staple in the early 20th century and meatloaf recipes gained wide circulation. As a topping, butter was usurped by tomato sauce until ketchup became popular in the 1920s. The Heinz company created a "House of Heinz" campaign to tout the gourmet appeal their products gave to everyday dishes such as meatloaf. Along with their ketchup, Heinz suggested incorporating other Heinz products, such as beefsteak sauce, chili sauce, and olives into meatloaf, or serving cubes of meatloaf with pickle slices for an easy hors d'oeuvre. For our meatloaf, we skipped the gourmet aspirations and unnecessary mix-ins for a stellar version of the 1950s favorite.

✓ WHY THIS RECIPE WORKS

Meatloaf and potatoes are an unbeatable combination, so frosted meatloaf—meatloaf coated in a layer of mashed potatoes—was an idea we could get behind. To perfect this nearly forgotten 1950s classic, we found that we had to broil the meatloaf in stages to keep the potatoes from slipping off: First, it was broiled to create a crust and then coated with a tangy, ketchup-based glaze for flavor and broiled again. After cooking through, the meatloaf was frosted with creamy mashed potatoes and broiled for a final stint to turn the fluffy crown of potatoes beautifully brown.

Frosted Meatloaf

SERVES 6 TO 8

If you don't have a ricer or a food mill, just mash the potatoes thoroughly.

¼	cup ketchup
1	tablespoon packed light brown sugar
1	tablespoon cider vinegar
½	teaspoon hot sauce
8	tablespoons unsalted butter
1	onion, chopped fine
3	garlic cloves, minced
17	square or 19 round saltines, crushed (⅔ cup)
1	cup whole milk
1	pound ground pork
2	large eggs plus 1 large yolk
⅓	cup minced fresh parsley
2	teaspoons Dijon mustard
2	teaspoons Worcestershire sauce
	Salt and pepper
½	teaspoon dried thyme
1	pound 90 percent lean ground beef
2	pounds russet potatoes, peeled and cut into 1-inch pieces

1. Adjust oven racks to upper-middle and lower-middle positions and heat broiler. Line rimmed baking sheet with aluminum foil, set wire rack in sheet, and place 14 by 6-inch piece of foil in center of rack. Whisk ketchup, sugar, vinegar, and hot sauce together in bowl; set aside glaze.

2. Melt 2 tablespoons butter in 10-inch skillet over medium heat. Add onion and cook until just softened, 3 to 5 minutes. Add garlic and cook until fragrant, about 30 seconds. Set aside off heat.

3. Combine saltines and ⅓ cup milk in large bowl and mash with fork until chunky paste forms. Add pork, eggs and yolk, parsley, mustard, Worcestershire, 1 teaspoon salt, ¾ teaspoon pepper, thyme, and onion mixture and knead with your hands until mostly combined. Add beef and knead until combined.

4. Transfer meat mixture to foil rectangle on wire rack and form into 9 by 6-inch loaf. Broil on upper-middle oven rack until well browned, 5 to 7 minutes. Brush glaze over top and sides of meatloaf, return to upper-middle rack, and broil until glaze begins to brown, 3 to 5 minutes. Move meatloaf to lower-middle oven rack, adjust oven temperature to 350 degrees, and bake until meatloaf registers 160 degrees, 40 to 45 minutes. Remove from oven.

5. Meanwhile, bring potatoes and 2 quarts water to boil in Dutch oven over high heat. Reduce heat to medium-low and simmer until potatoes are tender, 20 to 25 minutes; drain potatoes thoroughly in colander. Set ricer or food mill over now-empty pot and press or mill potatoes into pot. Stir 1 teaspoon salt, remaining 6 tablespoons butter, and remaining ⅔ cup milk into potatoes until combined.

6. Using offset spatula, spread mashed potatoes evenly over top and sides of meatloaf. Heat broiler and return meatloaf to lower-middle oven rack. Broil until potatoes are browned, about 15 minutes. Using foil as sling, transfer meatloaf to carving board and let rest for 15 minutes. Slice and serve.

REVIVING COMFORT FOOD

During World War II, meat was rationed. Americans were encouraged to extend short supplies through many means, boosting meatloaf's popularity. In the '50s, this classic was reinvented as a centerpiece for entertaining, topped with garnishes, glazes, sauces, and, of course, mashed potatoes.

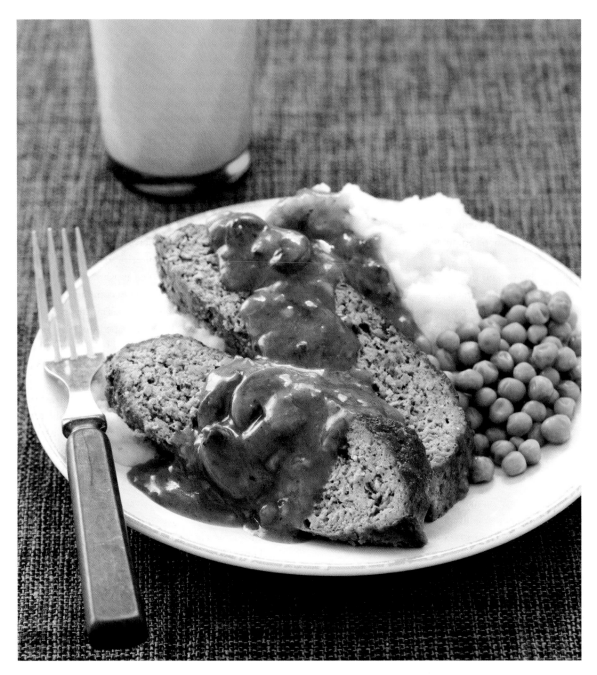

☑ WHY THIS RECIPE WORKS

As much as we love classic meatloaf, a recipe for a rustic meatloaf with a deep brown crust and hearty mushroom gravy piqued our interest. Sliced button mushrooms plus minced porcini gave the gravy an earthy richness. To further boost the flavor of the meatloaf itself, we added the porcini soaking liquid and more button mushrooms, which we ground in a food processor and sautéed. To keep the procedure simple, we baked the meatloaf in the same skillet. Then, while the loaf was resting, we used the skillet and the meat drippings to build our gravy.

Meatloaf with Mushroom Gravy

SERVES 6 TO 8

If you're short the 2 tablespoons of meatloaf drippings needed to make the gravy, supplement the drippings with melted butter or vegetable oil.

1	cup water
¼	ounce dried porcini mushrooms, rinsed
16	saltines
10	ounces white mushrooms, trimmed
1	tablespoon vegetable oil
1	onion, chopped fine
	Salt and pepper
4	garlic cloves, minced
1	pound ground pork
2	large eggs
1	tablespoon plus ¾ teaspoon Worcestershire sauce
1	pound 85 percent lean ground beef
¾	teaspoon minced fresh thyme
¼	cup all-purpose flour
2½	cups chicken broth

1. Adjust oven rack to middle position and heat oven to 375 degrees. Microwave water and porcini in covered bowl until steaming, about 1 minute. Let sit until softened, about 5 minutes. Strain porcini through fine-mesh strainer lined with coffee filter, reserving liquid. Mince and reserve porcini.

2. Process saltines in food processor until finely ground, about 30 seconds; transfer to large bowl and reserve. Pulse 5 ounces of white mushrooms in processor until finely ground, 8 to 10 pulses.

3. Heat oil in 12-inch nonstick skillet over medium-high heat until shimmering. Add onion and cook until browned, 6 to 8 minutes. Stir in processed mushrooms and ¼ teaspoon salt and cook until liquid evaporates and mushrooms begin to brown, about 5 minutes. Add garlic and cook until fragrant, about 30 seconds. Transfer to bowl with saltines and let cool to room temperature, about 15 minutes. Wipe out skillet with paper towels.

4. Add pork, ¼ cup reserved porcini liquid, eggs, 1 tablespoon Worcestershire, 1 teaspoon salt, and ¾ teaspoon pepper to cooled mushroom-saltine mixture and knead gently until nearly combined. Add beef and knead until well combined. Transfer meat mixture to now-empty skillet and shape into 10 by 6-inch loaf. Bake until meatloaf registers 160 degrees, 45 to 55 minutes. Transfer meatloaf to carving board and tent loosely with aluminum foil.

5. Slice remaining 5 ounces white mushrooms. Discard any solids in skillet and pour off all but 2 tablespoons fat. Heat fat over medium-high heat until shimmering. Add sliced mushrooms and reserved porcini and cook, stirring occasionally, until deep golden brown, 6 to 8 minutes. Stir in thyme and ¼ teaspoon salt and cook until fragrant, about 30 seconds. Add flour and cook, stirring frequently, until golden, about 2 minutes. Slowly whisk in broth, ½ cup reserved porcini liquid, and remaining ¾ teaspoon Worcestershire, scraping up any browned bits, and bring to boil. Reduce heat to medium and simmer, whisking occasionally, until thickened, 10 to 15 minutes. Season with salt and pepper to taste. Slice meatloaf and serve with gravy.

ONE SKILLET, START TO FINISH

ON THE STOVE
We brown the onion and ground mushrooms for robust flavor.

INTO THE OVEN
We shape and bake the meatloaf in the same skillet.

BACK TO THE STOVE
While the meatloaf rests, we use its drippings to make the gravy.

✓ WHY THIS RECIPE WORKS

The point of Swiss steak is to transform a tough, inexpensive cut of meat into a delicate meal so tender you can almost eat it with a spoon. Many recipes called for tenderizing the meat by pounding it before cooking, but we know from experience that pounding meat does nothing to tenderize it. Instead we relied on a slow braise to create the ideal texture. To flavor the Swiss steak gravy, we found a combination of sautéed onion, diced tomatoes, and sun-dried tomatoes was ideal.

Swiss Steak with Tomato Gravy

SERVES 6 TO 8

Top blade roast may also be labeled chuck roast first cut, top chuck roast, flat iron roast, or simply blade roast.

1	**(3½- to 4-pound) boneless top blade roast, trimmed**
	Salt and pepper
2	**tablespoons vegetable oil**
1	**onion, halved and sliced thin**
2	**tablespoons tomato paste**
1	**tablespoon all-purpose flour**
3	**garlic cloves, minced**
½	**teaspoon dried thyme**
1	**(14.5-ounce) can diced tomatoes**
1½	**cups chicken broth**
1	**tablespoon sun-dried tomatoes packed in oil, rinsed, patted dry, and minced**
1	**tablespoon minced fresh parsley**

1. Adjust oven rack to middle position and heat oven to 300 degrees. Cut roast crosswise into quarters and remove center line of gristle from each quarter to yield 8 steaks.

2. Pat steaks dry with paper towels and season lightly with salt and pepper. Heat 1 tablespoon oil in Dutch oven over medium-high heat just until smoking. Brown 4 steaks on both sides, about 6 minutes. Transfer to plate and repeat with remaining oil and steaks.

3. Add onion to empty pot and cook until softened, about 5 minutes. Add tomato paste, flour, garlic, and thyme and cook until fragrant, about 1 minute. Stir in diced tomatoes and broth and bring to boil.

4. Return steaks and any accumulated juices to pan. Cover, transfer to oven and cook until steaks are fork-tender, about 2 hours. Transfer steaks to platter, tent with aluminum foil, and let rest for 5 minutes. Skim fat from sauce. Stir in sun-dried tomatoes and parsley. Season with salt and pepper to taste. Pour sauce over steaks. Serve.

PREPARING BLADE ROAST FOR SWISS STEAK

Top blade roast, a shoulder cut with great flavor, has a pesky line of gristle that runs horizontally through its center. Follow these simple steps to remove it and cut perfect Swiss steaks.

1. Place roast on cutting board and cut crosswise into 4 even pieces.

2. One piece at a time, turn meat on its side to expose line of gristle that runs through its center.

3. Remove by slicing through meat on either side of gristle to yield 2 "steaks." Repeat with remaining pieces of blade roast to yield total of 8 steaks.

✅ WHY THIS RECIPE WORKS

We wanted to rescue this American classic from the frozen foods aisle for a great weeknight option. We started by mixing a panade (a milk and bread paste) into ground beef to help bind the meat and preserve moisture, but this trick made the dish taste too much like meatloaf. On a lark, we added mashed potatoes as seen in one recipe and were impressed with the silky texture and great flavor of the patties. To make the dish easier, we swapped in instant potato flakes. We browned the patties on both sides and let them finish cooking in the extra-rich mushroom and onion sauce, which kept the beef tender.

Salisbury Steak

SERVES 4

When shaping the patties in step 1, be sure to wet your hands to prevent sticking. Tawny port or dry sherry can be substituted for the ruby port. Do not use potato granules, which add an off-flavor.

½	cup milk
7	tablespoons instant potato flakes
1	pound 90 percent lean ground beef
	Salt and pepper
4	tablespoons unsalted butter
1	onion, halved and sliced thin
1	pound white mushrooms, trimmed and sliced thin
1	tablespoon tomato paste
2	tablespoons all-purpose flour
1¾	cups beef broth
¼	cup ruby port

1. Whisk milk and potato flakes in large bowl. Add beef, ½ teaspoon salt, and ½ teaspoon pepper and knead until combined. Shape into four ½-inch-thick oval patties and transfer to parchment paper–lined plate. Refrigerate for at least 30 minutes or up to 4 hours.

2. Melt 1 tablespoon butter in 12-inch nonstick skillet over medium-high heat. Cook patties until well browned on each side, about 10 minutes. Transfer to plate.

3. Add onion and remaining 3 tablespoons butter to now-empty skillet and cook until onion is softened, about 5 minutes. Add mushrooms and ½ teaspoon salt and cook until liquid has evaporated, 5 to 7 minutes. Stir in tomato paste and flour and cook until browned, about 2 minutes. Slowly stir in broth and port and bring to simmer. Return patties to skillet, cover, and simmer over medium-low heat until cooked through, 12 to 15 minutes. Season sauce with salt and pepper to taste. Serve.

TAKE 2 ASPIRIN–OR HAVE SOME SALISBURY STEAK

It's hard to imagine that chopped steak could be considered health food, but that's just what Dr. James Henry Salisbury had in mind when he invented his eponymous dish as a "meat cure" for wounded and ill Civil War soldiers (who were instructed to eat it three times a day—with no vegetables allowed).

Some 60 years later, during the period of World War I food rations, restaurateurs ground up their lean beef scraps, shaped them into patties, dressed the cooked patties with a rich mushroom cream sauce, and called it Salisbury steak. Around this time, recipes for Salisbury steak began showing up in cookbooks, but with a nod toward the original recipe, instructions indicated that invalids should skip the sauce. During World War II, Salisbury steak again enjoyed popularity because it was a great way to stretch meat: cream of wheat, oats, and soy grits were common fillers. And in 1965, Salisbury steak really hit the big time when Swanson introduced it in a special three-course TV dinner. Impressed by its storied past, we couldn't resist resurrecting this American classic.

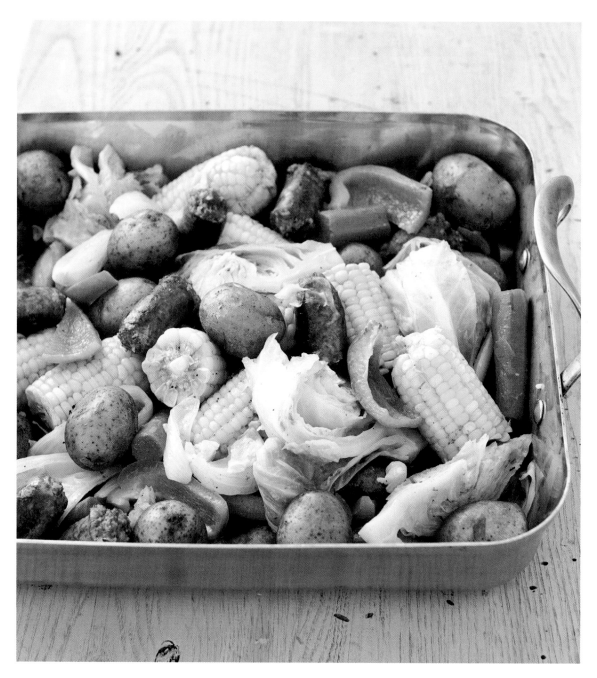

✔ WHY THIS RECIPE WORKS

Traditionally, cowboys layered vegetables and meat (usually sausage) into a giant milk can, then cooked it over an open fire to feed large groups of cowhands. To bring this all-in-one dish into the home kitchen, we opted to use a Dutch oven but keep the basic technique of layering ingredients according to cooking time. Browning the Bratwurst first created flavorful fond. We lined the bottom of the pot with sturdy red potatoes to protect the other vegetables from burning, and we added the quick-cooking green bell peppers halfway through cooking. Traditional lager as a cooking liquid gave our meat-and-potatoes meal toasty depth.

Milk-Can Supper

SERVES 6 TO 8

If your Dutch oven is slightly smaller than 8 quarts, the lid may not close all the way when you start cooking. But as the contents of the pot cook, they will decrease in volume, so you'll soon be able to clamp on the lid. Use small red potatoes, measuring 1 to 2 inches in diameter. Light-bodied American lagers, such as Budweiser, work best in this recipe.

1	tablespoon vegetable oil
2½	pounds bratwurst (10 sausages)
2	pounds small red potatoes, unpeeled
1	head green cabbage (2 pounds), cored and cut into 8 wedges
3	ears corn, husks and silk removed, ears cut into 3 pieces
6	carrots, peeled and cut into 2-inch pieces
1	onion, halved and cut through root end into 8 wedges
4	garlic cloves, peeled and smashed
10	sprigs fresh thyme
2	bay leaves
	Salt and pepper
1½	cups beer
2	green bell peppers, stemmed, seeded, and cut into 1-inch-wide strips

1. Heat oil in 8-quart Dutch oven over medium heat until shimmering. Add bratwurst and cook until browned all over, 6 to 8 minutes. Remove pot from heat. Transfer bratwurst to cutting board and halve crosswise.

2. Place potatoes in single layer in now-empty Dutch oven. Arrange cabbage wedges in single layer on top of potatoes. Layer corn, carrots, onion, garlic, thyme, bay leaves, 1 teaspoon salt, and ½ teaspoon pepper over cabbage. Pour beer over vegetables and arrange browned bratwursts on top.

3. Bring to boil over medium-high heat (wisps of steam will be visible). Cover, reduce heat to medium, and simmer for 15 minutes. Add bell peppers and continue to simmer, covered, until potatoes are tender, about 15 minutes. (Use long skewer to test potatoes for doneness.)

4. Transfer bratwurst and vegetables to large serving platter (or roasting pan, if your platter isn't large enough); discard thyme sprigs and bay leaves. Pour 1 cup cooking liquid over platter. Season with salt and pepper to taste. Serve, passing remaining cooking liquid separately.

TRAIL TALK

Food often outlasts the culture that created it. Milk-can supper, for example, originated as a way of feeding cowhands after a long day of work. It is still popular in parts of the West and upper Midwest, but the food lingo of the cowboys who once ate this dish has faded away. Some names for individual dishes, such as calf slobber (for meringue), reflected the coarseness of trail language. Perhaps most revealing was the name for the 5- or 10-gallon can that served as an all-purpose cooking utensil throughout a thousand-mile cattle drive: It was called the squirrel can, the uncomplimentary moniker coming from the idea that it was never emptied during the course of the entire drive but instead became the receptacle for whatever the cook found to add to it. In her 1933 article "Ranch Diction of the Texas Panhandle," author Mary Dale Buckner declared, "It is true that when a spoon, cup, dipper or some small object was dropped into [the squirrel can], usually no one bothered to remove it." We'll stick with the milk can.

✓ WHY THIS RECIPE WORKS

Not all pork chops are created alike—for pan-frying, we found that center-cut or bone-in pork chops worked best. The bone added valuable flavor to the meat and prevented it from drying out. Simply dredging the pork chops in flour, as most recipes instructed, produced a spotty, insubstantial crust that wouldn't stay put. We have had success letting floured chicken rest before re-dredging and frying, and we wondered if the same treatment would work for pork. Sure enough, our double-dipped chops emerged from the pan with a hefty, crisp, golden-brown crust.

Pan-Fried Pork Chops

SERVES 4

Chops between ¾ and 1 inch thick will work in this recipe.

1	teaspoon garlic powder
½	teaspoon paprika
½	teaspoon salt
½	teaspoon pepper
¼	teaspoon cayenne pepper
1	cup all-purpose flour
4	(8- to 10-ounce) bone-in pork rib or center-cut chops, about ¾ inch thick, trimmed
3	slices bacon, chopped
½	cup vegetable oil

1. Combine garlic powder, paprika, salt, pepper, and cayenne in bowl. Place flour in shallow dish. Pat chops dry with paper towels. Cut 2 slits about 2 inches apart through fat and connective tissue on edge of each chop. Season both sides of chops with spice mixture, then dredge chops lightly in flour (do not discard flour). Transfer to plate and let rest for 10 minutes.

2. Meanwhile, cook bacon in 12-inch nonstick skillet over medium heat until fat renders and bacon is crisp, 5 to 7 minutes. Using slotted spoon, transfer bacon to paper towel–lined plate and reserve for another use. Do not wipe out pan.

3. Add oil to fat in pan and heat over medium-high heat until just smoking. Return chops to flour dish and turn to coat chops again. Cook chops until well browned on each side, 6 to 8 minutes. Serve.

BBQ PAN-FRIED PORK CHOPS

Replace first 5 ingredients with 3 tablespoons light brown sugar, 1 teaspoon chili powder, 1 teaspoon paprika, ½ teaspoon salt, ½ teaspoon dry mustard, ¼ teaspoon ground cumin, and ¼ teaspoon cayenne pepper.

HERBED PAN-FRIED PORK CHOPS

Replace first 5 ingredients with ½ teaspoon dried marjoram, ½ teaspoon dried thyme, ¼ teaspoon dried basil, ¼ teaspoon dried rosemary (crumbled), ¼ teaspoon dried sage, pinch ground fennel, and ½ teaspoon salt.

PREVENTING CURLY CHOPS

Pork chops—especially thin-cut chops—have a tendency to curl as they cook. When exposed to the high heat of the pan, the ring of fat and connective tissue that surrounds the exterior tightens, causing the meat to buckle and curl. To prevent it, we cut two slits about 2 inches apart through the fat and connective tissue on each chop.

BUCKLED CHOP
No slits

FLAT CHOP
Slits cut

✔ WHY THIS RECIPE WORKS

Bone-in chops were a must for smothered pork chops, because the bone kept the meat moist and added flavor to the sauce. Caramelizing the onions made the sauce too sweet and took almost an hour. We had better luck cooking them in butter until they were lightly browned. We swapped out chicken broth in favor of meatier beef broth, which greatly improved the flavor of our sauce. Adding dried thyme, bay leaf, and cider vinegar bumped up the flavor even more. To thicken our broth, we made a cornstarch-and-broth slurry. The results? A silky sauce that clung to our chops.

Smothered Pork Chops

Chops thicker than ½ inch won't be fully tender in the allotted cooking time.

1	teaspoon onion powder
½	teaspoon paprika
	Salt and pepper
¼	teaspoon cayenne pepper
4	(8- to 10-ounce) bone-in blade-cut pork chops, about ½ inch thick, trimmed
1½	tablespoons vegetable oil
1	tablespoon unsalted butter
2	onions, halved and sliced ¼ inch thick
2	garlic cloves, minced
¼	teaspoon dried thyme
¾	cup plus 1 tablespoon beef broth
1	bay leaf
1	teaspoon cornstarch
1	teaspoon cider vinegar

1. Adjust oven rack to middle position and heat oven to 300 degrees. Combine onion powder, paprika, ½ teaspoon salt, ½ teaspoon pepper, and cayenne in small bowl. Pat chops dry with paper towels. Cut 2 slits about 2 inches apart through fat and connective tissue on edge of each chop. Rub chops with spice mixture.

2. Heat oil in large skillet over medium-high heat until just smoking. Brown chops on both sides, 6 to 8 minutes, and transfer to plate. Melt butter in now-empty skillet over medium heat. Cook onions until browned, 8 to 10 minutes. Add garlic and thyme and cook until fragrant, about 30 seconds. Stir in ¾ cup broth and bay leaf, scraping up any browned bits, and bring to boil. Return chops and any accumulated juices to pan, cover, and transfer to oven. Cook until chops are completely tender, about 1½ hours.

3. Transfer chops to platter and tent with aluminum foil. Discard bay leaf. Strain contents of skillet through fine-mesh strainer into large liquid measuring cup; reserve onions. Let liquid settle, then skim fat. Return 1½ cups defatted pan juices to now-empty skillet and bring to boil. Reduce heat to medium and simmer until sauce is reduced to 1 cup, about 5 minutes.

4. Whisk remaining 1 tablespoon broth and cornstarch in bowl until no lumps remain. Whisk cornstarch mixture into sauce and simmer until thickened, 1 to 2 minutes. Stir in reserved onions and vinegar. Season with salt and pepper to taste. Serve.

PORK CHOP PERFECTION

You might think smothered pork chops were born in a diner somewhere. You'd be wrong. "Smother" is an English term that refers to a method of cooking meat, poultry, or game slowly in a covered vessel. This method, essentially a braise, goes back at least to the 16th century. Recipes for smothers first came to the United States from England during the Revolutionary War. Amelia Simmons's *American Cookery*, written in 1796, includes a recipe for smothering a chicken with oysters, though onions are the most common smothering agent. It is believed onions in smothers were used to tone down the gaminess of meat or hide off-flavors. Sailors smothered their salt beef and salt pork rations with onions and potatoes when out to sea. Regional variations soon developed throughout the country: New Englanders often made smothers with fresh pork; in the South, Creole cooking advised against smothering pork, but recommended it for beef, chicken, and veal; and while other traditions in the Deep South did smother pork, it was more typically tails, chitterlings, or other tough or gamy parts—the parts of the pig most available to African-American slaves. Eventually, pork chops did make it into the pot, and we're glad they did.

☑ WHY THIS RECIPE WORKS

The apple flavor in cider-braised pork chops can be fleeting. We wanted tender, juicy chops infused with deep, rich cider flavor. Tasters preferred 1-inch blade chops for their heft, silky meat, and rich taste. Patting the chops dry before adding them to the heated Dutch oven helped them develop a flavorful crust. Apple cider lent both sweetness and tartness to the braising mixture and sauce, while a bit of fresh thyme provided a heady herbal component. Jarred apple butter added further apple flavor, and its natural pectin gave the sauce a thick, glossy consistency. A splash of cider vinegar provided brightness.

Cider-Braised Pork Chops

SERVES 6

Do not use chops thinner than 1 inch. In step 3, a fat separator makes quick work of defatting the sauce.

6 (8- to 10-ounce) bone-in blade-cut pork chops, about 1 inch thick, trimmed
  Salt and pepper
2 tablespoons vegetable oil
1 onion, chopped
¼ cup apple butter
2 tablespoons all-purpose flour
3 garlic cloves, minced
1 cup apple cider
1 sprig fresh thyme
1 teaspoon cider vinegar
1 tablespoon finely chopped fresh parsley

1. Adjust oven rack to lower-middle position and heat oven to 300 degrees. Pat chops dry with paper towels. Cut 2 slits about 2 inches apart through fat and connective tissue on edge of each chop. Season chops with salt and pepper. Heat oil in Dutch oven over medium-high heat until just smoking. Brown 3 chops on each side, about 8 minutes; transfer to plate, and then repeat with remaining 3 chops.

2. Pour off all but 1 tablespoon fat from pot and cook onion over medium heat until softened, about 5 minutes. Stir in 2 tablespoons apple butter, flour, and garlic and cook until onion is coated and mixture is fragrant, about 1 minute. Stir in cider and thyme, scraping up any browned bits with wooden spoon, and bring to boil. Add browned chops and any accumulated juices to pot, cover, and transfer to oven. Braise until chops are completely tender, about 1½ hours.

3. Transfer chops to serving platter. Strain sauce, then skim off fat. Whisk in vinegar, parsley, and remaining 2 tablespoons apple butter. Season with salt and pepper to taste. Serve, passing sauce at table. (Pork chops and sauce can be refrigerated separately for up to 2 days. To serve, reheat sauce and chops together over medium heat until chops are warmed through.)

---

3 KEYS TO BETTER APPLE FLAVOR

Cider alone won't provide much apple flavor. To pack the taste of apples into our pork chops, we settled on a triple helping of apple products.

APPLE BUTTER
Apple butter provides intense apple and warm spice flavor. It also helps thicken the sauce.

CIDER VINEGAR
Finishing with a splash of cider vinegar adds brightness and complexity to the sauce.

CIDER
Sweet-tart cider provides most of the liquid for the braising mixture and sauce.

✔ WHY THIS RECIPE WORKS

Forget the boxed varieties in the frozen foods aisle—our homemade fish sticks are fresh and crisp, and fry up in just minutes. Our recipe calls for cod, but halibut, haddock, and catfish are all worthy substitutes. Eggs beaten with mayonnaise helped our coating of crisp saltines and fresh bread crumbs adhere to the fish. We pan-fried the fish in two batches to ensure they cooked up even and crisp.

Crispy Fish Sticks with Tartar Sauce

Be sure to rinse the capers, otherwise the tartar sauce will be too salty. Halibut, haddock, or catfish can be substituted for the cod.

4	slices hearty white sandwich bread, torn into quarters
16	saltines
½	cup all-purpose flour
2	large eggs
1	cup mayonnaise
2	pounds skinless cod, cut into 1-inch-thick strips
	Salt and pepper
¼	cup finely chopped dill pickles, plus 1 tablespoon pickle juice
1	tablespoon capers, rinsed and minced
1	cup vegetable oil

1. Adjust oven rack to middle position and heat oven to 200 degrees. Pulse bread and saltines in food processor to fine crumbs, about 15 pulses; transfer to shallow dish. Place flour in second shallow dish. Beat eggs with ¼ cup mayonnaise in third shallow dish.

2. Pat fish dry with paper towels and season with salt and pepper. One at a time, coat fish strips lightly with flour, dip in egg mixture, and then dredge in crumbs, pressing on both sides to adhere. Transfer breaded fish to plate. Combine remaining ¾ cup mayonnaise, pickles, pickle juice, and capers in small bowl and set aside.

3. Heat ½ cup oil in large 12-inch nonstick skillet over medium heat until just smoking. Fry half of fish strips until deep golden and crisp on both sides, about 4 minutes. Drain on paper towel–lined plate and transfer to oven to keep warm. Discard oil, wipe out skillet, and repeat with remaining ½ cup oil and remaining fish. Serve with tartar sauce.

FISH STICKS—PIONEERING THE FROZEN FOOD LANDSCAPE

Commercial freezing brought fish to the people, but it was the fish stick, introduced in 1953 by Birds Eye, that got them interested in eating fish. Why? Fish sticks have always appealed on a few levels. The breading helps prevent the fish from sticking to the pan; their mild flavor and crunchy crust appeal to children; and conveniently, fish sticks require minimal cleanup. Over the years, neither the expanded market created by freezing nor the wild popularity of fish sticks did much to boost the nation's overall fish consumption. But fish sticks did fire up the frozen foods market, both in terms of the creativity of producers and the enthusiasm of consumers for new, convenient heat-and-eat food products. Before fish sticks went commercial in the frozen foods industry, they were found at fish markets and delis along the East Coast. And of course, they were made at home. Homemade might not be as convenient as the frozen type, but we still aimed for a recipe that was easy enough for a weeknight.

✔ WHY THIS RECIPE WORKS

This tri-layer Midwestern specialty doesn't much resemble salad, but the sweet-salty, creamy-crunchy combination grabbed our attention. We knew we could make this slightly offbeat potluck favorite shine with some homemade elements. We replaced the "whipped topping" with real cream, which we whipped into softened cream cheese with some sugar for a tangy, not-too-sweet middle layer. The top layer, traditionally made from boxed Jell-O, got an upgrade to plain gelatin flavored with real pureed strawberry juice and sliced frozen berries. The time it took to make these elements from scratch was well worth the extra effort.

Strawberry Pretzel Salad

For a sturdier crust, use (thinner) pretzel sticks not (fatter) rods. Thaw the strawberries in the refrigerator the night before you begin the recipe. You'll puree 2 pounds of the strawberries and slice the remaining 1 pound.

6½	ounces pretzel sticks
2¼	cups (15¾ ounces) sugar
12	tablespoons unsalted butter, melted and cooled
8	ounces cream cheese
1	cup heavy cream
3	pounds (10½ cups) frozen strawberries, thawed
¼	teaspoon salt
4½	teaspoons unflavored gelatin
½	cup cold water

1. Adjust oven rack to middle position and heat oven to 400 degrees. Spray 13 by 9-inch baking pan with vegetable oil spray. Pulse pretzels and ¼ cup sugar in food processor until coarsely ground, about 15 pulses. Add melted butter and pulse until combined, about 10 pulses. Transfer pretzel mixture to prepared pan. Using bottom of measuring cup, press crumbs into bottom of pan. Bake until crust is fragrant and beginning to brown, about 10 minutes, rotating pan halfway through baking. Set aside crust, letting it cool slightly, about 20 minutes.

2. Using stand mixer fitted with whisk, whip cream cheese and ½ cup sugar on medium speed until light and fluffy, about 2 minutes. Increase speed to medium-high and, with mixer still running, slowly add cream in steady stream. Continue to whip until soft peaks form, scraping down bowl as needed, about 1 minute longer. Spread whipped cream cheese mixture evenly over cooled crust. Refrigerate until set, about 30 minutes.

3. Meanwhile, process 2 pounds strawberries in now-empty food processor until pureed, about 30 seconds. Strain mixture through fine-mesh strainer set over medium saucepan, using underside of small ladle to push puree through strainer. Add remaining 1½ cups sugar and salt to strawberry puree in saucepan and cook over medium-high heat, whisking occasionally, until bubbles begin to appear around sides of pan and sugar is dissolved, about 5 minutes; remove from heat.

4. Sprinkle gelatin over water in large bowl and let sit until gelatin softens, about 5 minutes. Whisk strawberry puree into gelatin. Slice remaining strawberries and stir into strawberry-gelatin mixture. Refrigerate until gelatin thickens slightly and starts to cling to sides of bowl, about 30 minutes. Carefully pour gelatin mixture evenly over whipped cream cheese layer. Refrigerate salad until gelatin is fully set, at least 4 hours or up to 24 hours. Serve.

SALAD DAYS

Baked beans, marshmallows, fruit cocktail, flavored gelatin, grated American cheese, ginger ale, sauerkraut . . . Do the words "salad fixings" spring to mind?

Probably not, but then you aren't a well-bred, middle-class lady living in the first half of the 20th century. Had you been reared on the tenets of the domestic science movement that dominated American cooking at that time, such a list would indeed have suggested salad. As a "progressive housekeeper," you would have cringed at the very idea of what we call salad today.

As culinary historian Laura Shapiro has detailed in *Perfection Salad: Women and Cooking at the Turn of the Century*, vegetables had to be tamed, and the very best way to render untidy raw vegetables harmless was to encase them in gelatin. After molding and chilling her salad, she could gild the lily with a few stuffed prunes, rococo swirls of thinned mayonnaise, and a carved tomato tulip.

Pretzel salad is a direct descendent of such "Festive for Special Occasions Salads," as *Betty Crocker's New Picture Cook Book* grouped similar concoctions as late as 1961. Even today, despite the Cool Whip and the strawberry Jell-O, pretzel salad is not dessert—it's a salad.

CHAPTER 2

FORK-IN-THE-ROAD FAVORITES

WHEN MOST OF US THINK OF EATING ON THE ROAD, WE THINK OF diners, drive-ins, fast-food joints, and the like—most of which were the result of the rise of the automobile and the highways that followed. But before automobiles, trains were the preferred mode of travel for long journeys. Sure, trains often have dining cars—but that wasn't always the case. Just after the Civil War, newly freed slaves, looking for a living in Gordonsville, Virginia, hit on the idea of feeding hungry train passengers passing through town. As John T. Edge describes in *Fried Chicken: An American Story* (2004), a group of enterprising African-American women began selling batter-fried chicken (brined, dunked in a plain flour-water batter, and fried in lard), coffee, and pie to passengers through the windows of idling trains. They carried trays laden with food from their homes to the tracks. This informal concession continued for some 60 years. What better reason for the test kitchen to resurrect this American favorite for today?

Colorful stories and great road food aren't just limited to fried chicken, of course. The test kitchen's other stops include Baltimore, for their incomparable pit roast beef sandwich made with shaved barbecued beef slathered with tiger sauce (a garlicky, creamy sauce spiked with horseradish); St. Louis, for wafer-thin pizza topped with gooey, smoky cheese; and Cincinnati for its famous chili. What—you didn't know Cincinnati boasts some of the country's best chili? That's the delight of road food; you just don't know what's coming around the corner until you get there.

✅ WHY THIS RECIPE WORKS

The old-fashioned method of batter-fried chicken calls for dipping chicken parts in a batter not unlike pancake batter before frying. For juicy meat, we brined our chicken. To ensure a crisp crust, we replaced the milk in our initial batters with plain old water. With milk, the sugars in the milk solids browned too fast and produced a soft crust. Using equal parts cornstarch and flour in the batter also helped ensure a crisp crust on the chicken. And baking powder added lift and lightness without doughiness.

Batter-Fried Chicken

SERVES 4 TO 6

You will need at least a 6-quart Dutch oven for this recipe.

CHICKEN AND BRINE

- ¼ **cup salt**
- ¼ **cup sugar**
- 4 **pounds bone-in chicken pieces, breasts halved crosswise and leg quarters separated into thighs and drumsticks, trimmed**

BATTER

- 1 **cup all-purpose flour**
- 1 **cup cornstarch**
- 5 **teaspoons pepper**
- 2 **teaspoons baking powder**
- 1 **teaspoon salt**
- 1 **teaspoon paprika**
- ½ **teaspoon cayenne pepper**
- 1¾ **cups cold water**
- 3 **quarts peanut or vegetable oil**

1. FOR THE CHICKEN AND BRINE: Dissolve salt and sugar in 1 quart cold water in large container. Submerge chicken in brine, cover, and refrigerate for 30 minutes or up to 1 hour.

2. FOR THE BATTER: Meanwhile, combine flour, cornstarch, pepper, baking powder, salt, paprika, and cayenne in large bowl, add water, and whisk until smooth. Refrigerate batter while chicken is brining.

3. Set wire rack in rimmed baking sheet. Add oil to large Dutch oven until it measures about 2 inches deep and heat over medium-high heat to 350 degrees. Using tongs, remove chicken from brine and pat dry with paper towels. Rewhisk batter. Transfer half of chicken to batter and turn to coat. Remove chicken from batter, 1 piece at a time, allowing excess to drip back into bowl, and transfer to oil. Fry chicken, adjusting burner as necessary to maintain oil temperature between 300 and 325 degrees, until deep golden brown and breasts register 160 degrees and thighs and drumsticks register 175 degrees, 12 to 15 minutes. Drain chicken on prepared baking sheet. Return oil to 350 degrees and repeat with remaining chicken. Serve.

KEYS TO BEST BATTER-FRIED CHICKEN

1. Whisk together water, flour, baking powder, spices, and cornstarch to make thin batter for crisp crust.

2. After dipping chicken in batter, let excess drip off (back into bowl) to avoid doughy coating.

3. To prevent chicken pieces from sticking together in oil, don't crowd pot. Fry chicken in 2 batches.

✔ WHY THIS RECIPE WORKS

Really good honey fried chicken is juicy and tender on the inside with a crispy, sticky, honey-flavored coating. To keep the meat moist, we brined the chicken first. For the coating, we dusted the chicken in cornstarch and dipped it in a thin cornstarch-and-water batter. The hardest part was glazing the fried chicken in honey without making the crust soggy. We found that the key was to double-fry the chicken: We partially fried the chicken, let it rest to allow moisture from the skin to evaporate, then fried it again for an incredibly crunchy crust that stayed crispy when dunked in a glaze of warm honey and hot sauce.

Honey Fried Chicken

SERVES 4

If using kosher chicken, do not brine. You will need at least a 6-quart Dutch oven for this recipe.

BRINE AND CHICKEN

- ½ cup salt
- ½ cup sugar
- 3 pounds bone-in chicken pieces (split breasts cut in half, drumsticks, and/or thighs), trimmed

BATTER

- 1½ cups cornstarch
- ¾ cup cold water
- 2 teaspoons pepper
- 1 teaspoon salt
- 3 quarts peanut or vegetable oil

HONEY GLAZE

- ¾ cup honey
- 2 tablespoons hot sauce

1. FOR THE BRINE AND CHICKEN: Dissolve salt and sugar in 2 quarts cold water in large container. Submerge chicken in brine, cover, and refrigerate for 30 minutes to 1 hour.

2. FOR THE BATTER: While chicken is brining, whisk 1 cup cornstarch, water, pepper, and salt together in large bowl until smooth. Refrigerate batter.

3. Set wire rack inside rimmed baking sheet. Sift remaining ½ cup cornstarch into shallow bowl. Remove chicken from brine and dry thoroughly with paper towels. Working with 1 piece at a time, coat chicken thoroughly with cornstarch, shaking to remove excess; transfer to platter.

4. Add oil to large Dutch oven until it measures about 2 inches deep and heat over medium-high heat to 350 degrees. Whisk batter to recombine. Using tongs, transfer half of chicken to batter and turn to coat. Remove chicken from batter, 1 piece at a time, allowing excess to drip back into bowl, and transfer to hot oil. Fry chicken, stirring to prevent pieces from sticking together, until slightly golden and just beginning to crisp, 5 to 7 minutes. Adjust burner, if necessary, to maintain oil temperature between 325 and 350 degrees. (Chicken will not be cooked through at this point.) Transfer parcooked chicken to platter. Return oil to 350 degrees and repeat with remaining raw chicken and batter. Let each batch of chicken rest for 5 to 7 minutes.

5. Return oil to 350 degrees. Return first batch of chicken to oil and fry until breasts register 160 degrees and thighs/drumsticks register 175 degrees, 5 to 7 minutes. Transfer to prepared baking sheet. Return oil to 350 degrees and repeat with remaining chicken.

6. FOR THE HONEY GLAZE: Combine honey and hot sauce in large bowl and microwave until hot, about 1½ minutes. Add chicken pieces to honey mixture, one at a time, and turn to coat. Return to baking sheet, skin side up, to drain. Serve.

MAKING A BEELINE WEST

The common honeybee (*Apis mellifera L.*) is not native to North America. British settlers bound for Virginia brought hives aboard ships, along with peacocks, pigeons, and rabbits, as the author of a letter from the Virginia Company recorded in 1621. During the next 200 years, the bee population slowly rolled westward, pollinating the prairies and the settlers' crops and providing pioneers with honey, wax, candles, and medicine. Native Americans called the honeybee the "white man's fly," and they saw the bees that swarmed ahead of the settlers as a threat. "The Indians . . . consider them the harbinger of the white man," Washington Irving wrote as he traveled through the Oklahoma Territory in 1832. "As the bee advances, the Indian and the buffalo retire." Similarly, after visiting members of the Osage tribe in the Missouri Territory in 1836, writer Alphonso Wetmore reported that "the Indians held a day of mourning because a swarm of bees had been found."

✔ WHY THIS RECIPE WORKS

Creole fried chicken recipes should turn out meat that is deeply seasoned with the complex, lively heat of black, white, and cayenne pepper. We built depth of flavor in our fried chicken with a three-step approach: After brining the chicken, we sprinkled it with homemade Creole seasoning for added flavor without the dusty saltiness of packaged spice blends. We also added seasoning to the chicken's flour coating to lend a potent punch. And for a peppery finish, we sprinkled the hot chicken with more seasoning when it came out of the oil.

Creole Fried Chicken

SERVES 4 TO 6

In step 1, do not soak the chicken longer than eight hours, or it will be too salty. You will need at least a 6-quart Dutch oven for this recipe.

SEASONED BRINE AND CHICKEN

¼	cup sugar
3	tablespoons Worcestershire sauce
3	tablespoons hot sauce
2	tablespoons salt
1	tablespoon garlic powder
4	pounds bone-in chicken pieces, breasts halved crosswise and leg quarters separated into thighs and drumsticks, trimmed

CREOLE SEASONING

1	tablespoon pepper
1	tablespoon dried oregano
1	tablespoon garlic powder
2	teaspoons onion powder
2	teaspoons cayenne pepper
1	teaspoon white pepper
1	teaspoon celery salt
2	cups all-purpose flour
3	quarts peanut or vegetable oil

1. FOR THE SEASONED BRINE AND CHICKEN: Dissolve sugar, Worcestershire, hot sauce, salt, and garlic powder in 1 quart cold water in large container. Submerge chicken in brine, cover, and refrigerate for 1 hour or up to 8 hours.

2. FOR THE CREOLE SEASONING: Combine pepper, oregano, garlic powder, onion powder, cayenne, white pepper, and celery salt in large bowl; reserve ¼ cup spice mixture. Add flour to bowl with remaining spice mixture and stir to combine. Set wire rack in rimmed baking sheet.

3. Remove chicken from brine and pat dry with paper towels. Sprinkle chicken with 3 tablespoons reserved spice mixture and toss to coat. Dredge chicken pieces in flour mixture. Shake excess flour from chicken and transfer to wire rack. (Do not discard flour mixture.)

4. Adjust oven rack to middle position and heat oven to 200 degrees. Set clean wire rack in rimmed baking sheet. Add oil to large Dutch oven until it measures about 2 inches deep and heat over medium-high heat to 375 degrees. Return chicken pieces to flour mixture and turn to coat. Fry half of chicken, adjusting burner as necessary to maintain oil temperature between 300 and 325 degrees, until deep golden brown and breasts register 160 degrees and thighs and drumsticks register 175 degrees, 10 to 12 minutes. Transfer chicken to prepared baking sheet and place in oven. Return oil to 375 degrees and repeat with remaining chicken. Sprinkle crisp chicken with remaining 1 tablespoon spice mixture. Serve.

SECRETS TO BOLDLY FLAVORED CREOLE FRIED CHICKEN

1. Soaking chicken in brine of salt, sugar, Worcestershire, hot sauce, and garlic powder seasons chicken fully.

2. After brining, homemade Creole seasoning adds flavor without dusty saltiness of packaged spice blends.

3. The homemade Creole seasoning also lends potent punch to chicken's flour coating.

4. For peppery finish, sprinkle hot chicken with more homemade Creole seasoning when it comes out of oil.

WHY THIS RECIPE WORKS:

For well-seasoned, extra-crunchy fried chicken we started by brining the chicken in heavily salted buttermilk. For the crunchy coating, we combined flour with a little baking powder, then added buttermilk to make a thick slurry, which clung tightly to the meat. Frying the chicken with the lid on the pot for half the cooking time contained the spatter-prone oil and kept it hot.

Extra-Crunchy Fried Chicken

SERVES 4

Keeping the oil at the correct temperature is essential to producing crunchy fried chicken that is neither too brown nor too greasy. You will need at least a 6-quart Dutch oven for this recipe. If you want to produce a slightly lighter version of this recipe, you can remove the skin from the chicken before soaking it in the buttermilk. The chicken will be slightly less crunchy.

- 2 tablespoons salt
- 2 cups plus 6 tablespoons buttermilk
- 1 (3½-pound) whole chicken, cut into 8 pieces and trimmed (4 breast pieces, 2 drumsticks, 2 thighs), wings discarded
- 3 cups all-purpose flour
- 2 teaspoons baking powder
- ¾ teaspoon dried thyme
- ½ teaspoon pepper
- ¼ teaspoon garlic powder
- 1 quart peanut or vegetable oil

1. Dissolve salt in 2 cups buttermilk in large container. Submerge chicken in brine, cover, and refrigerate for 1 hour.

2. Whisk flour, baking powder, thyme, pepper, and garlic powder together in large bowl. Add remaining 6 tablespoons buttermilk; with your fingers rub flour and buttermilk together until buttermilk is evenly incorporated into flour and mixture resembles coarse, wet sand. Set wire rack inside rimmed baking sheet.

3. Dredge chicken pieces in flour mixture and turn to coat thoroughly, gently pressing flour mixture onto chicken. Shake excess flour from each piece of chicken and transfer to prepared baking sheet.

4. Line platter with triple layer of paper towels. Add oil to large Dutch oven until it measures about ¾ inch deep and heat over medium-high heat to 375 degrees. Place chicken pieces skin side down in oil, cover, and fry until deep golden brown, 8 to 10 minutes. Remove lid after 4 minutes and lift chicken pieces to check for even browning; rearrange if some pieces are browning faster than others. Adjust burner, if necessary, to maintain oil temperature between 300 and 315 degrees. Turn chicken pieces over and continue to fry, uncovered, until chicken pieces are deep golden brown on second side and breasts register 160 degrees and thighs and drumsticks register 175 degrees, 6 to 8 minutes. Using tongs, transfer chicken to prepared platter; let stand for 5 minutes. Serve.

EXTRA-SPICY, EXTRA-CRUNCHY FRIED CHICKEN

Add ¼ cup hot sauce to buttermilk-salt mixture in step 1. Replace dried thyme and garlic powder with 2 tablespoons cayenne pepper and 2 teaspoons chili powder in step 2.

STEPS TO AN EXTRA-CRUNCHY COATING

1. Soak chicken in buttermilk-salt mixture.

2. Coat chicken with buttermilk-moistened flour.

3. Add chicken to hot oil and cover pot to capture steam.

4. Use tongs to flip chicken and finish cooking with cover off.

✔ WHY THIS RECIPE WORKS

Mimicking the heat of this Nashville hot fried chicken was harder than we anticipated. We created a spicy exterior to the chicken by "blooming" the spices (cooking them in oil for a short period) to create a complex yet still lip-burning spicy flavor. We also added a healthy amount of hot sauce to our brine to inject spicy flavor into the chicken, making the flavor more than skin deep.

Nashville Hot Fried Chicken

SERVES 4 TO 6

Chicken quarters take longer to cook than smaller pieces. To ensure that the exterior doesn't burn before the inside cooks through, keep the oil temperature between 300 and 325 degrees while the chicken is frying. You will need at least a 6-quart Dutch oven for this recipe. Serve the chicken as they do in Nashville, on white bread with pickles.

BRINE AND CHICKEN

- ½ cup hot sauce
- ½ cup salt
- ½ cup sugar
- 1 (3½- to 4-pound) whole chicken, quartered

COATING

- 3 quarts peanut or vegetable oil
- 1 tablespoon cayenne pepper
- ½ teaspoon paprika
- ½ teaspoon sugar
- ¼ teaspoon garlic powder
  Salt and pepper
- 2 cups all-purpose flour

1. FOR THE BRINE AND CHICKEN: Dissolve hot sauce, salt, and sugar in 2 quarts cold water in large container. Submerge chicken in brine, cover, and refrigerate for 30 minutes or up to 1 hour.

2. FOR THE COATING: Heat 3 tablespoons oil in small saucepan over medium heat until shimmering. Add cayenne, paprika, sugar, garlic powder, and ½ teaspoon salt and cook until fragrant, about 30 seconds. Transfer to small bowl.

3. Set wire rack in rimmed baking sheet. Remove chicken from brine and pat with paper towels. Combine flour, ½ teaspoon salt, and ½ teaspoon pepper in large bowl. Dredge chicken pieces two at a time in flour mixture. Shake excess flour from chicken and transfer to prepared baking sheet. (Do not discard seasoned flour.)

4. Adjust oven rack to middle position and heat oven to 200 degrees. Set clean wire rack in rimmed baking sheet. Add remaining oil to large Dutch oven until it measures about 2 inches deep and heat over medium-high heat to 350 degrees. Return chicken pieces to flour mixture and turn to coat. Fry half of chicken, adjusting burner as necessary to maintain oil temperature between 300 and 325 degrees, until deep golden brown and breast meat registers 160 degrees and legs register 175 degrees, 20 to 25 minutes. Drain chicken on prepared baking sheet and place in oven. Return oil to 350 degrees and repeat with remaining chicken. Stir spicy oil mixture to recombine and brush over both sides of chicken. Serve.

NASHVILLE EXTRA-HOT FRIED CHICKEN

For spiced oil in step 2, increase oil to ¼ cup, cayenne to 3½ tablespoons, and sugar to ¾ teaspoon and add 1 teaspoon dry mustard. Continue with recipe as directed.

QUARTERING A CHICKEN

1. Slice between drumstick and breast. Use hands to bend back leg and pop out joint.

2. Cut through leg joint. Do not separate thigh from drumstick. Repeat steps 1 and 2 for other leg quarter.

3. To separate breast from backbone, cut through ribs with kitchen shears on each side of backbone.

4. Cut through breastbone to separate breast and wing section into halves.

✓ WHY THIS RECIPE WORKS

Some chicken nuggets recipes take the least desirable parts of the chicken and put them through a grinder. We opted for boneless, skinless chicken breasts. Brining the chicken prevented it from drying out, and seasoning the breast meat combated its inherently bland flavor. Ground-up panko (Japanese-style bread crumbs) combined with flour and a pinch of baking soda provided a crispy brown exterior for our nuggets. Using whole eggs to adhere the coating made the nuggets too eggy. Egg whites alone didn't have enough binding power, but we found that resting the nuggets before frying solved the problem.

Chicken Nuggets

Do not brine the chicken longer than 30 minutes or it will be too salty. To crush the panko, place it inside a zipper-lock bag and lightly beat it with a rolling pin. You will need at least a 6-quart Dutch oven for this recipe. This recipe doubles easily and freezes well.

- 4 (6-ounce) boneless, skinless chicken breasts, trimmed
- 2 cups water
- 2 tablespoons Worcestershire sauce
- Salt and pepper
- 1 cup all-purpose flour
- 1 cup panko bread crumbs, crushed
- 2 teaspoons onion powder
- ½ teaspoon garlic powder
- ½ teaspoon baking soda
- 3 large egg whites
- 1 quart peanut or vegetable oil
- 1 recipe dipping sauce (recipes follow)

1. Cut each chicken breast diagonally into thirds, then cut each third diagonally into ½-inch-thick pieces. Whisk water, Worcestershire, and 1 tablespoon salt in large bowl until salt dissolves. Add chicken pieces, cover, and refrigerate for 30 minutes.

2. Remove chicken from brine and pat dry with paper towels. Combine flour, panko, onion powder, 1 teaspoon salt, ¾ teaspoon pepper, garlic powder, and baking soda in shallow dish. Whisk egg whites in second shallow dish until foamy. Coat half of chicken with egg whites and dredge in flour mixture, pressing gently to adhere. Transfer to plate and repeat with remaining chicken (don't discard flour mixture). Let sit for 10 minutes.

3. Adjust oven rack to middle position and heat oven to 200 degrees. Set wire rack in rimmed baking sheet. Add oil to large Dutch oven until it measures about ¾ inch deep and heat over medium-high heat to 350 degrees.

Return chicken pieces to flour mixture and turn to coat, pressing flour mixture gently to adhere. Fry half of chicken until deep golden brown, about 3 minutes, turning halfway through cooking. Transfer chicken to prepared baking sheet and place in oven. Return oil to 350 degrees and repeat with remaining chicken. Serve with dipping sauce.

TO MAKE AHEAD: Let fried nuggets cool, transfer to zipper-lock bag, and freeze for up to 1 month. To serve, adjust oven rack to middle position and heat oven to 350 degrees. Place nuggets on rimmed baking sheet and bake, flipping once, until heated through, about 15 minutes.

HONEY-MUSTARD SAUCE
MAKES ¾ CUP, ENOUGH FOR 1 RECIPE CHICKEN NUGGETS

- ½ cup yellow mustard
- ⅓ cup honey
- Salt and pepper

Whisk mustard and honey in medium bowl until smooth. Season with salt and pepper to taste.

SWEET AND SOUR SAUCE
MAKES ¾ CUP, ENOUGH FOR 1 RECIPE CHICKEN NUGGETS

- ¾ cup apple, apricot, or hot pepper jelly
- 1 tablespoon white vinegar
- ½ teaspoon soy sauce
- ⅛ teaspoon garlic powder
- Pinch ground ginger
- Pinch cayenne pepper
- Salt and pepper

Whisk jelly, vinegar, soy sauce, garlic powder, ginger, and cayenne in medium bowl until smooth. Season with salt and pepper to taste.

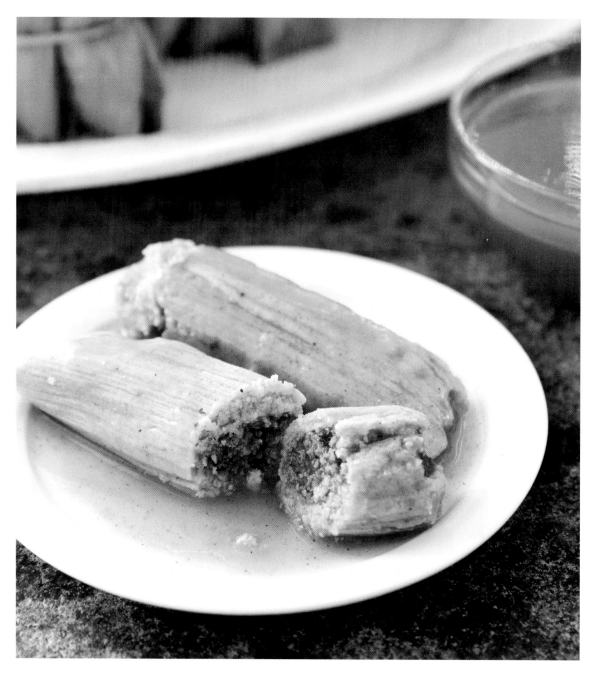

✓ WHY THIS RECIPE WORKS

Hot tamales—rich, spicy meat wrapped in flavorful corn dough—are a favorite in the Mississippi delta. A bit of this cornmeal mixture stirred into the uncooked ground beef kept the filling moist and baking soda was the trick for a more tender bite. We used butter instead of the traditional lard with coarsely ground cornmeal for a more balanced taste. We cooked the tamales in groups of six for more stability in the pot and made a spicy, glazy sauce with the seasoned stewing liquid and a cornstarch slurry. This was as close as we could come to being in the delta without a plane ticket.

Delta Hot Tamales

SERVES 6 TO 8

Use a saucepan that holds 4 quarts or more, with at least 5-inch sides. Corn husks can be found in the international aisle of grocery stores.

24	corn husks
1½	tablespoons chili powder
1	tablespoon paprika
1	tablespoon salt
2	teaspoons ground cumin
2	teaspoons sugar
¾	teaspoon pepper
¾	teaspoon cayenne pepper
2½	cups (12½ ounces) yellow cornmeal
1	tablespoon baking powder
12	tablespoons unsalted butter, cut into 12 pieces
½	teaspoon baking soda
1	pound 85 percent lean ground beef
2	garlic cloves, minced
2	tablespoons cornstarch combined with 2 tablespoons cold water

1. Place husks in large bowl and cover with hot water; soak until pliable, about 30 minutes. Combine chili powder, paprika, salt, cumin, sugar, pepper, and cayenne in bowl.

2. Pulse cornmeal and baking powder in food processor until combined, about 3 pulses. Add butter and 1½ tablespoons spice mixture and pulse to chop butter into small pieces, about 8 pulses. Add 1¼ cups water and process until dough forms, about 30 seconds. Reserve ½ cup cornmeal mixture. Divide remaining cornmeal mixture into 24 equal portions, about 1½ tablespoons each, and place on plate.

3. Dissolve baking soda in 2 tablespoons water in large bowl. Add beef, garlic, reserved ½ cup cornmeal mixture, and 1½ tablespoons spice mixture and knead with your hands until thoroughly combined. Divide meat mixture into 24 equal portions, about 1½ tablespoons each, and place on plate.

4. Remove husks from water and pat dry with dish towel. Working with 1 husk at a time, lay husk on counter, smooth side up, with long side parallel to counter edge and wide end oriented toward right. Using small offset spatula, spread 1 portion of cornmeal mixture in 3½-inch square over lower right corner of husk, flush to bottom edge but leaving ¼-inch border on right edge.

5. Place 1 portion of meat mixture in log across center of cornmeal (end to end), parallel to long side of husk. Roll husk away from you and over meat mixture so cornmeal mixture surrounds meat and forms cylinder; continue rolling to complete tamale. Fold tapered end (left side) of tamale up leaving top open. Using scissors, trim tapered end of tamale to align with filled end (if tapered end hangs over). Set tamales aside seam side down.

6. Stack tamales on their sides in groups of 6 and tie into bundles with kitchen twine. Add remaining 2 tablespoons spice mixture to large saucepan. Stand tamales, open ends up, in pot (walls of pot should clear tops of tamales). Add about 5½ cups water to pot to come within 1 inch of tops of tamales, being careful not to pour water into tamales.

7. Bring tamales to boil. Cover, reduce heat to low to maintain gentle simmer, and cook until tamales are firm and beginning to pull away from husks, about 30 minutes. Using tongs and slotted spoon, carefully transfer tamales to serving platter and remove twine.

8. Return liquid to simmer over medium heat. Whisk in cornstarch slurry and cook until slightly thickened, about 1 minute. Serve sauce with tamales.

COOKING WITH CORN HUSKS

Cooking the tamales in corn husks—which are available in most supermarkets near the dried chiles—adds a subtle depth of flavor. Working with the husks is actually quite easy, as they become pliable when soaked in hot water.

✓ WHY THIS RECIPE WORKS

Our biggest challenge in making gumbo was finding an easier way to prepare the dark brown roux, the fat and flour paste that thickens the stew and adds flavor. We created a relatively hands-off roux by toasting the flour on the stovetop, adding the oil, and finishing the roux in the oven. For the soup base, we started by making our own shrimp stock, but the process was time-consuming. Instead, we switched to store-bought chicken broth fortified with fish sauce. Tasters preferred meaty chicken thighs to breasts because they had more flavor.

Gumbo

SERVES 6 TO 8

A heavy cast-iron Dutch oven yields the fastest oven roux. If a lightweight pot is all you've got, increase the oven time by 10 minutes. The chicken broth must be at room temperature to prevent lumps from forming. Fish sauce lends an essential savory quality. Since the salt content of fish sauce varies among brands, taste the finished gumbo before seasoning with salt.

¾	cup plus 1 tablespoon all-purpose flour
½	cup vegetable oil
1	onion, chopped fine
1	green bell pepper, stemmed, seeded, and chopped
1	celery rib, chopped fine
5	garlic cloves, minced
1	teaspoon minced fresh thyme
¼	teaspoon cayenne pepper
1	(14.5-ounce) can diced tomatoes, drained
3¾	cups chicken broth, room temperature
¼	cup fish sauce
	Salt and pepper
2	pounds bone-in chicken thighs, skin removed, trimmed
8	ounces andouille sausage, halved lengthwise and sliced thin
2	cups frozen okra, thawed (optional)
2	pounds extra-large shrimp (21 to 25 per pound), peeled and deveined

1. Adjust oven rack to lowest position and heat oven to 350 degrees. Toast ¾ cup flour in Dutch oven over medium heat, stirring constantly, until just beginning to brown, about 5 minutes. Off heat, whisk in oil until smooth. Cover, transfer pot to oven, and cook until mixture is deep brown and fragrant, about 45 minutes. (Roux can be refrigerated for 1 week. To use, heat in Dutch oven over medium-high heat, whisking constantly, until just smoking, and continue with step 2.)

2. Transfer Dutch oven to stovetop and whisk cooked roux to combine. Add onion, bell pepper, and celery and cook over medium heat, stirring frequently, until vegetables are softened, about 10 minutes. Stir in remaining 1 tablespoon flour, garlic, thyme, and cayenne and cook until fragrant, about 1 minute. Add tomatoes and cook until dry, about 1 minute. Slowly whisk in broth and fish sauce until smooth. Season chicken with pepper. Add chicken to vegetable mixture and bring to boil.

3. Reduce heat to medium-low and simmer, covered, until chicken is tender, about 30 minutes. Skim fat and transfer chicken to plate. When chicken is cool enough to handle, cut into bite-size pieces and return to pot; discard bones.

4. Stir in sausage and okra, if using, and simmer until heated through, about 5 minutes. Add shrimp and simmer until cooked through, about 5 minutes. Season with salt and pepper to taste. Serve. (Gumbo can be refrigerated for 1 day.)

TO MAKE AHEAD: Gumbo can be made through step 3 and refrigerated for 3 days. To serve, bring gumbo to simmer, covered, in Dutch oven. Remove lid and proceed with recipe as directed.

NEWCOMER TO THE BAYOU

Asian fish sauce? Admittedly, it's an unconventional idea. And here's the cool part: New Orleans has a well-established Vietnamese community; it began after the fall of Saigon. As far as we know, we're the first to put fish sauce in gumbo, but there's no question that these new immigrants to New Orleans are having an impact on the city's storied food traditions: They've tossed lemon grass into crawfish boils, organized a farmers' market with such exotic items as *ngo gai* (an herb), banana buds, and longan fruit, and put the *banh mi* sandwich on the city's must-eat food list, right there next to the city's signature po' boys.

✓ WHY THIS RECIPE WORKS

Named for the "barbecue" color rather than the cooking method, this New Orleans skillet shrimp dish relies on a velvety, butter-based sauce to flavor peel-on shrimp. To achieve perfectly cooked shrimp, we started by searing them first to partially cook them and then later returned the shrimp to the finished sauce to gently cook through. By using a roux to thicken the sauce and sautéing the aromatics with tomato paste, we were able to create a silky, flavorful sauce that clung perfectly to the shrimp. We replaced time-consuming seafood stock with bottled clam juice, a technique the test kitchen has used before.

New Orleans Barbecue Shrimp

SERVES 4

Although authentic barbecue shrimp is always made with shell-on shrimp, peeled and deveined shrimp may be used. Light- or medium-bodied beers work best here. Serve with Tabasco sauce and French bread, if desired.

2	pounds extra-large (21–25 per pound) shrimp
½	teaspoon salt
½	teaspoon cayenne pepper
2	tablespoons vegetable oil
6	tablespoons unsalted butter, cut into 6 pieces
2	teaspoons all-purpose flour
1	teaspoon tomato paste
1	teaspoon minced fresh rosemary
1	teaspoon minced fresh thyme
½	teaspoon dried oregano
3	garlic cloves, minced
¾	cup bottled clam juice
½	cup beer
1	tablespoon Worcestershire sauce

1. Pat shrimp dry with paper towels and sprinkle with salt and cayenne. Heat 1 tablespoon oil in large skillet over medium-high heat until just smoking. Cook half of shrimp, without moving, until spotty brown on one side, about 1 minute; transfer to large plate. Repeat with remaining oil and shrimp.

2. Melt 1 tablespoon butter in empty skillet over medium heat. Add flour, tomato paste, rosemary, thyme, oregano, and garlic and cook until fragrant, about 30 seconds. Stir in clam juice, beer, and Worcestershire, scraping up any browned bits, and bring to boil. Return shrimp and any accumulated juices to skillet. Reduce heat to medium-low and simmer, covered, until shrimp are cooked through, about 2 minutes. Off heat, stir in remaining butter until incorporated. Serve.

NOT YOUR AVERAGE BARBECUE SAUCE

Barbecue sauce conjures up an image of a thick, sticky tomato-based mop, but New Orleans Barbecue Shrimp is bathed in a spicy herbed butter sauce made with these ingredients.

CLAM JUICE
The briny bite makes a simple replacement for fish stock.

BEER
The mellow, slightly hoppy bitterness balances the rich butter.

WORCESTERSHIRE
Often used to add bold, ultrasavory flavor to dishes.

BUTTER
Adding butter twice makes a rich, satiny sauce.

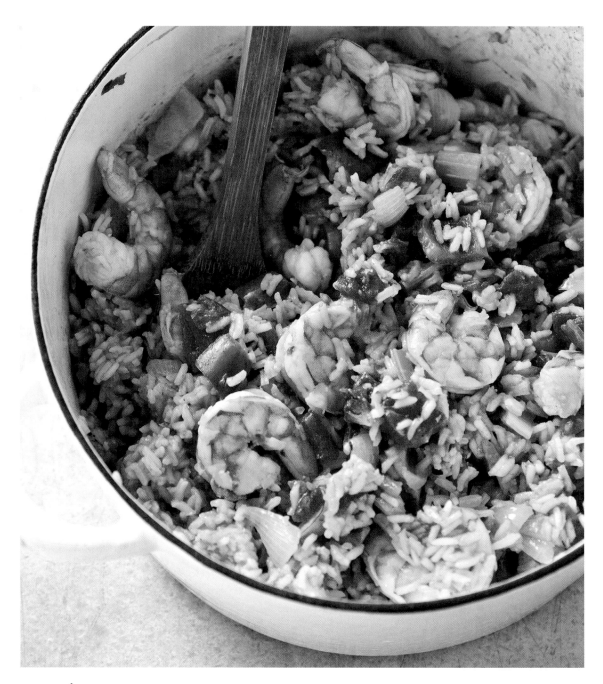

✔ WHY THIS RECIPE WORKS

Perloo (pronounced "PUHR-low"), a staple in South Carolina's Low Country, is a tomatoey rice dish simmered in broth. To start, we went the classic route and used reserved shrimp shells to create and flavor shrimp stock, which is surprisingly easy and practical to make from scratch. For the rice, we stuck to the traditional flavor base of onions, celery, and bell pepper. Sautéing the rice with the vegetables firmed up the grains' exterior and prevented mushiness. Just before removing the rice from the heat, we folded in the shrimp and let them rest, covered, for perfectly cooked shrimp and tender rice in a delicious one-pot meal.

Charleston Shrimp Perloo

SERVES 4 TO 6

After adding the shrimp to the pot, fold it in gently; stirring the rice too vigorously will make it mushy. Any extra stock can be refrigerated for three days or frozen for up to one month. Serve with hot sauce.

5	tablespoons unsalted butter
1½	pounds extra-large shrimp (21 to 25 per pound), peeled and deveined, shells reserved
2	onions, chopped
4	celery ribs, chopped
	Salt
4	cups water
1	tablespoon peppercorns
5	sprigs fresh parsley
2	bay leaves
1	green bell pepper, stemmed, seeded, and chopped
2	cups long-grain white rice
2	garlic cloves, minced
1	teaspoon minced fresh thyme
¼	teaspoon cayenne pepper
1	(14.5-ounce) can diced tomatoes

1. Melt 1 tablespoon butter in large saucepan over medium heat. Add shrimp shells, 1 cup onion, ½ cup celery, and 1 teaspoon salt and cook, stirring occasionally, until shells are spotty brown, about 10 minutes. Add water, peppercorns, parsley, and bay leaves. Increase heat to high and bring to boil. Reduce heat to low, cover, and simmer for 30 minutes. Strain shrimp stock through fine-mesh strainer set over large bowl, pressing on solids to extract as much liquid as possible; discard solids.

2. Melt remaining 4 tablespoons butter in Dutch oven over medium heat. Add bell pepper, remaining onion and celery, and ½ teaspoon salt and cook until vegetables are beginning to soften, 5 to 7 minutes. Add rice, garlic, thyme, and cayenne and cook until fragrant and rice is translucent, about 2 minutes. Stir in tomatoes and their juice and 3 cups shrimp stock (reserve remainder for another use) and bring to boil. Reduce heat to low, cover, and cook for 20 minutes.

3. Gently fold shrimp into rice until evenly distributed, cover, and continue to cook 5 minutes longer. Remove pot from heat and let sit, covered, until shrimp are cooked through and all liquid is absorbed, about 10 minutes. Serve.

PEELING AND DEVEINING SHRIMP

1. Break shell under swimming legs, which will come off as shell is removed. Leave tail intact if desired, or tug tail to remove shell.

2. Use paring knife to make shallow cut along back of shrimp to expose vein. Use tip of knife to lift out vein. Discard vein by wiping blade against paper towel.

✓ WHY THIS RECIPE WORKS

We aimed to give this stale chain restaurant classic a fresh makeover. The salad-bar pile ons, from chow mein noodles to snow peas to water chestnuts, got the ax. Instead, we started with crisp romaine lettuce, napa cabbage, bell peppers, cilantro, and scallions. To keep the chicken from tasting like an afterthought, we eschewed rotisserie chicken. We poached boneless, skinless chicken breasts in a flavorful mixture of soy sauce, orange juice, rice vinegar, and ginger, setting aside some of the mixture to whisk with sesame and vegetable oils for a bold dressing. We finished the dish with fresh oranges and roasted peanuts.

Chinese Chicken Salad

SERVES 6

You can substitute 1 minced clove of garlic and ¼ teaspoon of cayenne pepper for the Asian chili-garlic sauce.

2	oranges
¼	cup rice vinegar
¼	cup soy sauce
3	tablespoons grated fresh ginger
3	tablespoons sugar
1	tablespoon Asian chili-garlic sauce
3	tablespoons vegetable oil
2	tablespoons toasted sesame oil
4	(6- to 8-ounce) boneless, skinless chicken breasts, trimmed
2	romaine lettuce hearts (12 ounces), sliced thin
½	small head napa cabbage, cored and sliced thin (6 cups)
2	red bell peppers, stemmed, seeded, and cut into 2-inch-long matchsticks
1	cup fresh cilantro leaves
1	cup salted, dry-roasted peanuts, chopped
6	scallions, sliced thin

1. Cut thin slice from top and bottom of each orange, exposing fruit. Slice off rind and pith, cutting from top to bottom. Working over bowl, cut orange segments from thin membrane and transfer segments to second bowl; set aside. Squeeze juice from membrane into first bowl (juice should measure ¼ cup).

2. Combine orange juice, vinegar, soy sauce, ginger, sugar, and chili-garlic sauce in bowl. Transfer ½ cup of orange juice mixture to 12-inch skillet. Slowly whisk vegetable oil and sesame oil into remaining orange juice mixture to make vinaigrette; set aside.

3. Bring orange juice mixture in skillet to boil. Add chicken, reduce heat to medium-low, cover, and simmer until meat registers 160 degrees, 10 to 15 minutes, flipping halfway through cooking. Transfer chicken to plate and let rest for 5 to 10 minutes.

4. Meanwhile, boil pan juices until reduced to ¼ cup, 1 to 3 minutes, and set aside. Using 2 forks, shred chicken into bite-size pieces. Off heat, add chicken, any accumulated juices, and 2 tablespoons vinaigrette to skillet. Toss to coat and let sit for 10 minutes.

5. Toss lettuce, cabbage, bell peppers, cilantro, peanuts, and scallions with remaining vinaigrette in large bowl. Transfer to serving platter and top with chicken and oranges. Serve.

SHOPPING FOR AROMATIC ASIAN INGREDIENTS

Consider keeping these three versatile ingredients on hand to add authentic Asian flavor to a variety of dishes, including our Chinese Chicken Salad.

RICE VINEGAR
This Japanese vinegar is sweet and mild.

ASIAN CHILI-GARLIC SAUCE
If you like garlic and heat, you'll reach for this bottle often.

TOASTED SESAME OIL
This aromatic, boldly flavored oil is made from roasted sesame seeds. Its flavor doesn't hold up to cooking, so add it off heat.

WHY THIS RECIPE WORKS

Like many dishes you'll find in America's Chinese restaurants, chow mein has deep roots in China, where *chao mian* ("fried noodles") has been around for centuries. But this takeout standard often features dry meat and a bland, pasty sauce. To help the chicken retain moisture, we soaked sliced chicken in water and baking soda followed by a quick soak in Chinese rice wine and cornstarch. For the chow mein's sauce, oyster sauce added meaty notes, and more rice wine added sweet brightness. To avoid a gloppy sauce, we used just a bit of cornstarch as thickener then added plenty of bean sprouts for fresh crunch.

Chicken Chow Mein

Purchase thin, round fresh Chinese egg noodles, not flat and/or dried noodles, or substitute 6 ounces of dried chow mein, ramen, or wheat vermicelli.

1	**(9-ounce) package fresh Chinese noodles**
1	**tablespoon toasted sesame oil**
1	**teaspoon baking soda**
2	**(6-ounce) boneless, skinless chicken breasts, trimmed and cut crosswise into ¼-inch-thick slices**
3	**tablespoons Chinese rice wine or dry sherry**
1	**tablespoon cornstarch**
½	**cup chicken broth**
3	**tablespoons soy sauce**
3	**tablespoons oyster sauce**
¼	**teaspoon white pepper**
2	**tablespoons vegetable oil**
6	**ounces shiitake mushrooms, stemmed and sliced thin**
1	**carrot, peeled and cut into 2-inch matchsticks**
2	**celery ribs, cut on bias into ¼-inch-thick slices**
4	**scallions, white and green parts separated and sliced thin**
3	**garlic cloves, minced**
1	**tablespoon grated fresh ginger**
4	**ounces (2 cups) mung bean sprouts**

1. Bring 4 quarts water to boil in large pot. Add noodles to boiling water and cook until tender, 2 to 4 minutes. Drain noodles, rinse thoroughly with cold water, then drain again. Toss noodles with sesame oil in bowl; set aside.

2. Meanwhile, dissolve baking soda in ½ cup cold water in bowl. Add chicken and let sit at room temperature for 15 minutes. Drain chicken, rinse under cold water, then drain again. Pat chicken dry with paper towels. Combine 1 tablespoon rice wine, 2 teaspoons cornstarch, and chicken in bowl; set aside.

3. Whisk broth, soy sauce, oyster sauce, pepper, remaining 2 tablespoons rice wine, and remaining 1 teaspoon cornstarch together in bowl; set aside.

4. Heat oil in 12-inch nonstick skillet over high heat until just smoking. Add chicken and cook, stirring frequently, until opaque, about 2 minutes. Add mushrooms and carrot and cook, stirring frequently, until tender, about 2 minutes. Add celery and cook until crisp-tender, about 1 minute. Add scallion whites, garlic, and ginger and cook until fragrant, about 30 seconds.

5. Whisk broth mixture to recombine, then add to skillet and cook until thickened and chicken is cooked through, about 2 minutes. Add bean sprouts and noodles and toss until sauce evenly coats noodles, about 1 minute. Transfer to platter and sprinkle with scallion greens. Serve.

FRESH EGG NOODLES

You'll find chow mein in Chinese restaurants prepared with wheat noodles, Italian pastas, ramen noodles, or egg noodles. But our tasters preferred fresh Chinese egg noodles, available in the Asian section of most grocery stores.

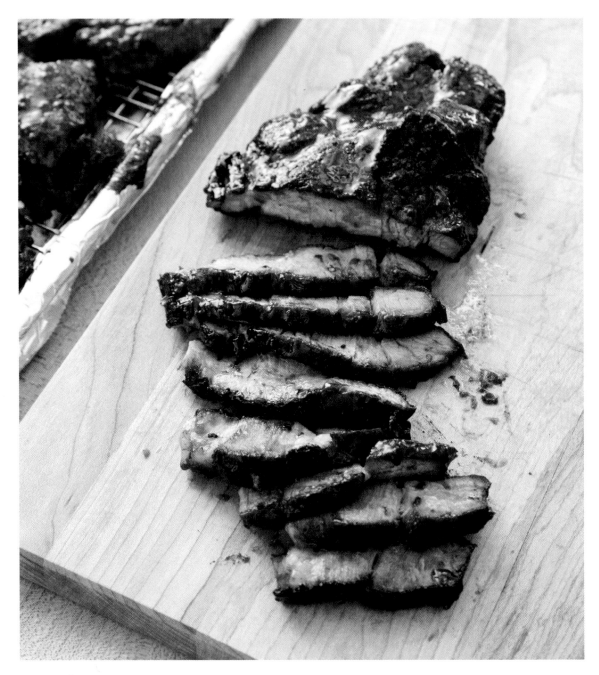

✓ WHY THIS RECIPE WORKS

Unlike what we typically think of as barbecue, Chinese barbecued pork is made neither on a grill nor in a smoker: It's usually cooked (and then glazed) in an oven. But we made this dish even more convenient— by adapting it to the slow cooker. Boneless pork butt renders lots of flavorful fat and pork juices as it cooks. Because this fat diluted any sauce we tried, we instead used a dry rub and then cooked the pork with a glazy sauce under the broiler. The finished "barbecued" pork was tender with a shiny, slightly charred exterior that tasted even better than it looked, earning it the nickname "meat candy" in the test kitchen.

Slow-Cooker Chinese Barbecued Pork

SERVES 8

Pork butt roast is often labeled Boston butt in the supermarket. Look for five-spice powder and hoisin sauce in the international aisle at your supermarket.

1½	teaspoons salt
1½	teaspoons five-spice powder
½	teaspoon pepper
1	(5- to 6-pound) boneless pork butt roast, trimmed and sliced crosswise into 1-inch-thick steaks
⅓	cup hoisin sauce
⅓	cup honey
¼	cup sugar
¼	cup soy sauce
¼	cup ketchup
2	tablespoons dry sherry
1	tablespoon toasted sesame oil
1	tablespoon grated fresh ginger
2	garlic cloves, minced

1. Combine salt, ¾ teaspoon five-spice powder, and pepper in bowl. Rub spice mixture all over pork and transfer to slow cooker. Cover and cook on low until pork is just tender, 5 to 6 hours.

2. When pork is nearly done, combine hoisin, honey, sugar, soy sauce, ketchup, sherry, oil, ginger, garlic, and remaining ¾ teaspoon five-spice powder in bowl. Set wire rack inside aluminum foil–lined rimmed baking sheet. Pour 1 cup water into sheet. Adjust oven rack 4 inches from broiler element and heat broiler.

3. Using tongs, transfer pork from slow cooker to prepared wire rack in single layer. Brush pork with one-third of hoisin mixture and broil until lightly caramelized, 5 to 7 minutes. Flip pork, brush with half of remaining hoisin mixture, and broil until lightly caramelized on second side, 5 to 7 minutes. Brush pork with remaining hoisin mixture and broil until deep mahogany and crispy around edges, about 3 minutes. Transfer to carving board and let rest for 10 minutes. Slice crosswise into thin strips. Serve.

PORK BUTT (BLADE SHOULDER)

This large, flavorful cut (often labeled Boston butt or pork shoulder at markets) can weigh as much as 8 pounds when sold with the bone in. Many markets take out the bone and sell this cut in smaller chunks, often wrapped in netting to hold the roast together. This cut is ideal for slow roasting, barbecuing, stewing, or braising.

WHY THIS RECIPE WORKS

Because the ground beef patty for patty melts is traditionally cooked twice—browned once in butter and a second time while the sandwich is griddled—many recipes produce something resembling dried-out hockey pucks. To solve the problem, we incorporated a panade (a paste of bread and milk) into the meat. To bump up the flavor of our burgers, we used rye bread and onion powder in the panade. Covering the cooking onions with the patties trapped some of the steam and helped the onions to soften quicker. This also allowed the flavors of the meat to seep into the onions and vice versa.

Patty Melts

SERVES 4

To make sure the melts hold together, use rye bread that's sliced about ½ inch thick.

10	slices hearty rye sandwich bread
2	tablespoons whole milk
¾	teaspoon onion powder
	Salt and pepper
1½	pounds 85 percent lean ground beef
3	tablespoons unsalted butter
2	onions, halved and sliced thin
8	ounces Swiss cheese, shredded (2 cups)

1. Adjust oven rack to middle position and heat oven to 200 degrees. Tear 2 pieces of bread into ½-inch pieces. Using potato masher, mash torn bread, milk, onion powder, ¾ teaspoon salt, and ½ teaspoon pepper in large bowl until smooth. Add beef and gently knead until well combined. Divide meat into 4 equal portions. Shape each portion into 6 by 4-inch oval.

2. Melt 1 tablespoon butter in 12-inch nonstick skillet over medium-high heat. Cook 2 patties until well browned on first side, about 5 minutes. Transfer to large plate, browned side up, and repeat with remaining 2 patties.

3. Pour off all but 1 teaspoon fat from pan. Add onions and ½ teaspoon salt and cook, stirring occasionally, until golden brown, 5 to 7 minutes. Arrange patties, browned side up, on top of onions, pouring any accumulated juices into pan. Reduce heat to medium and cook, shaking pan occasionally, until onions are tender and burgers are cooked through, about 5 minutes.

4. Divide 1 cup cheese among 4 slices bread. Top with patties, onions, remaining cheese, and remaining bread. Wipe out skillet with paper towels. Melt 1 tablespoon butter in now-empty skillet over medium heat. Cook 2 sandwiches until golden brown and cheese is melted, 3 to 4 minutes per side. Transfer to rimmed baking sheet and keep warm in oven. Repeat with remaining 1 tablespoon butter and remaining 2 sandwiches. Serve.

HEYDAY OF THE SANDWICH

When it comes to inventive sandwiches, you can't top 1920s America. Just a decade earlier, New Yorkers were said to eat only six types of sandwich: sardine, tongue, roast beef, Swiss cheese, liverwurst, and egg, according to William Grimes's book *Appetite City: A Culinary History of New York*. But three factors—Prohibition, the newfound popularity of automobiles, and women's increasing independence—had created a tearoom craze across the country, making sandwiches so popular that one New Yorker counted nearly 1,000 different types. In these newly minted salons of sandwiches, customers chose among dubious combinations like cheese-ketchup, lemon-prune, and baked bean–celery. Cookbooks reflected the trend, offering other odd partnerships, such as peanut butter and chili sauce, not to mention shredded coconut, cucumber, and mayonnaise. Makes Elvis's prized sandwich of fried peanut butter, banana, and bacon sound almost tame.

WHY THIS RECIPE WORKS

This Oklahoma specialty features a thin patty of ground beef topped with a crispy crust of caramelized onions cooked on a griddle. Served on a buttery grilled bun with yellow mustard, dill pickles, and a slice of American cheese, this exceptional burger is well worth a road trip. To make them at home, we sliced and salted the onions, then squeezed out their excess moisture so they'd brown quickly and stick to the burgers. We mashed the onions into the burgers, then put the burgers on a buttered skillet onion side down to brown the onions. Then we flipped the burgers and turned up the heat to finish cooking and get a nice sear.

Oklahoma Fried Onion Burgers

SERVES 4

A mandoline makes quick work of slicing the onion thinly. Squeeze the salted onion slices until they're as dry as possible, or they won't adhere to the patties. These burgers are traditionally served with yellow mustard and slices of dill pickle.

1	large onion, halved and sliced ⅛ inch thick
	Salt and pepper
12	ounces 85 percent lean ground beef
1	tablespoon unsalted butter
1	teaspoon vegetable oil
4	slices American cheese (4 ounces)
4	hamburger buns, buttered and toasted

1. Combine onion and 1 teaspoon salt in bowl and toss to combine. Transfer to colander and let sit for 30 minutes, tossing occasionally. Using tongs, transfer onion to clean dish towel, gather edges, and squeeze onion dry. Sprinkle with ½ teaspoon pepper.

2. Divide onion mixture into 4 separate mounds on rimmed baking sheet. Form beef into 4 lightly packed balls and season with salt and pepper. Place beef balls on top of onion mounds and flatten beef firmly so onion adheres and patties measure 4 inches in diameter.

3. Melt butter with oil in 12-inch nonstick skillet over medium heat. Using spatula, transfer patties to skillet, onion side down, and cook until onion is deep golden brown and beginning to crisp around edges, 6 to 8 minutes. Flip burgers, increase heat to high, and cook until well browned on second side, about 2 minutes. Place 1 slice cheese on each bottom bun. Place burgers on buns, add desired toppings, and serve.

KEYS TO FRIED ONION BURGERS

A few tricks helped the onions adhere to the burgers and caramelize rather than burn.

1. After you've salted the onions and squeezed them dry, divide into four piles, place the beef balls on top, and press.

2. Brown the onion side over gentler medium heat. Then flip the burgers and turn up the heat to sear the beef side.

✓ WHY THIS RECIPE WORKS

Atlanta brisket is a southern braise featuring onion soup mix, ketchup, and Atlanta's own Coca-Cola. We wanted to keep the regional charm but update the convenience-product flavor. To season the brisket, we pierced it with a fork, salted it, and let it sit overnight. For a great crust, we seared the brisket weighed down with a heavy pot. Finally, for the characteristic braising liquid, we mixed cola and ketchup and replaced the artificial-tasting soup mix with our own blend of sautéed onions, onion and garlic powders, brown sugar, and dried thyme. The mixture both flavored the meat and became a sweet, tangy sauce for serving.

Atlanta Brisket

SERVES 6

Parchment paper provides a nonreactive barrier between the cola-based braising liquid and the aluminum foil. A whole brisket is comprised of two smaller roasts: the flat cut and the point cut. For this recipe, we prefer the flat cut, which is rectangular in shape and leaner than the knobby, well-marbled point cut. The flat cut is topped with a thick fat cap; make sure that the fat cap isn't overtrimmed.

1	(3½-pound) beef brisket, flat cut, fat trimmed to ¼ inch thick
	Salt and pepper
4	teaspoons vegetable oil
1	pound onions, halved and sliced ½ inch thick
2	cups cola
1½	cups ketchup
4	teaspoons onion powder
2	teaspoons packed dark brown sugar
1	teaspoon garlic powder
1	teaspoon dried thyme

1. Using fork, poke holes all over brisket. Rub entire surface of brisket with 1 tablespoon salt. Wrap brisket in plastic wrap and refrigerate for at least 6 or up to 24 hours.

2. Adjust oven rack to lower-middle position and heat oven to 325 degrees. Pat brisket dry with paper towels and season with pepper. Heat 2 teaspoons oil in 12-inch nonstick skillet over medium-high heat until just smoking. Place brisket fat side down in skillet; weigh down brisket with heavy Dutch oven or cast-iron skillet and cook until well browned on bottom, about 4 minutes. Remove pot, flip brisket, and replace pot on top of brisket. Cook on second side until well browned, about 4 minutes longer. Transfer brisket to plate.

3. Heat remaining 2 teaspoons oil in now-empty skillet over medium heat until shimmering. Add onions and cook, stirring occasionally, until soft and golden brown, 10 to 12 minutes. Transfer onions to 13 by 9-inch baking dish and spread out in even layer.

4. Combine cola, ketchup, onion powder, sugar, garlic powder, thyme, 1 teaspoon salt, and 1 teaspoon pepper in bowl. Place brisket fat side up on top of onions and pour cola mixture over brisket. Place parchment paper over brisket and cover dish tightly with aluminum foil. Bake until tender and fork slips easily in and out of meat, 3½ to 4 hours. Let brisket rest in liquid, uncovered, for 30 minutes.

5. Transfer brisket to carving board. Skim any fat from top of sauce with large spoon. Slice brisket against grain into ¼-inch-thick slices and return to baking dish. Serve brisket with sauce.

TO MAKE AHEAD: Follow recipe through step 4. Allow brisket to cool in sauce, cover, and refrigerate overnight or up to 24 hours. To serve, slice brisket, return to sauce, and cover with parchment paper. Cover baking dish with aluminum foil and cook in 350-degree oven until heated through, about 1 hour.

GETTING A GREAT SEAR

Brisket is a flat cut of meat that curls up when you try to sear it. We fixed this problem by weighing down the brisket with a heavy Dutch oven (wrapped in foil to make cleanup easier) to ensure a more even sear.

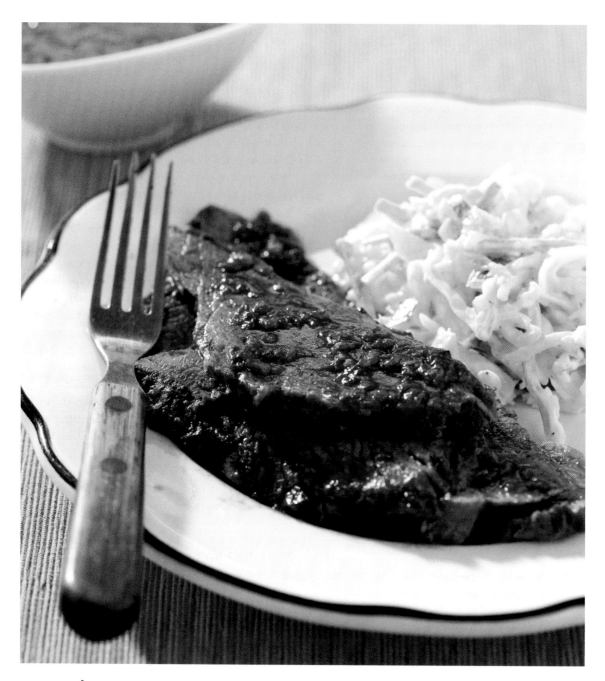

WHY THIS RECIPE WORKS

Barbecued brisket in the slow cooker? You bet. To minimize the moisture absorbed by the brisket (which traditionally isn't cooked directly in liquid), we came up with an unorthodox solution: elevating the meat off the bottom of the slow cooker with an inverted loaf pan. The liquid exuded from the meat during cooking was drawn under the loaf pan by a vacuum effect, which meant that the slow cooker more closely mimicked the dry heat of real barbecue. To bump up the flavor of this liquid, we added sautéed onion, garlic, tomato paste, and chipotle chiles.

Slow-Cooker BBQ Beef Brisket

Scoring the fat on the brisket at ½-inch intervals will allow the rub to penetrate the meat. Two disposable aluminum loaf pans stacked inside one another can be substituted for the metal loaf pan.

SPICE RUB AND BRISKET

- ½ cup packed dark brown sugar
- 2 tablespoons minced canned chipotle chile in adobo sauce
- 1 tablespoon ground cumin
- 1 tablespoon paprika
- 2 teaspoons pepper
- 1 teaspoon salt
- 1 (4- to 5-pound) brisket roast, fat trimmed to ¼ inch thick and scored lightly

AROMATICS AND SAUCE

- 3 tablespoons vegetable oil
- 1 onion, chopped fine
- 2 tablespoons tomato paste
- 1 tablespoon chili powder
- 1 tablespoon minced canned chipotle chile in adobo sauce
- 2 garlic cloves, minced
- ½ cup water, plus extra as needed
- ¼ cup ketchup
- 1 tablespoon cider vinegar
- ¼ teaspoon liquid smoke
  Salt and pepper

1. FOR THE SPICE RUB AND BRISKET: Combine sugar, chipotle, cumin, paprika, pepper, and salt in bowl. Rub sugar mixture all over brisket. Cover with plastic wrap and let sit at room temperature for 1 hour or refrigerate for up to 24 hours.

2. FOR THE AROMATICS AND SAUCE: Heat oil in 12-inch skillet over medium-high heat until shimmering. Cook onion until softened, about 5 minutes. Add tomato paste and cook until beginning to brown, about 1 minute. Stir in chili powder, chipotle, and garlic and

cook until fragrant, about 30 seconds. Mound onion mixture in center of slow cooker, arrange inverted metal loaf pan over onion mixture, and place brisket fat side up on top of loaf pan. Add water to slow cooker, cover, and cook on high until fork inserted in brisket can be removed with no resistance, 7 to 8 hours (or cook on low for 10 to 12 hours).

3. Transfer brisket to 13 by 9-inch baking dish, cover with aluminum foil, and let rest for 30 minutes. Carefully remove loaf pan from slow cooker. Pour onion mixture and accumulated juices into large bowl and skim fat. (You should have about 2 cups defatted juices; if you have less, supplement with water.)

4. Transfer brisket to carving board, slice thin against grain, and return to baking dish. Pour 1 cup reserved defatted juices over sliced brisket. Whisk ketchup, vinegar, and liquid smoke into remaining juices. Season with salt and pepper to taste. Serve, passing sauce at table.

TO MAKE AHEAD: In step 3, wrap brisket tightly in foil and refrigerate for up to 3 days. (Refrigerate juices separately.) To serve, transfer foil-wrapped brisket to baking dish and heat in 350-degree oven until brisket is heated through, about 1 hour. Reheat juices in microwave or saucepan set over medium heat. Continue with recipe as directed.

PREVENTING WATERLOGGED BRISKET

To minimize the moisture absorbed by the brisket, we place the meat on top of a loaf pan. The juices exuded by the meat are drawn under the pan by a vacuum effect, creating less moisture directly below the meat.

1. Pile onion mixture under inverted loaf pan and place brisket on top.

2. After cooking, remove loaf pan to release juices, which make a flavorful base for barbecue sauce.

✔ WHY THIS RECIPE WORKS

We wanted a foolproof recipe for this southern specialty. We started by making a whiskey-flavored marinade, then steeped the chops in it for at least one hour prior to cooking. We cooked the chops in a hot skillet and then used the same pan to prepare the glaze—browned bits left behind by the chops in the pan added deep, meaty flavor. Allowing the cooked chops to sit in the pan in the glaze for a few minutes before serving helped ensure it clung to the meat.

Tennessee Whiskey Pork Chops

SERVES 4

Bourbon tastes fine, but we think it's worth purchasing the real deal—Jack Daniel's Tennessee Whiskey—for this recipe. Watch the glaze closely during the last few minutes of cooking—the bubbles become very small as it approaches the right consistency.

½ cup Jack Daniel's Tennessee Whiskey or bourbon

½ cup apple cider

2 tablespoons packed light brown sugar

4 teaspoons cider vinegar

1 tablespoon Dijon mustard

½ teaspoon vanilla extract

⅛ teaspoon cayenne pepper

4 (8- to 10-ounce) bone-in, center-cut pork chops, about 1 inch thick, trimmed

2 teaspoons vegetable oil

Salt and pepper

1 tablespoon unsalted butter

1. Whisk whiskey, cider, sugar, 2 teaspoons vinegar, mustard, vanilla, and cayenne together in bowl. Transfer ¼ cup whiskey mixture to 1-gallon zipper-lock bag, add pork chops, press air out of bag, and seal. Turn bag to coat chops with marinade and refrigerate 1 to 2 hours. Reserve remaining whiskey mixture separately.

2. Remove chops from bag, pat dry with paper towels, and discard marinade. Heat oil in 12-inch skillet over medium-high heat until just beginning to smoke. Season chops with salt and pepper and cook until well browned on both sides and a peek into thickest part of a chop using paring knife yields still-pink meat ¼ inch from surface, 6 to 8 minutes, flipping chops halfway through cooking. Transfer chops to plate and cover tightly with aluminum foil.

3. Add reserved whiskey mixture to skillet and bring to boil, scraping up any browned bits with wooden spoon. Cook until reduced to thick glaze, 3 to 5 minutes. Reduce heat to medium-low and, holding on to chops, tip plate to add any accumulated juices back to skillet. Add remaining 2 teaspoons vinegar, whisk in butter, and simmer glaze until thick and sticky, 2 to 3 minutes. Remove pan from heat.

4. Return chops to skillet and let rest in pan, turning chops occasionally to coat both sides, until sauce clings to chops and meat registers 145 degrees, about 5 minutes. Transfer chops to platter and spoon sauce over. Serve.

BREAK OUT THE GOOD STUFF

Bourbon was fine, but we loved the deep, caramel-flavored glaze we got when using Jack Daniel's in this recipe. Tennessee whiskey differs from Kentucky bourbon because of a distiller's trick called the Lincoln County process, in which the distilled whiskey is filtered over hard maple charcoal. Then, like bourbon, it is aged in charred oak barrels, where it picks up its distinctive caramel color and smoky flavor.

✓ WHY THIS RECIPE WORKS

For these saucy Memphis wet ribs, a potent spice rub performs double duty, seasoning the meat and creating the backbone for our barbecue sauce. Tying two racks together allowed us to double our yield and cook four hefty racks of ribs at once. To keep the ribs moist, we grilled them over indirect heat and basted them with a traditional "mop" of juice and vinegar. After a few hours of smoking on the grill, we brushed the ribs with our flavorful barbecue sauce and transferred them to the steady, even heat of the oven to finish tenderizing.

Memphis-Style Wet Ribs for a Crowd

SERVES 8 TO 12

SPICE RUB

- ¼ cup paprika
- 2 tablespoons packed brown sugar
- 2 tablespoons salt
- 2 teaspoons pepper
- 2 teaspoons onion powder
- 2 teaspoons granulated garlic

BARBECUE SAUCE AND MOP

- 1½ cups ketchup
- ¾ cup apple juice, plus ½ cup for mop
- ¼ cup molasses
- ¼ cup cider vinegar, plus ¼ cup for mop
- ¼ cup Worcestershire sauce
- 2 tablespoons yellow mustard, plus 1 tablespoon for mop
- 2 teaspoons pepper

RIBS

- 4 (2½- to 3-pound) racks St. Louis–style spareribs, trimmed, membrane removed
- 2 cups wood chips, soaked in water for 15 minutes and drained
- 1 (13 by 9-inch) disposable aluminum roasting pan (if using charcoal) or 1 (8½ by 6-inch) disposable aluminum pan (if using gas)

1. FOR THE SPICE RUB: Combine all ingredients in bowl.

2. FOR THE BARBECUE SAUCE AND MOP: Combine ketchup, ¾ cup apple juice, molasses, ¼ cup vinegar, Worcestershire, 2 tablespoons mustard, and 2 tablespoons spice rub in medium saucepan and bring to boil over medium heat. Reduce heat to medium-low and simmer until thickened and reduced to 2 cups, about 20 minutes. Off heat, stir in pepper; set aside. For the mop, whisk ½ cup apple juice, ¼ cup vinegar, 1 tablespoon mustard, and ¼ cup barbecue sauce together in bowl.

3. FOR THE RIBS: Pat ribs dry with paper towels and season with remaining spice rub. Place 1 rack of ribs, meaty side down, on cutting board. Place second rack of ribs, meaty side up, directly on top of first rack, arranging thick end over tapered end. Tie racks together at 2-inch intervals with kitchen twine. Repeat with remaining 2 racks of ribs for two bundles. Using large piece of heavy-duty aluminum foil, wrap soaked chips in foil packet and cut several vent holes in top.

4A. FOR A CHARCOAL GRILL: Open bottom vent halfway and place disposable roasting pan on 1 side of grill. Fill pan with 2 quarts water. Arrange 3 quarts unlit charcoal briquettes on other side of grill. Light large chimney starter half filled with charcoal briquettes (3 quarts). When top coals are partially covered with ash, pour evenly over unlit coals. Place wood chip packet on coals. Set cooking grate in place, cover, and open lid vent halfway. Heat grill until hot and wood chips are smoking, about 5 minutes.

4B. FOR A GAS GRILL: Place wood chip packet and disposable pan over primary burner and fill pan with 2 cups water. Turn primary burner to high (leave other burners off), cover, and heat grill until hot and wood chips are smoking, about 15 minutes. (Adjust primary burner as needed to maintain grill temperature of 275 to 300 degrees.)

5. Clean and oil cooking grate. Place ribs on cooler side of grill and baste with one-third of mop. Cover (positioning lid vent over ribs for charcoal) and cook for 2 hours, flipping and switching positions of ribs and basting again with half of remaining mop halfway through cooking.

6. Adjust oven racks to upper-middle and lower-middle positions and heat oven to 300 degrees. Line 2 rimmed baking sheets with foil. Cut kitchen twine from racks. Transfer 2 racks, meaty side up, to each sheet. Baste with remaining mop and bake for 2 hours, switching and rotating sheets halfway through baking.

7. Remove ribs from oven and brush evenly with ½ cup barbecue sauce. Return to oven and continue to bake until tender, basting with ½ cup barbecue sauce and switching and rotating sheets twice during baking, about 45 minutes. (Ribs do not need to be flipped and should remain meaty side up during baking.) Transfer ribs to carving board. Brush evenly with remaining ½ cup barbecue sauce, tent loosely with foil, and let rest for 20 minutes. Cut ribs in between bones to separate. Serve.

WHY THIS RECIPE WORKS

Baltimore is known for its pit beef, replete with a well-seasoned, charred crust and a rosy pink interior. The meat is shaved paper thin, piled onto a kaiser roll, topped with a horseradish-y mayo known as tiger sauce, and finally covered with sliced onions. We started by cutting a beefy top sirloin roast in half and slow-cooked the meat on the cool side of the grill—a foil shield provided maximum protection so the meat didn't dry out. Then for maximum char, we generously seared both pieces all over.

Baltimore Pit Beef

SERVES 10

When shopping for the prepared horseradish, buy the brined (not creamy) variety and, if necessary, drain it.

TIGER SAUCE

- ½ cup mayonnaise
- ½ cup hot prepared horseradish
- 1 teaspoon lemon juice
- 1 garlic clove, minced
- Salt and pepper

PIT BEEF

- 4 teaspoons kosher salt
- 1 tablespoon paprika
- 1 tablespoon pepper
- 1 teaspoon garlic powder
- 1 teaspoon dried oregano
- ¼ teaspoon cayenne pepper
- 1 (4- to 5-pound) boneless top sirloin roast, trimmed and halved crosswise
- 10 kaiser rolls
- 1 onion, sliced thin

1. FOR THE TIGER SAUCE: Whisk mayonnaise, horseradish, lemon juice, and garlic together in bowl. Season with salt and pepper to taste. (Sauce can be refrigerated for up to 2 days.)

2. FOR THE PIT BEEF: Combine salt, paprika, pepper, garlic powder, oregano, and cayenne in bowl. Pat roasts dry with paper towels and rub with 2 tablespoons seasoning mixture. Wrap meat tightly with plastic wrap and refrigerate for 6 to 24 hours.

3A. FOR A CHARCOAL GRILL: Open bottom vent halfway. Light large chimney starter filled with charcoal briquettes (6 quarts). When top coals are partially covered with ash, pour evenly over half of grill. Set cooking grate in place, cover, and open lid vent halfway. Heat grill until hot, about 5 minutes.

3B. FOR A GAS GRILL: Turn all burners to high, cover, and heat grill until hot, about 15 minutes. Leave primary burner on high and turn other burner(s) off.

4. Clean and oil cooking grate. Unwrap roasts and place end to end on long side of 18 by 12-inch sheet of aluminum foil. Loosely fold opposite long side of foil around top of roasts. Place meat on cool part of grill with foil-covered side closest to heat source. Cover (positioning lid vent over meat if using charcoal) and cook until meat registers 100 degrees, 45 minutes to 1 hour.

5. Transfer roasts to plate and discard foil. Turn all burners to high if using gas. If using charcoal, carefully remove cooking grate and light large chimney starter three-quarters filled with charcoal briquettes (4½ quarts). When top coals are partially covered with ash, pour evenly over spent coals. Set cooking grate in place and cover. Heat grill until hot, about 5 minutes.

6. Pat roasts dry with paper towels and rub with remaining spice mixture. Place meat on hot part of grill. Cook (covered if using gas), turning occasionally, until charred on all sides and meat registers 120 to 125 degrees (for medium-rare), 10 to 20 minutes. Transfer meat to carving board, tent loosely with foil, and let rest for 15 minutes. Slice meat thin against grain. Transfer sliced beef to rolls, top with onion slices, and drizzle with sauce. Serve.

PREVENTING PIT BEEF FROM DRYING OUT

Even with indirect heat, the sides of the roasts closest to the fire can overcook. A simple foil shield protects them.

WHY THIS RECIPE WORKS

Warm spices and a host of unexpected garnishes lend Cincinnati chili recipes their unique flavors—but can sometimes muddle the dish. To recreate this Midwestern recipe in our own kitchen, we narrowed our ingredient list to four spices. Tomato paste added richness to our chili, while dark brown sugar gave it a sweet tang. Boiling the beef in water kept it extremely tender during cooking—we cooked ours directly in our spices and liquid to infuse the meat with their intense flavor. Serving our chili over spaghetti, and a combination of cheese, onions, red beans, and oyster crackers, gave us the true Cincinnati chili experience.

Cincinnati Chili

SERVES 6 TO 8

Use canned tomato sauce for this recipe—do not use jarred spaghetti sauce.

1	tablespoon vegetable oil
2	onions, chopped fine
2	tablespoons tomato paste
2	tablespoons chili powder
1	tablespoon dried oregano
1½	teaspoons ground cinnamon
1	garlic clove, minced
	Salt and pepper
¼	teaspoon ground allspice
2	cups chicken broth
2	cups canned tomato sauce
2	tablespoons cider vinegar
2	teaspoons packed dark brown sugar
1½	pounds 85 percent lean ground beef

1. Heat oil in Dutch oven over medium-high heat until shimmering. Cook onions until soft and browned around edges, about 8 minutes. Add tomato paste, chili powder, oregano, cinnamon, garlic, 1 teaspoon salt, ¾ teaspoon pepper, and allspice and cook until fragrant, about 1 minute. Stir in chicken broth, tomato sauce, vinegar, and sugar.

2. Add beef and stir to break up meat. Bring to boil, reduce heat to medium-low, and simmer until chili is deep brown and slightly thickened, 15 to 20 minutes. Season with salt to taste and serve. (Chili can be refrigerated for up to 3 days or frozen for up to 2 months.)

FIVE WAYS TO CINCINNATI

Those in the know can order their chili without a second thought, but for the uninitiated, here's a quick guide to the five ways of Cincinnati chili. The chili is almost never served on its own (one-way). Just don't forget the oyster crackers!

TWO-WAY CHILI
Served over spaghetti.

THREE-WAY CHILI
Served over spaghetti and topped with cheese.

FOUR-WAY CHILI
Served over spaghetti and topped with onions and cheese.

FIVE-WAY CHILI
Served over spaghetti and topped with onions, red beans, and cheese.

✓ WHY THIS RECIPE WORKS

This popular southwestern dish boasts rich bites of pork in a sauce dominated by green chiles. For our version, we used a combination of Anaheim and jalapeño peppers. To achieve the cohesive flavor and mild vegetal taste that we liked, we used canned, diced tomatoes and more than 2 pounds of chiles, along with 3 pounds of boneless pork butt—our preferred cut for its rich meatiness. To reduce the hands-on time, we started the pork with water in a covered pan to render the fat, then let the even heat of the oven cook the chili. Adding the jalapeños just before serving gave a fresh hit of heat.

Colorado Green Chili

SERVES 6

The chiles can be roasted and refrigerated up to 24 hours in advance.

- 3 pounds boneless pork butt roast, trimmed and cut into 1-inch pieces
  Salt
- 2 pounds (10 to 12) Anaheim chiles, stemmed, halved lengthwise, and seeded
- 3 jalapeño chiles
- 1 (14.5-ounce) can diced tomatoes
- 1 tablespoon vegetable oil
- 2 onions, chopped fine
- 8 garlic cloves, minced
- 1 tablespoon ground cumin
- ¼ cup all-purpose flour
- 4 cups chicken broth
  Cayenne pepper
  Lime wedges

1. Combine pork, ½ cup water, and ½ teaspoon salt in Dutch oven over medium heat. Cover and cook for 20 minutes, stirring occasionally. Uncover, increase heat to medium-high, and continue to cook, stirring frequently, until liquid evaporates and pork browns in its own fat, 15 to 20 minutes. Transfer pork to bowl and set aside.

2. Meanwhile, adjust 1 oven rack to lowest position and second rack 6 inches from broiler element. Heat broiler. Line rimmed baking sheet with aluminum foil and spray with vegetable oil spray. Arrange Anaheims, skin side up, and jalapeños in single layer on prepared sheet. Place sheet on upper rack and broil until chiles are mostly blackened and soft, 15 to 20 minutes, rotating sheet and flipping only jalapeños halfway through broiling. Place Anaheims in large bowl and cover with plastic wrap; let cool for 5 minutes. Set aside jalapeños. Heat oven to 325 degrees.

3. Remove skins from Anaheims. Chop half of Anaheims into ½-inch pieces and transfer to bowl. Process remaining Anaheims in food processor until smooth, about 10 seconds; transfer to bowl with chopped Anaheims. Pulse tomatoes and their juice in now-empty food processor until coarsely ground, about 4 pulses.

4. Heat oil in now-empty Dutch oven over medium heat until shimmering. Add onions and cook until lightly browned, 5 to 7 minutes. Stir in garlic and cumin and cook until fragrant, about 30 seconds. Stir in flour and cook for 1 minute. Stir in broth, Anaheims, tomatoes, and pork with any accumulated juices and bring to simmer, scraping up any browned bits. Cover pot, transfer to lower oven rack, and cook until pork is tender, 1 to 1¼ hours.

5. Without peeling, stem and seed jalapeños and reserve seeds. Finely chop jalapeños and stir into chili. Season chili with salt, cayenne, and reserved jalapeño seeds to taste. Serve with lime wedges.

EASIER ROASTED CHILES

Roasting chiles whole and then seeding them—the usual procedure— makes a mess: the wet seeds stick to everything. We halve and seed the raw Anaheims. It's neater and lets us skip the usual flipping step. We leave the jalapeños whole; they soften but don't deeply roast.

READY FOR ROASTING
Arrange the chiles head to foot for the best fit.

✔ WHY THIS RECIPE WORKS

Similar to Latin American empanadas, these deep-fried hand pies from Louisiana are filled with savory ground meat and spices. For the filling, we used equal parts ground beef and pork along with the classic Creole combination of onions, green bell peppers, and a pinch of cayenne for heat. Chicken broth and flour made the filling cohesive. Using chicken broth rather than milk in the dough gave the crust a subtle savory flavor. After a few minutes in hot oil, they emerged with a crisp, flaky crust and piping-hot filling.

Natchitoches Meat Pies

MAKES 16 PIES

You can make the dough and the filling up to 24 hours ahead and refrigerate them separately. You can also shape and fill the pies, refrigerating them for up to 24 hours before frying. Use a Dutch oven that holds 6 quarts or more.

FILLING

- 5 teaspoons vegetable oil
- ¾ pound 85 percent lean ground beef
- ¾ pound ground pork
- Salt and pepper
- 1 onion, chopped fine
- 1 green bell pepper, stemmed, seeded, and minced
- 6 scallions, white parts minced, green parts sliced thin
- 3 garlic cloves, minced
- ¼ teaspoon cayenne pepper
- 2 tablespoons all-purpose flour
- 1 cup chicken broth

DOUGH

- 4 cups (20 ounces) all-purpose flour
- 2 teaspoons salt
- 1 teaspoon baking powder
- 8 tablespoons vegetable shortening, cut into ½-inch pieces
- 1 cup chicken broth
- 2 large eggs, lightly beaten
- 1 quart vegetable oil for frying

1. FOR THE FILLING: Heat 2 teaspoons oil in 12-inch skillet over medium-high heat until just smoking. Add beef, pork, 1 teaspoon salt, and ½ teaspoon pepper and cook, breaking up pieces with spoon, until no longer pink, 8 to 10 minutes. Transfer meat to bowl.

2. Add remaining 1 tablespoon oil to now-empty skillet and heat over medium-high heat until shimmering. Add onion, bell pepper, scallion whites, ½ teaspoon salt, and ½ teaspoon pepper and cook until vegetables are just starting to brown, 3 to 5 minutes. Stir in garlic and cayenne and cook until fragrant, about 30 seconds.

3. Return meat and any accumulated juices to skillet with vegetables. Sprinkle flour over meat and cook, stirring constantly, until evenly coated, about 1 minute. Add broth, bring to boil, and cook until slightly thickened, about 3 minutes. Transfer filling to bowl and stir in scallion greens. Refrigerate until completely cool, about 1 hour. (Filling can be refrigerated for up to 24 hours.)

4. FOR THE DOUGH: Process flour, salt, and baking powder in food processor until combined, about 3 seconds. Add shortening and pulse until mixture resembles coarse cornmeal, 6 to 8 pulses. Add broth and eggs and pulse until dough just comes together, about 5 pulses. Transfer dough to lightly floured counter and knead until dough forms smooth ball, about 20 seconds. Divide dough into 16 equal pieces. (Dough can be covered and refrigerated for up to 24 hours.)

5. Line rimmed baking sheet with parchment paper. Working with 1 piece of dough at a time, roll into 6-inch circle on lightly floured counter. Place ¼ cup filling in center of dough round. Brush edges of dough with water and fold dough over filling. Press to seal, trim any ragged edges, and crimp edges with tines of fork. Transfer to prepared sheet. (Filled pies can be covered and refrigerated for up to 24 hours.)

6. Adjust oven rack to middle position and heat oven to 200 degrees. Set wire rack in second rimmed baking sheet. Add oil to large Dutch oven until it measures about ¾ inch deep and heat over medium-high heat to 350 degrees. Place 4 pies in oil and fry until golden brown, 3 to 5 minutes per side, using slotted spatula or spider to flip. Adjust burner, if necessary, to maintain oil temperature between 325 and 350 degrees. Transfer pies to prepared wire rack and place in oven to keep warm. Return oil to 350 degrees and repeat with remaining pies. Serve.

✅ WHY THIS RECIPE WORKS

With its wafer-thin crust, thick, sweet tomato sauce, and gooey Provel cheese, St. Louis–style pizza is unmistakable. Adding cornstarch to the dough absorbed moisture and allowed the crust to crisp in a conventional oven. We doctored a simple pizza sauce by adding sugar, tomato paste, dried oregano, and fresh basil. The fresh herb wasn't typical, but it gave the pizza a flavorful lift. Smoky, melty Provel cheese was difficult to find outside the St. Louis area, so we crafted a respectable substitute with American cheese, Monterey Jack, and liquid smoke.

St. Louis–Style Pizza

MAKES TWO 12-INCH PIZZAS

If you can find Provel cheese, use 10 ounces in place of the American cheese, Monterey Jack cheese, and liquid smoke.

SAUCE AND CHEESES

- 1 (8-ounce) can tomato sauce
- 3 tablespoons tomato paste
- 2 tablespoons chopped fresh basil
- 1 tablespoon sugar
- 2 teaspoons dried oregano
- 8 ounces white American cheese, shredded (2 cups)
- 2 ounces Monterey Jack cheese, shredded (½ cup)
- 3 drops liquid smoke

DOUGH

- 2 cups (10 ounces) all-purpose flour
- 2 tablespoons cornstarch
- 2 teaspoons sugar
- 1 teaspoon baking powder
- 1 teaspoon salt
- ½ cup plus 2 tablespoons water
- 2 tablespoons olive oil

1. FOR THE SAUCE AND CHEESES: Whisk together tomato sauce, tomato paste, basil, sugar, and oregano in small bowl; set aside. Toss cheeses with liquid smoke in medium bowl; set aside.

2. FOR THE DOUGH: Combine flour, cornstarch, sugar, baking powder, and salt in large bowl. Combine water and olive oil in liquid measuring cup. Stir water mixture into flour mixture until dough starts to come together. Turn dough onto lightly floured surface and knead 3 or 4 times, until cohesive.

3. Adjust oven rack to lower-middle position, place baking stone (or inverted baking sheet) on rack, and heat oven to 475 degrees. Divide dough into 2 equal pieces. Working with 1 piece of dough at a time, press into small circle and transfer to parchment paper dusted lightly with flour. Using rolling pin, roll and stretch dough to form 12-inch circle, rotating parchment as needed. Lift parchment and pizza off work surface onto inverted baking sheet.

4. Top each piece of dough with half of sauce and half of cheese. Carefully pull parchment paper and pizza off baking sheet onto hot baking stone. Bake until underside is golden brown and cheese is completely melted, 9 to 12 minutes. Remove pizza and parchment from oven. Transfer pizza to wire rack and let cool briefly. Assemble and bake second pizza. Cut into 2-inch squares. Serve.

TO MAKE AHEAD: The dough can be made in advance. At end of step 2, tightly wrap ball of dough in plastic wrap and refrigerate for up to 2 days.

MEET ME IN ST. LOUIS

You can make terrific pizza without yeast. It may sound crazy to most of us, but folks in St. Louis have been doing it for years.

With its wafer-thin crust; thick, sweet tomato sauce; gooey Provel cheese (another local secret); and signature square slices, St. Louis–style pizza is unmistakable. Imo's, a popular local chain, is credited with creating it, and it's said that founder Ed Imo, a former tile-layer, subconsciously cut the circular pizza into tile-shaped squares (the "square beyond compare," as the jingle goes). The chain and its pizza have since crossed into Illinois and Kansas.

☑ WHY THIS RECIPE WORKS

We wanted a recipe for fast-food-style crunchy potato wedges that we could prepare at home. Microwaving the potatoes in a tightly covered bowl helped them obtain perfectly cooked interiors and nicely crisped exteriors. For the coating, adding baking soda to buttermilk and replacing some of the flour with cornstarch resulted in crunchy, deep-golden-brown wedges. Finally, seasoning our crunchy potato wedges with a spice blend as they precooked in the microwave, then tossing the wedges in the seasonings when they came out of the oil, produced potatoes that were flavored from the inside out.

Crunchy Potato Wedges

SERVES 6

If you don't have buttermilk, substitute 1 cup milk mixed with 1 tablespoon lemon juice. Let the mixture sit 15 minutes before using. You will need at least a 6-quart Dutch oven for this recipe.

- 4 teaspoons kosher salt
- 2 teaspoons onion powder
- 1 teaspoon garlic powder
- 1 teaspoon dried oregano
- ¾ teaspoon cayenne pepper
- ½ teaspoon pepper
- 3 large russet potatoes (about 1¾ pounds), cut into ¼-inch wedges
- ¼ cup peanut or vegetable oil, plus 3 quarts for frying
- 1½ cups all-purpose flour
- ½ cup cornstarch
- 1 cup buttermilk
- ½ teaspoon baking soda

1. Combine salt, onion powder, garlic powder, oregano, cayenne, and pepper in small bowl.

2. Toss potato wedges with 4 teaspoons spice mixture and ¼ cup oil in large bowl; cover. Microwave until potatoes are tender but not falling apart, 7 to 9 minutes, shaking bowl to redistribute potatoes halfway through cooking. Uncover and drain potatoes. Arrange potatoes on rimmed baking sheet and let cool until potatoes firm up, about 10 minutes. (Potatoes can be held at room temperature for up to 2 hours.)

3. Set wire rack in rimmed baking sheet and line second baking sheet with triple layer of paper towels. Add remaining 3 quarts oil to large Dutch oven until it measures about 2 inches deep and heat over medium-high heat to 340 degrees. Meanwhile, combine flour and cornstarch in medium bowl and whisk buttermilk and baking soda together in large bowl. Working in 2 batches, dredge potato wedges in flour mixture, shaking off excess. Dip in buttermilk mixture, allowing excess to drip back into bowl, then coat again in flour mixture. Shake off excess and place on wire rack. (Potatoes can be coated up to 30 minutes in advance.)

4. When oil is ready, add half of coated wedges and fry until deep golden brown, 4 to 6 minutes. Transfer wedges to large bowl and toss with 1 teaspoon spice mixture. Drain wedges on paper towel–lined baking sheet. Return oil to 340 degrees and repeat with second batch of wedges. Serve with extra spice mixture on side.

TO MAKE AHEAD: Our Crunchy Potato Wedges freeze very well. Follow steps 1 through 4, frying each batch of wedges until they are light golden brown, 2 to 3 minutes. Do not toss with seasoning, and drain and cool potatoes completely on baking sheet lined with paper towels. Freeze wedges on baking sheet until completely frozen, about 2 hours, then transfer potatoes to zipper-lock bag for up to 2 months. When ready to eat, heat 3 quarts oil to 340 degrees and cook in 2 batches until deep golden brown, about 3 minutes. Toss with seasonings, drain, and serve.

CREAMY BBQ SAUCE
MAKES 1¼ CUPS, ENOUGH FOR 1 RECIPE CRUNCHY POTATO WEDGES

Combine ¾ cup mayonnaise, ¼ cup barbecue sauce, 3 tablespoons cider vinegar, 1 minced garlic clove, ¼ teaspoon pepper, and ⅛ teaspoon salt in small bowl.

BUFFALO BLUE CHEESE SAUCE
MAKES 1½ CUPS, ENOUGH FOR 1 RECIPE CRUNCHY POTATO WEDGES

Combine ¾ cup mayonnaise, ¼ cup blue cheese salad dressing, 3 tablespoons hot sauce, 1 minced garlic clove, ¼ teaspoon pepper, and ⅛ teaspoon celery salt in small bowl.

CURRIED CHUTNEY SAUCE
MAKES 1¼ CUPS, ENOUGH FOR 1 RECIPE CRUNCHY POTATO WEDGES

Combine ¾ cup mayonnaise, ¼ cup yogurt, ¼ cup minced fresh cilantro, 3 tablespoons mango chutney, 2 teaspoons curry powder, ¼ teaspoon pepper, and ⅛ teaspoon salt in small bowl.

✓ WHY THIS RECIPE WORKS

Let's face it, frozen potato tots don't live up to our childhood memories. And many recipes simply mix coarsely ground potato with flour and egg, which fry up into raw, dense nuggets. We found that par-cooking the chopped potato in the microwave was a step in the right direction, but the tots were still too heavy. Reducing the flour and omitting the egg helped, but the tots were still not light and fluffy. To minimize the gluey texture of potato starch, we tried processing the potatoes with water. Perfection. This step rinsed off the excess starch, and a small amount of salt in the mixture kept the interior downy white.

Crispy Potato Tots

MAKES 4 DOZEN

If any large pieces of potato remain after processing, chop them coarsely by hand. To make handling the uncooked tots easier, use a wet knife blade and wet hands. Once the tots are added to the hot oil, they may stick together; resist the temptation to stir and break them apart until after they have browned and set. You will need at least a 6-quart Dutch oven for this recipe.

2¼	teaspoons salt
2½	pounds russet potatoes, peeled and cut into 1½-inch pieces
1½	tablespoons all-purpose flour
½	teaspoon pepper
1	quart peanut or vegetable oil

1. Whisk 1 cup water and salt together in bowl until salt dissolves. Pulse potatoes and salt water in food processor until coarsely ground, 10 to 12 pulses, stirring occasionally. Drain mixture in fine-mesh strainer, pressing potatoes with rubber spatula until dry (liquid should measure about 1½ cups); discard liquid. Transfer potatoes to bowl and microwave, uncovered, until dry and sticky, 8 to 10 minutes, stirring halfway through cooking.

2. Stir flour and pepper into potatoes. Spread potato mixture into thin layer over large sheet of aluminum foil and let cool for 10 minutes. Push potatoes to center of foil and place foil and potatoes in 8-inch square baking pan. Push foil into corners and up sides of pan, smoothing it flush to pan. Press potato mixture tightly and evenly into pan. Freeze, uncovered, until firm, about 30 minutes.

3. Meanwhile, adjust oven rack to middle position and heat oven to 200 degrees. Set wire rack in rimmed baking sheet. Add oil to large Dutch oven until it measures about ¾ inch deep and heat over high heat until 375 degrees. Using foil overhang, lift potatoes from pan and cut into 48 pieces (5 cuts in 1 direction and 7 in other). Fry half of potato tots until golden brown and crisp, 5 to 7 minutes, stirring only after they are browned and set. Transfer to prepared baking sheet and place in oven. Return oil to 375 degrees and repeat with remaining potato tots. Serve.

TO MAKE AHEAD: Let fried potato tots cool, transfer to zipper-lock bag, and freeze for up to 1 month. To serve, adjust oven rack to middle position and heat oven to 400 degrees. Place potato tots on rimmed baking sheet and bake until heated through, 12 to 15 minutes.

CRISPY POTATO TOTS FOR A CROWD

Double all ingredients for Crispy Potato Tots. Process and drain potato mixture in 2 batches. Microwave entire potato mixture for 12 to 14 minutes, stirring halfway through cooking. Spread potato mixture over large sheet of foil to cool and press into 13 by 9-inch baking pan. After freezing, cut potato rectangle in half crosswise before cutting into potato tots per recipe. Fry in 4 batches.

BACON-RANCH POTATO TOTS

Stir 1 tablespoon cider vinegar into potatoes after microwaving. Add 4 slices finely chopped cooked bacon, 1 teaspoon onion powder, ½ teaspoon garlic powder, and ½ teaspoon dried dill to potatoes with flour in step 2.

PARMESAN-ROSEMARY POTATO TOTS

Stir 2 minced garlic cloves into drained potatoes before microwaving. Add 1 cup grated Parmesan cheese and 2 tablespoons minced fresh rosemary to potatoes with flour in step 2.

SOUTHWESTERN POTATO TOTS

Add ½ cup shredded smoked gouda cheese, 3 tablespoons minced fresh cilantro, and 2 tablespoons minced jarred jalapeños to potatoes with flour in step 2.

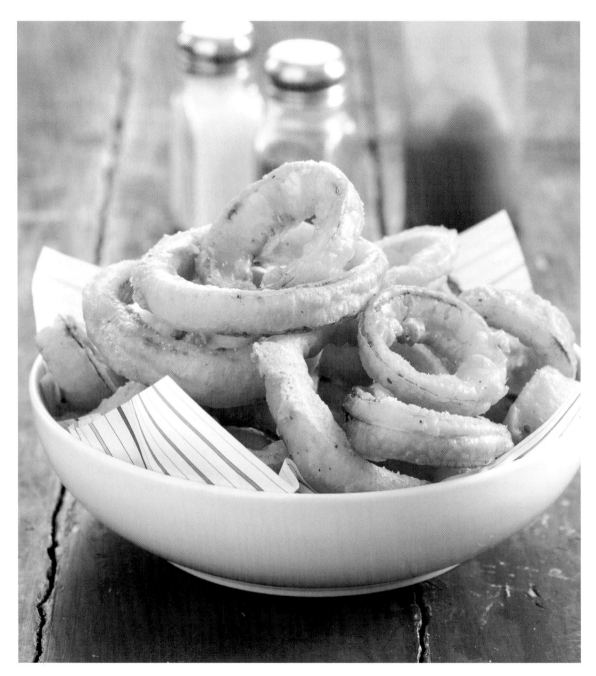

✓ WHY THIS RECIPE WORKS

We wanted sweet, tender onions for our Beer-Battered Onion Rings. We found that sweet onions worked best, and after testing many different batters, we settled on a beer, flour, salt, pepper, baking powder, and cornstarch batter. The beer gave the coating flavor, and the carbonation also provided lift to the batter. Baking powder yielded a coating that was thick and substantial, yet light, while cornstarch added crunch to the coating. Before frying our onion rings, we soaked the onions in a mixture of beer, malt vinegar, and salt to soften them and build flavor.

Beer-Battered Onion Rings

SERVES 4 TO 6

In step 1, do not soak the onion rounds longer than two hours or they will turn soft and become too saturated to crisp properly. Ordinary yellow onions will produce acceptable rings here. Cider vinegar can be used in place of malt vinegar. You will need at least a 6-quart Dutch oven for this recipe.

- 2 **sweet onions, peeled and sliced into ½-inch-thick rounds**
- 3 **cups beer**
- 2 **teaspoons malt vinegar**
  Salt and pepper
- 2 **quarts peanut or vegetable oil**
- ¾ **cup all-purpose flour**
- ¾ **cup cornstarch**
- 1 **teaspoon baking powder**

1. Place onion rounds, 2 cups beer, vinegar, ½ teaspoon salt, and ½ teaspoon pepper in 1-gallon zipper-lock bag; refrigerate for 30 minutes or up to 2 hours.

2. Line rimmed baking sheet with triple layer of paper towels. Add oil to large Dutch oven until it measures about 1½ inches deep and heat over medium-high heat to 350 degrees. While oil is heating, combine flour, cornstarch, baking powder, ½ teaspoon salt, and ¼ teaspoon pepper in large bowl. Slowly whisk in ¾ cup beer until just combined (some lumps will remain). Whisk in remaining beer as needed, 1 tablespoon at a time, until batter falls from whisk in steady stream and leaves faint trail across surface of batter.

3. Adjust oven rack to middle position and heat oven to 200 degrees. Remove onions from refrigerator and pour off liquid. Pat onion rounds dry with paper towels and separate into rings. Transfer one-third of rings to batter. One at a time, carefully transfer battered rings to oil. Fry until rings are golden brown and crisp, about 5 minutes, flipping halfway through frying. Drain rings on prepared baking sheet, season with salt and pepper to taste, and transfer to oven. Return oil to 350 degrees and repeat 2 more times with remaining onion rings and batter. Serve.

TROUBLESHOOTING ONION RINGS

1. To prevent raw, crunchy onions, soak rings in combination of beer, vinegar, and salt, which softens and flavors raw onion.

2. If batter is too thick, rings will be doughy; too thin and it will run off. Add beer gradually until batter falls from whisk to form ribbon trail.

3. To prevent fused rings, fry battered onion rings in small batches and transfer them one at a time to hot oil so they don't stick together.

STEAKHOUSE SPECIALS

AMERICA HAS LONG BEEN A MEAT AND POTATOES nation, but our love of steak (and all things beef) originated in Britain. In England there were men's dining clubs called beefsteak clubs, and of course, the Beefeaters, the colorfully costumed guards at the Tower of London who were paid 24 pounds of beef per month. Nice work if you can get it! British colonists in the 1700s brought their love of beef to America with them. In the U.S., steakhouses started to proliferate in the 1880s, especially in New York. Refrigerated railroad cars made it possible to safely transport meat from Chicago back east and to other parts of the country. The first steakhouses were a far cry from the sometimes posh and often family-friendly steakhouses of today. Think plenty of drinking and cursing and no women or children in sight. This men's

club atmosphere didn't last long and eventually steakhouses became the restaurant of choice for generations of Americans. In this chapter, we offer up not just recipes for steakhouse favorites like steak and potatoes, but other popular dishes that have made their way onto menus over the years, such as French Onion Soup, Chicken Cordon Bleu, and Baked Stuffed Shrimp.

✔️ WHY THIS RECIPE WORKS

The sizzling arrival of cast-iron plates of marinated steakhouse steak tips is often the most exciting part about them, because in reality, the first bite reveals chewy meat in an overly sweet marinade. For tender tips with great beefy flavor, we relied on sirloin steak tips. As for the marinade, we replaced the usual culprits—ketchup, barbecue sauce, and cola—with a mixture of soy sauce, oil, dark brown sugar, and tomato paste for enhanced meaty flavor and maximum char.

Grilled Steakhouse Steak Tips

Sirloin steak tips are often labeled "flap meat" and are sold as whole steaks, strips, and pieces. For even pieces, buy a whole steak of uniform size and cut it up yourself.

⅓ **cup soy sauce**

⅓ **cup vegetable oil**

3 **tablespoons packed dark brown sugar**

5 **garlic cloves, minced**

1 **tablespoon tomato paste**

1 **tablespoon paprika**

½ **teaspoon pepper**

¼ **teaspoon cayenne pepper**

2½ **pounds sirloin steak tips, trimmed**

1. Whisk soy sauce, oil, sugar, garlic, tomato paste, paprika, pepper, and cayenne together in bowl until sugar dissolves; transfer to zipper-lock bag. Pat beef dry with paper towels. Prick beef all over with fork and cut into 2½-inch pieces. Add meat to bag with soy sauce mixture and refrigerate for at least 2 or up to 24 hours, turning occasionally.

2A. FOR A CHARCOAL GRILL: Open bottom vent completely. Light large chimney starter filled with charcoal briquettes (6 quarts). When top coals are partially covered with ash, pour evenly over grill. Set cooking grate in place, cover, and open lid vent completely. Heat grill until hot, about 5 minutes. Leave burners on high.

2B. FOR A GAS GRILL: Turn all burners to high, cover, and heat grill until hot, about 15 minutes.

3. Clean and oil cooking grate. Grill beef (covered if using gas) until charred and registers 130 to 135 degrees (for medium), 8 to 10 minutes. Transfer meat to platter, tent loosely with aluminum foil, and let rest for 5 to 10 minutes. Serve.

COMMON INGREDIENTS, UNCOMMON RESULTS

We engineered our marinade to give the steak tips maximum meaty flavor and satisfying texture. These familiar ingredients make a strong team, each with its own part to play.

DARK BROWN SUGAR
Delivers depth, complexity, and a caramelized, crusty char.

VEGETABLE OIL
Distributes flavors and activates oil-soluble flavor compounds, such as those found in garlic.

TOMATO PASTE
Adds background savor and enough body to help the marinade cling.

SOY SAUCE
Its salt penetrates to deeply season the meat. Its glutamates boost meaty flavor.

✔ WHY THIS RECIPE WORKS

We usually rely on a red-hot skillet or the grill for our recipes that include putting a crusty sear on steaks, but we wondered if our oven's broiler could do the job just as well. Starting the steaks at a moderate temperature took the chill off, and letting them rest before putting them under the broiler produced evenly cooked meat. Covering the bottom of the pan with salt helped absorb the grease from the meat and greatly minimized smoking. To ensure a good sear on our steaks, we placed a wire rack over a 3-inch disposable pan, to bring the meat closer to the heating element.

Broiled Steaks

SERVES 4

To minimize smoking, be sure to trim as much exterior fat and gristle as possible from the steaks before cooking. Try to purchase steaks of a similar size and shape for this recipe. Note that you will need 2 cups of salt to line the roasting pan; the salt will absorb drippings from the steak and minimize smoking.

- 4 tablespoons unsalted butter, softened
- 1 teaspoon minced fresh thyme
- 1 teaspoon Dijon mustard
  Salt and pepper
- 1 (13 by 9-inch) disposable aluminum roasting pan, 3 inches deep
- 4 strip, rib-eye, or tenderloin steaks, 1 to 2 inches thick, trimmed

1. Adjust oven racks to upper-middle and lower-middle positions and heat oven to 375 degrees. Beat butter, thyme, mustard, ¼ teaspoon salt, and ¼ teaspoon pepper in bowl and refrigerate.

2. Spread 2 cups salt over bottom of aluminum pan. Pat steaks dry with paper towels, season with salt and pepper, and transfer to wire rack. Set rack over aluminum pan and transfer to lower oven rack. Cook 6 to 10 minutes, then remove pan from oven. Flip steaks, pat dry with paper towels, and let rest for 10 minutes.

3. Heat broiler. Transfer pan to upper oven rack and broil steaks, flipping every 2 to 4 minutes, until meat registers 120 to 125 degrees (for medium-rare), 6 to 16 minutes, depending on thickness of steaks (see chart). Transfer steaks to platter, top with reserved butter mixture, and tent with aluminum foil. Let rest for 5 minutes. Serve.

PERFECTLY BROILED STEAKS

The first step to perfectly broiled steaks is knowing exactly how thick your steaks are. Using a ruler, measure each steak and then follow the guidelines below.

STEAK THICKNESS	PRECOOK	BROIL
1 inch	6 minutes	Turn steaks every 2 minutes
1½ inches	8 minutes	Turn steaks every 3 minutes
2 inches	10 minutes	Turn steaks every 4 minutes

BROILER PREP

Since oven-rack positioning varies greatly from model to model, we suggest you ensure correct positioning with a dry run before turning on your oven.

Before preheating your oven and with your oven racks adjusted to the upper-middle and lower-middle positions, place a wire rack on top of a 3-inch-deep disposable aluminum pan and place it on the upper-middle rack. Place the steaks on top of the rack and use a ruler to measure the distance between the top of the steaks and the heating element of the broiler. For optimal searing, there should be ½ inch to 1 inch of space.

If there is more than 1 inch of space, here's how to close the gap: Elevate the aluminum pan by placing it on an inverted rimmed baking sheet; use a deeper-sided disposable aluminum pan; or stack multiple aluminum pans inside one another. If there's less than ½ inch of space, adjust the oven rack or use a shallower pan.

HOW HOT IS YOUR BROILER?

It's good to know if your broiler runs relatively hot, average, or cold. This information allows you to adjust the cooking time for this recipe (and others) accordingly. To see how your broiler stacks up, heat it on high and place a slice of white sandwich bread directly under the heating element on the upper-middle rack. If the bread toasts to golden brown in 30 seconds or less, your broiler runs very hot, and you will need to reduce the cooking time by a minute or two. If the bread toasts perfectly in one minute, your broiler runs about average. If the bread takes two minutes or longer to toast, your broiler runs cool and you may need to increase the cooking time by a minute or two.

WHY THIS RECIPE WORKS

In order to achieve a respectable crust on our restaurant-style grilled steak, the exterior of the meat must be dry. After trying numerous drying-out methods, including salting and aging, we considered the freezer. The freezer's intensely dry environment sufficiently dehydrated the steaks' exteriors, and since we were only freezing them for a short time, the interiors remained tender and juicy. We rubbed the steaks with a mixture of salt and cornstarch before freezing. The salt ensured they were well seasoned, and cornstarch, a champ at absorbing moisture, allowed us to cut the freezing time in half.

Char-Grilled Steaks

SERVES 4

Serve with one of the sauces that follow, if desired.

- 1 **teaspoon salt**
- 1 **teaspoon cornstarch**
- 4 **strip, rib-eye, or tenderloin steaks, about 1½ inches thick, trimmed**
- **Pepper**

1. Combine salt and cornstarch. Pat steaks dry with paper towels and rub with salt mixture. Arrange on wire rack set in rimmed baking sheet and freeze until steaks are firm and dry to touch, at least 30 minutes or up to 1 hour.

2A. FOR A CHARCOAL GRILL: Open bottom vent completely. Light large chimney starter filled with charcoal briquettes (6 quarts). When top coals are partially covered with ash, pour evenly over grill. Set cooking grate in place, cover, and open lid vent completely. Heat grill until hot, about 5 minutes.

2B. FOR A GAS GRILL: Turn all burners to high, cover, and heat grill until hot, about 15 minutes. Leave burners on high.

3. Clean and oil cooking grate. Season steaks with pepper. Grill (covered if using gas) until meat registers 120 to 125 degrees (for medium-rare), 8 to 16 minutes, flipping steaks halfway through cooking. Transfer to plate, tent with aluminum foil, and let rest for 5 minutes. Serve.

CLASSIC STEAK SAUCE

MAKES 1¼ CUPS, ENOUGH FOR 1 RECIPE GRILLED STEAKS

Raisins add depth and sweetness to this sauce.

- ½ **cup boiling water**
- ⅓ **cup raisins**
- ¼ **cup ketchup**
- 3 **tablespoons Worcestershire sauce**
- 2 **tablespoons Dijon mustard**
- 2 **tablespoons distilled white vinegar**
- **Salt and pepper**

Combine water and raisins in bowl and let sit, covered, until raisins are plump, about 5 minutes. Puree raisin mixture, ketchup, Worcestershire, mustard, and vinegar in blender until smooth, 30 seconds to 1 minute. Season with salt and pepper to taste. (Sauce can be refrigerated for 1 week.)

SPICY RED PEPPER STEAK SAUCE

MAKES 1¼ CUPS, ENOUGH FOR 1 RECIPE GRILLED STEAKS

This peppery sauce is a simplified version of the Spanish classic, romesco.

- 1 **slice hearty white sandwich bread, toasted until golden and torn into pieces**
- 2 **tablespoons slivered almonds, toasted**
- 1 **cup jarred roasted red peppers, drained**
- 1 **plum tomato, seeded and chopped**
- 2 **teaspoons red wine vinegar**
- 1 **garlic clove, minced**
- ⅛ **teaspoon cayenne pepper**
- 1 **tablespoon extra-virgin olive oil**
- **Salt**

Process bread and almonds in food processor until finely ground, about 10 seconds. Add red peppers, tomato, vinegar, garlic, and cayenne and process until smooth, about 1 minute. Season with salt to taste. (Sauce can be refrigerated for 1 week.)

GARLIC-PARSLEY STEAK SAUCE

MAKES 1¼ CUPS, ENOUGH FOR 1 RECIPE GRILLED STEAKS

A little of this aromatic vinaigrette goes a long way.

- ½ **cup finely chopped fresh parsley**
- ¼ **cup minced red onion**
- ¼ **cup red wine vinegar**
- 2 **garlic cloves, minced**
- ⅛ **teaspoon red pepper flakes**
- ¼ **cup extra virgin olive oil**
- **Salt and pepper**

Combine parsley, onion, vinegar, garlic, and pepper flakes in bowl. Slowly whisk in oil. Season with salt and pepper to taste. (Sauce can be refrigerated for 1 week.)

✔ WHY THIS RECIPE WORKS

Oversized cowboy-cut rib eyes offer big, beefy flavor, but cooking the huge steaks all the way through while achieving a flavorful seared crust is challenging. We used a bare minimum of seasonings—salt, pepper, and oil—to highlight the flavor of the steaks. To cook them, we opted for a low and slow approach to start. To keep the fire burning long enough, we layered unlit coals under lit ones. We let the steaks come to room temperature before grilling to cut down on cooking time, and then slow-roasted the steaks on the cooler side of the grill until they were almost done. A quick sear over hot coals gave them a flavorful dark crust.

Grilled Cowboy-Cut Rib Eyes

SERVES 4 TO 6

Don't start grilling until the steaks' internal temperatures have reached 55 degrees. Otherwise, the times and temperatures in this recipe will be inaccurate. You will need a wire rack and a rimmed baking sheet for this recipe.

2   (1¼- to 1½-pound) double-cut bone-in
    rib-eye steaks, 1¾ to 2 inches thick, trimmed
4   teaspoons kosher salt
2   teaspoons vegetable oil
2   teaspoons pepper

1. Set wire rack inside rimmed baking sheet. Pat steaks dry with paper towels and sprinkle all over with salt. Place steaks on prepared rack and let stand at room temperature until meat registers 55 degrees, about 1 hour. Rub steaks with oil and sprinkle with pepper.

2A. FOR A CHARCOAL GRILL: Open bottom vent halfway. Arrange 4 quarts unlit charcoal briquettes in even layer over half of grill. Light large chimney starter one-third filled with charcoal briquettes (2 quarts). When top coals are partially covered with ash, pour evenly over unlit coals. Set cooking grate in place, cover, and open lid vent halfway. Heat grill until hot, about 5 minutes.

2B. FOR A GAS GRILL: Turn all burners to high, cover, and heat grill until hot, about 15 minutes. Turn primary burner to medium-low and turn off other burner(s). Adjust primary burner as needed to maintain grill temperature of 300 degrees.

3. Clean and oil cooking grate. Place steaks on cooler side of grill with bones facing fire. Cover and cook until steaks register 75 degrees, 10 to 20 minutes. Flip steaks, keeping bones facing fire. Cover and continue to cook until steaks register 95 degrees, 10 to 20 minutes.

4. If using charcoal, slide steaks to hotter part of grill. If using gas, remove steaks from grill, turn primary burner to high, and heat until hot, about 5 minutes; place steaks over primary burner. Cover and cook until well browned and steaks register 120 degrees (for medium-rare), about 4 minutes per side. Transfer steaks to clean wire rack set in rimmed baking sheet, tent loosely with foil, and let rest for 15 minutes. Transfer steaks to carving board, cut meat from bone, and slice into ½-inch-thick slices. Serve.

IN PRAISE OF COWBOY STEAKS

Rib-eye steaks are deeply marbled, tender, and beefy—they're from the same part of the steer that's used for prime rib. Bone-in steaks (like these) have more flavor than boneless, and the bone protects against overcooking. Of special interest is the exterior band of fat and meat on a rib eye called the deckle; connoisseurs say it is the most flavorful part of the cow.

BIGGER IS BETTER

Cowboy-cut rib eyes are double-thick bone-in steaks. They take longer to cook than single-serving rib eyes, so they have more time to soak up smoky grill flavor.

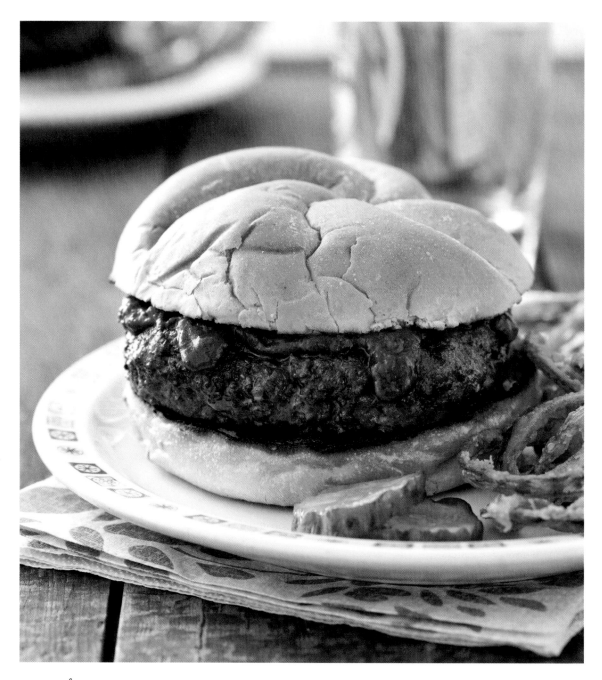

✅ WHY THIS RECIPE WORKS

We wanted a burger with the big beefy flavor and crusty char of a grilled steak. Ground sirloin, the most flavorful ground beef, was a natural choice, but unfortunately it's also quite lean. A seasoned butter added richness to the sirloin, but something was missing. Steak sauce! In about five minutes, we simmered up our own intensely flavored sauce, perfect for serving with the burger, smearing on the bun, and even mixing into the beef before cooking.

Grilled Steak Burgers

SERVES 4

Use kaiser rolls or other hearty buns for these substantial burgers.

BURGERS

8	tablespoons unsalted butter
2	garlic cloves, minced
2	teaspoons onion powder
1	teaspoon pepper
½	teaspoon salt
2	teaspoons soy sauce
1½	pounds 90 percent lean ground sirloin
4	hamburger buns

STEAK SAUCE

2	tablespoons tomato paste
⅔	cup beef broth
⅓	cup raisins
2	tablespoons soy sauce
2	tablespoons Dijon mustard
2	tablespoons balsamic vinegar
1	tablespoon Worcestershire sauce

1. FOR THE BURGERS: Melt butter in 8-inch skillet over medium-low heat. Add garlic, onion powder, pepper, and salt and cook until fragrant, about 1 minute. Pour all but 1 tablespoon butter mixture into bowl and let cool for about 5 minutes.

2. FOR THE STEAK SAUCE: Meanwhile, add tomato paste to skillet and cook over medium heat until paste begins to darken, 1 to 2 minutes. Stir in broth, raisins, soy sauce, mustard, vinegar, and Worcestershire and simmer until raisins plump, about 5 minutes. Process sauce in blender until smooth, about 30 seconds; transfer to bowl.

3. Add 5 tablespoons cooled butter mixture and soy sauce to ground beef and gently knead until well combined. Shape into four ¾-inch-thick patties and press shallow divot in center of each. Brush each patty all over with 1 tablespoon steak sauce. Combine remaining 2 tablespoons cooled butter mixture with 2 tablespoons steak sauce; set aside.

4A. FOR A CHARCOAL GRILL: Open bottom vent completely. Light large chimney starter filled with charcoal briquettes (6 quarts). When top coals are partially covered with ash, pour evenly over grill. Set cooking grate in place, cover, and open lid vent completely. Heat grill until hot, about 5 minutes.

4B. FOR A GAS GRILL: Turn all burners to high, cover, and heat grill until hot, about 15 minutes. Leave burners on high.

5. Clean and oil cooking grate. Grill burgers (covered if using gas) until meat registers 120 to 125 degrees (for medium-rare), 3 to 4 minutes per side, or 130 to 135 degrees (for medium), 4 to 5 minutes per side. Transfer burgers to plate, tent loosely with aluminum foil, and let rest for 5 to 10 minutes. Brush cut side of buns with butter–steak sauce mixture. Grill buns, cut side down, until golden, 2 to 3 minutes. Place burgers on buns. Serve with remaining steak sauce.

BUTTER MAKES IT BETTER

Why are our steakhouse burgers so good? Yep, butter. Ground sirloin has great flavor, but it's a little dry: Butter helps keep the burgers moist. Butter also gives richness and body to our homemade steak sauce. And we slather butter on the buns before toasting them on the grill.

FLAVORED BUTTER
For the meat, sauce, and buns.

✔ WHY THIS RECIPE WORKS

There are often two problems with baked stuffed shrimp: mushy, bland stuffing and shrimp as chewy as rubber bands. We wanted a recipe that produced crisp, flavorful stuffing and perfectly cooked shrimp. For the stuffing, tasters preferred the sweet flavor of fresh bread crumbs, toasted to ensure crispness. Butterflying the shrimp allowed us to press the stuffing into the shrimp—as the shrimp contracted in the oven, the stuffing was sealed into place. To prevent overcooked shrimp, yet still achieve crisp stuffing, we cooked the shrimp for a longer time at a lower temperature.

Baked Stuffed Shrimp

SERVES 4 TO 6

In a pinch, chicken broth can be substituted for the clam juice. A sturdy rimmed baking sheet can be used in place of the broiler pan bottom. Shrimp that are labeled U12 contain 12 or less shrimp per pound.

4	slices hearty white sandwich bread, torn into quarters
½	cup mayonnaise
¼	cup bottled clam juice
¼	cup finely chopped fresh parsley
4	scallions, chopped fine
1	tablespoon Dijon mustard
2	garlic cloves, minced
2	teaspoons grated lemon zest plus 1 tablespoon juice
⅛	teaspoon cayenne pepper
	Salt
1¼	pounds colossal shrimp (U12), peeled and deveined

1. Adjust oven rack to upper-middle position and heat oven to 375 degrees. Pulse bread in food processor to coarse crumbs, about 10 pulses. Transfer crumbs to broiler pan bottom and bake until golden and dry, 8 to 10 minutes, stirring halfway through cooking time. Remove crumbs from oven and reduce temperature to 275 degrees.

2. Combine toasted bread crumbs, mayonnaise, clam juice, parsley, scallions, mustard, garlic, lemon zest and juice, cayenne, and ¼ teaspoon salt in bowl.

3. Pat shrimp dry with paper towels and season with salt. Grease empty broiler pan bottom. To butterfly shrimp, use sharp paring knife to cut along (but not through) vein line, then open up shrimp like a book. Using tip of paring knife, cut 1-inch opening through center of shrimp. Arrange shrimp cut side down on prepared pan. Divide bread-crumb mixture among shrimp, pressing to adhere. Bake until shrimp are opaque, 20 to 25 minutes.

4. Remove shrimp from oven and heat broiler. Broil shrimp until crumbs are deep golden brown and crispy, 1 to 3 minutes. Serve.

CREOLE BAKED STUFFED SHRIMP WITH SAUSAGE

The smoky, meaty flavor of kielbasa is a nice foil to the sweet shrimp in this variation.

Omit cayenne and add 1 teaspoon Creole seasoning in step 2. Fold 4 ounces kielbasa sausage, chopped fine, into filling and proceed as directed.

EASY STEPS TO BAKED STUFFED SHRIMP

Cutting a hole clear through the center of each butterflied shrimp may seem like a mistake, but it actually gives the shrimp a way of holding on to the stuffing. The shrimp are butterflied on the convex side before being flipped over onto the pan.

1. Use paring knife to cut along but not through vein line, then open up shrimp like a book. Cut 1-inch opening all the way through center of shrimp.

2. After shrimp have been butterflied and openings have been cut, flip shrimp over onto broiler pan so that they will curl around stuffing.

3. Divide stuffing among shrimp, firmly pressing stuffing into opening and to edges of shrimp.

✅ WHY THIS RECIPE WORKS

Making chicken cordon bleu can be fussy; we wanted an easier way. We found cutting a pocket into the breast to be much more efficient than the traditional method of pounding and rolling. To get the same swirl effect achieved by rolling the chicken around the ham and cheese, we simply rolled the ham slices into cylinders around shredded cheese and tucked the cylinders into each chicken breast. Adding a healthy dose of Dijon mustard to the egg wash boosted the flavor of our chicken, as did supplementing homemade bread crumbs with buttery Ritz cracker crumbs.

Foolproof Chicken Cordon Bleu

SERVES 4 TO 6

To help prevent the filling from leaking, thoroughly chill the stuffed breasts before breading. We like Black Forest ham here.

25   Ritz crackers (about ¾ sleeve)
4   slices hearty white sandwich bread,
      torn into quarters
6   tablespoons unsalted butter, melted
8   thin slices deli ham (8 ounces)
8   ounces Swiss cheese, shredded (2 cups)
4   (8-ounce) boneless, skinless chicken breasts,
      trimmed
      Salt and pepper
3   large eggs
2   tablespoons Dijon mustard
1   cup all-purpose flour

1. Adjust oven racks to lowest and middle positions and heat oven to 450 degrees. Pulse crackers and bread in food processor until coarsely ground, about 15 pulses. Drizzle in butter; pulse a few times to incorporate. Bake crumbs on rimmed baking sheet on middle rack, stirring occasionally, until light brown, 3 to 5 minutes. Transfer to shallow dish. Do not turn oven off.

2. Top each ham slice with ¼ cup cheese and roll tightly; set aside. Pat chicken dry with paper towels. Using paring knife, cut into thickest part of each chicken breast to create deep pocket with opening of 3 to 4 inches. Stuff each breast with 2 ham-and-cheese rolls and press closed. Season both sides of chicken with salt and pepper. Transfer chicken to plate, cover with plastic wrap, and refrigerate for at least 20 minutes.

3. Beat eggs and mustard in second shallow dish. Place flour in third shallow dish. One at a time, coat stuffed chicken lightly with flour, dip into egg mixture, and dredge in crumbs, pressing to adhere. (Breaded chicken can be refrigerated, covered, for 1 day.) Transfer chicken to clean rimmed baking sheet. Bake on lowest rack until bottom of chicken is golden brown, about 10 minutes, and then move baking sheet to middle rack and reduce oven temperature to 400 degrees. Bake until golden brown and chicken registers 160 degrees, 20 to 25 minutes. Transfer to platter, tent with aluminum foil, and let rest for 5 minutes. Serve.

STUFFING, STREAMLINED

1. Using paring knife, cut into thickest part of chicken breast to create deep pocket with opening of 3 to 4 inches.

2. Top each slice of ham with ¼ cup shredded cheese. Roll into tight cylinder.

3. Stuff each pocket with 2 ham-and-cheese rolls and seal. Refrigerate chicken for at least 20 minutes before breading.

✅ WHY THIS RECIPE WORKS

It can be a hassle to stand over a pot of caramelized onions when a craving for this French classic strikes. We looked to the slow cooker for simplification. Replicating the meaty flavor of the soup was more of a challenge, as the slow, long cooking can result in washed-out flavor. We found that soy sauce, sherry, and thyme added early on helped boost flavor and the addition of beef bones to store-bought chicken and beef broths reproduced the rich meatiness of the classic. Apple butter highlighted the flavor of the onions without drawing attention to itself and also helped make for a rich, silky broth.

Slow-Cooker French Onion Soup

SERVES 6 TO 8

After halving the onions, slice them through the root end for hearty slices that will hold up to long cooking. Beef bones are stocked in the frozen foods aisle of most supermarkets.

SOUP

2	pounds beef bones
4	tablespoons unsalted butter
4	pounds yellow onions, halved and sliced through root end into ¼-inch-thick slices
	Salt and pepper
1	tablespoon packed brown sugar
1	teaspoon minced fresh thyme
¾	cup apple butter
¾	cup dry sherry
5	tablespoons all-purpose flour
¼	cup soy sauce
2	cups chicken broth
2	cups beef broth

CHEESE CROUTONS

1	small baguette, cut into ½-inch slices
10	ounces Gruyère cheese, shredded (2½ cups)

1. FOR THE SOUP: Arrange beef bones on paper towel–lined plate. Microwave until well browned, 8 to 10 minutes. Meanwhile, set slow cooker to high. Add butter, cover, and cook until melted. Add onions, 2 teaspoons salt, 1 teaspoon pepper, brown sugar, and thyme. Stir apple butter, sherry, flour, and soy sauce together in small bowl until smooth. Pour over onions and toss to coat. Tuck bones under onions around edge of slow cooker. Cover and cook on high heat until onions are softened and deep golden brown, 10 to 12 hours (start checking onions after 8 hours). (Cooked onions can be refrigerated in airtight container for 1 day.)

2. Remove bones from slow cooker. Heat broths in microwave until beginning to boil. Stir into slow cooker. Season with salt and pepper to taste.

3. FOR THE CHEESE CROUTONS: Adjust oven rack to upper-middle position (about 6 inches from broiler element) and heat oven to 400 degrees. Arrange bread slices in single layer on baking sheet and bake until bread is golden at edges, about 10 minutes. Heat broiler. Divide cheese evenly among croutons and broil until melted and bubbly, 3 to 5 minutes.

4. Ladle soup into bowls and top each with 2 croutons. Serve.

SLICING ONIONS FOR FRENCH ONION SOUP

Most soup recipes start by chopping or mincing onions. For our Slow-Cooker French Onion Soup, we wanted slices that would retain their shape through 10 to 12 hours of gentle simmering. We found that cutting onions with the grain (rather than across it) yielded slices durable enough for the slow cooker.

1. Using chef's knife, trim off both ends of onion.

2. Turn onion onto cut end to steady it and slice in half, through root end.

3. Peel each half, place flat side down, and cut onion, lengthwise, into slices.

WHY THIS RECIPE WORKS

Making mashed potatoes isn't typically a quick endeavor—add roasted garlic to the mix and you've really got a project on your hands. We wanted a streamlined recipe. We cut the potatoes into small pieces to promote even, quicker cooking. The small pieces also meant the potatoes could better soak up garlicky flavor. To mimic the flavor of roasted garlic, we sprinkled in a little sugar while sautéing the garlic. Finally, we simmered the potatoes in half-and-half, butter, and the sautéed garlic to avoid the "washing away" of flavor that can come from boiling in just water.

Garlic Mashed Potatoes

SERVES 8 TO 10

Cutting the potatoes into ½-inch pieces ensures that the maximum surface area is exposed to soak up garlicky flavor.

4	pounds russet potatoes, peeled, quartered, and cut into ½-inch pieces
12	tablespoons unsalted butter, cut into pieces
12	garlic cloves, minced
1	teaspoon sugar
1½	cups half-and-half
½	cup water
	Salt and pepper

1. Place cut potatoes in colander. Rinse under cold running water until water runs clear. Drain thoroughly.

2. Melt 4 tablespoons butter in Dutch oven over medium heat. Cook garlic and sugar, stirring often, until sticky and straw colored, 3 to 4 minutes. Add rinsed potatoes, 1¼ cups half-and-half, water, and 1 teaspoon salt to pot and stir to combine. Bring to boil, then reduce heat to low and simmer, covered and stirring occasionally, until potatoes are tender and most of liquid is absorbed, 25 to 30 minutes.

3. Off heat, add remaining 8 tablespoons butter to pot and mash with potato masher until smooth. Using rubber spatula, fold in remaining ¼ cup half-and-half until liquid is absorbed and potatoes are creamy. Season with salt and pepper to taste. Serve.

FOLK REMEDIES FOR REMOVING GARLIC ODOR

We know firsthand that garlic odor is hard to remove from your hands. There are plenty of folk remedies for doing this: washing with baking soda, vinegar, lemon juice, salt, or toothpaste, or even rubbing your hands on stainless steel. Do any of these tricks work? To find out, we had five testers mince garlic and rub it on their hands, then try each of the methods listed above (plus washing with soap and water).

Washing with all of these substances lessened the odor at least a little, with baking soda and lemon juice outperforming the others, and rubbing one's hands on stainless steel succeeding just as well. Why? Some of the aromatic compounds in garlic are weak acids that can be neutralized by alkaline baking soda. Because not all aroma compounds are acidic, baking soda can't neutralize the odor 100 percent. Stainless steel removes some of the odor when iron atoms in the stainless steel exchange some of their electrons with sulfur atoms from the volatile aroma compounds, rendering them nonvolatile (nonstinky). Lemon juice contains lemon oils that dissolve the oil-soluble aroma compounds in garlic, plus its own fragrance masks the remaining odor. The bottom line? Lemon juice, baking soda, and stainless steel all help a little, but there is no magic cure for removing garlic smell from your hands.

SECRETS TO GREAT ROASTED GARLIC FLAVOR

1. Cook the minced garlic (and a little sugar) in butter until the garlic is sticky and straw-colored; this blooms the garlic's sweet flavor and tempers its harshness.

2. For deeply integrated garlic flavor, toss the raw potatoes with the garlic-butter mixture, add the half-and-half and water directly to the pot, cover, and gently cook until tender.

WHY THIS RECIPE WORKS

To revive this classic potato dish, we first focused on how to prep the potatoes. Boiled cubed potatoes won out over shredded because they held their texture better in the casserole. Next, we sautéed onion and garlic, added cream and chicken broth (to cut the richness of the cream), and cooked the cubed potatoes in this mixture. Lemon juice and zest brought the casserole welcome brightness. For the crusty topping, we turned to an unexpected ingredient: frozen shredded hash browns. We sautéed the thawed hash browns in butter, cream, and chicken broth to enhance their flavor before topping the casserole.

Delmonico Potato Casserole

SERVES 8 TO 10

We prefer the buttery flavor of Yukon Gold potatoes here, but all-purpose and red potatoes also work. Do not use russets—their high starch content will make the casserole gluey. For the topping, we had good results with Ore-Ida Country Style Hash Browns, available in the frozen foods aisle of most supermarkets.

3	tablespoons unsalted butter
1	onion, chopped fine
2	garlic cloves, minced
2½	cups heavy cream
1½	cups chicken broth
2½	pounds Yukon Gold potatoes, peeled and cut into ½-inch cubes
⅛	teaspoon ground nutmeg
	Salt and pepper
1	teaspoon grated lemon zest plus 2 teaspoons juice
5	cups frozen shredded hash brown potatoes, thawed and patted dry with paper towels
1½	ounces Parmesan cheese, grated (¾ cup)
¼	cup finely chopped fresh chives

1. Adjust oven rack to upper-middle position and heat oven to 450 degrees. Melt 1 tablespoon butter in Dutch oven over medium-high heat. Cook onion until softened, about 3 minutes. Stir in garlic and cook until fragrant, about 30 seconds. Stir in 2 cups cream, 1 cup broth, Yukon Golds, nutmeg, 2 teaspoons salt, and 1 teaspoon pepper. Bring to boil, then reduce heat to medium and simmer until potatoes are translucent at edges and mixture is slightly thickened, about 10 minutes. Off heat, stir in lemon zest and juice.

2. Transfer potato mixture to 13 by 9-inch baking dish and bake until bubbling around edges and surface is just golden, about 20 minutes. Meanwhile, melt remaining 2 tablespoons butter in 12-inch nonstick skillet over medium-high heat. Cook shredded potatoes until beginning to brown, about 2 minutes. Add remaining ½ cup cream, remaining ½ cup broth, and ½ teaspoon pepper to skillet and cook, stirring occasionally, until liquid has evaporated, about 3 minutes. Off heat, stir in ½ cup Parmesan and 2 tablespoons chives.

3. Remove baking dish from oven and top with shredded potato mixture. Sprinkle with remaining ¼ cup Parmesan and continue to bake until top is golden brown, about 20 minutes. Let cool for 15 minutes. Sprinkle with remaining 2 tablespoons chives. Serve.

TO MAKE AHEAD: Prepare through step 1, let cool completely, transfer to baking dish, and refrigerate, covered with plastic wrap, for 1 day. To serve, proceed as directed in step 2, increasing baking time to 25 to 30 minutes.

POTATOES WITH PANACHE

In 1837, Delmonico's opened in lower Manhattan and a restaurant star was born. Owned by two Swiss men, the restaurant served French-style cuisine and became the model for many other fashionable restaurants of the era. Its lavish dining room served such luxurious fare as lobster Newburg, baked Alaska, and their signature potato side dish, Delmonico potatoes. The potatoes were boiled, finely shredded, and cooked with milk and heavy cream. When an order came in, a serving of potatoes was sprinkled with Parmesan cheese and "gratinéed" under the broiler. The result was a potato gratin with a creamy interior and a crusty, cheesy topping. But look up a modern recipe for this dish and you'll most likely find a casserole made of overboiled chunks of potatoes baked in a creamy cheddar sauce and topped with more cheese. We wanted to bring back the simplicity and elegance of the original dish, but make it more practical to feed a crowd.

✓ WHY THIS RECIPE WORKS

Cooking red potatoes in a super-saturated salt solution gave them incredibly creamy, well-seasoned interiors. After the potatoes were parcooked, we smashed them to expose some of the potato flesh, brushed them with malt vinegar, and roasted them on a well-oiled baking sheet until the exposed surface was golden and crispy. A final brush with more vinegar when the potatoes came out of the oven reinforced the addictive salty-sour flavor of these spuds.

Roasted Salt-and-Vinegar Potatoes

SERVES 4

Use small red potatoes, measuring 1 to 2 inches in diameter. If you prefer to use kosher salt, you will need 1½ cups of Morton's or 2½ cups of Diamond Crystal. Cider vinegar is a good substitute for the malt vinegar.

6	**tablespoons olive oil**
2	**pounds small red potatoes**
1¼	**cups salt**
3	**tablespoons malt vinegar**
	Pepper

1. Adjust oven rack to upper-middle position and heat oven to 500 degrees. Set wire rack inside rimmed baking sheet. Brush second rimmed baking sheet evenly with oil. Bring 2 quarts water to boil in Dutch oven over medium-high heat. Stir in potatoes and salt and cook until just tender and paring knife slips easily in and out of potatoes, 20 to 30 minutes. Drain potatoes and transfer to wire rack; let dry for 10 minutes.

2. Transfer potatoes to oiled baking sheet. Flatten each potato with underside of measuring cup until ½ inch thick. Brush potatoes with half of vinegar and season with pepper. Roast until potatoes are well browned, 25 to 30 minutes. Brush with remaining vinegar. Transfer potatoes to platter, smashed side up. Serve.

SCRUB THE POTATOES

Because the skins will be in the finished dish, it's important to scrub the potatoes well before cooking.

SALT OF THE EARTH (AND SEA)

A variety of salts are available in supermarkets today: table, iodized, kosher, and sea salt. What's the difference? Table and iodized salt (simply table salt with iodine added) have fine grains and contain anticaking agents that help them flow freely. Kosher salt, so named because it is used in the koshering process, has larger crystals and typically contains no additives. Both table and kosher salts are considered "refined salts" because they are mined from rock salt deposits and then purified. Sea salt is harvested by evaporating seawater and therefore has a full, slightly mineral flavor. Though we use table salt in the vast majority of our recipes, the choice is a matter of preference—except when it comes to our Roasted Salt-and-Vinegar Potatoes. While table, kosher, and sea salts all performed equally well in this recipe, we advise against using iodized salt as it gives the potatoes a noticeably chemical flavor.

MALT VINEGAR SUBSTITUTES

For our salt-and-vinegar potatoes, we raided the English larder for a beloved condiment: malt vinegar. Britons commonly douse fish and chips with it, so we knew it would be a perfect match for roasted potatoes. The vinegar, which is made from sprouted barley grains, gives the potatoes a pleasantly malty, tangy taste. But if you don't have it, cider or white wine vinegars are good substitutes. Avoid balsamic and rice vinegars, which tasters found too sweet, and red wine and distilled white vinegars, which were too harsh.

✔ WHY THIS RECIPE WORKS

Our Super-Stuffed Baked Potatoes feature fluffy potato, garlic, herbs, and creamy cheese in crispy potato-skin shells. Precooking the potatoes in the microwave shaved an hour off the cooking time. And while most stuffed baked potato recipes call for cutting the potato in half, we preferred to lop off just the top quarter of the potato. Prepared this way, the potato shells held more filling. But after hollowing out the potatoes, there wasn't enough stuffing to fill each one and mound the filling on top. To make the filling go further, we cooked an extra potato and used its flesh to top off the other stuffed baked potatoes.

Super-Stuffed Baked Potatoes

SERVES 6

This recipe calls for seven potatoes but makes six servings; the remaining potato is used for its flesh.

- 7 large russet potatoes
- 3 tablespoons unsalted butter, melted, plus 3 tablespoons unsalted butter
  Salt and pepper
- 1 (5.2-ounce) package Boursin cheese, crumbled
- ½ cup half-and-half
- 2 garlic cloves, minced
- ¼ cup chopped fresh chives

1. Adjust oven rack to middle position and heat oven to 475 degrees. Set wire rack in rimmed baking sheet. Prick potatoes all over with fork, place on paper towel, and microwave until tender, 20 to 25 minutes, turning potatoes over after 10 minutes.

2. Slice and remove top quarter of each potato, let cool for 5 minutes, then scoop out flesh, leaving ¼-inch layer of potato on inside. Discard 1 potato shell. Brush remaining shells inside and out with 3 tablespoons melted butter and sprinkle interiors with ¼ teaspoon salt. Transfer potatoes, scooped side up, to prepared baking sheet and bake until skins begin to crisp, about 15 minutes.

3. Meanwhile, mix half of Boursin with half-and-half in bowl until blended. Cook remaining 3 tablespoons butter and garlic in saucepan over medium-low heat until garlic is straw-colored, 3 to 5 minutes. Stir in Boursin mixture until combined.

4. Set ricer or food mill over medium bowl and press or mill potatoes into bowl. Gently fold in warm Boursin mixture, 3 tablespoons chives, 1 teaspoon pepper, and ½ teaspoon salt until well incorporated. Remove potato shells from oven and fill with potato-cheese mixture. Top with remaining crumbled Boursin and bake until tops of potatoes are golden brown, about 15 minutes. Sprinkle with remaining chives. Serve.

BIGGER, BETTER STUFFED POTATOES

During testing for our Super-Stuffed Baked Potatoes, we found that most recipes called for the baked potatoes to be cut right in half before being filled. But these skimpy spuds were far from the super-stuffed garlic potatoes we were looking for. Instead, we found the best method was to cut off only the top quarter of the potato, leaving a much more substantial spud to stuff.

1. Slice off top quarter of microwaved potato.

2. Use spoon to scoop out interior of potato, being careful to leave ¼-inch layer of potato in shell.

✔️ WHY THIS RECIPE WORKS

For this showstopper side dish, we found that using the right kind of potato is key. The russet potato was the best choice because of its starchy flesh and fluffy texture. Taking the time to rinse the potatoes of surface starch after they were sliced prevented them from sticking together, while trimming off the end of each potato gave the remaining slices room to fan out. To prevent overcooking our spuds in the punishing oven heat, we precooked them in the microwave before baking. A topping of fresh bread crumbs, melted butter, two kinds of cheese, garlic powder, and paprika is the crowning touch.

Crispy Baked Potato Fans

SERVES 4

To ensure that the potatoes fan out evenly, look for uniformly shaped potatoes.

BREAD-CRUMB TOPPING

- 1 slice hearty white sandwich bread, torn into quarters
- 4 tablespoons unsalted butter, melted
- 2 ounces Monterey Jack cheese, shredded (½ cup)
- ¼ cup grated Parmesan cheese
- 1 teaspoon paprika
- ½ teaspoon garlic powder
  Salt and pepper

POTATO FANS

- 4 russet potatoes
- 2 tablespoons extra-virgin olive oil
  Salt and pepper

1. FOR THE BREAD-CRUMB TOPPING: Adjust oven rack to middle position and heat oven to 200 degrees. Pulse bread in food processor until coarsely ground, about 5 pulses. Bake bread crumbs on rimmed baking sheet until dry, about 20 minutes. Let cool for 5 minutes, then combine crumbs, butter, Monterey Jack, Parmesan, paprika, garlic powder, ¼ teaspoon salt, and ¼ teaspoon pepper in large bowl. (Bread-crumb topping can be refrigerated in zipper-lock bag for 2 days.)

2. FOR THE POTATO FANS: Heat oven to 450 degrees. Cut ¼ inch from bottom and ends of potatoes, then slice potatoes crosswise at ¼-inch intervals, leaving ¼ inch of potato intact. Gently rinse potatoes under running water, let drain, and transfer, sliced side down, to plate. Microwave until slightly soft to touch, 6 to 12 minutes, flipping potatoes halfway through cooking.

3. Line rimmed baking sheet with aluminum foil. Arrange potatoes, sliced side up, on prepared baking sheet. Brush potatoes all over with oil and season with salt and pepper. Bake until skin is crisp and potatoes are beginning to brown, 25 to 30 minutes. Remove potatoes from oven and heat broiler.

4. Carefully top potatoes with stuffing mixture, pressing gently to adhere. Broil until bread crumbs are deep golden brown, about 3 minutes. Serve.

BLUE CHEESE AND BACON BAKED POTATO FANS

In step 1, substitute ⅓ cup crumbled blue cheese for Monterey Jack. In step 4, sprinkle 4 slices bacon, cooked until crisp and then crumbled, over potatoes just prior to serving.

PREPPING BAKED POTATO FANS

These potatoes may look difficult to make, but we found a few simple tricks to ensure perfect potato fans every time.

1. Trim ¼-inch slices from bottom and ends of each potato to allow them to sit flat and to give slices extra room to fan out during baking.

2. Chopsticks provide a foolproof guide for slicing potato petals without cutting all the way through potato.

3. Gently flex open fans while rinsing under cold running water; this rids potatoes of excess starch that can impede fanning.

✓ WHY THIS RECIPE WORKS

Potato gratin is a notoriously heavy side dish, laden with cream and gooey cheese. We wanted to shift the focus of this classic side dish to the potatoes. We chose Yukon Gold potatoes for their rich flavor and moderate starch content, which helped them hold their shape when cooked. Tossing the potatoes with fruity, flavorful extra-virgin olive oil heightened the flavor of the potatoes but didn't overpower them. For a crisp, cheesy topping, we mixed more olive oil with panko bread crumbs and sprinkled the dish with sharp, salty Pecorino-Romano. For added depth, we added sautéed onions, fresh thyme, and garlic.

Olive Oil Potato Gratin

SERVES 6 TO 8

The test kitchen's favorite supermarket extra-virgin olive oil is Columela. We prefer to use a mandoline to create thin, even slices of potato.

2   **ounces Pecorino-Romano cheese, grated (1 cup)**
½   **cup extra-virgin olive oil**
¼   **cup panko bread crumbs**
    Salt and pepper
2   **onions, halved and sliced thin**
2   **garlic cloves, minced**
1   **teaspoon minced fresh thyme**
1   **cup low-sodium chicken broth**
3   **pounds Yukon Gold potatoes, peeled and sliced ⅛ inch thick**

1. Adjust oven rack to upper-middle position and heat oven to 400 degrees. Grease 13 by 9-inch baking dish. Combine Pecorino, 3 tablespoons oil, panko, and ½ teaspoon pepper in bowl; set aside.

2. Heat 2 tablespoons oil in 12-inch skillet over medium heat until shimmering. Add onions, ½ teaspoon salt, and ¼ teaspoon pepper and cook, stirring frequently, until browned, about 15 minutes. Add garlic and ½ teaspoon thyme and cook until fragrant, about 30 seconds. Add ¼ cup broth and cook until nearly evaporated, scraping up any browned bits, about 2 minutes. Remove from heat; set aside.

3. Toss potatoes, remaining 3 tablespoons oil, 1 teaspoon salt, ½ teaspoon pepper, and remaining ½ teaspoon thyme together in bowl. Arrange half of potatoes in prepared dish, spread onion mixture in even layer over potatoes, and distribute remaining potatoes over onions. Pour remaining ¾ cup broth over potatoes. Cover dish tightly with aluminum foil and bake for 1 hour.

4. Remove foil, top gratin with reserved Pecorino mixture, and continue to bake until top is golden brown and potatoes are completely tender, 15 to 20 minutes. Let cool for 15 minutes. Serve.

SLICING POTATOES

A mandoline makes quick work of thinly slicing potatoes, but if you don't own one, cut a slice off of one side of each potato to create a flat, stable surface for thin slicing.

✔ WHY THIS RECIPE WORKS

Roasting red peppers on the grill turns their juicy crunch smoky and tender. We tossed stemmed and cored peppers in garlic-infused olive oil, allowing the oil to soak into the interiors' exposed flesh. To prevent flare-ups, we grilled the peppers in a foil-covered disposable pan then drained them and placed them directly on the hot grates to char. After easily scraping the charred skins from the peppers, we tossed them in a vinaigrette made from the leftover oil and liquid released from the peppers. The finished peppers were tender, smoky, and infused with heady garlic flavor that complemented the intensified sweetness.

Grill-Roasted Peppers

SERVES 4

These peppers can be refrigerated for up to 5 days.

- ¼ **cup extra-virgin olive oil**
- 3 **garlic cloves, peeled and smashed**
  Salt and pepper
- 1 **(13 by 9-inch) disposable aluminum pan**
- 6 **red bell peppers**
- 1 **tablespoon sherry vinegar**

1. Combine oil, garlic, ½ teaspoon salt, and ¼ teaspoon pepper in disposable pan. Using paring knife, cut around stems of peppers and remove cores and seeds. Place peppers in pan and turn to coat with oil. Cover pan tightly with aluminum foil.

2A. FOR A CHARCOAL GRILL: Open bottom vent completely. Light large chimney starter filled with charcoal briquettes (6 quarts). When top coals are partially covered with ash, pour evenly over half of grill. Set cooking grate in place, cover, and open lid vent completely. Heat grill until hot, about 5 minutes.

2B. FOR A GAS GRILL: Turn all burners to high, cover, and heat grill until hot, about 15 minutes. Turn all burners to medium-high.

3. Clean and oil cooking grate. Place pan on grill (over hotter side for charcoal) and cook, covered, until peppers are just tender and skins begin to blister, 10 to 15 minutes, rotating and shaking pan halfway through cooking.

4. Remove pan from heat and carefully remove foil (reserve foil to use later). Using tongs, remove peppers from pan, allowing juices to drip back into pan, and place on grill (over hotter side for charcoal). Grill peppers, covered, turning every few minutes until skins are blackened, 10 to 15 minutes.

5. Transfer juices and garlic in pan to medium bowl and whisk in vinegar. Remove peppers from grill, return to now-empty pan, and cover tightly with foil. Let peppers steam for 5 minutes. Using spoon, scrape blackened skin off each pepper. Quarter peppers lengthwise, add to vinaigrette in bowl, and toss to combine. Season with salt and pepper to taste, and serve.

STEAM AND THEN SEAR

We first steam the peppers in garlicky olive oil and their own juices. Then we sear the peppers and serve them with a vinaigrette made from the infused oil.

WHY THIS RECIPE WORKS

Stuffed tomatoes always sound delicious, but too often you get tasteless tomatoes and a lackluster stuffing that falls out in a clump. To concentrate flavor and get rid of excess moisture, we seasoned hollowed-out tomato shells with salt and sugar and let them drain. Couscous proved the best base for the filling, and we rehydrated it with the reserved tomato juice, ensuring the savory tomato flavor we craved. A topping of panko bread crumbs—pretoasted for proper browning—mixed with more cheese added crunch and richness, and a drizzle of the cooking liquid mixed with red wine vinegar provided a piquant final touch.

Stuffed Tomatoes

SERVES 6

Look for large tomatoes, about 3 inches in diameter.

6	large vine-ripened tomatoes (8 to 10 ounces each)
1	tablespoon sugar
	Kosher salt and pepper
4½	tablespoons extra-virgin olive oil
¼	cup panko bread crumbs
3	ounces Gruyère cheese, shredded (¾ cup)
1	onion, halved and sliced thin
2	garlic cloves, minced
⅛	teaspoon red pepper flakes
8	ounces (8 cups) baby spinach, chopped coarse
1	cup couscous
½	teaspoon grated lemon zest
1	tablespoon red wine vinegar

1. Adjust oven rack to middle position and heat oven to 375 degrees. Cut top ½ inch off stem end of tomatoes and set aside. Using melon baller, scoop out tomato pulp and transfer to fine-mesh strainer set over bowl. Press on pulp with wooden spoon to extract juice; set aside juice and discard pulp. (You should have about ⅔ cup tomato juice; if not, add water as needed to equal ⅔ cup.)

2. Combine sugar and 1 tablespoon salt in bowl. Sprinkle each tomato cavity with 1 teaspoon sugar mixture, then turn tomatoes upside down on plate to drain for 30 minutes.

3. Combine 1½ teaspoons oil and panko in 10-inch skillet and toast over medium-high heat, stirring frequently, until golden brown, about 3 minutes. Transfer to bowl and let cool for 10 minutes. Stir in ¼ cup Gruyère.

4. Heat 2 tablespoons oil in now-empty skillet over medium heat until shimmering. Add onion and ½ teaspoon salt and cook until softened, 5 to 7 minutes. Stir in garlic and pepper flakes and cook until fragrant, about 30 seconds. Add spinach, 1 handful at a time, and cook until wilted, about 3 minutes. Stir in couscous, lemon zest, and reserved tomato juice. Cover, remove from heat, and let sit until couscous has absorbed liquid, about 7 minutes. Transfer couscous mixture to bowl and stir in remaining ½ cup Gruyère. Season with salt and pepper to taste.

5. Coat bottom of 13 by 9-inch baking dish with remaining 2 tablespoons oil. Blot tomato cavities dry with paper towels and season with salt and pepper. Pack each tomato with couscous mixture, about ½ cup per tomato, mounding excess. Top stuffed tomatoes with 1 heaping tablespoon panko mixture. Place tomatoes in prepared dish. Season reserved tops with salt and pepper and place in empty spaces in dish.

6. Bake, uncovered, until tomatoes have softened but still hold their shape, about 20 minutes. Using slotted spoon, transfer to serving platter. Whisk vinegar into oil remaining in dish, then drizzle over tomatoes. Place tops on tomatoes and serve.

STUFFED TOMATOES WITH BACON

Substitute shredded smoked cheddar for Gruyère. Stir 3 slices chopped, cooked bacon into cooked couscous mixture with cheddar in step 4.

STUFFED TOMATOES WITH CAPERS AND PINE NUTS

Substitute shredded mozzarella for Gruyère. Stir 2 tablespoons rinsed capers and 2 tablespoons toasted pine nuts into cooked couscous mixture with mozzarella in step 4.

STUFFED TOMATOES WITH CURRANTS AND PISTACHIOS

Substitute crumbled feta for Gruyère. Stir 2 tablespoons currants and 2 tablespoons chopped pistachios into cooked couscous mixture with feta in step 4.

STUFFED TOMATOES WITH OLIVES AND ORANGE

Substitute shredded Manchego for Gruyère. Substitute ¼ teaspoon grated orange zest for lemon zest. Stir ¼ cup pitted kalamata olives, chopped, into cooked couscous mixture with Manchego in step 4.

OUR SUNDAY BEST

IS SUNDAY DINNER A LOST TRADITION? MOST PEOPLE MIGHT SAY YES. You'd certainly think so from a *New York Times* article, "Sunday Dinner, Old and New," which lamented the death of the Sunday dinner. But here's the kicker: The article was published in 1929. The piece opines, "The pace of modern life is to blame, and two of its major problems are specifically responsible." The two major problems? Uppity servant girls wanting a day off and put-upon housewives unwilling to pick up the slack. If only women did what they were told!

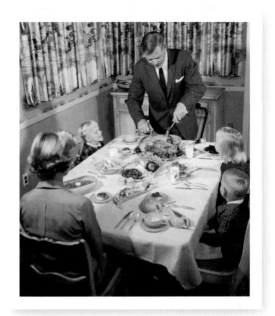

Class and gender issues aside, making time for a relaxing family meal will probably always be a challenge. Still, sitting down to enjoy a homemade meal with all the fixings is not a lost cause in our book. And preparing a Sunday dinner, especially a main course like our Sunday-Best Garlic Roast Beef, Cider-Baked Ham, or One-Pan Roast Chicken with Root Vegetables might just give you a leg up on weeknight meals. We say that's a tradition worth preserving.

✔️ WHY THIS RECIPE WORKS

For a roast turkey with moist, flavorful meat, we tried a number of options until we discovered a technique used for ages: barding. Similar to larding, it is a process of wrapping strips of lard (or other animal fat) around the meat so that it slowly releases flavor and moisture throughout roasting. After piercing the skin of the turkey breast and legs with a fork, we covered it with thin slices of salt pork before layering on cheesecloth that had been soaked in water and then aluminum foil. This insulated the meat and allowed the salt pork to slowly melt in the oven, basting the turkey with rich fat.

Old-Fashioned Roast Turkey with Gravy

SERVES 10 TO 12

You will need one 2-yard package of cheesecloth for this recipe. Because we layer the bird with salt pork, we prefer to use a natural turkey here; a self-basting turkey (such as a frozen Butterball) may become too salty. If using a self-basting turkey, omit the chicken broth in the gravy and increase the amount of water to 7 cups. Make sure to start the gravy as soon as the turkey goes into the oven.

TURKEY

- 1 **(2-yard) package cheesecloth**
- 4 **cups water**
- 1 **(12- to 14-pound) turkey, neck, giblets, and tailpiece removed and reserved for gravy**
- 1 **pound salt pork, cut into ¼-inch-thick slices**

GRAVY

- 1 **tablespoon vegetable oil**
- 1 **onion, chopped**
- 5 **cups water**
- 2 **cups chicken broth**
- 4 **sprigs fresh thyme**
- 1 **bay leaf**
- 6 **tablespoons all-purpose flour**
  Salt and pepper

1. FOR THE TURKEY: Adjust oven rack to lowest position and heat oven to 350 degrees. Fold cheesecloth into 18-inch square, place in large bowl, and cover with water. Tuck wings behind turkey and arrange, breast side up, on V-rack set in roasting pan. Prick skin of breast and legs of turkey all over with fork, cover breast and legs with salt pork, top with soaked cheesecloth (pouring any remaining water into roasting pan), and cover cheesecloth completely with heavy-duty aluminum foil.

2. Roast turkey until breast registers 140 degrees, 2½ to 3 hours. Remove foil, cheesecloth, and salt pork and discard. Increase oven temperature to 425 degrees. Continue to roast until breast registers 160 degrees and

thighs register 175 degrees, 40 minutes to 1 hour longer. Transfer turkey to carving board and let rest 30 minutes.

3. FOR THE GRAVY: Meanwhile, heat oil in large saucepan over medium-high heat until shimmering. Cook turkey neck and giblets until browned, about 5 minutes. Add onion and cook until softened, about 3 minutes. Stir in water, broth, thyme, and bay leaf and bring to boil. Reduce heat to low and simmer until reduced by half, about 3 hours. Strain mixture through fine-mesh strainer into 4-cup liquid measuring cup (you should have about 3½ cups), reserving giblets if desired.

4. Carefully strain contents of roasting pan into fat separator. Let liquid settle, then skim, reserving ¼ cup fat. Pour defatted pan juices into measuring cup with giblet broth to yield 4 cups liquid.

5. Heat reserved fat in empty saucepan over medium heat until shimmering. Stir in flour and cook until golden and fragrant, about 4 minutes. Slowly whisk in giblet broth and bring to boil. Reduce heat to medium-low and simmer until slightly thickened, about 5 minutes. Chop giblets and add to gravy, if desired, and season with salt and pepper to taste. Carve turkey and serve with gravy.

SALT PORK

Covering the breast and tops of the legs of the turkey with salt pork helps to season the meat and insulate it from overcooking. Don't confuse salt pork with bacon. Although both come from the belly of the pig and are salt-cured, bacon is heavily smoked and is typically leaner and meatier. Salt pork is unsmoked and used primarily as a flavoring agent (traditionally in dishes like baked beans) and is rarely actually consumed. We recommend buying blocks of salt pork (precut slices can dry out) and portioning it as needed. Look for salt pork that has at least a few streaks of meat throughout. Salt pork can be refrigerated for up to one month.

✓ WHY THIS RECIPE WORKS

We wanted a turkey stuffing rich enough to stand on its own without gravy. We found our answer in cornbread and sausage. Cornbread gives the stuffing more flavor than plain white bread. We wanted plenty of stuffing, so we chose to cook it in a Dutch oven, which is large enough to accommodate 10 to 12 portions. To compensate for the loss in richness and poultry flavor we didn't just rely on any sausage— we chose spicy andouille sausage. Adding chicken broth to the stuffing further boosted the meaty flavor of our stuffing and helped keep it from drying out.

Cornbread and Sausage Stuffing

SERVES 10 TO 12

We prefer spicy andouille sausage in this recipe, but chorizo or kielbasa work well, too. For the cornbread, use your favorite recipe, store-bought cornbread, or Betty Crocker Golden Corn Muffin and Bread Mix or Jiffy Corn Muffin Mix, both of which will work fine in stuffing.

12	cups prepared cornbread cut into ¾-inch cubes
1½	pounds andouille sausage, halved lengthwise and sliced into ¼-inch-thick half-moons
2	tablespoons unsalted butter
2	small onions, chopped fine
3	celery ribs, chopped fine
2	tablespoons minced fresh sage
3	garlic cloves, minced
1	teaspoon salt
1	teaspoon pepper
4	cups chicken broth

1. Adjust oven racks to upper-middle and lower-middle positions and heat oven to 400 degrees. Spread cornbread evenly over 2 rimmed baking sheets. Bake until slightly crisp, 15 to 20 minutes; let cool. Carefully remove upper-middle rack from oven.

2. Cook sausage in Dutch oven over medium-high heat until lightly browned, 5 to 7 minutes. Transfer to paper towel–lined plate and pour off fat left behind in pot. Melt butter over medium-high heat, add onions and celery, and cook until softened, about 5 minutes. Stir in sage, garlic, salt, and pepper and cook until fragrant, about 1 minute. Add broth and sausage, scraping up browned bits with wooden spoon. Add cornbread and gently stir until liquid is absorbed. Cover and set aside for 10 minutes. (Stuffing can be refrigerated for 1 day; let sit at room temperature for 30 minutes before baking.)

3. Remove lid and bake until top of stuffing is golden brown and crisp, about 30 minutes. Serve.

CORNBREAD AND BACON STUFFING

Substitute 1 pound bacon, chopped, for sausage, 3 cups fresh or frozen corn kernels for celery, and 3 thinly sliced scallions for sage.

DRYING CORNBREAD

Although cornbread gives stuffing great flavor, it also adds a lot of moisture, making a soggy baked mess. If you have the time, cube the cornbread, spread it out on baking sheets, and let it sit overnight on the counter. If you're in a hurry (and who isn't around the holidays?), pop the baking sheets holding the cornbread into a 400-degree oven until slightly crisp, 15 to 20 minutes.

✓ WHY THIS RECIPE WORKS

Developing a recipe for a classic herb roast chicken proved surprisingly tricky. Stuffing the chicken with fresh herbs delivered zero flavor, herb butter melted off the chicken, and infused oil failed to really penetrate the meat. Our solution was to slather the chicken with a thick paste of fresh herbs and garlic, processed until smooth, then let it rest to develop a pronounced herbal flavor. So that there was plenty of meat to go around, we used two whole chickens instead of one. For a simple pan sauce, while the chicken rested we whisked the drippings with chicken broth, white wine, cornstarch, butter, and additional herb paste.

Herb Roast Chicken

SERVES 6 TO 8

For even cooking, arrange the chickens side by side a few inches apart on the V-rack, with the legs pointing in opposite directions.

- 1   **cup chopped fresh parsley**
- 2   **tablespoons chopped fresh thyme**
- 1   **tablespoon chopped fresh rosemary**
- 2   **garlic cloves, minced**
-      **Salt and pepper**
- 2   **tablespoons olive oil**
- 2   **(3½- to 4-pound) whole chickens, giblets discarded**
- 1   **cup plus 2 tablespoons water**
- 2   **teaspoons cornstarch**
- 1¼ **cups chicken broth**
- ¼   **cup dry white wine**
- 2   **tablespoons unsalted butter, chilled**

1. Process parsley, thyme, rosemary, garlic, 2 teaspoons salt, and 1 teaspoon pepper in food processor until paste forms, about 30 seconds. Reserve 1 teaspoon herb paste for sauce. Combine 2 tablespoons herb paste with oil in bowl. Set aside herb-oil paste and remaining herb paste.

2. Adjust oven rack to middle position and heat oven to 450 degrees. Pat chickens dry with paper towels. Using your fingers, gently loosen skin covering breast and thighs. Rub remaining herb paste under skin of each chicken, making sure to coat breast, thigh, and leg meat. Rub herb-oil paste over outside of each chicken. Tuck wings behind back and tie legs together with kitchen twine. Transfer chickens to platter. Cover and refrigerate 1 hour.

3. Arrange chickens 2 inches apart, breast side down, on V-rack set inside large roasting pan. Roast until thigh meat registers 135 to 140 degrees, 35 to 40 minutes. Remove chickens from oven and, using 2 bunches of paper towels, flip breast side up (meat that was facing in should now be facing out). Pour 1 cup water into roasting pan. Return chickens to oven and roast until breast registers 160 degrees and thighs register 175 degrees, 25 to 30 minutes. Transfer to carving board and let rest for 20 minutes.

4. Whisk cornstarch with remaining 2 tablespoons water in bowl until no lumps remain. Pour pan juices and any accumulated chicken juices into liquid measuring cup; skim fat. Transfer ½ cup defatted pan juices to medium saucepan. Add broth and wine and bring to boil. Reduce heat to medium-low and simmer until sauce is slightly thickened and reduced to 1¼ cups, 8 to 10 minutes. Whisk in cornstarch mixture and simmer until thickened, 3 to 5 minutes. Off heat, whisk in butter and reserved herb paste. Season with salt and pepper to taste. Carve chickens and serve, passing sauce at table.

HERB FLAVOR TIMES THREE

To get deeply flavored roast chicken, we triple up on the herb paste.

1. Separate skin from meat and rub herb paste under skin.

2. Apply herb paste mixed with olive oil to exterior of each chicken.

3. Whisk teaspoon of herb paste into sauce for a fresh finish.

✓ WHY THIS RECIPE WORKS

The citrus flavor in roasted lemon chicken can be harsh or, on the flip side, totally absent. To infuse the meat with bright flavor, we combined lemon zest, sugar, and salt and rubbed it into the chicken under the skin. For even more lemon flavor, we roasted the chicken in a sauce of lemon juice mixed with water, more zest, and chicken broth. Roasting the bird at a high temperature ensured that the exposed skin became crisp. Before serving, we reduced the sauce to concentrate its flavor and thickened it with butter and cornstarch for sheen, body, and richness.

Roast Lemon Chicken

SERVES 3 TO 4

Avoid using nonstick or aluminum roasting pans in this recipe. The former can cause the chicken to brown too quickly, while the latter may react with the lemon juice, producing off-flavors.

- 1 **(3½- to 4-pound) whole chicken, giblets discarded**
- 3 **tablespoons grated lemon zest plus ⅓ cup juice (3 lemons)**
- 1 **teaspoon sugar**
  Salt and pepper
- 2 **cups chicken broth**
  Water
- 1 **teaspoon cornstarch**
- 3 **tablespoons unsalted butter**
- 1 **tablespoon finely chopped fresh parsley**

1. Adjust oven rack to middle position and heat oven to 475 degrees. Pat chicken dry with paper towels. Using kitchen shears, cut along both sides of backbone to remove it. Flatten breastbone and tuck wings behind back. Using your fingers, gently loosen skin covering breast and thighs. Combine lemon zest, sugar, and 1 teaspoon salt in small bowl. Rub 2 tablespoons zest mixture under skin of chicken. Season chicken with salt and pepper and transfer to roasting pan. (Seasoned chicken can be refrigerated for 2 hours.)

2. Whisk broth, 1 cup water, lemon juice, and remaining zest mixture in 4-cup liquid measuring cup, then pour into roasting pan. (Liquid should just reach skin of thighs. If it does not, add enough water to reach skin of thighs.) Roast until skin is golden brown and breast registers 160 degrees and thighs register 175 degrees, 40 to 45 minutes. Transfer to carving board and let rest for 20 minutes.

3. Carefully pour liquid from pan, along with any accumulated chicken juices, into saucepan (you should have about 1½ cups). Skim fat, then cook over medium-high heat until reduced to 1 cup, about 5 minutes. Whisk cornstarch with 1 tablespoon water in small bowl until no lumps remain, then whisk into saucepan. Simmer until sauce is slightly thickened, about 2 minutes. Off heat, whisk in butter and parsley and season with salt and pepper. Carve chicken and serve, passing sauce at table.

MORE LEMON FLAVOR IN LESS TIME

Butterflying the chicken may be unfamiliar, but this surprisingly simple process makes it easier to flavor the chicken with lemon—and it speeds roasting, too.

1. Use kitchen shears to cut out backbone. Flip bird over and press to flatten breastbone.

2. Carefully loosen skin, then rub zest mixture into breast, thigh, and leg meat.

3. Roast flattened chicken in lemony sauce so that its flavor can permeate meat.

✓ WHY THIS RECIPE WORKS

We had a tall order with our Apple Cider Chicken: It had to taste like apples, and it had to have super-crisp skin. Cooking the chicken in a skillet, skin side down, then moving it to a hot oven kept the skin exceptionally crisp. When it came to flavor, apple cider alone didn't do the trick. We also needed fresh apples, apple brandy, and cider vinegar to flavor the chicken with apple goodness. For the sauce, Granny Smith apples were too sour, while other varieties turned to mush when cooked. In the end, we preferred Golden Delicious, Cortland, or Jonagold apples, which held their shape and offered sweet flavor.

Apple Cider Chicken

SERVES 3 TO 4

Plain brandy, cognac, or Calvados (a French apple brandy) can be used in place of the apple brandy.

3	pounds bone-in chicken pieces, (split breasts halved crosswise, legs separated into thighs and drumsticks), trimmed
	Salt and pepper
2	teaspoons vegetable oil
1	onion, chopped fine
2	garlic cloves, minced
2	teaspoons minced fresh thyme
2	teaspoons all-purpose flour
1	large Golden Delicious, Cortland, or Jonagold apple (8 ounces), peeled, cored, and cut into ¾-inch pieces
1	cup apple cider
¼	cup apple brandy
1	teaspoon cider vinegar

1. Adjust oven rack to middle position and heat oven to 450 degrees. Pat chicken dry with paper towels and season with salt and pepper. Heat oil in 12-inch oven-proof skillet over medium-high heat until just smoking. Cook chicken skin side down until well browned, about 10 minutes. Flip and brown on second side, about 5 minutes. Transfer to plate.

2. Pour off all but 1 tablespoon fat from skillet. Add onion and cook until softened, about 5 minutes. Stir in garlic, thyme, and flour and cook, stirring frequently, until fragrant and flour is absorbed, about 1 minute. Add apple, apple cider, and 3 tablespoons apple brandy and bring to boil.

3. Nestle chicken skin side up into sauce and roast in oven until breasts register 160 degrees and thighs/ drumsticks register 175 degrees, about 10 minutes. Transfer chicken to platter. Stir vinegar and remaining 1 tablespoon brandy into sauce and season with salt and pepper to taste. Serve, passing sauce at table.

PREVENTING FLABBY SKIN

We avoid flabby skin with a hybrid technique that combines braising and pan roasting.

1. Brown chicken skin side down in skillet for 10 minutes until deep brown. Brown second side for 5 more minutes.

2. Finish chicken, skin side up and uncovered, in hot oven. Be sure liquid does not submerge chicken pieces.

APPLE CIDER VERSUS APPLE JUICE

To make cider, apples are simply cored, chopped, mashed, and then pressed to extract their liquid. Most cider is pasteurized before sale, though unpasteurized cider is also available. To make apple juice, manufacturers follow the same steps used to make cider, but they also filter the extracted liquid to remove pulp and sediment. Apple juice is then pasteurized, and potassium sorbate (a preservative) is often mixed in to prevent fermentation. Finally, apple juice is sometimes sweetened with sugar or corn syrup.

We tried using unsweetened apple juice in recipes for pork chops and glazed ham that call for cider. Tasters were turned off by excessive sweetness in the dishes made with apple juice, unanimously preferring those made with cider. This made sense: The filtration process used in making juice removes some of the complex, tart, and bitter flavors that are still present in cider. (When we tested the pH level of both liquids, the cider had a lower pH than the apple juice, confirming its higher level of acidity.) The bottom line: When it comes to cooking, don't swap apple juice for cider.

✔ WHY THIS RECIPE WORKS

Cooking vegetables and chicken together in the same pan often leads to unevenly cooked chicken and greasy, soggy vegetables. To get the chicken and vegetables to cook at the same rate, we used chicken parts, which contain less overall fat than a whole chicken and don't smother the vegetables underneath, which would cause them to steam. To ensure that the delicate white meat stayed moist while the darker meat cooked through, we placed the chicken breasts in the center of the pan, with the thighs and drumsticks around the perimeter.

One-Pan Roast Chicken with Root Vegetables

SERVES 4

We halve the chicken breasts crosswise for even cooking. Use Brussels sprouts no bigger than golf balls, as larger ones are often tough and woody.

12	ounces Brussels sprouts, trimmed and halved
12	ounces red potatoes, cut into 1-inch pieces
8	ounces shallots, peeled and halved
4	carrots, peeled and cut into 2-inch pieces, thick ends halved lengthwise
6	garlic cloves, peeled
4	teaspoons minced fresh thyme
1	tablespoon vegetable oil
2	teaspoons minced fresh rosemary
1	teaspoon sugar
	Salt and pepper
2	tablespoons unsalted butter, melted
3½	pounds bone-in chicken pieces (2 split breasts halved crosswise, 2 drumsticks, and 2 thighs), trimmed

1. Adjust oven rack to upper-middle position and heat oven to 475 degrees. Toss Brussels sprouts, potatoes, shallots, carrots, garlic, 2 teaspoons thyme, oil, 1 teaspoon rosemary, sugar, ¾ teaspoon salt, and ¼ teaspoon pepper together in bowl. Combine butter, remaining 2 teaspoons thyme, remaining 1 teaspoon rosemary, ¼ teaspoon salt, and ⅛ teaspoon pepper in second bowl; set aside.

2. Pat chicken dry with paper towels and season with salt and pepper. Place vegetables in single layer on rimmed baking sheet, arranging Brussels sprouts in center. Place chicken, skin side up, on top of vegetables, arranging breast pieces in center and leg and thigh pieces around perimeter of sheet.

3. Brush chicken with herb butter and roast until breasts register 160 degrees and thighs/drumsticks register 175 degrees, 35 to 40 minutes, rotating pan halfway through cooking. Transfer chicken to serving platter, tent loosely with aluminum foil, and let rest for 5 to 10 minutes. Toss vegetables in pan juices and transfer to platter with chicken. Serve.

ONE-PAN ROAST CHICKEN WITH FENNEL AND PARSNIPS

Replace Brussels sprouts and carrots with 1 fennel bulb, stalks discarded, bulb halved, cored, and sliced into ½-inch wedges, and 8 ounces (4 medium) parsnips, peeled and cut into 2-inch pieces.

PREPARING FENNEL

1. Cut off stalks and feathery fronds. Trim very thin slice from base and remove any tough or blemished outer layer.

2. Cut bulb in half through base. Use small sharp knife to remove pyramid-shaped cone.

3. Cut each half into ½-inch wedges.

WHY THIS RECIPE WORKS

For this convenient, one-pan meal, we were challenged to deliver tender potatoes and moist chicken at the same time. First, we quickly browned one side of the potatoes (an entire 2 pounds of potatoes fit into a 12-inch skillet when sliced into 1-inch-thick rounds). We placed the bird on top and moved everything to the oven where flavorful juices basted the potatoes. An hour later, the chicken was golden and juicy and the potatoes had a caramelized crust on the bottom. While the chicken rested, we returned the potatoes to the oven. By the time the chicken was ready to be served, the potatoes were soft and flavorful.

Skillet-Roasted Chicken and Potatoes

Use uniform, medium potatoes.

- **3 tablespoons olive oil**
- **2 teaspoons minced fresh thyme**
- **1½ teaspoons smoked paprika**
- **1½ teaspoons grated lemon zest, plus lemon wedges for serving**
- **Salt and pepper**
- **1 (4-pound) whole chicken, giblets discarded**
- **2 pounds Yukon Gold potatoes, peeled, ends squared off, and sliced into 1-inch-thick rounds**

1. Adjust oven rack to lower-middle position and heat oven to 400 degrees. Combine 2 tablespoons oil, thyme, paprika, lemon zest, 1 teaspoon salt, and ½ teaspoon pepper in bowl. Pat chicken dry with paper towels and use your fingers or handle of wooden spoon to carefully separate skin from breast. Rub oil mixture all over chicken and underneath skin of breast. Tie legs together with kitchen twine and tuck wingtips behind back.

2. Toss potatoes with remaining 1 tablespoon oil, 1½ teaspoons salt, and ½ teaspoon pepper. Arrange potatoes, flat sides down, in single layer in 12-inch ovensafe nonstick skillet. Place skillet over medium heat and cook potatoes, without moving them, until brown on bottom, 7 to 9 minutes (do not flip).

3. Place chicken, breast side up, on top of potatoes and transfer skillet to oven. Roast until breast registers 160 degrees and thighs register 175 degrees, 1 to 1¼ hours. Transfer chicken to carving board, tent loosely with aluminum foil, and let rest for 20 minutes.

4. Meanwhile, cover skillet, return potatoes to oven, and roast until tender, about 20 minutes. Carve chicken and serve with potatoes and lemon wedges.

KEYS TO POTATOES THAT ARE TENDER AND BROWN

Potatoes don't cook at the same rate as a chicken. Here's how we got the dish to work.

1. ON THE STOVE: Brown one side of the potatoes on the stovetop. Then top the spuds with the chicken and roast.

2. IN THE OVEN: Once the chicken is done, set it aside; cover the pan and return it to the oven to finish cooking the potatoes.

PREPPING FRESH THYME

For thin-stemmed thyme, chop the stems along with the leaves. If the stems are thick, hold the sprig upright and run your thumb and forefinger along the stem to release the leaves.

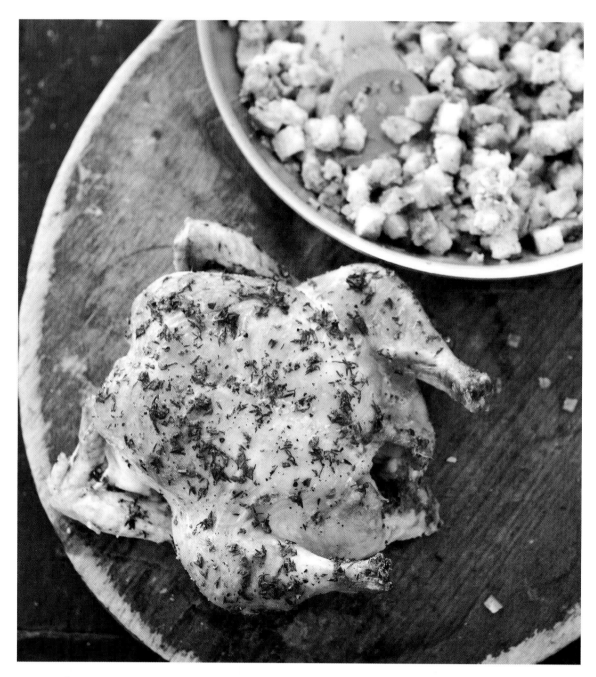

✔ WHY THIS RECIPE WORKS

To simplify Sunday-style stuffed chicken into a one-pan meal, we sped things up by taking the stuffing out of the chicken and making the entire dish in just one skillet. First we sautéed the aromatics for the stuffing, then we placed the chicken—brushed with a flavorful herb butter—right on top. We scattered the bread cubes around the bird and moved the skillet to the oven to simultaneously roast the chicken and toast the bread. As the chicken cooked, the bread soaked up its flavorful juices. Finally, while the chicken rested, a quick stir and a splash of broth mixed up the aromatics and moistened the stuffing.

Skillet-Roasted Chicken with Stuffing

SERVES 4

You can find Italian bread in the bakery section of your grocery store. Take care when stirring the contents of the skillet in steps 4 and 5, as the skillet handle will be very hot.

1	(4-pound) whole chicken, giblets discarded
6	tablespoons unsalted butter
2	tablespoons minced fresh sage
2	tablespoons minced fresh thyme
	Salt and pepper
2	onions, chopped fine
2	celery ribs, minced
7	ounces Italian bread, cut into ½-inch cubes (6 cups)
⅓	cup low-sodium chicken broth

1. Adjust oven rack to lower-middle position and heat oven to 375 degrees. Pat chicken dry with paper towels. Melt 4 tablespoons butter in small bowl in microwave, about 45 seconds. Stir in 1 tablespoon sage, 1 tablespoon thyme, 1 teaspoon salt, and ½ teaspoon pepper. Brush chicken with herb butter.

2. Melt remaining 2 tablespoons butter in 12-inch ovensafe skillet over medium heat. Add onions, celery, ½ teaspoon salt, and ½ teaspoon pepper and cook until softened, about 5 minutes. Add remaining 1 tablespoon sage and remaining 1 tablespoon thyme and cook until fragrant, about 1 minute. Off heat, place chicken, breast side up, on top of vegetables. Arrange bread cubes around chicken in bottom of skillet.

3. Transfer skillet to oven and roast until breasts register 160 degrees and thighs register 175 degrees, about 1 hour, rotating skillet halfway through roasting.

4. Carefully transfer chicken to plate and tent loosely with aluminum foil. Holding skillet handle with potholder (handle will be hot), stir bread and vegetables to combine, cover, and let stand for 10 minutes.

5. Add broth and any accumulated chicken juice from plate and cavity to skillet and stir to combine. Warm stuffing, uncovered, over low heat until heated through, about 3 minutes. Remove from heat, cover, and let sit while carving chicken. Transfer chicken to carving board, carve, and serve with stuffing.

CHOPPING ONIONS FINELY

1. Halve onion through root end, then peel onion and trim top. Make several horizontal cuts from one end of onion to other but don't cut through root end.

2. Make several vertical cuts. Be sure to cut up to but not through root end.

3. Rotate onion so root end is in back; slice onion thinly across previous cuts. As you slice, onion will fall apart into chopped pieces.

✔ WHY THIS RECIPE WORKS

A distant cousin to chicken and dumplings, chicken and slicks offers tender chicken in a rich, flavorful broth but swaps the traditional biscuit-style dumpling for a thick, chewy, noodlelike version. For a flavorful base, we browned the chicken before simmering it in the broth; bone-in pieces provided the best flavor. While authentic recipes call for lard in the slicks, we replaced it with more readily available vegetable oil, plus some of the rendered fat from our chicken. Cooking the slicks in an already thickened broth caused them to break apart, so we cooked them in the broth before adding toasted flour to thicken it.

Chicken and Slicks

SERVES 4 TO 6

If you're short on chicken fat at the end of step 1, supplement it with vegetable oil.

1½	pounds bone-in chicken thighs, trimmed
2	(12-ounce) bone-in split chicken breasts, halved crosswise and trimmed
	Salt and pepper
6	tablespoons plus 2 cups all-purpose flour
3	tablespoons vegetable oil
1	onion, chopped
2	teaspoons minced fresh thyme
7½	cups chicken broth
2	bay leaves
¼	cup chopped fresh parsley

1. Pat chicken dry with paper towels and season with salt and pepper. Toast 6 tablespoons flour in Dutch oven over medium heat, stirring constantly, until just beginning to brown, about 5 minutes. Transfer flour to medium bowl and wipe out pot. Heat 1 tablespoon oil in now-empty Dutch oven over medium-high heat until just smoking. Cook chicken until browned all over, about 10 minutes; transfer to plate. When chicken is cool enough to handle, remove and discard skin. Pour fat (you should have about 2 tablespoons) into small bowl; reserve.

2. Add onion and 1 tablespoon oil to now-empty pot and cook over medium heat until softened, about 5 minutes. Stir in thyme and cook until fragrant, about 30 seconds. Add 7 cups broth, chicken, and bay leaves and bring to boil. Reduce heat to low and simmer, covered, until breasts register 160 degrees and thighs register 175 degrees, 20 to 25 minutes. Remove from heat and transfer chicken to clean plate. When chicken is cool enough to handle, shred into bite-size pieces, discarding bones.

3. Meanwhile, combine remaining ½ cup chicken broth, reserved fat, and remaining 1 tablespoon oil in liquid measuring cup. Process remaining 2 cups flour and ½ teaspoon salt in food processor until combined. With processor running, slowly pour in broth mixture and process until mixture resembles coarse meal. Turn dough onto lightly floured surface and knead until smooth. Divide in half.

4. Roll each dough half into 10-inch square about ⅛ inch thick. Cut each square into twenty 5 by 1-inch rectangles. Place handful of noodles in single layer on parchment paper–lined plate, cover with another sheet of parchment, and repeat stacking with remaining noodles and additional parchment, ending with parchment. Freeze until firm, at least 10 minutes or up to 30 minutes.

5. Return broth to simmer and add noodles. Cook until noodles are nearly tender, 12 to 15 minutes, stirring occasionally to separate. Remove 1 cup broth from pot and whisk into reserved toasted flour. Stir broth-flour mixture into pot, being careful not to break up noodles, and simmer until slightly thickened, 3 to 5 minutes. Add shredded chicken and parsley and cook until heated through, about 1 minute. Season with salt and pepper to taste. Serve.

MAKING SLICKS

1. Roll each dough half into 10-inch square of ⅛ inch thickness. Then, using sharp knife, cut dough into twenty 5 by 1-inch rectangles.

2. Stack slicks between layers of parchment and freeze briefly before simmering.

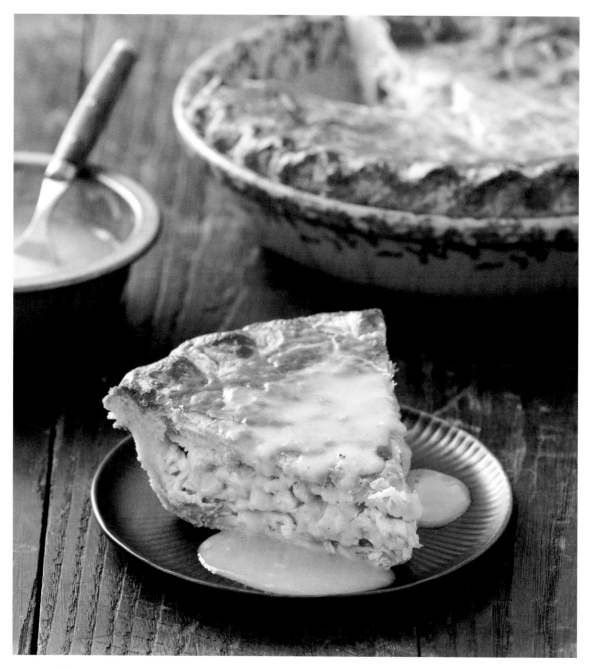

✓ WHY THIS RECIPE WORKS

Protestant immigrants from the Czech province Moravia settled in Pennsylvania and later North Carolina and brought with them such homey dishes as Moravian cake, cookies, and chicken pie, a satisfying double-crusted pie filled with shredded chicken and served with a rich gravy. Searing the chicken (a mix of breasts and thighs) helped to render its fat, which we used in a roux to thicken the gravy. For moist chicken, we poached it in chicken broth and used that broth to give our gravy flavor. As for the pie crust, we found that sour cream helped make for a rich, flaky crust that was remarkably easy to roll out.

Moravian Chicken Pie

SERVES 8

CRUST

- ½ cup sour cream, chilled
- 1 large egg, lightly beaten
- 2½ cups (12½ ounces) all-purpose flour
- 1½ teaspoons salt
- 12 tablespoons unsalted butter, cut into ½-inch pieces and chilled

PIE

- 2 (10- to 12-ounce) bone-in split chicken breasts, halved crosswise and trimmed
- 3 (5- to 7-ounce) bone-in chicken thighs, trimmed
  Salt and pepper
- 1 tablespoon vegetable oil
- 3 cups chicken broth
- 1 bay leaf
- 2 tablespoons unsalted butter
- ¼ cup all-purpose flour
- ¼ cup half-and-half
- 1 large egg, lightly beaten

1. FOR THE CRUST: Combine sour cream and egg in bowl. Process flour and salt in food processor until combined, about 3 seconds. Add butter and pulse until only pea-size pieces remain, about 10 pulses. Add half of sour cream mixture and pulse until combined, 5 pulses. Add remaining sour cream mixture and pulse until dough begins to form, about 10 pulses.

2. Transfer mixture to lightly floured counter and knead briefly until dough comes together. Divide dough in half and form each half into 4-inch disk. Wrap each disk in plastic wrap and refrigerate for at least 1 hour or up to 2 days.

3. Line rimmed baking sheet with parchment paper. Remove 1 dough disk from refrigerator and let sit for 10 minutes. Working on lightly floured counter, roll into 12-inch round and transfer to 9-inch pie plate, leaving ½-inch overhang all around. Repeat with second dough disk and transfer to prepared baking sheet. Cover both dough rounds with plastic wrap and refrigerate for 30 minutes.

4. FOR THE PIE: Pat chicken dry with paper towels and season with salt and pepper. Heat oil in large Dutch oven over medium-high heat until just smoking. Cook chicken until browned, about 10 minutes; transfer to plate. Pour fat (you should have 2 tablespoons; supplement with butter if necessary) into bowl; reserve. When chicken is cool enough to handle, remove and discard skin. Add broth, chicken, and bay leaf to now-empty pot and bring to boil. Reduce heat to low and simmer, covered, until breasts register 160 degrees and thighs register 175 degrees, 14 to 18 minutes. Transfer chicken to bowl. When chicken is cool enough to handle, shred into bite-size pieces, discarding bones. Pour broth through fine-mesh strainer into second bowl and reserve (you should have about 2¾ cups); discard bay leaf.

5. Adjust oven rack to lowest position and heat oven to 450 degrees. Heat butter and reserved fat in now-empty pot over medium heat until shimmering. Add flour and cook, whisking constantly, until golden, 1 to 2 minutes. Slowly whisk in 2 cups reserved broth and half-and-half and bring to boil. Reduce heat to medium-low and simmer gravy until thickened and reduced to 1¾ cups, 6 to 8 minutes. Season with salt and pepper to taste. Combine 1 cup gravy with shredded chicken; reserve remaining gravy for serving.

6. Transfer chicken mixture to dough-lined pie plate and spread into even layer. Top with second dough round, leaving at least ½-inch overhang all around. Fold dough under so that edge of fold is flush with rim of pie plate. Flute edges using thumb and forefinger or press with tines of fork to seal. Cut four 1-inch slits in top. Brush pie with egg and bake until top is light golden brown, 18 to 20 minutes. Reduce oven temperature to 375 degrees and continue to bake until crust is deep golden brown, 10 to 15 minutes. Let pie cool on wire rack for at least 45 minutes.

7. When ready to serve, bring remaining ¾ cup reserved gravy and remaining ¾ cup reserved broth to boil in medium saucepan. Simmer over medium-low heat until slightly thickened, 5 to 7 minutes. Season with salt and pepper to taste. Serve pie with gravy.

🥄 WHY THIS RECIPE WORKS

Guinness beef stew often captures only the bitterness and none of the deep, caramelized flavors of the beer. We found the trick to rich, malty flavor was to add some of the beer at the end of cooking so that the heat didn't dull the complex flavors. We also added a little brown sugar to balance some of the bitterness. We loved the idea of just dumping the meat into the pot without searing, but the flavor was lacking. To compensate, we first browned the onions and tomato paste, then cooked the stew uncovered so that the meat could brown in the oven.

Guinness Beef Stew

SERVES 6 TO 8

Use Guinness Draught, not Guinness Extra Stout, which is too bitter.

1	(3½- to 4-pound) boneless beef chuck-eye roast, pulled apart at seams, trimmed, and cut into 1½-inch pieces
	Salt and pepper
3	tablespoons vegetable oil
2	onions, chopped fine
1	tablespoon tomato paste
2	garlic cloves, minced
¼	cup all-purpose flour
3	cups chicken broth
1¼	cups Guinness Draught
1½	tablespoons packed dark brown sugar
1	teaspoon minced fresh thyme
1½	pounds Yukon Gold potatoes, unpeeled, cut into 1-inch pieces
1	pound carrots, peeled and cut into 1-inch pieces
2	tablespoons minced fresh parsley

1. Adjust oven rack to lower-middle position and heat oven to 325 degrees. Season beef with salt and pepper. Heat oil in Dutch oven over medium-high heat until shimmering. Add onions and ¼ teaspoon salt and cook, stirring occasionally, until well browned, 8 to 10 minutes.

2. Add tomato paste and garlic and cook until rust-colored and fragrant, about 2 minutes. Stir in flour and cook for 1 minute. Whisk in broth, ¾ cup Guinness, sugar, and thyme, scraping up any browned bits. Bring to simmer and cook until slightly thickened, about 3 minutes. Stir in beef and return to simmer. Transfer to oven and cook, uncovered, for 90 minutes, stirring halfway through cooking.

3. Stir in potatoes and carrots and continue cooking until beef and vegetables are tender, about 1 hour, stirring halfway through cooking. Stir in remaining ½ cup Guinness and parsley. Season with salt and pepper to taste and serve.

COOK IT UNCOVERED

Most stew recipes start by searing meat in batches on the stovetop. For an easier beef stew, we skip that step but keep the flavor by cooking the stew uncovered in the oven; the open pot allows the meat on top to take on flavorful browning. In addition, the liquid reduces, concentrating in flavor and texture, while the meat cooks.

PREPARING A CHUCK ROAST

1. Pull apart roast at its major seams (marked by lines of fat and silverskin). Use a knife as necessary.

2. With a sharp chef's knife or boning knife, trim off any thick layers of fat and silverskin. Cut meat into pieces as directed in recipe.

✔ WHY THIS RECIPE WORKS

Is there a more affordable roast beef alternative to pricey prime rib? One that is faster to cook and full of rich, beefy, tender flavor? In our testing, we found our answer with top sirloin. Skipping a stovetop sear, we browned the roast in the oven at a high temperature and then reduced the oven temperature to cook the roast through without losing too much moisture. And to give our roast an extra layer of savory flavor, we turned to garlic. A three-pronged attack yielded roast beef with great garlic flavor: We studded the roast beef with toasted garlic, rubbed it with garlic salt, and coated it while it cooked with a garlic paste.

Sunday-Best Garlic Roast Beef

SERVES 6 TO 8

Look for a top sirloin roast that has a thick, substantial fat cap still attached. The rendered fat will help to keep the roast moist. When making the jus, taste the reduced broth before adding any of the accumulated meat juices from the roast. The meat juices are well seasoned and may make the jus too salty. If you don't have a heavy-duty non-stick roasting pan, a broiler pan bottom works well, too.

BEEF

8	large garlic cloves, unpeeled
1	(4-pound) top sirloin roast, fat trimmed to ¼ inch

GARLIC-SALT RUB

3	large garlic cloves, minced
1	teaspoon dried thyme
½	teaspoon salt

GARLIC PASTE

½	cup olive oil
12	large garlic cloves, cut in half lengthwise
2	sprigs fresh thyme
2	bay leaves
½	teaspoon salt
	Pepper

JUS

1½	cups beef broth
1½	cups chicken broth

1. FOR THE BEEF: Toast garlic in 8-inch skillet over medium-high heat, tossing frequently, until spotty brown, about 8 minutes. Set aside. When cool enough to handle, peel and cut into ¼-inch slivers. Using paring knife, make 1-inch-deep slits all over roast and insert toasted garlic into slits.

2. FOR THE GARLIC-SALT RUB: Combine garlic, thyme, and salt in small bowl and rub all over roast. Place roast on large plate and refrigerate, uncovered, for at least 4 hours or preferably overnight.

3. FOR THE GARLIC PASTE: Heat oil, garlic, thyme, bay leaves, and salt in small saucepan over medium-high heat until bubbles start to rise to surface. Reduce heat to low and cook until garlic is soft, about 30 minutes. Let cool completely, then strain, reserving oil. Discard herbs and transfer garlic to small bowl. Mash garlic with 1 tablespoon garlic oil until paste forms. Cover and refrigerate paste until ready to use. Cover and reserve garlic oil.

4. Adjust oven rack to middle position, place nonstick roasting pan on rack, and heat oven to 450 degrees. Using paper towels, wipe garlic-salt rub off beef. Rub beef with 2 tablespoons reserved garlic oil and season with pepper. Transfer meat, fat side down, to preheated pan and roast, turning as needed until browned on all sides, 10 to 15 minutes.

5. Reduce oven temperature to 300 degrees. Remove pan from oven, turn roast fat side up, and, using spatula, coat top with garlic paste. Return meat to oven and roast until it registers 120 to 125 degrees (for medium-rare), 50 minutes to 1 hour, 10 minutes. Transfer to carving board, cover loosely with aluminum foil, and let rest for 20 minutes.

6. FOR THE JUS: Pour off fat from roasting pan and place pan over high heat. Add beef broth and chicken broth and bring to boil, scraping up browned bits with wooden spoon. Simmer, stirring occasionally, until reduced to 2 cups, about 5 minutes. Add accumulated juices from roast and cook for 1 minute, then pour through fine-mesh strainer. Slice roast crosswise into ¼-inch-thick slices. Serve with jus.

✓ WHY THIS RECIPE WORKS

For tender, juicy roast beef, we chose top sirloin roast with a thick fat cap, which rendered as the beef roasted and kept it moist. Searing each side before roasting helped to develop a flavorful crust. Though the right roasting temperature produced juicy meat (our roast having expelled very little liquid), it left precious few drippings in the roasting pan from which to make gravy. A good amount of beef broth, plus the rendered fat and fond left behind from searing the meat, provided volume and richness, while mushrooms, red wine, and Worcestershire sauce amped up the flavor.

Classic Roast Beef and Gravy

SERVES 6 TO 8

For the best flavor and texture, refrigerate the roast overnight after salting. If you don't have a V-rack, cook the roast on a wire rack set inside a rimmed baking sheet.

1	(4-pound) top sirloin roast, fat trimmed to ¼ inch
	Salt and pepper
1	tablespoon vegetable oil
8	ounces white mushrooms, trimmed and chopped
2	onions, chopped fine
1	carrot, peeled and chopped
1	celery rib, minced
1	tablespoon tomato paste
4	garlic cloves, minced
¼	cup all-purpose flour
1	cup red wine
4	cups beef broth
1	teaspoon Worcestershire sauce

1. Pat roast dry with paper towels. Rub 2 teaspoons salt evenly over meat. Cover with plastic wrap and refrigerate for at least 1 hour or up to 24 hours.

2. Adjust oven rack to lower-middle position and heat oven to 275 degrees. Pat roast dry with paper towels and rub with 1 teaspoon pepper. Heat oil in Dutch oven over medium-high heat until just smoking. Brown roast all over, 8 to 12 minutes, then transfer to V-rack set inside roasting pan (do not wipe out Dutch oven). Transfer to oven and cook until meat registers 120 to 125 degrees (for medium-rare), 1½ to 2 hours.

3. Meanwhile, add mushrooms to fat left in Dutch oven and cook until golden, about 5 minutes. Stir in onions, carrot, and celery and cook until browned, 5 to 7 minutes. Stir in tomato paste, garlic, and flour and cook until fragrant, about 2 minutes. Stir in wine and broth, scraping up any browned bits with wooden spoon. Bring to boil, then reduce heat to medium and simmer until thickened, about 10 minutes. Strain gravy, then stir in Worcestershire and season with salt and pepper; cover and keep warm.

4. Transfer roast to carving board, tent with aluminum foil, and let rest for 20 minutes. Slice roast crosswise into ½-inch-thick slices. Serve with gravy.

FLAVOR BUILDERS

A combination of sautéed mushrooms, tomato paste, beef broth, and Worcestershire sauce mimicked the roasted, beefy flavor of traditional gravy made with pan drippings.

TOP SIRLOIN—THE RIGHT CUT

Through extensive testing of every cut of beef, the test kitchen has settled on top sirloin as our favorite inexpensive roast. Look for a roast with at least a ¼-inch fat cap on top; the fat renders in the oven, basting the roast and helping to keep it moist.

WHY THIS RECIPE WORKS

For a roast beef dressed to impress without much effort, we turned to a swirl of herbs and mustard. To start, we combined fresh herbs with the mustard, butterflied the roast, and spread the herbs over the interior of the meat before folding it back together and securing it with twine. A simple herb butter, spread over the resting roast, melted and mingled with the natural juices of the meat, creating a flavorful sauce without the need to dirty another pan.

Herbed Roast Beef

SERVES 6 TO 8

For even deeper seasoning, refrigerate the roast overnight after filling it with the herb mixture in step 2.

- ⅓ cup minced fresh parsley
- 1 shallot, minced
- 2 tablespoons minced fresh thyme
- 2 tablespoons olive oil
- 1 tablespoon Dijon mustard
- 4 tablespoons unsalted butter, softened
- 1 (4-pound) top sirloin roast, fat trimmed to ¼ inch
- 1 tablespoon salt
- 1 tablespoon pepper

1. Combine parsley, shallot, and thyme in bowl. Transfer 2 tablespoons herb mixture to second bowl and stir in 1 tablespoon oil and mustard until combined. Add butter to remaining herb mixture and mash with fork until combined.

2. Butterfly roast by slicing horizontally through middle of meat, leaving about ½ inch of meat intact, and rub roast inside and out with salt and pepper. Spread herb-mustard mixture over interior of meat, fold roast back together, and tie securely with kitchen twine at 1-inch intervals. Refrigerate for at least 1 hour or up to 24 hours.

3. Adjust oven rack to middle position and heat oven to 275 degrees. Pat roast dry with paper towels. Heat remaining 1 tablespoon oil in 12-inch skillet over medium-high heat until just smoking. Brown roast all over, 8 to 12 minutes, then arrange on V-rack set inside roasting pan. Transfer to oven and roast until meat registers 120 to 125 degrees (for medium-rare), 1½ to 2 hours.

4. Transfer roast to carving board, spread with herb-butter mixture, tent with aluminum foil, and let rest for 20 minutes. Remove twine and slice roast crosswise into ¼-inch-thick slices. Serve.

HERBS GALORE

Fresh parsley and thyme flavor both the interior and exterior of our roast.

1. Butterfly roast by slicing horizontally through middle of the meat. Leave about ½ inch of meat intact, then open it like a book.

2. After seasoning meat, spread herb-mustard mixture over interior of meat.

3. Fold meat back to its original position, then tie securely at 1-inch intervals with kitchen twine.

4. For second hit of herb flavor after roast is cooked, spread it with herb butter.

FAST SEAR, SLOW ROAST FOR BEEF

To promote browning when roasting beef, you want the oven to be very hot. Unfortunately, even if you remove the roast when the center is pink, you'll find a thick, unsightly band of gray, overcooked meat at its edge; a low temperature does a better job of cooking the meat evenly. So we brown most beef roasts on the stovetop to build a flavorful crust, then roast them gently for a uniformly rosy, juicy interior.

1. Searing the roast assures a flavorful, deep brown crust.

2. Roasting at a low temperature (275 degrees) keeps the meat moist and succulent.

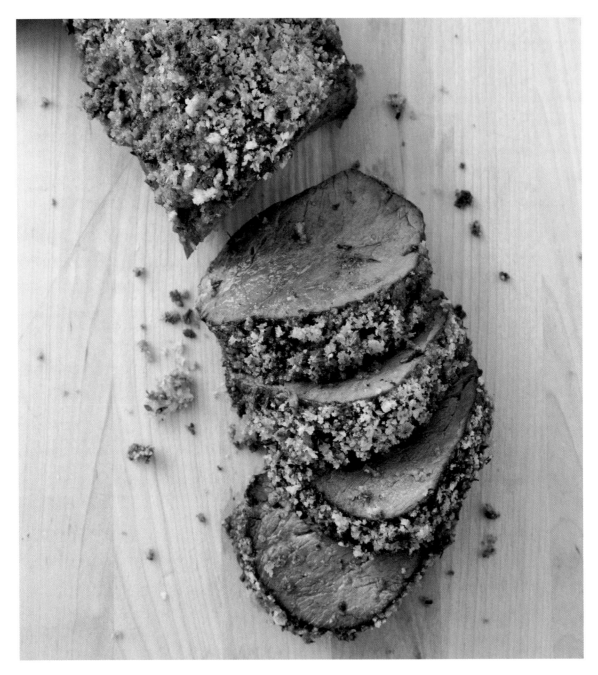

WHY THIS RECIPE WORKS

Though beef tenderloin offers incomparable tenderness, its flavor could often use some embellishment. To give the meat a flavor boost, we turned to a thick herbed crust. But herbs can burn easily, lose their flavor in a hot oven, or just fall off the meat. Cooking the roast in the oven at a high temperature for part of the time gave us a perfectly caramelized exterior that made applying an herb paste easy. Adding grated Parmesan cheese to the paste gave it nutty flavor and helped the paste adhere to the meat. Fresh parsley and thyme provided a flavorful coating and for a crisp texture, we relied on bread crumbs.

Herb-Crusted Beef Tenderloin

SERVES 12 TO 16

Make sure to begin this recipe two hours before you plan to put the roast in the oven. The tenderloin can be trimmed, tied, rubbed with the salt mixture, and refrigerated up to 24 hours in advance; make sure to bring the roast back to room temperature before putting it into the oven.

1	**(6-pound) whole beef tenderloin, trimmed, tail end tucked, and tied at 1½-inch intervals**
	Kosher salt and cracked peppercorns
2	**teaspoons sugar**
2	**slices hearty white sandwich bread, torn into pieces**
2½	**ounces Parmesan cheese, grated (1¼ cups)**
½	**cup chopped fresh parsley**
6	**tablespoons olive oil**
2	**teaspoons plus 2 tablespoons chopped fresh thyme**
4	**garlic cloves, minced**
1	**recipe Horseradish Cream Sauce**

1. Set wire rack in rimmed baking sheet. Pat tenderloin dry with paper towels. Combine 1 tablespoon salt, 1 tablespoon pepper, and sugar in small bowl and rub all over tenderloin. Transfer to prepared baking sheet and let sit at room temperature for 2 hours.

2. Meanwhile, pulse bread in food processor to fine crumbs, about 15 pulses. Transfer bread crumbs to medium bowl and toss with ½ cup Parmesan, 2 tablespoons parsley, 2 tablespoons oil, and 2 teaspoons thyme until evenly combined. Wipe out food processor with paper towels and process remaining ¾ cup Parmesan, 6 tablespoons parsley, ¼ cup oil, 2 tablespoons thyme, and garlic until smooth paste forms. Transfer herb paste to small bowl.

3. Adjust oven rack to upper-middle position and heat oven to 400 degrees. Roast tenderloin for 20 minutes and remove from oven. Using scissors, carefully cut kitchen twine and remove it. Coat tenderloin with herb paste, then bread-crumb topping. Roast until meat registers 120 to 125 degrees (for medium-rare) and topping is golden brown, 20 to 25 minutes. (If topping browns before meat reaches preferred internal temperature, lightly cover with aluminum foil for remainder of roasting time and remove while roast rests.) Let roast rest, uncovered, for 30 minutes on wire rack. Transfer to carving board and carve. Serve with Horseradish Cream Sauce.

HORSERADISH CREAM SAUCE
MAKES ABOUT 1 CUP

½	**cup sour cream**
½	**cup heavy cream**
¼	**cup prepared horseradish, drained**
2	**teaspoons Dijon mustard**
1	**garlic clove, minced**
¼	**teaspoon sugar**
	Salt and pepper

Mix all ingredients in bowl; add salt and pepper to taste. Cover and let stand at room temperature for 1 to 1½ hours to thicken. (Sauce can be refrigerated for up to 2 days.)

PREPARING HERB-CRUSTED BEEF TENDERLOIN

1. To ensure even cooking, fold thin, tapered end under roast, then tie entire roast with kitchen twine every 1½ inches. Roast for 20 minutes.

2. Remove roast from oven, snip twine with scissors, and remove before adding herb paste and bread-crumb mixture. Return to oven to finish cooking.

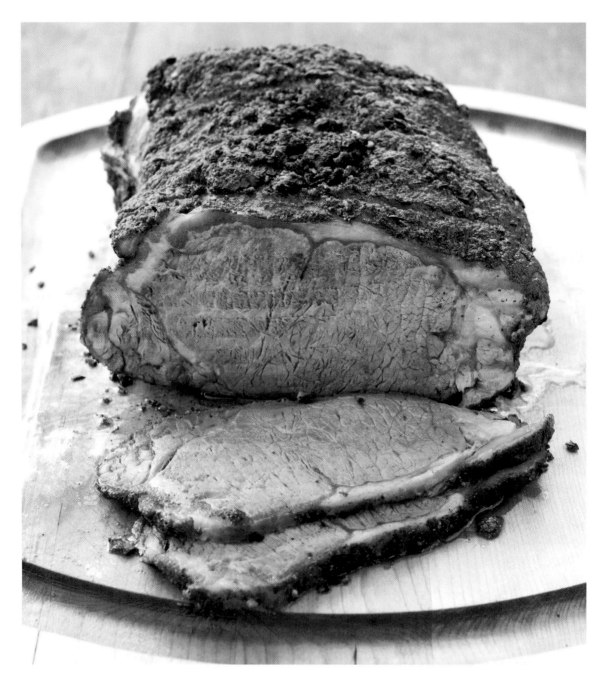

✅ WHY THIS RECIPE WORKS

For an occasion-worthy, beefy top-loin roast, we wanted a seared crust and a perfect medium-rare throughout, but most recipes we found could only give us one or the other. Gently roasting in a low oven until the meat was almost done and then setting it under the broiler for a few minutes achieved both results without the hassle of pan-searing. Scoring the fat cap before cooking helped the fat to render and the surface to crisp. We let the meat sit overnight with a spice and herb rub (and plenty of salt) to ensure a perfectly seasoned, flavorful roast, and served it with a bright, fresh salsa verde to complement the rich meat.

Holiday Strip Roast

SERVES 8 TO 10

Serve with Salsa Verde (recipe follows).

1	(5- to 6-pound) boneless top loin roast, fat trimmed to ¼ inch
2	tablespoons peppercorns
1	tablespoon coriander seeds
1	tablespoon yellow mustard seeds
3	tablespoons olive oil
2	tablespoons kosher salt
2	tablespoons chopped fresh rosemary
1	teaspoon red pepper flakes

1. Pat roast dry with paper towels. Using sharp knife, cut ½-inch crosshatch pattern through fat cap, ¼ inch deep. Tie kitchen twine around roast at 2-inch intervals. Grind peppercorns, coriander seeds, and mustard seeds to texture of coarse sand in spice grinder. Combine spice mixture, oil, salt, rosemary, and pepper flakes in bowl until thick paste forms. Rub paste all over roast and into crosshatch. Wrap roast with plastic wrap and refrigerate for 6 to 24 hours.

2. Set wire rack inside rimmed baking sheet. One hour before cooking, unwrap meat and place on prepared rack, fat side up. Adjust oven rack to middle position and heat oven to 275 degrees. Transfer roast to oven and cook until meat registers 115 degrees, about 90 minutes, rotating sheet halfway through cooking. Remove roast from oven and heat broiler.

3. Return roast to oven and broil on middle oven rack until fat cap is deep brown and interior of roast registers 125 degrees, 3 to 5 minutes. Transfer to carving board, tent loosely with aluminum foil, and let rest for 20 minutes. Remove twine and carve into thin slices. Serve.

SALSA VERDE

MAKES ABOUT 1½ CUPS

Mince the garlic before processing it, or it won't break down enough. This sauce can be prepared up to two days in advance and refrigerated. Before serving, bring it to room temperature and stir to recombine.

2	slices hearty white sandwich bread, torn into 1-inch pieces
1	cup extra-virgin olive oil
¼	cup lemon juice (2 lemons)
4	cups fresh parsley leaves
¼	cup capers, rinsed
4	anchovy fillets, rinsed
2	garlic cloves, minced
½	teaspoon kosher salt

Process bread, oil, and lemon juice in food processor until smooth, about 10 seconds. Add parsley, capers, anchovies, garlic, and salt and pulse until mixture is finely chopped, about 5 pulses, scraping down bowl as needed.

THE RIGHT GRIND

As part of the rub for the roast, we grind peppercorns with mustard seeds and coriander seeds to the texture of coarse sand. Since these ingredients are irregularly sized and of varying densities, the texture won't be uniform, which is OK. The correct grind looks like this.

COARSE AND IRREGULAR

✓ WHY THIS RECIPE WORKS

Our goal was to produce a recipe for holiday prime rib with roasted vegetables that was simple and fool-proof. We scored and salted a first-cut standing rib roast and refrigerated it for 24 hours for tender beef. A low-and-slow cooking method yielded evenly red and juicy meat, and an additional stint under the broiler turned the outside crispy and golden. Instead of forcing the vegetables to work in concert with the beef, we roasted them solo in the flavorful beef fat while the prime rib was resting. It was definitely a feast fit for a holiday—with only one pan to wash.

One-Pan Prime Rib and Roasted Vegetables

SERVES 8 TO 10

The roast must be salted and then refrigerated for at least 24 hours before cooking; salting and refrigerating for the full 96 hours results in the most tender, flavorful meat.

- 1 **(7-pound) first-cut beef standing rib roast (3 bones), fat trimmed to ¼ inch**
  Kosher salt and pepper
  Vegetable oil
- 2 **pounds carrots, peeled, cut into 2-inch lengths, halved or quartered lengthwise to create ½-inch-diameter pieces**
- 1 **pound parsnips, peeled and sliced ½ inch thick on bias**
- 1 **pound Brussels sprouts, trimmed and halved**
- 1 **red onion, halved and sliced through root end into ½-inch wedges**
- 2 **teaspoons minced fresh thyme**

1. Using sharp knife, cut through roast's fat cap in 1-inch crosshatch pattern, being careful not to cut into meat. Rub 2 tablespoons salt over entire roast and into crosshatch. Transfer to large plate and refrigerate, uncovered, for at least 24 hours or up to 96 hours.

2. Adjust oven rack to lower-middle position and heat oven to 250 degrees. Season roast with pepper and arrange, fat side up, on V-rack set in large roasting pan. Roast until meat registers 115 degrees for rare, 120 degrees for medium-rare, or 125 degrees for medium, 3 to 3½ hours. Transfer V-rack with roast to carving board, tent loosely with aluminum foil, and let rest for about 1 hour.

3. Meanwhile, increase oven temperature to 425 degrees. Pour off all but 2 tablespoons fat from pan. (If there isn't enough fat in pan, add vegetable oil to equal 2 tablespoons.) Toss carrots, parsnips, Brussels sprouts, onion, thyme, 1 teaspoon salt, and

½ teaspoon pepper with fat in pan. Roast vegetables, stirring halfway through roasting, until tender and browned, 45 to 50 minutes.

4. Remove pan from oven and heat broiler. Carefully nestle V-rack with roast among vegetables in pan. Broil roast until fat cap is evenly browned, rotating pan as necessary, about 5 minutes. Transfer roast to carving board, carve meat from bones, and cut into ¾-inch-thick slices. Season vegetables with salt and pepper to taste. Serve roast with vegetables.

BUY THE RIGHT ROAST

This recipe calls for a first-cut, bone-in standing rib roast, which contains ribs 9, 10, and 11 (the ribs that are closest to the tail of the steer; butchers often label this cut "loin-end"). First-cut roasts contain the largest eye of meat. While second-cut roasts are pretty good, too, they are slightly fattier and more irregular, making them more difficult to cook evenly. Since these cuts are often priced the same, it's worth your while to ask for the superior first-cut roast.

FIRST CUT
More meat, larger eye

SECOND CUT
More fat, smaller eye
(but still good)

CARVING A STANDING RIB ROAST

To carve a bone-in rib roast, simply hold the roast in place with a carving fork and cut parallel to the rib bones to remove the meat in one big piece. Then slice and serve the meat.

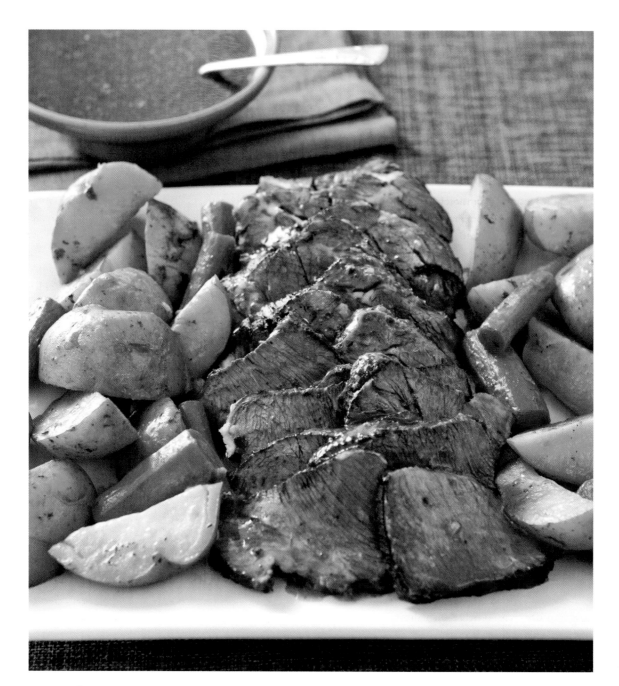

✔ WHY THIS RECIPE WORKS

Traditionally, this lazy cook's pot roast involves rubbing a chuck roast with onion soup mix, wrapping it in foil, and cooking it in the oven until tender. While we liked the ease of this dish, we weren't fans of its artificial, salty taste. To develop oniony flavor with ease, we started with onion powder and salt, but ditched the monosodium glutamate in favor of soy sauce, which enhanced the roast's beefy flavor. Brown sugar added sweetness and depth, while a surprise ingredient, a little espresso powder, provided toasty complexity. Dividing the roast into two halves allowed us to apply more of the flavorful spice rub to its exterior.

Chuck Roast in Foil

SERVES 4 TO 6

You will need an 18-inch-wide roll of heavy-duty aluminum foil for wrapping the roast. We prefer to use small red potatoes, measuring 1 to 2 inches in diameter, in this recipe.

RUB

3	tablespoons cornstarch
4	teaspoons onion powder
2	teaspoons packed light brown sugar
2	teaspoons salt
1	teaspoon pepper
1	teaspoon garlic powder
1	teaspoon instant espresso powder
1	teaspoon dried thyme
½	teaspoon celery seeds

CHUCK ROAST

1	(4-pound) boneless beef chuck-eye roast, pulled apart at seams, fat trimmed to ¼ inch, and tied at 1-inch intervals
2	onions, peeled and quartered
1	pound small red potatoes, quartered
4	carrots, peeled and cut into 1½-inch pieces
2	bay leaves
2	tablespoons soy sauce

1. FOR THE RUB: Adjust oven rack to lower-middle position and heat oven to 300 degrees. Combine all ingredients in small bowl.

2. FOR THE CHUCK ROAST: Pat roast dry with paper towels. Place two 30 by 18-inch sheets of heavy-duty aluminum foil perpendicular to each other inside large roasting pan. Place onions, potatoes, carrots, and bay leaves in center of foil and drizzle with soy sauce. Set roasts on top of vegetables. Rub roasts all over with rub.

Fold opposite corners of foil toward each other and crimp edges tightly to seal. Transfer pan to oven and cook until meat is completely tender, about 4½ hours.

3. Remove roasts from foil pouch and place on carving board. Tent meat with foil and let rest for 20 minutes. Remove onions and bay leaves. Using slotted spoon, place carrots and potatoes on serving platter. Strain contents of roasting pan through fine-mesh strainer into fat separator. Let liquid settle, then pour defatted pan juices into serving bowl.

4. Remove kitchen twine from roasts. Slice roasts thin against grain and transfer to platter with vegetables. Pour ½ cup pan juices over meat. Serve with remaining pan juices.

BACK IN FASHION

Family Circle magazine once asked Peg Bracken, author of the mega-bestselling *I Hate to Cook Book*, to select her greatest-hits list for the hate-to-cook set. Her list included such gems as Stayabed Stew ("For those days when you're en negligee, en bed, with a murder story and a box of bonbons") and the Basic I-Hate-to-Cook Muffin (made by combining beer and muffin mix). But one classic super-easy dish of the day was notably absent: chuck roast with instant onion soup. "Done to death," Bracken explained, adding, "I remember years ago when every working wife in the land was sprinkling a package of dried onion soup mix onto a chunk of chuck steak...the thing was bigger than a Hula-Hoop, and it died, of course, of overexposure." But guess what? The hula hoop is back, and in its new incarnation, chuck roast in foil is poised from a comeback, too.

✔ WHY THIS RECIPE WORKS

A crown roast—two bone-in pork loin roasts tied together in a round—can feed a holiday crowd and offers a dramatic presentation, but its shape presents serious challenges to even cooking. Simply roasting it yielded meat overcooked on the outside and undercooked around the inner circle. The solution? We turned the roast upside down to allow more air to circulate and to better expose the thickest part of the roast to the heat. For a side, we opted for potatoes, shallots, and apples roasted in the pan alongside the meat. Pureeing the apples into a rich pan sauce gave us both fruity flavor and a nice, thick consistency.

Crown Roast of Pork

SERVES 10 TO 12

A crown roast is two bone-in pork loin roasts tied into a crown shape, with the rib bones frenched and chine bones removed. This can be difficult to do, so ask your butcher to make this roast for you. We wrap extra kitchen twine around the widest part of the roast to provide more support when flipping. Use potatoes that measure 1 to 2 inches in diameter.

	Kosher salt and pepper
3	tablespoons minced fresh thyme
2	tablespoons minced fresh rosemary
5	garlic cloves, minced
1	(8- to 10-pound) pork crown roast
2	pounds small red potatoes
10	ounces shallots, peeled and halved
2	Golden Delicious apples, peeled, cored, and halved
8	tablespoons unsalted butter, melted
½	cup apple cider
1	cup chicken broth

1. Combine 3 tablespoons salt, 1 tablespoon pepper, thyme, rosemary, and garlic in bowl; reserve 2 teaspoons for vegetables. Pat pork dry with paper towels and rub with remaining herb salt. Wrap kitchen twine twice around widest part of roast and tie tightly. Refrigerate roast, covered, for 6 to 24 hours.

2. Adjust oven rack to lower-middle position and heat oven to 475 degrees. Place V-rack inside large roasting pan. Toss potatoes, shallots, apples, 4 tablespoons butter, and reserved herb salt in large bowl and transfer to pan. Arrange roast bone side down in V-rack and brush with remaining 4 tablespoons butter. Roast until meat is well browned and registers 110 degrees, about 1 hour.

3. Remove roast from oven and reduce oven temperature to 300 degrees. Using 2 bunches of paper towels, flip roast bone side up. Add apple cider to pan and return to oven, rotating direction of pan. Roast until meat registers 140 degrees, 30 to 50 minutes. Place meat on carving board, tent loosely with aluminum foil, and let rest for 15 to 20 minutes.

4. Transfer apple halves to blender and potatoes and shallots to bowl. Pour pan juices into fat separator, let liquid settle for 5 minutes, then pour into blender. Add chicken broth to blender with apples and pan juices and process until smooth, about 1 minute. Transfer sauce to medium saucepan and bring to simmer over medium heat. Season with salt and pepper to taste. Cover and keep warm. Remove twine from roast and slice meat between bones. Serve with vegetables and sauce.

COOKING CROWN ROAST OF PORK EVENLY

1. Using kitchen twine, make 2 loops around widest part of the roast and tie securely to help crown hold its shape when flipped.

2. Place pork bone side down on V-rack and adjust bones to steady roast. Roast about 1 hour, until meat registers 110 degrees.

3. Using paper towels to protect your hands, flip hot roast bone side up and set it back on V-rack to finish cooking in gentle oven.

✔ WHY THIS RECIPE WORKS

Pork shoulder's fat content and marbling mean it requires low and slow cooking to become tender—making it a natural for the slow cooker. For a full-flavored sauce, we browned the pork, then sautéed onions and garlic with tomato paste in the browned bits left behind before adding them to the slow cooker. A little instant tapioca produced just the right texture in the braising liquid. White wine added brightness and a splash of white wine vinegar, stirred in at the end of cooking, refreshed the wine flavor. Hearty root vegetables and diced tomatoes, which cooked along with the roast, balanced the flavors.

Slow-Cooker Pork Pot Roast

SERVES 8

This roast is sometimes sold in elastic netting that must be removed before cooking. If you cannot find 2½- to 3-pound pork picnic shoulder roasts, you can substitute one 6-pound pork picnic shoulder roast; cut it into two pieces and prepare as directed.

2	(2½- to 3-pound) boneless pork picnic shoulder roasts, trimmed
	Salt and pepper
2	tablespoons vegetable oil
2	onions, chopped
6	garlic cloves, minced
1	tablespoon tomato paste
½	cup white wine
1	(28-ounce) can diced tomatoes, drained
3	tablespoons instant tapioca
2	teaspoons minced fresh thyme
1	pound carrots, peeled, halved lengthwise, and cut into 2-inch pieces
1	pound parsnips, peeled, halved lengthwise, and cut into 2-inch pieces
2	teaspoons white wine vinegar

1. Open each roast and trim any excess fat, then tie each roast with kitchen twine at 1½-inch intervals and once around length of roasts. Pat roasts dry with paper towels and season with salt and pepper. Heat 2 teaspoons oil in 12-inch skillet over medium-high heat until just smoking. Brown roasts all over, about 10 minutes. Transfer to slow cooker.

2. Add onions and 2 teaspoons oil to now-empty skillet and cook until browned, about 5 minutes. Add garlic and tomato paste and cook until fragrant, about 1 minute. Stir in wine and simmer, scraping up browned bits with wooden spoon, until thickened, about 2 minutes. Stir in tomatoes, tapioca, and thyme; transfer to slow cooker.

3. Toss carrots, parsnips, ¼ teaspoon salt, ¼ teaspoon pepper, and remaining 2 teaspoons oil in bowl until vegetables are well coated. Scatter vegetable mixture over pork. Cover and cook on low until meat is tender, 9 to 10 hours (or cook on high 4 to 5 hours).

4. Transfer roasts to carving board, tent with aluminum foil, and let rest for 10 minutes. Remove twine from roasts and cut meat into ½-inch-thick slices; transfer to serving platter. Using slotted spoon, transfer carrots and parsnips to platter with pork. Stir vinegar into sauce and season with salt and pepper to taste. Serve, passing sauce separately.

TWO ROASTS ARE BETTER THAN ONE

We like to use two smaller roasts for this recipe, because the meat cooks more quickly and the small roasts are easier to manage in the slow cooker—and to find in the supermarket. Most boneless pork shoulder roasts come bound in string netting, which is difficult to remove after cooking. We prefer to cut the netting off before cooking, trim the roasts, and then tie each one with kitchen twine.

1. Remove netting from pork roasts. Open each roast and trim any excess fat.

2. Tie roasts separately. To ensure even cooking, fold smaller lobes under, then tie each roast with kitchen twine every 1½ inches around circumference and once around length.

WHY THIS RECIPE WORKS

For this Sunday dinner–worthy pork roast, we skipped lean loins and opted for a deeply flavored and inexpensive pork butt roast, which we flavored with a spice rub of cracked peppercorns, rosemary, sage, fennel seeds, and garlic. Cooking the roast in a low oven for seven hours rendered its fat and softened its tough connective tissue. For easy slicing, we refrigerated the cooked roast overnight until firm, then reheated it in the oven while we made a simple sauce from apple cider, apple jelly, and cider vinegar.

Old-Fashioned Roast Pork

SERVES 8

A heavy roasting pan with 3-inch sides is the best choice for this recipe, but a shallow broiler pan also works well. Boneless pork butt roast is often labeled Boston butt in the supermarket.

6	pounds boneless pork butt roast, fat trimmed to ⅛ inch, tied lengthwise and crosswise
3	garlic cloves, minced
2	teaspoons peppercorns, cracked
1½	teaspoons salt
1	tablespoon chopped fresh rosemary
1	tablespoon chopped fresh sage
1	tablespoon fennel seeds, chopped
2	large red onions, cut into 1-inch wedges
1	cup apple cider
¼	cup apple jelly
2	tablespoons cider vinegar

1. Adjust oven rack to lower-middle position and heat oven to 300 degrees. Pat pork dry with paper towels. Combine garlic, peppercorns, salt, rosemary, sage, and fennel seeds in small bowl. Rub roast with herb mixture.

2. Transfer to roasting pan and cook for 3 hours. Scatter onion wedges around roast, tossing onions in pan drippings to coat. (If roast has not produced any juices, toss onions with 1 tablespoon vegetable oil before adding to pan.) Continue roasting until meat is extremely tender and skewer inserted in center meets no resistance, 3½ to 4 hours. (Check pan juices every hour to make sure they have not evaporated. If necessary, add 2 cups water to pan and scrape up browned bits.)

3. Transfer roast to large baking dish, place onions in medium bowl, and pour pan drippings into 2-cup liquid measuring cup, adding enough water to measure 1½ cups. Let roast, onions, and drippings cool for 30 minutes, cover each with plastic wrap, and refrigerate overnight.

4. One hour before serving, adjust oven rack to middle position and heat oven to 300 degrees. Cut meat into ¼-inch slices and overlap in large baking dish. Skim off fat from pan drippings and transfer drippings and reserved onions to medium saucepan. Add cider, jelly, and vinegar and bring to boil over medium-high heat, then reduce to simmer. Spoon ½ cup sauce over pork slices and cover baking dish with aluminum foil. Place in oven and heat until very hot, 30 to 40 minutes.

5. Just before serving, reduce sauce until dark and thickened, 10 to 15 minutes. Serve pork, spooning onion mixture over meat or passing separately.

SECRETS TO OLD-FASHIONED FLAVOR

1. Trim any excess fat from pork, leaving behind ⅛-inch-thick layer. Tie trimmed roast tightly into uniform shape, lengthwise and then crosswise.

2. Rub mixture of rosemary, sage, fennel seeds, garlic, salt, and pepper over roast.

3. Roast pork for 3 hours, add onion wedges, and continue to roast until meat is extremely tender, 3½ to 4 hours more.

✔ WHY THIS RECIPE WORKS

Famous for its crispy skin, this Puerto Rican dish of long-cooked, heavily seasoned pork roast should result in flavorful meat along with its trademark crispy exterior. We rubbed a picnic shoulder with a salty sofrito (a paste of aromatics and herbs) the day before roasting, which kept the meat moist and packed a flavor punch. We then roasted the pork skin-side down, covered, which helped transform tough collagen into gelatin. Next, we removed the foil cover to ensure that our pork didn't taste steamed, and then turned the roast skin side up on a V-rack to dry the skin to prepare it for the last step—a quick roast at very high heat.

Puerto Rican Pork Roast

SERVES 8 TO 10

Depending on their size, you may need two bunches of cilantro. Crimp the foil tightly over the edges of the roasting pan in step 2 to minimize evaporation. Make sure to spray the V-rack in step 3.

1½	**cups chopped fresh cilantro leaves and stems**
1	**onion, chopped coarse**
¼	**cup kosher salt**
¼	**cup olive oil**
10	**garlic cloves, peeled**
2	**tablespoons pepper**
1	**tablespoon dried oregano**
1	**tablespoon ground cumin**
1	**(7-pound) bone-in pork picnic shoulder**
1	**tablespoon grated lime zest plus ⅓ cup juice (3 limes)**

1. Pulse 1 cup cilantro, onion, salt, oil, garlic, pepper, oregano, and cumin in food processor until finely ground, about 15 pulses, scraping down sides of bowl as needed. Pat pork dry with paper towels and rub sofrito all over. Wrap pork in plastic wrap and refrigerate for at least 12 hours or up to 24 hours.

2. Adjust oven rack to lower-middle position and heat oven to 450 degrees. Pour 8 cups water in large roasting pan. Unwrap pork and place skin side down in pan. Cover pan tightly with aluminum foil and roast for 90 minutes. Remove foil, reduce oven temperature to 375 degrees, and continue to roast for 2½ hours.

3. Remove pan from oven. Spray V-rack with vegetable oil spray. Gently slide metal spatula under pork to release skin from pan. Using folded dish towels, grasp ends of pork and transfer to V-rack, skin side up.

Wipe skin dry with paper towels. Place V-rack with pork in roasting pan. If pan looks dry, add 1 cup water. Return to oven and roast until pork registers 195 degrees, about 1 hour. (Add water as needed to keep bottom of pan from drying out.)

4. Line rimmed baking sheet with foil. Remove pan from oven. Transfer V-rack and pork to prepared sheet and return to oven. Immediately increase oven temperature to 500 degrees. Cook until pork skin is well browned and crispy (when tapped lightly with tongs, skin will sound hollow), 15 to 30 minutes, rotating sheet halfway through cooking. Transfer pork to carving board and let rest for 30 minutes.

5. Meanwhile, pour juices from pan into fat separator. Let liquid settle for 5 minutes, then pour off 1 cup defatted juices into large bowl. (If juices measure less than 1 cup, make up difference with water.) Whisk remaining ½ cup cilantro and lime zest and juice into bowl.

6. Remove crispy skin from pork in 1 large piece. Coarsely chop skin into bite-size pieces and set aside. Trim and discard excess fat from pork. Remove pork from bone and chop coarse. Transfer pork to bowl with cilantro-lime sauce and toss to combine. Serve pork, with crispy skin on side.

CREATING CRISPY SKIN

Elevating the roast on a V-rack to finish cooking crisps up the flavorful skin.

WHY THIS RECIPE WORKS

Ham glazed with sweet apple cider certainly sounds great, but most recipes lack serious apple flavor, not to mention they call for frequent basting. For a relatively hands-off ham that was infused with lots of apple flavor, we marinated the ham in apple cider spiked with warm spices. Baking the ham in an oven bag guarded against dried-out meat. And to give our ham a crusty, spicy-sweet exterior, we rolled back the bag once the ham was heated through, slathered on reduced apple cider, pressed a mixture of brown sugar and black pepper all over, and slid it back into the oven until caramelized.

Cider-Baked Ham

SERVES 16 TO 20

We prefer a bone-in, uncut, cured ham for this recipe, because the exterior layer of fat can be scored and helps create a nice crust. A spiral-sliced ham can be used instead, but there won't be much exterior fat, so skip the trimming and scoring in step 2. This recipe requires nearly a gallon of cider and a large oven bag. In step 4, be sure to stir the reduced cider mixture frequently to prevent scorching.

1	**cinnamon stick, broken into rough pieces**
¼	**teaspoon whole cloves**
3¼	**quarts apple cider**
8	**cups ice cubes**
1	**(7- to 10-pound) cured bone-in half ham, preferably shank end**
2	**tablespoons Dijon mustard**
1	**cup packed dark brown sugar**
1	**teaspoon pepper**
	Large oven bag

1. Toast cinnamon and cloves in large saucepan over medium heat until fragrant, about 3 minutes. Add 4 cups cider and bring to boil. Pour spiced cider into large stockpot or clean bucket, add 4 cups cider and ice, and stir until melted.

2. Meanwhile, remove skin from exterior of ham and trim fat to ¼-inch thickness. Score remaining fat at 1-inch intervals in crosshatch pattern. Transfer ham to container with chilled cider mixture (liquid should nearly cover ham) and refrigerate for at least 4 hours or up to 12 hours.

3. Discard cider mixture and transfer ham to large oven bag. Add 1 cup fresh cider to bag, tie securely, and cut 4 slits in top of bag. Transfer to large roasting pan and let stand at room temperature for 1½ hours.

4. Adjust oven rack to lowest position and heat oven to 300 degrees. Bake until ham registers 100 degrees, 1½ to 2½ hours. Meanwhile, bring remaining 4 cups cider and mustard to boil in saucepan. Reduce heat to medium-low and simmer, stirring often, until mixture is very thick and reduced to ⅓ cup, about 1 hour.

5. Combine sugar and pepper in bowl. Remove ham from oven and let rest for 5 minutes. Increase oven temperature to 400 degrees. Roll back oven bag and brush ham with reduced cider mixture. Using your fingers, carefully press sugar mixture onto exterior of ham. Return to oven and bake until dark brown and caramelized, about 20 minutes. Transfer ham to carving board, tent loosely with aluminum foil, and let rest for 15 minutes. Carve and serve.

SECRETS TO CIDER-BAKED HAM

1. Soaking ham in spice-infused cider lends concentrated flavor.

2. Baking ham with a cup of cider in oven bag keeps meat moist and lends even more cider flavor.

3. Brushing ham with sticky cider reduction provides big apple flavor and a base for crust.

4. Pressing mixture of brown sugar and pepper onto ham gives exterior spicy-sweet, crackly crust.

✔ WHY THIS RECIPE WORKS

Simply roasting asparagus and topping it with shaved Parmesan gives you limp spears and rubbery cheese. To get perfectly crisp-tender asparagus, we first salted it to rid it of excess moisture. For a cheesy coating that would stay put on the slender spears, we whipped a combination of honey and egg whites to soft peaks, dipped the asparagus in the mixture, then coated them with a mixture of bread crumbs and Parmesan. Finally, to reinforce the Parmesan flavor, we sprinkled the spears with more cheese at the end of roasting.

Parmesan-Crusted Asparagus

SERVES 4 TO 6

Avoid pencil-thin asparagus for this recipe. Work quickly when tossing the asparagus with the egg whites, as the salt on the asparagus will rapidly begin to deflate the whites.

- 2 pounds (½-inch-thick) asparagus, trimmed
  Salt and pepper
- 3 ounces Parmesan cheese, grated (1½ cups)
- ¾ cup panko bread crumbs
- 1 tablespoon unsalted butter, melted and cooled
  Pinch cayenne
- 2 large egg whites
- 1 teaspoon honey

1. Adjust oven rack to middle position and heat oven to 450 degrees. Line rimmed baking sheet with aluminum foil and spray with vegetable oil spray. Using fork, poke holes up and down stalks of asparagus. Toss asparagus with ½ teaspoon salt and let stand for 30 minutes on a paper towel–lined baking sheet.

2. Meanwhile, combine 1 cup Parmesan, panko, butter, ¼ teaspoon salt, ⅛ teaspoon pepper, and cayenne in bowl. Transfer half of panko mixture to shallow dish and reserve remaining mixture. Using stand mixer fitted with whisk, whip egg whites and honey on medium-low speed until foamy, about 1 minute. Increase speed to medium-high and whip until soft peaks form, 2 to 3 minutes. Scrape into 13 by 9-inch baking dish and toss asparagus in mixture. Working with 1 spear at a time, dredge half of asparagus in panko and transfer to aluminum foil–lined baking sheet. Refill shallow dish with reserved panko mixture and repeat with remaining half of asparagus.

3. Bake asparagus until just beginning to brown, 6 to 8 minutes. Sprinkle with remaining ½ cup Parmesan and continue to bake until cheese is melted and panko is golden brown, 6 to 8 minutes. Transfer to platter. Serve.

MAKING THE COATING STICK

1. Perforate and salt the asparagus to draw out excess moisture that could saturate the crumbs.

2. Whip egg whites to help crumbs adhere. Add honey for flavor and extra sticking power.

3. Work with 1 spear at a time to keep the bread crumbs from clumping.

✔ WHY THIS RECIPE WORKS

Raw Brussels sprout salad isn't as weird as it sounds: Brussels sprouts are very much like miniature cabbages in both texture and taste. To make this slaw-like salad, we thinly sliced the sprouts and tossed them with a bright, lemony vinaigrette with a touch of Dijon. We briefly marinated the salad in the vinaigrette to soften and season the sprouts. We topped the sprouts with toasted pine nuts and salty Pecorino Romano for a salad that's so delicious it can turn Brussels sprout loathers into Brussels sprout lovers.

Brussels Sprout Salad

Slice the sprouts as thin as possible. Shred the Pecorino Romano on the large holes of a box grater.

3	tablespoons lemon juice
2	tablespoons Dijon mustard
1	small shallot, minced
1	garlic clove, minced
	Salt and pepper
6	tablespoons extra-virgin olive oil
2	pounds Brussels sprouts, trimmed, halved, and sliced very thin
3	ounces Pecorino Romano cheese, shredded (1 cup)
½	cup pine nuts, toasted

1. Whisk lemon juice, mustard, shallot, garlic, and ½ teaspoon salt together in large bowl. Slowly whisk in oil until incorporated. Toss Brussels sprouts with vinaigrette and let sit for at least 30 minutes or up to 2 hours.

2. Fold in Pecorino and pine nuts. Season with salt and pepper to taste. Serve.

BRUSSELS SPROUT SALAD WITH CHEDDAR, HAZELNUTS, AND APPLE

Substitute 1 cup shredded sharp cheddar for Pecorino and ½ cup hazelnuts, toasted, skinned, and chopped, for pine nuts. Add 1 Granny Smith apple, cored and cut into ½-inch pieces.

BRUSSELS SPROUT SALAD WITH SMOKED GOUDA, PECANS, AND DRIED CHERRIES

Substitute 1 cup shredded smoked gouda for Pecorino and ½ cup pecans, toasted and chopped, for pine nuts. Add ½ cup chopped dried cherries.

HOW TO SLICE BRUSSELS SPROUTS

You can use the slicing disk of your food processor or slice the sprouts with a chef's knife. Follow these steps to do the latter safely and quickly.

1. TRIM: Trim the stem end of each sprout and then cut each sprout in half through the cut end.

2. SLICE: With the flat surface on the cutting board, thinly slice each half.

✔️ WHY THIS RECIPE WORKS

Conventional wisdom holds that anything but the gentlest treatment turns mashed potatoes into wallpaper paste, but we think our mixer-whipped spuds prove otherwise. For the lightest, fluffiest potatoes, we found high-starch russets worked best. Boiling the potatoes added extra water, resulting in a flat, not fluffy, finished dish. The best technique was to rinse excess starch from the raw potatoes, steam them, and then dry them in the pot on the stovetop over low heat. This process made them fluffier and better able to absorb the warm butter-and-milk mixture during whipping.

Whipped Potatoes

SERVES 8 TO 10

If your steamer basket has short legs (under 1¾ inches), the potatoes will sit in water as they cook and get wet. To prevent this, use balls of aluminum foil as steamer basket stilts. A stand mixer fitted with a whisk yields the smoothest potatoes, but a hand-held mixer may be used as well.

4	**pounds russet potatoes, peeled and cut into 1-inch pieces**
1½	**cups whole milk**
8	**tablespoons unsalted butter, cut into 8 pieces**
2	**teaspoons salt**
½	**teaspoon pepper**

1. Place cut potatoes in colander. Rinse under cold water until water runs clear, about 1 minute. Drain potatoes. Fill Dutch oven with 1 inch water and bring to boil. Place steamer basket in Dutch oven and fill with potatoes. Reduce heat to medium and cook, covered, until potatoes are tender, 20 to 25 minutes.

2. Heat milk, butter, salt, and pepper in small saucepan over medium-low heat, whisking until smooth, about 3 minutes; cover and keep warm.

3. Pour contents of Dutch oven into colander and return potatoes to dry pot. Stir over low heat until potatoes are thoroughly dried, about 1 minute. Using stand mixer fitted with whisk, break potatoes into small pieces on low speed, about 30 seconds. Add milk mixture in steady stream until incorporated. Increase speed to high and whip until potatoes are light and fluffy and no lumps remain, about 2 minutes. Serve.

CHOOSING YOUR MIXING METHOD

Don't try this recipe in your food processor—its sharp blades cut open the starch granules and turn the potatoes to glue. The beating motion of the mixer makes smooth, fluffy potatoes every time.

DON'T DO IT
A food processor's blade makes gluey mashed potatoes.

WHIP SMART
Use the mixer for light, fluffy whipped potatoes.

WHIP IT GOOD

In all likelihood, whipped potatoes owe their mid 20th-century fame to the Sunbeam Mixmaster. The appliance, first manufactured in 1930 and quickly enshrined as the must-have kitchen tool for American housewives, actually had a Mix-Finder Dial setting for whipped potatoes—speed 4 or 5, depending on the model. Whipping potatoes in the Mixmaster, the manufacturer claimed, saved "one-third the time usually taken by hand." But then, this machine promised time savings on just about every kitchen task. The 17 available attachments on early models included not only a slicer/shredder and an ice cream maker, but also a butter churn, a string bean slicer, and (our personal favorite) a pea sheller. It's no wonder this kitchen tool became perhaps the most famous appliance of the 20th century.

WHY THIS RECIPE WORKS

Duchess potatoes take mashed potatoes to the next level, enriching them with egg and piping them into decorative rosettes before baking. To cook our spuds, we tried boiling, but this made them water-logged; baking dried them out. Parcooking them in the microwave and finishing the rosettes in a hot oven proved best. For a potato mixture that was the right texture for piping, we stirred in butter, eggs, and cream while the potatoes were still hot, then added more butter once the potatoes had cooled. Baking powder ensured our picture-perfect Duchess Potatoes had the perfect airy, light texture to match.

Duchess Potatoes

SERVES 8

For the smoothest, most uniform texture, use a food mill or ricer to mash the potatoes. Choose potatoes of the same size so that they cook evenly.

3	pounds russet potatoes
1	cup heavy cream
6	tablespoons unsalted butter, cut into ¼-inch pieces and softened
1	large egg plus 1 large yolk, lightly beaten
1¼	teaspoons salt
½	teaspoon pepper
½	teaspoon baking powder
	Pinch nutmeg
	Vegetable oil spray

1. Adjust oven rack to upper-middle position and heat oven to 475 degrees. Meanwhile, prick potatoes all over with fork, place on plate, and microwave until tender, 18 to 25 minutes, turning potatoes over after 10 minutes.

2. Cut potatoes in half. When cool enough to handle, scoop flesh into large bowl and mash until no lumps remain. Add cream, 3 tablespoons butter, egg and yolk, salt, pepper, baking powder, and nutmeg and continue to mash until potatoes are smooth. Let cool to room temperature, about 10 minutes. Gently fold in remaining butter until pieces are evenly distributed.

3. Transfer potato mixture to piping bag fitted with ½-inch star tip. Pipe eight 4-inch-wide mounds of potato onto rimmed baking sheet. Spray lightly with vegetable oil spray and bake until golden brown, 15 to 20 minutes. Serve.

TO MAKE AHEAD: Once piped onto baking sheet, potatoes can be covered loosely with plastic wrap and refrigerated for 24 hours. Remove plastic and spray lightly with vegetable oil spray before baking.

TWO PATHS TO PERFECT PIPING

With a pastry bag fitted with a star tip, making beautiful duchess potatoes is child's play. If you don't have a pastry bag, don't worry: There's another easy way.

WITH PASTRY BAG: Pipe 4-inch circle of potato mixture onto baking sheet. Continue to pipe upward in circles to form 3-inch-high peak.

WITHOUT PASTRY BAG: Scoop potato mixture into zipper-lock bag, snip off 1 corner, and pipe as directed. Use tines of fork to create rippled surface.

FREEZER FRIENDLY

Our Duchess Potatoes freeze beautifully, which is handy, as they're ideal for a party. Pipe the mounds onto a rimmed baking sheet and then cover lightly with plastic wrap. Freeze for 2 hours until solid and transfer the potatoes to an airtight container (or leave them on the baking sheet if you've got the space). When you are ready to bake them, arrange on a rimmed baking sheet (or simply remove the plastic), spray lightly with vegetable oil spray, and bake according to our recipe. They can go straight from freezer to oven, and they won't even need any extra time.

Syracuse Salt Potatoes

SERVES 6 TO 8

You will need 1¼ cups of noniodized table salt, 1½ cups of Morton kosher salt, or 2½ cups of Diamond Crystal kosher salt to equal 14 ounces. We prefer to use small potatoes, measuring 1 to 2 inches in diameter, in this recipe.

8   **cups water**

14   **ounces salt**

3   **pounds small white or red potatoes**

8   **tablespoons unsalted butter, cut into 8 pieces**

2   **tablespoons minced fresh chives**

1   **teaspoon pepper**

1. Set wire rack in rimmed baking sheet. Bring water to boil in Dutch oven over medium-high heat. Stir in salt and potatoes and cook until potatoes are just tender, 20 to 30 minutes. Drain potatoes and transfer to prepared baking sheet. Let dry until salty crust forms, about 1 minute.

2. Meanwhile, microwave butter, chives, and pepper in medium bowl until butter is melted, about 1 minute. Transfer potatoes to serving bowl and serve, passing butter separately.

SALT MAGIC

Just out of the salty water, the potatoes will look like any other boiled potato.

One minute after they've been drained, the characteristic salt crust will appear on the potato skins.

The high salinity means the cooking water gets hotter than normal, resulting in extra-creamy potato flesh.

SELLING SALT POTATOES

Salt potatoes has its origins in the mid-1800s when Irish salt workers in the Syracuse area would cook unpeeled new potatoes in huge evaporation vats filled with boiling salt water. In 1914, John Hinerwadel, owner of an eponymous central New York clambake company, began offering salt potatoes on his menu. They became so popular that Mr. Hinerwadel started selling salt potato kits—complete with a sack of small white potatoes and a packet of salt—so people could make the potatoes at home. The red and white bags of potatoes with the signature red and yellow sun are still sold in the Syracuse area.

Mashed Potato Casserole

SERVES 8

The casserole may also be baked in a 13 by 9-inch pan.

4	pounds russet potatoes, peeled and cut into 1-inch chunks
12	tablespoons unsalted butter, cut into 12 pieces
½	cup half-and-half
½	cup chicken broth
2	teaspoons Dijon mustard
1	garlic clove, minced
2	teaspoons salt
4	large eggs
¼	cup finely chopped fresh chives

1. Adjust oven rack to upper-middle position and heat oven to 375 degrees. Bring potatoes and water to cover by 1 inch to boil in large pot over high heat. Reduce heat to medium and simmer until potatoes are tender, about 20 minutes.

2. Heat butter, half-and-half, broth, mustard, garlic, and salt in saucepan over medium-low heat until smooth, about 5 minutes. Keep warm.

3. Drain potatoes and transfer to large bowl. Using stand mixer fitted with paddle, beat potatoes on medium-low speed, slowly adding half-and-half mixture, until smooth and creamy, about 1 minute. Scrape down bowl; beat in eggs, 1 at a time, until incorporated, about 1 minute. Fold in chives.

4. Transfer potato mixture to greased 3-quart baking dish. Smooth surface of potatoes, then use fork to make peaked design on top of casserole. Bake until potatoes rise and begin to brown, about 35 minutes. Let cool for 10 minutes. Serve.

SECRETS TO PERFECT MASHED POTATO CASSEROLE

1. When poured into casserole dish, mashed potatoes will look very soupy. They will firm up and rise in oven.

2. For better browning and an impressive presentation, use fork to make peaked design on top of casserole.

CAN EVAPORATED MILK BE SUBSTITUTED FOR HALF-AND-HALF?

Sorry, the answer is no. We know this because we substituted evaporated milk (whole milk cooked to remove half the water, resulting in 8 percent milk fat) in a handful of our recipes—scalloped corn, mashed potatoes, vanilla pudding, and carrot soup—that call for half-and-half (a mixture of milk and cream that ranges from 10.5 percent to 18 percent milk fat). The savory dishes made with evaporated milk in place of half-and-half tasted tinny, and the desserts were too sweet.

Not willing to give up, we diluted the evaporated milk with water to approximate its pre-evaporated state (4 percent milk fat) and then used it in place of the half-and-half in our test recipes. Tasters didn't like that either, detecting a mildly cooked flavor. We tried other substitutes: Heavy cream, because of its high milk-fat content (at least 36 percent) muted the bright flavors in our recipes; whole milk made the food less rich, no surprise, but the flavors remained lively. We were able to best approximate our local brand of half-and-half by using either ⅔ cup skim milk plus ⅓ cup heavy cream or ¾ cup whole milk plus ¼ cup heavy cream. Of course, to do this you'll need to have heavy cream on hand.

If you have heavy cream and either skim or whole milk, you can mix up a good substitute for half-and-half. If you don't mind a slightly thinner consistency and lighter flavor, whole milk will work in most recipes.

⅓ CUP HEAVY CREAM + ⅔ CUP SKIM MILK =
1 CUP HALF-AND-HALF

¼ CUP HEAVY CREAM + ¾ CUP WHOLE MILK =
1 CUP HALF-AND-HALF

Creamy Mashed Sweet Potatoes

SERVES 4 TO 6

This recipe can be doubled and prepared in a Dutch oven, but the cooking time will need to be doubled as well.

- 2 **pounds sweet potatoes, peeled, quartered, and sliced ¼ inch thick**
- 4 **tablespoons unsalted butter, cut into 4 pieces**
- 3 **tablespoons heavy cream**
- 1 **teaspoon sugar**
  Salt and pepper

1. Combine sweet potatoes, butter, 2 tablespoons cream, sugar, ½ teaspoon salt, and ¼ teaspoon pepper in large saucepan. Cook, covered, over low heat until potatoes are fall-apart tender, 35 to 40 minutes.

2. Off heat, add remaining 1 tablespoon cream and mash sweet potatoes with potato masher. Serve.

HERBED MASHED SWEET POTATOES WITH CARAMELIZED ONION

If you prefer, substitute ¼ teaspoon dried thyme for the thyme sprig.

Add 1 sprig fresh thyme to saucepan in step 1. While sweet potatoes are cooking, melt 1 tablespoon butter in 8-inch nonstick skillet and add 1 small onion, chopped, ¼ teaspoon sugar, and ¼ teaspoon salt. Cook over low heat until onion is caramelized, about 15 minutes. Remove thyme and mash potatoes as directed. Stir in onion and 1 tablespoon sour cream.

SMOKEHOUSE MASHED SWEET POTATOES

Add ⅛ teaspoon cayenne pepper to saucepan in step 1. Mash sweet potatoes with ½ cup shredded smoked Gouda cheese and cover with lid until cheese melts, about 1 minute. Sprinkle with 6 slices chopped cooked bacon and 1 thinly sliced scallion.

NO-BOIL SWEET POTATOES

Boiling sweet potatoes in lots of liquid—as you would regular potatoes—is not a good idea. Sweet potatoes will soak up too much water, and the resulting mash will be a soggy mess. Better to cook them in a small amount of liquid. Just 2 tablespoons of heavy cream (plus a little butter), along with the water released from the sweet potatoes as they cook, is enough to steam them to tenderness.

THE SLICE IS RIGHT

It is imperative to cut the sweet potato into thin, even slices to ensure perfect cooking.

1. Quarter each peeled sweet potato lengthwise.

2. Cut each quarter into ¼-inch slices crosswise.

WHY THIS RECIPE WORKS

For a fluffy, soufflé-style sweet corn spoonbread with deep corn flavor, we focused on flavor, then texture. Sautéing the corn in butter, before steeping it in milk and pureeing it, ensured that the sweet corn flavor permeated our spoonbread. To make sure the cornmeal didn't impart a gritty texture, we soaked it in the milk beforehand. And to guarantee a stable foam and an impressive rise, we beat the egg whites with a bit of cream of tartar.

Sweet Corn Spoonbread

SERVES 6

You will need three ears of corn to yield 2 cups. Frozen corn, thawed and drained well, can be substituted for the fresh corn.

1	cup cornmeal
2¾	cups whole milk
4	tablespoons unsalted butter
2	cups fresh corn
1	teaspoon sugar
1	teaspoon salt
⅛	teaspoon cayenne pepper
3	large eggs, separated
¼	teaspoon cream of tartar

1. Adjust oven rack to middle position and heat oven to 400 degrees. Grease 1½-quart soufflé dish or 8-inch baking dish. Whisk cornmeal and ¾ cup milk in bowl until combined; set aside.

2. Melt butter in Dutch oven over medium-high heat. Cook corn until beginning to brown, about 3 minutes. Stir in remaining 2 cups milk, sugar, salt, and cayenne and bring to boil. Off heat, cover mixture and let steep for 15 minutes.

3. Transfer warm corn mixture to blender or food processor and puree until smooth. Return to pot and bring to boil. Reduce heat to low and add cornmeal mixture, whisking constantly, until thickened, 2 to 3 minutes; transfer to large bowl and let cool to room temperature, about 20 minutes. Once mixture is cool, whisk in egg yolks until combined.

4. Using stand mixer fitted with whisk, beat egg whites and cream of tartar on medium-low speed until foamy, about 1 minute. Increase speed to medium-high and whip until stiff peaks form, 3 to 4 minutes. Whisk one-third of whites into corn mixture, then gently fold in remaining whites until combined. Scrape mixture into prepared dish and transfer to oven. Reduce oven temperature to 350 degrees and bake until spoonbread is golden brown and has risen above rim of dish, about 45 minutes. Serve immediately.

INDIVIDUAL SPOONBREADS

To make individual spoonbreads, divide batter among 6 greased 7-ounce ramekins. Arrange ramekins on rimmed baking sheet and bake as directed, reducing cooking time to 30 to 35 minutes.

EGG WHITES 101

Egg whites are most easily whipped in a very clean metal bowl with a pinch of cream of tartar, which promotes stabilization.

SOFT PEAKS
Soft peaks will droop slightly downward from tip of whisk or beater.

STIFF PEAKS
Stiff peaks will stand up tall on their own.

OVERWHIPPED
Overwhipped egg whites will look curdled and separated; if you reach this point, start over with new whites and clean bowl.

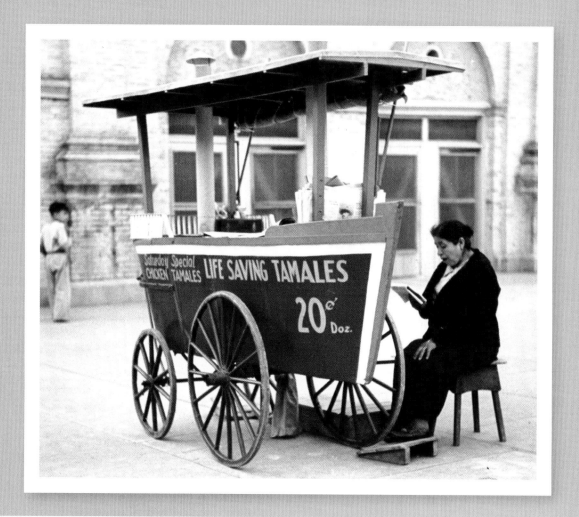

MEXICAN MIGRATION TO THE UNITED STATES BEGAN AT THE END OF the 19th century. As immigrants adapted to available foods and American tastes, Mexican food morphed into a new cuisine—less spicy and less labor-intensive. During the translation process, many of the Mexican originals became meatier and heavier. (A similar phenomenon occurred when Italian dishes were adapted in the U.S., with recipes becoming cheesier and richer.) For example, enchiladas and tacos, which had been commonly served in Mexico as street food (and eaten as a snack), made their way onto restaurant menus in new ways, slathered with sauce and cheese and rounded out with rice and beans. As Tex-Mex food became popular in all regions of the country, dishes were increasingly Americanized. Today, some might argue that Tex-Mex is the most popular American regional cuisine. Taco and enchilada kits have become supermarket staples, while burritos are as common on the fast-food scene as burgers.

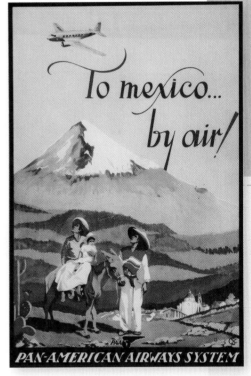

In general, our approach to Tex-Mex cooking is to honor the complex origins of these dishes and their unique cross-border heritage, while making sure the food is fresh and vibrant. We focus on several Tex-Mex favorites (no kits required), such as hearty beefy nachos, chicken tacos perfect for any weeknight, and stick-to-your ribs chili con carne that relies on supermarket ingredients but doesn't skimp on complex flavor.

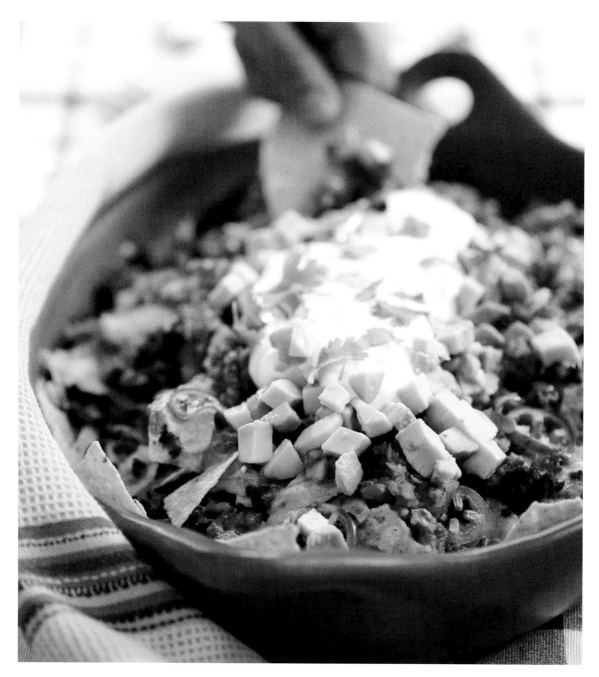

✓ WHY THIS RECIPE WORKS

Too often, nacho recipes produce soggy chips loaded down with bland, greasy beef, dry beans, and cold strings of cheese. Instead, we wanted hearty nachos that are crisp, flavorful, and fresh. Boldly seasoning our beef with a mixture of spices and other flavorings caused the flavor to pop. While many nacho recipes call for cheddar cheese, we found it didn't melt nearly as well as pepper Jack, which melted smoothly and added a kick, too.

Ultimate Spicy Beef Nachos

SERVES 8

In addition to our One-Minute Salsa (recipe follows), garnish the nachos with sour cream, chopped cilantro, and diced avocado.

REFRIED BEANS

- ½ cup canned refried beans
- 3 tablespoons shredded pepper Jack cheese
- 1 tablespoon chopped canned jalapeños

SPICY BEEF

- 2 teaspoons vegetable oil
- 1 small onion, chopped fine
- 3 garlic cloves, minced
- 1 tablespoon chili powder
- 1 teaspoon ground cumin
- ½ teaspoon dried oregano
- 1 teaspoon salt
- 1 pound 90 percent lean ground beef
- 2 tablespoons tomato paste
- 1 teaspoon packed brown sugar
- 1½ teaspoons minced canned chipotle chile in adobo sauce, plus 1 teaspoon adobo sauce
- ½ cup water
- 2 teaspoons lime juice

- 1 (9.5-ounce) bag tortilla chips
- 1 pound pepper Jack cheese, shredded (4 cups)
- 2 jalapeño chiles, sliced into thin rings
- 1 recipe One-Minute Salsa

1. Adjust oven rack to middle position and heat oven to 400 degrees.

2. **FOR THE REFRIED BEANS:** Pulse ingredients in food processor until smooth, about 10 pulses. Transfer to bowl and cover with plastic wrap.

3. **FOR THE SPICY BEEF:** Heat oil in large skillet over medium heat until shimmering. Cook onion until softened, about 4 minutes. Add garlic, chili powder, cumin, oregano, and salt and cook until fragrant, about 1 minute. Add beef and cook, breaking meat into small bits with wooden spoon and scraping pan bottom to prevent scorching, until no longer pink, about 5 minutes. Add tomato paste, sugar, chipotle, and adobo sauce and cook until paste begins to darken, about 1 minute. Add water, bring to simmer, and cook over medium-low until mixture is nearly dry, 5 to 7 minutes. Stir in lime juice and transfer mixture to plate lined with several layers of paper towels. Use more paper towels to blot up excess grease.

4. **TO ASSEMBLE:** Spread half of chips on large ovensafe serving platter or in 13 by 9-inch baking dish. Dollop half of bean mixture over chips, then spread evenly. Scatter half of beef mixture over beans, top with 2 cups cheese and half of jalapeños. Repeat with remaining chips, beans, beef, cheese, and jalapeños. Bake until cheese is melted and just beginning to brown, 12 to 14 minutes. Serve with salsa and other suggested garnishes.

ONE-MINUTE SALSA

MAKES ABOUT 1 CUP

Make sure to drain both the tomatoes and the jalapeños before processing. The salsa will keep for two days in the refrigerator. Season to taste before serving.

- ½ small red onion
- ¼ cup fresh cilantro leaves
- 2 tablespoons jarred jalapeños, drained
- 1 tablespoon lime juice
- 1 garlic clove, peeled
- ¼ teaspoon salt
- 1 (14.5-ounce) can diced tomatoes, drained

Pulse onion, cilantro, jalapeños, lime juice, garlic, and salt in food processor until roughly chopped, about 5 pulses. Add tomatoes and pulse until chopped, about 2 pulses. Transfer mixture to fine-mesh strainer and drain briefly. Serve.

✓ WHY THIS RECIPE WORKS

With bold Southwestern flavors and an appealing ingredient list, seven-layer dip recipes sound like a hit. But most versions of this party classic assume that guests won't notice the messy layers and tired flavors. In our version, canned black beans stood in for refried beans, while garlic, chili powder, and lime juice added flavor. We found that sour cream on its own quickly watered down our dip, but combining it with cheese gave this layer more structure.

Ultimate Seven-Layer Dip

SERVES 8 TO 10

This recipe is usually served in a clear dish so you can see the layers. For a crowd, double the recipe and serve in a 13 by 9-inch glass baking dish. If you don't have time to make fresh guacamole as called for, simply mash three avocados with 3 tablespoons lime juice and ½ teaspoon salt.

4 large tomatoes, cored, seeded, and chopped fine

2 jalapeño chiles, stemmed, seeded, and minced

3 tablespoons chopped fresh cilantro

6 scallions (2 minced, 4 with green parts sliced thin and white parts discarded)

2 tablespoons plus 2 teaspoons lime juice (2 limes)

Salt

1 (15-ounce) can black beans, drained but not rinsed

2 garlic cloves, minced

¾ teaspoon chili powder

1½ cups sour cream

1 pound pepper Jack cheese, shredded (4 cups)

1 recipe Chunky Guacamole (page 195)

Tortilla chips

1. Combine tomatoes, jalapeños, cilantro, minced scallions, and 2 tablespoons lime juice in medium bowl. Stir in ⅛ teaspoon salt and let stand until tomatoes begin to soften, about 30 minutes. Strain mixture into bowl and discard liquid.

2. Pulse black beans, garlic, remaining 2 teaspoons lime juice, chili powder, and ⅛ teaspoon salt in food processor until mixture resembles chunky paste, about 15 pulses. Transfer to bowl and wipe out food processor. Pulse sour cream and 2½ cups pepper Jack until smooth, about 15 pulses. Transfer to separate bowl.

3. Spread bean mixture evenly over bottom of 8-inch square baking dish or 1-quart glass bowl. Spread sour cream mixture evenly over bean layer and sprinkle evenly with remaining 1½ cups cheese. Spread guacamole over cheese and top with tomato mixture. Sprinkle with sliced scallion greens and serve with tortilla chips. (Dip can be refrigerated for up to 24 hours. Let dip stand at room temperature for 1 hour before serving.)

ULTIMATE SMOKY SEVEN-LAYER DIP

Cook 4 slices bacon in 10-inch skillet over medium-high heat until crisp, about 8 minutes. Drain on paper towel–lined plate and crumble. Pulse 1 to 3 teaspoons minced canned chipotle chile in adobo sauce with black beans in step 2. Garnish dip with crumbled bacon along with scallions.

PROCESSING YOUR PICO

Although the pico de gallo topping in our Ultimate Seven-Layer Dip adds lots of fresh flavor, chopping all the ingredients by hand takes some work. We found that a food processor gets the job done, but the texture won't be as perfectly uniform as pico made by hand. To make pico de gallo in the food processor, start by pulsing jalapeños with cilantro until finely chopped. Then add quartered, cored, and seeded tomatoes and pulse in 1-second bursts until the tomatoes are evenly chopped. Add minced scallions and lime juice. Strain as instructed.

SEEDING JALAPEÑOS

Most of the heat in a chile pepper is in the ribs and seeds. An easy way to remove both is simply to cut the pepper in half lengthwise, then, starting at the end opposite the stem, use a melon baller to scoop down the inside of each half. (You can also use the sharp edge of the melon baller to cut off the stem.)

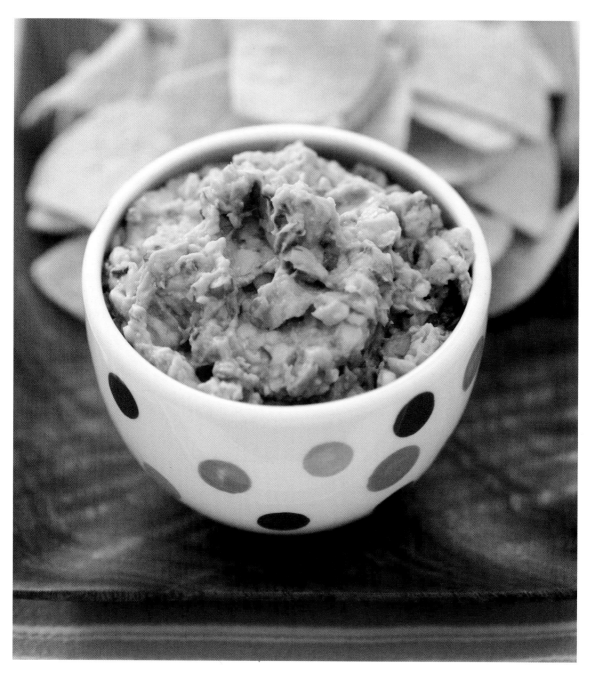

WHY THIS RECIPE WORKS

The best guacamole starts with ripe avocados, but other ingredients often overwhelm their delicate flavor. Tasters liked the flavor of minced garlic in guacamole, but thought raw onions were just too harsh. Instead, scallions lent a mellower onion flavor. Steeping them in lime juice for a few minutes before combining them with the avocados mellowed their flavor even more. To provide some textural contrast to our guacamole, we chopped the avocados and then mashed just two-thirds of the chunks.

Chunky Guacamole

MAKES ABOUT 3 CUPS

Preparing the guacamole ahead of time helps the flavors marry, but it should not be prepared more than one day in advance. To prevent the dip from turning brown, press a sheet of plastic wrap directly onto the surface and refrigerate until ready to use. We prefer pebbly Hass avocados to the smoother Fuerte variety.

2   **scallions, green and white parts separated and sliced thin**

1   **jalapeño chile, stemmed, seeded, and minced**

1   **small garlic clove, minced**

¼   **teaspoon finely grated lime zest plus 2 tablespoons juice**

3   **avocados, halved, pitted, and cubed**

3   **tablespoons chopped fresh cilantro**

    Salt

1. Combine scallion whites, jalapeño, garlic, and lime juice in large bowl. Let sit for 30 minutes.

2. Add two-thirds of avocado pieces to bowl with jalapeño mixture and mash with potato masher until smooth. Gently fold remaining avocado pieces into mashed avocado mixture. Gently stir in lime zest, scallion greens, and cilantro. Season with salt to taste. Serve.

RIPENING AVOCADOS

Avocados have a notoriously small window of perfect ripeness. To see if we could broaden this time frame, we bought a case of unripe avocados and ripened them at room temperature and in the refrigerator three ways: on the counter (or refrigerator shelf), enclosed in a paper bag, and enclosed in a paper bag with pieces of green apple (fruit gives off ethylene gas, which helps many fruits and vegetables ripen more quickly). We also tried two more esoteric techniques: burying the avocados at room temperature in flour and in rice. In the end, the only thing that mattered was the temperature at which the avocados were stored.

At room temperature, rock-hard avocados ripened within two days, but many of them ended up ripening unevenly, developing soft spots and air pockets on one side just as the other side was ripening. After completely ripening, they lasted two days on average if kept at room temperature (stored in the fridge after ripening, they lasted five days). Avocados ripened in the refrigerator, whether in a bag or out in the open, took around four days to soften, but did so evenly. Stored in the fridge, they lasted a full five days before starting to show signs of overripening.

The bottom line: If you need your avocados to ripen sooner rather than later, keep them on the counter. Otherwise, for better quality, you're better off putting them in the fridge and allowing them to ripen slowly. In either case, store the ripened fruit in the fridge to extend its shelf life.

PREPARING AVOCADO FOR GUACAMOLE

1. Halve avocado. Strike pit sharply with chef's knife. Twist blade to remove pit, then use dish towel to pull pit off blade.

2. Place avocado half on dish towel to secure it and make ½-inch crosshatch slices into flesh without cutting through skin.

3. Insert spoon between skin and flesh to separate the two. Gently scoop out avocado cubes.

✔ WHY THIS RECIPE WORKS

Huevos rancheros has made its way northward from Mexico, becoming common on breakfast menus around the United States. To make this crowd-pleasing but involved dish of fried eggs, cheese, and tomato-chile sauce manageable for a group, we roasted the sauce components to brown the vegetables and replicate the char from a cast-iron skillet. We then transferred everything to a casserole dish and nestled the eggs into the sauce so we could cook eight eggs at once. Moving this spicy dish of eggs and charred chiles to the oven gave us a perfectly timed meal that's not just for breakfast.

Huevos Rancheros

SERVES 4

Use a heavyweight rimmed baking sheet; flimsy sheets will warp. Our winning sheet is the Wear-Ever Half Size Heavy Duty Sheet Pan (13 gauge) by Vollrath. Serve with refried beans and hot sauce.

2	**(28-ounce) cans diced tomatoes**
1	**tablespoon packed brown sugar**
1	**tablespoon lime juice**
1	**onion, chopped**
½	**cup chopped canned green chiles**
¼	**cup extra-virgin olive oil**
3	**tablespoons chili powder**
4	**garlic cloves, sliced thin**
	Salt and pepper
4	**ounces pepper Jack cheese, shredded (1 cup)**
8	**large eggs**
1	**avocado, halved, pitted, and diced**
3	**scallions, sliced thin**
⅓	**cup minced fresh cilantro**
8	**(6-inch) corn tortillas, warmed**

1. Adjust oven rack to middle position and heat oven to 500 degrees. Line rimmed baking sheet with parchment paper. Drain tomatoes in fine-mesh strainer set over bowl, pressing with rubber spatula to extract as much juice as possible. Reserve 1¾ cups tomato juice and discard remainder. Whisk sugar and lime juice into reserved tomato juice and set aside.

2. In separate bowl, combine onion, chiles, oil, chili powder, garlic, ½ teaspoon salt, and drained tomatoes. Transfer tomato mixture to prepared baking sheet and spread in even layer to edges of sheet. Roast until charred in spots, 35 to 40 minutes, stirring and redistributing into even layer halfway through baking. Reduce oven temperature to 400 degrees.

3. Transfer roasted tomato mixture to 13 by 9-inch baking dish and stir in tomato juice mixture. Season with salt and pepper to taste, then spread into even layer. Sprinkle pepper Jack over tomato mixture. Using spoon, hollow out 8 holes in tomato mixture in 2 rows. Crack 1 egg into each hole. Season eggs with salt and pepper.

4. Bake until whites are just beginning to set but still have some movement when dish is shaken, 13 to 16 minutes. Transfer dish to wire rack, tent loosely with aluminum foil, and let sit for 5 minutes. Spoon avocado over top, then sprinkle with scallions and cilantro. Serve with warm tortillas.

TO MAKE AHEAD: The sauce can be made 24 hours in advance. Microwave until hot, about 2 minutes (stirring halfway), before transferring to baking dish and proceeding with recipe.

ROAST THE VEGETABLES; BAKE THE EGGS

To evoke the charred flavors in traditional huevos rancheros, we roast vegetables in a hot oven before layering them into a dish with cheese sprinkled over. Cracking eggs into wells in the mixture allows us to bake eight servings at once—no more standing at the stove frying egg after egg for an impatient crowd.

WHY THIS RECIPE WORKS

While each cuisine puts its own spin on the dish, Latin-style fried chicken is set apart by its garlicky-lime marinade and an extra-crunchy coating with lots of spice. Classic Latin fried chicken has a thin and crispy crust; we used a combination of flour cut with cornstarch for a nice, light coating and a little baking powder made it extra crisp. Refrigerating the marinated dredged chicken before frying made sure the coating set up nicely and thus stayed put on the chicken. Whether your idea of "South" is Savannah or San Salvador, this is one fried chicken recipe that you're definitely going to want to make.

Latin Fried Chicken

SERVES 4

Don't let the chicken marinate any longer than 2 hours or it will toughen from the lime juice. Use a Dutch oven that holds 6 quarts or more.

MARINADE

- 2   tablespoons kosher salt
- 6   garlic cloves, chopped coarse
- 1   tablespoon pepper
- 1   tablespoon ground cumin
- 2   teaspoons smoked paprika
- 2   teaspoons dried oregano
- 2   teaspoons grated lime zest plus ¼ cup juice (2 limes)
- 3   pounds bone-in chicken pieces (split breasts cut in half crosswise, drumsticks, thighs, and/or wings), trimmed

COATING

- 1¼ cups all-purpose flour
- ¾   cup cornstarch
- 1   tablespoon pepper
- 1   tablespoon granulated garlic
- 1   teaspoon baking powder
- 1   teaspoon white pepper
- 1   teaspoon kosher salt
- 1   teaspoon ground cumin
- ¼   teaspoon cayenne pepper
- 3   large egg whites, lightly beaten
- 3   quarts peanut or vegetable oil

1. FOR THE MARINADE: Combine salt, garlic, pepper, cumin, paprika, oregano, and lime zest and juice in bowl. Add chicken and turn to coat thoroughly. Cover with plastic wrap and refrigerate for at least 1 hour or up to 2 hours.

2. FOR THE COATING: Whisk flour, cornstarch, pepper, granulated garlic, baking powder, white pepper, salt, cumin, and cayenne together in bowl. Place egg whites in shallow dish.

3. Set wire rack in rimmed baking sheet. Remove chicken from marinade and scrape off solids. Pat chicken dry with paper towels. Working with 1 piece at a time, dip chicken into egg whites to thoroughly coat, letting excess drip back into dish. Dredge chicken in flour mixture, pressing to adhere. Transfer chicken to prepared wire rack and refrigerate for at least 30 minutes or up to 2 hours.

4. Add oil to large Dutch oven until it measures about 2 inches deep and heat over medium-high heat to 325 degrees. Add half of chicken to hot oil and fry until breasts register 160 degrees and drumsticks/thighs register 175 degrees, 13 to 16 minutes. Adjust burner, if necessary, to maintain oil temperature between 300 and 325 degrees. Transfer chicken to clean wire rack set in rimmed baking sheet. Return oil to 325 degrees and repeat with remaining chicken. Serve.

WHITE PEPPER

White peppercorns are fully ripe black peppercorns—the black outer husk is removed and the berries are dried. They lose much of their heat in this process but have a sharpness and a pronounced citrus flavor. Their taste is especially welcome in our spicy Latin Fried Chicken coating. Many chefs like the way that these peppercorns blend into white sauces, while Asian cooks use them in stir-fries and hot-and-sour soup.

WHY THIS RECIPE WORKS

We wanted our California-Style fish tacos to be light, fresh, and simple, with a perfect balance of flavors and textures. An ultrathin beer batter using a combination of flour, cornstarch, and baking powder proved to be ideal for getting a light, crispy coating on the delicate white fish. Quick-pickled onions and jalapeños added tart spiciness, and tossing shredded cabbage with the pickling liquid just before serving added flavor without overcomplicating the dish. Lime juice and sour cream added tang to the traditional creamy white sauce.

California-Style Fish Tacos

SERVES 6

Although this recipe looks involved, all the components are easy to execute and most can be made in advance. Light-bodied American lagers, such as Budweiser, work best here. Cut the fish on a slight bias if your fillets aren't quite 4 inches wide. You should end up with about 24 pieces of fish. Serve with green salsa, if desired.

PICKLED ONIONS

1	small red onion, halved and sliced thin
2	jalapeño chiles, stemmed and sliced into thin rings
1	cup white wine vinegar
2	tablespoons lime juice
1	tablespoon sugar
1	teaspoon salt

CABBAGE

3	cups shredded green cabbage
¼	cup pickling liquid from pickled onions
½	teaspoon salt
½	teaspoon pepper

WHITE SAUCE

½	cup mayonnaise
½	cup sour cream
2	tablespoons lime juice
2	tablespoons milk

FISH

2	pounds skinless whitefish fillets, such as cod, haddock, or halibut, cut crosswise into 4 by 1-inch strips
	Salt and pepper
¾	cup all-purpose flour
¼	cup cornstarch
1	teaspoon baking powder
1	cup beer
1	quart peanut or vegetable oil
24	(6-inch) corn tortillas, warmed
1	cup fresh cilantro leaves

1. FOR THE PICKLED ONIONS: Combine onion and jalapeños in medium bowl. Bring vinegar, lime juice, sugar, and salt to boil in small saucepan. Pour vinegar mixture over onion mixture and let sit for at least 30 minutes. (Pickled onions can be made and refrigerated up to 2 days in advance.)

2. FOR THE CABBAGE: Toss all ingredients together in bowl.

3. FOR THE WHITE SAUCE: Whisk all ingredients together in bowl. (Sauce can be made and refrigerated up to 2 days in advance.)

4. FOR THE FISH: Adjust oven rack to middle position and heat oven to 200 degrees. Set wire rack inside rimmed baking sheet. Pat fish dry with paper towels and season with salt and pepper. Whisk flour, cornstarch, baking powder, and 1 teaspoon salt together in large bowl. Add beer and whisk until smooth. Transfer fish to batter and toss until evenly coated.

5. Add oil to large Dutch oven until it measures about ¾ inch deep and heat over medium-high heat to 350 degrees. Working with 5 to 6 pieces at a time, remove fish from batter, allowing excess to drip back into bowl, and add to hot oil, briefly dragging fish along surface of oil to prevent sticking. Adjust burner, if necessary, to maintain oil temperature between 325 and 350 degrees. Fry fish, stirring gently to prevent pieces from sticking together, until golden brown and crispy, about 2 minutes per side. Transfer fish to prepared wire rack and place in oven to keep warm. Return oil to 350 degrees and repeat with remaining fish.

6. Divide fish evenly among tortillas. Top with pickled onions, cabbage, white sauce, and cilantro. Serve.

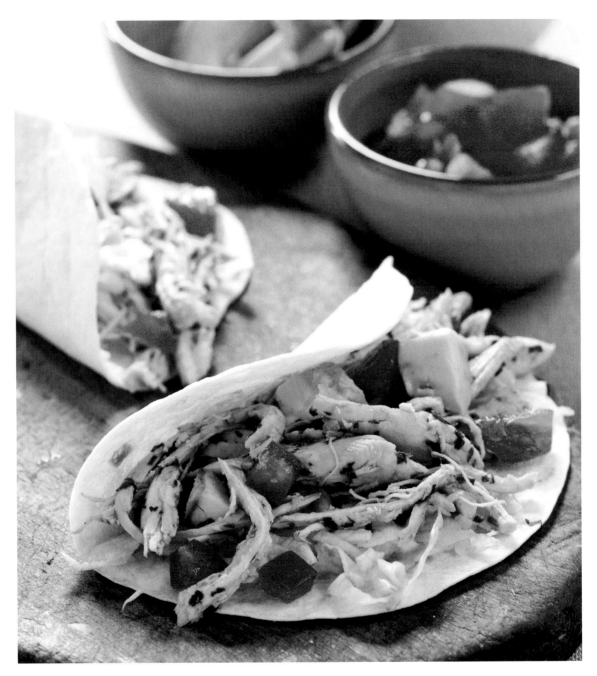

✔ WHY THIS RECIPE WORKS

We like the convenience of boneless, skinless chicken breasts in tacos, but they can be dry. After trying a variety of cooking methods, we found that poaching produced meat that was tender and moist. Chipotle chiles gave our poaching liquid a smoky, full-bodied flavor and orange juice offered a touch of sweetness that tempered its vivid acidity. For more robust flavor, we called on two kitchen staples: Worcestershire mimicked the complex flavor of dark meat, and mustard added sharpness that balanced the sweet orange juice and smoky chipotle.

Easy Chicken Tacos

SERVES 6

To warm the tortillas, wrap them in foil and heat them in a 350-degree oven for 15 minutes. Top the tacos with shredded lettuce, grated cheese, diced avocado, chopped tomato, and sour cream.

- 3   tablespoons unsalted butter
- 4   garlic cloves, minced
- 2   teaspoons minced canned chipotle chile in adobo sauce
- ¾   cup chopped fresh cilantro
- ½   cup orange juice
- 1   tablespoon Worcestershire sauce
- 4   (6-ounce) boneless, skinless chicken breasts, trimmed
- 1   teaspoon yellow mustard
-     Salt and pepper
- 12   (6-inch) flour tortillas

1. Melt butter in large skillet over medium-high heat. Add garlic and chipotle and cook until fragrant, about 30 seconds. Stir in ½ cup cilantro, orange juice, and Worcestershire and bring to boil. Add chicken and simmer, covered, over medium-low heat until meat registers 160 degrees, 10 to 15 minutes, flipping chicken halfway through cooking. Transfer to plate and tent with aluminum foil.

2. Increase heat to medium-high and cook until liquid is reduced to ¼ cup, about 5 minutes. Off heat, whisk in mustard. Using 2 forks, shred chicken into bite-size pieces and return to skillet. Add remaining ¼ cup cilantro to skillet and toss until well combined. Season with salt and pepper to taste. Serve with tortillas.

STORING CANNED CHIPOTLE CHILES

When a recipe uses just a teaspoon or two of chipotle chiles, here's how to store the rest of the can.

Canned chipotle chiles are jalapeños that have been ripened until red, smoked, and packed in a tangy tomato-based adobo sauce. Since the size of chipotles varies, in the test kitchen we measure them by minced teaspoons. Could we store leftovers in the freezer, or would they lose their potency? To see, we pureed several cans and froze measured teaspoons on a plastic wrap–covered plate. Once our "chipotle chips" were hard, we peeled them off the plastic and transferred them to a zipper-lock freezer bag.

Weeks later we made a salsa and a casserole with the frozen chipotles and compared them with the same dishes made with chiles from a newly opened can. Most tasters couldn't tell the two apart. The chipotles will keep for up to two months in the freezer and should be thawed before you use them. The chiles will also last for two weeks in the refrigerator.

SHREDDING CHICKEN

Hold one fork in each hand, with tines facing down. Insert tines into chicken and gently pull forks away from each other, breaking meat apart and into long thin shreds.

SURPRISE INGREDIENTS

In other recipes, you'd call these ordinary ingredients. But in a taco? Together, they add unexpected depth and dimension to our simple chicken tacos.

YELLOW MUSTARD, WORCESTERSHIRE SAUCE, ORANGE JUICE, AND BUTTER

✅ WHY THIS RECIPE WORKS

Forget about tasteless fillings. We simmer the chicken and rice for our chimichangas in a chipotle broth, infusing them with a smoky bite through and through. As for construction, we noticed that the standard burrito-style wrapping method left us with doughy tortilla ends and filling that fell out. We created an easy new folding technique that kept the filling put without any floury bites.

Easier Chicken Chimichangas

SERVES 4

If using a cast-iron Dutch oven, increase the broth to 1¾ cups, adding 1¼ cups in step 2. Serve with Smoky Salsa Verde (page 207).

1¼	cups chicken broth
1	tablespoon minced canned chipotle chile in adobo sauce
½	cup long-grain white rice
	Salt and pepper
2	(6-ounce) boneless, skinless chicken breasts, trimmed
1	tablespoon peanut or vegetable oil, plus 3 cups for frying
1	onion, chopped fine
2	garlic cloves, minced
1	teaspoon chili powder
½	teaspoon ground cumin
1	(15-ounce) can pinto beans, rinsed
4	ounces sharp cheddar cheese, shredded (1 cup)
⅓	cup chopped fresh cilantro
1	tablespoon all-purpose flour
1	tablespoon water
4	(10-inch) flour tortillas

1. Whisk broth and chipotle together in 2-cup liquid measuring cup. Combine ½ cup chipotle broth, rice, and ¼ teaspoon salt in bowl. Cover bowl and microwave until liquid is completely absorbed, about 5 minutes. Meanwhile, pat chicken dry with paper towels and season with salt and pepper.

2. Heat 1 tablespoon oil in Dutch oven over medium-high heat until just smoking. Add onion and cook until softened, about 5 minutes. Stir in garlic, chili powder, and cumin and cook until fragrant, about 30 seconds. Add remaining ¾ cup chipotle broth, parcooked rice, and beans and bring to boil.

3. Reduce heat to medium-low, add chicken, and cook, covered, until chicken registers 160 degrees and rice is tender, about 15 minutes, flipping chicken halfway

through cooking. Transfer chicken to cutting board and let rest for 5 to 10 minutes. Cut chicken into ½-inch pieces and combine with rice and bean mixture, cheddar, and cilantro in large bowl. Wash now-empty pot.

4. Whisk flour and water together in small bowl. Stack tortillas on plate and microwave, covered, until pliable, about 1 minute. Working one at a time, place one-quarter of chicken mixture in center of warm tortilla. Brush edges of tortilla with flour paste. Wrap top and bottom of tortilla tightly over filling. Brush ends of tortilla with paste and fold into center, pressing firmly to seal.

5. Set wire rack in rimmed baking sheet. Heat remaining 3 cups oil in clean pot over medium-high heat until 325 degrees. Place 2 chimichangas, seam side down, in oil. Fry, adjusting burner as necessary to maintain oil temperature between 300 and 325 degrees, until chimichangas are deep golden brown, about 4 minutes, turning them halfway through frying. Drain on prepared wire rack. Bring oil back to 325 degrees and repeat with remaining chimichangas. Serve.

GLUE AND FOLD

The usual burrito-style wrapping method left us between the devil and the deep blue sea: Either the filling leaked out in the pot of oil or the ends of the tortilla never crisped. Our new chimichanga folding technique solves both problems.

1. Place filling in middle of tortilla. Brush tortilla's circumference with flour-and-water paste. The paste acts as glue, letting you securely seal chimichanga.

2. After you've folded 2 opposing sides toward center and pressed them to seal, brush open flaps with more paste. Fold flaps in and again press firmly to seal chimichanga shut.

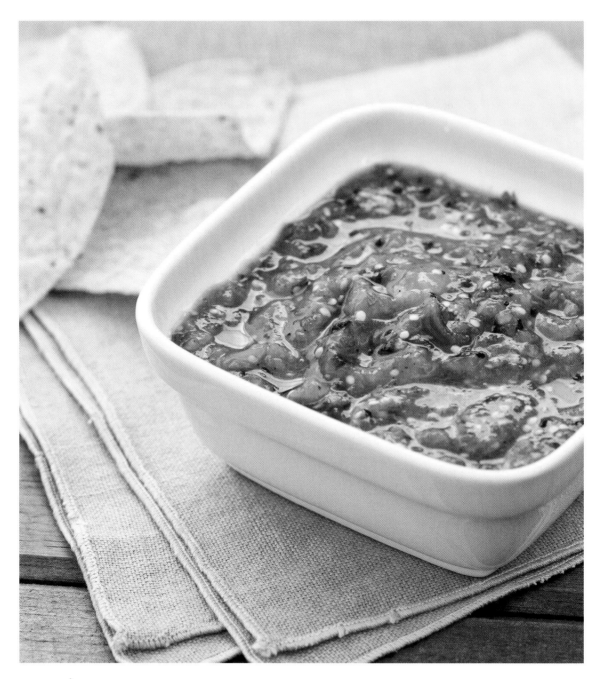

✓ WHY THIS RECIPE WORKS

Our recipe for salsa verde includes the typical ingredients: tomatillos, onions, garlic, jalapeño, and lots of cilantro. To temper their sharply acidic flavor, we broiled the tomatillos just until tender. We also broiled the other vegetables to provide subtle smokiness. Our recipe calls for a large amount of cilantro to ensure that its flavor stands out from the other ingredients.

Smoky Salsa Verde

MAKES 1 ¼ CUPS

This salsa is especially good served with our Easier Chicken Chimichangas (page 205), or try it with just about anything you'd serve salsa with, such as tortilla chips, grilled steak, or scrambled eggs.

1	**pound tomatillos, husks and stems removed, rinsed well and dried**
1	**small onion, quartered**
1	**jalapeño chile, stemmed, halved, and seeded**
1	**garlic clove, peeled**
1	**teaspoon olive oil**
½	**cup fresh cilantro leaves**
1	**tablespoon lime juice**
	Salt

1. Adjust oven rack 5 inches from broiler element and heat broiler. Toss tomatillos, onion, jalapeño, and garlic with oil and place on aluminum foil–lined rimmed baking sheet. Broil, shaking pan occasionally, until vegetables are lightly charred, 10 to 12 minutes. Cool slightly, about 5 minutes.

2. Add vegetables, cilantro, lime juice, and ¼ teaspoon salt to food processor and pulse until coarsely ground, 5 to 7 pulses. Season with salt to taste. Serve. (Salsa can be refrigerated for up to 3 days.)

TOMATILLOS

Called *tomates verdes* (green tomatoes) in much of Mexico, small green tomatillos have a tangier, more citrusy flavor than true green tomatoes. When choosing tomatillos, look for pale-green orbs with firm flesh that fills and splits open the fruit's outer papery husk, which must be removed before cooking. Avoid tomatillos that are too yellow and soft, as these specimens are past their prime and will taste sour and muted.

REVIVING TIRED HERBS

We rarely use an entire bunch of herbs at once, and inevitably a few days later they are looking less-than-fresh and we have to throw them out and start all over. Is there a way to revive tired herbs? With a little research, we found that soaking herbs in water restores the pressure of the cell contents against the cell wall, causing them to become firmer as the dehydrated cells plump up. So, after purposely letting several bunches of parsley, cilantro, and mint sit in the refrigerator until they became limp, sorry-looking versions of their former selves, we tried bringing the herbs back to life by soaking them in tepid and cold water. We found that soaking herbs (stems trimmed) for 10 minutes in cold water perks them up better than tepid water. These herbs had a fresher look and an improved texture.

✓ WHY THIS RECIPE WORKS

Tex-Mex cheese enchiladas are a wildly popular dish in the Lone Star State, beloved for their relative simplicity and their chile gravy, a red sauce that's a cross between beef gravy and Mexican enchilada sauce. We found that two toasted ancho chiles ground with a combination of spices gave the sauce smoky flavors that we brightened with a little white vinegar. We skipped frying the corn tortillas instead brushing them with oil and microwaving, resulting in soft, easy-to-roll tortillas without excess grease. For the cheesy filling, we combined sharp cheddar and Monterey Jack and used the oven to ensure melty, gooey cheese.

Tex-Mex Cheese Enchiladas

SERVES 6

Dried chiles vary in size and weight. You'll get a more accurate measure if you seed and tear them first; you need about ½ cup of prepped chiles. You'll lose some flavor, but you can substitute 2 tablespoons ancho chile powder and 1 tablespoon ground cumin for the whole ancho chiles and cumin seeds, decreasing the toasting time to 1 minute.

GRAVY

2	dried ancho chiles, stemmed, seeded, and torn into ½-inch pieces (½ cup)
1	tablespoon cumin seeds
1	tablespoon garlic powder
2	teaspoons dried oregano
3	tablespoons vegetable oil
3	tablespoons all-purpose flour
	Salt and pepper
2	cups chicken broth
2	teaspoons distilled white vinegar

ENCHILADAS

12	(6-inch) corn tortillas
1½	tablespoons vegetable oil
8	ounces Monterey Jack cheese, shredded (2 cups)
6	ounces sharp cheddar cheese, shredded (1½ cups)
1	onion, chopped fine

1. FOR THE GRAVY: Toast chiles and cumin in 12-inch skillet over medium-low heat, stirring frequently, until fragrant, about 2 minutes. Transfer to spice grinder and let cool for 5 minutes. Add garlic powder and oregano and grind to fine powder.

2. Heat oil in now-empty skillet over medium-high heat until shimmering. Whisk in flour, ½ teaspoon salt, ½ teaspoon pepper, and spice mixture and cook until fragrant and slightly deepened in color, about 1 minute.

Slowly whisk in broth and bring to simmer. Reduce heat to medium-low and cook, whisking frequently, until gravy has thickened and reduced to 1½ cups, about 5 minutes. Whisk in vinegar and season with salt and pepper to taste. Remove from heat, cover, and keep warm.

3. FOR THE ENCHILADAS: Adjust oven rack to middle position and heat oven to 450 degrees. Brush both sides of tortillas with oil. Stack tortillas, then wrap in damp dish towel. Place tortillas on plate and microwave until warm and pliable, about 1 minute.

4. Spread ½ cup gravy in bottom of 13 by 9-inch baking dish. Combine cheeses in bowl; set aside ½ cup cheese mixture for topping enchiladas. Place ¼ cup cheese mixture across center of each tortilla, then sprinkle each with 1 tablespoon onion. Tightly roll tortillas around filling and lay them seam side down in dish (2 columns of 6 tortillas will fit neatly across width of dish). Pour remaining 1 cup gravy over enchiladas, then sprinkle with reserved cheese mixture.

5. Cover dish with aluminum foil and bake until sauce is bubbling and cheese is melted, about 15 minutes. Let enchiladas cool for 10 minutes, then sprinkle with remaining onion. Serve.

TO MAKE AHEAD: The sauce can be made up to 24 hours in advance. To reheat, add 2 tablespoons water and microwave until loose, 1 to 2 minutes, stirring halfway through microwaving.

ENCHILADA ORIENTATION

The arrangement matters: After you have spread ½ cup of chile gravy in the 13 by 9-inch baking dish, fit the 12 enchiladas by creating two snug rows of six.

✓ WHY THIS RECIPE WORKS

Traditional beef enchiladas recipes require simmering steak for hours. Convenience recipes call for hamburger and canned sauce. We wanted to find a middle ground. For a deeply flavored sauce, we relied on chili powder and tomato sauce, along with onions, garlic, and spices. Slicing beefy, inexpensive blade steaks into small pieces cut our cooking time considerably. Authentic recipes fry the corn tortillas and then dip them in sauce to soften and season them. Instead, we softened the tortillas in the microwave. Once filled, topped with sauce and cheese, and baked, our enchiladas tasted like the real deal.

Authentic Beef Enchiladas

SERVES 4 TO 6

Cut back on the pickled jalapeños if you like your enchiladas on the mild side.

3	tablespoons chili powder
3	garlic cloves, minced
2	teaspoons ground coriander
2	teaspoons ground cumin
1	teaspoon sugar
	Salt
1¼	pounds top blade steaks, trimmed
1	tablespoon vegetable oil
2	onions, chopped
1	(15-ounce) can tomato sauce
½	cup water
8	ounces Monterey Jack or mild cheddar cheese, shredded (2 cups)
⅓	cup chopped fresh cilantro
¼	cup chopped canned jalapeños
12	(6-inch) corn tortillas

1. Combine chili powder, garlic, coriander, sugar, and 1 teaspoon salt in small bowl. Pat meat dry with paper towels and sprinkle with salt. Heat oil in Dutch oven over medium-high heat until shimmering. Cook meat until browned on both sides, about 6 minutes. Transfer meat to plate. Add onions to pot and cook over medium heat until golden, about 5 minutes. Stir in garlic mixture and cook until fragrant, about 1 minute. Add tomato sauce and water and bring to boil. Return meat and juices to pot, cover, reduce heat to low, and gently simmer until meat is tender and can be broken apart with wooden spoon, about 1½ hours.

2. Adjust oven rack to middle position and heat oven to 350 degrees. Strain beef mixture over medium bowl, breaking meat into small pieces; reserve sauce. Transfer meat to bowl and mix with 1 cup cheese, cilantro, and jalapeños.

3. Spread ¾ cup sauce in bottom of 13 by 9-inch baking dish. Place 6 tortillas on plate and microwave until soft, about 1 minute. Spread ⅓ cup beef mixture down center of each tortilla, roll tortillas tightly, and set in baking dish seam side down. Repeat with remaining tortillas and beef mixture (you may have to fit 2 or more enchiladas down the sides of the baking dish). Pour remaining sauce over enchiladas and spread to coat evenly. Sprinkle remaining 1 cup cheese evenly over enchiladas, wrap with aluminum foil, and bake until heated through, 20 to 25 minutes. Remove foil and continue baking until cheese browns slightly, 5 to 10 minutes. Serve.

TRIMMING BLADE STEAKS

After testing various beef cuts, we found that blade steaks (which are cut from the chuck) had enough marbling to produce silky, flavorful shredded beef for our enchiladas. The only trick is to cut away the center strip of gristle, which is very easy to do because the strip is in plain sight in the middle of each steak. Simply halve each steak lengthwise and then slice away the gristle, as shown here.

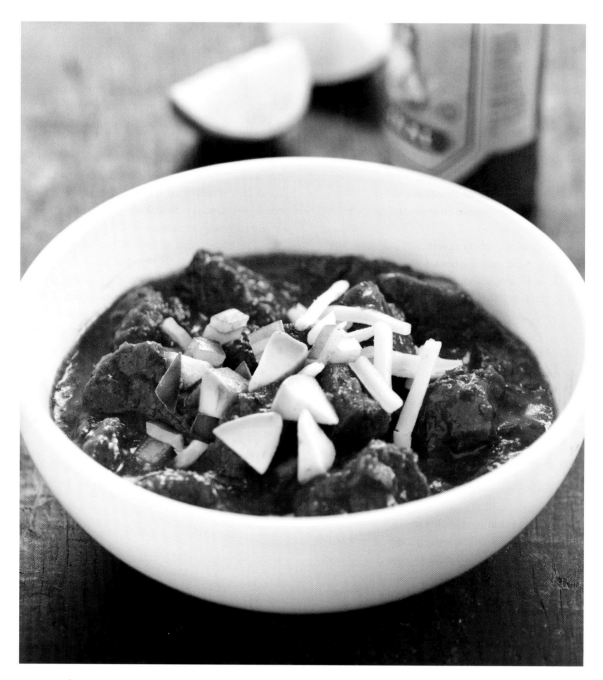

✔ WHY THIS RECIPE WORKS

Many chili con carne recipes call for toasting and grinding whole chiles. We wanted to create a simpler, authentic-tasting version. For the meat, we settled on beef chuck, our favorite cut for stews because its substantial marbling provides rich flavor and tender texture after prolonged cooking. To add a smoky meatiness to our chili, we browned the beef in bacon fat instead of oil. We added a jalapeño for brightness and heat and minced chipotle for smoky, spicy depth. A few tablespoons of corn muffin mix, in place of *masa harina* (corn flour), helped thicken our chili and gave it a silky texture.

Easy Chili con Carne

SERVES 6 TO 8

If the bacon does not render a full 3 tablespoons of fat in step 1, supplement it with vegetable oil. If desired, serve chili with chopped onion, avocado, shredded cheese, lime wedges, and/or hot sauce.

1	(14.5-ounce) can diced tomatoes
2	teaspoons minced canned chipotle chile in adobo sauce
4	slices bacon, chopped fine
1	(3½- to 4-pound) boneless beef chuck-eye roast, pulled apart at seams, trimmed, and cut into 1-inch pieces
	Salt and pepper
1	onion, chopped fine
1	jalapeño chile, stemmed, seeded, and chopped fine
3	tablespoons chili powder
4	garlic cloves, minced
1½	teaspoons ground cumin
½	teaspoon dried oregano
4	cups water
1	tablespoon packed brown sugar
2	tablespoons yellow corn muffin mix

1. Process tomatoes and chipotle in food processor until smooth. Cook bacon in Dutch oven over medium heat until crisp, about 8 minutes. Transfer bacon to paper towel–lined plate and reserve 3 tablespoons bacon fat.

2. Pat beef dry with paper towels and season with salt and pepper. Heat 1 tablespoon reserved bacon fat in now-empty Dutch oven over medium-high heat until just smoking. Brown half of beef, about 8 minutes. Transfer to bowl and repeat with 1 tablespoon bacon fat and remaining beef.

3. Add remaining 1 tablespoon bacon fat, onion, and jalapeño to again-empty Dutch oven and cook until softened, about 5 minutes. Stir in chili powder, garlic, cumin, and oregano and cook until fragrant, about 30 seconds. Stir in water, pureed tomato mixture, bacon, browned beef, and sugar and bring to boil. Reduce heat to low and simmer, covered, for 1 hour. Skim fat and continue to simmer uncovered until meat is tender, 30 to 45 minutes.

4. Ladle 1 cup chili liquid into medium bowl and stir in muffin mix; cover with plastic wrap. Microwave until mixture is thickened, about 1 minute. Slowly whisk mixture into chili and simmer until chili is slightly thickened, 5 to 10 minutes. Season with salt and pepper to taste. Serve. (Chili can be refrigerated for up to 3 days.)

SILKY SAUCE

Our chili gets silky texture and a hint of corn flavor from the addition of corn muffin mix.

THE SECRET INGREDIENT

✓ WHY THIS RECIPE WORKS

As the name implies, five-alarm chili should be spicy enough to make you break a sweat—but it has to have rich, complex chile flavor as well. We used a combination of dried anchos, smoky chipotle chiles in adobo sauce, fresh jalapeños, and chili powder to create layers of spicy flavor. Ground beef added meaty bulk, and pureeing the chiles along with canned tomatoes and corn chips added extra body and another layer of flavor. Mellowed with a bit of sugar and enriched with creamy pinto beans, our chili was well balanced and spicy without being harsh.

Five-Alarm Chili

SERVES 8 TO 10

Look for ancho chiles in the international aisle at the super-market. Light-bodied American lagers, such as Budweiser, work best here. Serve chili with lime, sour cream, diced tomato, diced avocado, scallions, and cornbread.

2 ounces (4 to 6) dried ancho chiles, stemmed, seeded, and cut into 1-inch pieces

3½ cups water

1 (28-ounce) can whole peeled tomatoes

¾ cup crushed corn tortilla chips

¼ cup canned chipotle chile in adobo sauce plus 2 teaspoons adobo sauce

2 tablespoons vegetable oil

2 pounds 85 percent lean ground beef
 Salt and pepper

2 pounds onions, chopped fine

2 jalapeño chiles, stemmed, seeds reserved, and minced

6 garlic cloves, minced

2 tablespoons ground cumin

2 tablespoons chili powder

1 tablespoon dried oregano

2 teaspoons ground coriander

2 teaspoons sugar

1 teaspoon cayenne pepper

1½ cups beer

3 (15-ounce) cans pinto beans, rinsed

1. Combine anchos and 1½ cups water in bowl and microwave until softened, about 3 minutes. Drain and discard liquid. Process anchos, tomatoes and their juice, remaining 2 cups water, tortilla chips, chipotle, and adobo sauce in blender until smooth, about 1 minute; set aside.

2. Heat 2 teaspoons oil in Dutch oven over medium-high heat until just smoking. Add beef, 1 teaspoon salt, and ½ teaspoon pepper and cook, breaking up pieces with spoon, until all liquid has evaporated and meat begins to sizzle, 10 to 15 minutes. Drain in colander and set aside.

3. Heat remaining 4 teaspoons oil in now-empty Dutch oven over medium-high heat until simmering. Add onions and jalapeños and seeds and cook until onions are lightly browned, about 5 minutes. Stir in garlic, cumin, chili powder, oregano, coriander, sugar, and cayenne and cook until fragrant, about 30 seconds. Pour in beer and bring to simmer. Stir in beans, reserved chile-tomato mixture, and reserved cooked beef and return to simmer. Cover, reduce heat to low, and cook, stirring occasionally, until thickened, 50 to 60 minutes. Season with salt to taste. Serve.

FIVE HITS FOR FIVE-ALARM CHILI

JALAPEÑO	**CHIPOTLE IN ADOBO**	**CHILI POWDER**	**CAYENNE**	**ANCHO**
Brings fresh vegetable flavor	Instant shortcut to smokiness	Wouldn't be chili without it	Adds raw heat	Adds depth, complexity, and mild heat

EVERYBODY LOVES ITALIAN

TODAY, SPAGHETTI AND MEATBALLS, LASAGNA, CHICKEN PARMESAN, and other Italian favorites seem just as at home on the American table as meatloaf and apple pie. But the popularity of Italian cuisine in the United States actually took many years to build. It began, of course, with Italian immigrants. Between 1890 and 1920, about 4 million Italian-born immigrants (almost one-quarter of all American immigrants) came to the States. World War I gave Italian food its first mainstream push, as newspapers and magazine articles at that time referred to Italian cuisine as "the food of our allies." Unfortunately, many pasta recipes of the day called for boiling pasta for 30 minutes until it was practically mush. But with Prohibition in the 1920s came speakeasies, many of which were run by Italians (or Sicilians) who knew what they were doing in the kitchen, and thus diners developed a taste for a properly cooked plate of pasta. Pasta with tomato sauce, an inexpensive meal, also fit right in on the American table during the tough times of the Depression. Later, American GIs returning from Italy post–World War II brought a love of Italian food back with them. And by this time Hollywood had jumped on the Italian food bandwagon—who can forget the charming spaghetti-eating scene in 1955's Lady and the Tramp—forever cementing the popularity of Italian food in American culture. In this chapter, we include several Italian favorites, including slow-cooker versions of meatballs and marinara and Sunday gravy along with easier and quicker approaches to lasagna, manicotti, and chicken Parmesan.

WHY THIS RECIPE WORKS

To translate a classic minestrone to the slow cooker, we needed to find a combination of vegetables that would cook through in the same amount of time. Green beans took too long to become tender. We scrapped cauliflower because its flavor overwhelmed the soup. Zucchini squash and Swiss chard won out for texture and their similar cooking times. Canned beans disintegrated in the soup, so we used dried white beans. We started cooking the beans in the soup along with some softened carrots and onions, then added the squash and chard and pasta toward the end of cooking so they would be perfectly tender.

Slow-Cooker Minestrone

We recommend using great Northern or cannellini beans here. Serve the minestrone with grated Parmesan cheese.

1	cup dried medium–size white beans, rinsed and picked over
6	tablespoons extra-virgin olive oil
2	onions, chopped fine
4	carrots, peeled and cut into ½-inch pieces
8	garlic cloves, minced
1	(28-ounce) can whole peeled tomatoes, coarsely crushed by hand
8	cups chicken broth
3	cups water
2	cups fresh basil leaves, chopped
1	teaspoon dried oregano
¼	teaspoon red pepper flakes
2	medium zucchini, quartered lengthwise, seeded, and sliced ¼ inch thick
8	ounces Swiss chard, stemmed and chopped
½	cup small dried pasta, such as ditalini, orzo, or small elbows
	Salt and pepper

1. Bring beans and enough water to cover by 1 inch to boil in medium saucepan over high heat. Reduce heat to low and simmer, covered, until beans are just beginning to soften, about 20 minutes. Drain beans and transfer to slow cooker.

2. Heat 3 tablespoons oil in Dutch oven over medium heat until shimmering. Add onions and carrots and cook until softened, about 5 minutes. Stir in garlic and cook until fragrant, about 30 seconds.

Add tomatoes and their juice and cook until pan is nearly dry, 8 to 12 minutes. Stir in broth, water, ½ cup basil, oregano, and pepper flakes and bring to boil; transfer to slow cooker. Cover and cook until beans are tender, 6 to 7 hours on low or 5 to 6 hours on high.

3. Stir zucchini, Swiss chard, and pasta into slow cooker and cook on high, covered, until pasta is tender, 20 to 30 minutes. Stir in remaining 1½ cups basil and remaining 3 tablespoons oil. Season with salt and pepper to taste and serve.

TO MAKE AHEAD: Soup can be made through step 2 and refrigerated for up to 2 days. To finish, bring to boil in Dutch oven. Stir in zucchini, chard, and pasta; reduce heat to low; and simmer until pasta is tender, about 10 minutes.

TIMING IS EVERYTHING

First the onions, carrots, and tomatoes go into the slow cooker with the broth to create a rich, long-simmered backbone of flavor. Then we add the quick-cooking zucchini, Swiss chard, and pasta toward the end so they don't overcook.

HEAD START
Sautéed vegetables and canned whole tomatoes season the broth.

LAST MINUTE
The more delicate vegetables are added with the pasta near the end of cooking.

WHY THIS RECIPE WORKS

We love the flavor and heartiness of Sunday gravy, but not the laundry list of ingredients or hours of monitoring the stovetop. For a streamlined recipe, we turned to our slow cooker and narrowed the meat selection down to three: flank steak, for meaty flavor; country-style spareribs, for tender, fall-off-the-bone meat; and sausage, for its spicy, sweet kick. Using the flavorful drippings left behind from browning the sausage to sauté our aromatics infused the whole dish with flavor. And a combination of drained diced tomatoes, canned tomato sauce, and tomato paste ensured a rich, thick sauce.

Slow-Cooker Italian Sunday Gravy

SERVES 8 TO 10

Most sausage has enough seasoning to make extra salt unnecessary. This recipe makes enough to sauce 2 pounds of pasta. We like rigatoni, ziti, or penne with this sauce.

1	tablespoon vegetable oil
1	pound sweet Italian sausage
1	pound hot Italian sausage
2	onions, chopped
12	garlic cloves, minced
2	teaspoons dried oregano
1	(6-ounce) can tomato paste
½	cup dry red wine
1	(28-ounce) can diced tomatoes, drained
1	(28-ounce) can tomato sauce
2	pounds bone-in country-style pork spareribs, trimmed
1	(1½-pound) flank steak, trimmed
3	tablespoons chopped fresh basil
	Pepper

1. Heat oil in Dutch oven over medium-high heat until just smoking. Add sweet sausage and cook until well browned and fat begins to render, about 8 minutes. Using slotted spoon, transfer sausage to paper towel–lined plate to drain, then place in slow cooker. Repeat with hot sausage; transfer to slow cooker.

2. Cook onions in rendered fat over medium heat until well browned, about 6 minutes. Stir in garlic and oregano and cook until fragrant, about 1 minute. Add tomato paste and cook until it begins to brown, about 5 minutes. Stir in wine and simmer, scraping up browned bits, until wine is slightly reduced, about 3 minutes. Transfer to slow cooker. Stir in diced tomatoes and tomato sauce.

3. Submerge spareribs and steak in sauce in slow cooker. Cover and cook until meat is tender, 8 to 10 hours on low or 4 to 5 hours on high.

4. About 30 minutes before serving, remove ribs, steak, and sausages and set aside until cool enough to handle. Shred ribs and steak into small pieces, discarding excess fat and bones; slice sausages in half crosswise. Skim fat from surface of sauce, then stir sausages and shredded meat back into sauce. Stir in basil and season with pepper to taste. Serve. (Gravy can be refrigerated for up to 3 days.)

TO MAKE AHEAD: Slow-Cooker Italian Sunday Gravy can be made in advance through step 2. After stirring in diced tomatoes and tomato sauce, add browned sausages and simmer over medium-low heat until cooked through, about 12 minutes. Refrigerate sausage and sauce in airtight container for up to 2 days. To cook gravy, warm sauce and sausages together over medium heat until heated through; transfer to slow cooker. Proceed with step 3.

THE MEAT MATTERS

For our easy Slow-Cooker Italian Sunday Gravy, we narrowed down the meat to the following combination, which offers the best taste and texture.

ITALIAN SAUSAGES	FLANK STEAK	COUNTRY-STYLE SPARERIBS
Browning the sausages in advance helps build deep flavor.	This lean cut adds beefy flavor without too much grease.	These meaty ribs become fall-apart tender in a slow cooker.

WHY THIS RECIPE WORKS

Earthy and intense, pork ragu takes pasta to a new level. Most recipes call for pork shoulder and a hard-to-find, bony cut like neck, shank, or feet. We tried using all baby back ribs and found the resulting ragu rich and meaty. For a classic Italian flavor profile, fennel took the place of celery in the ragu's base and ground fennel rubbed into the ribs echoed the anise flavor. Simmering the garlic head whole right in the sauce yielded sweeter softened cloves that we squeezed back into the sauce when tender. With fresh herbs and red wine, our ragu tasted balanced and far more complex than its simple preparation would suggest.

Pork Ragu

MAKES ABOUT 8 CUPS

This recipe makes enough sauce to coat 2 pounds of pasta. Leftover sauce may be refrigerated for up to 3 days or frozen for up to 1 month.

2	(2¼- to 2½-pound) racks baby back ribs, trimmed and each rack cut into fourths
2	teaspoons ground fennel
	Kosher salt and pepper
3	tablespoons olive oil
1	large onion, chopped fine
1	large fennel bulb, stalks discarded, bulb halved, cored, and chopped fine
2	large carrots, peeled and chopped fine
¼	cup minced fresh sage
1½	teaspoons minced fresh rosemary
1	cup plus 2 tablespoons dry red wine
1	(28-ounce) can whole peeled tomatoes, drained and chopped coarse
3	cups chicken broth
1	garlic head, outer papery skins removed and top fourth of head cut off and discarded
1	pound pappardelle or tagliatelle
	Grated Parmesan cheese

1. Adjust oven rack to middle position and heat oven to 300 degrees. Sprinkle ribs with ground fennel and generously season with salt and pepper, pressing spices to adhere. Heat oil in Dutch oven over medium-high heat until just smoking. Add half of ribs, meat side down, and cook, without moving them, until meat is well browned, 6 to 8 minutes; transfer to plate. Repeat with remaining ribs; set aside.

2. Reduce heat to medium and add onion, fennel, carrots, 2 tablespoons sage, rosemary, and ½ teaspoon salt to now-empty pot. Cook, stirring occasionally and scraping up any browned bits, until vegetables are well browned and beginning to stick to pot bottom, 12 to 15 minutes.

3. Add 1 cup wine and cook until evaporated, about 5 minutes. Stir in tomatoes and broth and bring to simmer. Submerge garlic and ribs, meat side down, in liquid; add any accumulated juices from plate. Cover and transfer to oven. Cook until ribs are fork-tender, about 2 hours.

4. Remove pot from oven and transfer ribs and garlic to rimmed baking sheet. Using large spoon, skim any fat from surface of sauce. Once cool enough to handle, shred meat from bones; discard bones and gristle. Return meat to pot. Squeeze garlic from its skin into pot. Stir in remaining 2 tablespoons sage and remaining 2 tablespoons wine. Season with salt and pepper to taste.

5. Meanwhile, bring 4 quarts water to boil in large pot. Add pasta and 2 tablespoons salt and cook, stirring often, until al dente. Reserve ½ cup cooking water, then drain pasta and return it to pot. Add half of sauce and toss to combine, adjusting consistency with reserved cooking water as needed. Serve, passing Parmesan separately.

MAKING RAGU FROM BABY BACK RIBS

Baby back ribs are an unusual choice for ragu. But they make perfect culinary sense for this dish, as these ribs have great meaty flavor, contain lots of bone to contribute body to the sauce, and cook relatively quickly (compared to other bony cuts like shanks). We cut two racks into three-rib segments, brown them, then braise them in flavorful liquid. Two hours later, we remove the meat, shred it, and add it back to the sauce.

WHY THIS RECIPE WORKS

Toasting mellows, softens, and sweetens a head of garlic. But rather than waiting the hour or more it can take to roast garlic in the oven, we set out to develop a quick pasta dish that could harness the same great flavor in short order. We browned a whopping 50 whole cloves on the stovetop, and then poached the garlic in chicken broth seasoned with sweet, tangy balsamic vinegar. After a spin in the food processor, the final result was a complex and silky sauce that we combined with walnuts and spicy arugula. The best part? The whole thing took just 15 minutes—more than enough time to cook the pasta.

Pasta with Roasted Garlic Sauce, Arugula, and Walnuts

It takes about four heads of garlic to yield 50 cloves, but you can use prepeeled.

50	garlic cloves, peeled (1 cup)
3	tablespoons extra-virgin olive oil, plus extra for drizzling
1	cup chicken broth
2	teaspoons balsamic vinegar
	Salt and pepper
1	pound spaghetti, linguine, or fettuccine
8	ounces (8 cups) baby arugula
1	cup walnuts, toasted and chopped
	Grated Pecorino Romano cheese

1. Combine garlic and oil in medium saucepan over medium-low heat. Cover and cook, stirring occasionally, until garlic is browned all over, 6 to 8 minutes. Add broth, vinegar, ¾ teaspoon salt, and ½ teaspoon pepper and bring to boil. Reduce heat to low and simmer, uncovered, until garlic is fork-tender, 5 to 7 minutes. Pour garlic mixture into food processor and process until smooth, about 1 minute.

2. Meanwhile, bring 4 quarts water to boil in large pot. Add pasta and 1 tablespoon salt and cook, stirring often, until al dente. Reserve ½ cup cooking water, then drain pasta and return it to pot. Add garlic sauce, arugula, and walnuts to pasta and toss to combine. Adjust consistency with reserved cooking water as needed. Season with salt and pepper to taste. Serve, drizzling individual servings with extra oil and passing Pecorino separately.

SPEEDY STOVETOP "ROASTING"

We love the mellow sweetness of roasted garlic, but we don't always have an hour to make it. Our stovetop method takes just 15 minutes. We sauté 50 cloves of garlic in olive oil in a covered pan for just 6 minutes or so. Later, we add balsamic vinegar, which helps mimic the complex, sweet flavor of oven-roasted garlic.

✅ WHY THIS RECIPE WORKS

Meatballs and marinara sauce are the epitome of comfort food, except when you're the cook. Frying the meatballs can be messy and take a good chunk of time when working in batches. For an easier method, we turned to the oven and roasted our meatballs at a high temperature, which ensured they developed a nice, browned crust. To keep our meatballs moist and tender, we added a panade (a paste of milk and bread). In addition to ground beef, using Italian sausage for the pork gave the meatballs a flavor boost, as did simmering them in the sauce after baking.

Meatballs and Marinara

SERVES 8

To keep the recipe easy and streamlined, the meatballs and sauce start with the same onion mixture. This recipe makes enough to sauce 2 pounds of pasta.

ONION MIXTURE

¼	cup olive oil
3	onions, chopped fine
8	garlic cloves, minced
1	tablespoon dried oregano
¾	teaspoon red pepper flakes

MARINARA

1	(6-ounce) can tomato paste
1	cup dry red wine
1	cup water
4	(28-ounce) cans crushed tomatoes
1	ounce Parmesan cheese, grated (½ cup)
¼	cup chopped fresh basil
	Salt
1–2	teaspoons sugar

MEATBALLS

4	slices hearty white sandwich bread, torn into pieces
¾	cup milk
8	ounces sweet Italian sausage, casings removed
2	ounces Parmesan cheese, grated (1 cup)
½	cup chopped fresh parsley
2	large eggs
2	garlic cloves, minced
1½	teaspoons salt
2½	pounds 80 percent lean ground chuck

1. FOR THE ONION MIXTURE: Heat oil in Dutch oven over medium-high heat until shimmering. Cook onions until golden, 10 to 15 minutes. Add garlic, oregano, and pepper flakes and cook until fragrant, about 30 seconds. Transfer half of onion mixture to large bowl and set aside.

2. FOR THE MARINARA: Add tomato paste to remaining onion mixture in pot and cook until fragrant, about 1 minute. Add wine and cook until slightly thickened, about 2 minutes. Stir in water and tomatoes and simmer over low heat until sauce is no longer watery, 45 minutes to 1 hour. Stir in Parmesan and basil and season with salt and sugar to taste.

3. FOR THE MEATBALLS: Meanwhile, adjust oven rack to upper-middle position and heat oven to 475 degrees. Add bread and milk to bowl with reserved onion mixture and mash together until smooth. Add sausage, Parmesan, parsley, eggs, garlic, and salt to bowl and mash to combine. Add beef and knead with hands until well combined. Lightly shape mixture into 2½-inch round meatballs (about 16 meatballs total), place on rimmed baking sheet, and bake until well browned, about 20 minutes.

4. Transfer meatballs to pot with sauce and simmer for 15 minutes. Serve. (Meatballs and marinara can be frozen for up to 1 month.)

WELL-SEASONED MEATBALLS WITHOUT THE MESS

We bypassed the messy frying step and baked our meatballs in a super-hot oven instead to ensure a nicely brown crust. Simmering the meatballs in the sauce briefly allows the sauce to season the meat, and vice versa.

1. Bake meatballs in very hot oven to ensure browned crust.

2. Simmer meatballs in sauce for 15 minutes before serving for flavorful sauce and meatballs.

✅ WHY THIS RECIPE WORKS

To infuse our slow-cooker meatballs and marinara sauce with depth of flavor, we used lots of onion, garlic, and tomato paste and sautéed them before adding them to the slow cooker. Microwaving the meatballs before adding them to the slow cooker rendered just enough fat (which we discarded) to ensure the sauce wouldn't be greasy. To bind and moisten the meatballs, we traded in the usual panade (a paste of milk and bread), which caused them to break apart in the slow cooker, for cream and shredded mozzarella cheese.

Slow-Cooker Meatballs and Marinara

SERVES 6

Microwave the meatballs on a large plate or in a casserole dish to contain the rendering fat. This recipe makes enough to sauce 1½ pounds of pasta.

ONION MIXTURE

2	tablespoons olive oil
2	onions, chopped fine
1	(6-ounce) can tomato paste
6	garlic cloves, minced
1	tablespoon dried oregano
½	teaspoon red pepper flakes
¼	teaspoon salt

MARINARA

½	cup red wine
2	(28-ounce) cans crushed tomatoes

MEATBALLS

4	ounces Italian sausage, casings removed
2	ounces mozzarella cheese, shredded (½ cup)
1	ounce Parmesan cheese, grated (½ cup)
2	large eggs
2	garlic cloves, minced
¾	teaspoon salt
1¼	pounds 85 percent lean ground beef
3	tablespoons heavy cream
1	ounce Parmesan cheese, grated (½ cup)
2	tablespoons finely chopped fresh basil
	Salt

1. FOR THE ONION MIXTURE: Heat oil in Dutch oven over medium-high heat until shimmering. Add onions, tomato paste, garlic, oregano, pepper flakes, and salt and cook until softened and lightly browned, about 8 to 10 minutes. Transfer half of onion mixture to large bowl and set aside.

2. FOR THE MARINARA: Add wine to remaining onion mixture in pot and cook until slightly thickened, about 2 minutes. Stir in tomatoes, then transfer to slow cooker.

3. FOR THE MEATBALLS: Add sausage, mozzarella, Parmesan, eggs, garlic, and salt to bowl with reserved onion mixture. Mash with potato masher until smooth. Add beef and cream to bowl and knead with hands until well combined. Lightly shape mixture into 2-inch round meatballs (about 12 total). Microwave meatballs on large plate until fat renders and meatballs are firm, 4 to 7 minutes. Nestle meatballs into slow cooker, discarding rendered fat. Cover and cook until meatballs are tender and sauce is slightly thickened, 4 to 5 hours on low.

4. Let meatballs and sauce settle for 5 minutes, then skim fat from surface and stir in Parmesan and basil. Season with salt to taste. Serve.

TO MAKE AHEAD: Slow-Cooker Meatballs and Marinara can be made in advance through shaping meatballs in step 3. Uncooked meatballs and sauce can be refrigerated in separate airtight containers for up to 24 hours. When ready to cook, add sauce to slow cooker and proceed with microwaving meatballs in step 3.

MICROWAVING MEATBALLS

Instead of browning the meatballs on the stovetop or in the oven, we microwaved them. Just five minutes is enough to set the exterior and keep them from falling apart in the slow cooker. The precooking also rendered some of the fat, minimizing the grease in our marinara sauce.

WHY THIS RECIPE WORKS

Pasta in a slow cooker? You bet. But achieving well-cooked pasta and melty cheese in the slow cooker takes some strategy. Borrowing a technique from risotto was the key to perfect pasta—we stirred the raw pasta into the browned sausage and onion mixture, coating the starch in fat and preventing the pasta from bloating in the slow cooker. To get cheese that was evenly melted, we added it after cooking and let it sit in the residual warmth of the turned-off slow-cooker.

Slow-Cooker Baked Ziti

SERVES 6

Our favorite crushed tomatoes are Tuttorosso Crushed Tomatoes in Thick Puree with Basil.

2	tablespoons olive oil
1	pound hot or sweet Italian sausage, casings removed
1	onion, chopped
3	garlic cloves, minced
½	teaspoon dried oregano
½	teaspoon salt
½	teaspoon pepper
8	ounces (2½ cups) ziti
1	(28-ounce) can crushed tomatoes
1	(15-ounce) can tomato sauce
8	ounces (1 cup) whole-milk ricotta cheese
4	ounces mozzarella cheese, shredded (1 cup)
2	tablespoons thinly sliced fresh basil

1. Make aluminum foil collar for slow cooker by folding 2 (18-inch-long) pieces of foil to make 2 (18 by 4-inch) strips. Line perimeter of slow cooker with foil strips and spray with vegetable oil spray.

2. Heat oil in Dutch oven over medium-high heat until just smoking. Cook sausage, breaking up pieces with spoon, until well browned, 6 to 8 minutes. Add onion and cook until lightly browned, about 5 minutes. Stir in garlic, oregano, salt, and pepper and cook until fragrant, about 1 minute.

3. Reduce heat to medium-low. Add ziti and cook, stirring constantly, until edges of pasta become translucent, about 4 minutes. Off heat, stir in crushed tomatoes and tomato sauce, scraping up any browned bits. Transfer mixture to prepared slow cooker. Cover and cook on low until pasta is tender, about 3 hours.

4. Using tongs, remove foil collar from slow cooker. Dollop ricotta over ziti and sprinkle with mozzarella. Cover and let sit for 20 minutes to let cheeses melt. Garnish with basil and serve.

KEY STEPS TO GREAT SLOW-COOKER "BAKED" ZITI

1. To prevent burning, fold aluminum foil into two strips and use them to line the perimeter of the slow cooker.

2. After hours in the slow cooker, pasta turns slimy and bloated. To avoid that, we first sauté it with the sausage and onion.

WHY THIS RECIPE WORKS

To streamline chicken Parmesan and still keep its flavors and textures intact, we browned boneless, skinless chicken breasts, which we had sliced into cutlets, in a nonstick pan, then made a simple tomato sauce and simmered the chicken right in the sauce so it could absorb the flavors. For the cheesy layer, we supplemented the traditional mozzarella with provolone (preferably the sharp variety) for a much richer flavor. And rather than breading the chicken, we sprinkled the bread crumbs, which we toasted and seasoned with Parmesan and basil, over the finished dish so they stayed ultra-crisp.

Skillet Chicken Parmesan

SERVES 4

We like the assertive flavor of sharp provolone here, but mild provolone works well, too.

2	slices hearty white sandwich bread, torn into large pieces
3	tablespoons olive oil
2½	ounces Parmesan cheese, grated (1¼ cups)
¼	cup chopped fresh basil
1	(28-ounce) can crushed tomatoes
2	garlic cloves, minced
	Salt and pepper
4	(6-ounce) boneless, skinless chicken breasts, trimmed
½	cup all-purpose flour
3	tablespoons vegetable oil
3	ounces mozzarella cheese, shredded (¾ cup)
3	ounces provolone cheese, shredded (¾ cup)

1. Pulse bread in food processor to coarse crumbs, about 10 pulses. Toast bread crumbs in 12-inch non-stick skillet over medium-high heat until browned, about 5 minutes, and transfer to bowl. Toss with 1 tablespoon olive oil, ¼ cup Parmesan, and half of basil. In separate bowl, combine remaining 2 tablespoons olive oil, ¼ cup Parmesan, remaining basil, tomatoes, garlic, and salt and pepper to taste.

2. Using sharp knife, and holding chicken securely, slice each breast horizontally into 2 cutlets of even thickness. Place flour in shallow dish. Season chicken with salt and pepper and dredge in flour. Heat 2 tablespoons vegetable oil in now-empty skillet over medium-high heat until shimmering. Add 4 cutlets and cook until golden brown on both sides, about 5 minutes. Transfer to plate and repeat with remaining cutlets and remaining 1 tablespoon vegetable oil.

3. Reduce heat to medium-low and add tomato mixture to now-empty skillet. Return cutlets to pan in even layer, pressing down to cover with sauce. Sprinkle mozzarella, provolone, and remaining ¾ cup Parmesan over chicken. Cover and cook until cheese is melted, about 5 minutes. Sprinkle with bread-crumb mixture and serve.

MAKING CUTLETS

To make chicken cutlets from chicken breasts, use your hand to hold chicken breast in place, keeping your fingers straight and parallel to breast. Using sharp chef's knife, start at thickest part of breast and slice it in half horizontally, producing 2 even cutlets.

SHREDDING SEMISOFT CHEESE

Semisoft cheeses like mozzarella can be messy to grate. To keep the holes of the grater from clogging, lightly coat that side of the box grater with vegetable oil spray before shredding the cheese.

☑ WHY THIS RECIPE WORKS

To get our lasagna fix without spending hours in the kitchen, we made the entire dish, from start to finish, in a 12-inch skillet. After sautéing aromatics, we browned our meat in the pan, then added the noodles and sauce. Meatloaf mix (a blend of ground beef, pork, and veal) contributed deep, meaty flavor. Canned diced tomatoes and tomato sauce, thinned with water, provided ample liquid to cook our noodles and thickened to just the right consistency after a brief simmer. For a rich, creamy topping, we dropped big dollops of ricotta cheese over the noodles and covered the pan so they'd melt.

Skillet Lasagna

SERVES 4 TO 6

A 12-inch nonstick skillet with a tight-fitting lid works best for this recipe.

1   **(28-ounce) can diced tomatoes**
      Water
1   **tablespoon olive oil**
1   **onion, chopped fine**
      Salt and pepper
3   **garlic cloves, minced**
⅛   **teaspoon red pepper flakes**
1   **pound meatloaf mix**
10   **curly-edged lasagna noodles, broken into 2-inch lengths**
1   **(8-ounce) can tomato sauce**
1   **ounce Parmesan cheese, grated (½ cup), plus 2 tablespoons, grated**
8   **ounces (1 cup) whole-milk or part-skim ricotta cheese**
3   **tablespoons chopped fresh basil**

1. Place tomatoes in 4-cup liquid measuring cup. Add water until mixture measures 4 cups.

2. Heat oil in 12-inch nonstick skillet over medium heat until shimmering. Add onion and ½ teaspoon salt and cook until onion begins to brown, about 5 minutes. Stir in garlic and pepper flakes and cook until fragrant, about 30 seconds. Add meat and cook, breaking up meat into small pieces with wooden spoon, until it is no longer pink, about 4 minutes.

3. Scatter pasta over meat but do not stir. Pour tomato mixture and tomato sauce over pasta, cover, and bring to simmer. Reduce heat to medium-low and simmer, stirring occasionally, until pasta is tender, about 20 minutes.

4. Off heat, stir in ½ cup Parmesan and season with salt and pepper to taste. Dollop heaping tablespoons of ricotta over top, cover, and let sit for 5 minutes. Sprinkle with basil and remaining 2 tablespoons Parmesan. Serve.

SKILLET LASAGNA WITH SAUSAGE AND RED PEPPER

Substitute 1 pound Italian sausage, casings removed, for meatloaf mix. Add 1 chopped red bell pepper to skillet with onion.

SECRETS TO SKILLET LASAGNA

1. Sauté onion, garlic, and meat in skillet, then scatter broken lasagna noodles over meat.

2. Pour diced tomatoes and tomato sauce over noodles, cover, and cook until pasta is tender, about 20 minutes.

3. Stir in Parmesan and dollop with ricotta, then cover skillet and let cheese soften off heat.

WHY THIS RECIPE WORKS

To make a spinach lasagna worthy of its name, we increased the amount of spinach. Frozen spinach tasted just as good as fresh and cut down on kitchen time. For the most even texture, we used the food processor to chop the spinach. For extra spinach flavor we included some of the drained spinach liquid (we combined it with the ricotta in the food processor) but not enough to make the lasagna watery. To keep the spinach flavor front and center, we nixed the traditional creamy béchamel in favor of a fresh, herb-flecked tomato sauce but still layered in plenty of mozzarella and Parmesan for richness.

Spinach and Tomato Lasagna

SERVES 8 TO 10

Our favorite brand of no-boil lasagna noodles is Barilla. You can thaw the spinach overnight in the refrigerator instead of microwaving it, but be sure to warm the spinach liquid to help smooth the ricotta.

30	ounces frozen chopped spinach
2	tablespoons olive oil
1	onion, chopped fine
5	garlic cloves, minced
⅛	teaspoon red pepper flakes
2	(28-ounce) cans crushed tomatoes
	Salt and pepper
6	tablespoons chopped fresh basil
1½	pounds (3 cups) whole-milk or part-skim ricotta cheese
3	ounces Parmesan cheese, grated (1½ cups)
2	large eggs
12	no-boil lasagna noodles
12	ounces whole-milk mozzarella cheese, shredded (3 cups)

1. Adjust oven rack to middle position and heat oven to 375 degrees. Microwave spinach in covered large bowl until completely thawed, about 15 minutes, stirring halfway through cooking. Squeeze spinach dry, reserving ⅓ cup liquid. Pulse spinach in food processor until ground, 8 to 10 pulses, scraping down bowl every few pulses. Wipe out large bowl with paper towels. Transfer spinach to now-empty bowl; set aside.

2. Heat oil in large saucepan over medium heat until shimmering. Add onion and cook until softened, about 5 minutes. Stir in garlic and pepper flakes and cook until fragrant, about 30 seconds. Add tomatoes, ½ cup processed spinach, 1 teaspoon salt, and ½ teaspoon pepper and cook until slightly thickened, about 10 minutes. Off heat, stir in 3 tablespoons basil; set aside.

3. Process ricotta and reserved spinach liquid in food processor until smooth, about 30 seconds. Add Parmesan, remaining 3 tablespoons basil, eggs, 1½ teaspoons salt, and ½ teaspoon pepper and process until combined. Stir ricotta mixture into remaining processed spinach.

4. Cover bottom of 13 by 9-inch baking dish with 1¼ cups sauce. Top with 3 noodles and spread one-third of ricotta mixture evenly over noodles. Sprinkle with ⅔ cup mozzarella and cover with 1¼ cups sauce. Repeat twice, beginning with noodles and ending with sauce. Top with remaining 3 noodles, remaining sauce, and remaining 1 cup mozzarella.

5. Cover pan tightly with aluminum foil sprayed with vegetable oil spray and bake until bubbling around edges, about 40 minutes. Discard foil and continue to bake until cheese is melted, about 10 minutes. Let cool on wire rack for 30 minutes. Serve.

KEYS TO SPINACH FLAVOR

For lasagna that actually tastes like spinach, we took a three-pronged approach.

- Increasing the amount of spinach to triple the amount called for in most recipes guaranteed it had a distinct presence.
- Adding some of the spinach water, from squeezing the spinach dry to prevent a soggy lasagna, to the ricotta cheese ensured a creamy, spinach-flavored filling.
- Chopping the spinach in the food processor produced a fine, even texture that distributed nicely in both the cheese filling and the sauce.

✔ WHY THIS RECIPE WORKS

For fuss-free but flavorful manicotti, we started by substituting no-boil lasagna noodles for the manicotti tubes. Briefly soaking them in hot water made them pliable and easy to roll up. Using the food processor to break down the ground beef allowed its flavor to permeate the sauce quickly so it needed just a short simmer. For even more meaty flavor, we added a popular pizza topping—pepperoni—which gave the sauce a spicy backbone. To liven up the filling, we included assertive provolone, plus a portion of the processed ground beef and pepperoni; a single egg helped to bind it all together.

Baked Manicotti with Meat Sauce

SERVES 6 TO 8

You will need 16 no-boil lasagna noodles for this recipe. The test kitchen's preferred brand, Barilla, comes 16 noodles to a box, but other brands contain only 12. It is important to let the dish cool for 15 minutes after baking.

MEAT SAUCE

1	onion, chopped
6	ounces thinly sliced deli pepperoni
1	pound 85 percent lean ground beef
5	garlic cloves, minced
1	tablespoon tomato paste
¼	teaspoon red pepper flakes
2	(28-ounce) cans crushed tomatoes
	Salt and pepper

MANICOTTI

1½	pounds (3 cups) ricotta cheese
10	ounces mozzarella cheese, shredded (2½ cups)
6	ounces provolone cheese, shredded (1½ cups)
1	large egg, lightly beaten
¼	cup finely chopped fresh basil
½	teaspoon salt
½	teaspoon pepper
16	no-boil lasagna noodles

1. FOR THE MEAT SAUCE: Adjust oven rack to upper-middle position and heat oven to 375 degrees. Pulse onion and pepperoni in food processor until coarsely ground, about 10 pulses. Add beef and pulse until thoroughly combined, 5 to 8 pulses.

2. Transfer mixture to large saucepan and cook over medium heat, breaking up mixture with wooden spoon, until no longer pink, about 5 minutes. Using slotted spoon, transfer 1 cup meat mixture to paper towel–lined plate and reserve. Add garlic, tomato paste, and pepper flakes to pot and cook until fragrant, about 1 minute. Stir in tomatoes and simmer until sauce is slightly thickened, about 20 minutes. Season with salt and pepper to taste. (Meat sauce can be refrigerated for up to 3 days.)

3. FOR THE MANICOTTI: Combine ricotta, 2 cups mozzarella, 1 cup provolone, egg, basil, salt, pepper, and reserved meat mixture in large bowl. Pour 1 inch boiling water into 13 by 9-inch baking dish and slip noodles into water, one at a time. Let noodles soak until pliable, about 5 minutes, separating noodles with tip of knife to prevent sticking. Remove noodles from water and place in single layer on clean dish towels; discard water and dry off baking dish.

4. Spread half of meat sauce over bottom of baking dish. Spread ¼ cup ricotta mixture evenly over bottom of each noodle. Roll noodles up around filling and lay them seam side down in baking dish. Spread remaining sauce over top to cover pasta completely. Cover dish tightly with aluminum foil and bake until bubbling around edges, about 40 minutes. Remove foil and sprinkle with remaining ½ cup mozzarella and ½ cup provolone. Bake until cheese is melted, about 5 minutes. Let cool for 15 minutes. Serve.

MANICOTTI MADE EASY

Manicotti shells are hard to fill without tearing. For easy-to-fill manicotti, we found a better solution in no-boil lasagna noodles.

1. After soaking no-boil lasagna noodles briefly in hot water, spread filling across bottom of each and roll into tube.

2. Arrange rolled manicotti seam side down over sauce in baking dish.

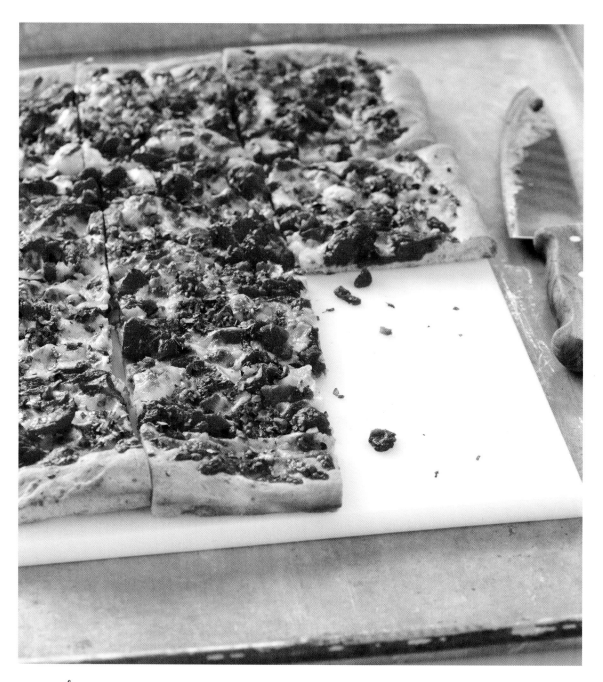

✔ WHY THIS RECIPE WORKS

Grandma pizza is a thin-crust pan pizza topped with a modest amount of cheese, then with chunks of tomatoes. To re-create this Long Island specialty, bread flour and lengthy kneading gave us the chewy crust we wanted, but the dough was difficult to stretch thin. Proofing the dough on the same sheet pan that we used to bake the pizza let it stretch on its own as it proofed. For a fresh, easy tomato topping that wouldn't make our crust soggy, we tossed drained diced tomatoes with salt, olive oil, garlic, and oregano. Baking the pizza on the lowest rack then cooling it on a wire rack perfectly crisped the bottom crust.

Grandma Pizza

SERVES 4

If the dough snaps back when you press it to the corners of the baking sheet, cover it, let it rest for 10 minutes, and try again.

DOUGH

3	tablespoons olive oil
¾	cup water
1½	cups (8¼ ounces) bread flour
2¼	teaspoons instant or rapid-rise yeast
1	teaspoon sugar
¾	teaspoon salt

TOPPING

1	(28-ounce) can diced tomatoes
1	tablespoon olive oil
2	garlic cloves, minced
1	teaspoon dried oregano
¼	teaspoon salt
8	ounces mozzarella cheese, shredded (2 cups)
¼	cup grated Parmesan cheese
2	tablespoons chopped fresh basil

1. FOR THE DOUGH: Coat rimmed baking sheet with 2 tablespoons oil. Combine water and remaining 1 tablespoon oil in 1-cup liquid measuring cup. Using stand mixer fitted with dough hook, mix flour, yeast, sugar, and salt on low speed until combined. With mixer running, slowly add water mixture and mix until dough comes together, about 1 minute. Increase speed to medium-low and mix until dough is smooth and comes away from sides of bowl, about 10 minutes.

2. Transfer dough to greased baking sheet and turn to coat. Stretch dough to 10 by 6-inch rectangle. Cover loosely with plastic wrap and let rise in warm place until doubled in size, 1 to 1½ hours. Stretch dough to corners of pan, cover loosely with plastic, and let rise in warm place until slightly puffed, about 45 minutes. Meanwhile, adjust oven rack to lowest position and heat oven to 500 degrees.

3. FOR THE TOPPING: Place tomatoes in colander and drain well. Combine drained tomatoes, oil, garlic, oregano, and salt in bowl. Combine mozzarella and Parmesan in second bowl. Sprinkle cheese mixture over dough, leaving ½-inch border around edges. Top with tomato mixture and bake until well browned and bubbling, about 15 minutes. Slide pizza onto wire rack, sprinkle with basil, and let cool for 5 minutes. Serve.

EASY RISE

Our method lets the dough proof right on the sheet. Spread dough on oiled baking sheet, then cover with plastic wrap and set it aside to rise.

WHERE WAS GRANDMA PIZZA BORN?

In a 2003 piece in the Long Island newspaper *Newsday*, writer Erica Marcus traced grandma pizza's origins to Umberto's Pizzeria in New Hyde Park. According to Marcus, in the early 1970s proprietor Umberto Corteo would ask his pizza man to create a simple pizza like the one his mother used to make in Italy. The Corteos opened a second pizzeria, King Umberto's, in nearby Elmont. It was later bought by two former Umberto's pizza makers, who built a best-selling item out of their former boss's favorite lunch, naming it grandma pizza sometime in the late 1980s. Within 10 years, other Long Island pizzerias were offering the pie, and a phenomenon was born.

✓ WHY THIS RECIPE WORKS

The bolder cousin of American-style pot roast, Italian Pot Roast trades the potatoes, carrots, and gravy for mushrooms, onion, and a thick sauce based on tomatoes, red wine, garlic, and herbs. For our version, we started with a chuck-eye roast for its beefy flavor and ample fat. Canned diced tomatoes, tomato sauce, and tomato paste gave us a thick, rich sauce; a double dose of red wine added depth and brightness. Simmering a whole head of garlic with our roast ensured the meat and sauce were infused with mellow garlic flavor.

Italian Pot Roast

SERVES 4 TO 6

Start checking the roast for doneness after two hours; if there is a little resistance when prodded with a fork, it's done. Light, sweeter red wines, such as a Merlot or Beaujolais, work especially well with this recipe.

1	(3½- to 4-pound) boneless beef chuck-eye roast, trimmed, tied at 1-inch intervals
	Salt and pepper
2	tablespoons vegetable oil
1	onion, chopped
1	celery rib, minced
1	pound cremini or white mushrooms, trimmed and quartered
2	tablespoons tomato paste
1	(14.5-ounce) can diced tomatoes
½	cup canned tomato sauce
½	cup water
1	cup red wine
2	teaspoons sugar
1	large garlic head, outer papery skins removed, halved
1	sprig fresh thyme
1	sprig fresh rosemary

GETTING THE GARLIC RIGHT

Here's how we tone down the garlic in our Italian Pot Roast so it offers mellow, not overpowering, flavor.

1. After slicing whole head of garlic in half, add it to pot to simmer with roast.

2. Once roast is done, squeeze garlic cloves from their skins and mash garlic with fork to form paste. Stir garlic paste back into sauce.

1. Adjust oven rack to middle position and heat oven to 300 degrees. Pat roast dry with paper towels and season with salt and pepper.

2. Heat oil in Dutch oven over medium-high heat until just smoking. Brown roast on all sides, 8 to 12 minutes. Transfer roast to large plate. Reduce heat to medium, add onion, celery, mushrooms, and tomato paste and cook until vegetables begin to soften, about 8 minutes. Add diced tomatoes, tomato sauce, water, ½ cup wine, sugar, garlic, and thyme. Add roast, with accumulated juices, to pot and bring to simmer over medium-high heat. Place piece of aluminum foil over pot, cover with lid, and transfer pot to oven.

3. Cook until roast is just fork-tender, 2½ to 3½ hours, turning roast after 1 hour. Remove lid and foil and let roast rest for 30 minutes, skimming fat from surface of liquid after 20 minutes. Transfer roast to carving board and tent with foil.

4. Remove and reserve garlic head and skim remaining fat. Add remaining ½ cup wine to pot, bring to boil over medium-high heat, and cook until sauce begins to thicken, about 12 minutes. Meanwhile, carefully squeeze garlic cloves from their skins and mash into paste. Add rosemary to pot and simmer until fragrant, about 2 minutes. Remove rosemary and thyme sprigs, stir in mashed garlic, and season with salt and pepper to taste.

5. Remove twine from roast and slice meat against grain into ½-inch-thick slices or pull apart into large pieces. Transfer meat to serving platter and pour ¾ cup sauce over meat. Serve, passing remaining sauce separately.

FIT TO BE TIED

A tied roast will cook evenly and won't fall apart during the long cooking time. If your roast doesn't come tied, simply tie pieces of kitchen twine around it at 1-inch intervals.

✓ WHY THIS RECIPE WORKS

Choosing the right pork chop and the right kind of peppers was essential to getting this dish right. We decided on thick-cut, bone-in rib chops, which we brined briefly to ensure seasoned and moist meat. Jarred sweet vinegar peppers held up to braising, and had a mild tang that we liked. To give long-cooked flavor to our quick-cooked braising sauce, we added a secret ingredient—anchovy fillets—which lent savory depth but did not impart any fishy flavor. We thickened the sauce in two ways: by flouring the chops (which also aided browning) and by reducing the sauce slightly after the pork was done.

Pork Chops with Vinegar Peppers

SERVES 4

Our favorite chicken broth is Swanson Chicken Stock.

3	tablespoons sugar
	Salt and pepper
4	(8- to 10-ounce) bone-in pork rib chops, 1 inch thick, trimmed
⅓	cup all-purpose flour
2	tablespoons olive oil
1	onion, halved and sliced thin
8	garlic cloves, lightly crushed and peeled
2	anchovy fillets, rinsed, patted dry, and minced
2	cups thinly sliced sweet green vinegar peppers
1	sprig fresh rosemary
1	cup chicken broth
½	cup red wine vinegar
1	tablespoon unsalted butter

1. Dissolve sugar and 3 tablespoons salt in 1½ quarts cold water in large container. Add chops, cover, and refrigerate for 30 minutes or up to 1 hour.

2. Place flour in shallow dish. Remove chops from brine. Pat chops dry with paper towels and season with pepper. Working with 1 chop at a time, dredge both sides in flour, shaking off excess. Heat 1 tablespoon oil in 12-inch skillet over medium-high heat until just smoking. Add chops and cook until well browned on first side, 5 to 7 minutes. Flip chops and cook on second side for 1 minute; transfer to plate, browned side up.

3. Reduce heat to medium and add remaining 1 tablespoon oil, onion, garlic, and anchovies to now-empty skillet. Cook, stirring frequently, until onion is softened and golden brown, 6 to 8 minutes. Add peppers and rosemary and cook until peppers begin to caramelize, about 5 minutes. Add broth and vinegar and bring to boil.

4. Arrange chops, browned side up, in skillet and add any accumulated juices from plate. Reduce heat to low, cover, and simmer until chops register 145 degrees, 6 to 10 minutes. Transfer chops to serving platter and tent loosely with aluminum foil.

5. Increase heat to high and boil sauce until slightly thickened, about 3 minutes. Off heat, stir in butter and season with salt and pepper to taste. Stir any accumulated juices from platter into sauce. Discard rosemary and spoon sauce over chops. Serve.

FINISHING A PAN SAUCE WITH BUTTER

Add butter to pan sauces off heat to prevent the butter from separating and leaving an oil slick on top. Butter gives our sauce richness and body.

THE STATE OF GRILLING

THE WAY WE COOK OUTDOORS TODAY IS DUE TO TWO ENTERPRISING Americans. The first was Henry Ford of the Ford Motor Company. In the early days of the automobile business when Ford manufactured the Model T, the car was partially built with wooden parts. The assembly process generated a lot of wood scraps. Not one to let things go to waste, Ford took advantage of a charcoal-making process that had been around since the 1890s—one in which wood could be burned to charcoal, mixed with a binder, and formed into briquettes. Ford put one of his relatives in charge of his new charcoal briquette–making business. The relative's name? E.G. Kingsford, a moniker that went on to become synonymous with briquettes.

The second American who made an unlikely contribution to the state of modern grilling was George Stephen, a metal worker who worked for Weber Brothers Metal in Chicago in the 1950s. Frustrated with the limited functionality of the flat, open grills of the time, called braziers, he began tinkering and eventually created the kettle grill. Stephen was actually working on a buoy at the metal shop when he became inspired by its shape and applied it to his grill project. The bottom half became the base of the grill and the top half the lid. After some experimentation, he realized that he needed to punch holes in the lid, to allow oxygen to enter and keep the flames going. This kettle design remains the standard for charcoal grills today. Of course, years later, gas grills have become popular. While gas is undeniably convenient, purists remain loyal to the authentically smoky flavor of food cooked on a charcoal grill.

Whichever grill you prefer to cook on, join us as we crisscross the United States to share all manner of grilling and barbecue recipes and a host of easy sides to complete your meal. Let's fire up the grill!

✔ WHY THIS RECIPE WORKS

Authentic Hawaiian huli huli chicken is typically something home cooks buy instead of make. The birds are continually basted with a sticky-sweet glaze and "huli"-ed, which means "turned" in Hawaiian. For the teriyaki-like glaze, we developed a version with soy sauce, rice vinegar, ginger, garlic, chili sauce, ketchup, brown sugar, and lots and lots of pineapple juice. We boiled the sauce down until it was thick, glossy, and sweet. To mimic a Hawaiian rotisserie, we spread the coals in a single layer. The direct heat rendered the fat and crisped the skin, but the chicken was far enough from the coals to avoid burning.

Huli Huli Chicken

SERVES 4 TO 6

When basting the chicken with the glaze in step 4, be careful not to drip too much of it onto the coals or flames or the grill may flare up.

CHICKEN

2	(3½- to 4-pound) whole chickens
2	quarts water
2	cups soy sauce
1	tablespoon vegetable oil
6	garlic cloves, minced
1	tablespoon grated fresh ginger

GLAZE

3	(6-ounce) cans pineapple juice
¼	cup packed light brown sugar
¼	cup soy sauce
¼	cup ketchup
¼	cup rice vinegar
4	garlic cloves, minced
2	tablespoons grated fresh ginger
2	teaspoons chili-garlic sauce
2	cups wood chips, soaked in water for 15 minutes and drained

1. FOR THE CHICKEN: Using kitchen shears, cut along both sides of backbone to remove it. Trim any excess fat or skin at neck. Flip chicken over and, using chef's knife, cut through breastbone to separate chicken into halves. Repeat with other chicken. Combine water and soy sauce in large bowl. Heat oil in large saucepan over medium-high heat until shimmering. Add garlic and ginger and cook until fragrant, about 30 seconds. Stir into soy sauce mixture. Add chicken and refrigerate, covered, for at least 1 hour or up to 8 hours.

2. FOR THE GLAZE: Combine pineapple juice, sugar, soy sauce, ketchup, vinegar, garlic, ginger, and chili-garlic sauce in empty saucepan and bring to boil. Reduce heat to medium and simmer until thick and syrupy (you should have about 1 cup), 20 to 25 minutes. Using large piece of heavy-duty aluminum foil, wrap soaked chips in foil packet and cut several vent holes in top.

3A. FOR A CHARCOAL GRILL: Open bottom vent halfway. Light large chimney starter three-quarters filled with charcoal briquettes (4½ quarts). When top coals are partially covered with ash, pour evenly over grill. Place foil packet on coals. Set cooking grate in place, cover, and open lid vent open halfway. Heat grill until hot and wood chips are smoking, about 5 minutes.

3B. FOR A GAS GRILL: Place wood chip packet directly on primary burner. Turn all burners to high, cover, and heat grill until hot and wood chips are smoking, about 15 minutes. Turn all burners to medium-low. (Adjust burners as needed to maintain grill temperature of 350 degrees.)

4. Clean and oil cooking grate. Remove chicken from brine and pat dry with paper towels. Place chicken skin side up on grill (do not place chicken directly above foil packet). Cover and cook chicken until well browned on bottom and thighs register 120 degrees, 25 to 30 minutes. Flip chicken skin side down and continue to cook, covered, until skin is well browned and crisp and thighs register 175 degrees, 20 to 25 minutes longer. Transfer chicken to platter, brush with half of glaze, and let rest for 5 minutes. Serve, passing remaining glaze at table.

TO MAKE AHEAD: Both brine and glaze can be made ahead and refrigerated for up to 3 days. Do not brine chicken for longer than 8 hours or it will become too salty.

HULI HISTORY LESSON

In 1955, Hawaiian chicken farmer Ernie Morgado served some local farmers barbecued chickens he'd made with his mom's homemade teriyaki-style sauce. They liked it so much that Morgado soon launched a catering business using specially designed barbecue troughs that held chicken halves between two grates. When the chickens were ready to turn, the workers would yell "Huli!" (turn, in Hawaiian), and all the chickens would be rotated in one go. Morgado named his sauce Huli Huli.

✔ WHY THIS RECIPE WORKS

Invented in the 1940s by Robert Baker, a Cornell University professor, this tangy, crisp-skinned grilled chicken recipe has been a star attraction at the New York State Fair ever since. Grilling two split chickens over gentle direct heat worked best here. To crisp the skin without burning it, we started the chicken skin side up to render the fat slowly, then flipped the chicken skin side down to brown until crisp. The traditional poultry seasoning worked great as a rub but tasted dusty in the sauce, so we replaced it with fresh rosemary and sage. Dijon mustard contributed even more flavor to the sauce and thickened it perfectly.

Cornell Barbecued Chicken

SERVES 4 TO 6

Do not brine the chicken longer than two hours or the vinegar will turn the meat mushy. Poultry seasoning is a mix of herbs and spices that can be found in the supermarket spice aisle.

CHICKEN

2	(3½- to 4-pound) whole chickens
¼	cup salt
3½	cups cider vinegar

SEASONING AND SAUCE

1	tablespoon ground poultry seasoning
	Salt and pepper
½	cup cider vinegar
3	tablespoons Dijon mustard
1	tablespoon chopped fresh sage leaves
1	tablespoon chopped fresh rosemary
½	cup olive oil

1. FOR THE CHICKEN: Using kitchen shears, cut along both sides of backbone to remove it. Trim any excess fat or skin at neck. Flip chicken over and, using chef's knife, cut through breastbone to separate chicken into halves. Repeat with other chicken. In large container, dissolve salt in vinegar and 2 quarts water. Submerge chickens in brine, cover, and refrigerate for 1 to 2 hours.

2. FOR THE SAUCE AND SEASONING: Combine poultry seasoning, 2 teaspoons salt, and 2 teaspoons pepper in small bowl; set aside. Process vinegar, mustard, sage, rosemary, ½ teaspoon salt, and ½ teaspoon pepper in blender until smooth, about 1 minute. With blender running, slowly add oil until incorporated. Transfer vinegar sauce to small bowl and reserve for basting chicken in steps 5 and 6.

3. Remove chickens from brine, pat dry with paper towels, and rub evenly with poultry seasoning mixture. Measure out ¾ cup vinegar sauce and set aside for cooking; reserve remaining sauce for serving.

4A. FOR A CHARCOAL GRILL: Open bottom vent completely. Light large chimney starter three-quarters filled with charcoal briquettes (4½ quarts). When top coals are partially covered with ash, pour evenly over grill. Set cooking grate in place, cover, and open lid vent halfway. Heat grill until hot, about 5 minutes.

4B. FOR A GAS GRILL: Turn all burners to high, cover, and heat grill until hot, about 15 minutes. Turn all burners to medium-low. (Adjust burners as needed to maintain grill temperature around 350 degrees.)

5. Clean and oil cooking grate. Place chicken skin side up on grill and brush with 6 tablespoons vinegar sauce for cooking. Cover and cook chicken until well browned on bottom and thighs register 120 degrees, 25 to 30 minutes, brushing with more sauce for cooking halfway through grilling.

6. Flip chicken skin side down and brush with remaining sauce for cooking. Cover and continue to cook chicken until skin is golden brown and crisp and breasts register 160 degrees and thighs register 175 degrees, 20 to 25 minutes longer.

7. Transfer chicken to carving board and let rest for 10 minutes. Carve chicken and serve with reserved sauce.

THE CHICKEN MAN OF CORNELL UNIVERSITY

Robert Baker (1921–2006) developed the recipe for Cornell chicken while employed at Pennsylvania State University, but his recipe didn't take off until he had moved on to the Animal Sciences Department at Cornell University (his alma mater) and published it in a school journal. This vinegary chicken wasn't Dr. Baker's only contribution to the culinary world: He also had a hand in developing the vacuum packaging still used by much of the poultry industry and was the inventor of chicken nuggets, turkey ham, and chicken hot dogs.

✅ WHY THIS RECIPE WORKS

For Alabama-inspired barbecued chicken, we ditched the tomato and slathered a mayonnaise-based sauce on hickory-smoked chicken. Smoking generally takes hours, but our recipe expedites the process by cutting the chickens in half and cooking them in the middle of the grill, sandwiched between piles of smoking coals topped with hickory chips. We coated our chickens with the traditional Alabama mixture of seasoned mayonnaise and vinegar two times during cooking so the hot chicken absorbed the sauce and was flavored through and through.

Alabama Barbecued Chicken

SERVES 4 TO 6

Hickory wood chips are traditional here; however, any type of wood chips will work fine. Two medium wood chunks, soaked in water for one hour, can be substituted for the wood chips on a charcoal grill.

SAUCE

- ¾ cup mayonnaise
- 2 tablespoons cider vinegar
- 2 teaspoons sugar
- ½ teaspoon prepared horseradish
- ½ teaspoon salt
- ½ teaspoon black pepper
- ¼ teaspoon cayenne pepper

CHICKEN

- 1 teaspoon salt
- 1 teaspoon black pepper
- ½ teaspoon cayenne pepper
- 2 (3½- to 4-pound) whole chickens
- 2 cups wood chips, soaked in water for 15 minutes and drained
- 1 (13 by 9-inch) disposable aluminum roasting pan (if using charcoal)

1. FOR THE SAUCE: Process ingredients in blender until smooth, about 1 minute. Refrigerate for at least 1 hour or up to 2 days.

2. FOR THE CHICKEN: Combine salt, pepper, and cayenne in small bowl. Using kitchen shears, cut along both sides of backbone to remove it. Trim any excess fat or skin at neck. Flip chicken over and, using chef's knife, cut through breastbone to separate chicken into halves. Repeat with other chicken. Pat chickens dry with paper towels and rub them evenly with spice mixture. Using large piece of heavy-duty aluminum foil, wrap soaked chips in foil packet and cut several vent holes in top.

3A. FOR A CHARCOAL GRILL: Open bottom vent halfway and place disposable pan in center of grill. Light large chimney starter filled with charcoal briquettes (6 quarts). When top coals are partially covered with ash, pour into 2 even piles on either side of pan. Place wood chip packet on 1 pile of coals. Set cooking grate in place, cover, and open lid vent halfway. Heat grill until hot and wood chips are smoking, about 5 minutes.

3B. FOR A GAS GRILL: Place wood chip packet directly on primary burner. Turn all burners to high, cover, and heat grill until hot and wood chips are smoking, about 15 minutes. Turn all burners to medium-low. (Adjust burners as needed to maintain grill temperature around 350 degrees.)

4. Clean and oil cooking grate. Place chicken skin side down on grill (in center of grill if using charcoal). Cover (positioning lid vent over chicken if using charcoal) and cook chicken until well browned on bottom and thighs register 120 degrees, 35 to 45 minutes.

5. Flip chicken skin side up. Cover and continue to cook chicken until skin is golden brown and crisp and breasts register 160 degrees and thighs register 175 degrees, 15 to 20 minutes longer.

6. Transfer chicken to carving board and brush with 2 tablespoons sauce. Tent chicken with foil and let rest for 10 minutes. Brush chicken with remaining sauce, carve, and serve.

KEEPING BBQ IN THE FAMILY

Big Bob Gibson's, famous for its white mayonnaise-based sauce, has been serving hickory-smoked barbecue in Decatur, Alabama, since 1925. Now run by Big Bob's grandchildren and great-grandchildren, the restaurant has expanded several times. The current pit smoker can cook 175 chickens, 110 slabs of ribs, and 60 whole turkeys at the same time. Although Big Bob used the sauce mostly on chicken, his grandson Don McLemore says nowadays people put it on everything from pork to potato chips.

Classic Barbecued Chicken

SERVES 4 TO 6

Don't try to grill more than 10 pieces of chicken at a time; you won't be able to line them up on the grill as directed in step 5.

QUICK BARBECUE SAUCE

- 3 **cups store-bought barbecue sauce**
- ½ **cup molasses**
- ½ **cup ketchup**
- ¼ **cup cider vinegar**
- 3 **tablespoons brown mustard**
- 2 **teaspoons onion powder**
- 1 **teaspoon garlic powder**

CHICKEN

- 1 **teaspoon salt**
- 1 **teaspoon pepper**
- ¼ **teaspoon cayenne pepper**
- 3 **pounds bone-in chicken pieces, breasts halved crosswise and leg quarters separated into thighs and drumsticks, trimmed**
- 1 **(13 by 9-inch) disposable aluminum roasting pan (if using charcoal)**

1. FOR THE QUICK BARBECUE SAUCE: Whisk all ingredients in medium saucepan and bring to boil over medium-high heat. Reduce heat to medium and cook until sauce is thick and reduced to 3 cups, about 20 minutes. (Sauce can be refrigerated in airtight container for up to 1 week.)

2. FOR THE CHICKEN: Combine salt, pepper, and cayenne in small bowl. Pat chicken dry with paper towels and rub evenly with spice mixture.

3A. FOR A CHARCOAL GRILL: Open bottom vent completely. Place disposable pan on 1 side of grill. Light large chimney starter filled with charcoal briquettes (6 quarts). When top coals are partially covered with ash, pour evenly over half of grill, opposite pan. Set cooking grate in place, cover, and open lid vent completely. Heat grill until hot, about 5 minutes.

3B. FOR A GAS GRILL: Turn all burners to high, cover, and heat grill until hot, about 15 minutes. Leave primary burner on high and turn other burner(s) off. (Adjust primary burner as needed to maintain grill temperature around 350 degrees.)

4. Clean and oil cooking grate. Place chicken, skin side down, on cool side of grill. Cover (positioning lid vent over chicken if using charcoal) and cook until chicken begins to brown, 30 to 35 minutes. Measure out 2 cups of sauce for brushing chicken.

5. Slide chicken into single line between hot and cool sides of grill and continue to cook, uncovered, flipping chicken and brushing with half of sauce for cooking every 5 minutes, until sticky, about 20 minutes.

6. Slide chicken to hot side of grill and continue to cook, flipping and brushing chicken with remaining sauce for cooking, until well glazed and breasts register 160 degrees and thighs/drumsticks register 175 degrees, about 5 minutes.

7. Transfer chicken to platter, tent loosely with aluminum foil, and let rest for 10 minutes. Serve with reserved sauce.

BARBECUED CHICKEN, SLOW AND LOW

First grill roasting, then basting over moderate heat, and finally finishing with more basting over higher heat ensures rendered, saucy, perfectly cooked chicken.

1. Cook chicken skin side down and covered on cool side of grill for about 30 minutes.

2. Move chicken into a single line near coals; baste and turn chicken. Then move pieces directly over coals to caramelize sauce.

✅ WHY THIS RECIPE WORKS

The combination of bourbon and smoke flavors sounded perfect, but first we had get the savory taste we wanted while keeping the chicken from drying out. The key was a mopping sauce: a sauce that is applied during long-grilling recipes to help keep the meat moist. And since smoke is attracted to moisture, keeping the chicken skin damp enhanced the smoky flavor. For even tastier chicken, we split them in half and cut slashes into the meat to create more surface area to soak up the flavor. By basting the chicken every 15 minutes, we ended up with moist, browned chicken with smokin' good bourbon taste.

Smoked Bourbon Chicken

SERVES 4

Use a bourbon you'd be happy drinking. Use all the basting liquid in step 5.

- 1¼ cups bourbon
- 1¼ cups soy sauce
- ½ cup packed brown sugar
- 1 shallot, minced
- 4 garlic cloves, minced
- 2 teaspoons pepper
- 2 (3½- to 4-pound) whole chickens, giblets discarded
- 1 cup wood chips
- 4 (12-inch) wooden skewers

1. Bring bourbon, soy sauce, sugar, shallot, garlic, and pepper to boil in medium saucepan over medium-high heat and cook for 1 minute. Remove from heat and let cool completely. Set aside ¾ cup bourbon mixture for basting chicken. (Bourbon mixture can be refrigerated up to 3 days in advance.)

2. With chickens breast side down, using kitchen shears, cut through bones on both sides of backbones; discard backbones. Flip chickens over and, using chef's knife, split chickens in half lengthwise through centers of breastbones. Cut ½-inch-deep slits across breasts, thighs, and legs, about ½ inch apart. Tuck wingtips behind backs. Divide chicken halves between two 1-gallon zipper-lock bags and divide remaining bourbon mixture between bags. Seal bags, turn to distribute marinade, and refrigerate for at least 1 hour or up to 24 hours, flipping occasionally.

3. Just before grilling, soak wood chips in water for 15 minutes, then drain. Using large piece of heavy-duty aluminum foil, wrap soaked chips in foil packet and cut several vent holes in top. Remove chicken halves from marinade and pat dry with paper towels; discard marinade. Insert 1 skewer lengthwise through thickest part of breast down through thigh of each chicken half.

4A. FOR A CHARCOAL GRILL: Open bottom vent halfway. Light large chimney starter filled with charcoal briquettes (6 quarts). When top coals are partially covered with ash, pour into steeply banked pile against side of grill. Place wood chip packet on coals. Set cooking grate in place, cover, and open lid vent halfway. Heat grill until hot and wood chips are smoking, about 5 minutes.

4B. FOR A GAS GRILL: Remove cooking grate and place wood chip packet directly on primary burner. Set grate in place, turn all burners to high, cover, and heat grill until hot and wood chips are smoking, about 15 minutes. Leave primary burner on high and turn off other burners. (Adjust primary burner as needed to maintain grill temperature between 350 to 375 degrees.)

5. Clean and oil cooking grate. Place chicken halves skin side up on cooler side of grill with legs pointing toward fire. Cover and cook, basting every 15 minutes with reserved bourbon mixture, until breasts register 160 degrees and thighs register 175 degrees, 75 to 90 minutes, switching placement of chicken halves after 45 minutes. (All of bourbon mixture should be used.) Transfer chicken to carving board, tent loosely with foil, and let rest for 20 minutes. Carve and serve.

HOW TO CUT A CHICKEN IN HALF

1. REMOVE BACKBONE:
Using poultry shears, cut through bones on both sides of backbone; discard backbone.

2. CUT THROUGH BREAST:
Flip chicken over and use chef's knife to halve chicken through center of breastbone.

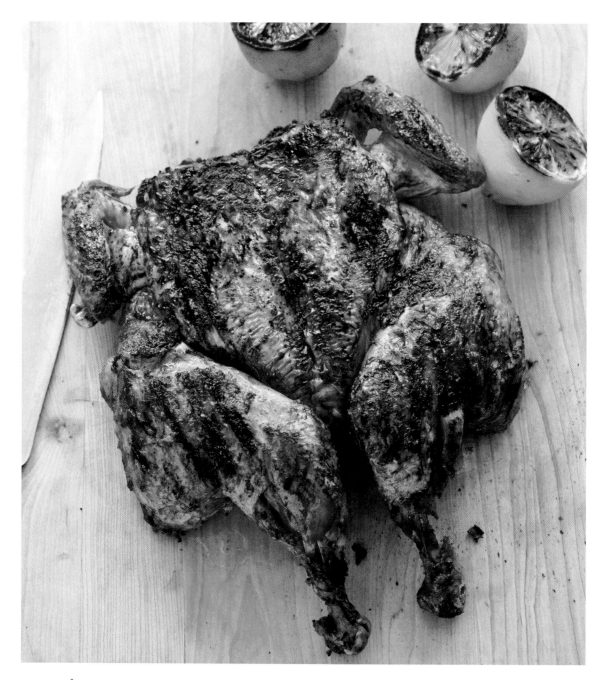

✔ WHY THIS RECIPE WORKS

For perfectly grilled butterflied lemon chicken, we banked all the coals on one side of the grill, placing the chicken opposite the coals and setting the lid on the grill. This allowed the fat under the chicken's skin to render slowly and the relatively gentle heat resulted in a moister bird. Placing the chicken on the grill skin side down reduced cooking time and allowed the most fat to render—a final sear directly over the dying coals at the end of cooking crisped and browned the skin nicely. To finish the chicken with intense lemon flavor, we caramelized lemon halves over the grill and made a sauce from their juice.

Grilled Butterflied Lemon Chicken

SERVES 8

CHICKEN AND RUB

2   (3½- to 4-pound) whole chickens

2   teaspoons grated lemon zest (reserve lemon
      for vinaigrette)

2   teaspoons salt

1   teaspoon pepper

1   (13 by 9-inch) disposable aluminum roasting pan

VINAIGRETTE

4   lemons, halved; plus zested, halved lemon
      from rub

2   tablespoons minced fresh parsley

2   teaspoons Dijon mustard

1   garlic clove, minced

1   teaspoon sugar

½   teaspoon salt

½   teaspoon pepper

⅔   cup extra-virgin olive oil

1. FOR THE CHICKEN AND RUB: Set wire rack in rimmed baking sheet. Using kitchen shears, cut along both sides of backbone to remove it. Flatten breastbone. Use your hands to loosen skin over breast and thighs and remove any excess fat. Repeat with other chicken. Combine lemon zest, salt, and pepper in bowl. Rub zest mixture under chicken skin and tuck wings behind back. Transfer chickens to prepared baking sheet and refrigerate, uncovered, for 30 minutes. (Chickens may be prepared up to this point 24 hours in advance; allow chickens to sit at room temperature for 30 minutes before grilling.)

2A. FOR A CHARCOAL GRILL: Open bottom vent completely and place disposable pan on 1 side of grill. Light large chimney starter filled with charcoal briquettes (6 quarts). When top coals are partially covered in ash, pour into steeply banked pile against side of grill (opposite disposable pan). Evenly scatter 20 unlit coals on top of hot coals. Set cooking grate in place, cover, and open lid vent completely. Heat grill until hot, about 5 minutes.

2B. FOR A GAS GRILL: Turn all burners to high, cover, and heat grill until hot, about 15 minutes. Leave primary burner on high and turn off other burner(s). (Adjust primary burner as needed to maintain grill temperature around 350 degrees.)

3. Clean and oil cooking grate. Place lemon halves, cut side down, on hot side of grill and cook until deep brown and caramelized, 5 to 8 minutes. Transfer to bowl.

4. Place chicken skin side down on cool side of grill, with legs closer to hot side. Cover (positioning lid vent over chicken if using charcoal) and cook until skin is well browned, 45 to 55 minutes.

5. Slide chicken to hot side of grill and continue to cook (covered if using gas) until deeply browned and breasts register 160 degrees and thighs register 175 degrees, about 5 minutes longer. Transfer chicken to carving board, tent loosely with aluminum foil, and let rest for 10 minutes.

6. FOR THE VINAIGRETTE: While chicken cooks, squeeze ⅓ cup juice from grilled lemons into bowl. Stir in parsley, mustard, garlic, sugar, salt, and pepper, then slowly whisk in oil until emulsified.

7. Carve chicken and transfer to serving platter. Pour ⅓ cup vinaigrette over chicken and serve, passing remaining vinaigrette separately.

BUTTERFLYING A WHOLE CHICKEN

1. Cut through bones on either side of backbone and trim any excess fat or skin at neck.

2. Flip chicken over and use heel of your hand to flatten breastbone.

🗸 WHY THIS RECIPE WORKS

To get crisp, well-rendered chicken wings, we tossed the wings in cornstarch (and spices) and grilled them over a gentle medium-low heat. We began grilling with the thicker skin side facing up so that the fat could slowly render, and then we flipped the wings at the end of cooking to crisp the skin. Also, though we normally cook white chicken meat to 160 degrees, wings are chock-full of collagen, which begins to break down upwards of 170 degrees. Cooking the wings to 180 degrees produced meltingly tender wings.

Grilled Chicken Wings

MAKES 24 WINGS

If you buy whole wings, cut them into two pieces before brining. Don't brine the wings for more than 30 minutes or they'll be too salty.

½	cup salt
2	pounds chicken wings, wingtips discarded, trimmed
1½	teaspoons cornstarch
1	teaspoon pepper

1. Dissolve salt in 2 quarts cold water in large container. Prick chicken wings all over with fork. Submerge chicken in brine, cover, and refrigerate for 30 minutes.

2. Combine cornstarch and pepper in bowl. Remove chicken from brine and pat dry with paper towels. Transfer wings to large bowl and sprinkle with cornstarch mixture, tossing until evenly coated.

3A. FOR A CHARCOAL GRILL: Open bottom vent completely. Light large chimney starter half filled with charcoal briquettes (3 quarts). When top coals are partially covered with ash, pour evenly over grill. Set cooking grate in place, cover, and open lid vent completely. Heat grill until hot, about 5 minutes.

3B. FOR A GAS GRILL: Turn all burners to high, cover, and heat grill until hot, about 15 minutes. Turn all burners to medium-low.

4. Clean and oil cooking grate. Grill wings (covered if using gas), thicker skin side up, until browned on bottom, 12 to 15 minutes. Flip chicken and grill until skin is crisp and lightly charred and meat registers 180 degrees, about 10 minutes. Transfer chicken to platter, tent loosely with aluminum foil, and let rest for 5 to 10 minutes. Serve.

BBQ GRILLED CHICKEN WINGS

Reduce pepper to ½ teaspoon. Add 1 teaspoon chili powder, 1 teaspoon paprika, ½ teaspoon garlic powder, ½ teaspoon dried oregano, and ½ teaspoon sugar to cornstarch mixture in step 2.

CREOLE GRILLED CHICKEN WINGS

Add ¾ teaspoon dried oregano, ½ teaspoon garlic powder, ½ teaspoon onion powder, ½ teaspoon white pepper, and ¼ teaspoon cayenne pepper to cornstarch mixture in step 2.

TANDOORI GRILLED CHICKEN WINGS

Reduce pepper to ½ teaspoon. Add 1 teaspoon garam masala, ½ teaspoon ground cumin, ¼ teaspoon garlic powder, ¼ teaspoon ground ginger, and ⅛ teaspoon cayenne pepper to cornstarch mixture in step 2.

PREPPING GRILLED CHICKEN WINGS

1. Puncturing each wing with a fork lets brine easily penetrate meat and gives rendered fat an escape route.

2. Quick saltwater brine seasons wings and keeps them juicy.

3. Right before grilling, dust wings with mixture of cornstarch (to prevent sticking) and black pepper.

WHY THIS RECIPE WORKS

Chicken leg quarters seem like a perfect candidate for the grill—the rich leg and thigh meat has plenty of skin to crisp up. But the thick joint takes longer to cook than the rest of the leg, so grilling often results in overcooking. To remedy this, we took a two-pronged approach. To prepare the chicken, we made slashes down to the bone, a technique often used for large cuts of meat. This helped the chicken cook evenly, and also ensured deep seasoning. We then used our two-level grilling technique, starting the chicken over a low flame, then searing it over a hot fire. A citrus-y dressing provided a welcome hit of brightness.

Grilled Chicken Leg Quarters

SERVES 4

A garlic press makes quick work of mincing the 6 cloves called for here. You can use 1 teaspoon of dried oregano in place of the fresh called for in the dressing. Do not (ever) use dried cilantro.

6	garlic cloves, minced
4	teaspoons kosher salt
1	tablespoon sugar
2	teaspoons grated lime zest plus 2 tablespoons juice
2	teaspoons plus ¼ cup extra-virgin olive oil
1½	teaspoons ground cumin
1	teaspoon pepper
½	teaspoon cayenne pepper
4	(10-ounce) chicken leg quarters, trimmed
2	tablespoons chopped fresh cilantro
2	teaspoons chopped fresh oregano

1. Combine garlic, salt, sugar, lime zest, 2 teaspoons oil, cumin, pepper, and cayenne in bowl and mix to form paste. Reserve 2 teaspoons garlic paste for dressing.

2. Position chicken skin side up on cutting board and pat dry with paper towels. Leaving drumsticks and thighs attached, make 4 parallel diagonal slashes in chicken: 1 across drumsticks, 1 across leg joints; and 2 across thighs (each slash should reach bone). Flip chicken over and make 1 more diagonal slash across back of drumsticks. Rub remaining garlic paste all over chicken and into slashes. Refrigerate chicken for at least 1 hour or up to 24 hours.

3A. FOR A CHARCOAL GRILL: Open bottom vent completely. Light large chimney starter filled with charcoal briquettes (6 quarts). When top coals are partially covered with ash, pour two-thirds evenly over half of grill, then pour remaining coals over other half of grill. Set cooking grate in place, cover, and open lid vent completely. Heat grill until hot, about 5 minutes.

3B. FOR A GAS GRILL: Turn all burners to high, cover, and heat grill until hot, about 15 minutes. Turn primary burner to medium and turn other burner(s) to low. (Adjust primary burner as needed to maintain grill temperature of 400 to 425 degrees.)

4. Clean and oil cooking grate. Place chicken on cooler side of grill, skin side up. Cover and cook until underside of chicken is lightly browned, 9 to 12 minutes. Flip chicken, cover, and cook until leg joint registers 165 degrees, 7 to 10 minutes.

5. Transfer chicken to hotter side of grill, skin side down, and cook (covered if using gas) until skin is well browned, 3 to 5 minutes. Flip chicken and continue to cook until leg joint registers 175 degrees, about 3 minutes longer. Transfer to platter, tent loosely with aluminum foil, and let rest for 5 to 10 minutes.

6. Meanwhile, whisk lime juice, remaining ¼ cup oil, cilantro, oregano, and reserved garlic paste together in bowl. Spoon half of dressing over chicken and serve, passing remaining dressing separately.

MAKING FLAVORFUL, WELL-COOKED CHICKEN LEG QUARTERS

1. SLASH: Make bone-deep slashes in each quarter so the seasonings can penetrate and the meat cooks more readily.

2. RUB: Massage the garlicky seasoning paste into the slashes and all over the chicken and refrigerate for up to 24 hours.

✔ WHY THIS RECIPE WORKS

Barbecuing is the perfect method for cooking fatty cuts of pork or beef, but relatively lean chicken is another story. For barbecued pulled chicken with a smoky flavor and moist, tender meat, we'd have to come up with some tricks. Brining the birds kept the white meat moist and juicy, and arranging the chickens on the grill with the breast meat farther from the heat source than the dark meat evened out the cooking times. We tweaked our favorite barbecue sauce to better complement the chicken, increasing the vinegar to balance the sweetness and swapping the root beer for coffee to boost the smoky flavor.

Barbecued Pulled Chicken

MAKES ENOUGH FOR 8 SANDWICHES

We prefer to halve the chickens ourselves, but you may be able to buy halved chickens from your butcher.

CHICKEN

- 1 cup salt
- 2 (4-pound) whole chickens, giblets discarded
   Pepper
- 2 cups wood chips, soaked in water for 15 minutes and drained

SAUCE

- 2 teaspoons vegetable oil
- 1 onion, chopped fine
- 4 cups chicken broth
- 1¼ cups cider vinegar
- 1 cup brewed coffee
- ¾ cup molasses
- ½ cup tomato paste
- ½ cup ketchup
- 2 tablespoons brown mustard
- 1 tablespoon hot sauce
- ½ teaspoon garlic powder
- ¼ teaspoon liquid smoke

1. FOR THE CHICKEN: Dissolve salt in 4 quarts cold water in large container. Remove backbones from chickens and split chickens in half lengthwise through center of breastbone. Using metal skewer, poke 20 holes all over each chicken half. Submerge chicken halves in brine, cover, and refrigerate for 1 hour. Remove chicken halves from brine, pat dry with paper towels, and season with pepper. Using large piece of heavy-duty aluminum foil, wrap soaked wood chips in foil packet and cut several vent holes in top.

2. FOR THE SAUCE: Meanwhile, heat oil in Dutch oven over medium-high heat until shimmering. Add onion and cook until softened, about 5 minutes. Whisk in broth, vinegar, coffee, molasses, tomato paste, ketchup, mustard, hot sauce, and garlic powder and bring to boil. Reduce heat to medium-low and simmer until mixture is thick and reduced to 4 cups, about 65 to 75 minutes. Stir in liquid smoke; reserve 1 cup sauce for serving. (Sauce can be refrigerated for up to 2 days.)

3A. FOR A CHARCOAL GRILL: Open bottom vent halfway. Light large chimney starter filled with charcoal briquettes (6 quarts). When top coals are partially covered with ash, pour into steeply banked pile against side of grill. Place wood chip packet on coals. Set cooking grate in place, cover, and open lid vent halfway. Heat grill until hot and wood chips are smoking, about 5 minutes.

3B. FOR A GAS GRILL: Place wood chip packet over primary burner. Turn all burners to high, cover, and heat grill until hot and wood chips are smoking, about 15 minutes. Leave primary burner on high and turn off other burner(s).

4. Clean and oil cooking grate. Place chicken halves skin side up on cool side of grill with legs closest to heat source. Cover and cook until breasts register 160 degrees and thighs register 175 degrees, 75 to 85 minutes. Transfer chicken to carving board, tent loosely with foil, and let rest until cool enough to handle, about 15 minutes. Remove and discard skin. Pull meat off bones, separating dark and light meat. Roughly chop dark meat into ½-inch pieces. Shred white meat into thin strands.

5. Add chicken to pot with sauce and cook over medium-low heat until chicken is warmed through, about 5 minutes. Serve on hamburger rolls, passing reserved sauce separately.

WHY THIS RECIPE WORKS

Real burnt ends are all about moist meat and plenty of flavorful, charred bark, but most pit masters use fatty point-cut brisket. To make the leaner (and more widely available) flat-cut brisket work, we cut it into strips and brine it for maximum moisture and flavor. Three hours of smoke on the grill—with a water pan for more moisture—followed by a few more hours in a low oven ensures fully tender brisket with plenty of char. We cut the meat into cubes before tossing it with a flavorful, homemade sauce. Home pit masters, take note.

Barbecued Burnt Ends

SERVES 8 TO 10

Look for a brisket with a significant fat cap. This recipe takes about 8 hours to prepare. The meat can be brined ahead of time, transferred to a zipper-lock bag, and refrigerated for up to a day. If you don't have ½ cup of juices from the rested brisket, supplement with beef broth.

BRISKET AND RUB

- 2 cups plus 1 tablespoon kosher salt
- ½ cup granulated sugar
- 1 (5- to 6-pound) beef brisket, flat cut, untrimmed
- ¼ cup packed brown sugar
- 2 tablespoons pepper
- 4 cups wood chips
- 1 (13 by 9-inch) disposable aluminum roasting pan (if using charcoal) or 2 (8½ by 6-inch) disposable aluminum pans (if using gas)

BARBECUE SAUCE

- ¾ cup ketchup
- ¼ cup packed brown sugar
- 2 tablespoons cider vinegar
- 2 tablespoons Worcestershire sauce
- 2 teaspoons granulated garlic
- ¼ teaspoon cayenne pepper

1. FOR THE BRISKET AND RUB: Dissolve 2 cups salt and granulated sugar in 4 quarts cold water in large container. Slice brisket with grain into 1½-inch-thick strips. Add brisket strips to brine, cover, and refrigerate for 2 hours. Remove brisket from brine and pat dry with paper towels.

2. Combine brown sugar, pepper, and remaining 1 tablespoon salt in bowl. Season brisket all over with rub. Just before grilling, soak wood chips in water for 15 minutes, then drain. Using 2 large pieces of heavy-duty aluminum foil, wrap soaked chips in 2 foil packets and cut several vent holes in tops.

3A. FOR A CHARCOAL GRILL: Open bottom vent halfway and place disposable pan filled with 2 quarts water

on one side of grill, with long side of pan facing center of grill. Arrange 3 quarts unlit charcoal briquettes on opposite side of grill and place 1 wood chip packet on coals. Light large chimney starter filled halfway with charcoal briquettes (3 quarts). When top coals are partially covered with ash, pour evenly over unlit coals and wood chip packet. Place remaining wood chip packet on lit coals. Set cooking grate in place, cover, and open lid vent halfway. Heat grill until hot and wood chips are smoking, about 5 minutes.

3B. FOR A GAS GRILL: Add ½ cup ice cubes to 1 wood chip packet. Remove cooking grate and place both wood chip packets directly on primary burner; place disposable pans each filled with 2 cups water directly on secondary burner(s). Set grate in place, turn all burners to high, cover, and heat grill until hot and wood chips are smoking, about 15 minutes. Leave primary burner on high and turn off other burner(s). (Adjust primary burner as needed to maintain grill temperature of 275 to 300 degrees.)

4. Clean and oil cooking grate. Arrange brisket on cooler side of grill as far from heat source as possible. Cover (positioning lid vent over brisket for charcoal) and cook without opening for 3 hours.

5. Adjust oven rack to middle position and heat oven to 275 degrees. Remove brisket from grill and transfer to rimmed baking sheet. Cover sheet tightly with foil. Roast until fork slips easily in and out of meat and meat registers 210 degrees, about 2 hours. Remove from oven, leave covered, and let rest for 1 hour. Remove foil, transfer brisket to carving board, and pour accumulated juices into fat separator.

6. FOR THE BARBECUE SAUCE: Combine ketchup, sugar, vinegar, Worcestershire, granulated garlic, cayenne, and ½ cup defatted brisket juices in medium saucepan. Bring to simmer over medium heat and cook until slightly thickened, about 5 minutes.

7. Cut brisket strips crosswise into 1- to 2-inch chunks. Combine brisket chunks and barbecue sauce in large bowl and toss to combine. Serve.

✔ WHY THIS RECIPE WORKS

Unlike other barbecue recipes, California barbecued tri-tip recipes call for cooking the meat (bottom sirloin roast) over high heat and seasoning it only with salt, pepper, garlic, and the sweet smoke of the grill. This consistently produces a charred exterior and very rare center—but we wanted the outside cooked less and the inside cooked more. To achieve this, we pushed all the coals in our grill to one side, which created a hot zone for cooking and a cooler one for finishing the meat slowly. To prevent the meat from tasting too smoky, we held off on the wood chips until after we'd seared the meat.

California Barbecued Tri-Tip

SERVES 4 TO 6

If you can't find tri-tip, bottom round steak will also work. Two medium wood chunks, soaked in water for one hour, can be substituted for the wood chips on a charcoal grill. Serve with Santa Maria Salsa (recipe follows) and California Barbecued Beans (page 309). We prefer this roast cooked medium-rare.

- 6 garlic cloves, minced
- 2 tablespoons olive oil
- ¾ teaspoon salt
- 1 (2-pound) tri-tip roast, trimmed
- 1 teaspoon pepper
- ¾ teaspoon garlic salt
- 2 cups wood chips, soaked in water for 15 minutes and drained

1. Combine garlic, oil, and salt in bowl. Pat meat dry with paper towels, poke it about 20 times on each side with fork, and rub it evenly with garlic mixture. Wrap meat in plastic wrap and let sit at room temperature for at least 1 hour or refrigerate for up to 24 hours. (If refrigerated, let sit at room temperature for 1 hour before grilling.) Before cooking, unwrap meat, wipe off garlic paste using paper towels, and rub it evenly with pepper and garlic salt. Using large piece of heavy-duty aluminum foil, wrap soaked chips in foil packet and cut several vent holes in top.

2A. FOR A CHARCOAL GRILL: Open bottom vent completely. Light large chimney starter filled with charcoal briquettes (6 quarts). When top coals are partially covered with ash, pour evenly over half of grill. Set cooking grate in place, cover, and open lid vent completely. Heat grill until hot, about 5 minutes.

2B. FOR A GAS GRILL: Turn all burners to high, cover, and heat grill until hot, about 15 minutes.

3. Clean and oil cooking grate. Grill meat on hot side of grill until well browned on both sides, about 10 minutes. Transfer meat to plate.

4. Place wood chip packet directly on coals or primary burner. If using gas, leave primary burner on high and turn other burner(s) off.

5. Place meat on cool side of grill. Cover (positioning lid vent over meat if using charcoal) and cook until meat registers 120 to 125 degrees (for medium-rare), about 20 minutes.

6. Transfer meat to carving board, tent loosely with aluminum foil, and let rest for 20 minutes. Slice meat thin against grain and serve.

SANTA MARIA SALSA

MAKES ABOUT 4 CUPS

The distinct texture of each ingredient is part of this salsa's identity and appeal, so we don't recommend using a food processor.

- 2 pounds tomatoes, cored and chopped
- 2 teaspoons salt
- 2 jalapeño chiles, stemmed, seeded, and chopped fine
- 1 small red onion, chopped fine
- 1 celery rib, chopped fine
- ¼ cup lime juice (2 limes)
- ¼ cup chopped fresh cilantro
- 1 garlic clove, minced
- ⅛ teaspoon dried oregano
- ⅛ teaspoon Worcestershire sauce

1. Place tomatoes in strainer set over bowl and sprinkle with salt; drain for 30 minutes. Discard liquid. Meanwhile, combine jalapeños, onion, celery, lime juice, cilantro, garlic, oregano, and Worcestershire in large bowl.

2. Add drained tomatoes to jalapeño mixture and toss to combine. Cover with plastic wrap and let stand at room temperature for 1 hour before serving. (Salsa can be refrigerated for up to 2 days.)

✔ WHY THIS RECIPE WORKS

For our Shredded Barbecued Beef, we cut a chuck roast into quarters. The smaller pieces of beef absorbed more smoke flavor and cooked much faster. After cooking the meat in a disposable roasting pan on the cooler side of the grill for a few hours, we flipped all 4 pieces, wrapped the pan in foil, and placed the roast in the oven to finish cooking. For a barbecue sauce with richer flavor, we sautéed the onions in beef fat from the pan. Chili powder and pepper added bite, while ketchup, vinegar, coffee, Worcestershire sauce, brown sugar, and the beef juices rounded out the flavors.

Shredded Barbecued Beef

SERVES 8 TO 10

If you prefer a smooth barbecue sauce, strain the sauce before tossing it with the beef in step 5. We like to serve this beef on white bread with plenty of pickle chips. Three medium wood chunks, soaked in water for one hour, can be substituted for the wood chips on a charcoal grill.

1	tablespoon salt
1	tablespoon pepper
1	teaspoon cayenne pepper
1	(5- to 6-pound) boneless beef chuck-eye roast, trimmed and quartered
1	(13 by 9-inch) disposable aluminum roasting pan
3	cups wood chips, soaked in water for 15 minutes and drained
1	onion, chopped fine
4	garlic cloves, minced
½	teaspoon chili powder
1¼	cups ketchup
¾	cup brewed coffee
½	cup cider vinegar
½	cup packed brown sugar
3	tablespoons Worcestershire sauce
½	teaspoon pepper

1. Combine salt, pepper, and cayenne in small bowl. Pat meat dry with paper towels and rub evenly with spice mixture. Wrap meat in plastic wrap and let sit at room temperature for at least 1 hour or refrigerate up to 24 hours. (If refrigerated, let sit at room temperature for 1 hour before grilling.) Before cooking, unwrap meat and transfer to disposable pan. Using 2 large pieces of heavy-duty aluminum foil, wrap soaked chips in 2 foil packets and cut several vent holes in tops.

2A. FOR A CHARCOAL GRILL: Open bottom vent completely. Light large chimney starter half filled with charcoal briquettes (3 quarts). When top coals are partially covered with ash, pour into steeply banked pile against 1 side of grill. Place wood chip packets on coals. Set cooking grate in place, cover, and open lid vent halfway. Heat grill until hot and wood chips are smoking, about 5 minutes.

2B. FOR A GAS GRILL: Place wood chip packets directly on primary burner. Turn all burners to high, cover, and heat grill until hot and wood chips are smoking, about 15 minutes. Leave primary burner on high and turn other burner(s) off. (Adjust primary burner as needed to maintain grill temperature between 250 and 300 degrees.)

3. Place pan of meat on cool side of the grill. Cover (positioning lid vent over meat if using charcoal) and cook until meat is deep red, about 2 hours. During final 20 minutes of grilling, adjust oven rack to lower-middle position and heat oven to 300 degrees.

4. Flip meat over in pan, cover pan tightly with foil, and roast beef in oven until fork slips easily in and out of beef, 2 to 3 hours.

5. Transfer meat to large bowl, tent loosely with foil, and let rest for 30 minutes. While meat rests, skim fat from accumulated juices in pan; reserve 2 tablespoons fat. Strain defatted juices; reserve ½ cup juice. Combine onion and reserved fat in medium saucepan and cook over medium heat until onion has softened, about 10 minutes. Add garlic and chili powder and cook until fragrant, about 30 seconds. Stir in ketchup, coffee, vinegar, sugar, Worcestershire, pepper, and any accumulated meat juices and simmer until thickened, about 15 minutes. Using 2 forks, pull meat into shreds, discarding any excess fat or gristle. Toss meat with ½ cup barbecue sauce. Serve, passing remaining sauce at table.

✅ WHY THIS RECIPE WORKS

Minneapolis taverns are famous for the Jucy Lucy, a moist beef burger stuffed with American cheese. Replicating the Jucy Lucy seemed easy enough—but our burgers, cooked to well-done to melt the cheese inside, were dry and tough or the cheese melted through the meat, leaving an empty cavern where the cheese had been. To keep the cheese in place, we created a double-sealed pocket by wrapping the cheese inside a small beef patty and then molding a second patty around it. Adding a mixture of bread and milk, mashed into a paste, to the ground beef kept the burgers moist and juicy.

Jucy Lucy Burgers

SERVES 4

Buy the American cheese from the deli counter, and ask them to slice it into a ½-inch slab from which you can cut four big cubes to fill the center of the burgers. One or two percent low-fat milk can be substituted for the whole milk. The cheesy center of these burgers is molten hot when first removed from the grill, so be sure to let the burgers rest for at least five minutes before serving.

2	**slices hearty white sandwich bread, torn into 1-inch pieces**
¼	**cup whole milk**
1	**teaspoon garlic powder**
¾	**teaspoon salt**
½	**teaspoon pepper**
1½	**pounds 85 percent lean ground beef**
1	**(½-inch-thick) piece deli American cheese, quartered**

1. In large bowl and using potato masher, mash bread, milk, garlic powder, salt, and pepper into smooth paste. Add beef and lightly knead mixture until well combined.

2. Divide meat into 4 equal portions. Using half of each portion of meat, encase cheese to form mini burger patty. Mold remaining half-portion of meat around mini patty and seal edges to form ball. Flatten ball with palm of your hand, forming ¾-inch-thick patty. Cover and refrigerate patties for at least 30 minutes or up to 24 hours.

3A. FOR A CHARCOAL GRILL: Open bottom vent completely. Light large chimney starter half filled with charcoal briquettes (3 quarts). When top coals are partially covered with ash, pour evenly over grill. Set cooking grate in place, cover, and heat grill until hot, about 5 minutes.

3B. FOR A GAS GRILL: Turn all burners to high, cover, and heat grill until hot, about 15 minutes. Turn all burners to medium.

4. Clean and oil cooking grate. Lay burgers on grill and cook, without pressing on them, until well browned on both sides and cooked through, 12 to 16 minutes, flipping burgers halfway through grilling. Transfer burgers to platter, tent loosely with aluminum foil, and let rest for 5 minutes before serving.

HOW TO FORM A JUCY LUCY

To avoid a burger blowout, it's essential to completely seal in the cheese.

1. Using half of each portion of meat, encase cheese to form mini burger patty.

2. Mold remaining half-portion of meat around mini patty and seal edges to form a ball and flatten to form ¾-inch patty.

THE GREAT LUCY DEBATE

A debate still rages as to where the Jucy Lucy was created. Two Minnesota taverns, Matt's Bar and the 5–8 Club, claim to have created the burger in the 1950s. As the story goes, a customer requested a burger with the cheese sealed in the middle. When he bit in, the hot cheese spurted out and he exclaimed, "That's one juicy Lucy!" As for the unusual spelling, that's still a mystery.

✅ WHY THIS RECIPE WORKS

For our version of New Mexico's green chile cheeseburgers—ground beef patties grilled to a crusty brown and topped with chopped fire-roasted chiles and a slice of cheese—we preferred the flavor and fat of 85 percent lean ground beef. For the topping, we used mild Anaheim chiles and spicy jalapeños for a complex chile flavor. We grilled the chiles with onions, then quickly chopped them with fresh garlic in the food processor. For even more chile flavor, we pureed some of the chile topping into a smooth paste and mixed it into the raw ground beef. This gave us burgers with satisfying heat through and through.

Green Chile Cheeseburgers

SERVES 4

In step 3, you may need to add a teaspoon or two of water to the food processor to help process the chile mixture. Pressing a shallow divot in the center of each burger patty keeps the burgers flat during grilling.

3	Anaheim chiles, stemmed, halved, and seeded
3	jalapeño chiles, stemmed, halved, and seeded
1	onion, sliced into ½-inch-thick rounds
1	garlic clove, minced
	Salt and pepper
1½	pounds 85 percent lean ground beef
4	slices deli American cheese

1A. FOR A CHARCOAL GRILL: Open bottom vent completely. Light large chimney starter filled with charcoal briquettes (6 quarts). When top coals are partially covered with ash, pour evenly over grill. Set cooking grate in place, cover, and open lid vent completely. Heat grill until hot, about 5 minutes.

1B. FOR A GAS GRILL: Turn all burners to high, cover, and heat grill until hot, about 15 minutes.

2. Clean and oil cooking grate. Place Anaheims, jalapeños, and onion on grill, cover, and cook until vegetables are lightly charred and tender, 4 to 6 minutes, flipping halfway through cooking. Transfer vegetables to bowl, cover, and let cool 5 minutes. Remove skins from chiles and discard; separate onion rounds into rings.

3. Transfer chiles and onion to food processor, add garlic, and pulse until coarsely chopped, about 5 pulses.

Transfer all but ¼ cup chopped chile mixture to empty bowl and season with salt and pepper; set aside. Process remaining mixture until finely chopped, about 45 seconds, scraping down bowl as needed.

4. Combine beef, finely chopped chile mixture, ½ teaspoon salt, and ¼ teaspoon pepper in large bowl and lightly knead until well combined. Shape into four ¾-inch-thick patties and press shallow depression in center of each.

5. Place burgers on grill, cover, and cook until well browned on first side, 3 to 5 minutes. Flip burgers, top with reserved coarsely chopped chile mixture and cheese, and continue to cook, covered, until cheese is melted and burgers are cooked to desired doneness, 3 to 5 minutes. Serve.

CHILE PINCH HITTER

For complex green chile flavor outside of New Mexico, we found that a combination of mild Anaheims and spicy jalapeños has a nice peppery balance.

MILD HEAT
Anaheim chiles add a mildly sweet, grassy flavor.

SPICE IS NICE
Jalapeño chiles have just enough heat to stand up to the beefiness of the burger.

✅ WHY THIS RECIPE WORKS

Chicago-style barbecued ribs recipes typically call for smoking the ribs at about 200 degrees for at least eight hours. This slow-and-low cooking method delivers the moist, tender meat that defines Chicago ribs. We wanted to replicate the same method at home. To shorten cooking time, we started our recipe on the grill—where the ribs picked up good color and smoke flavor—and finished them in the oven. Placing pans of water on the grill and in the oven steamed the ribs, making them extra moist and tender. For Chicago-style barbecue sauce, we used celery salt, allspice, and plenty of cayenne pepper.

Chicago-Style Barbecued Ribs

SERVES 4 TO 6

The dry spices are used to flavor both the rub and the barbecue sauce. One medium wood chunk, soaked in water for 1 hour, can be substituted for the wood chips on a charcoal grill. When removing the ribs from the oven, be careful to not spill the hot water in the bottom of the baking sheet.

SPICE RUB AND RIBS

1	tablespoon dry mustard
1	tablespoon paprika
1	tablespoon packed dark brown sugar
1½	teaspoons garlic powder
1½	teaspoons onion powder
1½	teaspoons celery salt
1	teaspoon cayenne pepper
½	teaspoon ground allspice
2	racks baby back ribs (about 1½ pounds each), trimmed
1	cup wood chips, soaked in water for 15 minutes and drained
1	(13 by 9-inch) disposable aluminum roasting pan

SAUCE

1¼	cups ketchup
¼	cup molasses
¼	cup cider vinegar
¼	cup water
⅛	teaspoon liquid smoke

1. FOR THE SPICE RUB AND RIBS: Combine dry mustard, paprika, sugar, garlic powder, onion powder, celery salt, cayenne, and allspice in bowl. Measure out and reserve 2 tablespoons spice mixture for sauce. To remove chewy membrane from ribs, loosen it with tip of paring knife and, with aid of paper towel, pull it off slowly in 1 big piece. Pat ribs dry with paper towels and rub evenly with spice mixture. Wrap meat in plastic wrap and let sit at room temperature for at least 1 hour or refrigerate for up to 24 hours. (If refrigerated, let sit at room temperature for 1 hour before grilling.)

2. FOR THE SAUCE: Whisk all ingredients with reserved 2 tablespoons spice rub in bowl. Using large piece of heavy-duty aluminum foil, wrap soaked chips in foil packet and cut several vent holes in top.

3A. FOR A CHARCOAL GRILL: Open bottom vent completely. Light large chimney starter filled with charcoal briquettes (6 quarts). Add 2 cups water to disposable pan and place it on 1 side of grill. When top coals are partially covered with ash, pour into steeply banked pile against other side of grill, opposite pan of water. Place wood chip packet on coals. Set cooking grate in place, cover, and open lid vent completely. Heat grill until hot and wood chips are smoking, about 5 minutes.

3B. FOR A GAS GRILL: Place wood chip packet directly on primary burner. Add 2 cups water to disposable pan and place it on secondary burner. Turn all burners to high, cover, and heat grill until hot and wood chips are smoking, about 15 minutes. Turn primary burner to medium and turn other burner(s) off. (Adjust primary burner as needed to maintain grill temperature around 325 degrees.)

4. Clean and oil cooking grate. Place ribs meat side down on grill over water-filled pan; ribs may overlap slightly. Cover (positioning lid vent over meat if using charcoal) and cook until ribs are deep red and smoky, about 1½ hours, flipping and rotating racks halfway through grilling. During final 20 minutes of grilling, adjust oven rack to middle position and heat oven to 250 degrees.

5. Set wire rack in rimmed baking sheet and add just enough water to cover pan bottom. Transfer ribs to rack and cover tightly with foil. Continue to cook ribs in oven until fork slips easily in and out of meat, 1½ to 2 hours.

6. Remove ribs from oven, tent with foil, and let rest for 30 minutes. Brush ribs evenly with half of sauce. Slice ribs between bones and serve with remaining sauce.

✔ WHY THIS RECIPE WORKS

Traditional Texas barbecued beef ribs are placed in pits for up to 10 hours. The smoke slowly permeates the meat, melting away fat, building flavor, and creating an unforgettable crust. We wanted a streamlined recipe. To speed things up, we first turned to steaming the ribs in the oven on a tray of water covered with aluminum foil, which tenderized the ribs. We then moved the ribs to the grill, where we smoked them over indirect heat (banking all the coals to one side of the grill and placing the ribs on the empty side) using wood chips. The surface of the meat dried and formed a spicy, crusty bark.

Texas Barbecued Beef Ribs

SERVES 4

Beef ribs are sold in slabs with up to seven bones, but slabs with three to four bones are easier to manage on the grill. If you cannot find ribs with a substantial amount of meat on the bones, don't bother making this recipe. One medium wood chunk, soaked in water for one hour, can be substituted for the wood chips on a charcoal grill.

TEXAS BARBECUE SAUCE

2	tablespoons unsalted butter
½	small onion, chopped fine
2	garlic cloves, minced
1½	teaspoons chili powder
1½	teaspoons pepper
½	teaspoon dry mustard
2	cups tomato juice
6	tablespoons distilled white vinegar
2	tablespoons Worcestershire sauce
2	tablespoons packed brown sugar
2	tablespoons molasses
	Salt

RIBS

3	tablespoons packed brown sugar
4	teaspoons chili powder
1	tablespoon salt
2	teaspoons pepper
½	teaspoon cayenne pepper
3–4	beef rib slabs (3 to 4 ribs per slab, about 5 pounds total), trimmed
1	cup wood chips, soaked in water for 15 minutes and drained

1. FOR THE TEXAS BARBECUE SAUCE: Melt butter in medium saucepan over medium heat. Add onion and cook until softened, about 5 minutes. Stir in garlic, chili powder, pepper, and dry mustard and cook until fragrant, about 30 seconds. Stir in tomato juice, vinegar, Worcestershire, sugar, and molasses and simmer until sauce is reduced to 2 cups, about 20 minutes. Season with salt to taste. (Sauce can be refrigerated in airtight container for 1 week.)

2. FOR THE RIBS: Combine sugar, chili powder, salt, pepper, and cayenne in bowl. Pat ribs dry with paper towels and rub them evenly with spice mixture. Cover ribs with plastic wrap and let sit at room temperature for 1 hour.

3. Adjust oven rack to middle position and heat oven to 300 degrees. Set wire rack set in rimmed baking sheet and add just enough water to cover pan bottom. Arrange ribs on rack and cover tightly with aluminum foil. Bake until fat has rendered and meat begins to pull away from bones, about 2 hours. Using large piece of heavy-duty foil, wrap soaked chips in foil packet and cut several vent holes in top.

4A. FOR A CHARCOAL GRILL: Open bottom vent halfway. Light large chimney starter filled with charcoal briquettes (6 quarts). When top coals are partially covered with ash, pour into steeply banked pile against 1 side of grill. Place wood chip packet on coals. Set cooking grate in place, cover, and open lid vent halfway. Heat grill until hot and wood chips are smoking, about 5 minutes.

4B. FOR A GAS GRILL: Place wood chip packet directly on primary burner. Turn all burners to high, cover, and heat grill until hot and wood chips are smoking, about 15 minutes. Leave primary burner on high and turn other burner(s) off. (Adjust primary burner as needed to maintain grill temperature between 250 and 300 degrees.)

5. Clean and oil cooking grate. Place ribs meat side down on cool side of grill; ribs may overlap slightly. Cover (positioning lid vent over meat if using charcoal) and cook until ribs are lightly charred and smoky, about 1½ hours, flipping and rotating racks halfway through grilling. Transfer to cutting board, tent with foil, and let rest for 10 minutes. Serve with barbecue sauce.

✔ WHY THIS RECIPE WORKS

Traditional vinegar-based Lexington-style pulled pork recipes take hours to prepare. We wanted to simplify this recipe without sacrificing flavor. To do so, we used a combination of grilling and oven roasting to reduce the cooking time from all day to just a few hours. To infuse our Lexington-style pulled pork with ample smoke flavor despite the abbreviated cooking time, we doubled the amount of wood chips we used.

Lexington-Style Pulled Pork

SERVES 8

Boneless pork butt (also labeled Boston butt) is often wrapped in elastic netting; be sure to remove the netting before rubbing the meat with the spices in step 1. Four medium wood chunks, soaked in water for one hour, can be substituted for the wood chips on a charcoal grill.

SPICE RUB AND PORK

- 2 tablespoons paprika
- 2 tablespoons pepper
- 2 tablespoons packed brown sugar
- 1 tablespoon salt
- 1 (4- to 5-pound) boneless pork butt roast, trimmed
- 4 cups wood chips, soaked in water for 15 minutes and drained

LEXINGTON BARBECUE SAUCE

- 1 cup water
- 1 cup cider vinegar
- ½ cup ketchup
- 1 tablespoon granulated sugar
- ¾ teaspoon salt
- ½ teaspoon pepper
- ½ teaspoon red pepper flakes

1. FOR THE SPICE RUB AND PORK: Combine paprika, pepper, sugar, and salt in bowl. Pat meat dry with paper towels and rub it evenly with spice mixture. Wrap meat in plastic wrap and let sit at room temperature for at least 1 hour or refrigerate for up to 24 hours. (If refrigerated, let sit at room temperature for 1 hour before grilling.) Using 2 large pieces of heavy-duty aluminum foil, wrap soaked chips in 2 foil packets and cut several vent holes in tops.

2A. FOR A CHARCOAL GRILL: Open bottom vent halfway. Light large chimney starter half filled with charcoal briquettes (3 quarts). When top coals are partially covered with ash, pour into steeply banked pile against 1 side of grill. Place wood chip packets on coals. Set cooking grate in place, cover, and open lid vent halfway. Heat grill until hot and wood chips are smoking, about 5 minutes.

2B. FOR A GAS GRILL: Place wood chip packets directly on primary burner. Turn all burners to high, cover, and heat grill until hot and wood chips are smoking, about 15 minutes. Turn primary burner to medium and turn other burner(s) off. (Adjust primary burner as needed to maintain grill temperature around 275 degrees.)

3. Clean and oil cooking grate. Place meat on cool side of grill. Cover (positioning lid vent over meat if using charcoal) and cook until pork has dark, rosy crust, about 2 hours. During final 20 minutes of grilling, adjust oven rack to lower-middle position and heat oven to 325 degrees.

4. Transfer pork to large roasting pan, cover pan tightly with foil, and roast pork in oven until fork slips easily into and out of meat, 2 to 3 hours. Remove pork from the oven and let rest, still covered with foil, for 30 minutes.

5. FOR THE SAUCE: Whisk together all ingredients until sugar and salt are dissolved. When cool enough to handle, unwrap pork and pull meat into thin shreds, discarding excess fat and gristle. Toss pork with ½ cup barbecue sauce, serving remaining sauce at table.

NORTH CAROLINA BARBECUE BATTLE

In the eastern part of North Carolina, it's just not barbecue unless it's a whole hog. Known as a pig pickin', this type of barbecue starts with a split hog and ends with succulent meat and crackling-crisp skin. The meat is then literally picked from the bones and lightly seasoned with a thin vinegar and pepper sauce. Western Carolinians eschew the whole hog and go straight for the pork shoulder—the most marbled and meatiest chunk of the animal. The pork shoulder is cooked just like the whole hog, but the sauce is enriched with just enough ketchup and sugar to take the edge off the acidity.

WHY THIS RECIPE WORKS

This regional recipe, nicknamed Carolina Gold, demands more than just a last-minute dose of bold flavors. A combination of grilling and oven roasting reduces the cooking time from all day to just four or five hours. We used a spice rub, which included dry mustard to jump-start the mustard flavor of the sauce. Most South Carolina barbecue sauce recipes use yellow mustard, which our tasters praised for its bright tang. Brushing the pork with the sauce before it went into the oven produced a second hit of mustard flavor; tossing the shredded pork with the remaining sauce gave the meat a final layer of mustard flavor.

South Carolina Pulled Pork

SERVES 8

Boneless pork butt (also labeled Boston butt) is often wrapped in elastic netting; be sure to remove the netting before rubbing the meat with the spices in step 1. The cooked meat can be shredded or chopped. Two wood chunks, soaked in water for 15 minutes, can be substituted for the wood chips on a charcoal grill.

SPICE RUB AND PORK

- 3 tablespoons dry mustard
- 2 tablespoons salt
- 1½ tablespoons packed light brown sugar
- 2 teaspoons pepper
- 2 teaspoons paprika
- ¼ teaspoon cayenne pepper
- 1 (4- to 5-pound) boneless pork butt roast, trimmed
- 4 cups wood chips, soaked in water for 15 minutes and drained

MUSTARD BARBECUE SAUCE

- ½ cup yellow mustard
- ½ cup packed light brown sugar
- ¼ cup distilled white vinegar
- 2 tablespoons Worcestershire sauce
- 1 tablespoon hot sauce
- 1 teaspoon salt
- 1 teaspoon pepper

1. FOR THE SPICE RUB AND PORK: Combine dry mustard, salt, sugar, pepper, paprika, and cayenne in bowl. Pat meat dry with paper towels and rub it evenly with spice mixture. Wrap meat in plastic wrap and let sit at room temperature for at least 1 hour or refrigerate up to 24 hours. (If refrigerated, let sit at room temperature for 1 hour before grilling.) Using 2 large pieces of heavy-duty aluminum foil, wrap soaked chips in 2 foil packets and cut several vent holes in tops.

2A. FOR A CHARCOAL GRILL: Open bottom vent completely. Light large chimney starter half filled with charcoal briquettes (3 quarts). When top coals are partially covered with ash, pour into steeply banked pile against 1 side of grill. Place wood chip packets on coals. Set cooking grate in place, cover, and open lid vent halfway. Heat grill until hot and wood chips are smoking, about 5 minutes.

2B. FOR A GAS GRILL: Place wood chip packets directly on primary burner. Turn all burners to high, cover, and heat grill until hot and wood chips are smoking, about 15 minutes. Turn primary burner to medium-high and turn other burner(s) off. (Adjust primary burner as needed to maintain grill temperature around 325 degrees.)

3. Clean and oil cooking grate. Place meat on cool side of grill. Cover (positioning lid vent over meat if using charcoal) and cook until pork has dark, rosy crust, about 2 hours. During final 20 minutes of grilling, adjust oven rack to lower-middle position and heat oven to 325 degrees.

4. FOR THE MUSTARD BARBECUE SAUCE: Whisk yellow mustard, sugar, vinegar, Worcestershire, hot sauce, salt, and pepper in bowl until smooth. Measure out ½ cup sauce and set aside for cooking, reserving remaining sauce for serving.

5. Transfer pork to roasting pan and brush evenly with sauce for cooking. Cover pan tightly with foil and roast pork in oven until fork slips easily in and out of meat, 2 to 3 hours.

6. Remove pork from oven and let rest, still covered with foil, for 30 minutes. When cool enough to handle, unwrap pork and pull meat into thin shreds, discarding excess fat and gristle. Toss pork with reserved sauce and serve.

WHY THIS RECIPE WORKS

Most grilled double-thick pork chop recipes result in a charred exterior and raw meat, or gray meat that tastes steamed. We wanted our pork chops to have great taste and tenderness. Cooking our pork chops over indirect heat made for juicy and tender meat. We used wood chips on the grill to infuse the pork with a nice level of smoke flavor. Coating the double-thick pork chops with a rub of brown sugar and potent herbs and spices helped produce a flavorful crust, and quick grilling over hot coals at the end of cooking gave the crust a crisp texture and rich mahogany color.

Smoked Double-Thick Pork Chops

SERVES 6 TO 8

We prefer blade chops, which have more fat to prevent drying out on the grill, but leaner loin chops will also work. Two medium wood chunks, soaked in water for one hour, can be substituted for the wood chips on a charcoal grill. These chops are huge. You may want to slice the meat off the bone before serving.

- ¼   cup packed dark brown sugar
- 1   tablespoon ground fennel
- 1   tablespoon ground cumin
- 1   tablespoon ground coriander
- 1   tablespoon paprika
- 1   teaspoon salt
- 1   teaspoon pepper
- 4   (1¼- to 1½-pound) bone-in blade-cut pork chops, about 2 inches thick, trimmed
- 2   cups wood chips, soaked in water for 15 minutes and drained

1. Combine sugar, fennel, cumin, coriander, paprika, salt, and pepper in bowl. Pat pork chops dry with paper towels and rub them evenly with spice mixture. Wrap chops in plastic wrap and refrigerate for at least 1 hour or up to 24 hours. Using large piece of heavy-duty aluminum foil, wrap soaked chips in foil packet and cut several vent holes in top.

2A. FOR A CHARCOAL GRILL: Open bottom vent halfway. Light large chimney starter filled with charcoal briquettes (6 quarts). When top coals are partially covered with ash, pour into pile on 1 side of grill. Place wood chip packet on coals. Set cooking grate in place, cover, and open lid vent halfway. Heat grill until hot and wood chips are smoking, about 5 minutes.

2B. FOR A GAS GRILL: Place wood chip packet directly on primary burner. Turn all burners to high, cover, and heat grill until hot and wood chips are smoking, about 15 minutes. Turn primary burner to medium and turn other burner(s) off. (Adjust primary burner as needed to maintain grill temperature around 275 degrees.)

3. Clean and oil cooking grate. Place pork chops on cool side of grill with bone sides facing hot side of grill. Cover (positioning lid vent over pork if using charcoal) and cook until meat registers 145 degrees, 50 minutes to 1 hour. Slide chops directly over fire (hot side on gas grill) and cook, uncovered, until well browned, about 4 minutes, flipping chops halfway through grilling. Transfer to platter and let rest for 20 minutes. Serve.

CUTTING YOUR OWN DOUBLE-THICK PORK CHOPS

We like juicy blade-end chops that are at least 2 inches thick for our Smoked Double-Thick Pork Chops recipe. If you can't find them prepackaged at your grocery store, just buy a 4½- to 5-pound bone-in blade roast and cut it into 2-inch portions yourself. If cutting your own chops, ask your butcher or meat department manager if the chine bone (a part of the backbone) has been removed from the base of the roast—this thick bone can make carving difficult. If the chine bone has not been removed, ask the butcher to cut the chops for you.

✔ WHY THIS RECIPE WORKS

Usually, by the time thin-cut pork chops pick up char on the grill, the insides have dried out. To ensure that our pork chops would brown quickly, we partially froze them to eliminate excess moisture from the exterior. Salting them first prevented them from drying out and allowed us to skip brining. A combination of softened butter and brown sugar spread over the chops resulted in a flavorful golden-brown crust when they came off the grill. And a chive- and mustard-spiked butter added even more flavor to the finished chops.

Grilled Thin-Cut Pork Chops

To prevent the chops from curling, cut two slits about 2 inches apart through the fat around the outside of each raw chop.

6	bone-in rib or center-cut pork chops, about ½ inch thick, trimmed
¾	teaspoon salt
4	tablespoons unsalted butter, softened
1	teaspoon packed brown sugar
½	teaspoon pepper
1	teaspoon minced fresh chives
½	teaspoon Dijon mustard
½	teaspoon grated lemon zest

1. Set wire rack in rimmed baking sheet. Pat chops dry with paper towels. Cut 2 slits, about 2 inches apart, through outer layer of fat and silverskin on each chop. Rub chops with salt. Arrange on prepared rack and freeze until chops are firm, at least 30 minutes but no more than 1 hour. Combine 2 tablespoons butter, brown sugar, and pepper in small bowl; set aside. Mix remaining 2 tablespoons butter, chives, mustard, and zest in second small bowl and refrigerate until firm, about 15 minutes. (Butter-chive mixture can be refrigerated, covered, for 1 day.)

2A. FOR A CHARCOAL GRILL: Open bottom vent completely. Light large chimney starter filled with charcoal briquettes (6 quarts). When top coals are partially covered with ash, pour evenly over grill. Set cooking grate in place, cover, and open lid vent completely. Heat grill until hot, about 5 minutes.

2B. FOR A GAS GRILL: Turn all burners to high, cover, and heat grill until hot, about 15 minutes.

3. Pat chops dry with paper towels. Spread softened butter-sugar mixture evenly over both sides of each chop. Grill, covered, over hot fire until well browned and meat registers 145 degrees, 6 to 8 minutes, flipping chops halfway through grilling. Transfer chops to platter and top with chilled butter-chive mixture. Tent with aluminum foil and let rest for 5 minutes. Serve.

SPICY THAI GRILLED THIN-CUT PORK CHOPS

Substitute 1½ teaspoons Asian chili-garlic sauce, 1 teaspoon minced fresh cilantro, and ½ teaspoon grated lime zest for chives, mustard, and lemon zest.

CARIBBEAN GRILLED THIN-CUT PORK CHOPS

Substitute 1 teaspoon grated fresh ginger, ½ teaspoon minced fresh thyme, and ½ teaspoon grated orange zest for chives, mustard, and lemon zest.

MEDITERRANEAN GRILLED THIN-CUT PORK CHOPS

Substitute 1½ teaspoons black olive tapenade and ½ teaspoon minced fresh oregano for chives and mustard.

THIN IS THE NEW THICK

For juicy, nicely charred chops, try our method: salting, freezing, and brushing with softened butter before grilling. Salting ensures juicy chops; freezing promotes crust formation by drying the exterior and adding valuable minutes to the cooking time; butter accelerates browning and adds richness to the lean meat.

WOULD YOU EAT THIS?
Grilled straight from the package, this chop is dry, pale, and bland.

NOW YOU'RE TALKING
Salted, frozen, buttered, then grilled, this chop is juicy, browned, and flavorful.

✔ WHY THIS RECIPE WORKS

St. Louis BBQ pork steaks are little-known in other parts of America, but in St. Louis, they are so popular that pork steaks are on permanent sale in family packs at the supermarket. We found there was no substitute for pork steak, so the only option was to cut our own. We ordered a boneless Boston butt and cut it in half crosswise, then turned each piece on end to slice 1-inch-thick steaks. Inspired by a test kitchen recipe for brats and beer, we used a method of sear, simmer, sear again. This untraditional process gives the steaks a nice char, candylike edges, and succulent, slightly chewy interiors.

St. Louis BBQ Pork Steaks

SERVES 4

Boneless pork butt is also labeled Boston butt. If pork steaks are available, use them and increase the cooking time in the sauce to 1 to 1½ hours. We use Budweiser in this recipe, since it's made in St. Louis, but any mild-tasting beer will do.

SPICE RUB AND PORK STEAKS

- 1 tablespoon packed brown sugar
- 1 tablespoon paprika
- 2 teaspoons dry mustard
- 2 teaspoons pepper
- 1 teaspoon onion powder
- 1 teaspoon garlic powder
- 1 teaspoon ground cumin
- 1 teaspoon salt
- ¼ teaspoon cayenne pepper
- 1 (5- to 6-pound) boneless pork butt roast, sliced crosswise, trimmed, and each half cut into three or four 1-inch-thick steaks

BARBECUE SAUCE

- 2 cups beer
- 1½ cups ketchup
- ¼ cup A.1. Steak Sauce
- ¼ cup packed dark brown sugar
- 2 tablespoons cider vinegar
- 2 tablespoons Worcestershire sauce
- 1 teaspoon garlic powder
- 1 teaspoon hot sauce
- 1 teaspoon liquid smoke
- 1 (13 by 9-inch) disposable aluminum roasting pan

1. FOR THE SPICE RUB AND PORK STEAKS: Combine sugar, paprika, dry mustard, pepper, onion powder, garlic powder, cumin, salt, and cayenne in bowl. Pat pork steaks dry with paper towels and rub them evenly with spice mixture. Wrap pork in plastic wrap and refrigerate for at least 1 hour or up to 24 hours.

2. FOR THE BARBECUE SAUCE: Whisk all ingredients together in bowl and transfer to disposable pan.

3A. FOR A CHARCOAL GRILL: Open bottom vent halfway. Light large chimney starter filled with charcoal briquettes (6 quarts). When top coals are partially covered with ash, pour evenly over grill. Set cooking grate in place, cover, and open lid vent halfway. Heat grill until hot, about 5 minutes.

3B. FOR A GAS GRILL: Turn all burners to high, cover, and heat grill until hot, about 15 minutes. Leave primary burner on high and turn other burner(s) off. (Adjust primary burner as needed to maintain grill temperature around 350 degrees.)

4. Clean and oil cooking grate. Place pork steaks on hot side of grill. Cook (covered if using gas) until well browned on both sides, about 10 minutes, flipping steaks halfway through grilling.

5. Transfer pork steaks to sauce in pan and coat thoroughly. Cover pan with aluminum foil and place on grill. Cover (positioning lid vent over pan if using charcoal) and cook steaks until fork-tender and they register 190 degrees, 45 minutes to 1 hour. Remove steaks from pan and grill until lightly charred around edges, 4 to 8 minutes, flipping steaks halfway through grilling.

6. Transfer steaks to serving platter, tent loosely with foil, and let rest for 10 minutes. Skim excess fat from sauce and serve with steaks.

MAKING PORK STEAKS

1. Slice pork crosswise in half and remove any large pieces of fat.

2. Rotate and stand each half of pork butt on its cut end and cut each half into three or four 1-inch-thick steaks.

✔ WHY THIS RECIPE WORKS

For an easy take on Chinese-style glazed and charred pork, we turned to the grill and opted for pork tenderloin, which cooks quickly over a hot fire. Butterflying and pounding the meat gave us maximum surface area for our glaze. A combination of thick, sweet apricot preserves and ketchup flavored with hoisin, fresh ginger, sesame oil, sherry, garlic, and five-spice powder gave us a salty-sweet sauce that acted as both marinade and glaze. Continuously flipping and glazing the pork creates a charred, caramelized—but not burnt—exterior.

Chinese-Style Glazed Pork Tenderloin

SERVES 4 TO 6

Leftover pork makes an excellent addition to fried rice or noodle soup.

2	(12- to 16-ounce) pork tenderloins, trimmed
½	cup soy sauce
½	cup apricot preserves
¼	cup hoisin sauce
¼	cup dry sherry
2	tablespoons grated fresh ginger
1	tablespoon toasted sesame oil
2	garlic cloves, minced
1	teaspoon five-spice powder
1	teaspoon pepper
¼	cup ketchup
1	tablespoon molasses
2	teaspoons vegetable oil

1. Lay tenderloins on cutting board with long side running parallel to counter edge. Cut horizontally down length of each tenderloin, stopping ½ inch from edge so tenderloin remains intact. Working with one at a time, open up tenderloins, place between 2 sheets of plastic wrap, and pound to ¾-inch thickness.

2. Combine soy sauce, preserves, hoisin, sherry, ginger, sesame oil, garlic, five-spice powder, and pepper in bowl. Reserve ¾ cup of marinade. Place pork in large zipper-lock bag and pour remaining marinade into bag with pork. Seal bag, turn to coat, and refrigerate for at least 30 minutes or up to 4 hours.

3. Combine reserved marinade, ketchup, and molasses in small saucepan. Cook over medium heat until syrupy and reduced to ¾ cup, 3 to 5 minutes. Reserve ¼ cup glaze for glazing cooked pork.

4A. FOR A CHARCOAL GRILL: Open bottom vent completely. Light large chimney starter filled with charcoal briquettes (6 quarts). When top coals are partially covered with ash, pour evenly over grill. Set cooking grate in place, cover, and open lid vent completely. Heat grill until hot, about 5 minutes.

4B. FOR A GAS GRILL: Turn all burners to high, cover, and heat grill until hot, about 15 minutes. Turn all burners to medium-high.

5. Clean and oil cooking grate. Pat pork dry with paper towels, then rub with vegetable oil. Grill pork (covered if using gas) until lightly charred on first side, about 2 minutes. Flip and brush grilled side of pork evenly with 2 tablespoons glaze. Continue grilling until lightly charred on second side, about 2 minutes. Flip and brush evenly with 2 more tablespoons glaze. Repeat flipping and glazing twice more, until pork registers 140 degrees and is thickly glazed, about 4 minutes longer. Transfer pork to cutting board and brush with reserved glaze. Tent loosely with aluminum foil and let rest for 5 minutes. Slice and serve.

PREPARING THE TENDERLOINS

1. Place tenderloins on cutting board and slice each down side, leaving ½ inch of meat uncut. Open each tenderloin like a book.

2. Place each butterflied tenderloin between two sheets of plastic wrap. Using meat pounder, pound each to ¾-inch thickness.

✔ WHY THIS RECIPE WORKS

We began our Chinese-Style Barbecue Spareribs by removing the tough membrane on the underside of the ribs. Instead of cooking the ribs on the grill the entire time, we found that cooking them in the sauce in the oven and then finishing them on the grill allowed for deeply seasoned Chinese-style ribs and eliminated the need to marinate them. Since the smoke from wood chips was overpowering, we replaced the wood chips with orange spice or Earl Grey tea bags soaked in water, wrapped in foil, and placed on the hot coals for a mellow, smoky flavor that complemented the Asian seasonings.

Chinese-Style Barbecued Spareribs

SERVES 6

Full-size spareribs are fatty, plus they're too large to fit on the grill. If you can't find St. Louis–style spareribs (which have been trimmed of the brisket bone and surrounding meat), substitute baby back ribs and begin to check for doneness after 1 hour on the grill. Cover the edges of the ribs loosely with foil if they begin to burn while grilling.

2	(2½- to 3-pound) racks St. Louis–style spareribs, trimmed
8	black tea bags, preferably orange spice or Earl Grey
1½	cups ketchup
1	cup soy sauce
1	cup hoisin sauce
1	cup sugar
½	cup dry sherry
6	garlic cloves, minced
2	tablespoons grated fresh ginger
2	teaspoons toasted sesame oil
1½	teaspoons cayenne pepper
1	(13 by 9-inch) disposable aluminum roasting pan
1	cup red currant jelly

1. To remove chewy membrane from ribs, loosen it with tip of paring knife and, with aid of paper towel, pull it off slowly in 1 big piece. Cut rib racks in half. Cover tea bags with water in small bowl and soak for 5 minutes. Squeeze water from tea bags. Using large piece of heavy-duty aluminum foil, wrap tea bags in foil packet and cut several vent holes in top.

2. Adjust oven rack to middle position and heat oven to 300 degrees. Whisk 1 cup ketchup, soy sauce, hoisin sauce, sugar, sherry, garlic, ginger, sesame oil, and cayenne in large bowl; reserve ½ cup for glaze. Arrange ribs, meaty side down, in disposable pan and pour remaining ketchup mixture over ribs. Cover pan tightly with foil and cook until fat has rendered and meat begins to pull away from bones, 2 to 2½ hours. Transfer ribs to large plate. Pour pan juices into fat separator. Let liquid settle and reserve 1 cup defatted pan juices.

3. Simmer reserved pan juices in medium saucepan over medium-high heat until reduced to ½ cup, about 5 minutes. Stir in jelly, reserved ketchup mixture, and remaining ½ cup ketchup and simmer until reduced to 2 cups, 10 to 12 minutes. Reserve one-third of glaze for serving.

4A. FOR A CHARCOAL GRILL: Open bottom vent completely. Light large chimney starter filled with charcoal briquettes (6 quarts). When top coals are partially covered with ash, pour evenly over half of grill. Place tea packet on coals. Set cooking grate in place, cover, and open lid vent completely. Heat grill until hot and tea is smoking, about 5 minutes.

4B. FOR A GAS GRILL: Place tea packet directly on primary burner. Turn all burners to high, cover, and heat grill until hot and tea is smoking, about 15 minutes. Leave primary burner on high and turn other burner(s) off.

5. Clean and oil cooking grate. Arrange ribs, meaty side down, on cool side of grill and cook, covered, until ribs are smoky and edges begin to char, about 30 minutes.

6. Brush ribs with glaze, flip, rotate, and brush again. Cover and cook, brushing with glaze every 30 minutes, until ribs are fully tender and glaze is browned and sticky, 1 to 1½ hours. Transfer ribs to cutting board, tent with foil, and let rest for 10 minutes. Serve with reserved glaze.

TO MAKE AHEAD: Ribs and glaze can be prepared through step 3 up to 2 days in advance. Once ribs are cool, wrap tightly in foil and refrigerate. Transfer glaze to microwave-safe bowl, cover with plastic wrap, and refrigerate. Before proceeding with step 4, allow ribs to stand at room temperature for 1 hour. Before proceeding with step 6, microwave glaze until warm, about 1 minute.

✔ WHY THIS RECIPE WORKS

Boneless country-style ribs present several cooking challenges. Each piece not only varies wildly from the next, but is also a mishmash of lean white meat and rich dark meat. Unfortunately, if the ribs are cooked to optimize the white meat, then the dark meat stays tough, and if they are cooked to optimize the dark meat, the white meat turns dry. To even out the cooking, we brined the ribs so that the white meat would stay juicy and pounded the ribs to an even ¾-inch thickness to "break down" the fattier dark meat. As for flavor, a double layer of barbecue spice and sauce and a quick smoke on the grill worked wonders.

Barbecued Country-Style Ribs

SERVES 4 TO 6

For easier pounding, cut any ribs that are longer than 5 inches in half crosswise.

1	tablespoon salt
2	pounds boneless country-style pork ribs, trimmed
¾	cup packed dark brown sugar
2	tablespoons chili powder
2	tablespoons paprika
1	tablespoon dry mustard
1	tablespoon onion powder
¾	teaspoon pepper
¼	teaspoon cayenne pepper
6	tablespoons ketchup
1	tablespoon cider vinegar
¼	cup wood chips, soaked in water for 15 minutes and drained

1. Dissolve salt in 2 cups cold water in large container. Place ribs, cut side down, between 2 sheets of plastic wrap and pound to ¾ inch thickness. Submerge pork in brine, cover, and refrigerate for 30 minutes to 1 hour.

2. Combine sugar, chili powder, paprika, dry mustard, onion powder, pepper, and cayenne in shallow dish. Transfer half of mixture to bowl and stir in ketchup and vinegar; set aside.

3. Remove pork from brine and pat dry with paper towels. Dredge pork in remaining spice mixture and transfer to plate. Using large piece of heavy-duty aluminum foil, wrap soaked chips in foil packet and cut several vent holes in top.

4A. FOR A CHARCOAL GRILL: Open bottom vent halfway. Light large chimney starter filled with charcoal briquettes (6 quarts). When top coals are partially covered with ash, pour evenly over half of grill. Place wood chip packet on coals. Set cooking grate in place, cover, and open lid vent halfway. Heat grill until hot and wood chips are smoking, about 5 minutes.

4B. FOR A GAS GRILL: Place wood chip packet directly on primary burner. Turn all burners to high, cover, and heat grill until hot and wood chips are smoking, about 15 minutes. Leave primary burner on high and turn other burner(s) off.

5. Clean and oil cooking grate. Place pork on cool side of grill, cover (positioning lid vent over meat if using charcoal), and cook until meat registers 125 degrees, 3 to 5 minutes. Brush pork with ketchup mixture and grill, brushed side down, over hot side of grill until lightly charred, 2 to 3 minutes. Brush second side of pork, flip, and grill until lightly charred and meat registers 145 degrees, 2 to 3 minutes. Transfer pork to platter, tent loosely with foil, and let rest for 5 to 10 minutes. Serve.

COUNTRY-STYLE RIBS

Country-style ribs aren't ribs at all. They're well-marbled pork chops cut from the blade end of the loin. We bought dozens of these chops while testing this recipe and found that they were inconsistently shaped and sized. What's more, these "ribs" had widely varying proportions of light and dark meat. To help level the culinary playing field and ensure even cooking, we pounded each piece into an even ¾ inch thickness.

MISMATCHED MEAT
Each "rib" contains both light and dark meat.

ENSURING EVEN COOKING

The white and dark meat in country-style ribs cook at different rates—the white meat cooks quickly, while the dark meat is slower to tenderize. To equalize them, we brined and pounded. Brining kept the white meat from drying out, while pounding the ribs thin let them cook faster, helpful since long cooking times accentuate differences in cooking. Think of a fast car and a slow car starting from a stoplight at the same time. Thirty seconds after the light turns green, the two cars won't be far apart. But after 10 minutes, they will be.

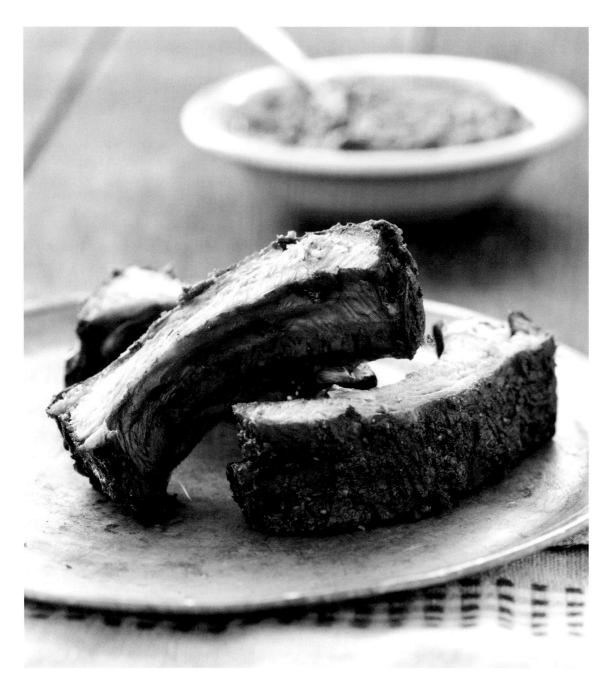

WHY THIS RECIPE WORKS

Corncob-smoking, a South Dakota specialty, may seem odd, but it gives meat a subtle smokiness hardwoods can't match. For barbecued ribs with mild, nutty sweetness, but without the complicated barbecuing rig, we layered charcoal on our grill with fresh corncobs (with the kernels removed) and a foil packet of cornmeal. The cornmeal gave the ribs an initial blast of smoky flavor, and the fresh cobs offered long-lasting smoke and a nutty aroma. We basted the ribs with a simple ketchup-based barbecue sauce with plenty of garlic and some celery seeds for sticky, sweet ribs that we couldn't get enough of.

South Dakota Corncob-Smoked Ribs

SERVES 4 TO 6

A gas grill can't do these corncob ribs justice, so please use charcoal. The test kitchen's favorite ketchup is Heinz Organic. To use up some of the leftover corn, try our recipe for Sweet Corn Spoonbread (page 187).

SAUCE

1	cup ketchup
¼	cup water
1	tablespoon pepper
1	tablespoon onion powder
1	tablespoon Worcestershire sauce
1	tablespoon light corn syrup
1	tablespoon granulated garlic
2	teaspoons celery seeds
½	teaspoon liquid smoke

RIBS

5	tablespoons packed light brown sugar
1	teaspoon salt
½	teaspoon pepper
2	(2½- to 3-pound) racks baby back pork ribs, trimmed and membrane removed
1	cup cornmeal
6	corncobs, kernels removed and reserved for another use
1	(13 by 9-inch) disposable aluminum roasting pan

1. FOR THE SAUCE: Whisk all ingredients together in medium bowl; set aside.

2. FOR THE RIBS: Combine sugar, salt, and pepper in bowl. Pat ribs dry with paper towels and rub with sugar mixture; set aside. Using large piece of heavy-duty aluminum foil, wrap cornmeal in foil packet and cut several vent holes in top.

3. Open bottom vents of charcoal grill halfway. Place disposable pan on 1 side of grill and fill pan with 2 quarts water. Arrange 3 quarts unlit charcoal briquettes on opposite side of grill. Place cobs on top of unlit briquettes. Light large chimney starter filled halfway with charcoal briquettes (3 quarts). When top coals are partially covered with ash, pour over cobs and unlit briquettes. Place cornmeal packet on coals. Set cooking grate in place, cover, and open lid vent halfway. Heat grill until hot and cornmeal is smoking, about 5 minutes.

4. Clean and oil cooking grate. Place ribs, meat side up, on cool part of grill opposite coals. Cover, positioning lid vent over ribs, and cook until ribs are deep red and tender, 3½ to 4 hours, rotating and switching ribs every hour. (Do not flip ribs.) During last 30 minutes of cooking, baste ribs every 10 minutes, rotating and switching ribs each time. Transfer ribs to carving board, tent loosely with foil, and let rest for 15 to 20 minutes. Cut ribs in between bones. Serve, passing remaining sauce separately.

FAILED CORNCOB TESTS

In South Dakota, bushels of dried, stripped corncobs impart a special flavor to ribs. To replicate it, we left no kernel unturned. It was A for effort, but these attempts were a bust.

Sooty: Unhusked ears of corn.	Sooty: Husked ears with the corn intact.	Too much work: Husked, stripped, and oven-dried.	Burnt taste: Popped popcorn.

✔ WHY THIS RECIPE WORKS

Two surefire ways to dress up a pork roast are to give it a flavorful, deeply caramelized crust on the grill and serve it with a savory-sweet mustard glaze. Our mustard-glazed pork loin has the best of both worlds. Leaving our roast untrimmed added moisture and flavor—and scoring the fat kept it from tasting too fatty. For the mustard glaze, apple jelly was a perfect complement to the spicy crunch of grainy mustard, and both married well with the other glaze ingredients—brown sugar, garlic, and fresh thyme. To fully infuse our pork loin with mustard flavor, we applied the glaze before, during, and after grilling.

Grilled Mustard-Glazed Pork Loin

SERVES 6 TO 8

Dijon and yellow mustards also work well in the glaze, but make certain to use apple jelly, not apple butter. Look for a pork roast with about ¼ inch of fat on top and tie the roast at 1-inch intervals to ensure an even shape.

½	**cup whole-grain mustard**
6	**tablespoons apple jelly**
2	**tablespoons packed dark brown sugar**
2	**tablespoons extra-virgin olive oil**
1	**large garlic clove, minced**
2	**teaspoons minced fresh thyme**
¾	**teaspoon pepper**
½	**teaspoon salt**
1	**boneless pork loin roast (2½ to 3 pounds), fat scored lightly, tied at 1-inch intervals**

1. Whisk mustard, jelly, sugar, oil, garlic, thyme, pepper, and salt together in bowl. Measure out ⅔ cup sauce and set aside for cooking; reserve remaining sauce for serving. Before grilling, pat pork loin dry with paper towels and coat it evenly with ⅓ cup sauce for cooking.

2A. FOR A CHARCOAL GRILL: Open bottom vent halfway. Light large chimney starter filled with charcoal briquettes (6 quarts). When top coals are partially covered with ash, pour evenly over half of grill. Set cooking grate in place, cover, and open lid vent halfway. Heat grill until hot, about 5 minutes.

2B. FOR A GAS GRILL: Turn all the burners to high, cover, and heat grill until hot, about 15 minutes.

Leave primary burner on high and turn other burner(s) off. (Adjust primary burner as needed to maintain grill temperature around 350 degrees.)

3. Clean and oil cooking grate. Place pork loin on hot side of grill. Cook (covered if using gas) until well browned on all sides, 12 to 15 minutes, turning as needed.

4. Flip pork loin fat side up and slide to cool side of grill. Brush pork with 2 tablespoons sauce for cooking. Cover (positioning lid vent over pork if using charcoal) and continue to cook until meat registers 140 degrees, 25 to 40 minutes longer, brushing every 10 minutes with remaining sauce for cooking.

5. Transfer pork loin to carving board, tent loosely with aluminum foil, and let rest for 15 minutes. Remove twine, cut meat into ¼-inch-thick slices, and transfer to serving platter. Whisk any accumulated juices into reserved sauce, spoon over meat, and serve.

THE BENEFITS OF SCORING

Scoring fat means using a sharp knife to cut a shallow crosshatch pattern into the fat layer. Use gentle pressure and avoid cutting through the fat and into the meat, which will result in moisture loss. Scoring helps the fat to render (basting the meat and keeping it moist as it cooks) and creates an uneven surface that holds the glaze.

✓ WHY THIS RECIPE WORKS

To create the flavor of cedar planks in our wood-grilled salmon (without having to mail-order them), we settled on wood chips and made individual aluminum foil trays to hold the chips and salmon. To prevent the salmon from sticking to the wood chips, we left the skin on, as it easily separated from the cooked fish. Poking a few slits in the bottom of the foil allowed more heat to reach the wood chips, which caused them to release more of their woodsy—but not overly smoky—flavor. Coating each fillet with a thin layer of olive oil and a light sprinkling of granulated sugar produced a golden, mildly sweet exterior.

Wood-Grilled Salmon

SERVES 4

Any variety of wood chips will work here, but aromatic woods such as cedar and alder give the most authentic flavor.

- 1½ teaspoons sugar
- ½ teaspoon salt
- ¼ teaspoon pepper
- 4 (6- to 8-ounce) skin-on salmon fillets, about 1¼ inches thick
- 1 tablespoon olive oil
- 2 cups wood chips, soaked in water for 15 minutes and drained

1. Combine sugar, salt, and pepper in bowl. Pat salmon fillets dry with paper towels, then brush flesh sides with oil and rub evenly with sugar mixture. Using 4 large sheets of heavy-duty aluminum foil, crimp edges of each sheet to make 4 trays, each measuring 7 by 5 inches. Perforate bottom of each tray with tip of paring knife. Divide wood chips among trays and lay 1 fillet skin side down on top of wood chips in each tray.

2A. FOR A CHARCOAL GRILL: Open bottom vent completely. Light large chimney starter filled with charcoal briquettes (6 quarts). When top coals are partially covered with ash, pour evenly over grill. Set cooking grate in place, cover, and open lid vent completely. Heat grill until hot, about 5 minutes.

2B. FOR A GAS GRILL: Turn all burners to high, cover, and heat grill until hot, about 15 minutes.

3. Clean and oil cooking grate. Place trays on grill. Cook (covered if using gas) until center is still translucent when checked with tip of paring knife and registers 125 degrees (for medium-rare), about 10 minutes.

4. Transfer trays to wire rack, tent loosely with foil, and let rest for 5 minutes. Slide metal spatula between skin and flesh of fish, transfer fish to platter, and serve.

BARBECUED WOOD-GRILLED SALMON

Add ¾ teaspoon chili powder and ¼ teaspoon cayenne pepper to sugar mixture and substitute 1 tablespoon Dijon mustard mixed with 1 tablespoon maple syrup for oil in step 1.

LEMON-THYME WOOD-GRILLED SALMON

Add 2 teaspoons minced fresh thyme and 1½ teaspoons grated fresh lemon zest to sugar mixture and substitute 2 tablespoons Dijon mustard for oil in step 1.

AN EASIER WAY TO PLANKED SALMON

Cooking salmon on a cedar plank infuses it with gentle wood flavor rather than overwhelming smokiness. Here's how to get the same great taste, minus the mail-order plank.

1. Crimp 4 sheets of foil to make trays. Using paring knife, poke small slits in bottom of trays.

2. Place soaked wood chips in foil trays and arrange salmon skin side down directly on top of wood chips.

3. Once salmon is cooked, slide metal spatula between flesh and skin; fish should release easily.

✔ WHY THIS RECIPE WORKS

Salmon steaks are a common choice for grilling: Their bone and thickness make them a far sturdier cut than a fillet. But the steak's thickness can also work against it, making it difficult for the interior and exterior to finish cooking at the same time. We began by tucking the belly flaps in toward the center of the steak and tying them to create medallions that would cook evenly and be easily maneuvered. To make sure our steaks were packed with flavor, we finished cooking them in a pan of zesty sauce on the cooler part of the grill. When they were done, our salmon steaks were flavorful, juicy, and moist.

Grilled Salmon Steaks with Lemon-Caper Sauce

SERVES 4

Before eating, lift out the small circular bone from the center of each steak.

- **4** (10-ounce) salmon steaks, 1 to 1½ inches thick
  Salt and pepper
- **2** tablespoons olive oil
- **1** teaspoon grated lemon zest and 6 tablespoons juice (2 lemons)
- **1** shallot, minced
- **3** tablespoons unsalted butter, cut into 3 pieces
- **1** tablespoon capers, rinsed
- **2** tablespoons minced fresh parsley
- **1** (13 by 9-inch) disposable aluminum pan

1. Pat salmon steaks dry with paper towels. Working with 1 steak at a time, carefully trim 1½ inches of skin from 1 tail. Tightly wrap other tail around skinned portion and tie steaks with kitchen twine. Repeat with remaining salmon steaks. Season salmon steaks with salt and pepper and brush both sides with oil. Combine lemon zest, lemon juice, shallot, butter, capers, and ⅛ teaspoon salt in disposable pan.

2A. FOR A CHARCOAL GRILL: Open bottom vent completely. Light large chimney starter filled with charcoal briquettes (6 quarts). When top coals are partially covered with ash, pour evenly over half of grill. Set cooking grate in place, cover, and open lid vent completely. Heat grill until hot, about 5 minutes.

2B. FOR A GAS GRILL: Turn all burners to high, cover, and heat grill until hot, about 15 minutes. Leave primary burner on high and turn off other burner(s).

3. Clean and oil cooking grate. Place salmon medallions on hot part of grill. Cook until browned, 2 to 3 minutes per side. Meanwhile, set pan on cool part of grill and cook until butter has melted, about 2 minutes. Transfer medallions to pan and gently turn to coat. Cook (covered if using gas) until center is still translucent when checked with tip of paring knife and registers 125 degrees (for medium-rare), 6 to 14 minutes, flipping salmon and rotating pan halfway through grilling. Remove twine and transfer salmon to platter. Off heat, whisk parsley into sauce and drizzle sauce over salmon. Serve.

PREPPING SALMON MEDALLIONS

1. For salmon steaks that are sturdy enough to grill easily, remove 1½ inches of skin from one tail of each steak.

2. Next, tuck the skinned portion into the center of the steak, wrap the other tail around it, and tie with kitchen twine.

WHY THIS RECIPE WORKS

We wanted tender, juicy, shrimp with a smoky, charred crust and chile flavor that was more than just superficial. To achieve this, we sprinkled one side of the shrimp with sugar to promote browning and grilled this side over the hot side of the grill for a few minutes and then flipped the skewers to finish gently cooking on the cool side of the grill. Creating a flavorful marinade that doubled as a sauce gave our shrimp skewers a spicy, assertive kick. And butterflying the shrimp before marinating and grilling them opened up more shrimp flesh for the marinade and finishing sauce to flavor.

Grilled Jalapeño and Lime Shrimp Skewers

SERVES 4

We prefer flat metal skewers that are at least 14 inches long for this recipe.

MARINADE

1–2	jalapeño chiles, stemmed, seeded, and chopped
3	tablespoons olive oil
6	garlic cloves, minced
1	teaspoon grated lime zest plus 5 tablespoons juice (3 limes)
½	teaspoon ground cumin
¼	teaspoon cayenne pepper
½	teaspoon salt

SHRIMP

1½	pounds extra-large shrimp (21 to 25 per pound), peeled and deveined
½	teaspoon sugar
1	tablespoon minced fresh cilantro

1. FOR THE MARINADE: Process all ingredients in food processor until smooth, about 15 seconds. Reserve 2 tablespoons marinade; transfer remaining marinade to medium bowl.

2. FOR THE SHRIMP: Pat shrimp dry with paper towels. To butterfly shrimp, use paring knife to make shallow cut down outside curve of shrimp. Add shrimp to bowl with marinade and toss to coat. Cover and refrigerate for at least 30 minutes or up to 1 hour.

3A. FOR A CHARCOAL GRILL: Open bottom vent completely. Light large chimney starter filled with charcoal briquettes (6 quarts). When top coals are partially covered with ash, pour evenly over half of grill. Set cooking grate in place, cover, and open lid vent completely. Heat grill until hot, about 5 minutes.

3B. FOR A GAS GRILL: Turn all burners to high, cover, and heat grill until hot, about 15 minutes.

4. Clean and oil cooking grate. Thread marinated shrimp on skewers. (Alternate direction of each shrimp as you pack them tightly on skewer to allow about a dozen shrimp to fit snugly on each skewer.)

Sprinkle 1 side of skewered shrimp with sugar. Grill shrimp, sugared side down, over hot side of grill (covered if using gas), until lightly charred, 3 to 4 minutes. Flip skewers and move to cool side of grill (if using charcoal) or turn all burners off (if using gas), and cook, covered, until other side of shrimp is no longer translucent, 1 to 2 minutes. Using tongs, slide shrimp into clean medium bowl and toss with reserved marinade. Sprinkle with cilantro and serve.

GRILLED RED CHILE AND GINGER SHRIMP SKEWERS

Replace marinade with 1 to 3 seeded and chopped small red chiles (or jalapeños), 1 minced scallion, 3 tablespoons rice vinegar, 2 tablespoons soy sauce, 1 tablespoon toasted sesame oil, 1 tablespoon grated fresh ginger, 2 teaspoons sugar, and 1 minced garlic clove. Prepare and grill shrimp as directed. Replace cilantro with 1 thinly sliced scallion and serve with lime wedges.

GRILLED CARIBBEAN SHRIMP SKEWERS

Replace marinade with 1 to 2 seeded and chopped habanero or serrano chiles, ¼ cup pineapple juice, 2 tablespoons olive oil, 1 tablespoon white wine vinegar, 3 minced garlic cloves, 1 teaspoon grated fresh ginger, 1 teaspoon packed brown sugar, 1 teaspoon dried thyme, ½ teaspoon salt, and ¼ teaspoon ground allspice. Prepare and grill shrimp as directed. Replace cilantro with 1 tablespoon minced fresh parsley.

HOW TO SKEWER SHRIMP

1. Make shallow cut down outside curve of shrimp to open up flesh.

2. Alternate direction of each shrimp as you pack them tightly on skewer.

WHY THIS RECIPE WORKS:

Grilling corn sounds like a simple proposition—but our research found dozens of variations on the cooking method for this classic summer vegetable. For a recipe that produced corn with a distinctly grilled taste and lightly charred kernels, we grilled the corn unhusked. (Tasters didn't like the grassy flavor the corn took on when we grilled it in its husk.) The grill imparted great flavor to our grilled corn, but also made the kernels tough and dry. To avoid this, we soaked the husked corn in salted water before grilling, which kept the kernels moist and seasoned them as well.

Grilled Corn on the Cob

SERVES 4 TO 6

If your corn isn't as sweet as you'd like, stir ½ cup of sugar into the water along with the salt. Avoid soaking the corn for more than 8 hours, or it will become overly salty.

> Salt and pepper
>
> 8 ears corn, husks and silks removed
>
> 8 tablespoons unsalted butter, softened, or 1 recipe flavored butter

1. In large pot, stir ½ cup salt into 4 quarts cold water until dissolved. Add corn and let soak for at least 30 minutes or up to 8 hours.

2A. FOR A CHARCOAL GRILL: Open bottom vent completely. Light large chimney starter filled with charcoal briquettes (6 quarts). When top coals are partially covered with ash, pour evenly over grill. Set cooking grate in place, cover, and open lid vent completely. Heat grill until hot, about 5 minutes.

2B. FOR A GAS GRILL: Turn all burners to high, cover, and heat grill until hot, about 15 minutes.

3. Clean and oil cooking grate. Grill corn, turning every 2 to 3 minutes, until kernels are lightly charred all over, 10 to 14 minutes. Remove corn from grill, brush with softened butter, and season with salt and pepper. Serve.

CHESAPEAKE BAY BUTTER

MAKES ABOUT 8 TABLESPOONS, ENOUGH FOR 8 EARS OF CORN

Using fork, beat 8 tablespoons softened, unsalted butter with 1 tablespoon hot sauce, 1 teaspoon Old Bay seasoning, and 1 minced garlic clove.

LATIN-SPICED BUTTER

MAKES ABOUT 8 TABLESPOONS, ENOUGH FOR 8 EARS OF CORN

Using fork, beat 8 tablespoons softened, unsalted butter with 1 teaspoon chili powder, ½ teaspoon ground cumin, ½ teaspoon grated lime zest, and 1 minced garlic clove. (Sprinkle cobs with ½ cup grated Parmesan, if desired.)

BASIL PESTO BUTTER

MAKES ABOUT 8 TABLESPOONS, ENOUGH FOR 8 EARS OF CORN

Using fork, beat 8 tablespoons softened, unsalted butter with 1 tablespoon basil pesto and 1 teaspoon lemon juice.

BARBECUE-SCALLION BUTTER

MAKES ABOUT 8 TABLESPOONS, ENOUGH FOR 8 EARS OF CORN

Using fork, beat 8 tablespoons softened, unsalted butter with 2 tablespoons barbecue sauce and 1 minced scallion.

A GOOD SOAK

The grill imparts great flavor but can make corn tough and dry. Soaking the husked corn in salted water keeps the kernels moist and seasons them, too.

WHY THIS RECIPE WORKS

California barbecued beans recipes use a bean variety and chili sauce rarely found outside of California. We wanted to re-create this recipe with nationally available supermarket ingredients. Pink kidney beans proved to be a good stand-in for the hard-to-find pinquito beans. Some recipes suggest using jarred taco sauce alone if the original recipe's requisite red chili sauce can't be found, but we found its taste and texture too thin. Instead, augmenting the sauce with a combination of fried bacon, ham, onion, and garlic with tomato puree, brown sugar, and dry mustard perfectly captured the chili sauce's bite.

California Barbecued Beans

SERVES 4 TO 6

If you can find them, pinquito beans (a variety grown in the Santa Maria Valley) are traditional in this dish. Bottled taco sauce is available in the Mexican aisle of most grocery stores. Don't add the tomato puree, taco sauce, brown sugar, and salt before the beans have simmered for an hour; they will hinder the proper softening of the beans.

4	slices bacon, chopped fine
½	pound deli ham, chopped fine
1	onion, chopped fine
4	garlic cloves, minced
1	pound pink kidney beans, soaked in 6 cups water overnight and drained
6	cups water
1	cup canned tomato puree
½	cup bottled taco sauce
5	tablespoons packed light brown sugar
1	tablespoon dry mustard
	Salt
¼	cup chopped fresh cilantro
2	tablespoons cider vinegar

1. Cook bacon and ham in Dutch oven over medium heat until fat renders and bacon and ham are lightly browned, 5 to 7 minutes. Add onion and cook until softened, about 5 minutes. Stir in garlic and cook until fragrant, about 30 seconds. Add beans and water and bring to simmer. Reduce heat to medium-low, cover, and cook until beans are just soft, about 1 hour.

2. Stir in tomato puree, taco sauce, sugar, dry mustard, and 2 teaspoons salt. Continue to simmer, uncovered, until beans are completely tender and sauce is thickened, about 1 hour. (If mixture becomes too thick, add water.) Stir in cilantro and vinegar and season with salt. Serve. (Beans can be refrigerated for up to 4 days.)

SORTING DRIED BEANS

It is important to rinse and pick over dried beans to remove any stones or debris before cooking. To make the task easier, sort dried beans on a large white plate or on a white, rimmed cutting board. The neutral background makes any unwanted matter a cinch to spot and discard.

QUICK-SOAKING BEANS

If you don't want to soak the beans overnight, there is a faster way. Simply cover the beans with water in a Dutch oven, bring them to a boil over high heat, and let them boil for 5 minutes. Remove the beans from the heat and allow them to sit, covered, in the hot water for 1 hour. Drain the beans and proceed with the recipe as directed. The quick-soaked beans taste just as good as beans that are soaked overnight.

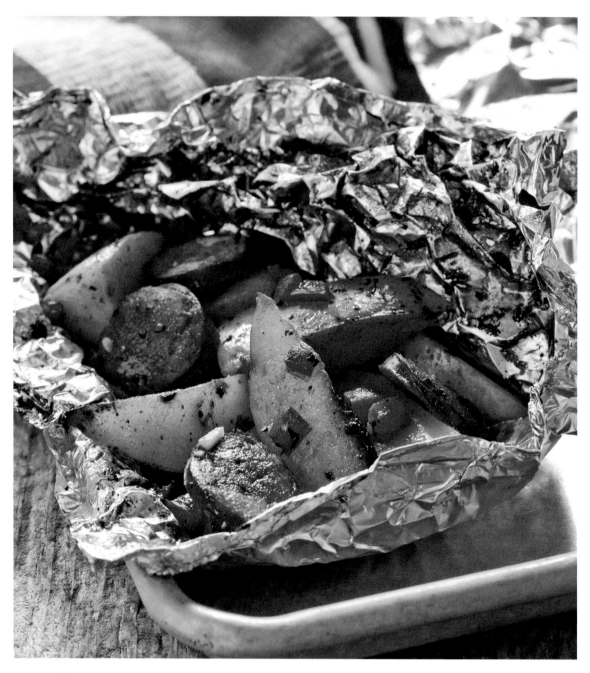

✓ WHY THIS RECIPE WORKS

We wanted to rescue this campfire classic, which too often results in unevenly cooked spuds. After multiple tests, we found that Yukon Golds were preferred to starchy, mealy russets and "slippery" red potatoes. To ensure evenly grilled potatoes, we cut them into evenly sized wedges and microwaved them for a few minutes before grilling them. Tossing the potatoes with a little oil prevented them from sticking to the foil.

Grilled Potato Hobo Packs

SERVES 4

To keep the packs from tearing, use heavy-duty aluminum foil or two layers of regular foil. Also, scrape the cooking grate clean before grilling.

2	pounds Yukon Gold potatoes (about 3 large), scrubbed
1	tablespoon olive oil
2	garlic cloves, peeled and chopped
1	teaspoon minced fresh thyme
1	teaspoon salt
½	teaspoon pepper

1. Cut each potato in half crosswise, then cut each half into 8 wedges. Place potatoes in large bowl and wrap tightly with plastic wrap. Microwave until edges of potatoes are translucent, 4 to 7 minutes, shaking bowl (without removing plastic) to redistribute potatoes halfway through cooking. Carefully remove plastic and drain well. Gently toss potatoes with oil, garlic, thyme, salt, and pepper.

2. Cut four 14 by 10-inch sheets of heavy-duty aluminum foil. Working with 1 at a time, spread one-quarter of potato mixture over half of foil, fold foil over potatoes, and crimp edges tightly to seal.

3A. FOR A CHARCOAL GRILL: Open bottom vent completely. Light large chimney starter filled with charcoal briquettes (6 quarts). When top coals are partially covered with ash, pour evenly over grill. Set cooking grate in place, cover, and open lid vent completely. Heat grill until hot, about 5 minutes.

3B. FOR A GAS GRILL: Turn all burners to medium-high, cover, and heat grill until hot, about 15 minutes.

4. Grill hobo packs over hot fire, covered, until potatoes are completely tender, about 10 minutes, flipping packs halfway through cooking. Cut open foil and serve.

SPANISH-STYLE GRILLED POTATO HOBO PACKS

Prepare Grilled Potato Hobo Packs, adding 6 ounces thinly sliced cured chorizo sausage, 1 seeded and chopped red bell pepper, and 1 teaspoon paprika to cooked potatoes as they are tossed in step 1.

VINEGAR AND ONION GRILLED POTATO HOBO PACKS

Prepare Grilled Potato Hobo Packs, microwaving 1 halved and thinly sliced small onion with potatoes in step 1. Add 2 tablespoons white wine or red wine vinegar to cooked potatoes as they are tossed in step 1.

SPICY HOME FRY GRILLED POTATO HOBO PACKS

Prepare Grilled Potato Hobo Packs, omitting chopped garlic. Add 1 teaspoon paprika, ½ teaspoon garlic powder, ½ teaspoon onion powder, and ¼ teaspoon cayenne pepper to cooked potatoes as they are tossed in step 1.

MAKING POTATO HOBO PACKS

1. Microwave potatoes first to help them cook quickly on the grill.

2. Arrange microwaved potatoes on foil, fold over, and crimp.

3. Flip packs halfway through grilling for evenly charred potatoes.

☑ WHY THIS RECIPE WORKS

Grilled salad may seem like an oxymoron, but we were intrigued by the idea of the flavors of a classic Caesar salad enriched with the smoky char of the grill. We found that compact romaine hearts held their shape better than whole heads. We halved them lengthwise to increase their surface area, making sure to keep the core intact so the leaves didn't fall apart on the grill. To prevent sticking, we brushed the leaves with dressing. Just 1 to 2 minutes over a hot grill gave us a smoky and charred (not wilted) exterior. To keep things simple, we replaced the croutons with slices of crusty bread grilled alongside the lettuce.

Grilled Caesar Salad

SERVES 6

Our favorite Parmesan cheese is Boar's Head Parmigiano-Reggiano.

DRESSING

1	tablespoon lemon juice
1	garlic clove, minced
½	cup mayonnaise
½	ounce Parmesan cheese, grated (¼ cup)
1	tablespoon white wine vinegar
1	tablespoon Worcestershire sauce
1	tablespoon Dijon mustard
2	anchovy fillets, rinsed
½	teaspoon salt
½	teaspoon pepper
¼	cup extra-virgin olive oil

SALAD

1	(12-inch) baguette, cut on bias into 5-inch-long, ½-inch-thick slices
3	tablespoons extra-virgin olive oil
1	garlic clove, peeled
3	romaine lettuce hearts (18 ounces), halved lengthwise through cores
½	ounce Parmesan cheese, grated (¼ cup)

1. FOR THE DRESSING: Combine lemon juice and garlic in bowl and let stand for 10 minutes. Process mayonnaise, Parmesan, lemon-garlic mixture, vinegar, Worcestershire, mustard, anchovies, salt, and pepper in blender for about 30 seconds. With blender running, slowly add oil. Reserve 6 tablespoons dressing for brushing romaine.

2A. FOR A CHARCOAL GRILL: Open bottom vent completely. Light large chimney starter filled with charcoal briquettes (6 quarts). When top coals are partially covered with ash, pour evenly over half of grill. Set cooking grate in place, cover, and open lid vent completely. Heat grill until hot, about 5 minutes.

2B. FOR A GAS GRILL: Turn all burners to high, cover, and heat grill until hot, about 15 minutes. Leave all burners on high.

3. FOR THE SALAD: Clean and oil cooking grate. Brush bread with oil and grill (over coals if using charcoal), uncovered, until browned, about 1 minute per side. Transfer to platter and rub with garlic clove. Brush cut sides of romaine with reserved dressing; place half of romaine, cut side down, on grill (over coals if using charcoal). Grill, uncovered, until lightly charred, 1 to 2 minutes. Move to platter with bread. Repeat. Drizzle romaine with remaining dressing. Sprinkle with Parmesan. Serve.

SALAD PREP FOR GRILLED CAESAR

We get twice the flavor by using the dressing before and after grilling.

1. Brush homemade Caesar dressing onto halved romaine hearts before grilling.

2. Grill dressed romaine halves on just one side to keep lettuce from wilting.

3. Once charred lettuce comes off grill, finish it with more Caesar dressing.

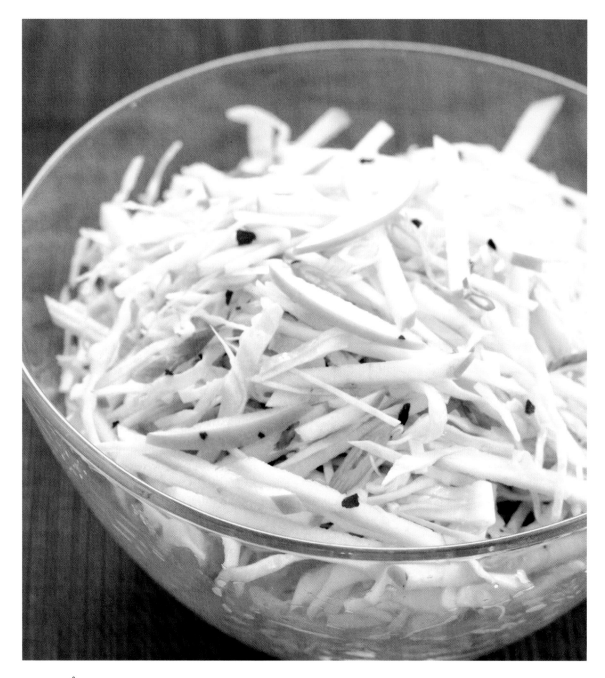

✓ WHY THIS RECIPE WORKS

We wanted to discover the secrets to tender cabbage, crunchy apples, and the sweet and spicy dressing that brings them together in this Southern barbecue side dish. Because cabbage is relatively watery, we salted the cut cabbage to draw out excess moisture before dressing it, which prevented moisture from diluting the dressing later and leaving us with a watery slaw. Granny Smith apples work best in this slaw recipe—tasters loved their sturdy crunch and tart bite. Cider vinegar gave the dressing a fruity flavor, while red pepper flakes, chopped scallions, and mustard added some punch.

Tangy Apple Cabbage Slaw

SERVES 6 TO 8

In step 1, the salted, rinsed, and dried cabbage can be refrigerated in a zipper-lock bag for up to 24 hours. To prep the apples, cut the cored apples into ¼-inch-thick planks, then stack the planks and cut them into thin matchsticks.

1	medium head green cabbage (2 pounds), cored and chopped fine (12 cups)
2	teaspoons salt
2	Granny Smith apples, cored and cut into thin matchsticks
2	scallions, sliced thin
6	tablespoons vegetable oil
½	cup cider vinegar
½	cup sugar
1	tablespoon Dijon mustard
¼	teaspoon red pepper flakes

1. Toss cabbage and salt in colander set over medium bowl. Let stand until wilted, about 1 hour. Rinse cabbage under cold water, drain, dry well with paper towels, and transfer to large bowl. Add apples and scallions and toss to combine.

2. Bring oil, vinegar, sugar, mustard, and pepper flakes to boil in saucepan over medium heat. Pour over cabbage mixture and toss to coat. Cover with plastic wrap and refrigerate at least 1 hour or up to 1 day. Serve.

CUTTING APPLES FOR SLAW

1. Cut cored apples into ¼-inch-thick planks.

2. Stack planks and cut them into thin matchsticks.

VINEGAR PRIMER

Although cider vinegar and white vinegar are made by the same process, the similarities end there. Vinegar is made by turning fermented liquid into acetic acid by adding certain bacteria to the liquid. Cider and distilled vinegars are made by the same process but start with different liquids: Cider vinegar begins with apple cider and distilled vinegar with ethyl alcohol (also known as grain alcohol). Although both vinegars are commonly used in pickle recipes (and are often substituted for each other), they do have distinctly different flavors. We like to use sweeter cider vinegar in sweet pickles, reserving white vinegar for applications such as sour pickles, where we want acidity without added flavor. While cider vinegar is fine in a sweet salad dressing, we don't think distilled vinegar adds much to any dressing. In general, we find that vinegars that start with wine are the best choice for salad dressings.

CIDER VINEGAR
Sweet cider vinegar begins with apple cider.

DISTILLED VINEGAR
Acidic distilled vinegar begins with ethyl alcohol.

WHY THIS RECIPE WORKS

The high water content of cabbage is typically to blame for watery slaws. We salted our cabbage to draw out the excess moisture. Memphis Chopped Coleslaw is usually studded with celery seeds and crunchy green peppers and tossed with an unapologetically sugary mustard dressing that's balanced by a bracing hit of vinegar. To ensure our slaw boasted brash, balanced flavor, we quickly cooked the spicy dressing to meld the flavors and tossed the hot dressing with the cabbage. The salted cabbage absorbed the dressing and became seasoned inside and out.

Memphis Chopped Coleslaw

SERVES 8 TO 10

In step 1, the salted, rinsed, and dried cabbage mixture can be refrigerated in a zipper-lock bag for up to 24 hours.

- 1   **head green cabbage (2 pounds), cored and chopped fine (12 cups)**
- 1   **jalapeño chile, stemmed, seeded, and minced**
- 1   **carrot, peeled and shredded on box grater**
- 1   **small onion, peeled and shredded on box grater**
- 2   **teaspoons salt**
- ¼   **cup yellow mustard**
- ¼   **cup chili sauce**
- ¼   **cup mayonnaise**
- ¼   **cup sour cream**
- ¼   **cup cider vinegar**
- 1   **teaspoon celery seeds**
- ⅔   **cup packed light brown sugar**

1. Toss cabbage, jalapeño, carrot, onion, and salt in colander set over medium bowl. Let stand until wilted, about 1 hour. Rinse cabbage mixture under cold water, drain, dry well with paper towels, and transfer to large bowl.

2. Bring mustard, chili sauce, mayonnaise, sour cream, vinegar, celery seeds, and sugar to boil in saucepan over medium heat. Pour over cabbage and toss to coat. Cover with plastic wrap and refrigerate 1 hour or up to 1 day. Serve.

HOW TO CHOP CABBAGE

1. Cut the cabbage into quarters, then trim and discard the hard core.

2. Separate the cabbage into small stacks of leaves that flatten when pressed.

3. Cut each stack of cabbage leaves into ¼-inch strips.

4. Cut the strips into ¼-inch pieces.

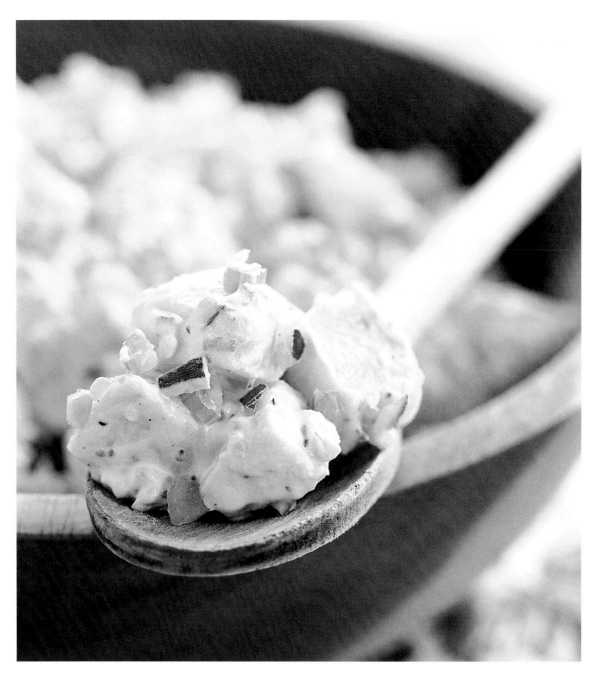

✓ WHY THIS RECIPE WORKS

For flavorful all-American potato salad, we decided to use firm-textured Yukon Gold potatoes because they hold their shape after cooking and won't turn mushy in the salad. Our recipe benefited from the sweetness of an unexpected ingredient: pickle juice. We drizzled the still-warm potatoes with a mixture of pickle juice and mustard. The hot potatoes easily absorbed the acidic liquid and tasted seasoned through to the middle. A combination of mayonnaise and sour cream formed the base of our creamy dressing, seasoned with classic additions like celery seeds, celery, and chopped hard-cooked eggs.

All-American Potato Salad

Make sure not to overcook the potatoes or the salad will be quite sloppy. Keep the water at a gentle simmer and use the tip of a paring knife to judge the doneness of the potatoes. If the knife inserts easily into the potato pieces, they are done.

2	**large eggs**
	Salt
2	**pounds Yukon Gold potatoes, peeled and cut into ¾-inch cubes**
3	**tablespoons dill pickle juice, plus ¼ cup finely chopped dill pickles**
1	**tablespoon yellow mustard**
¼	**teaspoon pepper**
½	**teaspoon celery seeds**
½	**cup mayonnaise**
¼	**cup sour cream**
½	**small red onion, chopped fine**
1	**celery rib, chopped fine**

1. Bring eggs, 1½ teaspoons salt, and 1 quart water to boil in small saucepan. Remove pan from heat, cover and let sit for 10 minutes. Transfer eggs to bowl filled with ice water and let cool for 5 minutes, then peel and chop coarse.

2. Place potatoes in large saucepan with cold water to cover by 1 inch. Bring to boil over high heat, add 1 teaspoon salt, reduce heat to medium-low, and simmer until potatoes are tender, 10 to 15 minutes.

3. Drain potatoes thoroughly, then spread out on rimmed baking sheet. Mix 2 tablespoons pickle juice and mustard together in small bowl, drizzle pickle juice mixture over hot potatoes, and toss until evenly coated. Refrigerate until cooled, about 30 minutes.

4. Mix remaining tablespoon pickle juice, chopped pickles, ½ teaspoon salt, pepper, celery seeds, mayonnaise, sour cream, red onion, and celery in large bowl. Toss in cooled potatoes, cover, and refrigerate until well chilled, about 30 minutes. (Salad can be refrigerated for up to 2 days.) Gently stir in eggs, just before serving.

DON'T THROW OUT THE JUICE

Pickle juice tossed with just-cooked potatoes gives them a tangy flavor that's not as harsh as straight vinegar and has a gentle sweetness, too.

WHY THIS RECIPE WORKS

For a summery potato salad cooked on the grill from start to finish featuring smoky, tender potatoes with crispy outsides, we began with halved, unpeeled red potatoes: The skin helped them to stay intact, and their firm, waxy texture stood up to the heat of the grill. Prior to grilling, we coated the potatoes with flavorful bacon fat. For even more smokiness, we grilled rounds of onions along with the potatoes. A spicy, smoky vinaigrette with a touch of mayo, chipotle, and crumbled bacon was a the perfect match for this backyard-ready potato salad.

Smoky Potato Salad

SERVES 8

Use small red potatoes 1½ to 2 inches in diameter. If you don't have 2 tablespoons of fat in the skillet after frying the bacon, add olive oil to make up the difference.

- 6 slices bacon
- 3 tablespoons red wine vinegar
- 2 tablespoons mayonnaise
- 2 teaspoons minced canned chipotle chile in adobo sauce
- Salt and pepper
- 3 tablespoons olive oil, plus extra for brushing
- 3 pounds small red potatoes, unpeeled, halved
- 1 large onion, sliced into ½-inch-thick rounds
- 4 scallions, sliced thin

1. Cook bacon in 12-inch skillet over medium heat until crisp, 7 to 9 minutes; transfer to paper towel–lined plate. Set aside 2 tablespoons bacon fat. When cool enough to handle, crumble bacon and set aside. Whisk vinegar, mayonnaise, chile, ½ teaspoon salt, and ½ teaspoon pepper together in large bowl. Slowly whisk in 3 tablespoons oil until combined; set aside.

2A. FOR A CHARCOAL GRILL: Open bottom vent completely. Light large chimney starter three-quarters filled with charcoal briquettes (4½ quarts). When top coals are partially covered with ash, pour evenly over grill. Set cooking grate in place, cover, and open lid vent completely. Heat grill until hot, about 5 minutes.

2B. FOR A GAS GRILL: Turn all burners to high, cover, and heat grill until hot, about 15 minutes. Turn all burners to medium.

3. Clean and oil cooking grate. Toss potatoes with reserved bacon fat and ½ teaspoon salt. Push a tooth-pick horizontally through each onion round to keep rings intact while grilling. Brush onion rounds lightly with extra oil and season with salt and pepper. Place potatoes, cut side down, and onion rounds on grill and cook, covered, until charred on first side, 10 to 14 minutes.

4. Flip potatoes and onion rounds and continue to cook, covered, until well browned all over and potatoes are easily pierced with tip of paring knife, 10 to 16 minutes longer. Transfer potatoes and onion rounds to rimmed baking sheet and let cool slightly.

5. When cool enough to handle, halve potatoes; remove toothpicks and coarsely chop onion rounds. Add potatoes, onion, scallions, and bacon to dressing and toss to combine. Season with salt and pepper to taste. Serve warm or at room temperature.

✓ WHY THIS RECIPE WORKS

Amish potato salad is distinct for its creamy cooked dressing and sweet-and-sour flavor. We modernized this recipe by ditching the labor-intensive dressing, which is traditionally enriched with eggs and gently cooked over a double-boiler. To keep the rich taste with less work, we processed a hard-cooked egg yolk into the dressing base of vinegar and sugar. Sprinkling a few tablespoons of the tangy dressing over the hot potatoes infused them with flavor. Then we tossed the cooled potatoes with the rest of the dressing, enriched with sour cream, for a cool, creamy potato salad with great old-fashioned flavor.

Amish Potato Salad

SERVES 8

You can substitute an equal amount of celery salt for the celery seed, but if you do, eliminate the table salt from the dressing. Make sure to use sturdy Yukon Golds here; fluffy russets will fall apart in the salad.

3	pounds Yukon Gold potatoes, peeled and cut into ¾-inch chunks
	Salt and pepper
⅓	cup cider vinegar
¼	cup sugar
2	tablespoons yellow mustard
4	large hard-cooked eggs, peeled (recipe follows)
½	teaspoon celery seed
¾	cup sour cream
1	celery rib, chopped fine

1. Bring potatoes, 1 tablespoon salt, and enough water to cover by 1 inch to boil in large pot over high heat. Reduce heat to medium and simmer until potatoes are just tender, about 10 minutes.

2. Meanwhile, microwave vinegar and sugar in small bowl until sugar dissolves, about 30 seconds. Process vinegar mixture, mustard, 1 hard-cooked egg yolk (reserve white), celery seed, and ½ teaspoon salt in food processor until smooth, about 30 seconds. Transfer to medium bowl.

3. Drain potatoes thoroughly and transfer to large bowl. Drizzle 2 tablespoons dressing over hot potatoes and, using rubber spatula, gently toss until evenly coated. Refrigerate until cooled, at least 30 minutes, stirring gently once to redistribute dressing.

4. Whisk sour cream into remaining dressing. Add remaining egg white and 3 hard-cooked eggs to dressing and, using potato masher, mash until only small pieces remain. Add dressing and celery to cooled potatoes, tossing gently to combine. Cover and refrigerate until chilled, about 30 minutes. Season with salt and pepper to taste. Serve. (Salad can be refrigerated for up to 2 days.)

FOOLPROOF HARD-COOKED EGGS

MAKES 4 EGGS

You can double or triple this recipe as long as you use a pot large enough to hold the eggs in a single later, covered by an inch of water.

4	large eggs

Bring eggs and enough water to cover by 1 inch to boil in medium saucepan over high heat. Remove pan from heat, cover, and let sit 10 minutes. Meanwhile, fill medium bowl with 4 cups water and 1 tray of ice cubes. Transfer eggs to ice water bath with slotted spoon; let sit for 5 minutes. Peel eggs.

SWEET ON SWEET-AND-SOUR

Like most other resourceful Colonial Americans, the Amish turned to pickling as a way to preserve fruits and vegetables for long (prerefrigeration) winters. It wasn't just practicality that drove them to pickling, however. The Amish people's penchant for these sweet-and-sour flavors is also rooted in the group's native Germany, where rich dishes are often finished with a splash of vinegar or served with vinegar-spiked sides, such as sauerkraut. The Amish table, it's said, is incomplete without "seven sweets and seven sours." A cornucopia of delicious foods reflects this Amish predilection, from watermelon rind and cantaloupe pickles to chow chow, pickled beets and eggs, and Amish potato salad, which is seasoned with plenty of vinegar and sugar.

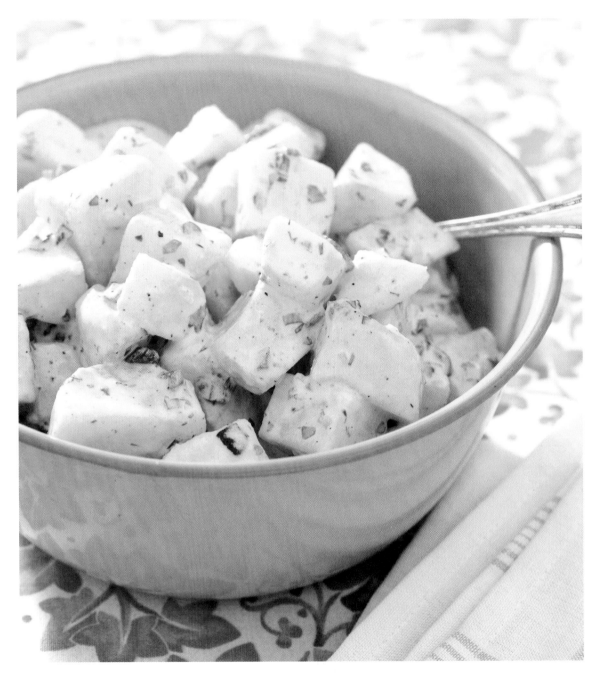

WHY THIS RECIPE WORKS

Bottled ranch dressing sounds like a quick way to dress up potato salad, but many recipes are surprisingly dull and bland. We found that peeling the potatoes (we liked red spuds)allowed them to absorb more dressing. For the dressing, we doubled the amount of cilantro used in most recipes and added fresh garlic and scallions for a welcome bite. Dijon mustard and vinegar provided acidity and bite, while chopped roasted red peppers made a sweet counterpoint. To better season the potatoes, we tossed the hot spuds first with just the Dijon mustard and vinegar. And just a dash of dried dill lent more herb flavor.

Ranch Potato Salad

We prefer white wine vinegar here, but white and cider vinegars are acceptable substitutes.

3	pounds red potatoes, peeled and cut into ¾-inch chunks
	Salt
¾	cup mayonnaise
½	cup buttermilk
¼	cup white wine vinegar
¼	cup drained jarred roasted red peppers, chopped fine
3	tablespoons finely chopped fresh cilantro
3	scallions, chopped fine
1	garlic clove, minced
⅛	teaspoon dried dill
2	teaspoons pepper
2	tablespoons Dijon mustard

1. Bring potatoes, 1 tablespoon salt, and enough water to cover potatoes by 1 inch to boil in large pot over high heat. Reduce heat to medium and simmer until potatoes are just tender, about 10 minutes. While potatoes simmer, whisk mayonnaise, buttermilk, 2 tablespoons vinegar, red peppers, cilantro, scallions, garlic, dill, 1 teaspoon salt, and pepper in large bowl.

2. Drain potatoes thoroughly, then spread out on rimmed baking sheet. Whisk mustard and remaining vinegar in small bowl. Drizzle mustard mixture over hot potatoes and toss until evenly coated. Refrigerate until cooled, about 30 minutes.

3. Transfer cooled potatoes to bowl with mayonnaise mixture and toss to combine. Cover and refrigerate until well chilled, about 30 minutes. Serve. (Salad can be refrigerated for up to 2 days.)

BETTER POTATO TEXTURE, AND FASTER, TOO

We discovered some interesting information about boiling potatoes while developing our recipe for Ranch Potato Salad. Most recipes for boiled potatoes call for starting the spuds in cold water so that they will come up to temperature slowly and cook evenly throughout. In an attempt to shorten the cooking time, we tried letting the water boil before adding the potatoes. In a side-by-side test, we weren't surprised that tasters preferred the potatoes started in cold water for their uniformly creamy texture. We were surprised, however, to find that the total cooking time for potatoes started in cold water was less than for those started in boiling water.

HIDDEN VALLEY RANCH DRESSING

The original ranch dressing first became popular at the Hidden Valley Guest Ranch near Santa Barbara, Calif., in the late 1950s. It began as a dried herb mixture that Steve Henson, the ranch's owner, combined with mayonnaise and buttermilk to make a creamy, tangy dressing for the ranch's house salad. It was so well received that guests clamored for bottles of the dressing to take home with them. Recognizing the potential of his concoction, Henson began marketing the mix in small packets, and the rest is culinary history. The little packets are still around, but the dressing really took off in 1983 when manufacturers figured out how to bottle this creamy dressing in a shelf-stable format.

✔ WHY THIS RECIPE WORKS

We wanted potato salad with vibrant dill flavor through and through. To do so, we seasoned our potato salad with three rounds of dill: first as an herb sachet while the potatoes simmered, next as a piquant dill vinegar, and finally as a fresh sprinkle. A dressing based on a combination of creamy mayonnaise and tangy sour cream, accented with Dijon mustard, provided the perfect backdrop for our dill flavor to shine.

Dill Potato Salad

SERVES 8

Use both dill stems and chopped leaves (sometimes called fronds) in the herb sachet. Trois Petits Cochons is our favorite brand of Dijon mustard.

- ¼ **cup white wine vinegar**
- 3 **tablespoons minced fresh dill, plus ½ cup leaves and stems, chopped coarse**
- 3 **pounds Yukon Gold potatoes, peeled and cut into ¾-inch pieces**
- **Salt and pepper**
- ½ **cup mayonnaise**
- ¼ **cup sour cream**
- 1 **tablespoon Dijon mustard**
- 3 **scallions, green parts only, sliced thin**

1. Combine vinegar and 1 tablespoon minced dill in bowl and microwave until steaming, 30 to 60 seconds. Set at room temperature until cool, 15 to 20 minutes.

2. Meanwhile, place chopped dill inside disposable coffee filter and tie closed with kitchen twine. Bring potatoes, dill sachet, 1 tablespoon salt, and enough water to cover potatoes by 1 inch to boil in large pot over high heat. Reduce heat to medium and simmer until potatoes are just tender, about 10 minutes.

3. Drain potatoes thoroughly, then transfer to large bowl; discard sachet. Drizzle 2 tablespoons dill vinegar over hot potatoes and gently toss until evenly coated. Refrigerate until cooled, about 30 minutes, stirring once.

4. Whisk mayonnaise, sour cream, remaining dill vinegar, mustard, ½ teaspoon salt, and ¼ teaspoon pepper together until smooth. Add dressing to cooled potatoes. Stir in scallions and remaining 2 tablespoons minced dill. Cover and refrigerate to let flavors meld, about 30 minutes. Season with salt and pepper to taste. Serve. (Salad can be refrigerated for up to 2 days.)

DILL THREE WAYS

Three rounds of fresh dill season our Dill Potato Salad.

INFUSE
We add a packet of chopped dill to the water in which the potatoes simmer.

MARINATE
We steep vinegar with minced dill and use it to dress the hot potatoes.

MINCE
We sprinkle extra minced dill over the dressed potato salad.

✔ WHY THIS RECIPE WORKS

Texans take their potato salad up a notch with a hefty dose of mustard and spicy chopped jalapeños. For our version, we started with classic potato salad, using firm Yukon Gold potatoes, which have a rich earthy flavor and hold their shape after cooking, and a mayonnaise-based dressing seasoned with onion, celery seeds, and dill pickles. To this we added plenty of bold yellow mustard and spicy jalapeños. We tempered the jalapeños' raw bite by quick-pickling them in a mixture of vinegar, sugar, and mustard seeds. We used the leftover pickling solution to flavor the hot potatoes. A pinch of cayenne added extra kick.

Texas Potato Salad

SERVES 8

Annie's Naturals Organic Yellow Mustard is our favorite brand of yellow mustard.

½	cup red wine vinegar
1½	tablespoons sugar
	Salt and pepper
1	teaspoon yellow mustard seeds
½	small red onion, sliced thin
2	jalapeño chiles (1 sliced into thin rings; 1 stemmed, seeded, and minced)
3	pounds Yukon Gold potatoes, peeled and cut into ¾-inch pieces
6	tablespoons mayonnaise
6	tablespoons yellow mustard
¼	teaspoon cayenne pepper
2	large hard-cooked eggs, cut into ¼-inch pieces
1	celery rib, minced

1. Combine vinegar, sugar, 1½ teaspoons salt, and mustard seeds in bowl and microwave until steaming, about 2 minutes. Whisk until sugar and salt are dissolved. Add onion and jalapeños and set aside until cool, 15 to 20 minutes. Strain onion and jalapeños through fine-mesh strainer set over bowl. Reserve pickled vegetables and vinegar mixture separately.

2. Meanwhile, combine potatoes, 8 cups water, and 1 tablespoon salt in Dutch oven and bring to boil over high heat. Reduce heat to medium and simmer until potatoes are just tender, 10 to 15 minutes.

3. Drain potatoes thoroughly, then transfer to large bowl. Drizzle 2 tablespoons reserved vinegar mixture over hot potatoes and toss gently until evenly coated. (Reserve remaining vinegar mixture for another use.) Refrigerate until cool, about 30 minutes, stirring once halfway through chilling.

4. Whisk mayonnaise, mustard, ½ teaspoon pepper, and cayenne together in bowl until combined. Add mayonnaise mixture, reserved pickled vegetables, eggs, and celery to potatoes and stir gently to combine. Season with salt and pepper to taste. Cover and refrigerate to let flavors blend, about 30 minutes. Serve. (Salad can be refrigerated for up to 2 days.)

KEEPING POTATO SALAD SAFE

Though mayonnaise is often blamed for spoiled potato salads, it is rarely the problem. In fact, it's the potatoes that are more likely to go bad. The bacteria usually responsible for spoiled potato salad is found in soil and dust, and it thrives on starchy foods like potatoes. No matter what kind of dressing you use, don't leave any potato salad out for more than two hours (one hour if the temperature is above 90 degrees), and promptly refrigerate any leftovers in a covered container.

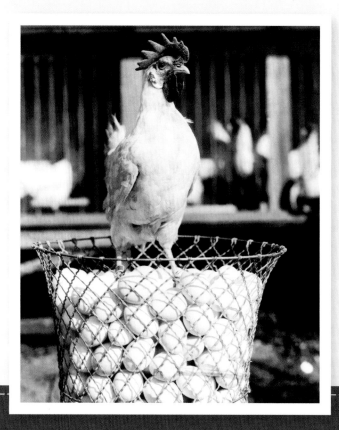

CHAPTER 8

RISE-AND-SHINE BREAKFAST AND BREADS

IN THE RUSH TO GET OUT THE DOOR MOST MORNINGS, MANY Americans turn to a quick, easy breakfast like a bowl of cereal or a grab-and-go breakfast bar. Sit-down, hot breakfasts are reserved for leisurely weekend mornings. Our forebears, however, often required a substantial breakfast to fuel them through a labor-intensive morning—and there was little leisure associated with it. In her 1869 novel *Oldtown Folks*, Harriet Beecher Stowe described breakfast from the perspective of one of the characters, who was recalling a breakfast from the Revolutionary War period in Massachusetts: "...I can inform all whom it may concern that rye and Indian bread smoking hot, on a cold winter morning, together with savory sausages, pork, and beans, formed a breakfast fit for a king, if the king had earned it by getting up in a cold room, washing in ice-water, tumbling through snow-drifts, and foddering cattle."

Toward the end of the 19th century, American breakfast began to change significantly as the nation industrialized and its citizens sought work in cities. An increasing awareness of the health consequences of a meat-heavy diet, paired with a less active lifestyle, helped to drive the success of prepared breakfast cereals, which also fulfilled another concern of the industrial age—convenience.

In this chapter, we skip breakfast cereal and instead take a look at some more satisfying tried-and-true breakfast favorites such as pancakes (with a nod to convenience, we create a recipe as easy as a mix, but far tastier), a diner-style omelet (why go out for breakfast when we can show you how to get the same results at home?), and buttery, sweet morning buns (just like those from your favorite bakery, but so much easier). Put on the coffee and get ready to rise and shine.

✓ WHY THIS RECIPE WORKS

For a tall, fluffy diner-worthy omelet, we ditched the whisk for an electric mixer, which helped us incorporate air into the eggs. Cream added richness, but when we added it to the whipped eggs, the omelet lost its fluffiness. Combining the cream and eggs before whipping didn't work either—the fat in the cream made it impossible to whip air into the eggs. Instead, we whipped the dairy first, then folded it into the whipped eggs. After letting the bottom of the omelet set on the stovetop, we popped the skillet into a preheated oven, and just six minutes later had a puffy, fluffy omelet, cooked to perfection.

Fluffy Diner-Style Cheese Omelet

SERVES 2

Although this recipe will work with a stand mixer, a hand-held mixer makes quick work of whipping such a small amount of cream. To make two omelets, double this recipe and cook the omelets simultaneously in two skillets. If you have only one skillet, prepare a double batch of ingredients and set half aside for the second omelet. Be sure to wipe out the skillet in between omelets.

- 3 tablespoons heavy cream, chilled
- 5 large eggs, room temperature
- ¼ teaspoon salt
- 2 tablespoons unsalted butter
- 2 ounces sharp cheddar cheese, shredded (½ cup)
- 1 recipe omelet filling (optional) (recipes follow)

1. Adjust oven rack to middle position and heat oven to 400 degrees. Using stand mixer fitted with whisk, whip cream on medium-low speed until foamy, about 1 minute. Increase speed to high and whip until soft peaks form, 1 to 3 minutes. Set whipped cream aside. Using dry, clean bowl and whisk attachment, whip eggs and salt on high speed until frothy and eggs have tripled in size, about 2 minutes. Gently fold whipped cream into eggs.

2. Melt butter in ovensafe 10-inch nonstick skillet over medium-low heat, swirling pan to coat bottom and sides. Add egg mixture and cook until edges are nearly set, 2 to 3 minutes. Sprinkle with ¼ cup cheddar and half of omelet filling, if using, and transfer to oven. Bake until eggs are set and edges are beginning to brown, 6 to 8 minutes.

3. Carefully remove pan from oven (handle will be very hot), sprinkle eggs with remaining ¼ cup cheddar and remaining omelet filling, if using, and let sit, covered, until cheese begins to melt, about 1 minute. Tilt pan and, using rubber spatula, push half of omelet onto cutting board, then fold omelet over itself to form half-moon shape. Cut omelet in half and serve.

SAUSAGE AND PEPPER FILLING
MAKES ENOUGH FOR 1 RECIPE FLUFFY DINER-STYLE OMELET

- 4 ounces hot or sweet Italian sausage, casings removed
- 1 tablespoon unsalted butter
- 1 small onion, chopped
- ½ red bell pepper, chopped
  Salt and pepper

Cook sausage in 10-inch nonstick skillet over medium heat, breaking up clumps with wooden spoon, until browned, about 6 minutes. Transfer to paper towel–lined plate. Add butter, onion, and bell pepper to now-empty skillet and cook until softened, about 10 minutes. Stir in sausage and season with salt and pepper to taste.

LOADED BAKED POTATO FILLING
MAKES ENOUGH FOR 1 RECIPE FLUFFY DINER-STYLE OMELET

- 1 large Yukon Gold potato, peeled and cut into ½-inch pieces
- 4 slices bacon, chopped
- 2 scallions, sliced thin
  Salt and pepper

Microwave potato, covered, in large bowl until just tender, 2 to 5 minutes. Cook bacon in 10-inch nonstick skillet over medium heat until crisp, about 8 minutes. Transfer bacon to paper towel–lined plate; pour off all but 1 tablespoon bacon fat. Add potato to skillet and cook until golden brown, about 6 minutes. Transfer potato to bowl, add cooked bacon, and stir in scallions. Season with salt and pepper to taste.

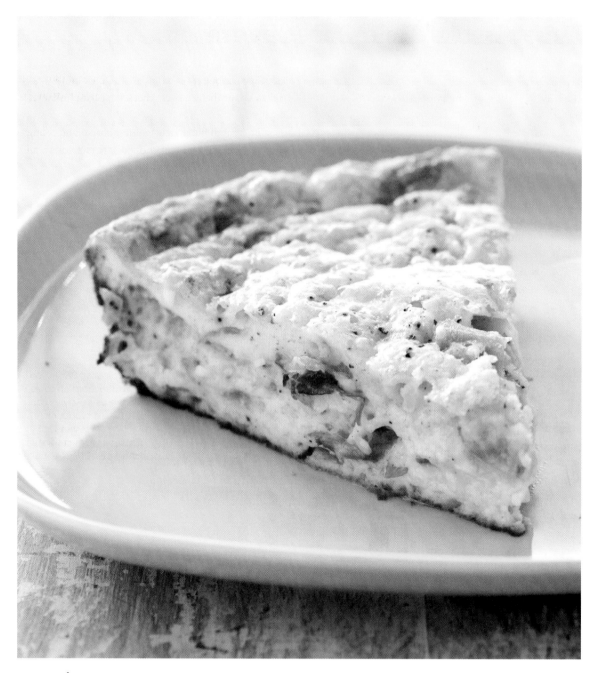

☑ WHY THIS RECIPE WORKS

"Impossible" pie is a 1970s phenomenon that promises a pie "crust" without rolling out finicky dough. Traditionally, a simple Bisquick batter was whisked with eggs and poured over vegetables, meat, and cheese and baked. To give our "crust" a crispy, browned exterior, we buttered the pie dish and coated it with Parmesan cheese. We replaced the Bisquick with a simple batter of flour, baking powder, eggs, and creamy half-and-half. Doubling the number of eggs made for a richer, custardy pie. For the filling, we chose ingredients that required a minimum of prep work: scallions, diced deli ham, and Gruyère cheese.

"Impossible" Ham-and-Cheese Pie

SERVES 8

Use a rasp-style grater or the smallest holes on a box grater for the Parmesan.

1	tablespoon unsalted butter, softened, plus 2 tablespoons melted
3	tablespoons finely grated Parmesan cheese
8	ounces Gruyère cheese, shredded (2 cups)
4	ounces thickly sliced deli ham, chopped
4	scallions, minced
½	cup (2½ ounces) all-purpose flour
¾	teaspoon baking powder
½	teaspoon pepper
¼	teaspoon salt
1	cup half-and-half
4	large eggs, lightly beaten
2	teaspoons Dijon mustard
⅛	teaspoon ground nutmeg

1. Adjust oven rack to lowest position and heat oven to 350 degrees. Grease 9-inch pie plate with softened butter, then coat plate evenly with Parmesan.

2. Combine Gruyère, ham, and scallions in bowl. Sprinkle cheese-and-ham mixture evenly in bottom of prepared pie dish. Combine flour, baking powder, pepper, and salt in now-empty bowl. Whisk in half-and-half, eggs, melted butter, mustard, and nutmeg until smooth. Slowly pour batter over cheese-and-ham mixture in pie dish.

3. Bake until pie is light golden brown and filling is set, 30 to 35 minutes. Let cool on wire rack for 15 minutes. Slice into wedges. Serve warm.

FINGER FOOD

To serve our "Impossible" Ham-and-Cheese Pie as an hors d'oeuvre at your next party, forgo the pie plate and instead bake it in an 8-inch square baking dish. Slice it into 1-inch squares and serve warm or at room temperature.

GRATING HARD CHEESE

When grating Parmesan and other hard cheeses, we use a rasp-style grater because it produces lighter, fluffier shreds of cheese that melt seamlessly into all kinds of dishes.

✔ WHY THIS RECIPE WORKS

Commercially made breakfast sausage always disappoints when it comes to flavor, tasting either too sweet or salty, or too bland or highly seasoned, so we decided to make our own. We started with ground pork with some fat in it (lean meat was neither fatty nor flavorful enough) and amped up its mild flavor with classic breakfast sausage flavors: garlic, sage, thyme, and cayenne pepper. A spoonful of maple syrup sweetened the patties nicely. To combine the meat mixture, we kneaded it gently with our hands, but were careful not to overmix it, which would toughen the meat.

Homemade Breakfast Sausage

SERVES 8

Avoid lean or extra-lean ground pork; it makes the sausage dry, crumbly, and less flavorful.

2	pounds ground pork
1	tablespoon maple syrup
1	garlic clove, minced
2	teaspoons dried sage
1½	teaspoons pepper
1	teaspoon salt
½	teaspoon dried thyme
⅛	teaspoon cayenne pepper
2	tablespoons unsalted butter

1. Combine pork, maple syrup, garlic, sage, pepper, salt, thyme, and cayenne in large bowl. Gently mix with hands until well combined. Using greased ¼-cup measure, divide mixture into 16 patties and place on rimmed baking sheet. Cover patties with plastic wrap, then gently flatten each one to ½-inch thickness.

2. Melt 1 tablespoon butter in 12-inch nonstick skillet over medium heat. Cook half of patties until well browned and cooked through, 6 to 10 minutes. Transfer to paper towel–lined plate and tent with aluminum foil. Wipe out skillet. Repeat with remaining butter and patties. Serve.

TO MAKE AHEAD: Follow recipe through step 1. Refrigerate uncooked patties for up to 1 day or freeze for up to 1 month. To serve, proceed as directed in step 2, increasing cooking time to 14 to 18 minutes.

DRIED HERBS

We use plenty of dried herbs in the test kitchen, but we don't use every dried herb. That's because delicate leafy herbs, such as basil, parsley, chives, mint, and cilantro, become musty and stale-tasting when dried. But heartier herbs, such as oregano, sage, and thyme, dry well and are good substitutes for fresh in most recipes—especially those in which the herbs will cook in liquid (such as stews and sauces). We've found that two herbs, tarragon and dill, fall into a middle category: They do add flavor in their dried form, but that flavor is more muted than that provided by other dried herbs.

A few general rules: Use only half as much dried herbs as fresh, and add them at the same time as you would add fresh. Dried herbs lose their potency 6 to 12 months after opening; you can test dried herbs for freshness by rubbing them between your fingers—if they don't smell bright, throw them away and buy a new jar.

Here are the dried herbs we use in the test kitchen and our favorite uses for each:

OREGANO

Great in tomato sauces, chili, Mexican and Latin dishes, and sprinkled on pizza. Dried oregano does not have the same sharp bite as fresh, but it does have a distinct and recognizable floral element.

SAGE

We prefer rubbed (or finely crumbled) sage to the ground or chopped kinds. Use with poultry, stuffings, pork, and full-flavored vegetables (like squash), and in butter sauces.

ROSEMARY

Works well in long-cooked dishes (especially those with Italian flavors) like soups, stews, and braises. Too much dried rosemary can turn a dish bitter, so use sparingly.

THYME

Good for long-cooked soups and stews and roasted meats and poultry; pairs especially well with the flavors of mustard and lemon.

✔ WHY THIS RECIPE WORKS

Though a commercial-grade griddle helps our local diner serve up home fries with a perfectly crispy exterior, the real secret is precooking the potatoes. Roasting or boiling our spuds took too much time for a quick breakfast side, so we turned to the microwave to jump-start their cooking before frying them in a large skillet. We found that packing the potatoes down with a spatula and cooking them a few minutes before turning them and then repeating these steps ensured they were evenly browned and extra-crunchy. Finally, we stirred in some sautéed onion and garlic salt to give our home fries a deep, savory flavor.

Short-Order Home Fries

Although we prefer the sweetness of Yukon Gold potatoes, other medium-starch potatoes, such as red potatoes, can be substituted. If you want to spice things up, add a pinch of cayenne pepper.

1½	pounds Yukon Gold potatoes, cut into ¾-inch pieces
4	tablespoons unsalted butter
1	onion, chopped fine
½	teaspoon garlic salt
½	teaspoon salt
	Pepper

1. Place potatoes and 1 tablespoon butter in large bowl and microwave, covered, until edges of potatoes begin to soften, 5 to 7 minutes, stirring halfway through cooking.

2. Meanwhile, melt 1 tablespoon butter in 12-inch nonstick skillet over medium heat. Add onion and cook until softened and golden brown, 8 to 10 minutes. Transfer to small bowl.

3. Melt remaining 2 tablespoons butter in now-empty skillet over medium heat. Add potatoes and pack down with spatula. Cook, without moving, until bottoms of potatoes are brown, 5 to 7 minutes. Turn potatoes, pack down again, and continue to cook until well browned and crisp, 5 to 7 minutes. Reduce heat to medium-low and continue to cook until potatoes are crusty, 9 to 12 minutes, stirring occasionally. Stir in onion, garlic salt, and salt and season with pepper to taste. Serve.

GREEK DINER-STYLE HOME FRIES

Omit garlic salt and add 1 tablespoon lemon juice, 2 minced garlic cloves, and ½ teaspoon dried oregano to potatoes along with onion in step 3.

HOME FRIES WITH FRESH HERBS

Add 1 teaspoon each chopped fresh basil, parsley, thyme, and tarragon to potatoes along with onion in step 3.

THE RIGHT SPUDS FOR HOME FRIES

High-starch, low-moisture potatoes, such as russets, may be great for baking and mashing, but when it comes to home fries, they are not the best choice. The fluffy flesh of these potatoes breaks down in the skillet, leaving nothing but a greasy pool of stodgy spuds. For tender tubers that retain their texture, we prefer medium-starch varieties, such as Yukon Gold and red potatoes. They hold their shape in the skillet, develop a great crust, and fry up to a beautiful golden brown.

RUSSET POTATOES
A falling-apart mess

YUKON GOLD POTATOES
Intact, crisp, and browned

✔ WHY THIS RECIPE WORKS

For our take on pancake mix that delivers both store-bought ease and from-scratch taste, we combined all-purpose flour with cake flour; this duo yielded sturdy yet tender cakes. To give pancakes made from our mix complexity and depth, we added an unusual ingredient, malted milk powder, which imparted a sweet, nutty flavor. Though most mixes call for shortening, we opted for butter, which gave us moister, more flavorful pancakes. Using buttermilk instead of milk when mixing the batter gave us high-rising pancakes—the acid of the buttermilk reacts with the baking soda, causing the batter to bubble and rise.

Better-Than-the-Box Pancake Mix

MAKES ABOUT 6 CUPS, ENOUGH FOR 24 PANCAKES

Malted milk powder might seem odd here, but it gives the pancakes a deeper, more complex flavor.

2	cups (10 ounces) all-purpose flour
2	cups (8 ounces) cake flour
1	cup (3 ounces) nonfat dry milk powder
¾	cup (3⅓ ounces) malted milk powder
⅓	cup (2⅓ ounces) sugar
2	tablespoons baking powder
1	teaspoon baking soda
1	tablespoon salt
12	tablespoons unsalted butter, cut into ½-inch pieces

Process all ingredients in food processor until no lumps remain and mixture resembles wet sand, about 2 minutes. (Pancake mix can be frozen for up to 2 months.)

BETTER-THAN-THE-BOX PANCAKES

To make 8 pancakes, whisk 2 cups Better-Than-the-Box Pancake Mix, 2 lightly beaten large eggs, and ½ cup buttermilk in large bowl until smooth. Using ¼-cup measure, portion batter into lightly oiled 12-inch nonstick skillet or griddle in 4 places and cook over medium-low heat until golden brown, about 2 minutes per side. Repeat with remaining batter. Serve. (If you don't have buttermilk, whisk 1½ teaspoons lemon juice or white vinegar into ½ cup whole or low-fat milk and let sit until slightly thickened, about 10 minutes.)

NOT JUST FOR MILKSHAKES

To give our pancakes complexity and depth, we added malted milk powder to the mix. This product is made from malted barley that has been evaporated and pulverized, and sometimes includes flour or evaporated milk powder. Though it is more commonly used to make milkshakes, we found it added a sweet, nutty flavor to the pancakes made from our Better-Than-the-Box Pancake Mix.

IS THE PAN READY FOR PANCAKES?

A properly heated pan or griddle is essential to making perfect, golden-brown, fluffy pancakes. A skillet that has not been properly heated and is too cool will produce pale, gummy pancakes. Here's a test to make sure your pan is hot enough: Drop a tablespoon of batter in its center. If, after one minute, the pancake is golden brown on the bottom, the pan is ready. If it remains blond—or is close to burning—adjust the heat accordingly.

PALE, GUMMY PANCAKE

PERFECT, FLUFFY PANCAKE

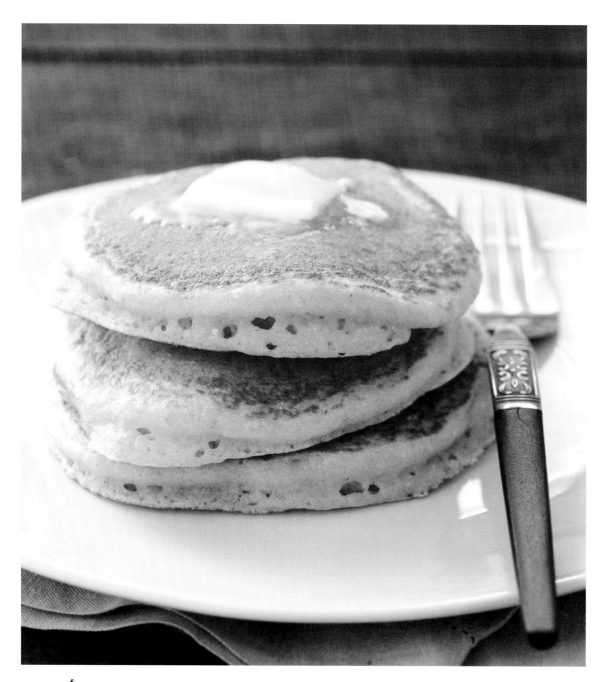

✔ WHY THIS RECIPE WORKS

Getting the height and lightness of traditional pancakes with the robust flavor and texture of cornmeal pancakes is tougher than it seems. Coarsely ground cornmeal can be sandy, and it lacks the gluten necessary to support a fluffy internal structure. We found that we could use more cornmeal by heating it with some of the buttermilk to soften it first. Soaking the cornmeal also thickened the batter, helping it ride higher in the pan instead of spreading out. Letting the batter sit for a few minutes before griddling the cakes allowed the buttermilk to react with the baking soda, which resulted in fluffier, airier pancakes.

Fluffy Cornmeal Pancakes

MAKES ABOUT 15 (4-INCH) PANCAKES

Our favorite cornmeal is Arrowhead Mills Whole-Grain Cornmeal.

1¾	cups buttermilk
1¼	cups (6¼ ounces) cornmeal
2	tablespoons unsalted butter, cut into ¼-inch pieces
¾	cup (3¾ ounces) all-purpose flour
2	tablespoons sugar
1¾	teaspoons baking powder
½	teaspoon baking soda
½	teaspoon salt
2	large eggs
2½	teaspoons vegetable oil

1. Adjust oven rack to middle position and heat oven to 200 degrees. Set wire rack inside rimmed baking sheet and place in oven. Whisk 1¼ cups buttermilk and cornmeal together in medium bowl. Stir in butter, cover, and microwave until slightly thickened around edges, about 90 seconds, stirring once halfway through cooking. Let sit, covered, for 5 minutes.

2. Whisk flour, sugar, baking powder, baking soda, and salt in large bowl. Beat eggs and remaining ½ cup buttermilk together in 1-cup liquid measuring cup. Whisk egg mixture into cornmeal mixture. Whisk cornmeal mixture into flour mixture. Let sit for 10 minutes.

3. Heat ½ teaspoon oil in 12-inch nonstick skillet over medium-low heat until shimmering. Using paper towels, carefully wipe out oil, leaving thin film on bottom of pan. Using level ¼-cup measure for each pancake, drop batter for 3 pancakes into pan. Cook until edges are set and bubbles begin to form on tops of pancakes, about 90 seconds. Flip, then cook until second side is golden brown, about 2 minutes longer. Transfer to prepared baking sheet in oven, cover loosely with aluminum foil, and repeat with remaining oil and batter. Serve.

THE VIRTUES OF PANCAKE PATIENCE

For the fluffiest pancakes, let the finished batter sit for 10 minutes before griddling the cakes. The rest gives the baking soda extra time to react and form large air bubbles, lightening the batter, ergo the pancakes. With a hearty whole grain like cornmeal, you want all the lift you can get. This trick works with any pancake batter made with whole grains.

CHOOSING THE RIGHT CORNMEAL

Cornmeal, or ground processed corn kernels, is available in all manner of sizes for use in different applications. In most cases, we recommend choosing stone-ground over commercially produced cornmeal on two counts: First of all, stone-ground cornmeal has a more rustic texture because of the stone's rough grinding surface (companies like Quaker use smooth steel rollers that produce very fine, uniform cornmeal). And secondly, stone-ground cornmeal has a fuller flavor because it contains both the hull and oil-rich germ of the corn kernel, which commercial producers extract for better shelf life.

WHY THIS RECIPE WORKS

A big, puffy pancake, a Dutch baby puffs and rises as it bakes, then falls in the center a few minutes out of the oven, resulting in a bowl-shaped breakfast treat with crisp sides and a thin, custardy bottom. For our version we started with a 12-inch skillet; its gently sloping walls promoted an even rise. Brushing the pan with oil and preheating it in the oven helped ensure the sides had the texture we wanted and jump-started the pancake's rise. Since fats tend to make baked goods tender rather than crisp, we used skim milk in our batter. For even more crispness, we replaced some of the flour with cornstarch.

Dutch Baby

SERVES 4

You can use whole or low-fat milk instead of skim, but the texture won't be as crisp. Serve with an assortment of berries and lightly sweetened whipped cream, if desired.

2	tablespoons vegetable oil
1	cup (5 ounces) all-purpose flour
¼	cup cornstarch
2	teaspoons grated lemon zest plus 2 tablespoons juice
1	teaspoon salt
3	large eggs
1¼	cups skim milk
1	tablespoon unsalted butter, melted and cooled
1	teaspoon vanilla extract
3	tablespoons confectioners' sugar

1. Adjust oven rack to middle position and heat oven to 450 degrees. Brush bottom and sides of 12-inch skillet with oil. Heat skillet in oven until oil is shimmering, about 10 minutes.

2. Meanwhile, combine flour, cornstarch, lemon zest, and salt in large bowl. Whisk eggs in second bowl until frothy and light, about 1 minute. Whisk milk, butter, and vanilla into eggs until incorporated. Whisk one-third of milk mixture into flour mixture until no lumps remain, then slowly whisk in remaining milk mixture until smooth.

3. Carefully pour batter into skillet and bake until edges are deep golden brown and crisp, about 20 minutes. Transfer skillet to wire rack, sprinkle pancake with lemon juice and confectioners' sugar, and cut into wedges. Serve.

EASY STEPS TO MAKING A DUTCH BABY PANCAKE

1. Brush bottom and sides of pan with vegetable oil to guarantee crisp exterior.

2. Heat greased pan before carefully pouring in batter to initiate rise.

3. Bake in hot 450-degree oven to ensure high rise.

4. Sprinkle deflated pancake with lemon juice and confectioners' sugar before serving.

WHY THIS RECIPE WORKS

To replicate the crisp, airy texture and tangy flavor of these classic New Orleans doughnuts, we began by using plenty of yeast, kick-starting it with warm water and sugar to develop its flavor. We added extra water for a super-hydrated dough, so that as soon as the wet dough hit the hot oil, it created lots of steam, giving our beignets an open, honeycombed structure. Since wet dough is tricky to roll out, we let it rise in the refrigerator to firm it up. A few minutes of frying and a shower of powdered sugar, and our beignets were ready to be enjoyed, Big Easy style.

Beignets

MAKES 24 BEIGNETS

This dough is very wet and sticky, so flour the counter and baking sheet generously. You'll need a least a 6-quart Dutch oven for this recipe.

1	cup water, heated to 110 degrees
3	tablespoons granulated sugar
1	tablespoon instant or rapid-rise yeast
3	cups (15 ounces) all-purpose flour
¾	teaspoon salt
2	large eggs
2	tablespoons plus 2 quarts vegetable oil
	Confectioners' sugar

1. Combine water, 1 tablespoon granulated sugar, and yeast in large bowl and let sit until foamy, about 5 minutes. Combine flour, remaining 2 tablespoons granulated sugar, and salt in second bowl. Whisk eggs and 2 tablespoons oil into yeast mixture. Add flour mixture and stir vigorously with rubber spatula until dough comes together. Cover bowl with plastic wrap and refrigerate until nearly doubled in size, about 1 hour.

2. Set wire rack inside rimmed baking sheet. Line second sheet with parchment paper and dust generously with flour. Place half of dough on well-floured counter and pat into rough rectangle with floured hands, flipping to coat with flour. Roll dough into ¼-inch-thick rectangle (roughly 12 by 9 inches). Using pizza wheel, cut dough into twelve 3-inch squares and transfer to floured baking sheet. Repeat with remaining dough.

3. Add remaining oil to large Dutch oven until it measures about 1½ inches deep and heat over medium-high heat to 350 degrees. Fry 6 beignets, adjusting burner as necessary to maintain oil temperature between 325 and 350 degrees, until golden brown, about 3 minutes, flipping halfway through frying. Using slotted spoon or tongs, transfer beignets to prepared baking sheet. Return oil to 350 degrees and repeat with remaining beignets. Dust beignets with confectioners' sugar and serve immediately.

FORMING BEIGNETS

This dough is very wet, which allows a network of delicate holes to develop in the beignets. However, wet dough can be tricky to work with. Here's how to easily shape and cut the beignets:

1. Dust counter and rolling pin generously with flour before you roll out chilled beignet dough.

2. Cut 3-inch squares with pizza wheel.

A FASTER WAY TO FLAVOR

Starting with a full tablespoon of yeast and proofing it in warm water jump-starts the fermentation process, giving our beignets complex flavor after just a 1-hour rise.

✓ WHY THIS RECIPE WORKS

A good cornmeal biscuit combines the tender, fluffy crumb of a traditional biscuit with the distinct corn-meal flavor of cornbread. To make the dough, we used a food processor to cut chilled butter quickly into our dry ingredients. So our biscuits would taste like cornmeal, but wouldn't have its dry, gritty texture, we soaked the cornmeal in buttermilk; just 10 minutes was enough to soften it. A bit of honey provided a subtle sweetness that drew out the corn flavor even more. Kneading the dough briefly prior to cutting out rounds ensured evenly textured biscuits that rose to an impressive height.

Cornmeal Biscuits

MAKES 12 BISCUITS

If you don't have buttermilk, you can substitute clabbered milk; whisk 1 tablespoon lemon juice into 1¼ cups of milk and let the mixture sit until slightly thickened, about 10 minutes. Avoid coarsely ground cornmeal, which makes gritty biscuits.

1	cup (5 ounces) cornmeal
1¼	cups buttermilk
1	tablespoon honey
2	cups (10 ounces) all-purpose flour
1	tablespoon baking powder
½	teaspoon baking soda
1	teaspoon salt
12	tablespoons unsalted butter, cut into ½-inch pieces and chilled

1. Adjust oven rack to middle position and heat oven to 450 degrees. Line rimmed baking sheet with parchment paper. Whisk cornmeal, buttermilk, and honey together in large bowl; let sit for 10 minutes.

2. Pulse flour, baking powder, baking soda, and salt in food processor until combined, about 3 pulses. Scatter butter evenly over top and continue to pulse until mixture resembles coarse meal, about 15 pulses. Add flour mixture to buttermilk mixture and stir until dough forms.

3. Turn dough out onto lightly floured counter and knead until smooth, 8 to 10 times. Pat dough into 9-inch circle, about ¾ inch thick. Using 2½-inch biscuit cutter dipped in flour, cut out rounds and transfer to prepared baking sheet, dipping cutter in flour after each cut. Pat remaining dough into ¾-inch-thick circle, cut rounds from dough, and transfer to baking sheet.

4. Bake until biscuits begin to rise, about 5 minutes, then reduce oven temperature to 400 degrees and bake until golden brown, 8 to 12 minutes longer, rotating baking sheet halfway through baking. Let biscuits cool on baking sheet for 5 minutes, then transfer to wire rack. Serve warm or let cool to room temperature. (Biscuits can be stored at room temperature for up to 2 days.)

STEPS TO TENDER, FLUFFY CORNMEAL BISCUITS

Our Cornmeal Biscuits have the moist, flavor-packed crumb of cornbread and the fluffy stature of a stamped biscuit.

1. Soak cornmeal in buttermilk for soft crumb without too much cornmeal grit before mixing together dough.

2. Transfer dough to lightly floured counter and knead briefly before patting into 9-inch circle.

3. Use biscuit cutter to cut dough into rounds, dipping cutter into flour between cuts.

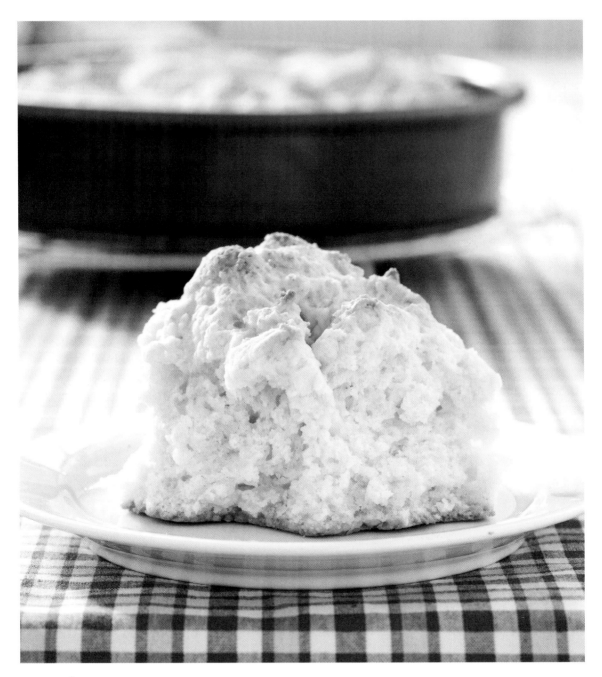

✔ WHY THIS RECIPE WORKS

As big as a cat's head, these tender, moist biscuits that originated in the Appalachian region boast a golden-brown, craggy top and downy, soft sides. Many Southern bakers rely on White Lily flour to ensure a tender texture, but since this flour isn't readily available everywhere, we substituted an equal mix of cake flour and all-purpose flour. For biscuits with a fluffy texture, we relied on softened butter and shortening, worked in with warm hands. Scooping the dough into a round cake pan, so the mounds were touching, gave us baked biscuits with tender, soft sides.

Cat Head Biscuits

MAKES 6 BISCUITS

If you don't have buttermilk, you can substitute clabbered milk; whisk 1 tablespoon lemon juice into 1¼ cups milk and let the mixture sit until slightly thickened, about 10 minutes. The recipe will also work with 3 cups White Lily flour in place of both the all-purpose and cake flours.

1½	cups (7½ ounces) all-purpose flour
1½	cups (6 ounces) cake flour
1	tablespoon baking powder
½	teaspoon baking soda
1	teaspoon salt
8	tablespoons unsalted butter, cut into ½-inch pieces and softened
4	tablespoons vegetable shortening, cut into ½-inch pieces
1¼	cups buttermilk

1. Adjust oven rack to upper-middle position and heat oven to 425 degrees. Grease 9-inch round cake pan. Combine all-purpose flour, cake flour, baking powder, baking soda, and salt in large bowl. Using fingertips, rub butter and shortening into flour mixture until mixture resembles coarse meal. Stir in buttermilk until combined.

2. Using greased ½-cup measure or large spring-loaded ice cream scoop, transfer 6 heaping portions of dough into prepared pan, placing five around edge and one in center.

3. Bake until puffed and golden brown, 20 to 25 minutes, rotating pan halfway through baking. Let biscuits cool in pan for 10 minutes, then transfer to wire rack. Serve. (Biscuits can be stored at room temperature for up to 2 days.)

FORMING CAT HEAD BISCUITS

Many biscuits are kneaded, rolled, stamped out, and then baked on sheet pans. For Cat Head Biscuits, we instead scoop the sticky, shaggy dough and nestle the biscuits in a cake pan. (A spring-loaded ice cream scoop does the job neatly and quickly.) All snuggled together, they're forced to rise, rather than spread, and the sides stay soft and white.

FLOUR MIXOLOGY

Southern bakers swear by White Lily all-purpose flour, which they say makes biscuits soft and downy, exactly the texture we sought for our Cat Head Biscuits. But what if you don't live in the South and can't easily get your hands on a bag? We found we could replicate it by combining equal amounts of ordinary all-purpose flour (made from a mix of high- and low-gluten wheats) and cake flour (a soft, fine-textured flour).

ALL-PURPOSE FLOUR
Contributes structure

CAKE FLOUR
Contributes softness

WHITE LILY
The soft and fluffy standard-bearer

WHY THIS RECIPE WORKS

Savory skillet-baked Southern-style cornbread should boast hearty corn flavor, a sturdy, moist crumb, and a dark brown crust. For the right texture, we used finely ground cornmeal. Toasting it in the oven for a few minutes intensified the corn flavor. Buttermilk added a sharp tang that worked well with the corn, and soaking the cornmeal in the buttermilk helped to soften it so our cornbread was moist and tender. When it came to the fat, a combination of butter (for flavor) and vegetable oil (which can withstand high heat without burning) worked best, and greasing the pan with both delivered the crisp crust we were after.

Southern-Style Skillet Cornbread

SERVES 12

If you don't have buttermilk, you can substitute clabbered milk; whisk 2 tablespoons lemon juice into 2 cups of milk and let the mixture sit until slightly thickened, about 10 minutes. We prefer a cast-iron skillet here, but any ovensafe 10-inch skillet will work fine. Avoid coarsely ground cornmeal, as it will make the cornbread gritty.

2¼	cups (11¼ ounces) cornmeal
2	cups buttermilk
¼	cup vegetable oil
4	tablespoons unsalted butter, cut into 4 pieces
2	large eggs
1	teaspoon baking powder
1	teaspoon baking soda
¾	teaspoon salt

1. Adjust oven racks to lower-middle and middle positions and heat oven to 450 degrees. Heat 10-inch cast-iron skillet on middle rack for 10 minutes. Spread cornmeal over rimmed baking sheet and bake on lower-middle rack until fragrant and color begins to deepen, about 5 minutes. Transfer hot cornmeal to large bowl and whisk in buttermilk; set aside.

2. Carefully add oil to hot skillet and continue to bake until oil is just smoking, about 5 minutes. Remove skillet from oven and add butter, carefully swirling pan until butter is melted. Pour all but 1 tablespoon oil mixture into cornmeal mixture, leaving remaining oil mixture in pan. Whisk eggs, baking powder, baking soda, and salt into cornmeal mixture.

3. Pour cornmeal mixture into hot skillet and bake until top begins to crack and sides are golden brown, 12 to 16 minutes, rotating pan halfway through baking. Let cornbread cool in pan for 5 minutes, then turn out onto wire rack. Serve.

SECRETS TO SAVORY SOUTHERN-STYLE SKILLET CORNBREAD

1. Toast cornmeal to give bread richer corn flavor.

2. Soak cornmeal in buttermilk to soften cornmeal and ensure tender yet sturdy crumb.

3. Grease and thoroughly heat skillet to create crisp crust.

✔ WHY THIS RECIPE WORKS

For golden-brown popovers that really popped, we used bread flour instead of all-purpose flour in the batter—the bread flour's higher protein content ensured the highest rise and crispiest crust. Resting the batter before baking prevented the popovers from setting up too quickly. We first baked our popovers at a high temperature to jump-start the initial rise, then turned the oven down so they would cook through evenly. To let steam escape (which can cause popovers to collapse), we poked a hole in the top of each one when they were almost done baking, and then again as they cooled.

Perfect Popovers

MAKES 6 POPOVERS
Greasing the pan with shortening ensures the best release, but vegetable oil spray may be substituted; do not use butter. Bread flour makes for the highest and sturdiest popovers, but 2 cups (10 ounces) of all-purpose flour may be substituted.

3	large eggs
2	cups 1 percent or 2 percent low-fat milk, heated to 110 degrees
3	tablespoons unsalted butter, melted and cooled
2	cups (11 ounces) bread flour
1	teaspoon salt
1	teaspoon sugar

1. Adjust oven rack to lower-middle position and heat oven to 450 degrees. Grease 6-cup popover pan with shortening, then flour pan lightly. Whisk eggs until light and foamy in medium bowl. Slowly whisk in milk and butter until incorporated.

2. Combine flour, salt, and sugar in large bowl. Whisk three-quarters of milk mixture into flour mixture until no lumps remain, then whisk in remaining milk mixture. Transfer batter to 4-cup liquid measuring cup, cover with plastic wrap, and let sit at room temperature for 1 hour. (Alternatively, batter can be refrigerated for up to 1 day. Bring to room temperature before proceeding.)

3. Whisk batter to recombine, then pour into prepared pan (batter will not reach top of cups). Bake until just beginning to brown, about 20 minutes. Without opening oven door, decrease oven temperature to 300 degrees and continue to bake until popovers are golden brown, 35 to 40 minutes longer. Poke small hole in top of each popover with skewer and continue to bake until deep golden brown, about 10 minutes longer. Transfer pan to wire rack, poke popovers again with skewer, and let cool for 2 minutes. Remove from pan and serve.

TO MAKE AHEAD: Cooled popovers can be stored at room temperature for up to 2 days. To serve, adjust oven rack to middle position and heat oven to 400 degrees. Heat popovers on rimmed baking sheet until crisp and heated through, 5 to 8 minutes.

MUFFIN TIN POPOVERS

If you don't have a popover pan, you can bake the popovers in a 12-cup muffin tin—with a sacrifice in stature. To ensure even cooking, use only the outer 10 cups of the tin.

Grease and flour outer 10 cups of muffin tin, then fill ¼ inch from the top (you may have some batter left over). Reduce initial baking time in step 3 to 15 minutes, and reduce secondary baking time to 20 to 25 minutes after oven temperature has been lowered. Poke popovers as directed and continue to bake for another 10 minutes.

POPOVERS GONE WRONG

POP NEVER
Short, squat popovers occur when the recipe calls for cake flour, which doesn't provide enough structure to the batter. Using too little batter can also make for squat popovers, as can an oven that's not hot enough.

POP UNDER
Deflated popovers occur when they aren't baked long enough to set up properly or aren't poked during baking to allow the steam to escape.

POP UGLY
Misshapen popovers are caused by using a preheated, oiled pan. The batter that first hits the pan immediately rises up through the wet batter, resulting in an ugly shape.

✓ WHY THIS RECIPE WORKS

When it comes to baking with whole wheat, the benefits—added fiber, bran, and nutty sweetness—are often trumped by the drawbacks—dense texture and squat appearance. To use one hundred percent whole wheat, we had to revise our standard blueberry muffin recipe. The resulting whole-wheat muffins were light and tender thanks to two leaveners and several high-moisture ingredients (buttermilk, eggs, blueberries, melted butter, and oil). As a final step we added a crumbly streusel topping to round out our now light and delicate muffins with hearty whole-wheat flavor.

Whole-Wheat Blueberry Muffins

MAKES 12 MUFFINS

Do not overmix the batter. You can substitute frozen (unthawed) blueberries for fresh in this recipe.

STREUSEL

- 3 tablespoons granulated sugar
- 3 tablespoons packed brown sugar
- 3 tablespoons whole-wheat flour
- Pinch salt
- 2 tablespoons unsalted butter, melted

MUFFINS

- 3 cups (16½ ounces) whole-wheat flour
- 2½ teaspoons baking powder
- ½ teaspoon baking soda
- 1 teaspoon salt
- 1 cup (7 ounces) granulated sugar
- 2 large eggs
- 4 tablespoons unsalted butter, melted
- ¼ cup vegetable oil
- 1¼ cups buttermilk
- 1½ teaspoons vanilla extract
- 7½ ounces (1½ cups) blueberries

1. FOR THE STREUSEL: Combine granulated sugar, brown sugar, flour, and salt in bowl. Add melted butter and toss with fork until evenly moistened and mixture forms large chunks with some pea-size pieces throughout; set aside.

2. FOR THE MUFFINS: Adjust oven rack to middle position and heat oven to 400 degrees. Spray 12-cup muffin tin, including top, generously with vegetable oil spray. Whisk flour, baking powder, baking soda, and salt together in large bowl. Whisk sugar, eggs, melted butter, and oil together in separate bowl until combined, about 30 seconds. Whisk buttermilk and vanilla into sugar mixture until combined.

3. Stir sugar mixture into flour mixture until just combined. Gently stir in blueberries until incorporated. Using a heaping ¼-cup dry measuring cup, divide batter evenly among prepared muffin cups (cups will be filled to rim); sprinkle evenly with streusel.

4. Bake until golden brown and toothpick inserted in center comes out with few crumbs attached, 18 to 20 minutes, rotating muffin tin halfway through baking. Let muffins cool in muffin tin on wire rack for 5 minutes. Remove muffins from muffin tin and let cool 5 minutes longer. Serve.

DON'T MAKE THIS MISTAKE: HEAVY AND DENSE MUFFINS

You can't simply swap whole-wheat flour into any muffin recipe and expect it to work. But if you know the science behind baking and account for the variables, you can make great blueberry muffins using 100 percent whole-wheat flour.

✔ WHY THIS RECIPE WORKS

Morning glory muffins are chock-full of nuts, fruit, carrots, and spices. But all these tempting add-ins can make for heavy, dense muffins, so our first move was to strain the fruit and press out the extra juice to prevent our muffins from being soggy. To keep the bright, fruity flavor intact, we simply saved the released fruit juice, reduced it on the stovetop, and added the concentrated syrup back to the batter. To keep the nuts and coconut from becoming mealy or soggy in the finished muffins, we toasted and processed them. At last, our muffins were truly glorious.

Morning Glory Muffins

MAKES 12 MUFFINS

Though we prefer golden raisins here, ordinary raisins will work, too.

¾	cup (2¼ ounces) sweetened shredded coconut, toasted
½	cup walnuts, toasted
2¼	cups (11¼ ounces) all-purpose flour
¾	cup (5¼ ounces) sugar
1½	teaspoons baking soda
½	teaspoon baking powder
1	teaspoon ground cinnamon
¾	teaspoon salt
1	(8-ounce) can crushed pineapple
1	Granny Smith apple, peeled, cored, and shredded
8	tablespoons unsalted butter, melted
3	large eggs
1	teaspoon vanilla extract
1½	cups shredded carrots (2 to 3 carrots)
1	cup golden raisins

1. Adjust oven rack to middle position and heat oven to 350 degrees. Spray 12-cup muffin tin with vegetable oil spray. Process coconut and walnuts in food processor until finely ground, 20 to 30 seconds. Add flour, sugar, baking soda, baking powder, cinnamon, and salt and pulse until combined. Transfer mixture to large bowl.

2. Place pineapple and shredded apple in fine-mesh strainer set over liquid measuring cup. Press fruit dry (you should have about 1 cup juice). Bring juice to boil in 12-inch skillet over medium-high heat and cook until reduced to ¼ cup, about 5 minutes. Let cool slightly. Whisk melted butter, cooled juice, eggs, and vanilla together until smooth. Stir wet mixture into dry mixture until combined. Stir in pineapple-apple mixture, carrots, and raisins.

3. Divide batter evenly among muffin cups. Bake until toothpick inserted in center comes out clean, 24 to 28 minutes, rotating pan halfway through baking. Let muffins cool in muffin tin on wire rack for 10 minutes. Remove muffins from tin and let cool for at least 10 minutes before serving. (Muffins can be stored at room temperature for up to 3 days.)

SECRETS TO GLORIOUS MORNING GLORY MUFFINS

1. Toasting the coconut and walnuts heightens their flavor, and processing them in a food processor until finely ground prevents soggy, stringy coconut and mealy nuts.

2. Pressing the juice out of the shredded apple and pineapple before stirring them into the batter keeps the muffins from being gummy and wet.

3. Reducing the released fruit juice on the stovetop (down from 1 cup to ¼ cup) and adding the syrup to the batter provides a bright, fruity flavor without adding too much moisture.

✅ WHY THIS RECIPE WORKS

To capture the best of breakfast baking, we set out to create a muffin that tasted like a cake doughnut in disguise with a tender crumb, a crisp exterior, and a buttery spiced coating. Adding an extra yolk and cutting all-purpose flour with cornstarch gave the muffins a tender crumb that wouldn't break apart. To replicate a fried exterior, we turned up the oven temperature, which crisped the crust nicely. Lastly we brushed the muffins with butter and rolled them in cinnamon sugar. From coating to crumb, these doughnut muffins combined the essence of a doughnut and the ease of a muffin (without a deep fryer in sight).

Muffin Tin Doughnuts

MAKES 12 DOUGHNUTS

In step 3, brush the doughnuts generously, using up all the melted butter. Use your hand to press the cinnamon sugar onto the doughnuts to coat them completely.

DOUGHNUTS

2¾	cups (13¾ ounces) all-purpose flour
1	cup (7 ounces) sugar
¼	cup cornstarch
1	tablespoon baking powder
1	teaspoon salt
½	teaspoon ground nutmeg
1	cup buttermilk
8	tablespoons unsalted butter, melted
2	large eggs plus 1 large yolk

COATING

1	cup sugar
2	teaspoons ground cinnamon
8	tablespoons unsalted butter, melted

1. FOR THE DOUGHNUTS: Adjust oven rack to middle position and heat oven to 400 degrees. Spray 12-cup muffin tin with vegetable oil spray. Whisk flour, sugar, cornstarch, baking powder, salt, and nutmeg together in bowl. Whisk buttermilk, melted butter, and eggs and yolk together in separate bowl. Add wet ingredients to dry ingredients and stir with rubber spatula until just combined.

2. Scoop batter into prepared tin. Bake until doughnuts are lightly browned and toothpick inserted in center comes out clean, 19 to 22 minutes. Let doughnuts cool in tin for 5 minutes.

3. FOR THE COATING: Whisk sugar and cinnamon together in bowl. Remove doughnuts from tin. Working with 1 doughnut at a time, brush all over with melted butter, then roll in cinnamon sugar, pressing lightly to adhere. Transfer to wire rack and let cool for 15 minutes. Serve.

BRUSH WITH BUTTER

We brush the warm muffins liberally with melted butter before rolling them in the cinnamon sugar. The butter helps the coating stick and makes the muffins taste more fried.

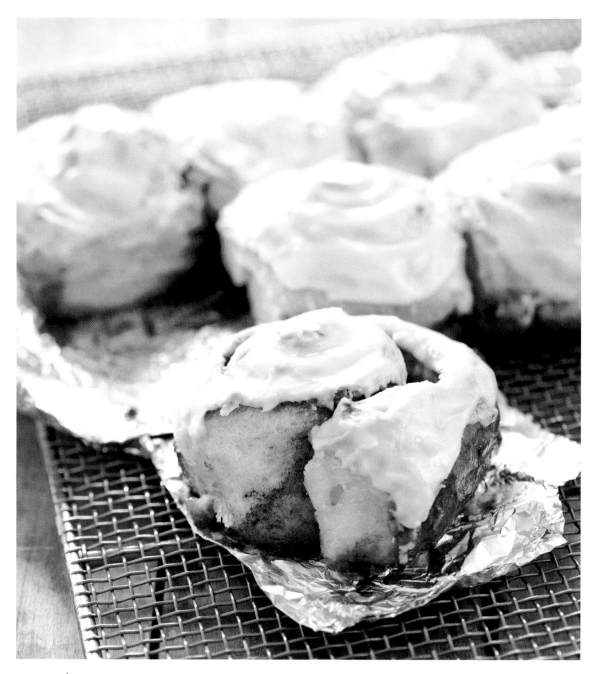

✔ WHY THIS RECIPE WORKS

Gooey softball-size cinnamon buns are the ultimate breakfast treat. For the base of ours, we turned to a buttery, tender brioche dough. Adding cornstarch to the all-purpose flour in the dough made the buns especially tender. For a filling with great flavor, we combined a good amount of cinnamon—no other spices necessary—with brown sugar. Softened butter helped keep the filling from spilling out as we rolled up the dough. Baked together, the butter and cinnamon sugar turned into a rich, gooey filling. A thick, tangy glaze of cream cheese, confectioners' sugar, and milk ensured our buns really looked the part.

Ultimate Cinnamon Buns

MAKES 8 BUNS

For smaller cinnamon buns, cut the dough into 12 pieces in step 3.

DOUGH

¾	cup whole milk, heated to 110 degrees
2¼	teaspoons instant or rapid-rise yeast
3	large eggs, room temperature
4¼	cups (21¼ ounces) all-purpose flour
½	cup cornstarch
½	cup (3½ ounces) granulated sugar
1½	teaspoons salt
12	tablespoons unsalted butter, cut into 12 pieces and softened

FILLING

1½	cups packed (10½ ounces) light brown sugar
1½	tablespoons ground cinnamon
¼	teaspoon salt
4	tablespoons unsalted butter, softened

GLAZE

1½	cups confectioners' sugar
4	ounces cream cheese, softened
1	tablespoon whole milk
1	teaspoon vanilla extract

1. FOR THE DOUGH: Make foil sling for 13 by 9-inch baking pan by folding 2 long sheets of aluminum foil; first sheet should be 13 inches wide and second sheet should be 9 inches wide. Lay sheets of foil in pan perpendicular to each other, with extra foil hanging over edges of pan. Push foil into corners and up sides of pan, smoothing foil flush to pan. Grease foil. Whisk milk and yeast together in liquid measuring cup until yeast dissolves, then whisk in eggs.

2. Adjust oven rack to middle position and place loaf or cake pan on bottom of oven. Using stand mixer fitted with dough hook, mix flour, cornstarch, sugar, and salt on low speed until combined. Add warm milk mixture in steady stream and mix until dough comes together, about 1 minute. Increase speed to medium and add butter, 1 piece at a time, until incorporated. Continue to mix until dough is smooth and comes away from sides of bowl, about 10 minutes (if dough is still wet and sticky, add up to ¼ cup flour, 1 tablespoon at a time, until it releases from bowl). Turn dough out onto counter and knead to form smooth, round ball. Transfer dough to medium greased bowl, cover with plastic wrap, and transfer to middle rack of oven. Pour 3 cups boiling water into loaf pan in oven, close oven door, and let dough rise until doubled in size, about 2 hours.

3. FOR THE FILLING: Combine sugar, cinnamon, and salt in small bowl. Remove dough from oven and turn out onto lightly floured counter. Roll dough into 18-inch square and, leaving ½-inch border around edges, spread with butter, then sprinkle evenly with sugar mixture and lightly press sugar mixture into dough. Starting with edge closest to you, roll dough into tight cylinder, pinch lightly to seal seam, and cut into 8 pieces. Transfer pieces, cut side up, to prepared pan. Cover with plastic and let rise in oven until doubled in size, about 1 hour.

4. FOR THE GLAZE AND TO BAKE: Remove buns and water pan from oven and heat oven to 350 degrees. Whisk all glaze ingredients together in medium bowl until smooth. Remove plastic and bake buns until deep golden brown and filling is melted, 35 to 40 minutes, rotating pan halfway through baking. Transfer to wire rack, top buns with ½ cup glaze, and let cool for 30 minutes. Using foil overhang, lift buns from pan and top with remaining glaze. Serve.

TO MAKE AHEAD: Follow recipe through step 3, skipping step of letting buns rise. Place buns in pan, cover with plastic wrap, and refrigerate for up to 1 day. To bake, let sit at room temperature for 1 hour. Remove plastic and proceed with step 4.

✔ WHY THIS RECIPE WORKS

Rich, gooey, homemade cinnamon buns can take upwards of 3 hours to prepare. We wanted the same tender, yeasty results in half the time. For a quicker rise, we supplemented the yeast (which we proofed in warm milk for extra speed) with baking powder. A mere 2 minutes of hand-kneading and a single 30-minute rise were enough to give us the flavor and texture we were looking for. We used a cooler-than-normal oven to give the yeast time to rise and develop flavor before the tops of the buns set. Brown sugar and butter in the filling and a touch of vanilla in our tangy cream cheese glaze made these buns ultra-rich and indulgent.

Quicker Cinnamon Buns

MAKES 8 BUNS

Since the filling, dough, and glaze all require melted butter, it's easier to melt all 10 tablespoons in a liquid measuring cup and divvy it up as needed. Stir the melted butter before each use to redistribute the milk solids. We developed this recipe using a dark cake pan, which produces deeply caramelized buns. If your cake pan is light-colored, adjust the oven rack to the lowest position, heat the oven to 375 degrees, and increase the baking time to 29 to 32 minutes.

FILLING

- ¾ cup packed (5¼ ounces) light brown sugar
- ¼ cup (1¾ ounces) granulated sugar
- 1 tablespoon ground cinnamon
- ⅛ teaspoon salt
- 2 tablespoons unsalted butter, melted
- 1 teaspoon vanilla extract

DOUGH

- 1¼ cups whole milk, room temperature
- 4 teaspoons instant or rapid-rise yeast
- 2 tablespoons granulated sugar
- 2¾ cups (13¾ ounces) all-purpose flour
- 2½ teaspoons baking powder
- ¾ teaspoon salt
- 6 tablespoons unsalted butter, melted

GLAZE

- 3 ounces cream cheese, softened
- 2 tablespoons unsalted butter, melted
- 2 tablespoons whole milk
- ½ teaspoon vanilla extract
- ⅛ teaspoon salt
- 1 cup (4 ounces) confectioners' sugar, sifted

1. FOR THE FILLING: Combine brown sugar, granulated sugar, cinnamon, and salt in bowl. Stir in melted butter and vanilla until mixture resembles wet sand; set aside.

2. FOR THE DOUGH: Grease dark 9-inch round cake pan, line with parchment paper, and grease parchment. Pour ¼ cup milk in small bowl and microwave until 110 degrees, 15 to 20 seconds. Stir in yeast and 1 teaspoon sugar and let sit until mixture is bubbly, about 5 minutes.

3. Whisk flour, baking powder, salt, and remaining 5 teaspoons sugar together in large bowl. Stir in 2 tablespoons butter, yeast mixture, and remaining 1 cup milk until dough forms (dough will be sticky). Transfer dough to well-floured counter and knead until smooth ball forms, about 2 minutes.

4. Roll dough into 12 by 9-inch rectangle, with long side parallel to counter edge. Brush dough all over with 2 tablespoons butter, leaving ½-inch border on far edge. Sprinkle dough evenly with filling, then press filling firmly into dough. Using bench scraper or metal spatula, loosen dough from counter. Roll dough away from you into tight log and pinch seam to seal.

5. Roll log seam side down and cut into 8 equal pieces. Stand buns on end and gently re-form ends that were pinched during cutting. Place 1 bun in center of prepared pan and others around perimeter of pan, seam sides facing in. Brush tops of buns with remaining 2 tablespoons butter. Cover buns loosely with plastic wrap and let rise for 30 minutes. Adjust oven rack to middle position and heat oven to 350 degrees.

6. Discard plastic and bake buns until edges are well browned, 23 to 25 minutes. Loosen buns from sides of pan with paring knife and let cool for 5 minutes. Invert large plate over cake pan. Using potholders, flip plate and pan upside down; remove pan and parchment. Reinvert buns onto wire rack, set wire rack inside parchment-lined rimmed baking sheet, and let cool for 5 minutes.

7. FOR THE GLAZE: Place cream cheese in large bowl and whisk in butter, milk, vanilla, and salt until smooth. Whisk in sugar until smooth. Pour glaze evenly over tops of buns, spreading with spatula to cover. Serve.

WHY THIS RECIPE WORKS

Morning buns rely on a complicated croissantlike dough that requires both substantial effort and time. For an easier path, we switched to a quick dough closer to puff pastry. Instead of rolling the butter into the dry ingredients on the counter, we moved it all to a zipper-lock bag and rolled everything right in the bag. To produce multiple layers in this rich pastry, we rolled the dough into a rectangle, then into a cylinder, and gently patted it flat. A blend of brown and white sugar added a subtle molasses flavor to the filling, while orange zest instilled it with bright citrus notes.

Morning Buns

MAKES 12 BUNS

If the dough becomes too soft to work with at any point, refrigerate it until it's firm enough to easily handle.

DOUGH

3	cups (15 ounces) all-purpose flour
1	tablespoon sugar
2¼	teaspoons instant or rapid-rise yeast
¾	teaspoon salt
24	tablespoons (3 sticks) unsalted butter, cut into ¼-inch-thick slices and chilled
1	cup sour cream, chilled
¼	cup orange juice, chilled
3	tablespoons ice water
1	large egg yolk

FILLING

½	cup (3½ ounces) granulated sugar
½	cup packed (3½ ounces) light brown sugar
1	tablespoon grated orange zest
2	teaspoons ground cinnamon
1	teaspoon vanilla extract

1. FOR THE DOUGH: Combine flour, sugar, yeast, and salt in large zipper-lock bag. Add butter to bag, seal, and shake to coat. Press air out of bag and reseal. Roll over bag several times with rolling pin, shaking bag after each roll, until butter is pressed into large flakes. Transfer mixture to large bowl and stir in sour cream, orange juice, water, and egg yolk until combined.

2. Turn dough onto floured counter and knead briefly to form smooth, cohesive ball. Roll dough into 20 by 12-inch rectangle. Starting with short edge, roll dough into tight cylinder. Pat cylinder flat to 12 by 4-inch rectangle and transfer to parchment paper–lined rimmed baking sheet. Cover with plastic wrap and freeze for 15 minutes.

3. FOR THE FILLING: Line 12-cup muffin tin with paper or foil liners and spray with vegetable oil spray. Combine granulated sugar, brown sugar, orange zest, cinnamon, and vanilla in medium bowl. Remove dough from freezer and place on lightly floured counter.

Roll dough into 20 by 12-inch rectangle and sprinkle evenly with filling, leaving ½-inch border around edges. Starting at long edge, roll dough into tight cylinder and pinch lightly to seal seam. Trim ½ inch dough from each end and discard. Cut dough into 12 pieces and transfer, cut side up, to prepared tin. Cover loosely with plastic and refrigerate for at least 4 hours or up to 1 day.

4. Adjust oven rack to middle position and place loaf or cake pan on bottom of oven. Remove plastic from buns and place in oven. Pour 3 cups boiling water into loaf pan in oven, close oven door, and let buns rise until puffed and doubled in size, 20 to 30 minutes. Remove buns and water pan from oven and heat oven to 425 degrees. Bake until buns begin to rise, about 5 minutes, then reduce oven temperature to 325 degrees. Bake until deep golden brown, 40 to 50 minutes, rotating pan halfway through baking. Let buns cool in muffin tin on wire rack for 5 minutes, then transfer to wire rack and discard liners. Serve warm.

TO MAKE AHEAD: Follow recipe through step 3, skipping step of refrigerating buns. Freeze buns, in muffin tin, until firm, about 30 minutes. Transfer buns, with liners, to zipper-lock bag and freeze for up to 1 month. To bake, return buns to muffin tin, cover with plastic, and refrigerate for at least 8 hours or up to 1 day. Proceed with step 4.

KEY STEPS TO FLAKY PASTRY

1. Flatten flour-coated butter into long flakes by pressing air out of bag, sealing it, and rolling over it a few times with rolling pin.

2. Add butter-flour mixture to bowl and stir in sour cream, orange juice, water, and egg yolk. Then mix and knead briefly before rolling dough.

WHY THIS RECIPE WORKS

Brought to Texas by Czech immigrants, kolaches are palm-size rounds of sweetened bread with dollops of sweet cheese or fruit filling in the center and a streusel topping. We discovered that long mixing with a dough hook developed plenty of stretchy gluten, making the finished pastries light and pleasantly chewy. For a Texas-style filling, a combination of tangy cream cheese and milkier, slightly salty ricotta created a perfect base, while a little sugar and lemon zest balanced the flavor. At the end of the day, our kolaches were subtly sweet, tender, buttery, and . . . gone.

Kolaches

Do not use nonfat ricotta cheese in this recipe. In step 1, if the dough hasn't cleared the sides of the bowl after 12 minutes, add more flour, 1 tablespoon at a time, up to 2 tablespoons. In step 6, to prevent sticking, reflour the bottom of the measuring cup (or drinking glass) after making each indentation.

DOUGH

1	cup whole milk
10	tablespoons unsalted butter, melted
1	large egg plus 2 large yolks
3½	cups (17½ ounces) all-purpose flour
⅓	cup (2⅓ ounces) sugar
2¼	teaspoons instant or rapid-rise yeast
1½	teaspoons salt

CHEESE FILLING

6	ounces cream cheese, softened
3	tablespoons sugar
1	tablespoon all-purpose flour
½	teaspoon grated lemon zest
6	ounces (¾ cup) whole-milk or part-skim ricotta cheese

STREUSEL

2	tablespoons plus 2 teaspoons all-purpose flour
2	tablespoons plus 2 teaspoons sugar
1	tablespoon unsalted butter, cut into 8 pieces and chilled
1	large egg beaten with 1 tablespoon milk

1. FOR THE DOUGH: Grease large bowl. Whisk milk, melted butter, and egg and yolks together in 2-cup liquid measuring cup (butter will form clumps). Whisk flour, sugar, yeast, and salt together in bowl of stand mixer. Fit stand mixer with dough hook, add milk mixture to flour mixture, and knead on low speed until no dry flour remains, about 2 minutes. Increase speed to medium and knead until dough clears sides of bowl but still sticks to bottom, 8 to 12 minutes.

2. Transfer dough to greased bowl and cover with plastic wrap. Adjust oven racks to upper-middle and lower-middle positions. Place dough on lower-middle rack and place loaf pan on bottom of oven. Pour 3 cups boiling water into loaf pan, close oven door, and let dough rise until doubled, about 1 hour.

3. FOR THE CHEESE FILLING: Using stand mixer fitted with paddle, beat cream cheese, sugar, flour, and lemon zest on low speed until smooth, about 1 minute. Add ricotta and beat until just combined, about 30 seconds. Transfer to bowl, cover with plastic, and refrigerate until ready to use.

4. FOR THE STREUSEL: Combine flour, sugar, and butter in bowl and rub between fingers until mixture resembles wet sand. Cover with plastic and refrigerate until ready to use.

5. Line 2 rimmed baking sheets with parchment paper. Punch down dough and place on lightly floured counter. Divide into quarters and cut each quarter into 4 equal pieces. Form each piece into rough ball by pulling dough edges underneath so top is smooth. On unfloured counter, cup each ball in your palm and roll into smooth, tight ball. Arrange 8 balls on each prepared sheet and cover loosely with plastic. Place sheets on oven racks. Replace water in loaf pan with 3 cups boiling water, close oven door, and let dough rise until doubled, about 90 minutes.

6. Remove sheets and loaf pan from oven. Heat oven to 350 degrees. Grease and flour bottom of ⅓-cup measuring cup (or 2¼-inch-diameter drinking glass). Make deep indentation in center of each dough ball by slowly pressing until cup touches sheet. (Perimeter of balls may deflate slightly.)

7. Gently brush kolaches all over with egg-milk mixture. Divide filling evenly among kolaches (about 1½ tablespoons per kolache) and smooth with back of spoon. Sprinkle streusel over kolaches, avoiding filling. Bake until golden brown, about 25 minutes, switching and rotating sheets halfway through baking. Let kolaches cool on pans for 20 minutes. Serve warm.

WHY THIS RECIPE WORKS

It might have a funny name, but monkey bread is a soft, sweet, sticky, ultra-cinnamony treat (its moniker probably refers to how it's pulled apart and stuffed into eager mouths). To expedite the rising and proofing of the dough, and ensure our bread had plenty of yeasty flavor, we used a good amount of instant yeast. Butter and milk helped keep the dough rich and moist, and a little sugar made the bread sweet enough to eat on its own. A dip in butter and cinnamon sugar gave the monkey bread a thick, caramel-like coating after its stint in the oven. And a drizzle of a simple glaze finished it off.

Monkey Bread

Make sure to use light brown sugar in the coating mix; dark brown sugar has a stronger molasses flavor that can be overwhelming. After baking, don't let the bread cool in the pan for more than 5 minutes or it will stick to the pan and come out in pieces. Monkey bread is best served warm.

DOUGH

2	tablespoons unsalted butter, softened, plus 2 tablespoons melted
1	cup milk, heated to 110 degrees
⅓	cup water, heated to 110 degrees
¼	cup (1¾ ounces) granulated sugar
2¼	teaspoons instant or rapid-rise yeast
3¼	cups (16¼ ounces) all-purpose flour
2	teaspoons salt

BROWN SUGAR COATING

1	cup packed (7 ounces) light brown sugar
2	teaspoons ground cinnamon
8	tablespoons unsalted butter, melted

GLAZE

1	cup (4 ounces) confectioners' sugar
2	tablespoons milk

1. FOR THE DOUGH: Grease 12-cup nonstick Bundt pan with softened butter; set aside. Combine milk, water, melted butter, sugar, and yeast in 2-cup liquid measuring cup.

2. Adjust oven rack to middle position and place loaf or cake pan on bottom of oven. Using stand mixer fitted with dough hook, mix flour and salt on low speed. Slowly add milk mixture and mix until dough comes together (if dough is too wet and doesn't come together, add up to 2 tablespoons more flour). Increase speed to medium and knead until dough is shiny and smooth, 6 to 7 minutes. Turn dough onto lightly floured counter and knead briefly to form smooth, round ball. Place dough in large greased bowl, coat surface with vegetable oil spray, and transfer to oven.

Pour 3 cups boiling water into loaf pan in oven, close oven door, and let dough rise until doubled in size, 50 minutes to 1 hour.

3. FOR THE BROWN SUGAR COATING: While dough rises, combine sugar and cinnamon in small bowl. Place melted butter in second bowl. Set aside.

4. TO FORM THE BREAD: Gently remove dough from bowl and pat into rough 8-inch square. Using bench scraper or knife, cut square into quarters, then cut each quarter into 16 pieces. Roll each piece of dough into a ball. Working with one at a time, dip each ball in melted butter, allowing excess butter to drip off, then roll in sugar mixture. Layer dough balls in prepared pan, staggering seams where dough balls meet. Cover pan tightly with plastic wrap, transfer to oven, and let rest until dough balls are puffy and have risen 1 to 2 inches from top of pan, 50 minutes to 1 hour, 10 minutes.

5. Remove dough balls and water pan from oven; adjust oven rack to medium-low position and heat oven to 350 degrees. Remove plastic and bake until top of dough is deeply browned and caramel begins to bubble around edges, 30 to 35 minutes, rotating pan halfway through baking. Let monkey bread cool in pan for 5 minutes, then turn out on platter and let cool slightly, about 10 minutes.

6. FOR THE GLAZE: Meanwhile, whisk sugar and milk together in small bowl until smooth. Using whisk, drizzle glaze over warm monkey bread, letting it run over top and sides of bread. Serve warm.

FORMING MONKEY BREAD

After forming dough balls, dip each one in melted butter and sugar and then place in greased Bundt pan, staggering seams where dough balls meet.

WHY THIS RECIPE WORKS

With their chewy interiors, crunchy crusts, and craggy texture, English muffins are a treat—but they're also a lot of work. For a no-fuss recipe without the kneading, rolling, cutting, or griddling, we made a simple loaf bread with the flavor and texture of English muffins. Protein-rich bread flour gave the loaf a chewy yet light consistency, and baking soda created the all-important honeycombed texture. Heating the milk before mixing the dough activated the yeast and shortened the rising time. We simply mixed the dough, let it rise, then baked it in loaf pans until the crust was well browned and the interior was perfectly craggy.

English Muffin Bread

MAKES 2 LOAVES

Serve this bread with butter and jam.

	Cornmeal
5	cups (27½ ounces) bread flour
4½	teaspoons instant or rapid-rise yeast
1	tablespoon sugar
2	teaspoons salt
1	teaspoon baking soda
3	cups whole milk, heated to 120 degrees

1. Grease two 8½ by 4½-inch loaf pans and dust with cornmeal. Combine flour, yeast, sugar, salt, and baking soda in large bowl. Stir in hot milk until combined, about 1 minute. Cover dough with greased plastic wrap and let rise in warm place for 30 minutes, or until dough is bubbly and has doubled.

2. Stir dough and divide between prepared loaf pans, pushing into corners with greased rubber spatula. (Pans should be about two-thirds full.) Cover pans with greased plastic and let dough rise in warm place until it reaches edges of pans, about 30 minutes. Adjust oven rack to middle position and heat oven to 375 degrees.

3. Discard plastic and transfer pans to oven. Bake until loaves are well browned and register 200 degrees, about 30 minutes, rotating and switching pans halfway through baking. Turn loaves out onto wire rack and let cool completely, about 1 hour. Slice, toast, and serve.

TRICKS TO THE RIGHT TEXTURE

To give our English Muffin Bread the proper chew and porous texture, we needed a few tricks. High-protein bread flour allows more gluten to develop in the batter for a satisfyingly chewy loaf. Stirring baking soda in with the other dry ingredients gives the bread extra rise for an appropriately coarse, honeycombed texture.

A WELL-DRESSED TABLE

By the end of the 19th century, the English were losing their taste for English-style muffins, but in the U.S. they had become such a popular breakfast bread that the properly set breakfast table required special dishes for serving them. Victorians, of course, were ardent believers that the correct home environment shaped correct behavior; proper dining and tableware, especially, equated with proper civilization. So wealthy families had specific dishware for everything, from glass or silver vases for celery to custom dishes to hold bananas to specialized vessels and utensils for serving sardines. And don't forget asparagus forks.

✅ WHY THIS RECIPE WORKS

For a brown soda bread with good wheaty flavor but without a gummy, dense texture, we started by finding the right ratio of whole-wheat to all-purpose flour. Toasted wheat germ played up the sweet, nutty flavor of the whole wheat. To keep the texture light, we needed plenty of leavening; baking soda alone gave the bread a soapy taste, so we used a combination of baking soda and baking powder. Just a touch of sugar and a few tablespoons of butter kept our bread wholesome but not "health foody," and brushing a portion of the melted butter on the loaf after baking gave it a rich crust.

Brown Soda Bread

MAKES 1 LOAF

Toasted wheat germ is sold in jars at well-stocked supermarkets.

2	cups (10 ounces) all-purpose flour
1½	cups (8¼ ounces) whole-wheat flour
½	cup toasted wheat germ
3	tablespoons sugar
1½	teaspoons salt
1	teaspoon baking powder
1	teaspoon baking soda
1¾	cups buttermilk
3	tablespoons unsalted butter, melted

1. Adjust oven rack to lower-middle position and heat oven to 400 degrees. Line rimmed baking sheet with parchment paper. Whisk all-purpose flour, whole-wheat flour, wheat germ, sugar, salt, baking powder, and baking soda together in large bowl. Combine buttermilk and 2 tablespoons melted butter in 2-cup liquid measuring cup.

2. Add wet ingredients to dry ingredients and stir with rubber spatula until dough just comes together. Turn out dough onto lightly floured counter and knead until cohesive mass forms, about 8 turns. Pat dough into 7-inch round and transfer to prepared baking sheet. Using sharp serrated knife, make ¼-inch-deep cross about 5 inches long on top of loaf. Bake until skewer inserted in center comes out clean and loaf registers 195 degrees, 45 to 50 minutes, rotating baking sheet halfway through baking.

3. Remove bread from oven. Brush with remaining 1 tablespoon melted butter. Transfer loaf to wire rack and let cool for at least 1 hour. Serve.

BROWN SODA BREAD WITH CURRANTS AND CARAWAY

Add 1 cup dried currants and 1 tablespoon caraway seeds to dry ingredients in step 1.

FASTEST. BREAD. EVER.

No yeast, no rise time, and almost no kneading or shaping.

Measure and whisk dry ingredients	5 minutes
Measure and combine wet ingredients	2 minutes
Stir wet into dry	1 minute
Knead briefly	1 minute
Shape simply	1 minute
Total work time	**10 minutes**

MIMICKING WHOLE-MEAL FLOUR

Classic brown Irish soda bread is robust and moist with a delicious wheaty sweetness. Traditionally, this bread adds coarse, whole-meal flour to the all-purpose flour used in the more familiar Irish soda bread to get that uniquely wheaty flavor. But whole-meal flour is hard to find in the United States. Many recipes simply substitute ordinary whole-wheat flour, while others skip the white flour entirely, combining the whole-wheat flour with practically the entire contents of a natural foods store. Predictably, the former produced loaves with wan wheat flavor, while the latter made loaves with great taste but heavy, crumbly textures.

To get the right flavor and texture, we tried various ratios of all-purpose and whole-wheat flours until we landed on 2 cups of white flour combined with 1½ cups of whole-wheat for a loaf with nice wheat flavor and mild sweetness. To round out that flavor and play up the toasty, nutty aspects, we tried adding by turns wheat germ (the embryo of the wheat berry), wheat bran (the outer layer of the grain that's removed to make white flour), and oatmeal (which we toasted and ground to make oat flour). All of them gave our loaf the complex wheatiness we were after, but the bran required a trip to a specialty store, while the oats needed both toasting and processing. Toasted wheat germ is sold in convenient jars at the supermarket, so that's what we use to enrich our wheaty loaf.

A combination of whole-wheat flour, toasted wheat germ, and all-purpose flour give our loaf both robust flavor and tender, moist texture.

✔ WHY THIS RECIPE WORKS

This hearty loaf from the breadbasket of America usually contains a daunting variety of flours and seeds. We shortened the ingredient list by using seven-grain cereal mix. This one easy addition gave our loaf hearty texture and complex flavor. To round it out, we stirred some seeds into the batter and sprinkled more on top of the loaf. Starting the bread in a hot oven created an initial "spring," giving the loaf a lighter crumb, then lowering the temperature prevented the seeds from burning. High-protein bread flour allowed our loaf to rise high, and a pan of water in the oven prevented the crust from setting before the bread had fully risen.

Dakota Bread

MAKES ONE 10-INCH LOAF

In step 2, if the dough is still sticking to the sides of the mixing bowl after 2 minutes, add more flour 1 tablespoon at a time, up to 3 tablespoons. Be sure to use hot cereal mix, not boxed cold breakfast cereals, which may also be labeled "seven-grain."

2	cups warm water (110 degrees)
1½	cups (7½ ounces) seven-grain hot cereal mix
2	tablespoons honey
2	tablespoons vegetable oil
3½	cups (19¼ ounces) bread flour
1¾	teaspoons salt
1	teaspoon instant or rapid-rise yeast
3	tablespoons raw, unsalted pepitas
3	tablespoons raw, unsalted sunflower seeds
1	teaspoon sesame seeds
1	teaspoon poppy seeds
1	large egg, lightly beaten

1. Grease large bowl. Line rimmed baking sheet with parchment paper. In bowl of stand mixer, combine water, cereal, honey, and oil and let sit for 10 minutes.

2. Add flour, salt, and yeast to cereal mixture. Fit stand mixer with dough hook and knead on low speed until dough is smooth and elastic, 4 to 6 minutes. Add 2 tablespoons pepitas and 2 tablespoons sunflower seeds to dough and knead for 1 minute longer. Turn out dough onto lightly floured counter and knead until seeds are evenly distributed, about 2 minutes.

3. Transfer dough to greased bowl and cover with plastic wrap. Let dough rise at room temperature until almost doubled in size and fingertip depression in dough springs back slowly, 60 to 90 minutes.

4. Gently press down on center of dough to deflate. Transfer dough to lightly floured counter and shape into tight round ball. Place dough on prepared sheet. Cover dough loosely with plastic and let rise at room temperature until almost doubled in size, 60 to 90 minutes.

5. Adjust oven racks to upper-middle and lowest positions and heat oven to 425 degrees. Combine remaining 1 tablespoon pepitas, remaining 1 tablespoon sunflower seeds, sesame seeds, and poppy seeds in small bowl. Using sharp knife, make ¼-inch-deep cross, 5 inches long, on top of loaf. Brush loaf with egg and sprinkle seed mixture evenly over top.

6. Place 8½ by 4½-inch loaf pan on lowest oven rack and fill with 1 cup boiling water. Place baking sheet with dough on upper-middle rack and reduce oven to 375 degrees. Bake until crust is dark brown and bread registers 200 degrees, 40 to 50 minutes. Transfer loaf to wire rack and let cool completely, about 2 hours. Serve.

THE RIGHT MIX

Our Dakota Bread recipe calls for bread flour (for an appropriately chewy texture) supplemented with seven-grain hot cereal mix, which provides the bread with nutty depth. Don't confuse seven-grain hot cereal with seven-grain cold cereal; the latter will harm the texture of the loaf.

HOT TO TROT
Seven-grain hot cereal

GREAT AMERICAN
CAKES AND COOKIES

WHEN MOST OF US THINK OF CAKE, WE THINK OF LIGHT, MOIST LAYER cakes swathed in fluffy frosting or rich, fine-crumbed pound cakes, but these cakes are mostly a 20th-century innovation. Prior to 1850, most cakes were leavened with eggs (and/or yeast) and were often packed with dried fruit and nuts—think traditional fruitcake and you're on the right track. They required a strong arm to mix and were heavy, dense affairs. Chemical leaveners such as cream of tartar, baking powder, and baking soda revolutionized cake making in the late 19th century, cutting out not only much of the labor and preparation time but also the cost—eggs could be very expensive. Case in point: A recipe for Plain White Cake from *Dixie Cookery* (1867) instructs the reader to "cream a pound and a quarter of butter, and beat it into a pound and a half of sugar and a pound and a half of flour alternately with the beaten whites of thirty eggs." Thirty eggs!

In this chapter we include a wide variety of beloved cakes, including ethereal Angel Food Cake and its easier cousin, Chiffon Cake (whose inventor used vegetable oil as the secret ingredient), as well as vibrant Red Velvet Cake (with its tangy cream cheese frosting), Strawberry Poke Cake (a cake borne of a marketing campaign for Jell-O), and many more.

Cookies get their due here, too. In contrast to the labor and time involved in preparing a cake (even a modern one), it's a cinch to make most cookies and they're in and out of the oven in minutes—making their appeal to children undeniable. In keeping with their kid-friendly qualities, it's no wonder so many cookies have fanciful names. In the following pages, we include recipes for such cookies as Fairy Gingerbread, Joe Froggers, Melting Moments, and more. So pour yourself a glass of cold milk and join us as we re-create classic cakes and cookies that adults and kids alike will enjoy.

✓ WHY THIS RECIPE WORKS

Although the exact origins of this cake are muddled, the appeal of a tender, shockingly bright red cake swathed in fluffy cream cheese frosting is undeniable. For a cake with an extra-tender crumb, we used two unexpected ingredients: buttermilk and vinegar. They reacted with our recipe's baking soda to create a fine, tender crumb. We also zeroed in on the perfect amount of cocoa that would add a dark hue to our cake as well as lending it a pleasant cocoa flavor.

Red Velvet Cake

SERVES 12

This recipe must be prepared with natural cocoa powder. Dutch-processed cocoa will not yield the proper color or rise.

CAKE

2¼	cups (11¼ ounces) all-purpose flour
1½	teaspoons baking soda
	Pinch salt
1	cup buttermilk
2	large eggs
1	tablespoon distilled white vinegar
1	teaspoon vanilla extract
2	tablespoons cocoa
2	tablespoons (1 ounce) red food coloring
12	tablespoons unsalted butter, softened
1½	cups (10½ ounces) granulated sugar

FROSTING

16	tablespoons unsalted butter, softened
4	cups (16 ounces) confectioners' sugar
16	ounces cream cheese, cut into 8 pieces, softened
1½	teaspoons vanilla extract
	Pinch salt

1. FOR THE CAKE: Adjust oven rack to middle position and heat oven to 350 degrees. Grease two 9-inch round cake pans, line with parchment paper, grease parchment, then flour pans. Whisk flour, baking soda, and salt in medium bowl. Whisk buttermilk, eggs, vinegar, and vanilla in 4-cup liquid measuring cup. Mix cocoa with food coloring in small bowl until smooth paste forms.

2. Using stand mixer fitted with paddle, beat butter and sugar together on medium high speed until pale and fluffy, about 3 minutes. Reduce speed to medium-low and add flour mixture in 3 additions, alternating with buttermilk mixture in 2 additions, scraping down bowl as needed. Add cocoa mixture and beat on medium speed until completely incorporated, about 30 seconds. Give batter final stir by hand. Scrape batter into prepared pans and bake until toothpick inserted in center comes out clean, about 25 minutes. Let cakes cool in pans on wire rack for 10 minutes. Remove cakes from pans, discarding parchment, and let cool completely on rack, about 2 hours. (Cooled cakes can be wrapped tightly in plastic wrap and kept at room temperature for up to 1 day.)

3. FOR THE FROSTING: Using stand mixer fitted with paddle, beat butter and sugar on medium-high speed until pale and fluffy, about 2 minutes. Add cream cheese, 1 piece at a time, and beat until incorporated, about 30 seconds. Beat in vanilla and salt. Refrigerate until ready to use.

4. When cakes are cooled, cover edges of cake platter with strips of parchment. Place 1 cake layer on platter. Spread 2 cups frosting evenly over top, right to edge of cake. Top with second cake layer, press lightly to adhere, then spread remaining frosting evenly over top and sides of cake. Carefully remove parchment strips before serving. (Cake can be refrigerated for up to 3 days.)

LOST AND FOUND

Red velvet cake fell out of fashion in the 1970s amidst health scares relating to red dye #2 (a similar fate befell red M&Ms, even though the candies never contained the dye in question). Once consumers were convinced that other red dyes were safe, red candies made it back into the M&Ms assortment (in 1987) and red velvet cakes started a comeback in bakeries.

🗸 WHY THIS RECIPE WORKS

Chocolate blackout cake, a tender chocolate layer cake sandwiched together with a puddinglike filling and covered with cake crumbs, was created by the now-shuttered Ebinger's bakery in Brooklyn. We set out to create our own version. We started by adding cocoa powder to the butter we were already melting for the cake. Heating the cocoa in the butter produced a cake that was dark and rich. And to complement the chocolate flavor of the cake, we made a chocolaty, dairy-rich pudding with a combination of milk and half-and-half, which gave it a velvety, lush quality.

Chocolate Blackout Cake

SERVES 10 TO 12

Be sure to give the pudding and the cake enough time to cool or you'll end up with runny pudding and gummy cake.

PUDDING

- 1¼ cups (8¾ ounces) granulated sugar
- ¼ cup cornstarch
- ½ teaspoon salt
- 2 cups half-and-half
- 1 cup whole milk
- 6 ounces unsweetened chocolate, chopped
- 2 teaspoons vanilla extract

CAKE

- 1½ cups (7½ ounces) all-purpose flour
- 2 teaspoons baking powder
- ½ teaspoon baking soda
- ½ teaspoon salt
- 8 tablespoons unsalted butter
- ¾ cup (2¼ ounces) Dutch-processed cocoa
- 1 cup brewed coffee
- 1 cup buttermilk
- 1 cup packed (7 ounces) light brown sugar
- 1 cup (7 ounces) granulated sugar
- 2 large eggs
- 1 teaspoon vanilla extract

1. FOR THE PUDDING: Whisk sugar, cornstarch, salt, half-and-half, and milk in large saucepan. Set pan over medium heat. Add chocolate and whisk constantly until chocolate melts and mixture begins to bubble, 2 to 4 minutes. Stir in vanilla and transfer pudding to large bowl. Place plastic wrap directly on surface of pudding and refrigerate until cold, at least 4 hours or up to 1 day.

2. FOR THE CAKE: Adjust oven rack to middle position and heat oven to 325 degrees. Grease two 8-inch round cake pans, line with parchment paper, grease parchment, then flour pans. Whisk flour, baking powder, baking soda, and salt in bowl.

3. Melt butter in large saucepan over medium heat. Stir in cocoa and cook until fragrant, about 1 minute. Off heat, whisk in coffee, buttermilk, brown sugar, and granulated sugar until dissolved. Whisk in eggs and vanilla, then slowly whisk in flour mixture.

4. Divide batter evenly between prepared pans and bake until toothpick inserted in center comes out clean, 30 to 35 minutes. Let cakes cool in pans on wire rack for 15 minutes. Remove cakes from pans, discarding parchment, and let cool completely on wire rack, about 2 hours.

5. TO ASSEMBLE THE CAKE: Working with 1 cake layer at a time, cut cakes horizontally into 2 layers using long, serrated knife. Crumble 1 cake layer into medium crumbs and set aside. Cover edges of cake platter with strips of parchment. Place 1 cake layer on platter. Spread 1 cup pudding over top, right to edge of cake. Top with second layer; press lightly to adhere. Repeat with 1 cup pudding and last cake layer. Spread remaining pudding evenly over top and sides of cake. Sprinkle cake crumbs evenly over top and sides of cake, pressing lightly to adhere crumbs. Carefully remove parchment strips before serving. (Cake can be refrigerated for up to 2 days.)

LOST ICON

Ebinger's Baking Company opened in 1898 on Flatbush Avenue in Brooklyn and grew into a chain of more than 60 stores before going bankrupt in 1972. Started by Arthur Ebinger, a baker who emigrated from Germany with a vast collection of recipes, the business grew to include his wife and their three sons. During its heyday, Ebinger's was a point of bragging rights for Brooklynites, as celebrities and the well-to-do from Manhattan never went to Brooklyn without taking home a cake or one of Ebinger's other specialties, which included challah, rye bread, pumpkin pie, Othellos (filled mini sponge cakes covered in chocolate), and crumb buns.

WHY THIS RECIPE WORKS

We wanted to resurrect the classic childhood favorite tunnel of fudge cake without the benefit of a prepackaged cake mix. Dutch-processed cocoa gave our cake deep chocolate flavor. Adding melted chocolate to the batter made our cake moister and contributed more chocolate punch. Slightly under-baking the cake was the first step toward achieving the ideal consistency for the tunnel. Replacing some of the granulated sugar with brown sugar and cutting back on the flour and butter provided the perfect environment for the fudgy interior to form.

Tunnel of Fudge Cake

SERVES 12 TO 14

For an accurate measurement of boiling water, bring a full kettle of water to a boil, then measure out the desired amount. Do not use a cake tester, toothpick, or skewer to test the cake—the fudgy interior won't give an accurate reading. Instead, remove the cake from the oven when the sides just begin to pull away from the pan and the surface of the cake springs back when pressed gently with your finger.

CAKE

- ¾ cup (2¼ ounces) Dutch-processed cocoa, plus extra for dusting pan
- ½ cup boiling water
- 2 ounces bittersweet chocolate, chopped
- 2 cups (10 ounces) all-purpose flour
- 2 cups pecans or walnuts, chopped fine
- 2 cups (8 ounces) confectioners' sugar
- 1 teaspoon salt
- 5 large eggs, room temperature
- 1 tablespoon vanilla extract
- 20 tablespoons (2½ sticks) unsalted butter, softened
- 1 cup (7 ounces) granulated sugar
- ¾ cup packed (5¼ ounces) light brown sugar

CHOCOLATE GLAZE

- ¾ cup heavy cream
- ¼ cup light corn syrup
- 8 ounces bittersweet chocolate, chopped
- ½ teaspoon vanilla extract

1. FOR THE CAKE: Adjust oven rack to lower-middle position and heat oven to 350 degrees. Grease 12-cup Bundt pan and dust with cocoa powder. Pour boiling water over chocolate in medium bowl and whisk until smooth. Let cool to room temperature. Whisk cocoa, flour, pecans, confectioners' sugar, and salt in large bowl. Whisk eggs and vanilla in 4-cup liquid measuring cup.

2. Using stand mixer fitted with paddle, beat butter, granulated sugar, and brown sugar on medium-high speed until light and fluffy, about 2 minutes. On low speed, add egg mixture until combined, about 30 seconds. Add chocolate mixture and beat until incorporated, about 30 seconds. Beat in flour mixture until just combined, about 30 seconds.

3. Scrape batter into prepared pan, smooth batter, and bake until edges are beginning to pull away from pan, about 45 minutes. Let cool in pan on wire rack for 1½ hours, then invert onto serving plate and let cool completely, at least 2 hours.

4. FOR THE CHOCOLATE GLAZE: Heat cream, corn syrup, and chocolate in small saucepan over medium heat, stirring constantly, until smooth. Stir in vanilla and set aside until slightly thickened, about 30 minutes. Drizzle glaze over cake and let set for at least 10 minutes. Serve. (Cake can be stored at room temperature for up to 2 days.)

BIRTH OF THE BUNDT PAN

Metallurgical engineer H. David Dalquist invented the Bundt pan in 1950 at the request of bakers in Minneapolis who were using old-fashioned ceramic pans of the same design. Dalquist turned to cast aluminum to produce a pan that was much lighter and easier to use. Sales of his Bundt pan (a name he trademarked) were underwhelming until Ella Helfrich's Tunnel of Fudge Cake made its debut in 1966. The Pillsbury Company quickly received over 200,000 requests for the pan, and to meet demand Dalquist's company, NordicWare, went into 24-hour production. Over 50 million Bundt pans have been sold worldwide.

SPECIAL OFFER!
TEFLON BUNDT PAN and nylon spatula
Authentic pan for "Tunnel-of-Fudge" Cake
ONLY $3 with two Land O'Lakes guarantee panels

$5.00 VALUE

WHY THIS RECIPE WORKS

Lane cake is a tall, fluffy, snow-white cake filled with a rich, sweet mixture of egg whites, butter, raisins, and "a wineglass full of good whiskey." Our simplified recipe capped the number of layers at two, and using a food processor streamlined much of the tedious prep work. Replacing sugar with boiled corn syrup in our frosting quickly brought the whipped egg whites to a safe temperature without resorting to a candy thermometer or complicated (and unreliable) guesswork.

Lane Cake

SERVES 10 TO 12

CAKE

1	cup whole milk, room temperature
6	large egg whites, room temperature
2	teaspoons vanilla extract
2¼	cups (9 ounces) cake flour
1¾	cups (12¼ ounces) sugar
4	teaspoons baking powder
1	teaspoon salt
12	tablespoons unsalted butter, cut into 12 pieces and softened

FILLING

5	tablespoons bourbon
1	tablespoon heavy cream
1	teaspoon cornstarch
	Pinch salt
⅓	cup sweetened shredded coconut
¾	cup pecans
¾	cup golden raisins
4	tablespoons unsalted butter
¾	cup sweetened condensed milk
½	teaspoon vanilla extract

FROSTING

2	large egg whites, room temperature
¼	teaspoon cream of tartar
¼	cup (1¾ ounces) sugar
⅔	cup light corn syrup
1	teaspoon vanilla extract

1. FOR THE CAKE: Adjust oven rack to middle position and heat oven to 350 degrees. Grease two 9-inch round cake pans, line with parchment paper, grease parchment, then flour pans. Whisk milk, egg whites, and vanilla in 4-cup liquid measuring cup. Using stand mixer fitted with paddle, mix flour, sugar, baking powder, and salt on low speed until combined. Add butter, 1 piece at a time, and beat until only pea-size pieces remain. Add half of milk mixture, increase speed to medium-high, and beat until light and fluffy, about 1 minute. Reduce speed to medium-low, add remaining milk mixture, and beat until incorporated, about 30 seconds. Give batter final stir by hand.

2. Scrape batter into prepared pans and bake until toothpick inserted in center comes out clean, 20 to 25 minutes. Let cakes cool in pans on wire rack for 10 minutes. Remove cakes from pans, discarding parchment, and let cool completely on racks, about 2 hours. (Cooled cakes can be tightly wrapped in plastic wrap and stored at room temperature for up to 2 days.)

3. FOR THE FILLING: Whisk bourbon, cream, cornstarch, and salt in bowl until smooth. Process coconut in food processor until finely ground, about 15 seconds. Add pecans and raisins and pulse until coarsely ground, about 10 pulses. Melt butter in large skillet over medium-low heat. Add processed coconut mixture and cook, stirring occasionally, until golden brown and fragrant, about 5 minutes. Stir in bourbon mixture and bring to boil. Remove from heat and add condensed milk and vanilla. Transfer to medium bowl and let cool to room temperature, about 30 minutes. (Filling can be refrigerated in airtight container for 2 days. Bring filling to room temperature before using.)

4. FOR THE FROSTING: Using stand mixer fitted with whisk, whip egg whites and cream of tartar on medium-high speed until frothy, about 30 seconds. With mixer running, slowly add sugar and whip until soft peaks form, about 2 minutes; set aside. Bring corn syrup to boil in small saucepan over medium-high heat and cook until large bubbles appear around perimeter of pan, about 1 minute. With mixer running, slowly pour hot syrup into whites (avoid pouring syrup onto beaters or it will splash). Add vanilla and beat until mixture has cooled and is very thick and glossy, 3 to 5 minutes.

5. Cover edges of cake platter with strips of parchment. Place 1 cake layer on platter. Spread filling over cake, then top with second cake layer, pressing lightly to adhere. Spread remaining frosting evenly over top and sides of cake. Carefully remove parchment strips before serving. (Cake can be refrigerated for up to 2 days.)

✔ WHY THIS RECIPE WORKS

Strange as it may seem, the vast majority of existing strawberry cake recipes turn to strawberry Jell-O for flavor. Hoping to avoid this artificial solution, we performed test after test to figure out the best way to flavor our cake with actual strawberries. Any strawberry solids wreaked havoc on the tender cake, but strained and reduced strawberry juices kept our cake light and packed a strawberry punch. Not to be left behind, the reserved strawberry solids enriched the frosting with more berry flavor.

Strawberry Dream Cake

SERVES 8 TO 10

Be sure to allow the cream cheese to soften so that it blends into a smooth frosting.

CAKE

10	ounces frozen whole strawberries (2 cups)
¾	cup whole milk, room temperature
6	large egg whites, room temperature
2	teaspoons vanilla extract
2¼	cups (9 ounces) cake flour
1¾	cups (12¼ ounces) granulated sugar
4	teaspoons baking powder
1	teaspoon salt
12	tablespoons unsalted butter, cut into 12 pieces and softened

FROSTING

10	tablespoons unsalted butter, softened
2¼	cups (9 ounces) confectioners' sugar
12	ounces cream cheese, cut into 12 pieces and softened
	Pinch salt
8	ounces fresh strawberries, hulled and sliced thin (about 1½ cups)

1. FOR THE CAKE: Adjust oven rack to middle position and heat oven to 350 degrees. Grease two 9-inch round cake pans, line with parchment paper, grease parchment, then flour pans.

2. Transfer strawberries to bowl, cover, and microwave until strawberries are soft and have released their juices, about 5 minutes. Place in fine-mesh strainer set over small saucepan. Firmly press fruit dry (juice should measure at least ¾ cup); reserve strawberry solids. Bring juice to boil over medium-high heat and cook, stirring occasionally, until syrupy and reduced to ¼ cup, 6 to 8 minutes. Whisk milk into juice until combined.

3. Whisk strawberry-milk mixture, egg whites, and vanilla in bowl. Using stand mixer fitted with paddle, mix flour, sugar, baking powder, and salt on low speed until combined. Add butter, 1 piece at a time, and mix until only pea-size pieces remain, about 1 minute. Add half of milk mixture, increase speed to medium-high, and beat until light and fluffy, about 1 minute. Reduce speed to medium-low, add remaining milk mixture, and beat until incorporated, about 30 seconds. Give batter final stir by hand.

4. Scrape batter into prepared pans and bake until toothpick inserted in center comes out clean, 20 to 25 minutes, rotating pans halfway through baking. Let cakes cool in pans on wire rack for 10 minutes. Remove cakes from pans, discarding parchment, and let cool completely on rack, about 2 hours. (Cooled cakes can be tightly wrapped with plastic wrap and stored at room temperature for up to 2 days.)

5. FOR THE FROSTING: Using stand mixer fitted with paddle, mix butter and sugar on low speed until combined, about 30 seconds. Increase speed to medium-high and beat until pale and fluffy, about 2 minutes. Add cream cheese, 1 piece at a time, and beat until incorporated, about 1 minute. Add reserved strawberry solids and salt and mix until combined, about 30 seconds. Refrigerate until ready to use, up to 2 days.

6. Pat strawberries dry with paper towels. Cover edges of cake platter with strips of parchment. Place 1 cake layer on platter. Spread ¾ cup frosting evenly over top, right to edge of cake. Press 1 cup strawberries in even layer over frosting and cover with additional ¾ cup frosting. Top with second cake layer, press lightly to adhere, then spread remaining frosting evenly over top and sides of cake. Garnish with remaining strawberries. Carefully remove parchment strips before serving. (Cake can be refrigerated for up to 2 days.)

✔ WHY THIS RECIPE WORKS

Strawberry poke cake was invented in 1969 as a way to increase Jell-O sales. It quickly became popular thanks to its festive look and easy assembly. But we encountered two problems: dull strawberry flavor and soggy box-mix cake. For a sturdier cake that would hold up to hot gelatin, we opted to make our own white cake from scratch. And to improve the strawberry flavor of the Jell-O, we combined it with the juice from cooked strawberries. Making a homemade "jam" from the berry solids and spreading the mixture on top of the cake gave our cake an extra layer of flavor.

Strawberry Poke Cake

SERVES 12

The top of the cake will look slightly overbaked—this keeps the crumb from becoming too soggy after the gelatin is poured on top.

CAKE

2¼	cups (11¼ ounces) all-purpose flour
4	teaspoons baking powder
1	teaspoon salt
1	cup whole milk
2	teaspoons vanilla extract
6	large egg whites
12	tablespoons unsalted butter, softened
1¾	cups (12¼ ounces) sugar

SYRUP AND TOPPING

4	cups frozen strawberries
½	cup water
6	tablespoons (2⅔ ounces) sugar
2	tablespoons orange juice
2	tablespoons strawberry-flavored gelatin
2	cups heavy cream, chilled

1. FOR THE CAKE: Adjust oven rack to middle position and heat oven to 350 degrees. Grease 13 by 9-inch baking pan, line with parchment paper, grease parchment, then flour pan. Whisk flour, baking powder, and salt in bowl. Whisk milk, vanilla, and egg whites in 4-cup liquid measuring cup.

2. Using stand mixer fitted with paddle, beat butter and sugar on medium-high speed until pale and fluffy, about 2 minutes, scraping down bowl as needed. Reduce speed to low and add flour mixture in 3 additions, alternating with milk mixture in 2 additions, beating after each addition until combined, about 30 seconds each time, scraping down bowl as needed. Give batter final stir by hand. Scrape into prepared pan and bake until toothpick inserted in center comes out clean, about 35 minutes. Let cake cool completely in pan, at least 1 hour. Once cool, cake can be wrapped in plastic wrap and kept at room temperature for up to 2 days.

3. FOR THE SYRUP AND TOPPING: Heat 3 cups strawberries, water, 2 tablespoons sugar, and orange juice in medium saucepan over medium-low heat. Cover and cook until strawberries are softened, about 10 minutes. Strain liquid into bowl, reserving solids, then whisk gelatin into liquid. Let cool to room temperature, at least 20 minutes.

4. Meanwhile, poke 50 deep holes all over top of cake with skewer. Evenly pour cooled liquid over top of cake. Wrap with plastic wrap and refrigerate until gelatin is set, at least 3 hours or up to 2 days.

5. Pulse reserved strained strawberries, 2 tablespoons sugar, and remaining 1 cup strawberries in food processor until mixture resembles strawberry jam, about 15 pulses. Spread mixture evenly over cake. Using stand mixer fitted with whisk, whip cream with remaining 2 tablespoons sugar on medium-low speed until foamy, about 1 minute. Increase speed to high and whip until soft peaks form, 1 to 3 minutes. Spread cream over strawberries. Serve. (Cake can be refrigerated for up to 2 days.)

PERFECTING THE POKE

Finding the right poking device wasn't as simple as you might think. Toothpicks were too small, while straws, handles of wooden spoons, pencils, and fingers were too big. A wooden skewer finally did the trick. But just poking didn't create a large enough hole for the liquid to seep into. In order to create deep lines of red color against the white crumb, we had to poke and then twist the skewer to really separate the crumb.

1. Using skewer, poke about 50 deep holes over cake, being careful not to poke through to bottom. Twist skewer to enlarge holes.

2. Slowly pour cooled gelatin mixture evenly over surface of cake and it will slowly soak into cake.

✓ WHY THIS RECIPE WORKS

Texas sheet cake is a huge, pecan-topped chocolate-glazed cake. For the cake, we relied on a combination of butter and vegetable oil, which produced a dense, brownielike texture. To increase the fudgy chocolate flavor, we used both cocoa powder and melted semisweet chocolate. Replacing milk with heavy cream gave the icing more body, while adding corn syrup produced a lustrous finish. The key to creating the signature fudgy layer between cake and icing was to let the warm icing soak into the hot cake. We poured the icing over the sheet cake straight out of the oven and smoothed it with a spatula.

Texas Sheet Cake

SERVES 24

Toast the pecans in a dry skillet over medium heat, shaking the pan occasionally, until golden and fragrant, about five minutes.

CAKE

2	cups (10 ounces) all-purpose flour
2	cups (14 ounces) granulated sugar
½	teaspoon baking soda
½	teaspoon salt
2	large eggs plus 2 large yolks
¼	cup sour cream
2	teaspoons vanilla extract
8	ounces semisweet chocolate, chopped
¾	cup vegetable oil
¾	cup water
½	cup (1½ ounces) Dutch-processed cocoa
4	tablespoons unsalted butter

CHOCOLATE ICING

8	tablespoons unsalted butter
½	cup heavy cream
½	cup (1½ ounces) Dutch-processed cocoa
1	tablespoon light corn syrup
3	cups (12 ounces) confectioners' sugar
1	tablespoon vanilla extract
1	cup pecans, toasted and chopped

1. FOR THE CAKE: Adjust oven rack to middle position and heat oven to 350 degrees. Grease 18 by 13-inch rimmed baking sheet. Combine flour, sugar, baking soda, and salt in large bowl. Whisk eggs and yolks, sour cream, and vanilla in another bowl until smooth.

2. Heat chocolate, oil, water, cocoa, and butter in large saucepan over medium heat, stirring occasionally, until smooth, 3 to 5 minutes. Whisk chocolate mixture into flour mixture until incorporated. Whisk egg mixture into batter, then pour into prepared baking pan. Bake until toothpick inserted into center comes out clean, 18 to 20 minutes. Transfer to wire rack.

3. FOR THE CHOCOLATE ICING: About 5 minutes before cake is done, heat butter, cream, cocoa, and corn syrup in large saucepan over medium heat, stirring occasionally, until smooth. Off heat, whisk in sugar and vanilla. Spread warm icing evenly over hot cake and sprinkle with pecans. Let cake cool to room temperature on wire rack, about 1 hour, then refrigerate until icing is set, about 1 hour longer. Cut into 3-inch squares. Serve. (Cake can be refrigerated for up to 2 days.)

TIMING IS EVERYTHING

The key to perfectly moist Texas sheet cake is to let the warm icing soak into the hot cake. As soon as the cake comes out of the oven, pour the warm icing over the cake and use a spatula to spread the icing to the edges of the cake. This creates the fudgy layer between the icing and the cake.

✓ WHY THIS RECIPE WORKS

This no-bake dessert is typically made by layering a mixture of instant vanilla pudding and Cool Whip between graham crackers and topping it with chocolate frosting. We loved the convenience of these store-bought items, but our enthusiasm waned when confronted by their flavor. With a couple of easy techniques (a quick stovetop pudding, whipped cream, and a microwave-and-stir glaze) and very little active time, we produced a from-scratch version that easily trumped its inspiration.

Chocolate Éclair Cake

SERVES 15

Six ounces of finely chopped semisweet chocolate can be used in place of the chips.

1¼	**cups (8¾ ounces) sugar**
6	**tablespoons cornstarch**
1	**teaspoon salt**
5	**cups whole milk**
4	**tablespoons unsalted butter, cut into 4 pieces**
5	**teaspoons vanilla extract**
1¼	**teaspoons unflavored gelatin**
2	**tablespoons water**
2¾	**cups heavy cream, chilled**
14	**ounces graham crackers**
1	**cup semisweet chocolate chips**
5	**tablespoons light corn syrup**

1. Combine sugar, cornstarch, and salt in large saucepan. Whisk milk into sugar mixture until smooth and bring to boil, scraping bottom of pan with heatproof rubber spatula, over medium-high heat. Immediately reduce heat to medium-low and cook, continuing to scrape bottom, until thickened and large bubbles appear on surface, 4 to 6 minutes. Off heat, whisk in butter and vanilla. Transfer pudding to large bowl and place plastic wrap directly on surface of pudding. Refrigerate until cool, about 2 hours.

2. Sprinkle gelatin over water in bowl and let sit until gelatin softens, about 5 minutes. Microwave until mixture is bubbling around edges and gelatin dissolves, 15 to 30 seconds. Using stand mixer fitted with whisk, whip 2 cups cream on medium-low speed until foamy, about 1 minute. Increase speed to high and whip until soft peaks form, 1 to 3 minutes. Add gelatin mixture and whip until stiff peaks form, about 1 minute.

3. Whisk one-third of whipped cream into chilled pudding, then gently fold in remaining whipped cream, 1 scoop at a time, until combined. Cover bottom of 13 by 9-inch baking dish with layer of graham crackers, breaking crackers as necessary to line bottom of pan. Top with half of pudding–whipped cream mixture (about 5½ cups) and another layer of graham crackers. Repeat with remaining pudding–whipped cream mixture and remaining graham crackers.

4. Microwave chocolate chips, remaining ¾ cup cream, and corn syrup in bowl, on 50 percent power, stirring occasionally, until smooth, 1 to 2 minutes. Let glaze cool to room temperature, about 10 minutes. Cover graham crackers with glaze and refrigerate cake for 6 to 24 hours. Serve. (Cake can be refrigerated for up to 2 days.)

THE WORST COLLEGE FOOD EVER

The Reverend Sylvester Graham, the inventor of the graham cracker, wasn't quite as much fun as that crisp treat might have you believe. In fact, he was a food zealot, convinced that a diet of nothing but water and graham crackers—originally a "health food" made from whole-wheat flour and honey—would turn you into a better person. Some 170 years ago, the administrators at Oberlin College, a small liberal-arts school in Ohio, grew enamored of Graham's ideas and decided to feed students according to his principles. (And you think your college food was bad?) Oberlin students were encouraged to abstain from consuming meat, tea, and coffee—except for "crust coffee" made from toast and boiled water. They were discouraged from eating butter and pastries and even from seasoning their food. (As legend has it, a professor actually lost his job for bringing a pepper shaker to the dining-hall table.) Oberlin students complained so vociferously that the college was forced to abandon its dining plan, and the Graham diet (if not his eponymous cracker) faded into culinary history.

✔ WHY THIS RECIPE WORKS

This unique dessert combines a layer of fudgy chocolate cake and a layer of rich, caramel-coated flan that "magically" switch places as they bake. We started with an easy dump-and-stir cake recipe. The cake's flavor was great, but it was soggy due to the moisture from the flan. Cutting some of the butter-milk and sugar from the cake batter did the trick. To help our flan firm up, we swapped some of the egg yolks for whole eggs and added cream cheese. The cream cheese also lent the flan a tanginess that offset its sweetness. Convenient store-bought caramel sauce topped it all off.

Magic Chocolate Flan Cake

SERVES 16

It's worth using good-quality caramel sauce, such as Fat Toad Farm Goat's Milk Caramel. If your blender doesn't hold 2 quarts, process the flan in two batches. The cake needs to chill for at least 8 hours before you can unmold it.

CAKE

½	cup caramel sauce or topping
½	cup plus 2 tablespoons (3⅛ ounces) all-purpose flour
⅓	cup (1 ounce) cocoa powder
½	teaspoon baking soda
⅛	teaspoon salt
4	ounces bittersweet chocolate, chopped
6	tablespoons unsalted butter
½	cup buttermilk
½	cup (3½ ounces) sugar
2	large eggs
1	teaspoon vanilla extract

FLAN

2	(14-ounce) cans sweetened condensed milk
2½	cups whole milk
6	ounces cream cheese
6	large eggs plus 4 large yolks
1	teaspoon vanilla extract

1. FOR THE CAKE: Adjust oven rack to middle position and heat oven to 350 degrees. Grease 12-cup nonstick Bundt pan. Microwave caramel until easily pourable, about 30 seconds. Pour into pan to coat bottom. Combine flour, cocoa, baking soda, and salt in bowl; set aside. Combine chocolate and butter in large bowl and microwave at 50 percent power, stirring occasionally, until melted, 2 to 4 minutes. Whisk buttermilk, sugar, eggs, and vanilla into chocolate mixture until incorporated. Stir in flour mixture until just combined. Pour batter over caramel in pan.

2. FOR THE FLAN: Process all ingredients in blender until smooth, about 1 minute. Gently pour flan over cake batter in Bundt pan and place Bundt pan in large roasting pan. Place roasting pan on oven rack and pour warm water into roasting pan until it reaches halfway up side of Bundt pan. Bake until toothpick inserted in cake comes out clean and flan registers 180 degrees, 75 to 90 minutes. Transfer Bundt pan to wire rack. Let cool to room temperature, about 2 hours, then refrigerate until set, at least 8 hours. (Remove roasting pan from oven once water has cooled.)

3. Place bottom third of Bundt pan in bowl of hot tap water for 1 minute. Invert completely flat cake platter, place platter over top of pan, and gently turn platter and pan upside down. Slowly remove pan, allowing caramel to drizzle over top of cake. Serve.

MODULATE THE HEAT

A water bath, or bain-marie, makes for a more even, temperate baking environment. Simply place your baking vessel in a larger vessel (we use a roasting pan) and partially fill the latter with water.

WHY THIS RECIPE WORKS

A great tres leches cake—a sponge cake soaked with a mixture of "three milks" (heavy cream, evaporated milk, and sweetened condensed milk)—should be moist but not mushy and sweet but not sickeningly so. For an ideal version, we needed to make our cake sturdy enough to handle the milk mixture, so we used whipped whole eggs instead of the usual egg whites. Although some tres leches recipes use equal amounts of evaporated milk, sweetened condensed milk, and cream, we found that cutting back on the cream produced a thicker mixture that didn't oversaturate the cake.

Tres Leches Cake

SERVES 12

The cake is best frosted right before serving.

MILK MIXTURE

1	(14-ounce) can sweetened condensed milk
1	(12-ounce) can evaporated milk
1	cup heavy cream
1	teaspoon vanilla extract

CAKE

2	cups (10 ounces) all-purpose flour
2	teaspoons baking powder
1	teaspoon salt
½	teaspoon ground cinnamon
8	tablespoons unsalted butter
1	cup whole milk
4	large eggs, room temperature
2	cups (14 ounces) sugar
2	teaspoons vanilla extract

TOPPING

1	cup heavy cream
3	tablespoons corn syrup
1	teaspoon vanilla extract

1. FOR THE MILK MIXTURE: Pour condensed milk into large bowl. Microwave covered at 50 percent power, stirring every 3 to 5 minutes, until slightly darkened and thickened, 9 to 15 minutes. Remove from microwave and slowly whisk in evaporated milk, cream, and vanilla. Let cool to room temperature.

2. FOR THE CAKE: Adjust oven rack to middle position and heat oven to 325 degrees. Grease and flour 13 by 9-inch baking dish. Whisk flour, baking powder, salt, and cinnamon in bowl. Heat butter and milk in small saucepan over low heat until butter is melted; remove from heat and set aside.

3. Using stand mixer fitted with whisk, whip eggs on medium speed until foamy, about 30 seconds. Slowly add sugar and continue to whip until fully incorporated, 5 to 10 seconds. Increase speed to medium-high and whip until mixture is thick and glossy, 5 to 7 minutes. Reduce speed to low, add milk-butter mixture and vanilla, and mix until combined, about 15 seconds. Add flour mixture in 3 additions, mixing on medium speed after each addition and scraping down bowl as needed, until flour is fully incorporated, about 30 seconds. Using rubber spatula, scrape batter into prepared dish. Bake until toothpick inserted in center comes out clean, 30 to 35 minutes. Transfer cake to wire rack and let cool for 10 minutes.

4. Using skewer, poke holes at ½-inch intervals in top of cake. Slowly pour milk mixture over cake until completely absorbed. Let sit at room temperature for 15 minutes, then refrigerate, uncovered, for 3 hours or up to 24 hours.

5. FOR THE TOPPING: Remove cake from refrigerator 30 minutes before serving. Using stand mixer fitted with whisk, whip cream, corn syrup, and vanilla on medium-low speed until foamy, about 1 minute. Increase speed to high and whip until soft peaks form, 1 to 3 minutes. Spread over cake and cut into 3-inch squares. Serve.

WHY THIS RECIPE WORKS

The beauty of blitz torte is that you get five impressive layers—cake, meringue, fruit-and-cream filling, more cake, and more meringue—for about the same amount of work as a two-layer cake. That's because the recipe is incredibly clever: Each meringue layer is baked directly atop the yellow cake batter. The recipe is also pleasingly symmetrical: The egg yolks go into the cake, while the whites go into the meringue. For our filling, we mimicked the rich egginess of custard by folding store-bought lemon curd into whipped cream, stabilizing it with gelatin, and layering it with raspberries. Bliss torte is more like it!

Blitz Torte

SERVES 8 TO 10

If your pans are dark, reduce the baking time in step 6 to 30 to 35 minutes.

FILLING

1	teaspoon unflavored gelatin
2	tablespoons water
1	cup heavy cream, chilled
1	teaspoon vanilla extract
½	cup lemon curd
10	ounces (2 cups) raspberries
2	tablespoons orange liqueur
1	tablespoon sugar

CAKE

½	cup whole milk
4	large egg yolks
1½	teaspoons vanilla extract
1¼	cups (5 ounces) cake flour
1	cup (7 ounces) sugar
1½	teaspoons baking powder
½	teaspoon salt
12	tablespoons unsalted butter, cut into 12 pieces and softened

MERINGUE

4	large egg whites
¼	teaspoon cream of tartar
¾	cup (5¼ ounces) sugar
½	teaspoon vanilla extract
½	cup sliced almonds

1. FOR THE FILLING: Sprinkle gelatin over water in small bowl and let sit until gelatin softens, about 5 minutes. Microwave until mixture is bubbling around edges and gelatin dissolves, 15 to 30 seconds. Using stand mixer fitted with whisk, whip cream and vanilla on medium-low speed until foamy, about 1 minute. Increase speed to medium-high and whip until soft peaks form, about 2 minutes. Add gelatin mixture and whip until firm, stiff peaks form, about 1 minute.

2. Whisk lemon curd in large metal bowl to loosen.

Fold whipped cream mixture into curd. Refrigerate cream filling for at least 1½ hours or up to 3 hours.

3. FOR THE CAKE: Meanwhile, adjust oven rack to middle position and heat oven to 325 degrees. Grease 2 light-colored 9-inch round cake pans, line with parchment paper, grease parchment, and flour pans.

4. Beat milk, yolks, and vanilla together with fork. Using stand mixer fitted with paddle, mix flour, sugar, baking powder, and salt on low speed until combined, about 5 seconds. Add butter, 1 piece at a time, and mix until only pea-size pieces remain, about 1 minute. Add half of milk mixture, increase speed to medium-high, and beat until light and fluffy, about 1 minute. Reduce speed to medium-low, add remaining milk mixture, and beat until incorporated, about 30 seconds. Give batter final stir by hand. Divide batter evenly between prepared pans and spread into even layer using small offset spatula.

5. FOR THE MERINGUE: Using clean, dry stand mixer fitted with a whisk, whip egg whites and cream of tartar on medium-low speed until foamy, about 1 minute. Increase speed to medium-high and whip whites to soft, billowy mounds, 1 to 3 minutes. Gradually add sugar and whip until glossy, stiff peaks form, 3 to 5 minutes. Add vanilla and whip until incorporated.

6. Divide meringue evenly between cake pans and spread evenly over cake batter to edges of pan. Use back of spoon to create peaks in meringue. Sprinkle meringue with almonds. Bake cakes until meringue is golden and has pulled away from sides of pan, 50 to 55 minutes, switching and rotating pans halfway through baking. Let cakes cool completely in pans on wire rack. (Cakes can be baked up to 24 hours in advance and stored, uncovered, in pans at room temperature.)

7. To finish filling, 10 minutes before assembling cake, combine raspberries, liqueur, and sugar in bowl.

8. Gently remove cakes from pans, discarding parchment. Place 1 cake layer on platter, meringue side up. Spread half of cream filling evenly over top. Using slotted spoon, spoon raspberries evenly over filling. Gently spread remaining cream filling over raspberries, covering raspberries completely. Top with second cake layer, meringue side up. Serve cake within 2 hours of assembly.

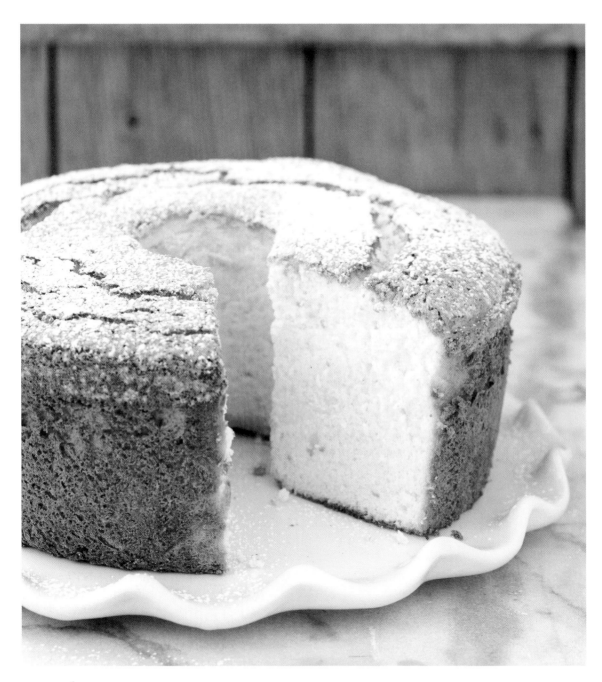

✅ WHY THIS RECIPE WORKS

The key to angel food cake is voluminous, stable egg whites. A mere speck of yolk precludes them from whipping to peaks. We had equal success with both cold and room-temperature egg whites. Cold whites achieved the same volume as room-temperature whites; they just took a few minutes longer. Cream of tartar offered some insurance against deflated whites because its acidity helped stabilize the egg whites. Cake flour was also important—all-purpose flour produced a chewy, gummy cake.

Angel Food Cake

SERVES 10 TO 12

Do not use all-purpose flour in this recipe as it will give the cake a breadlike texture. You will need a 12-cup tube pan with a removable bottom for this recipe. If your pan has "feet" that rise above the top edge of the pan, let the cake cool upside down; otherwise, invert the tube pan over a large metal kitchen funnel or the neck of a sturdy bottle. Cake can be served plain or dusted with confectioners' sugar.

1	cup plus 2 tablespoons (4½ ounces) cake flour
¼	teaspoon salt
1¾	cups (12¼ ounces) sugar
12	large egg whites
1½	teaspoons cream of tartar
1	teaspoon vanilla extract

1. Adjust oven rack to lower-middle position and preheat oven to 325 degrees. Whisk flour and salt in bowl. Process sugar in food processor until fine and powdery, about 1 minute. Reserve half of sugar in small bowl. Add flour mixture to food processor with remaining sugar and process until aerated, about 1 minute.

2. Using stand mixer fitted with whisk, whip egg whites and cream of tartar on medium-low speed until foamy, about 1 minute. Increase speed to medium-high. Slowly add reserved sugar and whip until soft peaks form, about 6 minutes. Add vanilla and mix until incorporated.

3. Sift flour-sugar mixture over egg whites in 3 additions, folding gently with rubber spatula after each addition until incorporated. Scrape mixture into 12-cup ungreased tube pan.

4. Bake until skewer inserted into center comes out clean and cracks in cake appear dry, 40 to 45 minutes. Let cool, inverted, to room temperature, about 3 hours. To unmold, run knife along interior of pan. Turn out onto platter. Serve.

CHOCOLATE-ALMOND ANGEL FOOD CAKE

Replace ½ teaspoon vanilla extract with ½ teaspoon almond extract in step 2. Fold 2 ounces finely grated bittersweet chocolate into batter following flour in step 3.

CAFÉ AU LAIT ANGEL FOOD CAKE

Add 1 tablespoon instant coffee or espresso powder to food processor along with flour in step 1. Replace ½ teaspoon vanilla with 1 tablespoon coffee liqueur in step 2.

KEY STEPS TO ANGEL FOOD CAKE

1. GRIND SUGAR: Process granulated sugar in food processor until powdery. It'll be fine, light, and won't deflate egg whites.

2. STABILIZE EGG WHITES: Add cream of tartar to egg whites at start of whipping. Once whites become foamy, add half of sugar—gradually.

3. SIFT FLOUR IN BATCHES: Gently sift flour-sugar mixture over beaten egg whites in additions to avoid deflating whites.

4. COOL UPSIDE DOWN: Invert cake until it is completely cool, about three hours. If you don't have pan with feet, invert it over neck of sturdy bottle.

✔ WHY THIS RECIPE WORKS

Chiffon cake should have the airy height of angel food cake with the richness of pound cake. For our chiffon cake recipe, we eliminated the unnecessary step of sifting the dry ingredients. We also perfected the method for beating our egg whites—slowly adding sugar once the eggs had been beaten to soft peaks and then continuing to beat them until just stiff and glossy—to avoid little pockets of cooked egg whites.

Chiffon Cake

SERVES 10 TO 12

Separate the eggs when they're cold; it's easier. You will need a 16-cup tube pan with a removable bottom for this recipe. If your pan has "feet" that rise above the top edge of the pan, let the cake cool upside down; otherwise, invert the tube pan over a large metal kitchen funnel or the neck of a sturdy bottle.

5	large eggs, separated
1	teaspoon cream of tartar
1½	cups (10½ ounces) sugar
1⅓	cups (5⅓ ounces) cake flour
2	teaspoons baking powder
½	teaspoon salt
¾	cup water
½	cup vegetable oil
1	tablespoon vanilla extract

1. Adjust oven rack to lower-middle position and heat oven to 325 degrees. Using stand mixer fitted with whisk, whip egg whites and cream of tartar on medium-high speed until soft peaks form, about 2 minutes. With mixer running, slowly add 2 tablespoons sugar and whip until just stiff and glossy, about 1 minute; set aside.

2. Combine flour, remaining sugar, baking powder, and salt in large bowl. Whisk water, oil, egg yolks, and vanilla in medium bowl until smooth. Whisk wet mixture into flour mixture until smooth. Whisk one-third whipped egg whites into batter, then gently fold in remaining whites, 1 scoop at a time, until well combined. Scrape mixture into 16-cup ungreased tube pan.

3. Bake until skewer inserted into center comes out clean and cracks in cake appear dry, 55 minutes to 1 hour, 5 minutes. Let cool, inverted, to room temperature, about 3 hours. To unmold, turn pan right side up and run flexible knife around tube and outer edge. Use tube to pull cake out of pan and set it on inverted baking pan. Cut bottom free. Invert cake onto serving plate and gently twist tube to remove. Serve.

ORANGE CHIFFON CAKE

Reduce total sugar to 1¼ cups. Replace water with ¾ cup orange juice and add 1 tablespoon grated orange zest along with vanilla in step 2. For glaze, whisk 3 tablespoons orange juice, 2 tablespoons softened cream cheese, and ½ teaspoon grated orange zest in medium bowl until smooth. Add 1½ cups confectioners' sugar and whisk until smooth. Pour glaze over cooled cake. Let glaze set for 15 minutes. Serve.

LET ME OUTTA HERE!

Like angel food cake, chiffon cake is baked in an ungreased pan. Why? The stiffly beaten egg whites need to cling to the pan to rise. If the pan were greased, they couldn't. Here's how to remove it from the pan.

1. When cake is cool, turn pan right side up and run flexible knife around tube and outer edge.

2. Use tube to pull cake out of pan and set it on inverted baking pan. Cut bottom free.

3. Invert cake onto serving plate and gently twist tube to remove.

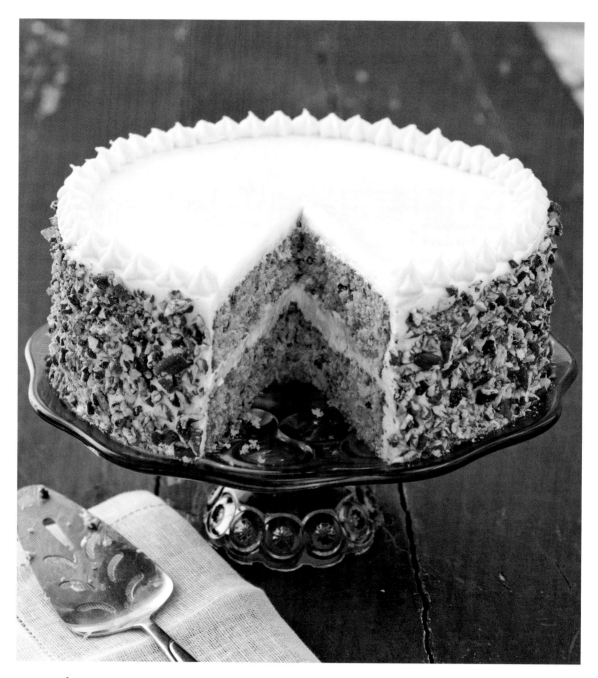

WHY THIS RECIPE WORKS

Although the name is a mystery (there's nothing Italian about this cake), the appeal of this Southern specialty is obvious: tender yellow cake with coconut and pecans, doused in tangy cream cheese frosting. But the recipes we found produced gummy cakes with weak coconut flavor. Cake flour made a more tender crumb, and heat-activated baking powder ensured the cake would rise evenly in the oven. To boost coconut flavor, we added it twice—pulverized, toasted coconut added flavor to the cake without drying it out, and cream of coconut amped up the frosting. Finally, we coated the sides in a blanket of toasted pecans.

Italian Cream Cake

SERVES 8 TO 10

Toast the coconut and nuts in a 350-degree oven until golden brown, 10 to 12 minutes. Watch carefully and stir occasionally to prevent burning.

CAKE

1½	cups sweetened shredded coconut, toasted
1	cup buttermilk, room temperature
2	teaspoons vanilla extract
2½	cups (10 ounces) cake flour
2	teaspoons baking powder
¾	teaspoon salt
½	teaspoon baking soda
12	tablespoons unsalted butter, cut into 12 pieces and softened
4	tablespoons shortening, cut into 4 pieces
1¾	cups (12¼ ounces) sugar
5	large eggs, room temperature
2	cups (8 ounces) pecans, toasted and chopped

FROSTING

12	tablespoons unsalted butter, softened
2¼	cups (9 ounces) confectioners' sugar
½	cup cream of coconut
½	teaspoon vanilla extract
	Pinch salt
16	ounces cream cheese, cut into 8 pieces and softened

1. FOR THE CAKE: Adjust oven rack to middle position and heat oven to 350 degrees. Grease two 9-inch round cake pans, line with parchment paper, grease parchment, then flour pans. Process coconut in food processor until finely ground, about 1 minute. Combine coconut, buttermilk, and vanilla in 2-cup liquid measuring cup and let sit until coconut is slightly softened, about 10 minutes; reserve.

2. Combine flour, baking powder, salt, and baking soda in bowl. Using stand mixer fitted with paddle, beat butter, shortening, and sugar on medium-high speed until pale and fluffy, about 3 minutes. Add eggs, one at a time, and beat until combined. Reduce speed to low and add flour mixture in 3 additions, alternating with 2 additions of reserved coconut-buttermilk mixture, scraping down bowl as needed. Add ¾ cup pecans and give batter final stir by hand.

3. Scrape equal amounts of batter into prepared pans and bake until toothpick inserted in center comes out clean, 28 to 32 minutes. Cool cakes in pans on wire rack for 10 minutes. Remove cakes from pans, discarding parchment, and cool completely, about 2 hours. (Cooled cakes can be wrapped with plastic wrap and stored at room temperature for up to 2 days.)

4. FOR THE FROSTING: Using stand mixer fitted with paddle, mix butter and sugar on low speed until combined, about 30 seconds. Increase speed to medium-high and beat until pale and fluffy, about 2 minutes. Add cream of coconut, vanilla, and salt and beat until smooth, about 30 seconds. Add cream cheese, one piece at a time, and beat until incorporated, about 1 minute. Refrigerate until ready to use.

5. When cakes are cooled, spread 1½ cups frosting over 1 cake round. Top with second cake round and spread remaining frosting evenly over top and sides of cake. Press remaining pecans onto sides of cake. Serve. (Cake can be refrigerated for up to 2 days. Bring to room temperature before serving.)

COCONUT: TOAST, GRIND, SOAK

To bring out the flavor of the shredded coconut, we toast it in a 350-degree oven until it is golden brown (about 10 minutes). To help the coconut flavor permeate the cake, we grind it to meal in the food processor. But toasted, ground coconut is hard and dry, a real problem in such a deliciously soft, moist cake. To moisten and soften the coconut meal, we soak it in buttermilk before adding it to the cake batter.

✓ WHY THIS RECIPE WORKS

In this delicious variation on classic pound cake, we added cream cheese for richness, tangy flavor, and an especially velvety texture. We let the pure flavors of eggs, butter, and the cream cheese take center stage, adding only a few teaspoons of vanilla and a moderate amount of sugar. To achieve a tight, fine crumb and a velvety texture, we left the leavener out altogether and used lower-protein cake flour. Extra egg yolks kept the cake moist and tender. Finally, a low oven took a little longer, but it produced a perfect golden-brown crust and a moist, tender interior.

Cream Cheese Pound Cake

SERVES 12 TO 14

If you do not have cake flour on hand, you can substitute ⅞ cup all-purpose flour and 2 tablespoons cornstarch for each cup of flour.

3	cups (12 ounces) cake flour
1	teaspoon salt
4	large eggs plus 2 large yolks, room temperature
¼	cup milk
2	teaspoons vanilla extract
3	cups (21 ounces) sugar
24	tablespoons (3 sticks) unsalted butter, softened
6	ounces cream cheese, softened

1. Adjust oven rack to middle position and heat oven to 300 degrees. Grease and flour 12-cup nonstick Bundt pan. Combine flour and salt in bowl. Whisk eggs and yolks, milk, and vanilla together in 2-cup liquid measuring cup.

2. Using stand mixer fitted with paddle, beat sugar, butter, and cream cheese on medium-high speed until pale and fluffy, about 3 minutes. Reduce speed to low and very slowly add egg mixture, mixing until incorporated (batter may look slightly curdled). Add flour mixture in 3 additions, scraping down bowl as needed. Give batter final stir by hand.

3. Scrape batter into prepared pan and gently tap pan on counter to release air bubbles. Bake until toothpick inserted in center comes out clean, 80 to 90 minutes, rotating pan halfway through baking. Cool cake in pan on wire rack for 15 minutes. Remove cake from pan and cool completely, about 2 hours. Serve. (Cake can be stored, wrapped in plastic wrap, at room temperature for 3 days.)

STRAWBERRY-RHUBARB COMPOTE

MAKES 4 CUPS

The compote can be refrigerated for up to one week. It's delicious drizzled on pound cake or ice cream or stirred into yogurt or oatmeal.

1	pound strawberries, hulled and chopped (3 cups)
1	cup (7 ounces) sugar
1	tablespoon lemon juice
1	pound rhubarb, sliced ¼-inch thick
	Pinch salt

1. Toss strawberries with ½ cup sugar and lemon juice in medium bowl. Transfer strawberry mixture to fine-mesh strainer set over medium saucepan and let stand, stirring occasionally, for 30 minutes. Do not wash bowl.

2. Return strawberries to bowl. Add rhubarb, remaining ½ cup sugar, and salt to strawberry juices in pan and bring to boil over medium-high heat. Reduce heat to medium-low and cook, stirring occasionally, until rhubarb is soft and liquid has thickened, 6 to 8 minutes.

3. Stir strawberries into pan and remove from heat. Transfer compote to bowl and let cool to room temperature, about 45 minutes. Serve.

PREPARING A BUNDT PAN

To ensure a clean release, make a simple paste from 1 tablespoon melted butter and 1 tablespoon flour (or cocoa powder for chocolate cakes) and apply it to pan with pastry brush.

✔ WHY THIS RECIPE WORKS

This thrifty pound cake, which was designed to save on gas by not requiring a preheated oven, is an especially tall cake and boasts a crisp crust. To create a light crumb, we used leaner whole milk instead of the heavy cream called for in most recipes. Swapping out all-purpose flour for cake flour yielded an even finer, more delicate crumb for our pound cake. We also used baking powder, which produced carbon dioxide bubbles that gave our cake its rise. Putting the pound cake into a cold oven, as is tradition, gave the carbon dioxide more time to produce greater rise.

Cold-Oven Pound Cake

SERVES 12

You'll need a 16-cup tube pan for this recipe; if not using a nonstick pan, make sure to thoroughly grease a traditional pan. In step 2, don't worry if the batter looks slightly separated.

3	cups (12 ounces) cake flour
½	teaspoon baking powder
1	teaspoon salt
1	cup whole milk
2	teaspoons vanilla extract
20	tablespoons (2½ sticks) unsalted butter, softened
2½	cups (17½ ounces) sugar
6	large eggs

1. Adjust oven rack to lower-middle position. Grease and flour 16-cup tube pan. Combine flour, baking powder, and salt in bowl. Whisk milk and vanilla in measuring cup.

2. Using stand mixer fitted with paddle, beat butter and sugar on medium-high speed until light and fluffy, about 2 minutes. Beat in eggs, one at a time, until combined. Reduce speed to low and add flour mixture in 3 additions, alternating with milk mixture in 2 additions, scraping down bowl as needed. Mix on low until smooth, about 30 seconds. Give batter final stir by hand.

3. Pour batter into prepared pan and smooth top. Place cake in cold oven. Adjust oven temperature to 325 degrees and bake, without opening oven door, until cake is golden brown and skewer inserted in center comes out clean, 1 hour, 5 minutes to 1 hour, 20 minutes.

4. Let cake cool in pan on wire rack for 15 minutes. Remove cake from pan and let cool completely on rack about 2 hours. Serve. (Cake can be stored at room temperature for up to 2 days.)

A COLD OVEN REALLY MAKES A DIFFERENCE

Curiosity led us to try baking our Cold-Oven Pound Cake in a preheated oven. The cake baked more quickly (no surprise), but it was squat and lacked the thick crust we'd come to expect. Evidently, the hot oven stopped the small amount of leavener in our recipe before its work was done. And it turns out the crust on our Cold-Oven Pound Cake is formed by moisture in the oven reacting with starch in the batter. A hot oven is drier than a cold oven (heat evaporates moisture), so there wasn't enough moisture in the preheated oven to form a nice, thick crust.

SQUAT CAKE
A preheated oven produces a squat, crustless cake with this recipe.

PERFECT CAKE
In contrast, a cold oven produces a high rise and a thick crust.

WHY PAY FOR PREHEATING?

Gas ovens became widely available in the United States during the first decades of the 20th century. Because these ovens were more expensive than their wood- and coal-fired counterparts, gas companies had to get creative in marketing them. One popular tactic was to develop and promote recipes started in a cold oven, with the hook that consumers could save money in their gas ovens by not paying for "needless" preheating. Hence: Cold-oven pound cake.

✓ WHY THIS RECIPE WORKS

Packaged chocolate cream cupcakes are a childhood treat. But try one today and you're met with wan chocolate cake encasing salty whipped vegetable shortening. We knew we could do better. Blooming cocoa in boiling water and adding chocolate chips and espresso powder gave our cupcakes plenty of chocolate depth. Combining marshmallow crème and the right amount of gelatin gave us the perfect creamy filling. To fill our cupcakes without a pastry bag, we used a paring knife to cut inverted cones from the tops of the cupcakes, added the frosting, and plugged the holes.

Chocolate Cream Cupcakes

MAKES 12 CUPCAKES

To ensure an appropriately thick filling, be sure to use marshmallow crème (such as Fluff or Kraft Jet-Puffed Creme), not marshmallow sauce. For an accurate measurement of boiling water, bring a full kettle of water to a boil, then measure out the desired amount.

CUPCAKES

1	cup (5 ounces) all-purpose flour
½	teaspoon baking soda
¼	teaspoon salt
½	cup boiling water
⅓	cup (1 ounce) cocoa
⅓	cup (2 ounces) semisweet chocolate chips
1	tablespoon instant espresso powder
¾	cup (5¼ ounces) sugar
½	cup sour cream
½	cup vegetable oil
2	large eggs
1	teaspoon vanilla extract

FILLING

¾	teaspoon unflavored gelatin
3	tablespoons water
4	tablespoons (½ stick) unsalted butter, softened
1	teaspoon vanilla extract
	Pinch salt
1¼	cups marshmallow crème

GLAZE

½	cup semisweet chocolate chips
3	tablespoons unsalted butter

1. FOR THE CUPCAKES: Adjust oven rack to middle position and heat oven to 325 degrees. Spray 12-cup muffin tin with vegetable oil spray and flour. Combine flour, baking soda, and salt in bowl. Whisk water, cocoa, chocolate chips, and espresso powder in large bowl until smooth. Add sugar, sour cream, oil, eggs, and vanilla and mix until combined. Whisk in flour mixture until incorporated. Divide batter evenly among muffin cups. Bake until toothpick inserted in center comes out with few dry crumbs attached, 18 to 22 minutes. Let cupcakes cool in tin on wire rack for 10 minutes, then turn out onto wire rack and let cool completely.

2. FOR THE FILLING: Sprinkle gelatin over water in large bowl and let sit until gelatin softens, about 5 minutes. Microwave until mixture is bubbling around edges and gelatin dissolves, about 30 seconds. Stir in butter, vanilla, and salt until combined. Let mixture cool until just warm to touch, about 5 minutes, then whisk in marshmallow crème until smooth; refrigerate until set, about 30 minutes. Transfer ⅓ cup marshmallow mixture to pastry bag fitted with small plain tip; reserve remaining mixture for filling cupcakes.

3. FOR THE GLAZE: Microwave chocolate and butter in small bowl, stirring occasionally, until smooth, about 30 seconds. Let glaze cool to room temperature, about 10 minutes.

4. Insert tip of paring knife at 45-degree angle and about ¼ inch from edge of cupcake, cut cone from top of each cupcake, and cut off all but top ¼ inch of cone, leaving circular disk of cake. Fill cupcakes with 1 tablespoon filling each. Replace tops, frost with 2 teaspoons cooled glaze, and let sit 10 minutes. Using pastry bag, pipe curlicues across glazed cupcakes. Serve. (Cupcakes can be stored at room temperature for up to 2 days.)

FILLING THE CUPCAKES

1. Insert tip of paring knife at 45-degree angle about ¼ inch from edge of cupcake. Cut out and remove cake cone. Cut off all but top ¼ inch of cone, leaving circular disk of cake.

2. Using spoon, fill each cupcake with marshmallow mixture and then top with reserved cake "plug." The glaze and the curlicues will hide your handiwork.

WHY THIS RECIPE WORKS

Most hot fudge pudding cakes end up looking rich and fudgy but have very little chocolate flavor. For chocolate pudding cake that tasted as good as it looked, we folded semisweet chocolate chips into the batter, which added another layer of chocolate flavor and ensured plenty of gooey pockets in the baked cake. Vegetable oil, which most recipes call for, was flavorless, and we found substituting melted butter improved our pudding cake's flavor. Using Dutch-processed cocoa, which is less acidic than natural cocoa powder, produced a richer chocolate taste.

Hot Fudge Pudding Cake

SERVES 6 TO 8

For an accurate measurement of boiling water, bring a full kettle of water to a boil, then measure out the desired amount. Do not overbake this cake or the pudding sauce will burn in the pan and the cake will be dry, not fudgy. Store leftovers, covered with plastic wrap, in the refrigerator. Reheat individual servings in a microwave on high power until hot (about one minute).

1	cup (7 ounces) sugar
½	cup (1½ ounces) Dutch-processed cocoa
1	cup (5 ounces) all-purpose flour
2	teaspoons baking powder
¼	teaspoon salt
½	cup milk
4	tablespoons unsalted butter, melted
1	large egg yolk
2	teaspoons vanilla extract
½	cup semisweet chocolate chips
1	cup boiling water
	Vanilla ice cream or whipped cream

1. Adjust oven rack to middle position and heat oven to 350 degrees. Spray 8-inch square baking pan with vegetable oil spray. Whisk ½ cup sugar with ¼ cup cocoa in small bowl.

2. Whisk flour, remaining ½ cup sugar, remaining ¼ cup cocoa, baking powder, and salt in large bowl. Whisk milk, butter, egg yolk, and vanilla in medium bowl until smooth. Stir milk mixture into flour mixture until just combined. Fold in chocolate chips (batter will be stiff).

3. Using rubber spatula, scrape batter into prepared pan and spread into corners. Sprinkle reserved cocoa mixture evenly over top. Gently pour boiling water over cocoa. Do not stir.

4. Bake until top of cake looks cracked, sauce is bubbling, and toothpick inserted into cakey area comes out with moist crumbs attached, about 25 minutes. Let cool in pan on wire rack for at least 10 minutes. To serve, scoop warm cake into individual serving bowls and top with vanilla ice cream or whipped cream.

BABY PUDDING CAKES

Put a fancy spin on this homey recipe by baking up individual pudding cakes.

Spray eight 6-ounce ovenproof ramekins or coffee cups with vegetable oil spray. Fill each with 2 tablespoons batter. Top each with 1½ tablespoons cocoa mixture, followed by 2 tablespoons boiling water. Arrange cups on rimmed baking sheet and bake until tops are just cracked, 20 to 25 minutes.

IS IT DONE YET?

This highly unconventional cake breaks most of the usual rules, including how to judge when it's ready to come out of the oven.

1. When the top is crackled like a brownie and the sauce is bubbling up from the bottom, it's time to start testing for doneness. For the most accurate test, insert the toothpick close to the edge, where the cake is firmest. (Don't insert the toothpick in the center, where the cake should be gooey.)

2. The toothpick should have large, moist crumbs—but no gooey batter—attached. Check at least two spots to be certain that what's sticking to the toothpick isn't just a melted chocolate chip.

WHY THIS RECIPE WORKS

For the brightest lemon flavor in our lemon pudding cake, we used a full half-cup of lemon juice. To coax even more flavor from the lemons, we creamed a bit of grated zest with the butter and sugar. A bit of cornstarch gently firmed the pudding layer without muddying the lemon flavor. To prevent the top layer of the cake from deflating, we beat sugar into the egg whites. This stabilized the whites and resulted in a high, golden, and fluffy cake. For the creamiest texture, it was important to bake the cake in a water bath. The hot water protected the pudding from cooking too quickly.

Lemon Pudding Cake

SERVES 8

This dessert is best served warm or at room temperature the same day it is made.

¼   **cup (1¼ ounces) all-purpose flour**

2   **teaspoons cornstarch**

1¼   **cups (8¾ ounces) sugar**

5   **tablespoons unsalted butter, softened**

2   **tablespoons grated zest and ½ cup juice from 4 lemons**

5   **large eggs, separated**

1¼   **cups whole milk, room temperature**

2   **quarts boiling water**

1. Adjust oven rack to lowest position and heat oven to 325 degrees. Grease 8-inch square baking dish. Whisk flour and cornstarch in bowl. Using stand mixer fitted with paddle, beat ½ cup sugar, butter, and lemon zest on medium-high speed until light and fluffy, about 2 minutes. Beat in egg yolks, 1 at a time, until incorporated. Reduce speed to medium-low. Add flour mixture and mix until incorporated. Slowly add milk and lemon juice, mixing until just combined.

2. Using clean bowl and whisk attachment, beat egg whites on medium-high speed until soft peaks form, about 2 minutes. With mixer running, slowly add remaining ¾ cup sugar until whites are firm and glossy, about 1 minute. Whisk one-third of whites into batter, then gently fold in remaining whites, 1 scoop at a time, until well combined.

3. Place clean dish towel in bottom of roasting pan and arrange prepared baking dish on towel. Spoon batter into prepared dish. Carefully place pan on oven rack and pour boiling water into pan until water comes halfway up sides of baking dish. Bake until surface is golden brown and edges are set (center should jiggle slightly when gently shaken), about 1 hour. Transfer dish to wire rack and let cool for at least 1 hour. To serve, scoop warm cake into individual serving bowls.

USING A WATER BATH

The water lowers the temperature surrounding the baking dish for gentle, even cooking.

1. To prevent baking dish from sliding, line bottom of roasting pan with clean dish towel.

2. Set roasting pan on oven rack and carefully pour boiling water into pan, halfway up sides of baking dish.

3. After baking, promptly remove baking dish from water. Let water cool before moving water bath.

WHY THIS RECIPE WORKS

In a baked cheesecake, tart lemon juice is mellowed by the heat of the oven. For our icebox version of lemon cheesecake, we needed to dial back the lemon juice to compensate for the lack of baking. Lemon curd, a rich, tangy spread made from eggs, butter, cream, sugar, and lemon juice, added crisp lemon flavor without the undesirable chewiness of zest or the processed flavor of lemon extract. Using lemon cookies instead of graham crackers for the crust created an additional layer of lemon flavor.

Lemon Icebox Cheesecake

Let the dissolved gelatin mixture cool down for a few minutes, or the gelatin will seize when combined with the filling. We tested our cheesecake with several store brands of lemon sandwich cookies; all worked well.

CRUST

10	lemon sandwich cookies, broken into pieces (about 1¼ cups)
2	tablespoons unsalted butter, melted
1	teaspoon grated lemon zest

CURD

¼	cup (1¾ ounces) sugar
1	large egg plus 1 large yolk
	Pinch salt
2	tablespoons lemon juice
1	tablespoon unsalted butter
1	tablespoon heavy cream

FILLING

2¾	teaspoons unflavored gelatin
¼	cup lemon juice (2 lemons)
1½	pounds cream cheese, cut into 1-inch pieces and softened
¾	cup (5¼ ounces) sugar
	Pinch salt
1¼	cups heavy cream, room temperature

1. FOR THE CRUST: Adjust oven rack to middle position and heat oven to 350 degrees. Process cookies in food processor until finely ground, about 30 seconds. Add butter and zest and pulse until combined, about 10 pulses. Press mixture into bottom of 9-inch springform pan. Bake until lightly browned and set, about 10 minutes. Let cool completely on wire rack, at least 30 minutes.

2. FOR THE CURD: While crust is cooling, whisk sugar, egg and yolk, and salt together in small saucepan. Add lemon juice and cook over medium-low heat, stirring constantly, until thick and puddinglike, about 3 minutes. Remove from heat and stir in butter and cream. Press through fine-mesh strainer into small bowl and refrigerate lemon curd until needed.

3. FOR THE FILLING: Sprinkle gelatin over lemon juice in small bowl and let stand until gelatin softens, about 5 minutes. Microwave until mixture is bubbling around edges and gelatin dissolves, about 30 seconds. Set aside.

4. Using stand mixer fitted with paddle beat cream cheese, sugar, and salt on medium speed until smooth and creamy, scraping down sides of bowl as needed, about 2 minutes. Slowly add cream and beat until light and fluffy, about 2 minutes. Add gelatin mixture and ¼ cup curd, increase speed to medium-high, and beat until smooth and airy, about 3 minutes.

5. Pour filling into cooled crust and smooth top. Pour thin lines of remaining curd on top of cake and lightly drag paring knife or skewer perpendicularly through lines to create marbled appearance. Refrigerate until set, at least 6 hours. Remove sides of pan. Serve. (Cheesecake can be refrigerated for up to 3 days.)

SWIRL SHOWSTOPPER

Making a swirl with the lemon curd on top of the cheesecake is absurdly easy and awfully impressive.

1. Use measuring cup to pour curd in 4 thin lines on top of cheesecake.

2. Drag paring knife or skewer perpendicularly through lines to create marbled design.

✔ WHY THIS RECIPE WORKS

These delicate butter cookies literally melt in your mouth, thanks to the generous amount of cornstarch in the dough. Unfortunately, the cornstarch leaves behind a chalky residue with each bite. After settling on the maximum amount of cornstarch we could use without detection, we scoured supermarket shelves in search of other low-protein dry ingredients to replace the remainder. We replaced all-purpose flour with cake flour and chose confectioners' sugar over granulated, but we still needed more bulk. The solution? Rice Krispies! The ground cereal added the volume we were looking for without toughening the crumb.

Melting Moments

MAKES ABOUT 70 COOKIES

If the dough gets too soft to slice, return it to the refrigerator to firm up.

½	cup Rice Krispies cereal
16	tablespoons unsalted butter, cut into 16 pieces and softened
3	tablespoons heavy cream
1	teaspoon vanilla extract
1¼	cups (5 ounces) cake flour
¼	cup (1¼ ounces) cornstarch
⅛	teaspoon salt
⅔	cup (2⅔ ounces) confectioners' sugar

1. Process Rice Krispies in blender until finely ground, about 30 seconds. Combine 4 tablespoons butter and cream in large bowl and microwave until butter is melted, about 30 seconds. Whisk in processed Rice Krispies and vanilla until combined. Let cool slightly, 5 to 7 minutes.

2. Combine flour, cornstarch, and salt in medium bowl; reserve. Whisk sugar into cooled butter mixture until incorporated. Add remaining 12 tablespoons butter, whisking until smooth. Stir in flour mixture until combined.

3. Working with half of dough at a time, dollop dough into 8-inch strip down center of 14 by 12-inch sheet of parchment paper. Fold 1 long side of parchment over dough. Using ruler, press dough into tight 1-inch-wide log. Repeat with remaining dough and another sheet of parchment. Refrigerate dough until firm, about 1 hour. (Dough can be wrapped in plastic wrap and aluminum foil and frozen for up to 1 month.)

4. Adjust oven racks to upper-middle and lower-middle positions and heat oven to 300 degrees. Line 2 baking sheets with parchment. Cut dough into ¼-inch slices and place 1 inch apart on prepared baking sheets. Bake until set but not brown, 18 to 22 minutes, switching and rotating baking sheets halfway through baking. Let cool completely on sheets, about 15 minutes. Repeat with remaining dough. Serve. (Cookies can be stored at room temperature for up to 2 days.)

CRESCENT COOKIES

After step 2, transfer dough to pastry bag fitted with ½-inch star tip. Pipe 1½-inch-long crescents onto prepared baking sheets. Refrigerate dough until firm, about 30 minutes. Bake as directed.

JAM THUMBPRINT COOKIES

After step 2, transfer dough to pastry bag fitted with ½-inch plain tip. Pipe 1-inch-wide and ½-inch-high dough rounds onto prepared baking sheets. Using back of ¼-teaspoon measuring spoon dipped in water, make indentation in center of each round. Refrigerate dough until firm, about 30 minutes. Bake until set, 18 to 20 minutes, switching and rotating sheets halfway through baking. Fill each dimple with ½ teaspoon jam and bake for 5 minutes.

ROUND SPRITZ COOKIES

After step 2, transfer dough to pastry bag fitted with ½-inch star tip. Pipe 1-inch-wide and ½-inch-high dough rounds onto prepared baking sheets. Refrigerate dough until firm, about 30 minutes. Bake as directed.

HANDLING SOFT DOUGH

The high proportion of butter to flour makes the dough for these cookies very soft and challenging to handle. With this technique, you can easily roll it into a log.

1. Dollop half of dough in strip down center of sheet of parchment.

2. Pulling parchment taut, use ruler to press dough into tight log

---

WHY THIS RECIPE WORKS

We set out to create a slice-and-bake cookie recipe that would combine both crispness and rich butter and vanilla flavor—in effect, shortbread shaped into a convenient slice-and-bake log. Using both granulated sugar and light brown sugar gave the cookies a richness and complexity that tasters liked. We used the food processor to combine our recipe ingredients quickly without whipping in too much air—our cookies had the fine, shortbreadlike texture we were after.

Slice-and-Bake Cookies

MAKES ABOUT 40 COOKIES

Be sure that the cookie dough is well chilled and firm so that it can be uniformly sliced.

⅓	cup (2⅓ ounces) granulated sugar
2	tablespoons packed light brown sugar
½	teaspoon salt
12	tablespoons unsalted butter, cut into pieces and softened
2	teaspoons vanilla extract
1	large egg yolk
1½	cups (7½ ounces) all-purpose flour

1. Process granulated sugar, brown sugar, and salt in food processor until no lumps of brown sugar remain, about 30 seconds. Add butter, vanilla, and yolk and process until smooth and creamy, about 20 seconds. Scrape down sides of bowl, add flour, and pulse until dough forms, about 15 seconds.

2. Turn out dough onto lightly floured counter and roll into 10-inch log. Wrap tightly with plastic wrap and refrigerate until firm, at least 2 hours or up to 3 days. (Dough can be wrapped in foil and frozen for up to 1 month.)

3. Adjust oven racks to upper-middle and lower-middle positions and heat oven to 350 degrees. Line 2 baking sheets with parchment paper. Slice chilled dough into ¼-inch rounds and place 1 inch apart on prepared baking sheets. Bake until edges are just golden, about 15 minutes, switching and rotating baking sheets halfway through baking. Let cool 10 minutes on sheets, then transfer to wire rack and let cool completely. Repeat with remaining dough. (Cookies can be stored in airtight container at room temperature for up to 1 week.)

COCONUT-LIME COOKIES

In step 1, add 2 cups sweetened shredded coconut and 2 teaspoons grated lime zest to food processor along with sugars and salt.

WALNUT-BROWN SUGAR COOKIES

In step 1, add 2 more tablespoons brown sugar and 1 cup chopped walnuts to food processor along with sugars and salt.

ORANGE-POPPY SEED COOKIES

In step 1, add ¼ cup poppy seeds and 1 tablespoon grated orange zest to food processor along with sugars and salt.

GLAZE ME

We love the simplicity of our Slice-and-Bake Cookies, but a confectioners' sugar glaze is an easy way to dress them up. If the glaze is too thick to spread, thin it with 1 tablespoon water. Each glaze makes enough for 1 recipe Slice-and-Bake Cookies.

GINGER-LIME GLAZE

Whisk 1 tablespoon softened cream cheese, 1 teaspoon ground ginger, and 2 tablespoons lime juice in medium bowl until combined. Whisk in 1½ cups confectioners' sugar until smooth.

MALTED MILK GLAZE

Whisk 1 tablespoon softened cream cheese, 1 tablespoon malted milk powder, 1 teaspoon vanilla extract, and 2 tablespoons milk in medium bowl until combined. Whisk in 1½ cups confectioners' sugar until smooth.

CAPPUCCINO GLAZE

Whisk 1 tablespoon softened cream cheese, 1 tablespoon instant espresso powder, and 2 tablespoons milk in medium bowl until combined. Whisk in 1½ cups confectioners' sugar until smooth.

PEANUT BUTTER AND JELLY GLAZE

Whisk 1 tablespoon creamy peanut butter, 2 tablespoons strawberry jelly, and 1 tablespoon water in medium bowl until combined. Whisk in 1½ cups confectioners' sugar until smooth.

WHY THIS RECIPE WORKS

Original recipes for fairy gingerbread, a cookie popular in the 19th century, melted in our mouths but were also severely lacking in flavor. A bit of vanilla extract and salt helped boost the flavor. Doubling the ginger added a much-needed kick, but without any competing flavors it was overwhelming. We cut back a little and toasted the ground ginger to bring out its natural flavor. Grating fresh ginger straight into the batter added even more intense ginger flavor. Switching from bread flour to all-purpose flour made the batter slightly easier to spread. A little baking soda helped retain the cookies' airy crispness.

Fairy Gingerbread

MAKES 60 COOKIES

Use cookie or baking sheets that measure at least 15 by 12 inches. Don't be disconcerted by the scant amount of batter: You really are going to spread it very thin. Use the edges of the parchment paper as your guide, covering the entire surface thinly and evenly. For easier grating, freeze a 2-inch piece of peeled ginger for 30 minutes, then use a rasp-style grater.

1½	teaspoons ground ginger
¾	cup plus 2 tablespoons (4⅜ ounces) all-purpose flour
½	teaspoon baking soda
¼	teaspoon salt
5	tablespoons unsalted butter, softened
9	tablespoons (4 ounces) packed light brown sugar
4	teaspoons grated fresh ginger
¾	teaspoon vanilla extract
¼	cup whole milk, room temperature

1. Adjust oven racks to upper-middle and lower-middle positions and heat oven to 325 degrees. Spray 2 rimless baking sheets (or inverted rimmed baking sheets) with vegetable oil spray and cover each with 15 by 12-inch sheet parchment paper. Heat ground ginger in small skillet over medium heat until fragrant, about 1 minute. Combine flour, toasted ginger, baking soda, and salt in medium bowl.

2. Using stand mixer fitted with paddle, beat butter and sugar on medium-high speed until light and fluffy, about 2 minutes. Add fresh ginger and vanilla and mix until incorporated. Reduce speed to low and add flour mixture in 3 additions, alternating with milk in 2 additions; scrape down bowl as needed.

3. Evenly spread ¾ cup batter to cover parchment on each prepared sheet (batter will be very thin). Bake until deep golden brown, 16 to 20 minutes, switching and rotating baking sheets halfway through baking. Immediately score cookies into 3 by 2-inch rectangles. Let cool completely, about 20 minutes. Using tip of paring knife, separate cookies along score marks. (Cookies can be stored in airtight container at room temperature for 3 days.)

MAKING FAIRY GINGERBREAD

While making several dozen batches of Fairy Gingerbread, we had time to perfect our technique. The cookies are made with an unusual method we'd never encountered before. Here's how:

1. To form cookies of requisite thinness, use small offset spatula to spread batter to edges of 15 by 12-inch sheet of parchment paper.

2. Immediately after removing cookies from oven, use chef's knife or pizza wheel to score 3 by 2-inch rectangles. Work quickly to prevent breaking.

3. Once cookies are cool, trace over scored lines with paring knife and gently break cookies apart along lines.

☑ WHY THIS RECIPE WORKS

Joe froggers, from a recipe that dates back more than 200 years, are incredibly moist, spicy, slightly salty cookies, found in bakeries along the North Shore of Massachusetts. We wanted to develop our own recipe. Dissolving salt into our recipe's rum and water gave the cookie its distinctive salty flavor. Ginger, allspice, nutmeg, and cloves contributed warm spice flavor. Many recipes we found in our research called for lard, but we found that using butter made for a more flavorful cookie.

Joe Froggers

MAKES 24 COOKIES

Place only six cookies on each baking sheet—they will spread. If you don't own a 3½-inch cookie cutter, use a drinking glass. Use mild (not robust or blackstrap) molasses. Make sure to chill the dough for a full 8 hours or it will be too hard to roll out.

⅓	cup dark rum (such as Myers's)
1	tablespoon water
1½	teaspoons salt
3	cups (15 ounces) all-purpose flour
¾	teaspoon ground ginger
½	teaspoon ground allspice
¼	teaspoon ground nutmeg
⅛	teaspoon ground cloves
1	cup molasses
1	teaspoon baking soda
8	tablespoons unsalted butter, softened but still cool
1	cup (7 ounces) sugar

1. Stir rum, water, and salt in small bowl until salt dissolves. Whisk flour, ginger, allspice, nutmeg, and cloves in medium bowl. Stir molasses and baking soda in liquid measuring cup (mixture will begin to bubble) and let sit until doubled in volume, about 15 minutes.

2. Using stand mixer fitted with paddle, beat butter and sugar on medium-high speed until fluffy, about 2 minutes. Reduce speed to medium-low and gradually beat in rum mixture. Add flour mixture in 3 additions, beating on medium-low until just incorporated, alternating with molasses mixture in 2 additions, scraping down sides of bowl as needed. Give dough final stir by hand (dough will be extremely sticky). Cover bowl containing dough with plastic wrap and refrigerate until stiff, at least 8 hours or up to 3 days.

3. Adjust oven racks to upper-middle and lower-middle positions and heat oven to 375 degrees. Line 2 baking sheets with parchment paper. Working with half of dough at a time on heavily floured counter, roll out to ¼-inch thickness. Using 3½-inch cookie cutter, cut out 12 cookies. Transfer 6 cookies to each baking sheet, spacing cookies about 1½ inches apart. Bake until cookies are set and just beginning to crack, about 8 minutes, switching and rotating baking sheets halfway through baking time. Let cookies cool on sheets on wire rack 10 minutes, then transfer cookies to rack to cool completely. Repeat with remaining dough. (Cookies may be stored in airtight container for up to 1 week.)

SALTY HISTORY

Joe froggers date back more than 200 years to Black Joe's Tavern, located in Marblehead, Massachusetts, a seaside town north of Boston. A freed slave and Revolutionary War veteran, Joseph Brown (known as Old Black Joe), and his wife, Lucretia (affectionately known as Auntie Cresse), opened the tavern in a part of Marblehead called Gingerbread Hill. Besides serving drinks (mostly rum), Joe and Auntie Cresse baked cookies: large, moist molasses and rum cookies made salty by the addition of Marblehead seawater. These cookies were popular sustenance on long fishing voyages, as they had no dairy to spoil and the combination of rum, molasses, and seawater kept them chewy for weeks.

According to Samuel Roads Jr.'s *History and Traditions of Marblehead*, published in 1879, the funny name for these cookies referred to the lily pads (similar in size and shape to the cookies) and large croaking frogs that would fill the pond behind Joe's tavern. Thus the cookies became known as Joe froggers.

✔ WHY THIS RECIPE WORKS

These cakey cookies are a deli favorite in New York, but rarely do they live up to the hype. We wanted to improve upon the classic chocolate-vanilla combination. To get the "cookie" just right, we made several small but high-impact adjustments. We dialed back the amount of baking soda and baking powder to get rid of unwanted air bubbles, added more vanilla extract to heighten the flavor, and used just enough sour cream to make the cookies tender but not sticky. Corn syrup made the glaze thick and shiny, while milk made it creamy and spreadable. Cocoa powder kept the chocolate glaze flavorful and simple.

Black and White Cookies

MAKES 12 COOKIES

Twelve cookies doesn't sound like much, but these cookies are huge. You'll get neater cookies if you spread on the vanilla glaze first. This recipe provides a little extra glaze, just in case.

COOKIES

1¾	cups (8¾ ounces) all-purpose flour
½	teaspoon baking powder
¼	teaspoon baking soda
⅛	teaspoon salt
10	tablespoons unsalted butter, softened
1	cup (7 ounces) granulated sugar
1	large egg
2	teaspoons vanilla extract
⅓	cup sour cream

GLAZE

5	cups (20 ounces) confectioners' sugar, sifted
7	tablespoons whole milk
2	tablespoons corn syrup
1	teaspoon vanilla extract
½	teaspoon salt
3	tablespoons Dutch-processed cocoa powder, sifted

1. FOR THE COOKIES: Adjust oven racks to upper-middle and lower-middle positions and heat oven to 350 degrees. Line 2 baking sheets with parchment paper. Combine flour, baking powder, baking soda, and salt in bowl.

2. Using stand mixer fitted with paddle, beat butter and sugar on medium-high speed until pale and fluffy, about 2 minutes. Add egg and vanilla and beat until combined. Reduce speed to low and add flour mixture in 3 additions, alternating with 2 additions of sour cream, scraping down bowl as needed. Give dough final stir by hand.

3. Using greased ¼-cup measure, drop cookie dough 3 inches apart onto prepared baking sheets. Bake until edges are lightly browned, 15 to 18 minutes, switching and rotating sheets halfway through baking. Let cookies cool on sheets for 5 minutes, then transfer to wire rack to cool completely, about 1 hour.

4. FOR THE GLAZE: Whisk sugar, 6 tablespoons milk, corn syrup, vanilla, and salt together in bowl until smooth. Transfer 1 cup glaze to small bowl; reserve. Whisk cocoa and remaining 1 tablespoon milk into remaining glaze until combined.

5. Working with 1 cookie at a time, spread 1 tablespoon vanilla glaze over half of underside of cookie. Refrigerate until glaze is set, about 15 minutes. Cover other half of cookies with 1 tablespoon chocolate glaze and let cookies sit at room temperature until glaze is firm, at least 1 hour. Serve. (Cookies can be stored at room temperature for up to 2 days.)

GLAZING BLACK AND WHITE COOKIES

1. Using a butter knife or offset mini spatula, glaze half of the underside of each cookie with vanilla glaze. Chill the cookies in the refrigerator for 15 minutes so the glaze can start to harden.

2. Glaze the other half of each cookie with chocolate glaze, and let the cookies sit until the glaze sets, about one hour.

WHY THIS RECIPE WORKS

We wanted a light, airy cake for our whoopie pies, so we used the creaming mixing method, blending the butter and sugar with a mixer until fluffy and nearly white in color. We also used lots of Dutch-processed cocoa powder and vanilla in our recipe for full flavor and a deep, dark-colored crumb. And for a cleaner, fuller flavor, we replaced the shortening (or lard) found in most recipes with butter.

Whoopie Pies

MAKES 6 PIES
Don't be tempted to bake all the cakes on one baking sheet; the batter needs room to spread in the oven.

CAKES

2	cups (10 ounces) all-purpose flour
½	cup (1½ ounces) Dutch-processed cocoa powder
1	teaspoon baking soda
½	teaspoon salt
8	tablespoons unsalted butter, softened but still cool
1	cup packed (7 ounces) light brown sugar
1	large egg, room temperature
1	teaspoon vanilla extract
1	cup buttermilk

FILLING

12	tablespoons unsalted butter, softened but still cool
1¼	cups (5 ounces) confectioners' sugar
1½	teaspoons vanilla extract
⅛	teaspoon salt
2½	cups marshmallow crème

1. FOR THE CAKES: Adjust oven racks to upper-middle and lower-middle positions and heat oven to 350 degrees. Line 2 baking sheets with parchment paper. Whisk flour, cocoa powder, baking soda, and salt in medium bowl.

2. Using stand mixer fitted with paddle, beat butter and sugar on medium-high speed until fluffy, about 4 minutes. Beat in egg until incorporated, scraping down sides of bowl as necessary, then beat in vanilla. Reduce speed to low and beat in flour mixture in 3 additions, alternating with buttermilk in 2 additions. Give batter final stir by hand.

3. Using ⅓-cup measure, scoop 6 mounds of batter onto each baking sheet, spacing mounds about 3 inches apart. Bake until cakes spring back when pressed, 15 to 18 minutes, switching and rotating baking sheets halfway through baking. Let cool completely on baking sheets, at least 1 hour.

4. FOR THE FILLING: Using stand mixer fitted with paddle, beat butter and sugar on medium speed until fluffy, about 2 minutes. Beat in vanilla and salt. Beat in marshmallow crème until incorporated, about 2 minutes. Refrigerate filling until slightly firm, about 30 minutes. (Bowl can be wrapped and refrigerated for up to 2 days.)

5. Dollop ⅓ cup filling on center of flat side of 6 cakes. Top with flat side of remaining 6 cakes and gently press until filling spreads to edge of cake. Serve. (Whoopie pies can be refrigerated for up to 3 days.)

WHAT'S UP, WHOOPIE PIE?

Where did whoopie pies originate? Both Maine and Pennsylvania—the Pennsylvania Dutch of Lancaster County, to be specific—claim whoopie pies as their own. Maine's earliest claim dates back to 1925, when Labadie's Bakery in Lewiston first sold whoopie pies to the public. Some research showed that the Berwick Cake Company began manufacturing Whoopie! Pies (the exclamation point was part of the name) in 1927. These sources claim that whoopie pies were named after the musical *Whoopie; Whoopie* had its debut in Boston in 1927. In addition, Marshmallow Fluff, a key ingredient in many whoopie pie recipes, had been invented in nearby Lynn seven years earlier.

What about Pennsylvania's claim on whoopie pies? We found an article in a copy of the *Gettysburg Times* from 1982 that spoke of a chocolate cake sandwich with a fluffy cream center. These sandwiches were called gobs and were sold by the Dutch Maid Bakery of Geistown. While the name was different, the description (and a huge picture) showed that these were no doubt whoopie pies. The Dutch Maid Bakery purchased the rights to the gob in 1980 from the Harris and Boyer Baking Company also of Pennsylvania, which had started manufacturing gobs in 1927. Maine might have a few years on Pennsylvania when it comes to whoopie pies, but who's to know for sure?

WHILE FRESH FRUIT, LIKE A CRISP APPLE OR A JUICY PEACH, SHOULD SUFFICE for dessert, it so often doesn't. Enter thrifty, humble, but oh-so-satisfying American fruit desserts like dumplings, fritters, cobblers, and crisps. But what is American fruit? Blueberries and cranberries, sure. But apples and peaches are not as quintessentially American as you might think. Apples got their start in America from seeds brought by English colonists (the first apple orchard was planted on a slope in Boston in what is now Beacon Hill), while peaches got their foothold in Florida, Louisiana, and Georgia, courtesy of the Spanish explorers who arrived there in the late 16th century.

Of the myriad of apple desserts seen now, classic apple dumplings and apple fritters are two of our favorites. In the 19th century, every homemaker could toss together a biscuit or pie dough and deftly wrap it around stuffed apples. They tied up the dumplings in cheesecloth, boiled or steamed them, and served them with sauce; latter-day cooks prefer to bake them. We're not sure when apple dumplings fell out of favor, but we set out to resurrect them. The same goes for apple fritters. Today, these apple-studded pastries seem to be elbowing out muffins and scones at coffee shops, but we were sure we could do better. We wanted a fritter packed with warm-spiced apple flavor—crisp on the outside and moist, not greasy, within.

Among the simplest fruit desserts out there are cobblers, crisps, and the funny-named grunts. But soggy toppings, too-thick (or too-thin) fillings, and unbalanced fruit flavor were a few of the challenges we'd tackle in creating our versions. In this chapter, we'll show you how to make fruit desserts the best they can be.

✓ WHY THIS RECIPE WORKS

Apple dumplings are a homespun combination of warm pastry, concentrated apple flavor, raisins, butter, and cinnamon, but too often the apples turn too soft or are unevenly baked. The pastry can also turn gummy from the apples' juices. We found that biscuit dough was easier to work with than pie dough and did a great job of absorbing the liquid from the apples without getting mushy. Rather than baking the dumplings in syrup as some recipes instruct, we served our sauce on the side, which preserved the dumplings' texture.

Baked Apple Dumplings

MAKES 8 DUMPLINGS

Use a melon baller or a metal teaspoon measure to core the apples. Serve warm, with Cider Sauce (recipe follows).

DOUGH

2½	cups (12½ ounces) all-purpose flour
3	tablespoons sugar
2	teaspoons baking powder
¾	teaspoon salt
10	tablespoons unsalted butter, cut into ½-inch pieces and chilled
5	tablespoons vegetable shortening, cut into ½-inch pieces and chilled
¾	cup cold buttermilk

APPLE DUMPLINGS

6	tablespoons (2⅔ ounces) sugar
1	teaspoon ground cinnamon
3	tablespoons unsalted butter, softened
3	tablespoons golden raisins, chopped
4	Golden Delicious apples
2	egg whites, lightly beaten

1. FOR THE DOUGH: Process flour, sugar, baking powder, and salt in food processor until combined, about 15 seconds. Scatter butter and shortening over flour mixture and pulse until mixture resembles wet sand, about 10 pulses; transfer to bowl. Stir in buttermilk until dough forms. Turn out onto lightly floured work surface and knead briefly until dough is cohesive. Press dough into 8 by 4-inch rectangle. Cut in half, wrap each half tightly in plastic wrap, and refrigerate until firm, about 1 hour.

2. FOR THE APPLE DUMPLINGS: Adjust oven rack to middle position and heat oven to 425 degrees. Combine sugar and cinnamon in small bowl. In second bowl, combine butter, raisins, and 3 tablespoons cinnamon sugar mixture. Peel apples and halve through equator. Remove core and pack butter mixture into each apple half.

3. On lightly floured counter, roll each dough half into 12-inch square. Cut each 12-inch square into four 6-inch squares. Working with one at a time, lightly brush edges of dough square with egg white and place apple, cut side up, in center of each square. Gather dough 1 corner at a time on top of apple, crimping edges to seal. Using paring knife, cut vent hole in top of each dumpling.

4. Line rimmed baking sheet with parchment paper. Arrange dumplings on prepared baking sheet, brush tops with egg white, and sprinkle with remaining cinnamon sugar. Bake until dough is golden brown and juices are bubbling, 20 to 25 minutes. Let cool on baking sheet for 10 minutes. Serve.

CIDER SAUCE

MAKES ABOUT 1½ CUPS

1	cup apple cider
1	cup water
1	cup (7 ounces) sugar
½	teaspoon ground cinnamon
2	tablespoons unsalted butter
1	tablespoon lemon juice

Bring cider, water, sugar, and cinnamon to simmer in small saucepan and cook over medium-high heat until thickened and reduced to 1½ cups, about 15 minutes. Off heat, whisk in butter and lemon juice. Drizzle over dumplings to serve.

WRAPPING DUMPLINGS

1. Fold corners of dough up to enclose apple halves, overlapping and crimping to seal.

2. Arrange dumplings on baking sheet, brush with egg white, and sprinkle with cinnamon sugar.

✓ WHY THIS RECIPE WORKS

Apple fritters should be crisp on the outside, moist within, and sing out apple flavor. Too often, recipes for fritters produce leaden, soggy pastries with undercooked interiors. We found that the best solution was to dry the apples with paper towels and mix them with the dry ingredients. The dry ingredients absorbed the moisture that would otherwise have leached out during frying. As for the batter, we found that replacing the milk with apple cider reinforced the sweet apple flavor. And a quick glaze, spiked with more cider and warm spices and spooned over the warm fritters, added another layer of apple flavor.

Apple Fritters

We like Granny Smith apples in these fritters because they are tart and crisp. Apple juice doesn't have enough flavor—you really do need the cider.

FRITTERS

2	Granny Smith apples, peeled, cored, and cut into ¼-inch pieces
2	cups (10 ounces) all-purpose flour
⅓	cup (2⅓ ounces) granulated sugar
1	tablespoon baking powder
1	teaspoon salt
1	teaspoon ground cinnamon
¼	teaspoon ground nutmeg
¾	cup apple cider
2	large eggs, lightly beaten
2	tablespoons unsalted butter, melted
3	cups peanut or vegetable oil

GLAZE

2	cups (8 ounces) confectioners' sugar
¼	cup apple cider
½	teaspoon ground cinnamon
¼	teaspoon ground nutmeg

1. FOR THE FRITTERS: Spread prepared apples in single layer on paper towel–lined baking sheet and pat thoroughly dry with paper towels. Combine flour, sugar, baking powder, salt, cinnamon, and nutmeg in large bowl. Whisk cider, eggs, and melted butter in medium bowl until combined. Stir apples into flour mixture. Stir in cider mixture until incorporated.

2. Set wire rack in rimmed baking sheet. Heat oil in Dutch oven over medium-high heat to 350 degrees. Use ⅓-cup measure to transfer 5 heaping portions of batter to oil. Press batter lightly with back of spoon to flatten. Fry, adjusting burner as necessary to maintain oil temperature between 325 and 350 degrees, until deep golden brown, 2 to 3 minutes per side. Transfer fritters to prepared wire rack. Bring oil back to 350 degrees and repeat with remaining batter. Let fritters cool for 5 minutes.

3. FOR THE GLAZE: While fritters cool, whisk sugar, cider, cinnamon, and nutmeg in medium bowl until smooth. Top each fritter with 1 heaping tablespoon glaze. Let glaze set for 10 minutes. Serve.

FORMING FRITTERS

1. Use ⅓-cup measure and spoon to carefully and gently portion batter into hot oil.

2. Use spoon to gently press on each fritter. Flattened shape helps interior cook through.

WHY THIS RECIPE WORKS

Although it's hard to imagine that apple crisp needs much improving upon, we liked the tartness and texture that cranberries added to one of our favorite standard dessert recipes. Raw cranberries proved too bitter, but we found dried cranberries and cooked fresh berries made cranberry-apple crisp with the best taste and texture. And we used tapioca to thicken the fruit juices instead of cornstarch or flour.

Cranberry-Apple Crisp

SERVES 8 TO 10

If you can't find Braeburn apples, Golden Delicious will work. Serve with vanilla ice cream or whipped cream.

TOPPING

¾	cup (3¾ ounces) all-purpose flour
½	cup packed (3½ ounces) light brown sugar
½	cup (3½ ounces) granulated sugar
1	teaspoon ground cinnamon
12	tablespoons unsalted butter, cut into ½-inch pieces and chilled
¾	cup (2¼ ounces) old-fashioned rolled oats

FILLING

1	pound (4 cups) fresh or frozen cranberries
1¼	cups (8¾ ounces) granulated sugar
¼	cup water
2½	pounds Granny Smith apples, peeled, cored, halved, and cut into ½-inch pieces
2½	pounds Braeburn apples, peeled, cored, halved, and cut into ½-inch pieces
1	cup dried sweetened cranberries
3	tablespoons instant tapioca

1. FOR THE TOPPING: Adjust oven rack to middle position and heat oven to 400 degrees. Pulse flour, brown sugar, granulated sugar, cinnamon, and butter in food processor until mixture has texture of coarse crumbs (some pea-size pieces of butter will remain), about 12 pulses. Transfer to medium bowl, stir in oats, and use fingers to pinch topping into peanut-size clumps. Refrigerate while preparing filling.

2. FOR THE FILLING: Bring fresh cranberries, ¾ cup sugar, and water to simmer in Dutch oven over medium-high heat and cook until cranberries are completely softened and mixture is jamlike, about 10 minutes. Scrape mixture into bowl. Add apples, remaining ½ cup sugar, and dried cranberries to now-empty Dutch oven and cook over medium-high heat until apples begin to release their juices, about 5 minutes.

3. Off heat, stir cranberry mixture and tapioca into apple mixture. Pour into 13 by 9-inch baking dish set in rimmed baking sheet and smooth surface evenly with spatula.

4. TO ASSEMBLE: Mound topping over filling in center of dish, then use your fingers to rake topping out toward edges of dish and bake until juices are bubbling and topping is deep golden brown, about 30 minutes. (If topping is browning too quickly, loosely cover with piece of aluminum foil.) Let cool on wire rack for 10 minutes. Serve.

TO MAKE AHEAD: After pinching topping into small clumps in step 1, transfer mixture to zipper-lock bag and refrigerate for up to 5 days or freeze for up to 1 month. The cooked filling can be refrigerated for up to 2 days. To bake, sprinkle chilled topping evenly over chilled filling, loosely cover with foil, and bake for 20 minutes. Uncover and bake until juices are bubbling and topping is deep golden brown, 15 to 20 minutes longer.

CRISP ESSENTIALS

1. Cook cranberries, sugar, and water until mixture is thick and jammy.

2. Mound topping in center of dish, then use your fingers to rake topping out toward edges of dish.

WHY THIS RECIPE WORKS

This 19th-century fruit dessert boasts sweetened stewed berries covered with drop biscuit dough that is covered to steam and cook through. We found the idea of a simple stovetop fruit dessert appealing, but standard recipes produced washed-out fruit and a soggy topping. To improve the recipe, we cooked down half of the berries until jammy, and then stirred in the remaining berries. A bit of cornstarch further thickened the filling. For a fluffy biscuit topping, we placed a dish towel under the lid during cooking to absorb condensation. A sprinkle of cinnamon sugar over the finished dessert provided sweet crunch.

Maine Blueberry Grunt

Do not use frozen blueberries here, as they will make the filling watery. You will need a clean dish towel for this recipe.

FILLING

2½	pounds (8 cups) blueberries
½	cup (3½ ounces) sugar
½	teaspoon ground cinnamon
2	tablespoons water
1	teaspoon grated lemon zest plus 1 tablespoon juice
1	teaspoon cornstarch

TOPPING

¾	cup buttermilk
6	tablespoons unsalted butter, melted and cooled slightly
1	teaspoon vanilla extract
2¼	cups (11¼ ounces) all-purpose flour
1½	teaspoons baking powder
½	teaspoon baking soda
½	teaspoon salt
½	cup (3½ ounces) sugar
½	teaspoon ground cinnamon

1. FOR THE FILLING: Cook 4 cups blueberries, sugar, cinnamon, water, and lemon zest in Dutch oven over medium-high heat, stirring occasionally, until mixture is thick and jamlike, 10 to 12 minutes. Whisk lemon juice and cornstarch in small bowl, then stir into blueberry mixture. Add remaining 4 cups blueberries and cook until heated through, about 1 minute; remove pot from heat, cover, and keep warm.

2. FOR THE TOPPING: Combine buttermilk, butter, and vanilla in 2-cup liquid measuring cup. Whisk flour, baking powder, baking soda, salt, and 6 tablespoons sugar in large bowl. Slowly stir buttermilk mixture into flour mixture until dough forms.

3. Using small ice cream scoop or 2 large spoons, spoon golf ball–size dough pieces on top of warm berry mixture (you should have 14 pieces). Wrap lid of Dutch oven with clean dish towel (keeping towel away from heat source) and cover pot. Simmer gently until biscuits have doubled in size and toothpick inserted in center comes out clean, 16 to 22 minutes.

4. Combine remaining 2 tablespoons sugar and cinnamon in small bowl. Remove lid and sprinkle biscuit topping with cinnamon sugar. Serve immediately.

SECRETS TO GREAT GRUNT

1. Use small ice cream scoop to drop evenly sized balls of biscuit dough over warm filling.

2. A clean dish towel beneath lid absorbs condensation during cooking, keeping biscuit topping light and fluffy.

3. A sprinkling of cinnamon sugar adds crunchy contrast to steamed biscuits.

✔ WHY THIS RECIPE WORKS

We wanted a peach cobbler that avoided a watery filling and soggy topping. To do this, we turned to a skillet and concentrated the peach flavor by first sautéing the peaches in butter and sugar to release their juices, then cooking them down until all the liquid had evaporated. To keep the filling from being too mushy, we withheld some of the peaches from sautéing, adding them just before baking. We also made the biscuits sturdy enough to stand up to the fruit by mixing melted butter rather than cold butter into the dry ingredients.

Skillet Peach Cobbler

SERVES 6 TO 8

Four pounds of frozen sliced peaches can be substituted for fresh; there is no need to defrost them. Start step 2 when the peaches are almost done.

FILLING

4	tablespoons unsalted butter
5	pounds peaches, peeled, halved, pitted, and cut into ½-inch wedges
6	tablespoons (2⅔ ounces) sugar
⅛	teaspoon salt
1	tablespoon lemon juice
1½	teaspoons cornstarch

TOPPING

1½	cups (7½ ounces) all-purpose flour
6	tablespoons (2⅔ ounces) sugar
1½	teaspoons baking powder
¼	teaspoon baking soda
¼	teaspoon salt
¾	cup buttermilk
4	tablespoons unsalted butter, melted and cooled
1	teaspoon ground cinnamon

1. FOR THE FILLING: Adjust oven rack to middle position and heat oven to 425 degrees. Melt butter in 12-inch ovensafe nonstick skillet over medium-high heat. Add two-thirds of peaches, sugar, and salt and cook, covered, until peaches release their juices, about 5 minutes. Remove lid and simmer until all liquid has evaporated and peaches begin to caramelize, 15 to 20 minutes. Add remaining peaches and cook until heated through, about 5 minutes. Whisk lemon juice and cornstarch in small bowl, then stir into peach mixture. Cover skillet and set aside off heat.

2. FOR THE TOPPING: Meanwhile, whisk flour, 5 tablespoons sugar, baking powder, baking soda, and salt in medium bowl. Stir in buttermilk and butter until dough forms. Turn dough out onto lightly floured work surface and knead briefly until smooth, about 30 seconds.

3. Combine remaining 1 tablespoon sugar and cinnamon. Break dough into rough 1-inch pieces and space them about ½ inch apart on top of hot peach mixture. Sprinkle with cinnamon sugar and bake until topping is golden brown and filling is thickened, 18 to 22 minutes. Let cool on wire rack for 10 minutes. Serve.

PEELING PEACHES

1. With paring knife, score small X at base of each peach.

2. Lower peaches into boiling water and simmer until skins loosen, 30 to 60 seconds.

3. Transfer peaches immediately to ice water and let cool for about 1 minute.

4. Use paring knife to remove strips of loosened peel, starting at X on base of each peach.

WHY THIS RECIPE WORKS

Kuchen, the official state dessert of South Dakota, features a tender yeasted dough, peaches full of flavor, and a layer of smooth, delicately sweet custard. We created a buttery crust by slowly adding softened butter to the dough, letting the dough rise and then rest in the fridge. An extra egg yolk made our custard thick and rich, without the eggy flavor found in egg whites. Finally, to ready the peaches, we sprinkled them with sugar and let them sit in a colander to pull out their excess juice and prevent the kuchen from becoming soggy. This dessert might come from South Dakota, but it felt right at home in our kitchen.

Dakota Peach Kuchen

MAKES TWO 9-INCH KUCHENS

The dough will need 2 hours to rise plus 1 hour to chill in the refrigerator. We developed this recipe using dark cake pans; if your pans are light, increase the baking time in step 7 to 55 to 60 minutes.

CRUST

½	cup whole milk
2	large eggs
2½	cups (12½ ounces) all-purpose flour
1	tablespoon sugar
2	teaspoons instant or rapid-rise yeast
½	teaspoon salt
8	tablespoons unsalted butter, cut into 8 pieces and softened

FRUIT AND CUSTARD

1	pound fresh peaches, peeled, halved, pitted, and cut into ½-inch wedges or 12 ounces frozen sliced peaches, thawed
2	tablespoons plus ¾ cup (5¼ ounces) sugar
1	large egg plus 1 large yolk
¼	teaspoon salt
1¼	cups heavy cream
4	tablespoons unsalted butter, cut into 4 pieces
½	teaspoon vanilla extract
¼	teaspoon ground cinnamon

1. FOR THE CRUST: Grease large bowl. Whisk milk and eggs in 2-cup liquid measuring cup until combined. Using stand mixer fitted with dough hook, mix flour, sugar, yeast, and salt on medium-low speed until combined, about 5 seconds. With mixer running, slowly add milk mixture and knead until dough forms, about 1 minute.

2. With mixer still running, add butter 1 piece at a time until incorporated. Continue kneading until dough clears sides of bowl but still sticks to bottom, 8 to 12 minutes (dough should be soft and sticky).

3. Transfer dough to greased bowl, cover with plastic wrap, and let rise on counter until doubled in size, about 1 hour. Punch down dough and divide into 2 equal balls. Wrap each ball in plastic, transfer to refrigerator, and let rest for at least 1 hour or up to 24 hours.

4. Grease 2 dark-colored 9-inch round cake pans. Roll each chilled dough balls into a 9-inch disk on lightly floured counter. Transfer to prepared pans, pushing dough to edges of pans. Cover pans loosely with plastic and let rise on counter until puffy, about 1 hour. Adjust oven rack to middle position and heat oven to 350 degrees.

5. FOR THE FRUIT AND CUSTARD: Meanwhile, toss peaches with 2 tablespoons sugar in bowl, then transfer to colander set in sink; let sit for 25 minutes. Whisk remaining ¾ cup sugar, egg and yolk, and salt in medium bowl until combined. Heat cream in medium saucepan over medium heat until just beginning to simmer.

6. Slowly whisk hot cream into egg mixture. Transfer cream mixture back to saucepan and cook over medium-low heat, stirring constantly, until mixture thickens and coats back of spoon, 3 to 5 minutes. Strain custard through fine-mesh strainer set over medium bowl. Whisk in butter and vanilla and transfer to refrigerator to cool until dough is ready. (Custard can be made up to 24 hours in advance but does not need to be fully chilled before going into crust.)

7. Leaving 1-inch border all around, press down centers of doughs with bottom of dry measuring cup to deflate and create wells for peaches and custard. Arrange peaches, evenly spaced, in circular pattern in depressed dough bottoms, avoiding border. Pour custard evenly over peaches in each pan, about 1 cup per pan (you may have a few tablespoons extra). Sprinkle with cinnamon. Bake until crusts are golden brown and centers jiggle slightly when shaken, 35 to 40 minutes, switching and rotating pans halfway through baking. Let cool completely. Remove kuchens from pans using flexible spatula. Slice and serve.

WHY THIS RECIPE WORKS

We wanted our banana pudding to be rich and creamy, so we opted for half-and-half instead of milk in the pudding component. Roasting the bananas intensified their flavor and helped break them down so we could incorporate them more easily into the pudding. Adding a squeeze of lemon juice to the roasted bananas prevented them from browning in the refrigerator. Even whole cookies became sodden and pasty when layered with hot pudding. We solved the problem by simply waiting for the pudding to cool a little before assembling the dessert.

Banana Pudding

SERVES 12

If your food processor bowl holds less than 11 cups, puree half the pudding with the roasted bananas and lemon juice in step 3, transfer it to a large bowl, and whisk in the rest of the pudding.

PUDDING

7	slightly underripe large bananas (2½ pounds), unpeeled
1½	cups (10½ ounces) sugar
8	large egg yolks
6	tablespoons cornstarch
6	cups half-and-half
½	teaspoon salt
3	tablespoons unsalted butter
1	tablespoon vanilla extract
3	tablespoons lemon juice
1	(12-ounce) box vanilla wafers

WHIPPED TOPPING

1	cup heavy cream, chilled
1	tablespoon sugar
½	teaspoon vanilla extract

1. FOR THE PUDDING: Adjust oven rack to upper-middle position and heat oven to 325 degrees. Place 3 unpeeled bananas on baking sheet and bake until skins are completely black, about 20 minutes. Let cool for 5 minutes.

2. Meanwhile, whisk ½ cup sugar, egg yolks, and cornstarch in medium bowl until smooth. Bring half-and-half, remaining 1 cup sugar, and salt to simmer over medium heat in large saucepan. Whisk ½ cup simmering half-and-half mixture into egg yolk mixture to temper. Slowly whisk tempered yolk mixture into saucepan. Cook, whisking constantly, until mixture is thick and large bubbles appear at surface, about 2 minutes. Remove from heat and stir in butter and vanilla.

3. Transfer pudding to food processor. Add warm peeled roasted bananas and 2 tablespoons lemon juice and process until smooth. Scrape into large bowl and place plastic wrap directly on surface of pudding. Refrigerate until slightly cool, about 45 minutes.

4. Peel and cut remaining bananas into ¼-inch slices and toss in bowl with remaining 1 tablespoon lemon juice. Spoon one-quarter of pudding into 3-quart trifle dish and top with layer of cookies, layer of sliced bananas, and another layer of cookies. Repeat twice, ending with pudding. Place plastic wrap directly on surface of pudding and refrigerate until wafers have softened, at least 8 hours or up to 2 days.

5. FOR THE WHIPPED TOPPING: Using stand mixer fitted with whisk, whip cream, sugar, and vanilla on medium-low speed until foamy, about 1 minute. Increase speed to high and whip until stiff peaks form, 1 to 3 minutes. (Whipped cream can be refrigerated for 4 hours.) Top banana pudding with whipped cream. Serve.

TOASTED COCONUT BANANA PUDDING

Replace 2 cups half-and-half with one 16-ounce can unsweetened coconut milk in step 2. Sprinkle ¼ cup toasted sweetened shredded coconut over whipped cream–topped pudding before serving.

PEANUT-Y BANANA PUDDING

In step 4, sandwich 2 vanilla wafers around 1 banana slice and ½ teaspoon creamy peanut butter (you'll need ½ cup total). Assemble by alternating layers of pudding and cookie-banana sandwiches, ending with pudding. Sprinkle ¼ cup chopped salted dry-roasted peanuts over whipped cream–topped pudding before serving.

✓ WHY THIS RECIPE WORKS

The best bourbon bread pudding is a rich, "scoopable" custard that envelops the bread with a balance of sweet spiciness and robust bourbon flavor. Tearing a crusty baguette into ragged pieces, then toasting them, gave the pudding a rustic look and kept the bread from turning soggy in the custard. We used a mixture of 3 parts cream to 1 part milk and replaced the whole eggs with yolks for a rich, creamy custard that didn't curdle. Once the custard set up in the oven, we sprinkled cinnamon, sugar, and butter on top and let it bake until the topping was caramelized.

New Orleans Bourbon Bread Pudding

SERVES 8 TO 10

This bread pudding is great on its own, but for a little more punch, drizzle Bourbon Sauce over individual servings. A bakery-quality French baguette makes this dish even better.

1   **(18- to 20-inch) baguette, torn into 1-inch pieces (10 cups)**
1   **cup golden raisins**
¾   **cup bourbon**
6   **tablespoons unsalted butter, cut into 6 pieces and chilled, plus extra for baking dish**
8   **large egg yolks**
1½   **cups packed (10½ ounces) light brown sugar**
3   **cups heavy cream**
1   **cup whole milk**
1   **tablespoon vanilla extract**
1½   **teaspoons ground cinnamon**
¼   **teaspoon nutmeg**
¼   **teaspoon salt**
3   **tablespoons granulated sugar**

1. Adjust oven rack to middle position and heat oven to 450 degrees. Arrange bread in single layer on baking sheet and bake until crisp and browned, about 12 minutes, turning pieces over and switching baking sheets halfway through baking. Let bread cool. Reduce oven temperature to 300 degrees.

2. Meanwhile, heat raisins with ½ cup bourbon in small saucepan over medium-high heat until bourbon begins to simmer, 2 to 3 minutes. Strain mixture, reserving bourbon and raisins separately.

3. Butter 13 by 9-inch broiler-safe baking dish. Whisk egg yolks, brown sugar, cream, milk, vanilla, 1 teaspoon cinnamon, nutmeg, and salt together in large bowl. Whisk in reserved bourbon plus remaining ¼ cup bourbon. Add toasted bread and toss until evenly coated. Let mixture sit until bread begins to absorb custard, about 30 minutes, tossing occasionally. If majority of bread is still hard, continue to soak for 15 to 20 minutes.

4. Pour half of bread mixture into prepared baking dish and sprinkle with half of raisins. Pour remaining bread mixture into dish and sprinkle with remaining raisins. Cover with aluminum foil and bake for 45 minutes.

5. Meanwhile, mix granulated sugar and remaining ½ teaspoon cinnamon in small bowl. Using your fingers, cut 6 tablespoons butter into sugar mixture until size of small peas. Remove foil from pudding, sprinkle with butter mixture, and bake, uncovered, until custard is just set, 20 to 25 minutes. Remove pudding from oven and heat broiler.

6. Once broiler is heated, broil pudding until top forms golden crust, about 2 minutes. Transfer to wire rack and cool at least 30 minutes or up to 2 hours. Serve.

BOURBON SAUCE
MAKES ABOUT 1 CUP

1½   **teaspoons cornstarch**
¼   **cup bourbon**
¾   **cup heavy cream**
2   **tablespoons sugar**
   Pinch salt
2   **teaspoons unsalted butter, cut into 8 pieces**

Whisk cornstarch and 2 tablespoons bourbon in small bowl until well combined. Heat cream and sugar in small saucepan over medium heat until sugar dissolves. Whisk in cornstarch mixture and bring to boil. Reduce heat to low and cook until sauce thickens, 3 to 5 minutes. Off heat, stir in salt, butter, and remaining 2 tablespoons bourbon. Drizzle warm sauce over individual servings. (Sauce can be refrigerated for up to 5 days.)

✔ WHY THIS RECIPE WORKS

Although our initial tests of this traditional British "pudding" were fairly disastrous, we knew that good bread and fresh summer berries could make a delicious dessert. The rectangular shape of a loaf pan proved a more stable mold than traditional round bowls. We staled challah bread (our top choice for its flavor and texture) in the oven for added support. Since the moisture content of fresh berries can vary, we strained the juice from the filling and dipped the bread in it ourselves. Cooking only half of the berries and mixing the rest in later brightened the filling, and apricot preserves and gelatin helped the pudding keep its shape.

Summer Berry Pudding

SERVES 6

Fill in any gaps in pudding crusts with toast trimmings.

8	(¼-inch-thick) slices challah, crusts removed
12	ounces strawberries, hulled and chopped (2 cups)
8	ounces blackberries, halved (1½ cups)
8	ounces (1½ cups) blueberries
5	ounces (1 cup) raspberries
½	cup (3½ ounces) granulated sugar
1	teaspoon unflavored gelatin
2	tablespoons cold water
½	cup (5½ ounces) apricot preserves
1	cup heavy cream, chilled
1	tablespoon confectioners' sugar

1. Adjust oven rack to middle position and heat oven to 350 degrees. Line 8½ by 4½-inch loaf pan with plastic wrap, pushing plastic into corners and up sides of pan and allowing excess to overhang long sides. Make cardboard cutout just large enough to fit inside pan.

2. Place challah on wire rack set in rimmed baking sheet. Bake until dry, about 10 minutes, flipping challah and rotating sheet halfway through baking. Let challah cool completely.

3. Combine strawberries, blackberries, blueberries, and raspberries in bowl. Transfer half of mixture to medium saucepan, add granulated sugar, and bring to simmer over medium-low heat, stirring occasionally. Reduce heat to low and continue to cook until berries release their juices and raspberries begin to break down, about 5 minutes. Off heat, stir in remaining berries. After 2 minutes, strain berries through fine-mesh strainer set over medium bowl for 10 minutes, stirring berries once halfway through straining (do not press on berries). Reserve berry juice. (You should have ¾ to 1 cup.)

4. Sprinkle gelatin over water in bowl and let sit until gelatin softens, about 5 minutes. Microwave until mixture is bubbling around edges and gelatin dissolves, about 30 seconds. Whisk preserves and gelatin mixture together in large bowl. Fold in strained berries.

5. Trim 4 slices of challah to fit snugly side by side in bottom of loaf pan (you may have extra challah). Dip slices in reserved berry juice until saturated, about 30 seconds per side, then place in bottom of pan. Spoon berry mixture over challah. Trim remaining 4 slices of challah to fit snugly side by side on top of berries (you may have extra challah). Dip slices in reserved berry juice until saturated, about 30 seconds per side, then place on top of berries. Cover pan loosely with plastic and place in 13 by 9-inch baking dish. Place cardboard cutout on top of pudding. Top with 3 soup cans to weigh down pudding. Refrigerate pudding for at least 8 hours or up to 24 hours.

6. Using stand mixer fitted with whisk, whip cream and confectioners' sugar on medium-low speed until foamy, about 1 minute. Increase speed to high and whip until soft peaks form, 1 to 3 minutes. Transfer to serving bowl. Remove cans, cardboard, and plastic from top of pudding. Loosen pudding by pulling up on edges of plastic. Place inverted platter over top of loaf pan and flip platter and pan upside down to unmold pudding. Discard plastic. Slice pudding with serrated knife and serve with whipped cream.

CONSTRUCTING SUMMER BERRY PUDDING

1. Saturate dried, trimmed challah with reserved berry juices and place in bottom of plastic wrap–lined pan.

2. Spoon sweetened four-berry mixture over challah, and top with four more slices of saturated challah.

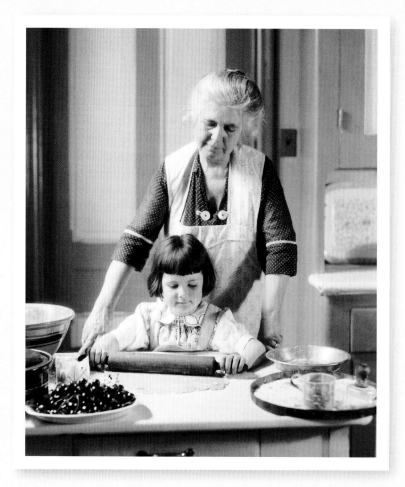

SAVE ROOM FOR PIE

ENGLISH SETTLERS WERE THE FIRST TO BRING THEIR LOVE OF PIES TO U.S. soil. The English had long enjoyed savory, meat-filled pies and on occasion, fruit pies. When faced with the abundance of berries and other fruit on American soil, settlers naturally filled their pies with what was on hand, such as pumpkin and cranberries. Over the years regional specialties began to develop.

HEARTY THANKSGIVING GREETINGS.

American pies like pecan pie were originally made with sorghum or maple syrup. In Texas, where everything is big, apple slab pie was created to feed a crowd. Shaker lemon pie was borne of the Shakers' frugal insistence on using every bit of the fruit: peel, pith, and all, and Key lime pie relies on Florida's plethora of Key limes—though we found that regular limes work just fine (and you don't have to juice as many!).

Early pie crusts were not the tender, flaky pastry we know today. In fact, English pies were called "coffers" or "coffins," as in "box," and the crust was a sturdy paste which served as a lid to keep the ingredients juicy and prevent scorching—it was not eaten. Luckily, times have changed. In this chapter, we offer not just traditional pastry dough, made with a combination of

butter and vegetable shortening for great flavor and tender, flaky texture, but a second variety of pie dough, which boasts the tang of cream cheese and requires no rolling—you simply pat the dough into a pie plate. We call it No-Fear Single-Crust Pie Dough. Now there's no excuse for you not to bake a fresh, homemade pie during the holidays or at any other time of year.

Double-Crust Pie Dough

MAKES ENOUGH FOR ONE 9-INCH PIE

2½	cups (12½ ounces) all-purpose flour
2	tablespoons sugar
1	teaspoon salt
8	tablespoons vegetable shortening, cut into ¼-inch pieces and chilled
12	tablespoons unsalted butter, cut into ¼-inch pieces and chilled
6–8	tablespoons ice water

1. Process flour, sugar, and salt in food processor until combined, about 5 seconds. Scatter shortening over top and process until mixture resembles coarse cornmeal, about 10 seconds. Scatter butter over top and pulse until mixture resembles coarse crumbs, about 10 pulses. Transfer to bowl.

2. Sprinkle 6 tablespoons water over flour mixture. Using rubber spatula, stir and press dough until it sticks together. If dough does not come together, stir in remaining water, 1 tablespoon at a time, until it does.

3. Divide dough into 2 even pieces and flatten each into 4-inch disk. Wrap disks tightly in plastic wrap and refrigerate for 1 hour. Let chilled dough soften slightly on counter before rolling.

Classic Single-Crust Pie Dough

MAKES ENOUGH FOR ONE 9-INCH PIE

1¼	cups (6¼ ounces) all-purpose flour
1	tablespoon sugar
½	teaspoon salt
4	tablespoons vegetable shortening, cut into ¼-inch pieces and chilled
6	tablespoons unsalted butter, cut into ¼-inch pieces and chilled
3–4	tablespoons ice water

1. Process flour, sugar, and salt in food processor until combined, about 5 seconds. Scatter shortening over top and process until mixture resembles coarse cornmeal, about 10 seconds. Scatter butter over top and pulse until mixture resembles coarse crumbs, about 10 pulses. Transfer to bowl.

2. Sprinkle 3 tablespoons water over flour mixture. Using rubber spatula, stir and press dough until it sticks together. If dough does not come together, add remaining 1 tablespoon water. Flatten dough into 4-inch disk, wrap tightly in plastic wrap, and refrigerate for 1 hour.

3. Let chilled dough soften slightly. Lightly flour counter, then roll dough into 12-inch circle and fit it into 9-inch pie plate. Trim, fold, and crimp edges of dough. Wrap dough-lined pie plate in plastic and place in freezer until dough is fully chilled and firm, about 30 minutes, before using.

ROLLING AND FITTING PIE DOUGH

1. Roll dough outward from its center into 12-inch circle. Between every few rolls, give dough quarter turn.

2. Toss additional flour underneath dough as needed to keep dough from sticking to counter.

3. Loosely roll dough around rolling pin, then gently unroll it over pie plate.

4. Lift dough and gently press it into pie plate, letting excess hang over plate.

No-Fear Single-Crust Pie Dough

MAKES ENOUGH FOR ONE 9-INCH PIE

Anyone can make this pat-in-the-pan pie dough—no rolling or transferring of dough to the dish required. Cream cheese helps make this dough easy to handle and helps ensure a tender crust. Make sure you press the dough evenly into a glass pie plate; if you hold the dough-lined plate up to the light, you will be able to clearly see any thick or thin spots.

    1¼   **cups (6¼ ounces) all-purpose flour**
    2   **tablespoons sugar**
    ¼   **teaspoon salt**
    8   **tablespoons unsalted butter, softened but still cool**
    2   **ounces cream cheese, softened but still cool**

1. Lightly coat 9-inch Pyrex pie plate with vegetable oil spray. Whisk flour, sugar, and salt together in bowl.

2. Using stand mixer fitted with paddle, beat butter and cream cheese on medium-high speed until completely homogeneous, about 2 minutes, stopping once or twice to scrape down beater and sides of bowl. Add flour mixture and mix on medium-low speed until mixture resembles coarse cornmeal, about 20 seconds. Scrape down sides of bowl. Increase mixer speed to medium-high and beat until dough begins to form large clumps, about 30 seconds. Reserve 3 tablespoons of dough. Turn remaining dough onto lightly floured counter, gather into ball, and flatten into 6-inch disk. Transfer disk to greased pie plate.

3. Press dough evenly over bottom of pie plate toward sides, using heel of your hand. Hold plate up to light to ensure that dough is evenly distributed. With your fingertips, continue to work dough over bottom of plate and up sides until evenly distributed.

4. On floured counter, roll reserved dough into 12-inch rope. Divide into 3 pieces and roll each piece into 8-inch rope. Arrange ropes, evenly spaced, around top of pie plate, pressing and squeezing to join them with dough in plate and form uniform edge. Use your fingers to flute edge of dough. Wrap dough-lined pie plate in plastic wrap and place in freezer until dough is fully chilled and firm, about 30 minutes, before using.

NO-FEAR PIE DOUGH

1. Hold pie plate up to light to check thickness of dough; it should be translucent, not opaque. Pay attention to curved edges.

2. Roll reserved dough into three 8-inch ropes. Arrange ropes around perimeter of pie plate, leaving small (about 1-inch) gaps between them.

3. Squeeze ropes together.

4. Create a fluted edge, dipping your fingers in flour if dough is sticky.

✔ WHY THIS RECIPE WORKS

Most Shaker lemon pie recipes mix lemon slices—peel and all—with sugar and eggs to form a custardy filling. But unless we macerated the lemon slices for 24 hours, the pie turned out bitter. We wanted to speed up this recipe for modern times. First, we squeezed the seeded lemon slices and reserved the juice for the filling. Then, we simmered the slices and then added them to the filling with the uncooked juice for bright lemon flavor without any macerating time.

Shaker Lemon Pie

SERVES 8

Have an extra lemon on hand in case the three sliced lemons do not yield enough juice. See page 454 for more information on rolling and fitting pie dough.

1	recipe Double-Crust Pie Dough (page 454)
3	large lemons, sliced thin and seeded
1¾	cups (12¼ ounces) sugar
⅛	teaspoon salt
1	tablespoon cornstarch
4	large eggs
1	tablespoon heavy cream

1. Roll 1 disk of dough into 12-inch circle on lightly floured counter, then fit it into 9-inch pie plate, letting excess dough hang over edge; cover with plastic wrap and refrigerate for 30 minutes. Roll other disk of dough into 12-inch circle on lightly floured counter, then transfer to parchment paper–lined baking sheet; cover with plastic and refrigerate for 30 minutes.

2. Adjust oven rack to lowest position and heat oven to 425 degrees. Squeeze lemon slices in fine-mesh strainer set over bowl; reserve juice (you should have 6 tablespoons). Bring drained slices and 2 cups water to boil in saucepan, then reduce heat to medium-low and simmer until slices are softened, about 5 minutes. Drain well and discard liquid. Combine softened lemon slices, sugar, salt, and ¼ cup reserved lemon juice in bowl; stir until sugar dissolves.

3. Whisk cornstarch and remaining 2 tablespoons lemon juice in large bowl. Whisk eggs into cornstarch mixture, then slowly stir in lemon slice mixture until combined. Pour into chilled pie shell. Brush edges of dough with 1 teaspoon cream. Loosely roll second piece of dough around rolling pin then gently unroll it over pie. Trim, fold, and crimp edges, and cut 4 vent holes in top. Brush top with remaining 2 teaspoons cream.

4. Bake until light golden, about 20 minutes, then decrease oven temperature to 375 degrees and continue to bake until golden brown, 20 to 25 minutes. Let pie cool on wire rack for at least 1 hour. Serve. (Pie can be refrigerated for 2 days.)

BUILDING BOLD, NOT BITTER, LEMON FLAVOR

Using sliced whole lemons, pith and all, can produce an overwhelmingly bitter filling. We found a few tricks to create bright lemon flavor while tempering the bitterness of the pith.

1. Squeeze seeded lemon slices and reserve juice for filling.

2. Simmer slices to mellow bitterness of pith and then add them to filling with uncooked juice.

THE SLICE IS RIGHT

While developing our recipe for Shaker Lemon Pie, we found that using a knife to evenly cut the lemons into paper-thin slices was a difficult and time-consuming task. We had better results with a mandoline (or V-slicer), which produced perfectly thin slices in no time at all. If you don't have a mandoline, we did find another piece of kitchen equipment that will make the process easier—the freezer. Popping the lemons into the freezer for about 30 minutes firms them up for better hand slicing, which is best accomplished with a serrated knife.

SHAKER COOKING

The Shakers' food was never ornate and was always healthy and hearty enough to support their industrious, hard-working lifestyle. Shakers scrubbed—rather than peeled—their vegetables (and, in the case of Shaker Lemon Pie, their citrus fruit) to minimize waste. They were also pioneers in using exact measurements in cooking at a time when many recipes called for a "dash," "glob," or "handful" of something.

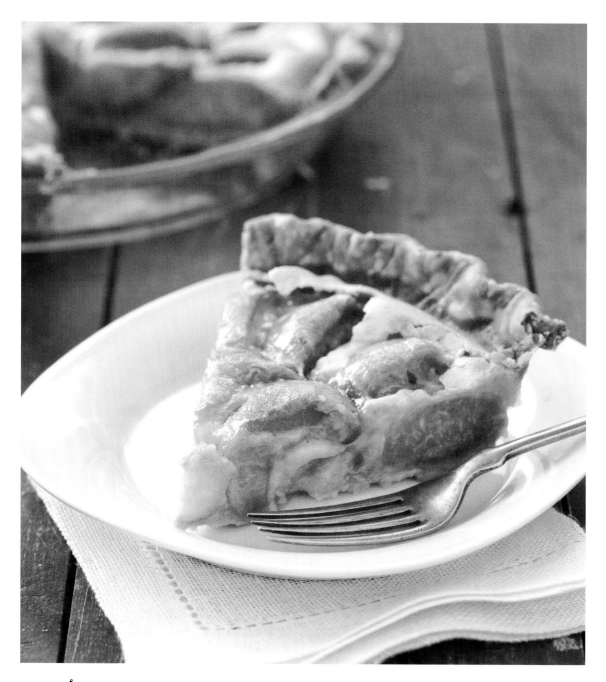

WHY THIS RECIPE WORKS

Old-fashioned recipes for this pie call for simply arranging peaches in a pie crust, dousing them with fresh cream, and baking. But today's commercial cream gave us a milky, lumpy, and bland puddle rather than a rich filling. To thicken the cream, we whisked in a little flour and two eggs yolks. But the juicy peaches wreaked watery havoc on our custardy pie filling. Roasting them in the oven evaporated their excess liquid, and a dusting of sugar encouraged caramelizing for even more flavor. Prebaking the crust ensured it would stay crisp and flaky after the roasted fruit and filling were added.

Peaches and Cream Pie

SERVES 8

Keep an eye on the peaches at the end of their baking time to ensure that they don't scorch. You can use Classic Single-Crust Pie Dough (page 454) or No-Fear Single-Crust Pie Dough (page 455) for this pie.

1   recipe single-crust pie dough, fitted into 9-inch pie plate and chilled
2   pounds ripe but firm peaches, peeled, halved, and pitted
2   tablespoons plus ½ cup (4⅓ ounces) sugar
3   tablespoons all-purpose flour
¼   teaspoon salt
⅓   cup heavy cream
2   large egg yolks
½   teaspoon vanilla extract

1. Adjust oven racks to upper-middle and lower-middle positions and heat oven to 375 degrees. Line chilled crust with double layer of aluminum foil and fill with pie weights.

2. Place peach halves cut side up on foil-lined rimmed baking sheet and sprinkle with 2 tablespoons sugar. Bake peaches on upper-middle rack until softened and juice is released, about 30 minutes, flipping halfway through baking.

3. After 30 minutes, place crust on lower-middle rack and, while peaches continue to roast, bake until edges are lightly browned, about 15 minutes. Remove crust from oven and carefully remove foil and weights. Continue to bake until bottom of crust is light golden brown and peaches are caramelized, about 5 minutes longer. Cool crust and peaches for 15 minutes.

4. Reduce oven temperature to 325 degrees. Cut peach halves lengthwise into quarters. Arrange peaches in single layer over crust. Combine remaining ½ cup sugar, flour, and salt in bowl. Whisk in cream, egg yolks, and vanilla until smooth. Pour cream mixture over peaches. Bake until filling is light golden brown and firm in center, 45 to 55 minutes. Cool pie on wire rack for at least 3 hours. Serve.

TWICE-BAKED PEACHES

Eat a peach out of hand, and its juiciness is no small part of what makes it so good. But cook the fruit, and that same high water content can ruin peach pie, especially when coupled with cream. To evaporate the peach juices and concentrate the peach flavor, we roasted the fruit before filling the pie. A sprinkle of sugar helps the peach halves caramelize. Plus, to save time, while you're roasting the fruit on one rack of the oven, you can prebake the crust on another.

BLIND BAKING A PIE CRUST

The crusts for many pies and tarts are baked before filling (this is called blind baking) so that they stay golden brown, crisp, and flaky once filled.

1. Line chilled pie crust with double layer of aluminum foil, covering edges to prevent burning.

2. Fill crust with pie weights or pennies and bake until lightly browned, about 15 minutes.

3. Remove pie weights and foil and continue to bake until light golden brown, about 5 minutes longer.

✓ WHY THIS RECIPE WORKS

Apple pie and cheddar cheese share a history, and we wanted to incorporate this sweet-savory pairing into a single recipe. For a flaky crust infused with cheesy flavor, extra-sharp cheddar and a teaspoon of dry mustard amped up the crust's savory qualities. Traditional apple filling got a kick from some cayenne, and precooking the filling allowed us to cram in twice as many apples. Starting with a hotter oven browned the bottom crust, and then reducing the heat kept the top from burning. The result: a moist, sweet-tart filling that perfectly complemented our flaky, cheesy crust.

Apple Pie with Cheddar Crust

SERVES 8

For the best flavor, be sure to use extra-sharp cheddar here. Freezing the butter for 15 minutes promotes flakiness in the crust—do not skip this step.

CRUST

2½	cups (12½ ounces) all-purpose flour
1	tablespoon granulated sugar
1	teaspoon salt
1	teaspoon dry mustard
⅛	teaspoon cayenne pepper
8	ounces extra-sharp cheddar cheese, shredded (2 cups)
8	tablespoons unsalted butter, cut into ¼-inch pieces and frozen for 15 minutes
⅓	cup ice water, plus extra as needed

FILLING

2	pounds Granny Smith, Empire, or Cortland apples, peeled, cored, halved, and sliced ¼-inch thick
2	pounds Golden Delicious, Jonagold, or Braeburn apples, peeled, cored, halved, and sliced ¼-inch thick
6	tablespoons (2⅔ ounces) granulated sugar
¼	cup packed (1¾ ounces) light brown sugar
½	teaspoon grated lemon zest plus 1 tablespoon juice
¼	teaspoon salt
⅛	teaspoon ground cinnamon

1. FOR THE CRUST: Process flour, sugar, salt, mustard, and cayenne in food processor until combined, about 5 seconds. Scatter cheddar and butter over top and pulse until butter is size of large peas, about 10 pulses.

2. Pour half of ice water over flour mixture and pulse until incorporated, about 3 pulses. Repeat with remaining ice water. Pinch dough with your fingers; if dough feels dry and does not hold together, sprinkle 1 to 2 tablespoons extra ice water over mixture and pulse until dough forms large clumps and no dry flour remains, 3 to 5 pulses.

3. Divide dough in half and form each half into 4-inch disk. Wrap disks tightly in plastic wrap and refrigerate for 1 hour. Let chilled dough sit on counter to soften slightly, about 10 minutes, before rolling. (Wrapped dough can be refrigerated for up to 2 days or frozen for up to 1 month. If frozen, let dough thaw completely on counter before rolling.)

4. FOR THE FILLING: Stir apples, granulated sugar, brown sugar, lemon zest, salt, and cinnamon together in Dutch oven. Cover and cook over medium heat, stirring frequently, until apples are just tender but still hold their shape, 10 to 15 minutes. Off heat, stir in lemon juice. Spread apple mixture on rimmed baking sheet and let cool completely, about 30 minutes. (Filling can be refrigerated for up to 24 hours.)

5. Roll 1 disk of dough into 12-inch circle between 2 sheets of parchment paper or plastic. Loosely roll dough around rolling pin and gently unroll it onto 9-inch pie plate, letting excess dough hang over edge. Ease dough into plate by gently lifting edge of dough with your hand while pressing into plate bottom with your other hand. Trim overhang to ½ inch beyond lip of pie plate. Wrap dough-lined pie plate loosely in plastic and refrigerate until dough is firm, about 15 minutes.

6. Adjust oven rack to lowest position and heat oven to 425 degrees. Fill pie shell with apple mixture. Roll other disk of dough into 12-inch circle between 2 sheets of parchment or plastic. Loosely roll dough around rolling pin and gently unroll it onto filling.

7. Trim overhang to ½ inch beyond lip of pie plate. Pinch edges of top and bottom crusts firmly together. Tuck overhang under itself; folded edge should be flush with edge of pie plate. Crimp dough around edge of pie plate using your fingers. Cut four 2-inch slits in top of dough.

8. Set pie on foil or parchment-lined baking sheet and bake for 20 minutes. Reduce oven temperature to 375 degrees and continue to bake until crust is deep golden brown and filling is bubbling, 35 to 45 minutes. Transfer pie to wire rack and let cool for at least 1½ hours. Serve.

WHY THIS RECIPE WORKS

Unlike a traditional apple pie, a slab pie is prepared in a baking sheet and can feed up to 20 people. Its filling is thickened to ensure neat slicing, and its crust is topped with a sugary glaze. But rolling out the dough for this mammoth pie proved problematic, as did making the filling thick enough to hold up to slicing. Gluing two sturdy store-bought crusts together with water and then rolling the dough into a large rectangle allowed us to get the crust into the large pan without a tear. To give the crust a sweet, buttery flavor, we rolled it in crushed animal crackers. Tapioca thickened the filling well without making it starchy.

Apple Slab Pie

SERVES 18 TO 20

We prefer an 18 by 13-inch nonstick rimmed baking sheet for this pie. If using a conventional baking sheet, coat it lightly with vegetable oil spray.

PIE

3½	pounds Granny Smith apples, peeled, cored, halved, and sliced thin
3½	pounds Golden Delicious apples, peeled, cored, halved, and sliced thin
1½	cups (10½ ounces) granulated sugar
½	teaspoon salt
1½	cups (4 ounces) animal crackers
2	(16-ounce) boxes refrigerated pie dough
4	tablespoons unsalted butter, melted and cooled
6	tablespoons instant tapioca
2	teaspoons ground cinnamon
3	tablespoons lemon juice

GLAZE

¾	cup reserved apple juice (from filling)
2	tablespoons lemon juice
1	tablespoon unsalted butter, softened
1¼	cups (5 ounces) confectioners' sugar

1. FOR THE PIE: Combine apples, 1 cup sugar, and salt in colander set over large bowl. Let sit, tossing occasionally, until apples release their juices, about 30 minutes. Press gently on apples to extract liquid and reserve ¾ cup juice. Adjust oven rack to lower-middle position and heat oven to 350 degrees.

2. FOR THE BOTTOM CRUST: Pulse crackers and remaining ½ cup sugar in food processor until finely ground, about 20 pulses. Dust counter with cracker mixture, brush half of 1 pie round with water, overlap with second pie round, and dust top with cracker mixture. Roll out dough to 19 by 14 inches and transfer to rimmed baking sheet. Brush dough with butter, cover loosely with plastic wrap and refrigerate.

3. FOR THE TOP CRUST: Roll remaining 2 dough rounds together with remaining cracker mixture to a 19 by 14-inch rectangle.

4. Toss drained apples with tapioca, cinnamon, and lemon juice and arrange evenly over bottom crust, pressing lightly to flatten. Brush edges of bottom crust with water and arrange top crust on pie. Press crusts together. Use paring knife to trim any excess dough. Use fork to crimp and seal outside edge of pie and then pierce top of pie at 2-inch intervals. Bake until pie is golden brown and juices are bubbling, about 1 hour. Let pie cool on wire rack for 1 hour.

5. FOR THE GLAZE: While pie is cooling, simmer reserved apple juice in saucepan over medium heat until syrupy and reduced to ¼ cup, about 6 minutes. Stir in lemon juice and butter and let cool to room temperature. Whisk in confectioners' sugar and brush glaze evenly over warm pie. Let pie cool completely, at least 1 hour longer. Serve. (Pie can be refrigerated for up to 1 day.)

HOW TO MAKE APPLE SLAB PIE

1. Use water to "glue" together 2 store-bought pie crusts.

2. Add flavor to the bottom crust by rolling it out in mixture of crushed cookie crumbs and sugar.

3. After transferring bottom crust to baking dish, brush it with melted butter for extra richness.

4. Top filled pie with second "double" crust and use fork to tightly seal edges of crust.

✓ WHY THIS RECIPE WORKS

The pecan pies of today bear little resemblance to their 19th-century inspiration. Could we re-create old-fashioned pecan pie without using modern-day processed corn syrup? Many traditional syrups (cane, sorghum) produced a great pie, but we had to mail away for those ingredients. In the end, combining maple syrup with brown sugar and molasses replicated the old-fashioned versions perfectly. We started the pie at a high oven temperature to ensure the bottom crust was crisp and golden brown and then dropped the temperature to finish baking.

Old-Fashioned Pecan Pie

SERVES 8 TO 10

Serve with Bourbon Whipped Cream (recipe follows), if desired. You can use Classic Single-Crust Pie Dough (page 454) or No-Fear Single-Crust Pie Dough (page 455) for this pie.

1	cup maple syrup
1	cup packed (7 ounces) light brown sugar
½	cup heavy cream
1	tablespoon molasses
4	tablespoons unsalted butter, cut into ½-inch pieces
½	teaspoon salt
6	large egg yolks, lightly beaten
1½	cups (6 ounces) pecans, toasted and chopped
1	recipe single-crust pie dough, fitted into 9-inch pie plate and chilled

1. Adjust oven rack to lowest position and heat oven to 450 degrees. Heat syrup, sugar, cream, and molasses in saucepan over medium heat, stirring occasionally, until sugar dissolves, about 3 minutes. Remove from heat and let cool for 5 minutes. Whisk butter and salt into syrup mixture until combined. Whisk in egg yolks until incorporated.

2. Scatter pecans in pie shell. Carefully pour filling over. Place pie in oven and immediately reduce oven temperature to 325 degrees. Bake until filling is set and center jiggles slightly when pie is gently shaken, 45 minutes to 1 hour. Let pie cool on rack for 1 hour, then refrigerate until set, about 3 hours or up to 1 day. Bring to room temperature before serving.

BOURBON WHIPPED CREAM

MAKES ABOUT 2 CUPS

Although any style of whiskey will work here, we like the smokiness of bourbon.

1	cup heavy cream
2	tablespoons bourbon
1½	tablespoons packed light brown sugar
½	teaspoon vanilla extract

Using stand mixer fitted with whisk, whip cream, bourbon, sugar, and vanilla on medium-low speed until foamy, about 1 minute. Increase speed to high and whip until stiff peaks form, about 2 minutes. (Whipped cream can be refrigerated for 4 hours.)

MOVE OVER, KARO

Before cloying Karo syrup monopolized the market, pies were made with many other, less processed types of syrup, including sorghum (made from a cereal grass) and cane (made from the boiled-down juice of the sugarcane plant). These syrups still exist, and you can mail-order them, or travel to places like Louisiana or Kentucky to find them. We tasted a range of such syrups, including Steen's 100% Pure Cane Syrup and Townsend's Sweet Sorghum, then tried to duplicate their complex flavors from products we could buy at the supermarket. In the end, a combination of three ordinary sweeteners created an old-fashioned flavor that easily bested Karo.

Molasses brings a robust, slightly bitter quality.

Light brown sugar adds warmth and caramel tones.

Maple syrup adds delicate complexity.

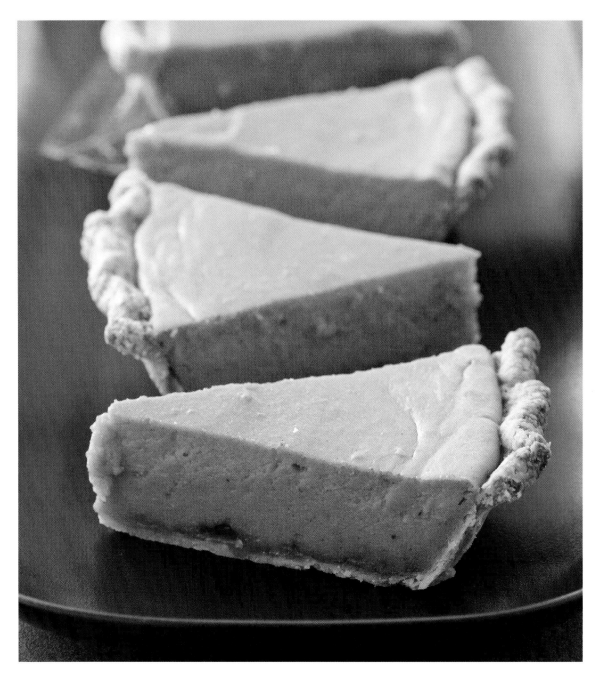

✅ WHY THIS RECIPE WORKS

Hoping to streamline this holiday dessert, we started by "baking" whole sweet potatoes in the microwave. A food processor made quick work of pureeing the flesh and lent a super-smooth texture. Sour cream added subtle tang while smoothing out the custard even more, and supplementing whole eggs with extra yolks added richness and helped with sliceability. We heated the spices in butter to intensify (or bloom) their flavor before adding them, along with some bourbon and vanilla, to the filling. First we sprinkled brown sugar onto the crust, which melted into a gooey faux caramel and took this pie to the next level.

Sweet Potato Pie

SERVES 8

The best pies use homemade crust. You can use Classic Single-Crust Pie Dough (page 454) or No-Fear Single-Crust Pie Dough (page 455) for this pie. If you're pressed for time, try our favorite store-bought crust, Wholly Wholesome 9" Certified Organic Traditional Bake at Home Rolled Pie Dough. Choose sweet potatoes that are about the same size so that they'll cook evenly. Serve with Bourbon Whipped Cream (page 465), if desired.

1	**(9-inch) single-crust pie dough**
1¼	**cups packed (8¾ ounces) light brown sugar**
1¾	**pounds sweet potatoes, unpeeled**
½	**teaspoon salt**
4	**tablespoons unsalted butter**
½	**teaspoon ground cinnamon**
¼	**teaspoon ground nutmeg**
1	**cup sour cream**
3	**large eggs plus 2 large yolks**
2	**tablespoons bourbon (optional)**
1	**teaspoon vanilla extract**

1. Adjust oven rack to middle position and heat oven to 375 degrees. Roll dough into 12-inch circle on lightly floured counter. Loosely roll dough around rolling pin and gently unroll it onto 9-inch pie plate, letting excess dough hang over edge. Ease dough into plate by gently lifting edge of dough with your hand while pressing into plate bottom with your other hand Trim overhang to ½ inch beyond lip of pie plate. Tuck overhang under itself; folded edge should be flush with edge of pie plate. Crimp dough evenly around edge of pie using your fingers. Wrap dough-lined pie plate loosely in plastic and freeze until dough is firm, about 15 minutes.

2. Line chilled pie shell with two 12-inch squares of parchment paper, letting parchment lie over edges of dough, and fill with pie weights. Bake until lightly golden around edges, 18 to 25 minutes. Carefully remove parchment and weights, rotate crust, and continue to bake until center begins to look opaque and slightly drier, 3 to 6 minutes. Remove from oven. Let crust cool completely. Sprinkle ¼ cup sugar over bottom of crust; set aside. Reduce oven temperature to 350 degrees.

3. Meanwhile, prick potatoes all over with fork. Microwave on large plate until potatoes are very soft and surface is slightly wet, 15 to 20 minutes, flipping every 5 minutes. Immediately slice potatoes in half to release steam. When cool enough to handle, scoop flesh into bowl of food processor. Add salt and remaining 1 cup sugar and process until smooth, about 60 seconds, scraping down sides of bowl as needed. Melt butter with cinnamon and nutmeg in microwave, 15 to 30 seconds; stir to combine. Add spiced butter, sour cream, eggs and yolks, bourbon, if using, and vanilla to potatoes and process until incorporated, about 10 seconds, scraping down sides of bowl as needed.

4. Pour potato mixture into prepared pie shell. Bake until filling is set around edges but center registers 165 degrees and jiggles slightly when pie is shaken, 35 to 40 minutes. Let pie cool completely on wire rack, about 2 hours. Serve.

✔ WHY THIS RECIPE WORKS

Authentic Key lime pie recipes used to be simple and uncooked—but they contained raw eggs, a no-no in modern times. We wanted to develop an eggless Key lime pie recipe as bright and custardy as the original. In lieu of using egg yolks, we found the right ratio of instant vanilla pudding, gelatin, and cream cheese to thicken our Icebox Key Lime Pie's filling into a perfect, smooth consistency. A full cup of fresh lime juice produced a pie with bracing lime flavor. Lime zest added another layer of flavor, and processing the zest with a little sugar offset its sourness and eliminated the annoying chewy bits.

Icebox Key Lime Pie

SERVES 8 TO 10

Use instant pudding, which requires no stovetop cooking, for this recipe. Do not be tempted to use bottled lime juice, which lacks depth of flavor.

CRUST

8	whole graham crackers, broken into small pieces
2	tablespoons sugar
5	tablespoons unsalted butter, melted

FILLING

¼	cup (1¾ ounces) sugar
1	tablespoon grated lime zest plus 1 cup juice (8 limes)
8	ounces cream cheese, softened
1	(14-ounce) can sweetened condensed milk
⅓	cup instant vanilla pudding mix
1¼	teaspoons unflavored gelatin
1	teaspoon vanilla extract

1. FOR THE CRUST: Adjust oven rack to middle position and heat oven to 350 degrees. Process crackers and sugar in food processor until finely ground, about 30 seconds. Add melted butter in steady stream while pulsing until crumbs resemble damp sand. Sprinkle mixture into 9-inch pie plate and use bottom of dry measuring cup to press crumbs firmly into bottom and sides. Bake until fragrant and browned around edges, 12 to 14 minutes. Let cool completely.

2. FOR THE FILLING: Process sugar and zest in clean food processor until sugar turns bright green, about 30 seconds. Add cream cheese and process until combined, about 30 seconds. Add condensed milk and pudding mix and process until smooth, about 30 seconds. Scrape down sides of bowl. Sprinkle gelatin over 2 tablespoons lime juice in small bowl and let sit until gelatin softens, about 5 minutes. Heat in microwave for 15 seconds; stir until dissolved. With processor running, pour in gelatin mixture, remaining lime juice, and vanilla and mix until thoroughly combined, about 30 seconds.

3. Pour filling into cooled crust, cover with plastic wrap, and refrigerate for at least 3 hours or up to 2 days. To serve, let pie sit at room temperature for 10 minutes before slicing.

BIGGER LIMES = LESS WORK

When developing our recipe for Icebox Key Lime Pie, we found the flavor of Key limes and regular supermarket limes (called Persian limes) to be almost identical in our pie recipe. But there was a big difference in squeezing time.

KEY LIMES
We had to squeeze 40 Key limes to yield 1 cup of juice.

PERSIAN LIMES
Just six to eight Persian limes gave us all the juice we needed.

A MYSTERY OF PIE HISTORY

Before Gail Borden invented sweetened condensed milk in 1856, drinking milk was a health risk, as there was no pasteurization or refrigeration for fresh milk. The shelf-stability and safety of sweetened condensed milk made it especially popular in areas like the Florida Keys, where the hot climate promoted rapid spoilage of anything perishable. Like many of our iconic foods, no one knows for sure when or by whom the first Key lime pie was made, but with canned milk in every pantry by the 1870s and an abundance of tiny Key limes throughout the area, it was only a matter of time. Most food historians trace the history of this pie back to the 1890s, but there are those—especially in the Keys—who claim the recipe is decades older.

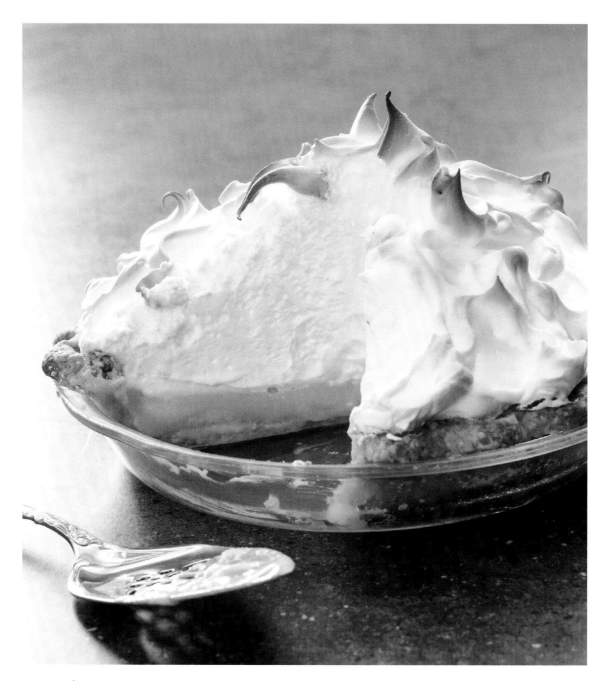

✅ WHY THIS RECIPE WORKS

We wanted a lemon meringue pie with an impressively tall and fluffy topping, so we made the meringue with a hot sugar syrup and added a bit of cream of tartar to the egg whites as we beat them. This ensured that the meringue was cooked through and stable enough to be piled high on top of the filling. For our pie's bright citrus flavor, we flavored the filling with lemon zest and lemon juice and then, to ensure the filling was silky smooth, we strained out the zest.

Mile-High Lemon Meringue Pie

SERVES 8 TO 10

You can use Classic Single-Crust Pie Dough (page 454) or No-Fear Single-Crust Pie Dough (page 455) for this pie. This pie is best served on the day it's made.

- 1   **recipe single-crust pie dough, fitted into 9-inch pie plate and chilled**

LEMON FILLING

- 1¼   **cups (8¾ ounces) sugar**
- 1   **cup lemon juice plus 2 tablespoons grated zest (5 lemons)**
- ½   **cup water**
- 3   **tablespoons cornstarch**
- ¼   **teaspoon salt**
- 8   **large egg yolks**
- 4   **tablespoons unsalted butter, cut into 4 pieces and softened**

MERINGUE

- 1   **cup (7 ounces) sugar**
- ½   **cup water**
- 4   **large egg whites**
     Pinch salt
- ½   **teaspoon cream of tartar**
- ½   **teaspoon vanilla extract**

1. Adjust oven rack to middle position and heat oven to 375 degrees. Line chilled crust with double layer of aluminum foil and fill with pie weights. Bake until pie dough looks dry and is light in color, 25 to 30 minutes. Remove weights and foil and continue to bake crust until deep golden brown, 10 to 12 minutes longer. Let crust cool on wire rack to room temperature.

2. **FOR THE FILLING:** Whisk sugar, lemon juice, water, cornstarch, and salt together in large saucepan until cornstarch is dissolved. Bring to simmer over medium heat, whisking occasionally until mixture becomes translucent and begins to thicken, about 5 minutes. Whisk in egg yolks until combined. Stir in lemon zest and butter.

Bring to simmer and stir constantly until mixture is thick enough to coat back of spoon, about 2 minutes. Strain through fine-mesh strainer into cooled pie shell and scrape filling off underside of strainer. Place plastic wrap directly on surface of filling and refrigerate until set and well chilled, at least 2 hours or up to 1 day.

3. **FOR THE MERINGUE:** Adjust oven rack to middle position and heat oven to 400 degrees. Combine sugar and water in small saucepan. Bring to vigorous boil over medium-high heat. Once syrup comes to rolling boil, cook 4 minutes (mixture will become slightly thickened and syrupy). Remove from heat and set aside while beating whites.

4. Using stand mixer fitted with whisk, whip egg whites in large bowl at medium-low speed until frothy, about 1 minute. Add salt and cream of tartar and whip, gradually increasing speed to medium-high, until whites hold soft peaks, about 2 minutes. With mixer running, slowly pour hot syrup into whites (avoid pouring syrup onto whisk or it will splash). Add vanilla and whip until meringue has cooled and becomes very thick and shiny, 5 to 9 minutes.

5. Using rubber spatula, mound meringue over filling, making sure meringue touches edges of crust. Use spatula to create peaks all over meringue. Bake until peaks turn golden brown, about 6 minutes. Let pie cool on wire rack to room temperature. Serve.

MAKING A MERINGUE MOUNTAIN

1. Use rubber spatula to press meringue onto edge of pie crust. This will keep meringue from shrinking.

2. Use spatula to make dramatic peaks and swirls all over meringue.

WHY THIS RECIPE WORKS

Raspberry chiffon pie can often be weak on berry flavor. We wanted to produce an intensely flavored pie, so we included a layer of sweetened, thickened fruit on the crust and beneath the chiffon. We also stiffened our recipe's chiffon filling by using extra gelatin and a little cream cheese, which enabled it to hold additional raspberry puree for even more flavor.

Raspberry Chiffon Pie

SERVES 8 TO 10

You can use Classic Single-Crust Pie Dough (page 454) or No-Fear Single-Crust Pie Dough (page 455) for this pie. The raspberry-flavored gelatin is important for the color and flavor of the chiffon layer; do not substitute unflavored gelatin. For an accurate measurement of boiling water, bring a full kettle of water to a boil, then measure out the desired amount.

<table>
<tr><td>1</td><td>recipe single-crust pie dough, fitted into 9-inch pie plate and chilled</td></tr>
</table>

FRUIT

12	ounces (2½ cups) frozen raspberries
3	tablespoons pectin (Sure-Jell)
1½	cups (10½ ounces) sugar
	Pinch salt
5	ounces (1 cup) fresh raspberries

CHIFFON

3	tablespoons raspberry-flavored gelatin
3	tablespoons boiling water
3	ounces cream cheese, softened
1	cup heavy cream, chilled

TOPPING

1¼	cups heavy cream, chilled
2	tablespoons sugar

1. Adjust oven rack to middle position and heat oven to 375 degrees. Line chilled crust with double layer of aluminum foil and fill with pie weights. Bake until pie dough looks dry and is light in color, 25 to 30 minutes. Remove weights and foil and continue to bake crust until deep golden brown, 10 to 12 minutes longer. Let crust cool on wire rack to room temperature.

2. **FOR THE FRUIT:** Cook frozen berries in medium saucepan over medium-high heat, stirring occasionally, until berries begin to give up their juice, about 3 minutes. Stir in pectin and bring to full boil, stirring constantly. Stir in sugar and salt and return to full boil. Cook, stirring constantly, until slightly thickened, about 2 minutes. Pour through fine-mesh strainer into medium bowl, pressing on solids to extract as much puree as possible. Scrape puree off underside of strainer into bowl.

3. Transfer ⅓ cup raspberry puree to small bowl and let cool to room temperature. Gently fold fresh raspberries into remaining puree. Spread fruit mixture evenly over bottom of cooled pie shell and set aside.

4. **FOR THE CHIFFON:** Dissolve gelatin in boiling water in bowl of stand mixer. Fit stand mixer with paddle, add cream cheese and reserved ⅓ cup raspberry puree, and beat on high speed, scraping down bowl once or twice, until smooth, about 2 minutes. Add cream and beat on medium-low speed until incorporated, about 30 seconds. Scrape down bowl. Increase speed to high and beat until cream holds stiff peaks, 1 to 2 minutes. Spread evenly over fruit in pie shell. Cover pie with plastic wrap. Refrigerate until set, at least 3 hours or up to 2 days.

5. **FOR THE TOPPING:** When ready to serve, fit stand mixer with whisk and whip cream and sugar on medium-low speed until foamy, about 1 minute. Increase speed to high and whip until stiff peaks form, 1 to 3 minutes. Spread or pipe over chilled filling. Serve.

TWO LAYERS, TWO THICKENERS

FOR THE FRUIT LAYER:
For the bottom layer, we used Sure-Jell (pectin) to achieve a concentrated raspberry flavor and texture. There are two formulations of Sure-Jell. We found that the original formula made the smoothest, thickest bottom layer of fruit.

FOR THE CHIFFON LAYER:
A few tablespoons of raspberry gelatin made for great stability and color in the creamy chiffon layer and reinforced the berry flavor.

✔ WHY THIS RECIPE WORKS

Frozen strawberries, which are great for cooking, form the base of our strawberry pie. We cooked them down in a dry saucepan until they released their juice and the mixture was thick, concentrated, and flavorful. Because strawberries are low in pectin, the natural thickener found in citrus fruits and many other plants, we added some lemon juice, which perked up the flavor and tightened the texture of the filling a little. To thicken the filling further, we added a bit of unflavored gelatin. Then we mixed in fresh strawberries for a fresh finish with big, berry flavor.

Icebox Strawberry Pie

SERVES 8

You can use Classic Single-Crust Pie Dough (page 454) or No-Fear Single-Crust Pie Dough (page 455) for this pie. In step 2, it is imperative that the cooked strawberry mixture measure 2 cups; any more and the filling will be loose. If your fresh berries aren't fully ripe, you may want to add extra sugar to taste in step 3.

- 1   **recipe single-crust pie dough, fitted into 9-inch pie plate and chilled**

FILLING

- 2   **pounds (7 cups) frozen strawberries**
- 1   **tablespoon unflavored gelatin**
- 2   **tablespoons lemon juice**
- 2   **tablespoons water**
- 1   **cup (7 ounces) sugar**
-      **Pinch salt**
- 1   **pound fresh strawberries, hulled and sliced thin**

TOPPING

- 4   **ounces cream cheese, softened**
- 3   **tablespoons sugar**
- ½   **teaspoon vanilla extract**
- 1   **cup heavy cream**

1. Adjust oven rack to middle position and heat oven to 375 degrees. Line chilled crust with double layer of aluminum foil and fill with pie weights. Bake until pie dough looks dry and is light in color, 25 to 30 minutes. Remove weights and foil and continue to bake crust until deep golden brown, 10 to 12 minutes longer. Let crust cool to room temperature on wire rack.

2. **FOR THE FILLING:** Cook frozen berries in large saucepan over medium-low heat until berries begin to release juice, about 3 minutes. Increase heat to medium-high and cook, stirring frequently, until thick and jamlike, about 25 minutes (mixture should measure 2 cups).

3. Sprinkle gelatin over lemon juice and water in small bowl. Let stand until gelatin is softened and mixture has thickened, about 5 minutes. Stir gelatin mixture, sugar, and salt into cooked berry mixture and return to simmer, about 2 minutes. Transfer to bowl and cool to room temperature, about 30 minutes.

4. Fold fresh berries into filling. Spread evenly in pie shell and refrigerate until set, about 4 hours. (Filled pie can be refrigerated for 24 hours.)

5. **FOR THE TOPPING:** Using stand mixer fitted with whisk, beat cream cheese, sugar, and vanilla on medium speed until smooth, about 30 seconds. With mixer running, add cream and whip until stiff peaks form, about 2 minutes. Dollop individual slices of pie with topping and serve.

DON'T MAKE THIS MISTAKE

In step 2, be sure to accurately measure the reduced strawberry mixture: You'll need exactly 2 cups. Scrape the strawberry mixture into a large liquid measuring cup. If it measures more than 2 cups, return it to the pan to cook down. It may seem fussy to stop to measure, but the pie will not set or slice properly if you have more than 2 cups of the strawberry mixture.

MEASURE METICULOUSLY

✔ WHY THIS RECIPE WORKS

This prize-wining icebox pie with a sophisticated name originally called for raw eggs. Testing showed that we could cook the eggs with sugar on the stovetop, almost like making a custard. Once the egg and sugar mixture was light and thick, we removed it from the heat and continued whipping it until it was fully cooled. Bittersweet chocolate folded into the cooled egg and sugar mixture made for a pie with more intense chocolate flavor. And to lighten the filling's texture, we incorporated whipped cream.

French Silk Chocolate Pie

SERVES 8 TO 10

You can use Classic Single-Crust Pie Dough (page 454) or No-Fear Single-Crust Pie Dough (page 455) for this pie. Serve with lightly sweetened whipped cream.

- 1 **recipe single-crust pie dough, fitted into 9-inch pie plate and chilled**
- 1 **cup heavy cream, chilled**
- 3 **large eggs**
- ¾ **cup (5¼ ounces) sugar**
- 2 **tablespoons water**
- 8 **ounces bittersweet chocolate, melted and cooled**
- 1 **tablespoon vanilla extract**
- 8 **tablespoons unsalted butter, cut into ½-inch pieces and softened**

1. Adjust oven rack to middle position and heat oven to 375 degrees. Line chilled crust with double layer of aluminum foil and fill with pie weights. Bake until pie dough looks dry and is light in color, 25 to 30 minutes. Remove weights and foil and continue to bake crust until deep golden brown, 10 to 12 minutes longer. Let crust cool on wire rack to room temperature.

2. Using stand mixer fitted with whisk, whip cream on medium-low speed until foamy, about 1 minute. Increase speed to high and whip until stiff peaks form, 1 to 3 minutes. Transfer whipped cream to small bowl and refrigerate.

3. Combine eggs, sugar, and water in large heatproof bowl set over medium saucepan filled with ½ inch barely simmering water (don't let bowl touch water). Using hand-held mixer set at medium speed, beat egg mixture until thickened and registers 160 degrees, 7 to 10 minutes. Remove bowl from heat and continue to beat egg mixture until fluffy and cooled to room temperature, about 8 minutes.

4. Add chocolate and vanilla to cooled egg mixture and beat until incorporated. Beat in butter, few pieces at a time, until well combined. Using spatula, fold in whipped cream until no streaks of white remain. Scrape filling into pie shell and refrigerate until set, at least 3 hours or up to 24 hours. Serve.

WHISKING CHOCOLATE INTO SILK

1. Beating eggs and sugar together in double boiler incorporates air and gives filling light, ethereal texture. When egg mixture reaches 160 degrees, it will be very thick. Remove it from heat.

2. Continue beating egg mixture until it is fluffy and cool. Then add melted chocolate and beat in softened butter for rich flavor and silky-smooth texture.

THE PILLSBURY BAKE-OFF

In 1949, General Mills launched the "Grand National Recipe and Baking Contest" (later known as the Pillsbury Bake-Off). It was held at the posh Waldorf-Astoria Hotel in New York. The grand-prize winner (for No-Knead Water Rising Twists) brought home $50,000; Eleanor Roosevelt was one of the luminaries on hand to present the awards. Since then, many prize-winning Pillsbury recipes have become part of our culinary heritage, among them French Silk Chocolate Pie (the exotic name reflects the international curiosity of postwar America), Open Sesame Pie in 1954 (which caused a run on sesame seeds nationwide), and Peanut Blossom Cookies (with a Hershey's Kiss in the middle).

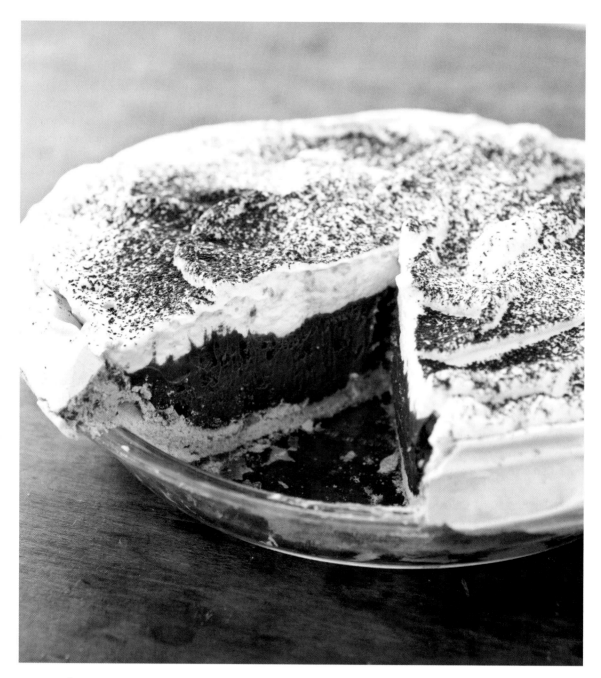

WHY THIS RECIPE WORKS

Chocolate angel pie is a lavish version of chocolate cream pie with creamy chocolate mousse, fluffy whipped cream, and an airy meringue crust. For a light, crisp crust, 2½ hours in a low oven was necessary. To prevent the crust from sticking to the pan, we relied on cornstarch, both in the egg whites and dusted over the pie plate. We loaded nearly a pound of chocolate into the filling by making a cooked custard. Using two kinds of chocolate lent depth and complexity. To finish, we topped the pie with lightly sweetened whipped cream and a sprinkling of cocoa powder for a decadent, supremely chocolaty dessert.

Chocolate Angel Pie

Serve the assembled pie within 3 hours of chilling.

FILLING

9	ounces milk chocolate, chopped fine
5	ounces bittersweet chocolate, chopped fine
3	large egg yolks
1½	tablespoons granulated sugar
½	teaspoon salt
½	cup half-and-half
1¼	cups heavy cream, chilled

MERINGUE CRUST

1	tablespoon cornstarch, plus extra for pie plate
½	cup (3½ ounces) granulated sugar
3	large egg whites
	Pinch cream of tartar
½	teaspoon vanilla extract

TOPPING

1⅓	cups heavy cream, chilled
2	tablespoons confectioners' sugar
	Unsweetened cocoa powder

1. FOR THE FILLING: Microwave milk chocolate and bittersweet chocolate in large bowl at 50 percent power, stirring occasionally, until melted, 2 to 4 minutes. Whisk egg yolks, sugar, and salt together in medium bowl until combined, about 1 minute. Bring half-and-half to simmer in small saucepan over medium heat. Whisking constantly, slowly add hot half-and-half to egg yolk mixture in 2 additions until incorporated. Return half-and-half mixture to now-empty saucepan and cook over low heat, whisking constantly, until thickened slightly, 30 seconds to 1 minute. Stir half-and-half mixture into melted chocolate until combined. Let cool slightly, about 8 minutes.

2. Using stand mixer fitted with whisk, whip cream on medium-low speed until foamy, about 1 minute. Increase speed to high and whip until soft peaks form, 1 to 3 minutes. Gently whisk one-third of whipped cream into cooled chocolate mixture. Fold in remaining whipped cream until no white streaks remain. Cover and refrigerate for at least 3 hours, or until ready to assemble pie. (Filling can be made up to 24 hours in advance.)

3. FOR THE MERINGUE CRUST: Adjust oven rack to lower-middle position and heat oven to 275 degrees. Grease 9-inch pie plate and dust well with extra cornstarch, using pastry brush to distribute evenly. Combine sugar and 1 tablespoon cornstarch in bowl. Using stand mixer fitted with whisk, whip egg whites and cream of tartar on medium-low speed until foamy, about 1 minute. Increase speed to medium-high and whip whites to soft, billowy mounds, 1 to 3 minutes. Gradually add sugar mixture and whip until glossy, stiff peaks form, 3 to 5 minutes. Add vanilla to meringue and whip until incorporated.

4. Spread meringue into prepared pie plate, following contours of plate to cover bottom, sides, and edges. Bake for 1½ hours. Rotate pie plate, reduce oven temperature to 200 degrees, and bake until completely dried out, about 1 hour longer. (Shell will rise above rim of pie plate; some cracking is OK.) Let cool completely, about 30 minutes.

5. FOR THE TOPPING: Spoon cooled chocolate filling into cavity of pie shell, distributing evenly. Using stand mixer fitted with whisk, whip cream and sugar on medium-low speed until foamy, about 1 minute. Increase speed to high and whip until stiff peaks form, 1 to 3 minutes. Spread whipped cream evenly over chocolate. Refrigerate until filling is set, about 1 hour. Dust with cocoa. Slice with sharp knife and serve.

BUSTED CRUST

The egg white crust is part of what distinguishes angel pie. To avoid a sticky, broken meringue shell, we added cornstarch to the whites, and we greased the pie plate and dusted it with more cornstarch.

MERINGUE MESS
Don't let this happen to you.

Shopping For Equipment

With a well-stocked kitchen, you'll be able to take on any recipe. But there's so much equipment out there on the market, how do you figure out what's what? Price often correlates with design, not performance. Over the years, our test kitchen has evaluated thousands of products. We've gone through copious rounds of testing and have identified the most important attributes in every piece of equipment, so when you go shopping you'll know what to look for. And because our test kitchen accepts no support from product manufacturers, you can trust our ratings. Prices in this chart are based on shopping at online retailers and will vary. See AmericasTestKitchen.com for updates to these testings.

KNIVES AND MORE	ITEM	WHAT TO LOOK FOR	TEST KITCHEN FAVORITES
MUST-HAVE ITEMS	**CHEF'S KNIFE**	• High-carbon stainless steel knife • Thin, curved 8-inch blade • Lightweight • Comfortable grip and nonslip handle	**Victorinox Fibrox 8-Inch Chef's Knife** (formerly Victorinox Forschner) $39.95
	PARING KNIFE	• 3- to 3½-inch blade • Thin, slightly curved blade with pointed tip • Comfortable grip	**Wüsthof Classic with PEtec 3½-Inch Paring Knife** (model #4066) $39.95 Best Buy: **Victorinox Fibrox 3¼-Inch Paring Knife** $4.95
	SERRATED KNIFE	• 10- to 12-inch blade • Long, somewhat flexible, slightly curved blade • Pointed serrations that are uniformly spaced and moderately sized	**Wüsthof Classic 10-Inch Bread Knife** $89.95 Best Buy: **Victorinox Fibrox 10¼-Inch Bread Knife** $24.95
	SLICING KNIFE	• Tapered 12-inch blade for slicing large cuts of meat • Oval scallops (called a granton edge) carved into blade • Fairly rigid blade with rounded tip	**Victorinox Fibrox 12-Inch Granton Edge Slicing Knife** $49.95
	STEAK KNIVES	• Super-sharp, straight-edged blade • Sturdy, not wobbly, blade	**Victorinox Rosewood Straight Edge Steak Knife Set** (model #46059) $169.99 for a set of six Best Buy: **Chicago Cutlery 4-Piece Walnut Tradition Steak Knife Set** $23.99 for a set of four

KNIVES AND MORE	ITEM	WHAT TO LOOK FOR	TEST KITCHEN FAVORITES
	SANTOKU KNIFE	• 6½-inch blade • Narrow, curved, and short blade • Comfortable grip	**MAC Superior 6½-Inch Santoku Knife** $74.95
	BONING KNIFE	• 6-inch blade • Narrow, highly maneuverable and razor-sharp blade • Comfortable grip and nonslip handle	**Victorinox Fibrox 6-Inch Straight Boning Knife** (Flexible) $19.95
	MEAT CLEAVER	• Razor-sharp blade • Balanced weight between handle and blade • Comfortable grip	**Global 6-Inch Meat Cleaver** $144.95 Best Buy: **LamsonSharp 7¼-Inch Meat Cleaver** $48
	HYBRID CHEF'S KNIFE	• High-carbon stainless steel knife • Lightweight • Thin blade that tapers from spine to cutting edge and from handle to tip	**Masamoto VG Gyutou, 8.2 Inches** $162.50
	ELECTRIC KNIFE	• Comfortable handle • Slices turkey skin without ripping and baked goods without crumbling	**Oster Electric Knife Set** $19.99
	MANDOLINE	• Razor-sharp blade(s) • Hand guard to shield fingers • Gripper prongs to grasp food • Measurement-marked dial for precision cuts • Storage for extra blades	**Swissmar Börner Original V-Slicer Plus Mandoline** $29.99 Best Buy: **Kyocera Adjustable Ceramic Mandoline Slicer** $26.96
	CARVING BOARD	• Heavy, sturdy board • Deep, wide trench to trap juices • Central well to hold meat snugly	**Williams-Sonoma Medium Maple Reversible Carving Board** $58

KNIVES AND MORE	ITEM	WHAT TO LOOK FOR	TEST KITCHEN FAVORITES
MUST-HAVE ITEM	CUTTING BOARD	• Roomy work surface at least 20 by 15 inches • Teak board for minimal maintenance • Durable edge-grain construction (wood grain runs parallel to surface of board)	**Proteak Edge Grain Teak Cutting Board** $84.99 Best Buy: **OXO Good Grips Carving and Cutting Board** $21.99
	INNOVATIVE CUTTING BOARD	• Sturdy, sink spanning bamboo board • Collapsible colander for easy multitasking	**Island Bamboo Over-the-Sink Cutting Board with Colander** $39.99
MUST-HAVE ITEM	KNIFE SHARPENER	• Diamond sharpening material for electric sharpeners • Easy to use and comfortable • Clear instructions	Electric: **Chef'sChoice Model 130 Professional Sharpening Station** $139.95 Manual: **AccuSharp Knife and Tool Sharpener** $7.99

POTS AND PANS	ITEM	WHAT TO LOOK FOR	TEST KITCHEN FAVORITES
MUST-HAVE ITEM	TRADITIONAL SKILLET	• Stainless steel interior and fully clad for even heat distribution • 12-inch diameter and flared sides • Comfortable, ovensafe handle • Cooking surface of at least 9 inches • Good to have smaller (8- or 10-inch) skillets too	**All-Clad Stainless 12-Inch Frypan** $135
	INEXPENSIVE SKILLET	• Fully clad with stainless steel interior for even heat distribution • 12-inch diameter and flared sides • Comfortable, ovensafe handle • Cooking surface of at least 9 inches	**Emeril Pro-Clad Stainless Steel Tri-Ply 12-Inch Fry Pan** $34.99
MUST-HAVE ITEM	NONSTICK SKILLETS	• Dark, nonstick surface • 12- or 12½-inch diameter, thick bottom • Comfortable, ovensafe handle • Cooking surface of at least 9 inches • Good to have smaller (8- or 10-inch) skillets too	**T-Fal Professional Total Non-Stick 12½-Inch Fry Pan** $34.99

POTS AND PANS	ITEM	WHAT TO LOOK FOR	TEST KITCHEN FAVORITES
	CAST-IRON SKILLET	• Thick bottom and straight sides • Roomy interior (cooking surface of 9¼ inches or more) • Preseasoned	**Lodge 12-Inch Skillet** $33.95
	ECO-FRIENDLY SKILLET	• PFOA-free (perfluorooctanoic acid) surfaces are nonstick and more durable than silicone coatings • Roomy interior (cooking surface of 9 inches or more) NOTE: We prefer our favorite nonstick skillet for its superior performance.	**Scanpan Professional 12½-Inch Fry Pan** $129.95
	DUTCH OVEN	• Enameled cast iron or stainless steel • Capacity of at least 6 quarts • Diameter of at least 9 inches • Tight-fitting lid • Wide, sturdy handles	**Le Creuset 7¼-Quart Round French Oven** $304.95 **All-Clad Stainless 8-Quart Stockpot** $279.95 Best Buy: **Lodge Color Enamel 6-Quart Dutch Oven** $49.97
	SAUCEPANS	• Large saucepan with 3- to 4-quart capacity and small nonstick saucepan with 2- to 2½-quart capacity • Tight-fitting lids • Pans with rounded corners that a whisk can reach into • Long, comfortable handles that are angled for even weight distribution	Large: **All-Clad Stainless 4-Quart Saucepan with Lid and Loop** $224.95 Best Buy: **Cuisinart MultiClad Unlimited 4-Quart Saucepan** $69.99 Small: **Calphalon Contemporary Nonstick 2½-Quart Shallow Saucepan** $39.95
	RIMMED BAKING SHEETS	• Light-colored surface (heats and browns evenly) • Thick, sturdy pan • Dimensions of 18 by 13 inches • Good to have at least two	**Wear-Ever 13-Gauge Half Size Heavy Duty Sheet Pan by Vollrath** (formerly Lincoln Foodservice) $14.99

MUST-HAVE ITEMS

POTS AND PANS	ITEM	WHAT TO LOOK FOR	TEST KITCHEN FAVORITES
	SAUTÉ PAN	• Aluminum core surrounded by layers of stainless steel • Hefty but well-balanced pan • 9½- to 10-inch diameter • Helper handle and tight-fitting lid	**All-Clad Stainless Steel 3-Quart Sauté Pan** $224.95 Best Buy: **Cuisinart MultiClad Pro Triple-Ply 3½-Quart Sauté Pan with Lid** $79.95
	OMELET PAN	• Gently sloped sides for easy turning and rolling of omelets • Nonstick finish • Heavy construction for durability and even heat distribution • 8-inch size for French omelets	**Original French Chef 8-Inch Black Nonstick Omelette Pan** $139.95
	STOCKPOT	• 12-quart capacity • Thick bottom to prevent scorching • Wide body for easy cleaning and storage • Flat or round handles that extend at least 1¾ inches	**All-Clad Stainless 12-Quart Stock Pot** $389.95 Best Buy: **Cuisinart Chef's Classic Stainless 12-Quart Stock Pot** $69.99
MUST-HAVE ITEM	ROASTING PAN	• At least 15 by 11 inches • Stainless steel interior with aluminum core for even heat distribution • Upright handles for easy gripping • Light interior for better food monitoring	**Calphalon Contemporary Stainless Roasting Pan with V-Rack** $99.99
	V-RACK	• Fixed, not adjustable, to provide sturdiness • Tall, vertical handles positioned on long side of rack	**All-Clad Nonstick Roasting Rack** $24.95

POTS AND PANS	ITEM	WHAT TO LOOK FOR	TEST KITCHEN FAVORITES
	COOKWARE SET	• Fully clad stainless steel with aluminum core for even heat distribution • Moderately heavy, durable construction • Lids included • Ideal mix of pans includes 12-inch skillet, 10-inch skillet, 2-quart saucepan, 4-quart saucepan, 8-quart stockpot	**All-Clad Stainless Steel 10-Piece Cookware Set** $799.95 Best Buy: **Tramontina 18/10 Stainless Steel TriPly-Clad 8-Piece Cookware Set** $144.97

HANDY TOOLS	ITEM	WHAT TO LOOK FOR	TEST KITCHEN FAVORITES
	KITCHEN SHEARS	• Take-apart scissors (for easy cleaning) • Super-sharp blades • Sturdy construction • Work for both right- and left-handed users	**Kershaw 1120M TaskMaster Kitchen Shears** $49.95 Best Buy: **J. A. Henckels International Kitchen Shears—Take Apart** $14.95
	TONGS	• Scalloped edges • Slightly concave pincers • Length of 12 inches (to keep your hand far from the heat) • Open and close easily	**OXO Good Grips 12-Inch Locking Tongs** $12.95
	WOODEN SPOON	• Slim yet broad bowl • Stain-resistant bamboo • Comfortable handle	**SCI Bamboo Wood Cooking Spoon** $2.40
	SLOTTED SPOON	• Deep bowl • Long handle • Enough holes for quick draining	**OXO Good Grips Nylon Slotted Spoon** $6.99
	BASTING SPOON	• Thin, shallow bowl • Handle at least 9 inches in length • Slight dip from handle to bowl	**Rösle Basting Spoon with Hook Handle** $28.95
	ALL-AROUND SPATULAS	• Head about 3 inches wide and 5½ inches long • 11 inches in length (tip to handle) • Long, vertical slots • Good to have a metal spatula to use with traditional cookware and plastic for nonstick cookware	Metal: **Wüsthof Gourmet Fish Spatula** $44.95 Plastic: **Matfer Bourgeat Pelton Spatula** $8.23

MUST-HAVE ITEMS

MUST-HAVE ITEM

HANDY TOOLS	ITEM	WHAT TO LOOK FOR	TEST KITCHEN FAVORITES
MUST-HAVE ITEM	RUBBER SPATULA	• Wide, stiff blade with a thin edge that's flexible enough to conform to the curve of a mixing bowl • Heat-resistant	**Rubbermaid Professional 13½-Inch High Heat Scraper** $18.99
	OFFSET SPATULAS	• Flexible blade offset from handle • Good to have a small spatula for icing cookies and cupcakes and a large one for layer cakes and sheet cakes	Large: **Ateco Offset Spatula** $5.75 Small: **Wilton 9-Inch Angled Spatula** $4.79
	COOKIE SPATULA	• Small, silicone blade with thin, flexible edge • Angled handle	**OXO Good Grips Cookie Spatula** $6.99
MUST-HAVE ITEMS	ALL-PURPOSE WHISK	• At least 10 wires • Wires of moderate thickness • Comfortable rubber handle • Balanced, lightweight feel	**OXO Good Grips 11-Inch Balloon Whisk** $9.99
	PEPPER MILL	• Easy-to-adjust, clearly marked grind settings • Efficient, comfortable grinding mechanism • Generous capacity	**Cole and Mason Derwent Gourmet Precision Pepper Mill** $40
	ONE-HANDED PEPPER MILL	• Grinds quickly and easily • Accurately grinds in five textures from fine to coarse • Long-lasting rechargeable battery	**Peppermills Supreme Electric Pepper Mill** $39.95
	SUGAR SHAKER	• Mesh head that produces a fine, even dusting • Narrow cylinder that fits comfortably in your hand	**Ateco Stainless Steel Fine Mesh Shaker** $3.88

HANDY TOOLS	ITEM	WHAT TO LOOK FOR	TEST KITCHEN FAVORITES
MUST-HAVE ITEMS	LADLE	• Stainless steel • Hook handle • Pouring rim to prevent dripping • Handle 9 to 10 inches in length	**Rösle Ladle with Pouring Rim** $31.95
	CAN OPENER	• Intuitive and easy to attach • Smooth turning motions • Dishwasher safe	**Fissler Magic Smooth-Edge Can Opener** $29
	JAR OPENER	• Strong, sturdy clamp grip • Adjusts quickly to any size jar	**Amco Swing-A-Way Comfort Grip Jar Opener** $6.99
MUST-HAVE ITEM	GARLIC PRESS	• Conical holes that press garlic through efficiently • Solid, stainless steel construction • Comfortable handle • Easy to clean	**Kuhn Rikon Stainless Steel Epicurean Garlic Press** $39.95
	GARLIC PEELER	• Thick, comfortable silicone sleeve • Removes skins without bruising • Easy to wash	**Zak! Designs E-Z Rol Garlic Peeler** $8.79
	SERRATED FRUIT PEELER	• Comfortable grip and nonslip handle • Sharp blade	**Messermeister Serrated Swivel Peeler** $5.50
MUST-HAVE ITEM	VEGETABLE PEELER	• Sharp, carbon steel blade • 1-inch space between blade and peeler to prevent jamming • Lightweight and comfortable	**Kuhn Rikon Original 4-Inch Swiss Peeler** $3.50
	RASP GRATER	• Sharp teeth (require little effort or pressure when grating) • Maneuverable over round shapes • Comfortable handle	**Microplane Classic 8.5-inch Zester/Grater** $12.95

	ITEM	WHAT TO LOOK FOR	TEST KITCHEN FAVORITES
MUST-HAVE ITEM	GRATER	• Paddle-style grater • Sharp, extra-large holes and generous grating plane • Rubber-lined feet for stability • Comfortable handle	**Rösle Coarse Grater** $35.95
	ROTARY GRATER	• Barrel at least 2 inches in diameter • Classic turn-crank design • Comfortable handle • Simple to disassemble for easy cleanup	**Zyliss All Cheese Grater** $19.95
	MANUAL JUICER	• Hand-held squeezer with comfortable handle • Sturdy, enameled aluminum construction • Sized specifically for lemons, limes, and oranges	**Amco Enameled Citrus Squeezers** $11.95, lime $12.95, lemon $15.95, orange
	PORTION SCOOP	• Perfect half-sphere shape for easy portioning of batter and dough • Easy-to-squeeze handles to eject dough • Size number indicates how many portions per quart	**Fante's Stainless Portion Scoop #16** (2-ounce) $15.99
	ICE CREAM SCOOP	• Stainless steel • Slim, comfortable handle • Thin bowl edge for easier scooping	**Rösle Ice Cream Scoop** $20
	MEAT POUNDER	• At least 1½ pounds in weight • Vertical handle for better leverage and control	**Norpro Grip-EZ Meat Pounder** $17.50
	BENCH SCRAPER	• Sturdy blade • Beveled edge for easy cutting and scraping • Comfortable handle with plastic, rubber, or nylon grip	**Dexter-Russell 6" Dough Cutter/Scraper–Sani-Safe Series** $7
	BOWL SCRAPER	• Curved shape with comfortable grip • Rigid enough to move dough but flexible enough to scrape up batter • Thin, straight edge doubles as dough cutter or bench scraper	**iSi Basics Silicone Scraper Spatula** $5.99

HANDY TOOLS	ITEM	WHAT TO LOOK FOR	TEST KITCHEN FAVORITES
MUST-HAVE ITEMS	ROLLING PIN	• Moderate weight (1 to 1½ pounds) • 19-inch straight barrel • Slightly textured wooden surface to grip dough for easy rolling	**J.K. Adams Plain Maple Rolling Dowel** $13.95
	MIXING BOWLS	• Good to have both stainless steel and glass (for mixing, microwaving, and holding prepped ingredients) • Sets of 6 to 9 nesting bowls ranging in capacity from about 1¼ ounces to 4 quarts (for glass) and 2 cups to 8 quarts (for stainless steel)	Stainless Steel: **Vollrath Economy Stainless Steel Mixing Bowls** $2.90–$6.90 Glass: **Pyrex Smart Essentials with Colored Lids** $27.98
	MINI PREP BOWLS	• Sturdy and somewhat heavy bowls to prevent tipping • Roomy 6-ounce capacity • Glass to resist stains and not absorb odors • Dishwasher- and microwave-safe	**Pyrex 6-Ounce Dessert Dishes, Set of 4** $6.99
MUST-HAVE ITEM	OVEN MITT	• Form-fitting and not overly bulky for easy maneuvering • Machine washable • Flexible, heat-resistant material	**Kool-Tek 15-Inch Oven Mitt by KatchAll** $44.95 Best Buy: **OrkaPlus Silicone Oven Mitt with Cotton Lining** $14.95
	COOKIE CUTTERS	• Metal cutters • Thin, sharp cutting edge and round or rubber-grip top • Depth of at least 1 inch	**Little difference among various brands**
	PASTRY BRUSH	• Silicone bristles (heat-resistant, durable, and easy to clean) • Perforated flaps (to trap liquid) • Angled head to reach tight spots • Comfortable handle	**OXO Good Grips Silicone Pastry Brush** $6.99
	SPLATTER SCREEN	• Diameter of at least 13 inches • Lollipop-shaped design • Tightly woven mesh face	**Amco 13-Inch Splatter Screen** $15.95

	ITEM	WHAT TO LOOK FOR	TEST KITCHEN FAVORITES
	BOUILLON STRAINER/ CHINOIS	• Conical shape • Depth of 7 to 8 inches • At least one hook on rim for stability	**Winco Reinforced Extra Fine Mesh Bouillon Strainer** $33.78
	COLANDER	• 4- to 7-quart capacity • Metal ring attached to bottom for stability • Many holes for quick draining • Small holes so pasta doesn't slip through	**RSVP International Endurance Precision Pierced 5-Quart Colander** $25.99
	FINE-MESH STRAINER	• At least 6 inches in diameter (measured from inside edge to inside edge) • Sturdy construction	**CIA Masters Collection 6¾ Inch Fine Mesh Strainer** $27.50
	SPIDER SKIMMER	• Long, angled metal handle • Woven wire basket • Shallow, flat basket lip	**WMF Profi Plus 13.5-cm Wok Mesh Strainer** $18
	FOOD MILL	• Interchangeable disks for fine, medium, and coarse purees • Stainless steel • Easy to turn	**Cuisipro Stainless Steel Food Mill** $105
	FAT SEPARATOR	• Pitcher-style • Wide-shaped spout for pouring • Strainer for catching solids • 4-cup capacity	**Trudeau Gravy Separator with Integrated Strainer** $11.41

MUST-HAVE ITEMS

HANDY TOOLS	ITEM	WHAT TO LOOK FOR	TEST KITCHEN FAVORITES
MUST-HAVE ITEM	POTATO MASHER	• Solid mashing disk with small holes • Comfortable grip	**WMF Profi Plus Stainless Steel Potato Masher** $15.99
MUST-HAVE ITEM	SALAD SPINNER	• Ergonomic and easy-to-operate hand pump • Wide base for stability • Flat lid for easy cleaning and storage	**OXO Good Grips Salad Spinner** $29.99
	STEAMER BASKET	• Collapsible stainless steel basket with feet • Adjustable and removable center rod for easy removal from pot and easy storage	**OXO Good Grips Pop-Up Steamer** $16.99
	MORTAR AND PESTLE	• Heavy, stable base with tall, narrow walls • Rough interior to help grip and grind ingredients • Comfortable, heavy pestle	**Frieling "Goliath" Mortar and Pestle Set** $49.95

MEASURING EQUIPMENT	ITEM	WHAT TO LOOK FOR	TEST KITCHEN FAVORITES
MUST-HAVE ITEMS	DRY MEASURING CUPS	• Stainless steel cups (hefty and durable) • Measurement markings that are visible even once the cup is full • Evenly weighted and stable • Long handles that are level with the rim of the cup	**Amco Houseworks Professional Performance 4-Piece Measuring Cup Set** $14.95
	LIQUID MEASURING CUPS	• Crisp, unambiguous markings that include ¼ and ⅓ cup measurements • Heatproof, sturdy cup with handle • Good to have in a variety of sizes (1, 2, and 4 cups)	**Pyrex 2-Cup Measuring Cup** $5.99

MEASURING EQUIPMENT	ITEM	WHAT TO LOOK FOR	TEST KITCHEN FAVORITES
	ADJUSTABLE MEASURING CUP	• Plungerlike bottom (with a tight seal between plunger and tube) that you can set to correct measurement, then push up to cleanly extract sticky ingredients (such as shortening or peanut butter) • 1- or 2-cup capacity • Dishwasher-safe	**KitchenArt Pro Adjust-A-Cup** $12.95
	MEASURING SPOONS	• Long, comfortable handles • Rim of bowl flush with handle (makes it easy to "dip" into a dry ingredient and "sweep" across the top for accurate measuring) • Slim design	**Cuisipro Stainless Steel Measuring Spoon Set** $11.95
	KITCHEN RULER	• Stainless steel and easy to clean • 18 inches in length • Large, easy-to-read markings	**Empire 18-Inch Stainless Steel Ruler** $8.49
	DIGITAL SCALE	• Easy-to-read display not blocked by weighing platform • At least 7-pound capacity • Accessible buttons • Gram-to-ounce conversion feature • Roomy platform	**OXO Food Scale** $49.99 Best Buy: **Soehnle 65055 Digital Scale** $29.75

Left margin: MUST-HAVE ITEMS

THERMOMETERS AND TIMERS	ITEM	WHAT TO LOOK FOR	TEST KITCHEN FAVORITES
	INSTANT-READ THERMOMETER	• Digital model with automatic shut-off • Quick-response readings in 10 seconds or less • Wide temperature range (-40 to 450 degrees) • Long stem that can reach interior of large cuts of meat • Water resistant	**ThermoWorks Splash-Proof Super-Fast Thermapen** $96 Best Buys: **ThermoWorks Super-Fast Pocket Thermometer** $19 **CDN ProAccurate Quick-Read Thermometer** $16.95
	OVEN THERMOMETER	• Clearly marked numbers for easy readability • Hang model or stable base • Large temperature range (up to 600 degrees)	**Cooper-Atkins Oven Thermometer** (model #24HP) $6

Left margin: MUST-HAVE ITEMS

THERMOMETERS AND TIMERS	ITEM	WHAT TO LOOK FOR	TEST KITCHEN FAVORITES
	CANDY THERMOMETER	• Digital model • Easy-to-read console • Mounting clip (to attach probe to the pan)	**Thermoworks ChefAlarm** $59
	BARBECUE THERMOMETER	• Simultaneously checks food and grill temperature • Easy to read • Heatproof finger-grip • Dishwasher-safe	**Polder Dual Sensor Meat and Oven Thermometer** $10
	REFRIGERATOR/ FREEZER THERMOMETER	• Clear digital display • Wire probe for monitoring refrigerator and freezer simultaneously	**Maverick Cold-Chek Digital Refrigerator/Freezer Thermometer** $19.99
	REMOTE THERMOMETER	• Bluetooth device connects quickly to smart phones and delivers accurate temperature readouts • Easy to use	**iDevices Kitchen Thermometer** $78
	KITCHEN TIMER	• Lengthy time range (1 second to at least 10 hours) • Ability to count up after alarm goes off • Easy to use and read	**Polder 3-in-1 Clock, Timer, and Stopwatch** (model #898-95) $15.12
	MULTI-EVENT KITCHEN TIMER	• Easy to read and set timers • Shows at a glance which timer is going off • Durable, solid construction	**American Innovative Chef's Quad Timer** $29.99

MUST-HAVE ITEM

BAKEWARE	ITEM	WHAT TO LOOK FOR	TEST KITCHEN FAVORITES
MUST-HAVE ITEM	GLASS BAKING DISH	• Dimensions of 13 by 9 inches • Large enough to hold casseroles and large crisps and cobblers • Handles	**Pyrex Bakeware 9 x 13-Inch Baking Dish** $12.99
	BROILER-SAFE BAKING DISH	• Large, easy-to-grip handles • Straight sides for easy serving • Lightweight porcelain	**HIC Porcelain Lasagna Baking Dish** $29.95
	METAL BAKING PAN	• Dimensions of 13 by 9 inches • Straight sides • Nonstick coating for even browning and easy release of cakes and bar cookies	**Williams-Sonoma Goldtouch Nonstick Rectangular Cake Pan** $32.95
	SQUARE BAKING PANS	• Straight sides • Light gold or dark nonstick surface for even browning and easy release of cakes • Good to have both 9-inch and 8-inch square pans	**Williams-Sonoma Nonstick Goldtouch Square Cake Pan** $26, 8-inch $27, 9-inch Best Buy: **Chicago Metallic Gourmetware 8-Inch Nonstick Square Cake Pan** $6
MUST-HAVE ITEMS	ROUND CAKE PANS Best all-around	• Best for cake • Straight sides • Light finish for tall, even baking • Nonstick surface for easy release	**Nordic Ware Naturals Nonstick 9-inch Round Cake Pan** $14.32
	Best for browning	• Dark finish is ideal for pizza and cinnamon buns • Nonstick	**Chicago Metallic Non-Stick 9" Round Cake Pan** $10.97
	PIE PLATES	• Glass promotes even browning and allows progress to be monitored • ½-inch rim (makes it easy to shape decorative crusts) • Shallow angled sides prevent crusts from slumping • Good to have two	**Pyrex Bakeware 9-Inch Pie Plate** $8.16

BAKEWARE	ITEM	WHAT TO LOOK FOR	TEST KITCHEN FAVORITES
MUST-HAVE ITEM	LOAF PANS	• Light gold or dark nonstick surface for even browning and easy release • Good to have both 8½ by 4½-inch and 9 by 5-inch pans	**Williams-Sonoma 8½ x 4½-Inch Nonstick Goldtouch Loaf Pan** $21 Best Buy: **Baker's Secret 9 x 5-Inch Nonstick Loaf Pan** $5
MUST-HAVE ITEMS	SPRINGFORM PAN	• Nonstick coated base • Tight seal between band and bottom of pan (prevents leakage) • Even browning	**Nordic Ware Pro Form 9-Inch LeakProof Springform Pan** $15
	COOKIE SHEET	• Thick aluminum heats and browns evenly • Won't warp with repeated use • Raised edges for easy maneuvering • Nonstick, spacious surface	**Vollrath Wear-Ever Cookie Sheet** (Natural Finish) $15.99
	MUFFIN PAN	• Nonstick surface for even browning and easy release • Wide, extended rims and raised lip for easy handling • Cup capacity of ½ cup	**Wilton Avanti Everglide Metal-Safe Nonstick 12-Cup Muffin Pan** $13.99
	COOLING RACK	• Grid-style rack with tightly woven, heavy-gauge bars • Should fit inside a standard 18 by 13-inch rimmed baking sheet • Dishwasher-safe	**CIA Bakeware 12 x 17-Inch Cooling Rack** $15.95 Best Buy: **Libertyware Half-Size Sheet Pan Grate** $5.25
	BAKER'S COOLING RACK	• Sturdy rack • Four collapsible shelves • Unit folds down for easy storage	**Linden Sweden Baker's Cooling Rack** $17.99
	BISCUIT CUTTERS	• Sharp edges • A set with a variety of sizes	**Ateco 11-Piece Plain Round Cutter Set** $14.99

BAKEWARE	ITEM	WHAT TO LOOK FOR	TEST KITCHEN FAVORITES
	BUNDT PAN	• Heavyweight cast aluminum • Silver platinum nonstick surface for even browning and easy release • Clearly defined ridges • 15-cup capacity	**Nordic Ware Anniversary Bundt Pan** (model #50037) $26.95
	TART PAN	• Tinned steel for even browning and easy release • Removable bottom • If you bake a lot, it's good to have multiple sizes, though 9 inches is standard	**Kaiser Tinplate 9-Inch Quiche Pan with Removable Bottom** $9
	TUBE PAN	• Heavy pan (at least 1 pound) • Heavy bottom for leak-free seal • Dark nonstick surface for even browning and easy release • 16-cup capacity • Feet on rim	**Chicago Metallic Professional Nonstick Angel Food Cake Pan** $19.95
	PULLMAN LOAF PAN	• Squared-off pan (4 by 4 inches) • Nonstick aluminized steel for easy cleanup • Light surface for even browning	**USA Pan 13 by 4-inch Pullman Loaf Pan and Cover** $33.95
	BAKER'S EDGE PAN	• Attached cutting grid • Dark nonstick surface for easy release	**Baker's Edge Brownie Pan** $34.95
	RAMEKINS	• Sturdy, high-fired porcelain (chip-resistant and safe for use in oven, broiler, microwave, and dishwasher) • For one all-purpose set, capacity of 6 ounces and diameter of 3 inches	**Apilco 6-Ounce Ramekins** $29 for a set of four
	BAKING STONE	• Substantial but not too heavy to handle • Dimensions of 16 by 14 inches • Clay, not cement, for evenly browned crusts	**The Baker's Catalogue Pizza Baking Stone by Old Stone Oven** $54.95

SMALL APPLIANCES	ITEM	WHAT TO LOOK FOR	TEST KITCHEN FAVORITES
MUST-HAVE ITEM	FOOD PROCESSOR	• 14-cup capacity • Sharp and sturdy blades • Wide feed tube • Should come with basic blades and discs: steel blade, dough blade, shredding/slicing disc	**Cuisinart Custom 14-Cup Food Processor** $199
	STAND MIXER	• Planetary action (stationary bowl and single mixing arm) • Powerful motor • Bowl size of at least 4½ quarts • Slightly squat bowl to keep ingredients in beater's range • Should come with basic attachments: paddle, dough hook, metal whisk	**Kitchen-Aid Pro Line Series 7-quart Bowl Lift Stand Mixer** $549.95 Best Buy: **KitchenAid Classic Plus Series 4.5-quart Tilt-Head Stand Mixer** $229.99
MUST-HAVE ITEMS	HAND-HELD MIXER	• Lightweight model • Slim wire beaters without a central post • Digital display • Separate ejector buttons (not part of the speed dial) • Variety of speeds	**Cuisinart Power Advantage 7-Speed Hand Mixer** $59.95
	BLENDER	• Mix of straight and serrated blades at different angles • Jar with curved base • At least 44-ounce capacity • Heavy base for stability	**Vitamix 5200** $449 Best Buy: **Breville BBL605XL Hemisphere Control Blender** $200
	IMMERSION BLENDER	• Easy to operate and lightweight • Detachable shaft for easy cleaning • Wide blade cage so food can circulate	**KitchenAid 3-Speed Hand Blender** $59.99
	ELECTRIC GRIDDLE	• Large cooking area (about 21 by 12 inches) • Attached pull-out grease trap (won't tip over) • Nonstick surface for easy cleanup	**BroilKing Professional Griddle** $99.99

SMALL APPLIANCES	ITEM	WHAT TO LOOK FOR	TEST KITCHEN FAVORITES
	ELECTRIC JUICER	• Ideal for making a large amount of fruit or vegetable juice • Centrifugal, not masticating, model for fresher-tasting juice • 3-inch-wide feed tube • Easy to assemble and clean	**Breville Juice Fountain Plus** $149.99
	ADJUSTABLE ELECTRIC KETTLE	• Heats water to a range of different temperatures • Automatic shutoff • Separate base for cordless pouring • Visible water level	**Zojirushi Micom Water Boiler & Warmer** $114.95 Best Buy: **Chef'sChoice 688 Electric Smart Kettle** $99.99
	COFFEE MAKER	• Thermal carafe that keeps coffee hot and fresh with capacity of at least 10 cups • Short brewing time (6 minutes is ideal) • Copper, not aluminum, heating element • Easy-to-fill water tank • Clear, intuitive controls	**Technivorm Moccamaster 10-Cup Coffee Maker with Thermal Carafe** $299 Best Buy: **Bonavita 8-Cup Coffee Maker** $149
	COFFEE MAKER, POD	• Fast and intuitive controls to set temperature of water • Ability to make "smooth" and full-bodied brews, including coffee, tea, and espresso	**Cuisinart Single Serve Brewing System by Keurig** $199.00
	MEAT GRINDER	• All-metal machine • Motorized grinder with reverse mode for unclogging stuck pieces • Easy to assemble	**Waring Pro Professional Meat Grinder** $199.99 Best Buy: **KitchenAid Food Grinder Attachment** $48.74

SMALL APPLIANCES	ITEM	WHAT TO LOOK FOR	TEST KITCHEN FAVORITES
	DEEP FRYER	• Large, wide basket ensures even heat exposure • Recovers heat quickly after food is added NOTE: We prefer to deep-fry in a Dutch oven for superior temperature control and larger capacity, but a deep fryer can be useful for French fries and other low-temperature fried foods.	**Waring Pro Professional Deep Fryer** $139.95
	PORTABLE INDUCTION BURNER	• Large cooking surface for even heating of pans • Basic push buttons and dial controls for ease of use	**Max Burton Induction Cook Top** $124.25
	ICE CREAM MAKER	• Minimum 1½-quart capacity • Removable canister and blade for easy cleaning	**Whynter SNÖ Professional Ice Cream Maker** $330.99 Best Buy: **Cuisinart Automatic Frozen Yogurt, Ice Cream, and Sorbet Maker** (model #ICE-21) $49.95
	PRESSURE COOKER	• Stainless steel rather than aluminum for more durable construction that doesn't react to acidic foods • Stovetop model with low sides and wide base for easy access and better browning and heat retention • Pressure indicator that is easy to see and interpret at a glance	**Fissler Vitaquick 8 Liter Pressure Cooker** (8.5 quart) $280 Best Buy: **Fagor Duo 8-Quart Pressure Cooker** $109.95
	SLOW COOKER	• At least 6-quart capacity (4-quart capacity for small slow cookers) • Insert handles • Clear lid to see progress of food • Dishwasher-safe insert • Intuitive controls with programmable timer and warming mode	Large: **KitchenAid 6-Quart Slow Cooker with Solid Glass Lid** $99.99 Small: **Cuisinart 4-Quart Cook Central 3-in-1 Multicooker** $129.95

SMALL APPLIANCES	ITEM	WHAT TO LOOK FOR	TEST KITCHEN FAVORITES
	TWO-SLOT TOASTER	• Quartz heating element for even heating • Clear window to monitor browning • Ample room for large or thick bread slices or bagels	**Magimix by Robot-Coupe Vision Toaster** $249.95 Best Buy: **KitchenAid 2 Slice Manual High-Lift Lever Toaster with LCD Display** $89.99
	TOASTER OVEN	• Quartz heating elements for steady, controlled heat • Roomy but compact interior • Simple to use	**The Smart Oven by Breville** $249.95 Best Buy: **Hamilton Beach Set & Forget Toaster Oven with Convection Cooking** $99.99
	TABLETOP GRILL	• Large grilling area • Easy to clean	**Delonghi Alfredo Healthy Indoor Grill** $53.99
	WAFFLE IRON	• Audible alert • Heat-resistant handles • Multiple doneness settings	**Chef'sChoice WafflePro Express** $69.95

GRILLING EQUIPMENT	ITEM	WHAT TO LOOK FOR	TEST KITCHEN FAVORITES
	GAS GRILL	• Large grilling area (at least 350 square inches) • Built-in thermometer • Two burners for varying heat levels (three is even better) • Attached table • Fat drainage system	**Weber Spirit E-210** $399
	CHARCOAL GRILL	• Sturdy construction to efficiently maintain heat • Well-designed cooking grate, handles, lids, and wheels • Generous cooking surface • Large charcoal capacity • Well-positioned air vents • Gas ignition to instantly and easily light coals • Ash catcher for easy cleanup	**Weber Performer Platinum 22.5-Inch Charcoal Grill with Touch-n-Go Gas Ignition** $349 Best Buy: **Weber One-Touch Gold 22.5-Inch Charcoal Grill** $149

GRILLING EQUIPMENT	ITEM	WHAT TO LOOK FOR	TEST KITCHEN FAVORITES
	PORTABLE CHARCOAL GRILL	• Ample cooking surface with raised lip • Cover that can be secured for travel • Lightweight but durable	**Weber Smokey Joe Gold Portable Charcoal Grill** $34.70
	SMOKER	• Large cooking area • Water pan • Multiple vents for precise temperature control	**Weber Smokey Mountain Cooker Smoker, 18½ Inch** $299
	CHIMNEY STARTER	• 6-quart capacity • Holes in canister so air can circulate around coals • Sturdy construction • Heat-resistant handle • Dual handle for easy control	**Weber Rapidfire Chimney Starter** $14.99
	GRILL TONGS	• 16 inches in length • Scalloped, not sharp and serrated, edges • Open and close easily • Lightweight • Moderate amount of springy tension	**OXO Good Grips 16-Inch Locking Tongs** $14.99
	GRILL BRUSH	• Long handle • Replaceable, long-lasting steel pads for scrubbing	**Grill Wizard 18-inch China Grill Brush** $31.50
	GRILL SPATULA	• Handle at least 12 inches in length • Sharp cutting edge	**Weber Original Stainless Steel Spatula** $14.99
	BASTING BRUSH	• Silicone bristles • Angled brush head • Handle between 8 and 13 inches • Heat-resistant	**Elizabeth Karmel's Grill Friends Super Silicone Angled Barbecue Basting Brush** $9.95
	BARBECUE GLOVES	• Excellent heat protection • Gloves, rather than mitts, for dexterity • Long sleeves to protect forearms	**Steven Raichlen Ultimate Suede Grilling Gloves** $29.99 per pair

GRILLING EQUIPMENT	ITEM	WHAT TO LOOK FOR	TEST KITCHEN FAVORITES
	SKEWERS	• Flat and metal • ³⁄₁₆ inch thick	**Norpro 12-Inch Stainless Steel Skewers** $6.85 for a set of six
	RIB RACK	• Sturdily supports six racks of ribs • Doubles as roasting rack (when flipped upside down) • Nonstick coating for easy cleanup	**Charcoal Companion Non-Stick Reversible Roasting/Rib Rack** $14.95
	GRILL LIGHTER	• Flexible neck • Refillable chamber with large, easy-to-read fuel window • Comfortable grip	**Zippo Flexible Neck Utility Lighter** $18.35
	ELECTRIC CHARCOAL STARTER	• Long, offset heating element • Quick-to-heat	**Grill Dome Rapid-Lite Electric Charcoal Starters** $34.95
	DISPOSABLE GRILL	• Kit includes aluminum pan, metal grate, and charcoal • Large grilling area (about 12 by 10 inches) • After use, can be thrown away or recycled	**EZ Grill Disposable Instant Grill, Large** $10.99
	OUTDOOR GRILL PAN	• Narrow slits and raised sides so food can't fall through or off • Sturdy construction with handles	**Weber Style 6435 Professional Grade Grill Pan** $19.99
	SMOKER BOX	• Cast iron for slow heating and steady smoke • Easy to fill, empty, and clean	**GrillPro Cast Iron Smoker Box made by Onward Manufacturing Company** $12.79

GRILLING EQUIPMENT	ITEM	WHAT TO LOOK FOR	TEST KITCHEN FAVORITES
	WOOD, FOR SMOKING	• Hickory wood for bold, smoky flavor • Long-lasting chunks for charcoal grills • Wood chips for gas grills	**Little difference among various brands**
	VERTICAL ROASTER	• Helps poultry cook evenly • 8-inch shaft keeps chicken above fat and drippings in pan • Attached basin catches drippings for pan sauce • Sturdy construction	**Norpro Vertical Roaster with Infuser** **$27.95** Best Buy: **Elizabeth Karmel's Grill Friends Porcelain Chicken Sitter Stand, 12 Inches** **$11.99**
	PROPANE INDICATOR	• Easy-to-read dial • Accurately measures propane by weight	**Grill Gauge Propane Tank Scale** **$13.99**

SPECIALTY PIECES	ITEM	WHAT TO LOOK FOR	TEST KITCHEN FAVORITES
	APPLE CORER	• Comfortable grip with offset handle • Sharp teeth • Wide blade diameter	**CuisiPro Apple Corer** **$9.95**
	APPLE SLICER	• Sharp, serrated corer with 1-inch diameter • Ability to cut 8 or 16 slices • Comfortable handle	**Williams-Sonoma Dial-a-Slice Apple Divider** **$19.95**
	CORN STRIPPER	• Safer than using chef's knife • Attached cup to catch kernels • Comfortable grip and sharp blade	**OXO Good Grips Corn Stripper** **$11.99**

SPECIALTY PIECES	ITEM	WHAT TO LOOK FOR	TEST KITCHEN FAVORITES
	TOMATO CORER	• Sharp teeth make easy, clean cuts • Lightweight, rounded-off plastic handle • Comfortable head-handle combination	**Norpro Tomato Core It** $2.99
	NUT CHOPPER	• Sharp, sturdy stainless steel chopping tines • Dishwasher-safe	**Progressive International Heavy Duty Nut Chopper** $8.89
	GRILL PAN	• Cast-iron pan with enamel coating for heat retention and easy cleanup • Tall ridges (4 to 5.5 mm high) to keep food above rendered fat • Generous cooking area	**Staub 12-Inch American Square Grill Pan and Press** $219.95 Best Buy: **Lodge Pre-Seasoned Square Grill Pan & Ribbed Panini Press** $18.97 (press sold separately for $14.58)
	STOVETOP GRIDDLE	• Anodized aluminum for even heating • Nonstick coating • Lightweight (about 4 pounds) • Heat-resistant loop handles • At least 17 by 9 inches (large enough to span two burners) • Pour spout for draining grease	**Anolon Advanced Double Burner Griddle** $48.95
	OYSTER KNIFE	• Sturdy, flat blade with slightly curved tip for easy penetration • Slim, nonstick handle for secure, comfortable grip	**R. Murphy New Haven Oyster Knife** $16.65
	SILICONE MICROWAVE LID	• Thin, silicone round to cover splatter-prone food during microwave heating • Easy to clean • Doubles as jar opener	**Piggy Steamer** $18

SPECIALTY PIECES	ITEM	WHAT TO LOOK FOR	TEST KITCHEN FAVORITES
	PASTRY BAG	• Plastic-coated canvas pastry bag (for durability and easy cleanup) or disposable bags • Large bag (about 18 inches in length) for easier gripping and twisting • Accommodates standard-size tips	**Ateco 18-Inch Plastic-Coated Pastry Bag** $4.45
	CHEESE WIRE	• Comfortable plastic handles • Narrow wire	**Fante's Handled Cheese Wire** $2.99
	PIZZA WHEEL	• Clear plastic wheel to prevent damage to pans • Comfortable, soft-grip handle	**OXO Good Grips 4-Inch Pizza Wheel** $12.99
	POTATO RICER	• Large hopper that can hold 1¼ cups sliced potatoes • Interchangeable fine and coarse disks • Sturdy, ergonomic handles	**RSVP International Potato Ricer** $13.95
	TORTILLA WARMER	• Triple-layered sides with two layers of fabric around sheet of insulating plastic • 12-inch diameter to fit large wraps	**IMUSA 12-Inch Cloth Tortilla Warmer** $5.99
	CUPCAKE AND CAKE CARRIER	• Fits both round and square cakes and cupcakes • Snap locks • Nonskid base • Collapses for easy storage	**Progressive Collapsible Cupcake and Cake Carrier** $29.99

SPECIALTY PIECES	ITEM	WHAT TO LOOK FOR	TEST KITCHEN FAVORITES
	CAKE LIFTER	• Sturdy but small and slightly flexible • Rounded corners for visibility • Comfortable offset handle	**Fat Daddio's Cake Lifter** $11.88
	REVOLVING CAKE STAND	• Elevated rotating stand so you can hold the spatula steady for easy frosting	**Ateco Professional Icing Turntable** $66.99 Best Buy: **Ateco Plastic Revolving Cake Stand** $19.95
	CREAM WHIPPER	• Slim canister for one-handed squeezing • Slender metal tip to make rosettes and mounds	**Liss Professional Polished Stainless Steel Cream Whipper** (1-pint) $149.95
	SPICE/COFFEE GRINDER	• Electric, not manual, grinders • Deep bowl to hold ample amount of coffee beans • Good to have two, one each for coffee grinding and spice grinding	**Capresso Cool Grind, Model 501** $19.99
	INNOVATIVE TEAPOT	• Contained ultrafine-mesh strainer keeps tea leaf dregs separate • One-piece design for easy cleaning	**Adagio Teas IngenuiTEA** $14.95
	TRAVEL MUG	• Simple, leakproof lid design • Good heat retention • Easy-to-clean and dishwasher safe	**Timolino Icon 16-Ounces Signature Vacuum Travel Mug** $28

SPECIALTY PIECES	ITEM	WHAT TO LOOK FOR	TEST KITCHEN FAVORITES
	WINE OPENER	• Easy-to-grip chrome body • Hinged fulcrum for leverage • Teflon-coated worm with zero friction	**Pulltap's Classic Evolution Corkscrew by Pulltex** $39.95
	ELECTRIC WINE OPENER	• Sturdy, quiet corkscrew • Broad base that rests firmly on bottle	**Waring Pro Professional Cordless Wine Opener** $39.95
	WINE AERATOR	• Long, tubelike design that exposes wine to air as it is being poured • Neat, hands-free aerating	**Nuance Wine Finer** $49.95
	COCKTAIL SHAKER	• Double-walled canister to prevent condensation for slip-free gripping • Convenient pop-up spout • Tight-sealing lid	**Metrokane Fliptop Cocktail Shaker** $29.95
	BEER SAVERS	• Fit both glass and plastic bottles • Preserve carbonation for up to 48 hours	**Savebrands Beer Savers** $6.99 for six-pack
	COOLER	• Insulating layer of plastic lining • Lightweight, durable, sturdy, and easy to move, even when full • Easy to clean	**California Cooler Bags T-Rex Large Collapsible Rolling Cooler** $75
	SELTZER MAKER	• Easy to use and easy to control level of fizz • CO_2 canisters are long lasting and convenient to exchange at retail stores	**SodaStream Source Start Kit** $99.95

SPECIALTY PIECES	ITEM	WHAT TO LOOK FOR	TEST KITCHEN FAVORITES
	VACUUM SEALER	• Countertop, heat-sealed model • Works well with wide variety of bags, canisters, and rolls	**Weston Professional Advantage Vacuum Sealer** $189.99 Best Buy: **Waring Pro Pistol Vac Professional Vacuum Sealer System** $69.95
	COMPOST BUCKET	• Plastic pail to collect food scraps for composter • Carbon filter prevents odors from escaping and allows oxygen to enter so decomposition can occur • Easy to open lid that latches securely in place • 2.4-gallon capacity	**Exaco Trading Kitchen Compost Waste Collector** $19.98
	FIRE EXTINGUISHER	• Easy to operate • Powerful, controlled spray	**Kidde Kitchen Fire Extinguisher** (model #21005753/FX10K) $18.97

KITCHEN SUPPLIES	ITEM	WHAT TO LOOK FOR	TEST KITCHEN FAVORITES
	PARCHMENT PAPER	• Sturdy paper for heavy doughs • Easy release of baked goods • At least 14 inches wide	
	PLASTIC WRAP	• Clings tightly and resticks well • Packaging with sharp teeth that aren't exposed (to avoid snags on clothing and skin) • Adhesive pad to hold cut end of wrap	**Glad Cling Wrap Clear Plastic** $2.59
	BUTTER SAVER	• Fits the end of standard-size stick of butter • Kept butter from picking up off-flavors for more than a week • Measures 1 tablespoon	**Savebrands Butter Saver** $4.99

MUST-HAVE ITEMS

KITCHEN SUPPLIES	ITEM	WHAT TO LOOK FOR	TEST KITCHEN FAVORITES
	PAPER PLATES	• Large surface area • Sturdy enough to support heavy food • Plastic-coated to repel grease and moisture	**Vanity Fair Impressions Dinner Plates, 11 Inches** $3.79 for 14 plates
	FOOD STORAGE CONTAINER	• Snap-style seal with ridge on underside to ensure tight seal • Low, flat rectangle for easy storage and more efficient heating and chilling • Made of plastic free of BPA (bisphenol-A)	**Snapware Airtight 8-Cup Rectangle Food Storage Container** $7.99
	DISH TOWEL	• Thin cotton for absorbency and flexibility • Dries glassware without steaks • Washes clean without shrinking	**Williams-Sonoma Striped Towels** $19.95 for set of 4
	APRONS	• Adjustable neck strap and long strings • Full coverage; chest area reinforced with extra layer of fabric • Stains wash out completely	**Bragard Travail Apron** $26.95
	LIQUID DISH DETERGENT	• High concentration of surfactants to wash away oil • Clean scent	**Mrs. Meyer's Clean Day Liquid Dish Soap, Lavender** $3.99 for 16 fluid ounces (25 cents per ounce)

Stocking Your Pantry

Using the best ingredients is one way to guarantee success in the kitchen. But how do you know what to buy? Shelves are filled with a dizzying array of choices—and price does not equal quality. Over the years, the test kitchen's blind tasting panels have evaluated thousands of ingredients, brand by brand, side by side, plain and in prepared applications, to determine which brands you can trust and which brands to avoid. In the chart that follows, we share the results, revealing our top-rated choices and the attributes that made them stand out among the competition. And because our test kitchen accepts no support from product manufacturers, you can trust our ratings. See AmericasTestKitchen.com for updates to these tastings.

	TEST KITCHEN FAVORITE	WHY WE LIKE IT	RUNNERS-UP
	ANCHOVIES **Ortiz Oil-Packed Spanish**	• Pleasantly fishy, salty flavor, not overwhelming or bland • Firm, meaty texture, not mushy • Already filleted and ready to use, unlike salt-packed variety	Flott Salt-Packed
	APPLESAUCE **Musselman's Lite**	• An unusual ingredient, sucralose, sweetens this applesauce without overpowering its fresh, bright apple flavor • Pinch of salt boosts flavor above weak, bland, and too-sweet competitors • Coarse, almost chunky texture, not slimy like applesauces sweetened with corn syrup	Musselman's Home Style
	BACON, SUPERMARKET **Farmland Thick Sliced Smoked**	• Good balance of saltiness and sweetness • Smoky and full flavored, not one-dimensional • Very meaty, not too fatty or insubstantial • Crisp yet hearty texture, not tough or dry	Boar's Head Brand Naturally Smoked Sliced and Hormel Black Label Original
	BARBECUE SAUCE **Bull's-Eye Original**	• Spicy, fresh tomato taste • Good balance of tanginess, smokiness, and sweetness • Robust flavor from molasses • Sweetened with sugar and molasses, not high-fructose corn syrup, which caramelizes and burns quickly	
	BEANS, CANNED BAKED **B&M Vegetarian**	• Firm and pleasant texture with some bite • Sweetened with molasses for complexity and depth	Bush's Best Original and Van Camp's Original

	TEST KITCHEN FAVORITE	WHY WE LIKE IT	RUNNERS-UP
	BEANS, CANNED BLACK **Bush's Best**	• Clean, mild, and slightly earthy flavor • Firm, almost al dente texture, not mushy or pasty • Good amount of salt	Goya and Progresso

	BEANS, CANNED
	CHICKPEAS
	Pastene
		• Firm yet tender texture bests pasty and dry
		  competitors
		• Clean chickpea flavor
		• Enough salt to enhance but not overwhelm
		  the flavor
			Goya

	BEANS, CANNED RED KIDNEY **Goya**	• Sweet with strong bean flavor • Beautiful red, plump beans • Smooth, creamy texture, not mushy, chalky, or too firm • Flavor boost from added sugar and salt	S&W
	BEANS, CANNED WHITE **Goya Cannellini**	• Clean, earthy flavor • Smooth, creamy interior with tender skins • Not full of broken beans like some competitors	Bush's Best Cannellini Beans White Kidney Beans
	BEANS, REFRIED **Taco Bell Home Originals**	• Well-seasoned mixture • Super-smooth texture, not overly thick, pasty, or gluey	Goya Traditional Refried Pinto Beans and Old El Paso
	BREAD, MULTIGRAIN **Nature's Own Specialty 12 Grain**	• Substantial, chewy slices • Nutty, hearty seeds throughout and topped with rolled oats • Uses no white flour	Arnold 12 Grain, Pepperidge Farm 15 Grain
	BREAD, WHITE SANDWICH **Arnold Country Classics**	• Subtle sweetness, not tasteless or sour • Perfect structure, not too dry or too soft	Pepperidge Farm Farmhouse Hearty White
	BREAD, WHOLE-WHEAT SANDWICH **Pepperidge Farm 100% Whole Wheat**	• Whole-grain, nutty, earthy flavor • Dense, chewy texture, not gummy or too soft • Not too sweet, contains no corn syrup and has low sugar level (unlike competitors) NOTE: Available only east of the Mississippi River.	Rudi's Organic Bakery Honey Sweet Whole Wheat

	TEST KITCHEN FAVORITE	WHY WE LIKE IT	RUNNERS-UP
	BREAD CRUMBS, PANKO **Ian's Panko**	• Crisp, with a substantial crunch • Not too delicate, stale, sandy, or gritty • Oil-free and without seasonings or undesirable artificial flavors	
	BROTH, BEEF **Rachael Ray Stock-in-a-Box All-Natural Beef Flavored Stock**	• Deep beefy profile with rich notes and gelatin-like body • Flavor-enhancing ingredients such as tomato paste and yeast extract	College Inn Bold Stock Tender Beef Flavor
	BROTH, CHICKEN **Swanson Chicken Stock**	• Strong chicken flavor, not watery, beefy, or vegetal • Hearty and pleasant aroma • Roasted notes, not sour, rancid, or salty like some competitors • Flavor-boosting ingredients include carrots, celery, and onions	Better Than Bouillon Chicken Base
	BROTH, VEGETARIAN **Orrington Farms Vegan Chicken Flavored Broth Base and Seasoning**	• Savory depth without off-tasting vegetable undertones • Easy to store • Yeast extract adds depth and richness	Swanson Certified Organic Vegetable Broth
	BROWNIE MIX **Ghirardelli Chocolate Supreme**	• Rich, balanced chocolate flavor from both natural and Dutch-processed cocoa • Moist, chewy, and fudgy with perfect texture	
	BUTTER, UNSALTED **Plugrá European-Style**	• Sweet and creamy • Complex tang and grassy flavor • Moderate amount of butterfat so that it's decadent and glossy but not so rich that baked goods are greasy	Land O'Lakes and Vermont Creamery European-Style
	CHEESE, AMERICAN, PRESLICED **Boar's Head**	• Strong cheesy flavor, unlike some competitors • Higher content of cheese culture contributes to better flavor	Kraft Deli Deluxe

	TEST KITCHEN FAVORITE	WHY WE LIKE IT	RUNNERS-UP
	CHEESE, ASIAGO **BelGioioso**	• Sharp, tangy, and complex flavor, not mild • Firm and not too dry • Melts, shreds, and grates well	
	CHEESE, BLUE For dressings and dips: **Stella**	• Sweet, balanced, and mild flavor, not too pungent • Wet and extremely crumbly texture similar to feta	Danish Blue
	For eating out of hand: **Stilton**	• Balance of buttery, nutty, sweet, and salty flavors • Fairly firm with sliceable yet crumbly texture	Roquefort
	CHEESE, CHEDDAR, EXTRA-SHARP **Cabot Private Stock**	• Balance of salty, creamy, and sweet flavors • Considerable but well-rounded sharpness, not overwhelming • Firm, crumbly texture, not moist, rubbery, or springy • Aged at least 12 months for complex flavor	Cabot Extra-Sharp, Grafton Village Cheese Company Premium, Cabot Sharp, and Tillamook Special Reserve
	CHEESE, CHEDDAR, PRESLICED **Tillamook Sharp**	• Slightly crumbly, not rubbery or processed, texture characteristic of block cheddar • Strong, tangy, and salty flavor, not bland or too mild	Cabot All Natural Sharp and Cracker Barrel Natural Sharp
	CHEESE, CHEDDAR, PREMIUM **Milton Creamery Prairie Breeze**	• Earthy complexity with nutty, buttery, and fruity flavors • Dry and crumbly with crystalline crunch, not rubbery or overly moist • Aged no more than 12 months to prevent overly sharp flavor	Cabot Clothbound, Tillamook Vintage White Extra Sharp, and Beecher's Flagship Reserve
	CHEESE, CHEDDAR, REDUCED-FAT **Cracker Barrel Reduced Fat Sharp**	• Ample creaminess • Strong cheesy flavor • Good for cooking	Cabot 50% Light Sharp
	CHEESE, CHEDDAR, SHARP **Cabot Private Stick Cheddar Cheese**	• Sharp, clean, and tangy flavor • Firm, crumbly texture, not moist, rubbery, or springy • Aged a minimum of 12 months for complex flavor	Tillamook Sharp, Cracker Barrel Sharp White, and Grafton Village Cheese Company
	CHEESE, COTTAGE **Hood Country Style**	• Rich, well-seasoned, and buttery flavor • Velvety, creamy texture • Pillowy curds	Friendship 4% California Style and Breakstone's 4% Small Curd

	TEST KITCHEN FAVORITE	WHY WE LIKE IT	RUNNERS-UP
	CHEESE, CREAM **Philadelphia**	• Rich, tangy, and milky flavor • Thick, creamy texture, not pasty, waxy, or chalky	Organic Valley
	CHEESE, FETA **Mt. Vikos Traditional Feta**	• Strong tangy, salty flavor • Creamy, dense texture • Pleasing crumbly texture	Valbreso Feta
	CHEESE, FONTINA For eating out of hand: **Fontina Val d'Aosta**	• Strong, earthy aroma • Somewhat elastic texture with small irregular holes • Grassy, nutty flavor—but can be overpowering in cooked dishes	
	For cooking: **BelGioioso Italian Fontina**	• Semisoft, super-creamy texture • Mildly tangy, nutty flavor • Melts well	
	CHEESE, GOAT **Laura Chenel's Chèvre**	• Rich-tasting, grassy, tangy flavor • Smooth and creamy both unheated and baked • High salt content	Vermont Creamery, Chevrion, Cypress Grove
	CHEESE, GRUYÈRE **Gruyère Reserve Wheel (Peney-Le-Jorat)**	• Grassy, salty flavor, not bland or pedestrian • Creamy yet dry texture, not plasticky like some competitors • Aged a minimum of 10 months for strong and complex flavor • Melts especially well	Gruyère Salé
	CHEESE, MOZZARELLA **Galbani (formerly Sorrento) Whole Milk**	• Creamy and buttery with clean dairy flavor • Soft, not rubbery, chew	Kraft Low-Moisture Part Skim, Boar's Head Whole-Milk Low Moisture, and Kraft Shredded Low-Moisture Part-Skim
	CHEESE, PARMESAN **Boar's Head Parmigiano-Reggiano**	• Rich and complex flavor balances tanginess and nuttiness • Dry, crumbly texture yet creamy with a crystalline crunch, not rubbery or dense • Aged a minimum of 12 months for better flavor and texture	Il Villagio Parmigiano-Reggiano and BelGioioso
	CHEESE, PEPPERJACK **Boar's Head Monterey Jack Cheese with Jalapeño**	• Buttery, tangy cheese • Clean, balanced flavor with assertive spice	Tillamook Pepper Jack Cheese

	TEST KITCHEN FAVORITE	WHY WE LIKE IT	RUNNERS-UP
	CHEESE, PROVOLONE **Provolone Vernengo**	• Bold, nutty, and tangy flavor, not plasticky or bland • Firm, dry texture	
	CHEESE, RICOTTA, PART-SKIM **Calabro**	• Clean, fresh flavor, not rancid or sour from addition of gums or stabilizers • Creamy texture with perfect curds, unlike chalky, grainy, and soggy competitors	Freshly made ricotta cheese without gums or stabilizers
	CHEESE, SWISS For cheese plate: **Edelweiss Creamery Emmenthaler**	• Subtle flavor with sweet, buttery, nutty, and fruity notes • Firm yet gently giving texture, not rubbery • Aged longer for better flavor, resulting in larger eyes • Mildly pungent yet balanced	Emmi Kaltbach
	For cheese plate or cooking: **Emmi Emmenthaler Cheese AOC**	• Creamy texture • Salty mildness preferable for grilled cheese sandwiches	For cooking only: Boar's Head Gold Label Imported
	CHICKEN, WHOLE **Mary's Free Range Air-Chilled**	• Great, savory chicken flavor • Very tender • Air-chilled for minimum water retention and cleaner flavor	
	Bell & Evans Air-Chilled Premium Fresh	• Firm and tender texture • Full chicken flavor • Moist and juicy	
	CHICKEN, BREASTS, BONELESS SKINLESS **Bell & Evans Air-Chilled**	• Juicy and tender with clean chicken flavor • Not salted or brined • Air-chilled • Aged on bone for at least six hours after slaughter for significantly more tender meat	Springer Mountain Farms and Eberly's Free Range Young Organic
	CHILI POWDER **Morton & Bassett**	• Bold, full-flavored heat • Multidimensional flavor from a blend of cayenne and other chiles • Spices that complement but don't overwhelm the chiles	Penzeys Spices

	TEST KITCHEN FAVORITE	WHY WE LIKE IT	RUNNERS-UP
	CHOCOLATE, DARK **Ghirardelli 60% Cacao** **Bittersweet Chocolate** **Premium Baking Bar**	• Creamy texture, not grainy or chalky • Complex flavor with notes of cherry and wine with slight smokiness • Balance of sweetness and bitterness	Callebaut Intense Dark L-60-40NV (60% Cacao)
	CHOCOLATE, MILK **Dove Silky Smooth**	• Intense, full, rich chocolate flavor • Super-creamy texture from abundant milk fat and cocoa butter • Not overwhelmingly sweet	Endangered Species All-Natural Smooth and Green & Black's Organic
	CHOCOLATE, MILK CHIPS **Hershey's**	• Bold chocolate flavor outshines too-sweet, weak chocolate flavor of other chips • Complex with caramel and nutty notes • Higher fat content makes texture creamier than grainy, artificial competitors	
	CHOCOLATE, **DARK CHIPS** **Ghirardelli 60% Cacao** **Bittersweet**	• Intense, complex flavor beats one-dimensional flavor of competitors • Low sugar content highlights chocolate flavor • High amount of cocoa butter ensures creamy, smooth texture, not gritty and grainy • Wider, flatter shape and high percentage of fat help chips melt better in cookies	Hershey's Special Dark Mildly Sweet
	CHOCOLATE, **UNSWEETENED** **Hershey's Unsweetened** **Baking Bar**	• Well-rounded, complex flavor • Assertive chocolate flavor and deep notes of cocoa	Valrhona Cacao Pate Extra 100% and Scharffen Berger Unsweetened Dark
	CHOCOLATE, WHITE **CHIPS** **Guittard Choc-Au-Lait**	• Creamy texture, not waxy or crunchy • Silky smooth meltability from high fat content • Complex flavor like high-quality real chocolate, no artificial or off-flavors	Ghirardelli Classic White
	CINNAMON **Penzeys Extra Fancy** **Vietnamese Cassia**	• Warm, fragrant aroma with clove, fruity, and slightly smoky flavors • Mellow start with spicy finish • Strong yet not overpowering • Not harsh, bitter, dusty, or gritty NOTE: Available through mail order, Penzeys (800-741-7787, www.penzeys.com).	Smith and Truslow Freshly Ground Organic and Adams Ground
	COCOA POWDER **Hershey's Natural** **Unsweetened**	• Full, strong chocolate flavor • Complex flavor with notes of coffee, cinnamon, orange, and spice	Droste

COCONUT MILK

For savory recipes:
Chaokoh

- Strong coconut flavor
- Smooth and creamy texture superior to competitors
- Not very sweet, ideal for savory recipes like soups and stir-fries

For sweet recipes:
Ka-Me

- Rich, velvety texture, not too thin or watery
- Fruity and complex flavor, not mild or bland
- Ideal sweetness for desserts

COFFEE, WHOLE BEAN, SUPERMARKET

Dark roast: **Millstone Colombian Supremo**

- Deep, complex, and balanced flavor without metallic, overly acidic, or otherwise unpleasant notes
- Smoky and chocolaty with a bitter, not burnt, finish

Starbucks Coffee House Blend

Medium roast: **Peet's Coffee Café Domingo**

- Extremely smooth but bold-tasting with a strong finish
- Rich chocolate and toast flavors
- Few defective beans, low acidity, and optimal moisture

Millstone Breakfast Blend

COFFEE, DECAF
Maxwell House Decaf Original Roast

- Smooth, mellow flavor without being acidic or harsh
- Complex, with a slightly nutty aftertaste
- Made with only flavorful Arabica beans

Peet's Decaf House Blend Ground and Starbucks Coffee Decaf House Blend

CORNMEAL
Arrowhead Mills Whole Grain

- Clean, pure corn flavor comes from using whole-grain kernels
- Ideal texture resembling slightly damp, fine sand, not too fine or too coarse

CURRY POWDER
Penzeys Sweet

- Balanced, neither too sweet nor too hot
- Complex and vivid earthy flavor, not thin, bland, or one-dimensional

NOTE: Available through mail order, Penzeys (800-741-7787, www.penzeys.com).

	TEST KITCHEN FAVORITE	WHY WE LIKE IT	RUNNERS-UP
	DINNER ROLLS, FROZEN **Pepperidge Farm Stone Baked Artisan French Dinner Rolls**	• Tender on the inside with crispy crust • Has only 7 ingredients • Tastes homemade, with a hint of salt	
	EGG WHITES, PROCESSED **Eggology 100% Egg Whites**	• Work well in egg white omelets • Pasteurized; safe for use in uncooked applications • Make satisfactory baked goods	
	FIVE-SPICE POWDER **Frontier Natural Products Co-op**	• Nice depth, not one-dimensional • Balanced heat and sweetness	Dynasty Chinese Five Spices, McCormick Gourmet Collection Chines Five Spice, Dean & DeLuca Five Spice Blend, and Morton & Bassett Chinese Five Spice
	FLOUR, ALL-PURPOSE **King Arthur Unbleached**	• Fresh, toasty flavor • No metallic taste or other off-flavors • Consistent results across recipes • Made tender, flaky pie crust, hearty biscuits, crisp cookies, and chewy, sturdy bread	Gold Medal Enriched Bleached Presifted, Gold Medal Unbleached, and Heckers/Ceresota Unbleached Enriched Presifted
	Pillsbury Unbleached Enriched	• Clean, toasty, and hearty flavor • No metallic or other off-flavors • Consistent results across recipes • Made flaky pie crust, chewy cookies, and tender biscuits, muffins, and cakes	
	FLOUR, WHOLE-WHEAT **King Arthur Premium**	• Finely ground for hearty but not overly coarse texture in bread and pancakes • Sweet, nutty flavor	Bob's Red Mill Organic
	FRENCH FRIES, FROZEN **Alexia Organic Yukon Select Fries**	• Crispy exteriors with fluffy, creamy interiors • Earthy, potato-y flavor	Ore-Ida Golden Fries

	TEST KITCHEN FAVORITE	WHY WE LIKE IT	RUNNERS-UP
	GIARDINIERA **Pastene**	• Sharp, vinegary tang • Crunchy mix of vegetables • Mellow heat that's potent but not overpowering	Scala Hot
	GNOCCHI **Gia Russa Gnocchi with Potato**	• Tender, pillowlike texture • Nice potato flavor • Slightly sour taste that disappears when paired with tomato sauce	De Cecco
	GRITS **Anson Mills**	• Full, ripe, fresh corn flavor • Nice chew while still thick and creamy	Arrowhead Mills, Bob's Red Mill
	HAM, BLACK FOREST DELI **Dietz & Watson**	• Good texture • Nice ham flavor	
	HAM, COUNTRY **Harper's Grand Champion Whole Country Ham**	• Aged 3 to 6 months • Porky and complex, with robust flavor and balanced salt levels • Available online or in some southern supermarkets	Burgers' Smokehouse Ready to Cook Country Ham; Edwards Virginia Traditions Uncooked Virginia Ham
	HAM, SPIRAL-SLICED, HONEY-CURED **Cook's Spiral Sliced Hickory Smoked Honey**	• Good balance of smokiness, saltiness, and sweetness • Moist, tender yet firm texture, not dry or too wet • Clean, meaty ham flavor	
	HOISIN SAUCE **Kikkoman**	• Balances sweet, salty, pungent, and spicy flavors • Initial burn mellows into harmonious and aromatic blend without bitterness	

	TEST KITCHEN FAVORITE	WHY WE LIKE IT	RUNNERS-UP
	HORSERADISH **Boar's Head Pure Horseradish**	• No preservatives, just horseradish, vinegar, and salt (found in refrigerated section) • Natural flavor and hot without being overpowering	Ba-Tampte Prepared Horseradish
	HOT DOGS **Nathan's Famous Beef Franks**	• Meaty, robust, and hearty flavor, not sweet, sour, or too salty • Juicy but not greasy • Firm, craggy texture, not rubbery, mushy, or chewy	Hebrew National Beef Franks
	HOT FUDGE SAUCE **Hershey's Hot Fudge Topping**	• True fudge flavor, not weak or overly sweet • Thick, smooth, and buttery texture	
	HOT SAUCE **Huy Fong Sriracha Hot Chili Sauce and Frank's RedHot Original**	• Right combination of punchy heat, saltiness, sweetness, and garlic • Full, rich flavor • Mild heat that's not too hot	Original Louisiana, Tapatio Salsa Picante
	ICE CREAM BARS **Dove Bar Vanilla Ice Cream with Milk Chocolate**	• Rich, prominent chocolate flavor • Thick, crunchy chocolate coating • Dense, creamy, ice cream with pure vanilla flavor • Milk chocolate, not coconut oil, listed first in coating ingredients	Häagen-Dazs Vanilla Milk Chocolate All Natural, Blue Bunny Big Alaska, and Good Humor Milk Chocolate
	ICE CREAM CONES **Joy Classic Waffle Cones**	• Lightly sweet, with vanilla, toasty, and nutty flavors • Crunchy and crisp but not overly hard • Individual paper jackets keep things neat	Joy Sugar Cones, Keebler Waffle Cones, Keebler Sugar Cones, Comet (Nabisco) Sugar Cones
	ICE CREAM, CHOCOLATE **Ben & Jerry's**	• Deep, concentrated chocolate flavor, not too light or sweet • Dense and creamy texture	Friendly's Rich & Creamy Classic Chocolate Ice Cream
	ICE CREAM, VANILLA **Ben & Jerry's**	• Complex yet balanced vanilla flavor from real vanilla extract • Sweetness solely from sugar, rather than corn syrup • Creamy richness from both egg yolks and small amount of stabilizers	Häagen-Dazs Vanilla

	TEST KITCHEN FAVORITE	WHY WE LIKE IT	RUNNERS-UP
	ICED TEA Loose leaf: **Tazo Iced Black Tea**	• Distinctive flavor with herbal notes • Balanced level of strength and astringency	Luzianne and Tetley Premium Blend
	Bottled, with lemon: **Lipton PureLeaf**	• Bright, balanced, and natural tea and lemon flavors • Uses concentrated tea leaves to extract flavor	Gold Peak
	JUICE, GRAPEFRUIT **Natalie's 100% Florida Grapefruit Juice**	• Balanced and bright flavor, not too sweet • Clean and refreshing crispness	Florida's Natural Ruby Red Grapefruit Juice
	JUICE, ORANGE **Natalie's Orchid Island Juice Company**	• Blend of Hamlin, Pineapple, and Valencia oranges • Fresh, sweet, and fruity flavor without overly acidic, sour, or from-concentrate taste • Gentler pasteurization helps retain fresh-squeezed flavor • Pleasant amount of light pulp	Tropicana Pure Premium 100% Pure and Natural with Some Pulp
	JUICE, FROZEN ORANGE CONCENTRATE **Minute Maid Original Frozen Concentrated Orange Juice**	• Full-bodied orange flavor • Good texture, includes some pulp	Tropicana 100% Juice Frozen Concentrated Orange Juice
	KETCHUP **Heinz Organic**	• Clean, pure sweetness from sugar, not high-fructose corn syrup • Bold, harmonious punch of saltiness, sweetness, tang, and tomato flavor	Hunt's and Simply Heinz
	LEMONADE **Natalie's Natural Lemonade**	• Natural-tasting lemon flavor from 20 percent real lemon juice, without artificial flavors or off-notes • Perfect balance of tartness and sweetness, unlike many overly sweet competitors	Simply Lemonade and Minute Maid Premium Frozen Concentrate

	TEST KITCHEN FAVORITE	WHY WE LIKE IT	RUNNERS-UP
	MACARONI & CHEESE **Kraft Homestyle Classic Cheddar**	• Reinforces flavor with blue and cheddar cheeses • Uses creamy, clingy liquid cheese sauce • Dry noodles, rather than frozen, for substantial texture and bite • Crunchy, buttery breadcrumb topping	Kraft Velveeta Original
	MAPLE SYRUP **Maple Grove Farms Grade A Dark Amber**	• Clean yet rich maple flavor, not too mild, harsh, or artificial in flavor • Moderate sweetness bests overwhelmingly sugary competitors • Ideal consistency, neither too thin nor too thick like pancake syrups made from corn syrup	Highland Sugarworks Grade B (especially in baking) and Camp Grade A Dark Amber
	MAYONNAISE **Hellmann's Real**	• Great balance of taste and texture • Richer, deeper flavor from using egg yolks alone (no egg whites) • Short ingredient list that's close to homemade NOTE: Hellmann's is known as Best Foods west of the Rockies.	Spectrum Organic
	MAYONNAISE, LIGHT **Hellmann's Light**	• Bright, balanced flavor close to full-fat counterpart, not overly sweet like other light mayos • Not as creamy as full-fat but passable texture NOTE: Hellmann's is known as Best Foods west of the Rockies.	Hellmann's Canola Cholesterol Free
	MIRIN (JAPANESE RICE WINE) **Mitoku Organic Mikawa Mirin Sweet Rice Seasoning**	• Roasted flavor that is caramel-like and rich • Subtle salty-sweet and balanced flavor	Sushi Chef Mirin Sweetened Sake and Kikkoman Aji-Mirin Sweet Cooking Rice Seasoning
	MOLASSES **Brer Rabbit All Natural Unsulphured Mild Flavor**	• Acidic yet balanced • Strong and straightforward raisin-y taste • Pleasantly bitter bite	Plantation Barbados Unsulphured and Grandma's Molasses Unsulphured Original
	MUSTARD, BROWN **Gulden's Spicy Brown Mustard**	• Complex flavor with both heat and gentle tang • Smooth, creamy texture that goes perfectly with hot dogs	French's Spicy Brown Mustard and Beaver Deli Mustard

	TEST KITCHEN FAVORITE	WHY WE LIKE IT	RUNNERS-UP
	MUSTARD, COARSE-GRAIN **Grey Poupon Harvest Coarse Ground**	• Spicy, tangy burst of mustard flavor • High salt content amplifies flavor • Contains no superfluous ingredients that mask mustard flavor • Big, round seeds add pleasant crunch • Just enough vinegar, not too sour or thin	Grey Poupon Country Dijon
	MUSTARD, DIJON **Trois Petits Cochons Moutarde de Dijon**	• Potent, bold, and very hot, not weak or mild • Good balance of sweetness, tanginess, and sharpness • Not overly acidic, sweet, or one-dimensional like competitors	Maille Dijon Originale Traditional and Roland Extra Strong
	MUSTARD, YELLOW **Annie's Naturals Organic**	• Lists mustard seeds second in the ingredients for rich mustard flavor • Good balance of heat and tang • Relatively low salt content	Gulden's, French's Classic, and Westbrae Natural
	OATS, ROLLED For hot cereal: **Bob's Red Mill Organic Extra Thick**	• Rich oat flavor with nutty, barley, and toasty notes • Creamy, cohesive texture • Plump grains with decent chew	
	Quick Oats: **Quaker Old-Fashioned**	• Plump, almost crunchy texture with a slight chew, not gluey or mushy • Hearty, oaty, and toasty flavor • Subtly sweet with a natural taste	
	OATS, STEEL-CUT **Bob's Red Mill Organic**	• Rich and complex oat flavor with buttery, earthy, nutty, and whole-grain notes • Creamy yet toothsome texture • Moist but not sticky NOTE: Not recommended for baking	Arrowhead Mills Organic Hot Cereal, Country Choice Organic, and Hodgson's Mill Premium
	OLIVE OIL, CALIFORNIA **California Olive Ranch Arbequina**	• Round and full, sweet olive flavor with little bitterness or pungency • Complex with fruity, nutty, and buttery notes and fresh, pure olive aftertaste	Sciabica's Sevillano Variety Fall Harvest

	TEST KITCHEN FAVORITE	WHY WE LIKE IT	RUNNERS-UP
	OLIVE OIL, EXTRA-VIRGIN **Columela**	• Buttery flavor that is sweet and full with a peppery finish • Aromatic and fruity, not bland or bitter • Clean taste, comparable to a fresh-squeezed olive, outshines bland, greasy competitors	Lucini Italia Premium Select and Colavita
	OLIVE OIL, REGULAR **Colavita**	• Peppery, fruity flavors • Bold flavor, not too bland or mild like some competitors • Loses most flavor when heated to 300 F, so not specifically recommended for cooking	Filippo Berio
	PANCAKE MIX **Hungry Jack Buttermilk Pancake and Waffle Mix**	• Flavorful balance of sweetness and tang well-seasoned with sugar and salt • Light, extra fluffy texture • Requires vegetable oil (along with milk and egg) to reconstitute the batter	Aunt Jemima Original
	PAPRIKA **The Spice House Hungarian Sweet**	• Complex flavor with earthy, fruity notes • Bright and bold, not bland and boring • Rich, toasty aroma NOTE: Available only through mail order, The Spice House (312-274-0378, www.thespicehouse.com).	Penzeys Hungary Sweet (available through mail order, Penzeys, 800-741-7787, www.penzeys.com)
	PASTA, CHEESE RAVIOLI **Rosetto**	• Creamy, plush, and rich blend of ricotta, Romano, and Parmesan cheeses • Pasta with nice, springy bite • Perfect dough-to-filling ratio	Buitoni Four Cheese and Celentano
	PASTA, CHEESE TORTELLINI **Barilla Three Cheese**	• Robustly flavored filling from combination of ricotta, Emmentaler, and Grana Padano cheeses • Tender pasta that's sturdy enough to withstand boiling but not so thick that it becomes doughy	Seviroli and Buitoni Three Cheese
	PASTA, EGG NOODLES **Pennsylvania Dutch Wide Egg Noodles**	• Balanced, buttery flavor with no off-flavors • Light and fluffy texture, not gummy or starchy	De Cecco Egg Pappardelle; Light 'n Fluffy Egg Noodles, Wide

	TEST KITCHEN FAVORITE	WHY WE LIKE IT	RUNNERS-UP
	PASTA, ELBOW MACARONI **Barilla**	• Rich flavor from egg yolks • Firm, chewy bite • Wide corkscrew shape	Mueller's
	PASTA, FRESH **Buitoni Fettuccine**	• Firm but yielding, slightly chewy texture, not too delicate, gummy, or heavy • Faint but discernible egg flavor with no chemical, plasticky, or otherwise unpleasant flavors • Rough, porous surface absorbs sauce better than dried pasta	
	PASTA, LASAGNA NOODLES No-boil: **Barilla**	• Taste and texture of fresh pasta • Delicate, flat noodles	Ronzoni and Pasta DeFino
	Whole-wheat: **Bionaturae Organic 100% Whole Wheat**	• Complex nutty, rich wheat flavor • Substantial chewy texture without any grittiness	DeLallo 100% Organic
	PASTA, PENNE **Mueller's Penne Rigate**	• Hearty texture, not insubstantial or gummy • Wheaty, slightly sweet flavor, not bland	Benedetto Cavalieri Penne Rigate and De Cecco
	PASTA, SPAGHETTI **De Cecco Spaghetti No. 12**	• Rich, nutty, wheaty flavor • Firm, ropy strands with good chew, not mushy, gummy, or mealy	Rustichella D'Abruzzo Pasta Abruzzese di Semola di Grano Duro, Garofalo, and DeLallo Spaghetti No. 4
	PASTA, SPAGHETTI, WHOLE-WHEAT **Bionaturae 100% Whole Wheat**	• Chewy, firm, and toothsome, not mushy or rubbery • Full and nutty wheat flavor	Barilla PLUS Multigrain
	PASTA SAUCE **Bertolli Tomato & Basil**	• Fresh-cooked, balanced tomato flavor, not overly sweet • Pleasantly chunky, not too smooth or pasty • Not overseasoned with dry herbs like competitors	Francesco Rinaldi Traditional Marinara, Prego Marinara Italian, and Barilla Marinara

	TEST KITCHEN FAVORITE	WHY WE LIKE IT	RUNNERS-UP
	PASTA SAUCE, PREMIUM **Victoria Marinara Sauce**	• Nice, bright acidity that speaks of real tomatoes • Robust flavor comparable to homemade	Classico Marinara with Plum Tomatoes and Olive Oil
	PEANUT BUTTER, CREAMY **Skippy**	• Smooth, creamy, and spreadable • Good balance of sweet and salty flavors	Jif Natural and Reese's
	PEPPERCORNS, BLACK **Kalustyan's Indian Tellicherry**	• Enticing and fragrant, not musty, aroma with flavor to back it up and moderate heat • Fresh, complex flavor at once sweet and spicy, earthy and smoky, fruity and floral NOTE: Available only by mail order, Kalustyan's (800-352-3451, www.kalustyans.com).	Morton & Bassett Organic Whole (widely available)
	PEPPERONI, SLICED **Margherita Italian Style**	• Nice balance of meatiness and spice • Tangy, fresh flavor with hints of fruity licorice and peppery fennel • Thin slices with the right amount of chew	Boar's Head
	PEPPERS, ROASTED RED **Dunbars Sweet**	• Balance of smokiness and sweetness • Mild, sweet, and earthy red pepper flavor • Firm texture, not slimy or mushy • Packed in simple yet strong brine of salt and water without distraction of other strongly flavored ingredients	Cento
	PICKLES, BREAD-AND-BUTTER **Bubbies**	• Subtle, briny tang • All-natural solution that uses real sugar, not high-fructose corn syrup	
	PICKLES, WHOLE KOSHER DILL **Boar's Head**	• Authentic, garlicky flavor and firm, snappy crunch • Balanced salty, sour, and garlic flavors • Fresh and refrigerated, not processed and shelf-stable	Claussen

	TEST KITCHEN FAVORITE	WHY WE LIKE IT	RUNNERS-UP
	PIE CRUST, READY-MADE **Wholly Wholesome 9" Certified Organic Traditional Bake at Home Rolled Pie Dough**	• Palm oil gives it a tender, flaky texture without artificial taste • Sold in sheets so you can use your own pie plate • Slightly sweet, rich flavor	
	PIZZA, PEPPERONI, FROZEN **Pizzeria! by DiGiorno Primo Pepperoni**	• Thick, crisp, and airy crust with a browned and charred bottom • Herby, zesty sauce. Very meaty pepperoni	Freschetta Brick Oven Crust Pepperoni and Italian Style Cheese and Red Baron Fire Baked Pepperoni Pizza
	PORK, PREMIUM **Snake River Farms American Kurobuta (Berkshire) Pork**	• Deep pink tint, which indicates higher pH level and more flavorful meat • Tender texture and juicy, intensely pork-y flavor	D'Artagnan Berkshire Pork Chops (Milanese-Style Cut) and Eden Farms French-Cut Kurobuta Pork
	POTATO CHIPS **Lay's Kettle Cooked Original**	• Big potato flavor, no offensive off-flavors • Perfectly salted • Slightly thick chips that aren't too delicate or brittle • Not too greasy	Herr's Crisp 'N Tasty and Utz
	POTATO CHIPS, REDUCED FAT **Cape Cod 40% Reduced Fat**	• Real potato flavor with excellent crunch and texture • Contain only potatoes, canola oil, and salt • With less sodium than many competitors, they have just the right balance of salt	Lay's Kettle Cooked Reduced Fat Extra Crunchy
	PRESERVES, PEACH **American Spoon Red Haven Peach Preserves**	• Bold, ripe peach taste and balanced sweetness • Loose and spreadable texture, similar to homemade preserves	Bonne Maman Peach Preserves and Smucker's Peach Preserves

	TEST KITCHEN FAVORITE	WHY WE LIKE IT	RUNNERS-UP
	PRESERVES, RASPBERRY **Smucker's**	• Clean, strong raspberry flavor, not too tart or sweet • Not overly seedy • Ideal, spreadable texture, not too thick, artificial, or overprocessed	Trappist Red Raspberry Jam
	PRESERVES, STRAWBERRY **Welch's**	• Big, distinct strawberry flavor • Natural-tasting and not overwhelmingly sweet • Thick and spreadable texture, not runny, slimy, or too smooth	Smucker's and Smucker's Simply Fruit Spreadable Fruit
	RELISH, SWEET PICKLE **Cascadian Farm**	• Piquant, sweet flavor, lacks out-of-place flavors such as cinnamon and clove present in competitors • Fresh and natural taste, free of yellow dye #5 and high-fructose corn syrup • Good texture, not mushy like competitors	Heinz Premium
	RICE, ARBORIO **RiceSelect**	• Creamier than competitors • Smooth grains • Characteristic good bite of Arborio rice in risotto where al dente is ideal	Riso Baricella and Rienzi
	RICE, BASMATI **Tilda Pure**	• Very long grains expand greatly with cooking, a result of being aged for a minimum of one year, as required in India • Ideal, fluffy texture, not dry, gummy, or mushy • Nutty taste with no off-flavors • Sweet aroma	Kohinoor Super
	RICE, BROWN **Lundberg Organic Long Grain Brown**	• Firm yet tender grains • Bold, toasty, nutty flavor	Goya Brown Rice
	RICE, LONG-GRAIN WHITE **Lundberg Organic Long Grain White Rice**	• Nutty, buttery, and toasty flavor • Distinct, smooth grains that offer some chew without being overly chewy	Carolina Enriched Extra Long-Grain and Canilla Extra Long-Grain Enriched

	TEST KITCHEN FAVORITE	WHY WE LIKE IT	RUNNERS-UP
	RICE, READY **Minute Ready to Serve White Rice**	• Parboiled long-grain white rice that is ready in less than 2 minutes • Toasted, buttery flavor • Firm grains with al dente bite	
	SALSA, JARRED GREEN **Frontera Tomatillo Salsa**	• Sweet and nuanced flavor with a roasted, smoky taste from charred tomatillo skins • A good amount of heat • Has no preservatives or stabilizers	Ortega Salsa Verde, Medium
	SALSA, HOT **Pace Hot Chunky**	• Good balance of bright tomato, chile, and vegetal flavors • Chunky, almost crunchy texture, not mushy or thin • Spicy and fiery but not overpowering	Newman's Own All Natural Chunky Hot and Herdez Hot Salsa Casera
	SALSA, MEDIUM **Chi-Chi's Medium Thick and Chunky Salsa**	• Fresh, balanced flavor; vegetables are firm and crunchy • Jalapeño chiles for medium-level heat	
	SALT **Maldon Sea Salt**	• Light and airy texture • Delicately crunchy flakes • Not so coarse as to be overly crunchy or gritty nor so fine as to disappear	Fleur de Sel de Camargue, Morton Coarse Kosher, and Diamond Crystal Kosher
	SAUSAGE, BREAKFAST **Jimmy Dean Fully Cooked Original Pork Sausage Links**	• Big pork flavor, not bland or overly spiced • Good balance of saltiness and sweetness with pleasantly lingering spiciness • Tender, super-juicy meat, not rubbery, spongy, or greasy	
	SOUP, CANNED CHICKEN NOODLE **Muir Glen Organic**	• Organic chicken and vegetables and plenty of seasonings give it a fresh taste and spicy kick • Firm, not mushy, vegetables and noodles • No off-flavors	Progresso Traditional

	TEST KITCHEN FAVORITE	WHY WE LIKE IT	RUNNERS-UP
	SOUP, CANNED TOMATO **Progresso Vegetable Classics Hearty**	• Includes fresh, unprocessed tomatoes, not just tomato puree like some competitors • Tangy, slightly herbaceous flavor • Balanced seasoning and natural sweetness • Medium body and slightly chunky texture	Imagine Organic Vine Ripened
	SOY SAUCE For cooking: **Lee Kum Kee Tabletop**	• Pleasantly salty yet sweet with high sodium and sugar content • Depth of flavor balances salty, sweet, roasted, and fruity notes • Aromatic in rice and teriyaki	
	For dipping: **Ohsawa Nama Shoyu Organic Unpasteurized**	• Lower sodium content allows clean, mellow taste to shine in uncooked applications • Rich and nuanced flavor with sweet, floral, and caramel notes resulting from traditional, slow-brewed production	
	STEAK SAUCE **Heinz 57 Sauce**	• Mellow, restrained flavor that doesn't overpower the meat • Fruity, sweet and tangy flavor with hints of heat and smoke • Smooth texture with enough body to cling to steak without being gluey	Lea & Perrins
	SWEETENED CONDENSED MILK **Borden Eagle Brand Whole Milk**	• Made with whole milk; creamier in desserts and balances more assertive notes from other ingredients	Nestlé Carnation
	TARTAR SAUCE **Legal Sea Foods**	• Creamy, nicely balanced sweet/tart base • Lots of vegetable chunks	McCormick Original
	TEA, BLACK For plain tea: **Twinings English Breakfast**	• Bright, bold, and flavorful yet not too strong • Fruity, floral, and fragrant • Smooth, slightly astringent profile preferred for tea without milk	PG Tips
	For tea with milk: **Tazo Awake**	• Clean, strong taste • Smoky and fruity with notes of clove, cinnamon, and vanilla • Aromatic but not overwhelming • Good balance of flavor and intensity • More astringent profile stands up to milk	Tetley Specialty English Breakfast

	TEST KITCHEN FAVORITE	WHY WE LIKE IT	RUNNERS-UP
	TERIYAKI SAUCE **Annie Chun's All Natural**	• Distinct teriyaki flavor without offensive or dominant flavors, unlike competitors • Smooth, rich texture, not too watery or gluey	
	TOMATOES, CANNED CRUSHED **Tuttorosso in Thick Puree with Basil**	• Chunky texture, not pasty, mushy, or watery • Bright, fresh tomato taste • Balance of saltiness, sweetness, and acidity NOTE: Available only in New England, Mid-Atlantic region, and Florida.	Muir Glen Organic with Basil and Hunt's Organic
	TOMATOES, CANNED DICED **Hunt's**	• Bright, fresh tomato flavor that balances sweet and tart • Firm yet tender texture	Muir Glen Organic Diced Tomatoes
	TOMATOES, CANNED PUREED **Muir Glen Organic Tomato Puree**	• Full tomato flavor without any bitter, sour, or tinny notes • Pleasantly thick, even consistency, not watery or thin	Hunt's, Progresso, and Cento
	TOMATOES, CANNED WHOLE **Muir Glen Organic**	• Pleasing balance of bold acidity and fruity sweetness • Firm yet tender texture, even after hours of simmering	Hunt's
	TOMATO PASTE **Goya**	• Bright, robust tomato flavors • Balance of sweet and tart flavors	Pastene and Contadina
	TORTILLA CHIPS **Santitas Authentic Mexican Style White Corn**	• Mild and pleasantly salty flavor, not bland, artificial, or rancid • Sturdy yet crunchy and crisp texture, not brittle, stale, or cardboardlike	Tostitos 100% White Corn Restaurant Style, Green Mountain Gringo All Natural, and Tostitos Natural Yellow Corn Restaurant Style

	TEST KITCHEN FAVORITE	WHY WE LIKE IT	RUNNERS-UP
	TORTILLAS, CORN **Maria and Ricado's Handmade Style Soft Corn Tortillas, Yellow**	• Soft and pliable, don't crack when rolled up • Light, cornlike sweetness with a hint of nuttiness • Wheat gluten added to dough makes tortilla more cohesive and elastic	
	TORTILLAS, FLOUR **Old El Paso 6-Inch Flour Tortillas**	• Thin and flaky texture, not doughy or stale • Made with plenty of fat and salt	Mission
	TOSTADAS, CORN **Mission Tostadas Estilo Casero**	• Crisp, crunchy texture • Good corn flavor • Flavor and texture that are substantial enough to stand up to hearty toppings	Charras
	TUNA, CANNED **Wild Planet Wild Albacore**	• Rich, fresh-tasting, and flavorful, but not fishy • Hearty, substantial chunks of tuna	American Tuna Pole Caught Wild Albacore and Starkist Selects Solid White Albacore
	TUNA, CANNED PREMIUM **Nardin Bonito Del Norte Ventresca Fillets**	• Creamy, delicate meat and tender yet firm fillets • Full, rich tuna flavor	Tonnino Tuna Ventresca Yellowfin in Olive Oil
	TURKEY, WHOLE **Empire Kosher**	• Moist and dense texture without being watery, chewy, or squishy • Meaty, full turkey flavor • Buttery white meat • Koshering process renders brining unnecessary	Good Shepherd Ranch Heritage (available through mail order, Good Shepherd Turkey Ranch Inc., 785-227-5149, www. reeseturkeys.net)

	TEST KITCHEN FAVORITE	WHY WE LIKE IT	RUNNERS-UP
	VANILLA BEANS **McCormick Madagascar**	• Moist, seed-filled pods • Complex, robust flavor with caramel notes	Spice Islands Bourbon
	VANILLA EXTRACT **McCormick Pure**	• Strong, rich vanilla flavor where others are weak and sharp • Complex flavor with spicy, caramel notes and a sweet undertone	Rodelle Pure and Gold Medal Imitation by C.F. Sauer Co.
	VEGETABLE OIL **Crisco Natural Blend Oil**	• Unobtrusive, mild flavor for stir-frying and sautéing and for use in baked goods and in uncooked applications such as mayonnaise and vinaigrette • Neutral taste and absence of fishy or metallic flavors when used for frying	Mazola Canola Oil
	VINEGAR, APPLE CIDER **Spectrum Naturals Organic Unfiltered**	• Deep, warm profile with sweet, mellow, and smooth cider flavor • Balance of richness and tanginess • Complex with notes of honey and caramel with clear apple flavor	
	VINEGAR, BALSAMIC **Lucini Gran Riserva Balsamico**	• Sweet, nuanced flavor lacking any harshness or astringency • Smooth and thick like traditional balsamic, not too thin or light • Balance of tanginess and sweetness with complexity and a slight acidic zing	Monari Federzoni of Modena and Ortalli of Modena
	VINEGAR, RED WINE **Laurent du Clos**	• Crisp red wine flavor balanced by stronger than average acidity and subtle sweetness • Complex yet pleasing taste from multiple varieties of grapes	Pompeian Gourmet and Spectrum Naturals Organic

	TEST KITCHEN FAVORITE	WHY WE LIKE IT	RUNNERS-UP
	VINEGAR, WHITE WINE For cooking: **Colavita Aged**	• Balance of tanginess and subtle sweetness, not overly acidic or weak • Fruity, bright, and perfumed	
	For vinaigrettes: **Spectrum Naturals Organic**	• Rich, dark flavor tastes fermented and malty, not artificial or harsh • Fruity flavor with caramel, earthy, and nutty notes	
	YOGURT, GREEK FULL-FAT **Olympus Traditional Greek Yogurt Strained, Plain 10% Fat**	• Rich taste and satiny texture, not thin, watery, or soupy • Buttery, tangy flavor	Greek Gods Traditional Plain and Fage Total
	YOGURT, GREEK NONFAT **Olympus Traditional Greek Nonfat Yogurt Strained, Plain**	• Smooth, creamy consistency, not watery or pudding like from added thickeners, such as pectin or gelatin • Pleasantly tangy, well-balanced flavor, not sour or metallic	Voskos Greek Plain Nonfat, Brown Cow Plain Greek 0% Fat, and Dannon Greek Plain 0% Fat
	YOGURT, LOW-FAT STRAWBERRY **Dannon Fruit on the Bottom**	• Good strawberry flavor, not too sweet, sour, or bland • Pleasantly thick, not watery or runny • No artificial, plasticky, or otherwise unwelcome flavors as in many competitors	Wallaby Organic Creamy Australian-Style and Fage 2% All Natural Greek Strained
	YOGURT, WHOLE-MILK **Brown Cow Cream Top Plain**	• Rich, well-rounded flavor, not sour or bland • Especially creamy, smooth texture, not thin or watery • Higher fat content contributes to flavor and texture	Stonyfield Farm Organic Plain

EPISODE DIRECTORY

SEASON ONE 2008

EPISODE 101
Forgotten Cakes
Strawberry Poke Cake 391
Chocolate Blackout Cake 383

EPISODE 102
Sunday Dinner
Sunday-Best Garlic Roast Beef 149
Mashed Potato Casserole 183

EPISODE 103
Feeding a Crowd, Italian-Style
Slow-Cooker Italian
Sunday Gravy 221
Meatballs and Marinara 227

EPISODE 104
Southern Regional Recipes
Lexington-Style Pulled Pork 281
Memphis Chopped Coleslaw 317

EPISODE 105
Autumn Supper
Old-Fashioned Roast Pork 167
Cranberry-Apple Crisp 439

EPISODE 106
All-American Picnic
Extra-Crunchy Fried Chicken 43
All-American Potato Salad 319

EPISODE 107
Easy as Pie
Raspberry Chiffon Pie 473
No-Fear Single-Crust Pie Dough 455

EPISODE 108
Steakhouse Favorites
Broiled Steaks 95
Super-Stuffed Baked Potatoes 115

EPISODE 109
Barbecued Chicken
Classic Barbecued Chicken 255
Best Potluck Macaroni and Cheese 5

EPISODE 110
Regional Chops
Tennessee Whiskey Pork Chops 71
Smoked Double-Thick Pork Chops 285

EPISODE 111
Midwestern Favorites
Chicago-Style Barbecued Ribs 277
Cincinnati Chili 77

EPISODE 112
California Grilling
California Barbecued Tri-Tip 269
California Barbecued Beans 309
Santa Maria Salsa 269

EPISODE 113
Diner Favorites
Fluffy Diner-Style Cheese Omelet 333
Short-Order Home Fries 339

SEASON TWO 2009

EPISODE 201
Old-Fashioned Roast Beef Dinner
Classic Roast Beef and Gravy 151
Perfect Popovers 355

EPISODE 202
Pucker-Up Pies
Mile-High Lemon Meringue Pie 471
Icebox Key Lime Pie 469

EPISODE 203
Rise And Shine
Ultimate Cinnamon Buns 363
Better-Than-the-Box
Pancake Mix 341

EPISODE 204
Surefire Seafood
Wood-Grilled Salmon 301
Baked Stuffed Shrimp 103
Grilled Jalapeño and Lime Shrimp
Skewers 305

EPISODE 205
Fudgy Cakes
Tunnel of Fudge Cake 385
Hot Fudge Pudding Cake 415

EPISODE 206
Texas Chili
Easy Chili Con Carne 213
Southern-Style Skillet Cornbread 353

CONVERSIONS AND EQUIVALENTS

SOME SAY COOKING IS A SCIENCE AND AN ART. WE would say that geography has a hand in it, too. Flour milled in the United Kingdom and elsewhere will feel and taste different from flour milled in the United States. So we cannot promise that the loaf of bread you bake in Canada or England will taste the same as a loaf baked in the States, but we can offer guidelines for converting weights and measures. We also recommend that you rely on your instincts when making our recipes. Refer to the visual cues provided. If the bread dough hasn't "come together in a ball," as described, you may need to add more flour—even if the recipe doesn't tell you to. You be the judge.

The recipes in this book were developed using standard U.S. measures following U.S. government guidelines. The charts below offer equivalents for U.S., metric, and imperial (U.K.) measures. All conversions are approximate and have been rounded up or down to the nearest whole number.

EXAMPLE:

1 teaspoon	=	4.9292 milliliters, rounded up to 5 milliliters
1 ounce	=	28.3495 grams, rounded down to 28 grams

VOLUME CONVERSIONS

U.S.	METRIC
1 teaspoon	5 milliliters
2 teaspoons	10 milliliters
1 tablespoon	15 milliliters
2 tablespoons	30 milliliters
¼ cup	59 milliliters
⅓ cup	79 milliliters
½ cup	118 milliliters
¾ cup	177 milliliters
1 cup	237 milliliters
1¼ cups	296 milliliters
1½ cups	355 milliliters
2 cups (1 pint)	473 milliliters
2½ cups	591 milliliters
3 cups	710 milliliters
4 cups (1 quart)	0.946 liter
1.06 quarts	1 liter
4 quarts (1 gallon)	3.8 liters

WEIGHT CONVERSIONS

OUNCES	GRAMS
½	14
¾	21
1	28
1½	43
2	57
2½	71
3	85
3½	99
4	113
4½	128
5	142
6	170
7	198
8	227
9	255
10	283
12	340
16 (1 pound)	454

CONVERSIONS FOR INGREDIENTS COMMONLY USED IN BAKING

Baking is an exacting science. Because measuring by weight is far more accurate than measuring by volume, and thus more likely to achieve reliable results, in our recipes we provide ounce measures in addition to cup measures for many ingredients. Refer to the chart below to convert these measures into grams.

INGREDIENT	OUNCES	GRAMS
1 cup all-purpose flour*	5	142
1 cup whole-wheat flour	5½	156
1 cup granulated (white) sugar	7	198
1 cup packed brown sugar (light or dark)	7	198
1 cup confectioners' sugar	4	113
1 cup cocoa powder	3	85
4 tablespoons butter† (½ stick, or ¼ cup)	2	57
8 tablespoons butter† (1 stick, or ½ cup)	4	113
16 tablespoons butter† (2 sticks, or 1 cup)	8	227

* U.S. all-purpose flour, the most frequently used flour in this book, does not contain leaveners, as some European flours do. These leavened flours are called self-rising or self-raising. If you are using self-rising flour, take this into consideration before adding leavening to a recipe.

† In the United States, butter is sold both salted and unsalted. We generally recommend unsalted butter. If you are using salted butter, take this into consideration before adding salt to a recipe.

OVEN TEMPERATURES

FAHRENHEIT	CELSIUS	GAS MARK (IMPERIAL)
225	105	¼
250	120	½
275	135	1
300	150	2
325	165	3
350	180	4
375	190	5
400	200	6
425	220	7
450	230	8
475	245	9

CONVERTING TEMPERATURES FROM AN INSTANT-READ THERMOMETER

We include doneness temperatures in many of the recipes in this book. We recommend an instant-read thermometer for the job. Refer to the above table to convert Fahrenheit degrees to Celsius. Or, for temperatures not represented in the chart, use this simple formula:

Subtract 32 degrees from the Fahrenheit reading, then divide the result by 1.8 to find the Celsius reading.

EXAMPLE:
"Roast chicken until thighs register 175 degrees."
To convert:

175°F − 32 = 143°
143° ÷ 1.8 = 79.44°C, rounded down to 79°C

INDEX

Note: Page references in *italics* indicate photographs.

G

Garlic
    Mashed Potatoes, *108*, *109*
    odor, removing from hands, *109*
    -Parsley Steak Sauce, *97*
    Roast Beef, Sunday-Best, *148*, *149*
    Roasted, Sauce, Arugula, and Walnuts, Pasta with, *224*, *225*
Ginger
    Fairy Gingerbread, *424*, *425*
    Joe Froggers, *426*, *427*
    -Lime Glaze, *423*
Glazed Meatloaf, *12*, *13*
Glazes
    Cappuccino, *423*
    Ginger-Lime, *423*
    Malted Milk, *423*
    Peanut Butter and Jelly, *423*
Gouda cheese
    Smokehouse Mashed Sweet Potatoes, *185*
    Southwestern Potato Tots, *87*
Graham crackers
    Chocolate Éclair Cake, *394*, *395*
    Icebox Key Lime Pie, *468*, *469*
Grains
    Charleston Shrimp Perloo, *54*, *55*
    Creamy Cheese Grits, *6*, *7*
    Dakota Bread, *376*, *377*
    Easier Chicken Chimichangas, *204*, *205*
    see also Cornmeal
Grandma Pizza, *240*, *241*
Gravy
    Classic Roast Beef and, *150*, *151*
    Mushroom, Meatloaf with, *16*, *17*
    Old-Fashioned Roast Turkey with, *126*, *127*
Greek Diner-Style Home Fries, *339*
Green Chile Cheeseburgers, *274*, *275*
Greens
    Chicken Florentine, *8*, *9*

Greens *(cont.)*
    Chinese Chicken Salad, *56*, *57*
    Grilled Caesar Salad, *312*, *313*
    Pasta with Roasted Garlic Sauce, Arugula, and Walnuts, *224*, *225*
    Slow-Cooker Minestrone, *218*, *219*
    Spinach and Tomato Lasagna, *236*, *237*
    Stuffed Tomatoes, *122*, *123*
    see also Cabbage
Grilled dishes
    Alabama Barbecued Chicken, *252*, *253*
    Baltimore Pit Beef, *74*, *75*
    Barbecued Burnt Ends, *266*, *267*
    Barbecued Country-Style Ribs, *294*, *295*
    Barbecued Pulled Chicken, *264*, *265*
    California Barbecued Beans, *308*, *309*
    California Barbecued Tri-Tip, *268*, *269*
    Char-Grilled Steaks, *96*, *97*
    Chicago-Style Barbecued Ribs, *276*, *277*
    Chinese-Style Barbecued Spareribs, *292*, *293*
    Chinese-Style Glazed Pork Tenderloin, *290*, *291*
    Classic Barbecued Chicken, *254*, *255*
    Cornell Barbecued Chicken, *250*, *251*
    Green Chile Cheeseburgers, *274*, *275*
    Grilled Butterflied Lemon Chicken, *258*, *259*
    Grilled Caesar Salad, *312*, *313*
    Grilled Chicken Leg Quarters, *262*, *263*
    Grilled Chicken Wings, *260*, *261*
        BBQ, *261*
        Creole, *261*
        Tandoori, *261*
    Grilled Corn on the Cob, *306*, *307*
    Grilled Cowboy-Cut Rib Eyes, *98*, *99*
    Grilled Mustard-Glazed Pork Loin, *298*, *299*
    Grilled Potato Hobo Packs, *311*
        Spanish-Style, *310*, *311*
        Spicy Home Fry, *311*
        Vinegar and Onion, *311*
    Grilled-Roasted Peppers, *120*, *121*

I

PHOTO CREDITS

Page vi: (left) Bob Landry/Time & Life Pictures/Getty Images, (right) H. Armstrong Roberts/Retrofile/Getty Images

Pages viii (top), 1, 9, 11, 15, 21, 34 (top right), 35, 83, 91 (top), 217, 331, 379, 385, 395, 411, 432 (left), 433, 453: The America's Test Kitchen Archive

Page xii: Nina Leen/Time & Life Pictures/Getty Images

Page 3: Photography Collection, Miriam and Ira D. Wallach Division of Art, Prints and Photographs, The New York Public Library, Astor, Lenox and Tilden Foundations

Page 34: (center) © DaZo Vintage Stock Photos/ Images.com/Corbis, (left) © Paul Edmondson/ Spaces Images/Corbis

Page 90: (left) Brand X Pictures/Getty Images, (right) © SuperStock/Corbis

Page 91: (bottom) Archive Holdings Inc./Archive Holdings/Getty Images

Page 111: Picture Collection, The New York Public Library, Astor, Lenox and Tilden Foundations

Page 124: Evans/Hulton Archive/Getty Images

Page 125: © H. Armstrong Roberts/ClassicStock/Corbis

Page 188: Carl Mydans/Time & Life Pictures/Getty Images

Page 189: © K.J. Historical/Corbis

Page 216: (left) Orlando/Hulton Archive/Getty Images, (right) SuperStock/Getty Images

Page 241: Courtesy Umberto's Pizzeria

Page 246: © ClassicStock/Corbis

Page 247: (top) From the collections of The Henry Ford, (bottom) Courtesy Weber-Stephen Products LLC

Page 273: Norton & Peel, Minnesota Historical Society

Page 325: © Catherine Karnow/Corbis

Page 330: © Minnesota Historical Society/Corbis

Page 378: Stringer/Hulton Archive/Getty Images

Page 432: (right) Fox Photos/Hulton Archive/Getty Images

Page 452: © H. Armstrong Roberts/Corbis